CRIMINAL LAW

CRITICAL LAW

The Fundamentals

SECOND EDITION

by
CHRISTINA MCALHONE
Senior Lecturer in Law,
University of Northumbria,
LLB (Hon.), Solicitor (non-practising),
PGCED.

and
REBECCA HUXLEY-BINNS
Reader in Legal Education,
Nottingham Law School,
LLB (Hon.), FHED.

THOMSON REUTERS

First Edition 2007
Second Edition 2010

Published in 2010 by
Thomson Reuters (Legal) Limited (Registered in England & Wales,
Company No. 1679046. Registered Office and address for service:
100 Avenue Road, Swiss Cottage,
London NW3 3PF).

For further information on our products and services, visit
http://www.sweetandmaxwell.thomson.com

Typeset by LBJ Typesetting Ltd of Kingsclere
Printed and bound in Great Britain by
Ashford Colour Press, Gosport, Hants

No natural forests were destroyed to make this product;
only farmed timber was used and replanted.

A CIP catalogue record of this book is available from the British Library.

ISBN: 978-0-41404-241-4

Dedication

To Daniel and Abigail
With love
Christina and Rebecca

Preface

Preface to the first edition

Criminal Law is one of the most dynamic of all law subjects. Criminal offences are often the focus of media and Government debate, and many students who choose to study law do so because of their notions of justice as portrayed in dramas about criminal trials. Even soap operas will have a criminal court case every now and again to keep their viewers mesmerised. Yet the substantive criminal law is technical and can be very demanding. There are inconsistent, complex and sometimes illogical decisions which have to be understood and analysed by the student of law. We have tried to make the law as accessible and understandable as possible, without losing any of the complexities and critical comments which ensure the higher marks. To assist, we have included flowcharts, grids, tables and summaries on a regular basis.

The book is designed to cover all the main topic areas on the ILEX Level 6, all undergraduate and post graduate conversion modules in criminal law.

Preface to this edition

We have updated this text taking into account feedback received from reviewers, colleagues and students, to whom we are grateful. We have expanded the explanations of some of the key cases, added further critical commentary and in particular have included more of the sexual offences in Ch.6. We have also taken into account many developments in the criminal law, including but not limited to:

- **Badza [2009] EWCA Crim 1363;**
- **Devonald [2008] EWCA 527;**
- **Evans [2009] 1 W.L.R. 1999;**
- **Jheeta [2007] EWCA Crim 1699;**
- **Kennedy [2008] 1 A.C. 269;**
- **Khan (Uzma) [2009] 1 W.L.R. 2036;**
- **R. v B [2007] 1 W.L.R. 1567;**
- **Rahman [2009] 1 A.C. 129;**
- **Raphael & Johnson [2008] Crim. L.R. 995;**
- **Stewart [2009] EWCA Crim 593;**
- **Taylor [2009] EWCA Crim 544;**
- **Wood [2009] 1 W.L.R. 496;**
- **Yemoh [2009] EWCA Crim 930;**
- as well as the provisions of the Serious Crime Act 2007, the Corporate Manslaughter and Corporate Homicide Act 2007, the Criminal Justice and Immigration Act 2008 and the Coroners and Justice Act 2009; and
- Law Commission proposals and views of academics where relevant to the law examined here.

We have also added new features including the "Over to you boxes" and end of chapter assessment questions and answers, which we hope you find useful.

The law is stated as we believe it to be on March 9, 2010.

Christina and Rebecca

Acknowledgements

Grateful acknowledgement is made for permission to reproduce from the undermentioned works:

SWEET & MAXWELL
Textbook of Criminal Law, 2nd edn, Williams.

"Justice Devlin's Legacy: Duffy-a battered women 'caught' in time" [2009] Crim. L.R. 851, Susan Edwards.

Qadir [1997] 9 Arch. News 1.

OXFORD UNIVERSITY PRESS
Criminal Law, Smith and Hogan, 12th edn.

Contents

Dedication   v
Preface   vii
Acknowledgments   ix
List of Figures   xxiii
Table of Cases   xxv
Table of Statutes   xlv
Guided Tour   li

1 : Introduction to Criminal Law   1

Introduction   2
Nature and Function of the Criminal Law   2
Subjectivism and Objectivism in the Criminal Law   3
Sources of Criminal Law   4
   The Doctrine of Precedent   5
The Human Rights Act 1998   5
Structure of the Courts and Appeals Against Conviction or Acquittal 6
Burden and Standard of Proof   8
   What the Prosecution must Prove   8
   The Burden on the Defendant   8
Reform of the Criminal Law   9

  ● Summary   10

2 : Actus Reus   11

Introduction   12
Definition of Actus Reus   12
Acts and Omissions   13
   Conduct Crimes   13
   Voluntary Conduct   13

Omissions 14

The Exception not the Rule 14

Offences Capable of Being Committed by Omission 15

Common Law Duties 16

Who Decides if There is a Duty 22

Statutory Duties 22

State of Affairs Offences 22

Circumstances 23

Causation 23

Result Crimes 23

Establishing the Chain of Causation 25

Factual Causation 25

Legal Causation 25

Breaking the Chain of Causation 26

Reform of Causation 36

Coincidence in Time of Mens Rea and Actus Reus 37

● **Summary** 38
● **End of Chapter Question** 41
● **Further Reading** 41
● **Self Test Questions** 42

3 | Mens Rea

43

Introduction 44

Determining the Mens Rea 44

Motive 45

Proof of Mens Rea 45

Common Forms of Mens Rea 46

Intention 46

Recklessness 60

Negligence 65

Other Forms of Mens Rea 65

The Doctrine of Transferred Malice 66

Limitations on Transferred Malice 67

Transferred Malice and Defences 67

Offences of Strict Liability 67

Absolute and Strict Liability 67

Strict Liability at Common Law 68

Strict Liability Under Statute 68

European Convention on Human Rights' Challenges 76

Can the Imposition of Strict Liability be Justified   76
The Alternatives   79

● **Summary**   79
● **End of Chapter Question**   80
● **Further Reading**   81
● **Self Test Questions**   81

4 Homicide   **83**

Introduction   84
The Actus Reus of Homicide   84
Jurisdiction   84
Murder   86
The Mens Rea of Murder   86
Reform of Murder   88
Manslaughter   88
Voluntary Manslaughter   89
Diminished Responsibility   91
Diminished Responsibility under the Coroners and Justice Act 2009   96
Provocation   98
Provocation and the Coroners and Justice Act 2009   109
Suicide Pact   114
Involuntary Manslaughter   114
Reckless Manslaughter   114
Gross Negligence Manslaughter   115
Constructive Manslaughter   121
Infanticide   126
Causing or Allowing the Death of a Child or Vulnerable Adult   127
Corporate Manslaughter   128

● **Summary**   132
● **End of Chapter Question**   134
● **Further Reading**   135
● **Self Test Questions**   136

5 Non-fatal Offences Against the Person   **137**

Introduction   138
The Offences of Assault and Battery   138

Assault   139
Battery   143
Assault Occasioning Actual Bodily Harm   145
The s.47 Offence   145
The Actus Reus of the s.47 Offence   145
The Mens Rea of the s.47 Offence   147
Offences Involving Wounding or Grievous Bodily Harm   147
The s.20 Offence   147
The Actus Reus of the s.20 Offence   147
The Mens Rea of the s.20 Offence   149
The s.18 Offence   150
The Actus Reus of the s.18 Offence   150
The Mens Rea of the s.18 Offence   150
Reform   151
Racially and Religiously Aggravated Assaults   152
Meaning of Racially or Religiously Aggravated   153
Stalking and Protection from Harassment Act 1997   155
Harassment   155
Putting People in Fear of Violence   156
The Mens Rea of the Harassment Offences   157
Specific Defences to Harassment   158
Consent   160
Is Consent a True Defence?   160
Valid Consent   160
The Public Interest and Valid Consent   161
The Public Interest and Invalid Consent   164

● **Summary**   168
● **End of Chapter Question**   168
● **Further Reading**   171
● **Self Test Questions**   172

6   Sexual Offences   173

Introduction   174
Rape   174
The Offence of Rape   174
The Actus Reus of Rape   175
The Mens Rea of Rape   176
Sexual Assault   177
The Offence of Sexual Assault   177

The Actus Reus of Sexual Assault   177
The Mens Rea of Sexual Assault   180
Assault by Penetration   181
The Offence of Assault by Penetration   181
The Actus Reus of Assault by Penetration   181
The Mens Rea of Assault by Penetration   182
Causing a Person to Engage in Sexual Activity   183
The Offence Under s.4 (Causing Another, etc.)   183
The Actus Reus of an Offence Under s.4 (Causing Another, etc.)   183
The Mens Rea of an Offence Under s.4 (Causing Another, etc.)   184
Sex With an Adult Relative: Penetration   184
The Offences Involving Sex with an Adult Relative   184
The Actus Reus of the s.64 Offence   185
The Mens Rea of the s.64 Offence   185
The Actus Reus of the s.65 Offence   185
The Mens Rea of the s.65 Offence   186
The Preparatory Offences   186
Administering a Substance with Intent   186
Committing an Offence with Intent to Commit a Sexual Offence   188
Trespass with Intent to Commit a Sexual Offence   188
Sexual Offences Involving Children   189
Sexual Offences Involving Children Under the Age of 13   189
Abuse of a Position of Trust   192
Offences Involving Sexual Grooming   194
Sex with a Child Relative   195
Consent   196
Background to the Provision in the 2003 Act   197
The Meaning of Consent—s.74   197
The Presumptions About Consent   198
The Intoxicated Complainant   202

● **Summary**   204
● **End of Chapter Question**   206
● **Further Reading**   207
● **Self Test Questions**   208

7   **Offences Against Property I—Theft**   **209**

Introduction   210
The Offence of Theft   210
The Actus Reus of Theft   211

Appropriation	211
Property	219
Belonging to Another	224
The Mens Rea of Theft	231
Dishonesty	231
Intention Permanently to Deprive	239
● **Summary**	243
● **End of Chapter Question**	244
● **Further Reading**	245
● **Self Test Questions**	246

8 Offences Against Property II — 247

Introduction	248
Robbery	248
The Offence	248
The Actus Reus of Robbery	248
The Mens Rea of Robbery	250
Assault with Intent to Rob	250
Burglary	251
The Offences	251
The Actus Reus of Burglary	252
The Mens Rea of Burglary	255
Aggravated Burglary	256
Blackmail	257
The Offence	257
The Actus Reus of Blackmail	257
The Mens Rea of Blackmail	259
Handling Stolen Goods	261
The Offence	261
The Actus Reus of Handling Stolen Goods	262
The Mens Rea of Handling Stolen Goods	271
Going Equipped for Stealing	272
The Offence	272
The Actus Reus of Going Equipped	272
The Mens Rea of Going Equipped	273
Possession of Articles for use in Frauds	274
Making Off Without Payment	274
The Offence	274

The Actus Reus of Making Off   275
The Mens Rea of Making Off   276
Fraud   277
The Old Deception Offences   277
Conspiracy to Defraud   278
The Fraud Act 2006   281
Dishonestly Obtaining Services   285

● **Summary**   287
● **End of Chapter Question**   289
● **Further Reading**   290
● **Self Test Questions**   290

9 : **Offences Involving Property III—Criminal Damage**   **291**

Introduction   292
The Criminal Damage Act 1971   292
The Simple (or Basic) Offence of Criminal Damage   292
The Actus Reus of Criminal Damage   293
The Mens Rea of Criminal Damage   297
Lawful Excuse   299
The Aggravated Offence   299
The Differences Between the Simple Offence and The Aggravated Offence   299
The Actus Reus of Aggravated Criminal Damage   299
The Mens Rea of Aggravated Criminal Damage   300
Lawful Excuse   301
Arson   301
The Charge   302
The Actus Reus of Arson   302
The Mens Rea of Arson   302
Lawful Excuse   302
Threatening to Destroy or Damage Property   303
Lawful Excuse   303
Possessing Anything with Intent to Destroy or Damage Property   304
Lawful Excuse   304
Racially or Religiously Aggravated Criminal Damage   305
Lawful Excuse   305
Belief in Consent   306
Belief in Protection of Property   307
Intoxication and Lawful Excuse   309

● **Summary** 309
● **End of Chapter Question** 310
● **Further Reading** 311
● **Self Test Questions** 311

10 : Inchoate Offences 313

Introduction 314
Attempt 314
What is an Attempt? 314
The Actus Reus of Attempt 314
The Mens Rea of Attempt 318
Attempts and Impossibility 320
Attempts and Reform 321
Conspiracy 323
Statutory Conspiracy 324
Incitement 328
Encouraging or Assisting Crime(s) 328
The Elements of the Part 2 Offences 329
Defence of Reasonableness 333
Limitation 334
Double Inchoate Liability 335
Impossibility 336

● **Summary** 336
● **End of Chapter Question** 337
● **Further Reading** 338
● **Self Test Questions** 338

11 : Participation in Criminal Offences 339

Introduction 340
Secondary Liability 340
Distinguishing Accessories from Principals 340
Principals and Innocent Agents 341
Who is an Accessory? 342
Liability of Accessories 345
Accessories and Transferred Malice 351
Joint Enterprise Liability 351

What is a Joint Enterprise? 351
Is Joint Enterprise a Separate Basis of Liability 352
Liability for Unintended Consequences 353
The Effect of the Acquittal or Reduction of Liability of the Principal 362
Where the Principal Lacked Mens Rea 362
Where the Principal has a Defence not Available to the Accessory 363
Can an Accessory be Liable for a Graver Offence than the Principal? 364
Withdrawal of Participation by an Accessory 364
What Constitutes an Effective Withdrawal? 364
Can a Victim be an Accessory? 367
Reform 367
Assistance After the Principal Offence 368
Vicarious Liability 369
What is Vicarious Liability in the Criminal Law? 369
Vicarious Liability for Crimes of Strict Liability 370
Vicarious Liability for Crimes with Mens Rea 372
Reform 373
Corporate Liability 374
Introduction 374
Vicarious or Corporate Liability 374
Acting Through its Officers 374
The Identification Doctrine 375

● **Summary** 377
● **End of Chapter Question** 380
● **Further Reading** 381
● **Self Test Questions** 382

12 Defences I—Defences Negating the Offence or Affecting Capacity — **383**

Introduction 384
Mistake 384
Introduction 384
Mistakes which Negate the Mens Rea 384
Mistakes which do not Negate the Mens Rea 385
Mistake as to the Need to Act in Self-defence or Prevention of Crime 386
Mistaken Belief in Consent 387
Mistake in Bigamy 387

Intoxication   388

  Introduction   388

  What is Intoxication?   389

  Voluntary Intoxication   389

  Involuntary Intoxication   401

  Intoxicated Mistaken Beliefs   403

  Intoxication Giving Rise to Automatism or Insanity   405

  Reform   405

Automatism   409

  Introduction   409

  What is Automatism?   409

  A Denial of Actus Reus or Mens Rea?   409

  Requirements for the Defence to Succeed   410

  Self-induced Automatism   411

  Reform   412

Insanity   413

  Introduction   413

  The Burden of Proof   413

  The Importance of the Distinction between Sane and Insane Automatism   413

  The Legal Definition of Insanity   414

  Irresistible Impulse   419

  Insane Delusions   419

  Criticism and Reform   419

Unfit to Plead   423

  Judge Determines the Defendant is Fit to Plead   423

  Judge Determines the Defendant is Unfit to Plead   423

Doli Incapax   423

● **Summary**   424

● **End of Chapter Question**   425

● **Further Reading**   426

● **Self Test Questions**   427

13 : Defences II—Defences which Justify or Excuse the Offence 429

Introduction   430

Consent   430

Self-defence and the Prevention of Crime   431

  Introduction   431

Duress   439

   Introduction   439

   Duress by Threats or of Circumstances   440

   The Elements of the Defence   441

   Availability of the Defence   448

   Reform of Duress   449

Necessity   451

   Medical Necessity   452

   Necessity and Murder   452

   Necessity and other Crimes   455

   Arguments against the Existence of the Defence of Necessity   455

   Why should the Defence be Recognised   456

Marital Coercion and Superior Orders   457

● **Summary**   457
● **End of Chapter Question**   458
● **Further Reading**   459
● **Self Test Questions**   459

Index   461

List of Figures

◀ ⋯⋯⋯⋯⋯⋯⋯⋯⋯⋯⋯⋯⋯⋯⋯⋯⋯⋯⋯⋯⋯⋯⋯⋯⋯⋯⋯⋯⋯⋯⋯⋯⋯⋯⋯⋯⋯

1	Illustration of the hierarchy of the criminal courts and the appeals process	7
2	Causation—Summary	40
3	Grid summarising the development of the law on oblique intent	55
3.1	The relationship between intention and foresight in homicide	58
4	The types of manslaughter	90
4.1	A comparison of provocation and the loss of self-control defence	113
5	Illustration of the different ways in which s.18 may be committed	151
5.1	Illustration of issues which arise when prosecuting stalking cases under the 1861 and 1997 Acts	158
5.2	Summary of liability	168
5.3	Summary of the effect of consent	169
6	Summary of consent issues in offence of rape	205
7	Summary of dishonesty	238
8	Illustration of the different ways in which burglary may be committed	256
8.1	The abolished deception offences	277
9	Illustration of the ways in which the simple and aggravated offences of criminal damage may be committed	301
10	When acts are merely preparatory	319
10.1	Requirements for an attempt	322
10.2	Encouraging or assisting crimes	329
10.3	The elements of the Serious Crime Act Offences	333
11	Summary of the four modes of secondary liability referred to in s.8 of the Accessories and Abettors Act 1861	344
11.1	Summary of the requirements of secondary liability	351
11.2	Over to you . . . Flowchart	360
11.3	Criminal Vicarious Liability	373

11.4 Summary of A's liability for the murder of V committed by P during a joint enterprise to commit offence X   379

12 Summary of mistake   388

12.1 Intoxication   402

12.2 Sane and Insane Automatism   422

13 The defence of self-defence   438

13.1 The requirements and limitations imposed in the defence of duress   450

Table of Cases

A (Children) (Conjoined Twins: medical treatment) (No.1), Re [2001] Fam. 147; [2001] 2 W.L.R. 480 CA   pp.54, 55, 58, 85, 86, 454, 456, 457, 459

A (Mental Patient: Sterilisation), Re [2000] 1 F.L.R. 549; [2000] 1 F.C.R. 193 CA   pp.452, 453

A (A Juvenile) v R. [1978] Crim. L.R. 689   p.293

Adams v R [1995] 1 W.L.R. 52; [1995] B.C.C. 376 PC (NZ)   p.280

Airedale NHS Trust v Bland [1993] A.C. 789; [1993] 2 W.L.R. 316 HL   pp.16, 58, 85, 452

Allchorn v Hopkins (1905) 69 J.P. 355   p.373

Allen v Whitehead [1930] 1 K.B. 211   p.372

Alphacell v Woodward [1972] A.C. 824; [1972] 2 W.L.R. 1320 HL   pp.73, 74, 78

Andrews v DPP [1937] A.C. 576; (1938) 26 Cr. App. R. 34 HL   pp.116, 122, 123

Attorney General for Jersey v Holley [2005] UKPC 23; [2005] 2 A.C. 580; [2005] 3 W.L.R.   pp.295, 105, 106, 107, 108, 112, 113

Attorney General for Northern Ireland v Gallagher [1963] A.C. 349; [1961] 3 W.L.R. 619 HL   pp.400, 402

Attorney General of Hong Kong v Chan Nai-Keung [1987] 1 W.L.R. 1339; (1987) 3 B.C.C. 403 PC (HK)   p.221

Attorney General's Reference (No.1 of 1974) [1974] Q.B. 744; [1974] 2 W.L.R. 891 CA   p.269

Attorney General's Reference (No.1 of 1975) [1975] Q.B. 773; [1975] 3 W.L.R. 11 CA   pp.342, 343, 344

Attorney General's References (Nos 1 and 2 of 1979) [1980] Q.B. 180; [1979] 3 W.L.R. 577 CA   pp.255, 320

Attorney General's Reference (No.6 of 1980) [1981] Q.B. 715; [1981] 3 W.L.R. 125 CA   pp.161, 162, 164

Attorney General's Reference (No.1 of 1982) [1983] Q.B. 751; [1983] 3 W.L.R. 72 CA   p.280

Attorney General's Reference (No.2 of 1982) [1984] Q.B. 624; [1984] 2 W.L.R. 447 CA   p.226

Attorney General's Reference (No.1 of 1983) [1985] Q.B. 182; [1984] 3 W.L.R. 686 CA   pp.229, 230

Attorney General's Reference (No.2 of 1983) [1984] Q.B. 456; [1984] 2 W.L.R. 465 CA   p.435

Attorney General's Reference (No.1 of 1985) [1986] Q.B. 491; [1986] 2 W.L.R. 733 CA   p.226

Attorney General's Reference (No.1 of 1992) [1993] 1 W.L.R. 274; [1993] 2 All E.R. 190 CA   pp.317, 319

Attorney General's Reference (No.2 of 1992) [1994] Q.B. 91; [1993] 3 W.L.R. 982 CA   p.410

Attorney General's Reference (No.3 of 1992) [1994] 1 W.L.R. 409; (1994) 98 Cr. App. R. 383 CA   p.320

Attorney General's Reference (No.3 of 1994) [1998] A.C. 245; [1997] 3 W.L.R. 421 HL   pp.66, 85, 125

Attorney General's Reference (No.2 of 1999) [2000] Q.B. 796; [2000] 3 W.L.R. 195 CA   pp.120, 128, 129, 377

Attorney General's Reference (No.3 of 2004) [2005] EWCA Crim 1882; [2006] Crim. L.R. 63   p.355

Atwal v Massey [1971] 3 All E.R. 881; (1972) 56 Cr. App. R. 6 DC   p.271

B (A Child) v DPP [2000] 2 A.C. 428; [2000] 2 W.L.R. 452 HL   pp.70, 71, 72, 160, 385, 387, 431

B and S v Leathley [1979] Crim. L.R. 314   p.255

Barnfather v Islington Education Authority [2003] EWHC 418 (Admin); [2003] 1 W.L.R. 2318; [2003] E.L.R. 263   p.76

Baron v Crown Prosecution Service Unreported June 13, 2000 DC   p.156

Beckford v R. [1988] A.C. 130; [1987] 3 W.L.R. 611 PC (Jamaica)   pp.86, 386, 437

Bedder v DPP [1954] 1 W.L.R. 1119; [1954] 2 All E.R. 801 HL   pp.102, 103

Blake v DPP [1993] Crim. L.R. 586; [1993] C.O.D. 374 DC   p.307

Boggeln v Williams [1978] 1 W.L.R. 873; [1978] 2 All E.R. 1061 QBD   p.234

Bratty v Attorney General of Northern Ireland [1963] A.C. 386; [1961] 3 W.L.R. 965 HL   pp.14, 409, 416

Bravery v Bravery [1954] 1 W.L.R. 1169; [1954] 3 All E.R. 59 CA   p.161

Broome v Perkins (1987) 85 Cr. App. R. 321; [1987] R.T.R. 321 DC   p.410

Brown v R. [2005] UKPC 18; [2006] 1 A.C. 1; [2005] 2 W.L.R. 1558 PC (Jamaica)   p.119

Buckoke v Greater London Council [1971] Ch. 655; [1971] 2 W.L.R. 760 CA   pp.455, 457

Burrell v Harmer [1967] Crim. L.R. 169; (1966) 116 N.L.J. 1658 DC   p.161

CR v United Kingdom. *See* SW v United Kingdom

Callow v Tillstone (1900) 83 L.T. 411; (1900) 64 J.P. 823   pp.67, 77, 345

Caurti v DPP [2001] EWHC Admin 867; [2002] Crim. L.R. 131   p.157

Chamberlain v Lindon [1998] 1 W.L.R. 1252; [1998] 2 All E.R. 538 DC   pp.308, 311

Chan Wing-Siu v R. [1985] A.C. 168; [1984] 3 W.L.R. 677 PC (HK)   p.353

Chi-Cheung v R [1995] 1 A.C. 111; [1994] 3 W.L.R. 514 PC (HK)   pp.45, 327

Clode v Barnes [1974] 1 W.L.R. 544; [1974] 1 All E.R. 1166 DC   p.370

Cobb v Williams [1973] R.T.R. 113; [1973] Crim. L.R. 243 DC   p.370

Collins v Wilcock [1984] 1 W.L.R. 1172; [1984] 3 All E.R. 374 DC   pp.143, 160

Comer v Bloomfield (1970) 55 Cr. App. R. 305   p.316

Commissioner of Police of the Metropolis v Charles [1977] A.C. 177; [1976] 3 W.L.R. 431 HL   p.282

Commissioner of Police of the Metropolis v Streeter (1980) 71 Cr. App. R. 113 DC   p.269

Coppen v Moore (No.2) [1898] 2 Q.B. 306   pp.370, 371

Corcoran v Anderton (1980) 71 Cr. App. R. 104; [1980] Crim. L.R. 385 DC   pp.212, 249

Corcoran v Whent [1977] Crim. L.R. 52 DC   p.227

Cox v Riley (1986) 83 Cr. App. R. 54; [1986] Crim. L.R. 460 QBD   p.294

Cresswell v DPP [2006] EWHC 3379 (Admin); (2007) 171 J.P. 233; (2007) 171 J.P.N. 500 DC   p.223

Davidge v Bunnett [1984] Crim. L.R. 297 DC   p.228

Dennis Clothier and Sons Ltd Unreported 2003   p.130

DPP v Armstrong [2000] Crim. L.R. 379; (1999) 96(45) L.S.G. 32 DC   p.336

DPP v Beard [1920] A.C. 479; (1920) 14 Cr. App. R. 159 HL   p.390

DPP v DA (A Child) [2001] Crim. L.R. 140 DC   p.149

DPP v Doot [1973] A.C. 807; [1973] 2 W.L.R. 532 HL   p.324

DPP v Gohill [2007] EWHC 239 (Admin)   p.235

DPP v Gomez [1993] A.C. 442; [1992] 3 W.L.R. 1067 HL   pp.213, 214, 215, 216, 217, 218, 219, 231, 232, 244, 245, 249, 250

DPP v Green [2004] EWHC 1225 (QB)   p.154

DPP v Harper [1997] 1 W.L.R. 1406; (1997) 161 J.P. 697 QBD   p.413

DPP v Howard [2008] EWHC 608 (Admin)   p.154

DPP v K [1997] 1 Cr. App. R. 36; [1997] Crim. L.R. 121 DC   p.363

DPP v K (A Minor) [1990] 1 W.L.R. 1067; [1990] 1 All E.R. 331 QBD   p.144

DPP v Lavender [1994] Crim. L.R. 297 DC   p.241

DPP v Little [1992] Q.B. 645; [1992] 2 W.L.R. 460 QBD   p.139

DPP v M [2004] EWHC 1453 (Admin); [2004] 1 W.L.R. 2758; [2005] Crim. L.R. 392   p.305

DPP v Majewski [1977] A.C. 443 [1976] 2 W.L.R. 623 HL   pp.390, 391, 392, 393, 394, 396, 397, 399, 400, 406, 407, 408, 411, 422, 424

DPP v Morgan [1976] A.C. 182; [1975] 2 W.L.R. 913 HL   pp.176, 385, 386, 387, 394, 436

DPP v Newbury [1977] A.C. 500; [1976] 2 W.L.R. 918 HL   pp.122, 123, 124, 125

DPP v Ramsdale [2001] EWHC Admin 106   p.156

DPP v Ray [1974] A.C. 370; [1973] 3 W.L.R. 359 HL   p.282

DPP v Rogers [1998] Crim. L.R. 202 DC   p.442

DPP v Santa-Bermudez [2003] EWHC 2908 (Admin); (2004) 168 J.P. 373; [2004] Crim. L.R. 471   pp.21, 144

DPP v Smith [1961] A.C. 290; [1960] 3 W.L.R. 546 HL   pp.45, 87, 146, 148

DPP v Stonehouse [1978] A.C. 55; [1977] 3 W.L.R. 143 HL   p.316

DPP for Northern Ireland v Lynch [1975] A.C. 653; [1975] 2 W.L.R. 641 HL   pp.343, 348, 441, 448

DPP for Northern Ireland v Maxwell [1978] 1 W.L.R. 1350; [1978] 3 All E.R. 1140 HL   p.350

Dobson v North Tyneside HA [1997] 1 W.L.R. 596; [1996] 4 All E.R. 474 CA   p.224

Drake v DPP (1994) 158 J.P. 828; [1994] R.T.R. 411 QBD   p.294

Edwards v Ddin [1976] 1 W.L.R. 942; [1976] 3 All E.R. 705 QBD   pp.227, 245

Edwards (alias David Christopher Murray) v R. [1973] A.C. 648; [1972] 3 W.L.R. 893 PC (Hong Kong)   p.100

Elliot v C (A Minor) [1983] 1 W.L.R. 939; [1983] 2 All E.R. 1005 DC   p.64

Environment Agency (formerly National Rivers Authority) v Empress Car Co (Aber-tillery) Ltd [1999] 2 A.C. 22; [1998] 2 W.L.R. 350 HL   pp.24, 28, 29, 37, 39, 135

F v West Berkshire HA [1990] 2 A.C. 1; [1989] 2 W.L.R. 1025 HL   pp.143, 452, 456

Fagan v Commissioner of Police of the Metropolis [1969] 1 Q.B. 439; [1968] 3 W.L.R. 1120 DC   pp.21, 37, 139, 140, 143, 144

Ferguson v Weaving [1951] 1 K.B. 814; [1951] 1 All E.R. 412 DC   pp.348, 373

Frenchay Healthcare NHS Trust v S [1994] 1 W.L.R. 601; [1994] 2 All E.R. 403   p.17

G v DPP [2004] EWHC 183 (Admin); (2004) 168 J.P. 313; (2004) 168 J.P.N. 417   p.154

Gammon (Hong Kong) Ltd v Attorney General of Hong Kong [1985] A.C. 1; [1984] 3 W.L.R. 437 PC (HK)   p.69

Gardener v Akeroyd [1952] 2 Q.B. 743; [1952] 2 All E.R. 306 DC   p.373

Gillick v West Norfolk and Wisbech AHA [1986] A.C. 112; [1985] 3 W.L.R. 830 HL   p.348

Governor of Pentonville Prison Ex p. Osman (No.1) [1990] 1 W.L.R. 277; [1989] 3 All E.R. 701 QBD   p.212

Gray's Haulage Co Ltd v Arnold [1966] 1 W.L.R. 534; [1966] 1 All E.R. 896 QBD   p.70

Griffiths v Studebakers Ltd [1924] 1 K.B. 102 KBD   p.371

H v United Kingdom (15023/89), April 4, 1990 ECtHR   p.9

HL Bolton Engineering Co Ltd v PJ Graham and Sons Ltd [1957] 1 Q.B. 159; [1956] 3 W.L.R. 804 CA   p.374

Hardman v Chief Constable of Avon and Somerset [1986] Crim. L.R. 330   pp.293, 310

Harrow LBC v Shah [2000] 1 W.L.R. 83; [1999] 3 All E.R. 302 QBD   pp.74, 75, 77, 371

Haughton v Smith [1975] A.C. 476; [1974] 2 W.L.R. 1 HL   p.268

Haystead v Chief Constable of Derbyshire [2000] 3 All E.R. 890; [2000] 2 Cr. App. R. 339 DC   pp.139, 144

Hill v Baxter [1958] 1 Q.B. 277; [1958] 2 W.L.R. 76 QBD   p.411

Hipgrave v Jones [2004] EWHC 2901 (QB); [2005] 2 F.L.R. 174 QBD   p.156

Hobson v Impett (1957) 41 Cr. App. R. 138 DC   p.262

Holmes v DPP [1946] A.C. 588; (1946) 31 Cr. App. R. 123 HL   p.99

Hui Chi-Ming v R. [1992] 1 A.C. 34; [1991] 3 W.L.R. 495 PC (HK)   p.354

Hyam v DPP [1975] A.C. 55; [1974] 2 W.L.R. 607 HL   pp.47, 56, 87

Invicta Plastics Ltd v Clare [1976] R.T.R. 251; [1976] Crim. L.R. 131 DC   p.328

JJC (A Minor) v Eisenhower [1984] Q.B. 331; [1983] 3 W.L.R. 537 QBD   pp.148, 171

Jaggard v Dickinson [1981] Q.B. 527; [1981] 2 W.L.R. 118 DC   pp.309, 403

James & Son v Smee [1955] 1 Q.B. 78; [1954] 3 W.L.R. 631 QBD   pp.72, 77

Johnson v Phillips [1976] 1 W.L.R. 65; [1975] 3 All E.R. 682 QBD   p.455

Johnson v Youden [1950] 1 K.B. 544; [1950] 1 All E.R. 300 DC   p.347

Kelly v DPP [2002] EWHC 1428 (Admin); (2002) 166 J.P. 621; [2003] Crim. L.R. 45   p.156

Knuller (Publishing, Printing and Promotions Ltd) v DPP 1973] A.C. 435; [1972] 3 W.L.R. 143 HL   p.4

Kokkinakis v Greece (1994) 17 E.H.R.R. 397 ECtHR   pp.76, 120

Laskey v United Kingdom (1997) 24 E.H.R.R. 39 ECtHR   p.165

Lau v DPP [2000] 1 F.L.R. 799; [2000] Crim. L.R. 580 DC   pp.156, 157

Lewis v Lethbridge [1987] Crim. L.R. 59 DC   p.228

Lister v Hesley Hall Ltd [2001] UKHL 22; [2002] 1 A.C. 215; [2001] 2 W.L.R. 1311   p.370

Logdon v DPP [1976] Crim. L.R. 121 DC   p.139

Low v Blease [1975] Crim. L.R. 513; (1975) 119 S.J. 695 DC   p.223

Luc Thiet Thuan v R. [1997] A.C. 131; [1996] 3 W.L.R. 45 PC (HK)   pp.104, 105, 106, 112

MacAngus v HM Advocate [2009] HCJAC 8; 2009 S.L.T. 137; 2009 S.C.L. 408; 2009 S.C.C.R. 238   p.34

McCann v United Kingdom (1995) 21 E.H.R.R. 97 ECtHR   p.439

Magna Plant Ltd v Mitchell [1966] Crim. L.R. 394; 116 N.L.J. 780 DC   p.376

Majrowski v Guy's and St Thomas's NHS Trust [2006] UKHL 34; [2007] 1 A.C. 224; [2006] 3 W.L.R. 125   p.370

Mancini v DPP [1942] A.C. 1; [1941] 3 All E.R. 272 HL   pp.102, 107

Mattis v Pollock (t/a Flamingos Nightclub) [2002] EWHC 2177 QB   p.370

Meli v R. [1954] 1 W.L.R. 228; [1954] 1 All E.R. 373 PC   p.37

Melias v Preston [1957] 2 Q.B. 380; [1957] 3 W.L.R. 42 DC   p.371

Meridian Global Funds Management Asia Ltd v Securities Commission [1995] 2 A.C. 500; [1995] 3 W.L.R. 413 PC (NZ)   p.377

Minor v DPP (1988) 86 Cr. App. R. 378; (1988) 152 J.P. 30 QBD   p.273

Moore v DPP Unreported February 2, 2010   pp.318, 319, 323

Morphitis v Salmon (1990) 154 J.P. 365; [1990] Crim. L.R. 48 DC   pp.293, 294

National Coal Board v Gamble [1959] 1 Q.B. 11; [1958] 3 W.L.R. 434 DC   pp.343, 347

National Rivers Authority (Southern Region) v Alfred McAlpine Homes East Ltd [1994] 4 All E.R. 286; [1994] Env. L.R. 198 QBD   p.372

Norfolk Constabulary v Seekings and Gould [1986] Crim. L.R. 167   p.255

Oxford v Moss (1979) 68 Cr. App. R. 183; [1979] Crim. L.R. 119 QBD   p.223

Palmer v R [1971] A.C. 814; [1971] 2 W.L.R. 831 PC (Jamaica)   pp.431, 434

Parry v DPP [2004] EWHC 3112 (Admin); [2005] A.C.D. 64   p.154

People v Beardsley (1907) 113 N.W. 1128   p.18

Pharmaceutical Society of Great Britain v Storkwain Ltd [1986] 1 W.L.R. 903; [1986] 2 All E.R. 635 HL   p.73

R. v Abdul-Hussain [1999] Crim. L.R. 570 CA   p.443

R. v Acott [1997] 1 W.L.R. 306; [1997] 1 All E.R. 706 HL   p.98

R. v Adomako [1995] 1 A.C. 171; [1994] 3 W.L.R. 288 HL   pp.63, 116, 117, 118, 119, 120, 121, 122, 131, 135

R. v Ahluwalia [1992] 4 All E.R. 889; (1993) 96 Cr. App. R. 133 CA   pp.93, 101, 108, 113

R. v Ahmad (1987) 84 Cr. App. R. 64; (1986) 18 H.L.R. 416 CA   p.16

R. v Aitkin [1992] 1 W.L.R. 1006; [1992] 4 All E.R. 541   pp.163, 398

R. v Ali (1994) 16 Cr. App. R. (S.) 692; [1995] Crim. L.R. 303 CA   p.446

R. v Allen [1985] A.C. 1029; [1985] 3 W.L.R. 107 HL   p.277

R. v Allen [1988] Crim. L.R. 698 CA   pp.393, 395

R. v Altham [2006] EWCA Crim 7; [2006] 1 W.L.R. 3287; [2006] 2 Cr. App. R. 8   p.455

R. v Anderson [1966] 2 Q.B. 110; [1966] 2 W.L.R. 1195 CA   p.353

R. v Anderson [1986] A.C. 27; [1985] 3 W.L.R. 268 HL   p.327

R. v Antoine [2001] 1 A.C. 340; [2000] 2 W.L.R. 703 HL   p.423

R. v Atakpu [1994] Q.B. 69; [1993] 3 W.L.R. 812 CA   pp.218, 219, 250

R. v Aziz [1993] Crim. L.R. 708 CA (Crim Div)   p.276

R. v B [2006] EWCA Crim 2945; [2007] 1 W.L.R. 1567; [2007] 1 Cr. App. R. 29   p.202

R. v Badza [2009] EWCA Crim 2695   p.349

R. v Bailey (1983) 77 Cr. App. R. 76   pp.390, 399, 401, 411, 412, 427

R. v Baillie [1995] 2 Cr. App. R. 31; [1995] Crim. L.R. 739 CA   pp.101, 112, 113

R. v Bainbridge [1960] 1 Q.B. 129; [1959] 3 W.L.R. 656 CA   pp.343, 344, 350

R. v Baker [1994] Crim. L.R. 444 CA   p.365

R. v Baker [1999] 2 Cr. App. R. 335 CA   p.447

R. v Baker [1997] Crim. L.R. 497 CA   pp.307, 442

R. v Baker   p.311

R. v Baker   p.383

R. v Ball [1989] Crim. L.R. 730 CA   p.124

R. v Barnard (1980) 70 Cr. App. R. 28; [1980] Crim. L.R. 235 CA   p.324

R. v Barnes [2004] EWCA Crim 3246; [2005] 1 W.L.R. 910; [2005] 2 All E.R. 113   pp.162, 164

R. v Bateman (1925) 19 Cr. App. R. 8   pp.115, 116

R. v Becerra (1975) 62 Cr. App. R. 212 CA   pp.364, 366, 383

R. v Belfon [1976] 1 W.L.R. 741; [1976] 3 All E.R. 46 CA   p.151

R. v Bell [1984] 3 All E.R. 842; [1985] R.T.R. 202 CA   p.14

R. v Benge (1865) 4 F. & F. 504   p.26

R. v Bennett [2007] EWCA Crim 2815   p.251

R. v Bentham [2005] UKHL 18; [2005] 1 W.L.R. 1057; [2005] 2 All E.R. 65   pp.249, 256

R. v Betts (1931) 22 Cr. App. R. 148   p.343

R. v Bevans (1988) 87 Cr. App. R. 64; [1988] Crim. L.R. 236 CA   p.260

R. v Bird [1985] 1 W.L.R. 816 [1985] 2 All E.R. 513 CA   p.435

R. v Blake [1997] 1 W.L.R. 1167; [1997] 1 All E.R. 963 CA   pp.75, 308

R. v Blaue [1975] 1 W.L.R. 1411; [1975] 3 All E.R. 446 CA   p.36

R. v Bloxham [1983] 1 A.C. 109; [1982] 2 W.L.R. 392 HL   p.264

R. v Bollom [2003] EWCA Crim 2846; [2004] 2 Cr. App. R. 6   p.148

R. v Bonner [1970] 1 W.L.R. 838; [1970] 2 All E.R. 97 (Note) CA   p.225

R. v Bourne (1952) 36 Cr. App. R. 125 CA   p.363

R. v Bournewood Community and Mental Health NHS Trust Ex p. L [1999] 1 A.C. 458; [1998] 3 W.L.R. 107 HL   p.452

R. v Bowen [1997] 1 W.L.R. 372; [1996] 4 All E.R. 837 CA   p.445

R. v Bowles and Bowles [2004] 8 Arch. News 2   pp.318, 319

R. v Boyea (1992) 156 J.P. 505; [1992] Crim. L.R. 574 CA   p.164

R. v Brady [2006] EWCA Crim 2413; [2007] Crim. L.R. 564   pp.64, 149, 298

R. v Bree [2007] EWCA Crim 804; [2008] Q.B. 131; [2007] 3 W.L.R. 600   pp.203, 207

R. v Briggs [2003] EWCA Crim 3662; [2004] 1 Cr. App. R. 34; [2004] Crim. L.R. 495   p.216

R. v Brindley [1971] 2 Q.B. 300; [1971] 2 W.L.R. 895 CA   p.369

R. v Brooks (1982) 76 Cr. App. R. 66; (1983) 2 Tr. L.R. 85 CA   p.275

R. v Brown (1776) 168 E.R. 177   p.108

R. v Brown [1972] 2 Q.B. 229; [1972] 3 W.L.R. 11 CA   p.107

R. v Brown [1985] Crim. L.R. 212 CA   p.252

R. v Brown [1994] 1 A.C. 212; [1993] 2 W.L.R. 556 HL   pp.3, 143, 160, 161, 162, 163, 164, 165, 431

R. v Brown [1998] Crim. L.R. 485   p.148

R. v Bryce [2004] EWCA Crim 1231; [2004] 2 Cr. App. R. 35   pp.342, 344, 347, 348, 352

R. v Bryson [1985] Crim. L.R. 669 CA   pp.57, 151

R. v Bundy [1977] 1 W.L.R. 914; [1977] 2 All E.R. 382 CA   p.273

R. v Burgess [1991] 2 Q.B. 92; [1991] 2 W.L.R. 1206 CA   pp.416, 417

R. v Burgess and McLean [1995] Crim. L.R. 425   p.99

R. v Burroughes Unreported November 29, 2000 CA   p.265

R. v Byrne [1960] 2 Q.B. 396; [1960] 3 W.L.R. 440 CA   pp.92, 93, 96

R. v C [2008] EWCA Crim 1155; [2009] 1 Cr. App. R. 15; (2008) 105(23) L.S.G. 26;   p.197

R. v C (Sean Peter) [2001] EWCA Crim 1251; [2001] 2 F.L.R. 757; [2001] 3 F.C.R. 409   p.157

R. v Cahill [1993] Crim. L.R. 141 CA   pp.240, 241

R. v Cairns [1999] 2 Cr. App. R. 137; [2000] R.T.R. 15 CA   p.444

R. v Cairns [2002] EWCA Crim 2838; [2003] 1 W.L.R. 796; [2003] 1 Cr. App. R. 38   p.457

R. v Cakmak [2002] EWCA Crim 500; [2002] 2 Cr. App. R. 10; [2002] Crim. L.R. 581   p.303

R. v Caldwell [1982] A.C. 341; [1981] 2 W.L.R. 509 HL   pp.4, 62, 63, 64, 65, 116, 282, 298, 394

R. v Calhaem [1985] Q.B. 808; [1985] 2 W.L.R. 826 CA   pp.343, 344

R. v Campbell (1991) 93 Cr. App. R. 350; [1991] Crim. L.R. 268 CA   pp.317, 319

R. v Campbell [1997] Crim. L.R. 495   p.91

R. v Camplin [1978] A.C. 705; [1978] 2 W.L.R. 679 HL   pp.103, 104, 105, 111, 112, 113

R. v Carey [2006] EWCA Crim 17; [2006] Crim. L.R. 842   p.124
R. v Cash [1985] Q.B. 801; [1985] 2 W.L.R. 735 CA   p.267
R. v Cato [1976] 1 W.L.R. 110; [1976] 1 All E.R. 260 CA   p.33
R. v Chan-Fook [1994] 1 W.L.R. 689; [1994] 2 All E.R. 552 CA   pp.146, 170
R. v Cheshire [1991] 1 W.L.R. 844; [1991] 3 All E.R. 670 CA   pp.24, 29, 135
R. v Chrastny (No.1) [1991] 1 W.L.R. 1381; [1992] 1 All E.R. 189 CA   p.325
R. v Church [1966] 1 Q.B. 59; [1965] 2 W.L.R. 1220 CA   pp.37, 123, 124
R. v Clarence (1888) 22 Q.B. 23   pp.166, 167
R. v Clark [2001] EWCA Crim 884; [2002] 1 Cr. App. R. 14; [2001] Crim. L.R. 572   p.221
R. v Clarke [1972] 1 All E.R. 219; (1972) 56 Cr. App. R. 225 CA   p.414
R. v Clarkson [1971] 1 W.L.R. 1402; [1971] 3 All E.R. 344   p.346
R. v Clear [1968] 1 Q.B. 670; [1968] 2 W.L.R. 122 CA   pp.258, 259
R. v Clegg [1995] 1 A.C. 482; [1995] 2 W.L.R. 80 HL   pp.436, 457
R. v Clouden [1987] Crim. L.R. 56 CA   p.249
R. v Codere (1917) 12 Cr. App. R. 21 CA   p.418
R. v Cogan [1976] Q.B. 217; [1975] 3 W.L.R. 316 CA   pp.342, 362
R. v Cole [1994] Crim. L.R. 582 CA   p.446
R. v Coleman (1986) 150 J.P. 175; [1986] Crim. L.R. 56 CA   p.266
R. v Coles (1980) 144 J.P.N. 528   p.94
R. v Collins [1973] Q.B. 100; [1972] 3 W.L.R. 243 CA   pp.252, 253
R. v Collister (1955) 39 Cr. App. R. 100 CA   p.258
R. v Concannon [2002] Crim. L.R. 213   p.354
R. v Coney (1882) 8 Q.B.D. 534   p.346
R. v Constanza [1997] 2 Cr. App. R. 492; [1997] Crim. L.R. 576 CA   pp.140, 141, 170
R. v Conway [1989] Q.B. 290; [1988] 3 W.L.R. 1238 CA   pp.440, 444, 458
R. v Coomber [2005] EWCA Crim 1113 CA   pp.187, 207
R. v Cooper [2004] EWCA Crim 1382 CA   p.298
R. v Corbett [1996] Crim. L.R. 594 CA   p.36
R. v Court [1989] A.C. 28; [1988] 2 W.L.R. 1071 HL   p.179
R. v Cunningham [1957] 2 Q.B. 396; [1957] 3 W.L.R. 76 CA   pp.61, 62
R. v Cunningham [1982] A.C. 566; [1981] 3 W.L.R. 223 HL   p.87
R. v Curtis [2010] EWCA Crim 123; [2010] 1 Cr. App. R. 31   p.156
R. v D [2006] EWCA Crim 1139; [2006] 2 Cr. App. R. 24; [2006] Crim. L.R. 923   p.146
R. v Dalby [1982] 1 W.L.R. 621; [1982] 1 All E.R. 916 CA   pp.33, 125
R. v Dalloway (1847) 2 Cox 273   p.25
R. v Davenport [1954] 1 W.L.R. 569; [1954] 1 All E.R. 602 CA   p.220
R. v Davies [1975] Q.B. 691; [1975] 2 W.L.R. 586 CA   pp.99, 112
R. v Davis (1881) 14 Cox C.C. 563   p.405
R. v Dawson (1976) 64 Cr. App. R. 170   p.249
R. v Dawson (1985) 81 Cr. App. R. 150; (1985) 149 J.P. 513 CA   pp.123, 124
R. v Day (1845) 1 Cox C.C. 207   p.143
R. v Day [2001] EWCA Crim 1594; [2001] Crim. L.R. 984   p.362

R. v Dear [1996] Crim. L.R. 595 CA   p.32

R. v Denton [1981] 1 W.L.R. 1446; [1982] 1 All E.R. 65 CA   p.306

R. v Devonald [2008] EWCA 527   p.202

R. v Dica [2004] EWCA Crim 1103; [2004] Q.B. 1257; [2004] 3 W.L.R. 213   pp.118, 148, 149, 166, 167

R. v Dietschmann [2003] UKHL 10; [2003] 1 A.C. 1209; [2003] 2 W.L.R. 613   p.94

R. v DPP [2007] EWHC 739 (Admin); (2007) 171 J.P. 404 DC   p.249

R. v Dix (1982) 74 Cr. App. R. 306; [1982] Crim. L.R. 302 CA   p.94

R. v Dougal Unreported November 2005   pp.202, 203

R. v Doughty (1986) 83 Cr. App. R. 319; [1986] Crim. L.R. 625 CA   pp.99, 113

R. v Doukas [1978] 1 W.L.R. 372; [1978] 1 All E.R. 1061 CA   p.273

R. v Drayton [2005] EWCA Crim 2013; (2005) 169 J.P. 593; [2006] Crim. L.R. 243   p.302

R. v Dudley [1989] Crim. L.R. 57 CA   p.301

R. v Dudley [2006] EWCA Crim 387; [2006] 2 Cr. App. R. (S.) 77   p.115

R. v Dudley and Stephens (1884–85) L.R. 14 Q.B.D. 273   pp.452, 453, 454, 455, 456, 458

R. v Duffy [1949] 1 All E.R. 932 CA   pp.98, 99, 100, 108, 113

R. v Dunbar [1958] 1 Q.B. 1; [1957] 3 W.L.R. 330 CA   p.91

R. v Dunnington [1984] Q.B. 472; [1984] 2 W.L.R. 125 CA   p.314

R. v Dytham [1979] Q.B. 722; [1979] 3 W.L.R. 467 CA   pp.15, 17

R. v Eagleton (1855) Dears. 515   p.316

R. v Easom [1971] 2 Q.B. 315; [1971] 3 W.L.R. 82 CA   p.243

R. v Ellames [1974] 1 W.L.R. 1391; [1974] 3 All E.R. 130 CA   p.273

R. v Emery (1993) 14 Cr. App. R. (S.) 394 CA   p.445

R. v Emmett, *The Times,* October 15, 1999 CA   pp.164, 165

R. v Enoch (1833) 5 Car. & P. 539   p.85

R. v Evans [2009] EWCA Crim 650; [2009] 1 W.L.R. 1999; [2010] 1 All E.R. 13   pp.20, 21, 22, 22, 34 118, 126

R. v Feely [1973] Q.B. 530; [1973] 2 W.L.R. 201 CA   pp.233, 234, 235, 236

R. v Fenton (1975) 61 Cr. App. R. 261; [1975] Crim. L.R. 712 CA   p.94

R. v Fernandes [1996] Cr. App. R. 175 CA   p.240

R. v Fiak [2005] EWCA Crim 2381; [2005] Po. L.R. 211   p.293

R. v Finlay [2003] EWCA Crim 3868   p.34

R. v Firth (1990) 91 Cr. App. R. 217; (1990) 154 J.P. 576 CA   pp.283, 284

R. v Fisher (1865) LR 1 CCR 7 DC   p.294

R. v Fitzmaurice [1983] Q.B. 1083; [1983] 2 W.L.R. 227 CA   p.336

R. v Fitzpatrick [1977] N.I. 20 CA   p.447

R. v Flatt [1996] Crim. L.R. 576 CA   p.446

R. v Flattery (1877) 2 Q.B.D. 410   pp.201, 202

R. v Forbes [2001] UKHL 40; [2002] 2 A.C. 512; [2001] 3 W.L.R. 428   p.386

R. v Forsyth [1997] 2 Cr. App. R. 299; [1997] Crim. L.R. 581 CA   pp.270, 271

R. v **Fotheringham** (1988) 88 Cr. App. R. 206; [1988] Crim. L.R. 846 CA   p.403
R. v **Francis** [1982] Crim. L.R. 363 CA   p.257
R. v **Franklin** (1883) 15 Cox C.C. 163   p.122
R. v **G** [2003] UKHL 50; [2004] 1 A.C. 1034; [2003] 3 W.L.R. 1060   pp.4, 61, 62, 63, 64, 298, 399, 412
R. v **G** [2008] UKHL 37; [2009] 1 A.C. 92; [2008] 1 W.L.R. 1379   p.189
R. v **G**   p.116
R. v **G**   p.310
R. v **Gallasso** (1994) 98 Cr. App. R. 284; [1993] Crim. L.R. 459 CA   p.215
R. v **Gamble** [1989] N.I. 268   pp.356, 361
R. v **Garwood** [1987] 1 W.L.R. 319; [1987] 1 All E.R. 1032 CA   p.259
R. v **Geddes** (1996) 160 J.P. 697; [1996] Crim. L.R. 894 CA   pp.317, 319, 323
R. v **George** [1956] Crim. L.R. 52   p.180
R. v **Ghosh** [1982] Q.B. 1053; [1982] 3 W.L.R. 110 CA   pp.45, 234, 235, 236, 237, 239, 244, 272, 276, 283, 287
R. v **Giannetto** [1997] 1 Cr. App. R. 1; [1996] Crim. L.R. 722 CA   pp.343, 345
R. v **Gibbins and Proctor** (1918) 13 Cr App. R. 134   p.18
R. v **Gilks** [1972] 1 W.L.R. 1341; [1972] 3 All E.R. 280 CA   p.229
R. v **Gilmartin** [1983] Q.B. 953; [1983] 2 W.L.R. 547 CA   p.282
R. v **Gilmour** [2000] N.I. 367; [2000] 2 Cr. App. R. 407 CA   pp.362, 364
R. v **Gingell** [2000] 1 Cr. App. R. 88; (1999) 163 J.P. 648 CA   p.265
R. v **Gittens** [1984] Q.B. 698; [1984] 3 W.L.R. 327 CA   p.94
R. v **Goodfellow** (1986) 83 Cr. App. R. 23; [1986] Crim. L.R. 468 CA   pp.123, 125
R. v **Gotts** [1992] 2 A.C. 412; [1992] 2 W.L.R. 284 HL   p.448
R. v **Gould** [1968] 2 Q.B. 65; [1968] 2 W.L.R. 643 CA   p.387
R. v **Graham** [1982] 1 W.L.R. 294; [1982] 1 All E.R. 801 CA   pp.441, 444, 445
R. v **Graham** [1997] 1 Cr. App. R. 302; [1997] Crim. L.R. 340 CA.   p.221
R. v **Grant** [2001] EWCA Crim 2611; [2002] Q.B. 1030; [2002] 2 W.L.R. 1409   p.423
R. v **Greatrex** [1999] 1 Cr. App. R. 126; [1998] Crim. L.R. 733 CA   pp.357, 383
R. v **Gregson** [2006] EWCA Crim 3364   pp.103l, 113
R. v **Griffiths** (1974) 60 Cr. App. R. 14 CA   pp.271, 272
R. v **Gross** (1913) 23 Cox CC 455   p.67
R. v **Grundy** [1977] Crim. L.R. 543 CA   pp.148, 365
R. v **Gullefer** [1990] 1 W.L.R. 1063; [1990] 3 All E.R. 882 CA   pp.316, 318, 319
R. v **H** [2005] EWCA Crim 732; [2005] 1 W.L.R. 2005; [2005] 2 All E.R. 859   pp.178, 179, 180
R. v **H** [2007] EWCA Crim 2056   pp.197, 204, 207
R. v **Haider Unreported** 1985 CA   p.263
R. v **Hale** [1978] Crim. L.R. 596   p.250
R. v **Hall** [1973] Q.B. 496; [1972] 3 W.L.R. 974 CA   p.228
R. v **Hall** (1985) 81 Cr. App. R. 260; [1985] Crim. L.R. 377 CA   p.271
R. v **Hallam** [1994] Crim. L.R. 323 CA   p.210

R. v Hancock [1986] A.C. 455; [1986] 2 W.L.R. 357 HL   pp.52, 53, 55

R. v Hardie [1985] 1 W.L.R. 64; [1984] 3 All E.R. 848 CA   pp.398, 399, 408, 411

R. v Harris (1976) 62 Cr. App. R. 28; [1976] Crim. L.R. 514 CA   pp.282, 289

R. v Harry [1974] Crim. L.R. 32   p.258

R. v Harvey (1981) 72 Cr. App. R. 139; [1981] Crim. L.R. 104 CA   p.259

R. v Hasan [2005] UKHL 22; [2005] 2 A.C. 467; [2005] 2 W.L.R.   pp.709, 386, 403,
    430, 440, 441, 443, 444, 447, 448, 449

R. v Hatton [2005] EWCA Crim 2951; [2006] 1 Cr. App. R. 16; [2006] Crim. L.R.
    353   p.404

R. v Hayward (1833) 6 Car. & P. 157   p.101

R. v Hayward (1908) 21 Cox C.C. 123   pp.35, 123

R. v Heard [2007] EWCA Crim 125; [2008] Q.B. 43; [2007] 3 W.L.R. 475 CA   pp.394,
    395, 396, 401

R. v Heath [2000] Crim. L.R. 109 CA   p.447

R. v Hegarty [1994] Crim. L.R. 353 CA   p.445

R. v Henderson and Battley Unreported November 24, 1984   p.293

R. v Hennessy [1989] 1 W.L.R. 287; [1989] 2 All E.R. 9 CA   pp.415, 416, 417, 427

R. v Hill (1988) 89 Cr. App. R. 74; [1989] Crim. L.R. 136 CA   pp.308, 311

R. v Hinks [2001] 2 A.C. 241; [2000] 3 W.L.R. 1590 HL   pp.214, 216, 217, 231, 244

R. v Hinton-Smith [2005] EWCA Crim 2575   p.184

R. v Hobson [1998] 1 Cr. App. R. 31; (1998) 43 B.M.L.R. 181 CA   p.94

R. v Holland (1841) 2 Mood. & R. 351   p.32

R. v Holloway [1994] Q.B. 302; [1993] 3 W.L.R. 927 CA   p.116

R. v Hood [2003] EWCA Crim 2772; [2004] 1 Cr. App. R. (S.) 73 CA   p.18

R. v Horne [1994] Crim. L.R. 584 CA   p.445

R. v Horrex [1999] Crim. L.R. 500   p.107

R. v Horseferry Road Magistrates Court Ex p. Siadatan [1991] 1 Q.B. 260; [1990] 3
    W.L.R. 1006 QBD   pp.141, 199

R. v Howe [1987] 1 A.C. 417; [1987] 2 W.L.R. 568 HL   pp.364, 441, 448

R. v Howells [1977] Q.B. 614; [1977] 2 W.L.R. 716 CA   p.72

R. v Hudson [1971] 2 Q.B. 202; [1971] 2 W.L.R. 1047 CA   p.446

R. v Hughes (1841) 9 Car. & P. 752   p.175

R. v Humphreys [1995] 4 All E.R. 1008; [1996] Crim. L.R. 431 CA   pp.104, 108

R. v Hunt (1978) 66 Cr. App. R. 105; [1977] Crim. L.R. 740 CA   pp.307, 311

R. v Ibrams (1982) 74 Cr. App. R. 154 CA   p.101

R. v Instan [1893] 1 Q.B. 450   p.19

R. v Ireland [1998] A.C. 147; [1997] 3 W.L.R. 534 HL   pp.139, 142, 148, 149, 155, 171

R. v Ismail [2005] EWCA Crim 397; [2005] 2 Cr. App. R. (S.) 88; [2005] Crim. L.R.
    491   p.175

R. v JF Alford Transport Ltd [1997] 2 Cr. App. R. 326; [1999] R.T.R. 51 CA   pp.346, 347

R. v JTB [2009] UKHL 20; [2009] 1 A.C. 1310; [2009] 2 W.L.R. 1088   p.424

R. v Jackson [1985] Crim. L.R. 444 CA   p.325

R. v Jackson [2009] UKPC 28 PC (Jamaica)   p.357

R. v Jackson Transport (Ossett) Ltd (1996) (November) H.S. at W. 4   p.130

R. v Jama [2004] EWCA Crim 960   p.93

R. v James [2006] EWCA Crim 14; [2006] Q.B. 588; [2006] 2 W.L.R. 887 CA (Crim Div)   pp.5, 106

R. v Jheeta [2007] EWCA Crim 1699; [2008] 1 W.L.R. 2582; [2007] 2 Cr. App. R. 34   pp.200, 202

R. v Johnson [1989] 1 W.L.R. 740; [1989] 2 All E.R. 839 CA   p.100

R. v Johnson [2007] EWCA Crim 1978; [2008] Crim. L.R. 132; (2007) 104(37) L.S.G. 35;   pp.418, 420

R. v Jones [1976] 1 W.L.R. 672; [1976] 3 All E.R. 54 CA   p.254

R. v Jones (1986) 83 Cr. App. R. 375; [1987] Crim. L.R. 123 CA   pp.163, 387

R. v Jones [1990] 1 W.L.R. 1057; [1990] 3 All E.R. 886 CA   pp.316, 319

R. v Jones [1997] Q.B. 798; [1997] 2 W.L.R. 792 CA   p.57

R. v Jones [2004] EWCA Crim 1981; [2005] Q.B. 259; [2004] 3 W.L.R. 1362 CA   p.307

R. v Jones [2007] EWCA Crim 1118; [2008] Q.B. 460; [2007] 3 W.L.R. 907   pp.191, 321

R. v Jordan (1956) 40 Cr. App. R. 152 CA   pp.29, 135

R. v Julien [1969] 1 W.L.R. 839; [1969] 2 All E.R. 856 CA   p.435

R. v K (Age of Consent: Reasonable Belief) [2001] UKHL 41; [2002] 1 A.C. 462; [2001] 3 W.L.R. 471   pp.72, 387

R. v Kanwar [1982] 1 W.L.R. 845; [1982] 2 All E.R. 528 CA   p.265

R. v Kelleher [2003] EWCA Crim 3525; (2003) 147 S.J.L.B. 1395   p.307

R. v Kelly (1992) 97 Cr. App. R. 245; [1993] Crim. L.R. 763 CA   p.257

R. v Kelly [1999] Q.B. 621; [1999] 2 W.L.R. 384 CA   pp.224, 225

R. v Kemp [1957] 1 Q.B. 399; [1956] 3 W.L.R. 724   p.414

R. v Kennedy [2007] UKHL 38; [2008] 1 A.C. 269; [2007] 3 W.L.R. 612   pp.33, 34, 125, 135

R. v Khan [1990] 1 W.L.R. 813; [1990] 2 All E.R. 783 CA   p.320

R. v Khan [1998] Crim L.R. 830 CA   pp.20, 118

R. v Khan [2009] EWCA Crim 2; [2009] 1 W.L.R. 2036; [2009] 4 All E.R. 544   pp.19, 22, 128

R. v Kimber [1983] 1 W.L.R. 1118; [1983] 3 All E.R. 316 CA   pp.160, 385, 431

R. v Kimsey [1996] Crim. L.R. 35   pp.26, 135

R. v Kingston [1995] 2 A.C. 355; [1994] 3 W.L.R. 519 HL   pp.390, 401, 406, 408

R. v Kite and OLL Ltd [1994] 144 N.L.J. 1735   p.130

R. v Klass [1998] 1 Cr. App. R. 453; (1998) 162 J.P. 105 CA   p.257

R. v Kohn (1979) 69 Cr. App. R. 395; [1979] Crim. L.R. 675 CA   p.221

R. v Konzani [2005] EWCA Crim 706; [2005] 2 Cr. App. R. 14; (2005) 149 S.J.L.B. 389   pp.118, 167

R. v Kopsch (1925) 19 Cr. App. R. 50   p.419

R. v Lamb [1967] 2 Q.B. 981; [1967] 3 W.L.R. 888 CA   pp.123, 139

R. v Lambert [2002] Q.B. 1112; [2001] 2 W.L.R. 211 CA   pp.9, 92

R. v Lambie [1982] A.C. 449; [1981] 3 W.L.R. 88 HL   p.282
R. v Larsonneur (1934) 24 Cr. App. R. 74 CA   p.68
R. v Latif [1996] 1 W.L.R. 104; [1996] 1 All E.R. 353 HL   pp.27, 135
R. v Latimer (1886) 17 Q.B.D. 359   pp.66, 135, 171
R. v Lawrence [1971] Crim. L.R. 645 CA   p.261
R. v Lawrence [1972] A.C. 626; [1971] 3 W.L.R. 225 HL   pp.213, 214, 245
R. v Lawrence [1982] A.C. 510; [1981] 2 W.L.R. 524 HL   p.63
R. v Le Brun [1992] Q.B. 61; [1991] 3 W.L.R. 653 CA   p.38
R. v Letenock (1917) 12 Cr. App. R. 221   p.108
R. v Lidar (1999) 4 Arch. News 3   p.115
R. v Linekar [1995] Q.B. 250; [1995] 2 W.L.R. 237 CA   p.202
R. v Lipman [1970] 1 Q.B. 152; [1969] 3 W.L.R. 819 CA   p.393
R. v Lloyd [1967] 1 Q.B. 175; [1966] 2 W.L.R. 13 CA   pp.94, 97
R. v Lloyd [1985] Q.B. 829; [1985] 3 W.L.R. 30 CA   pp.241, 242
R. v Longbottom (1849) 3 Cox C 439   p.25
R. v Loukes [1996] 1 Cr. App. R. 444; [1996] R.T.R. 164 CA   p.346
R. v Lowe [1973] Q.B. 702; [1973] 2 W.L.R. 481 CA   p.122
R. v Lyddaman [2006] EWCA 383   p.182
R. v McDavitt [1981] Crim. L.R. 843 CA   p.275
R. v McInnes [1971] 1 W.L.R. 1600; [1971] 3 All E.R. 295 CA   pp.432, 435
R. v McKechnie (1992) 94 Cr. App. R. 51; [1992] Crim. L.R. 194 CA   p.31
R. v McNamara and Bennett [2009] EWCA Crim 2530   p.51
R. v Mainwaring (1982) 74 Cr. App. R. 99 CA   p.228
R. v Malcherek [1981] 1 W.L.R. 690; [1981] 2 All E.R. 422 CA   pp.29, 85, 135
R. v Malone [1998] 2 Cr. App. R. 447; [1998] Crim. L.R. 834 CA   pp.197, 207
R. v Marjoram [2000] Crim. L.R. 372 CA   p.32
R. v Mark [2004] EWCA Crim. 2490   p.119
R. v Marshall [1998] 2 Cr. App. R. 282; (1998) 162 J.P. 489 CA   p.241
R. v Marston [2007] EWCA Crim 2477   p.198
R. v Martin (1881) 8 Q.B.D. 54   p.144
R. v Martin [1989] 1 All E.R. 652; (1989) 88 Cr. App. R. 343 CA   p.441
R. v Martin [2000] 2 Cr. App. R. 42; (2000) 164 J.P. 174 CA   p.444
R. v Martin [2001] EWCA Crim 2245; [2003] Q.B. 1; [2002] 2 W.L.R. 1   p.437
R. v Matthews [2003] 2 Cr. App. R. 461   pp.51, 54, 55, 56
R. v Meachen [2006] EWCA Crim 2414   pp.163, 164
R. v Mellor [1996] 2 Cr. App. R. 245; [1996] Crim. L.R. 743 CA   p.30
R. v Meredith [1973] Crim. L.R. 253   p.225
R. v Michael, 173 E.R. 867; (1840) 9 Car. & P. 356.   p.341
R. v Miller [1954] 2 Q.B. 282; [1954] 2 W.L.R. 138   p.146
R. v Miller, The Times, May 16, 1972   p.94
R. v Miller [1983] 2 A.C. 161; [1983] 2 W.L.R. 539 HL   pp.12, 16, 21, 21, 34, 118, 126, 144
R. v Millward (1994) 158 J.P. 1091; [1994] Crim. L.R. 527 CA   pp.345, 346, 363

R. v Misra [2004] EWCA 2375; [2005] 1 Cr. App. R. 21; [2005] Crim. L.R. 234   pp.119, 121, 126

R. v Mitchell [2008] EWCA Crim 2552; [2009] 1 Cr. App. R. 31; [2009] Crim. L.R. 287   p.366

R. v Mitchell [1995] Crim. L.R. 506   p.94

R. v Mitchell (1999) 163 J.P. 75; [1999] Crim. L.R. 496 CA   pp.365, 366

R. v M'Naghten (1843) 4 St. Tr. NS 847   pp.91, 405, 413, 414, 419, 422, 426

R. v Moloney [1985] A.C. 905; [1985] 2 W.L.R. 648 HL   pp.47, 50, 52, 53, 55, 56, 57, 59, 87, 135

R. v Moor Unreported May 11, 1999 Newcastle Crown Ct   p.58

R. v Morhall [1996] A.C. 90; [1995] 3 W.L.R. 330 HL   pp.101, 103, 104, 105, 107, 112, 113

R. v Morris [1984] A.C. 320; [1983] 3 W.L.R. 697 HL   pp.211, 212, 213, 214, 245, 249, 382

R. v Morrison (1989) 89 Cr. App. R. 17 CA   p.151

R. v Mowatt [1968] 1 Q.B. 421; [1967] 3 W.L.R. 1192 CA   p.150

R. v Moys (1984) 79 Cr. App. R. 72; [1984] Crim. L.R. 494 CA   p.271

R. v Muhamad [2002] EWCA Crim 1856; [2003] Q.B. 1031; [2003] 2 W.L.R. 1050   pp.71, 72, 76

R. v Nash [1999] Crim. L.R. 308   p.315

R. v Naviede [1997] Crim. L.R. 662   p.216

R. v Navvabi [1986] 1 W.L.R. 1311; [1986] 3 All E.R. 102 CA   p.213

R. v Nedrick [1986] 1 W.L.R. 1025; [1986] 3 All E.R. 1 CA   pp.52, 53, 55

R. v Ngan [1998] 1 Cr. App. R. 331; (1997) 94(33) L.S.G. 27 CA   p.212

R. v Nicholls (1874) 13 Cox C.C. 75   p.19

R. v Nicklin [1977] 1 W.L.R. 403; [1977] 2 All E.R. 444 CA   p.261

R. v O'Connor [1991] Crim. L.R. 135; (1992) 13 Cr. App. R. (S.) 188 QBD   p.404

R. v O'Flaherty [2004] EWCA Crim 526; [2004] 2 Cr. App. R. 20; [2004] Crim. L.R. 751   pp.365, 366

R. v O'Grady [1987] Q.B. 995; [1987] 3 W.L.R. 321 CA   pp.108, 404, 405

R. v O'Leary (1986) 82 Cr. App. R. 341 CA   p.257

R. v O'Toole [1987] Crim. L.R. 759 CA   p.320

R. v Olugboja [1982] Q.B. 320; [1981] 3 W.L.R. 585 CA   pp.198, 199

R. v Owino [1996] 2 Cr. App. R. 128; [1995] Crim. L.R. 743 CA   pp.432, 437

R. v Page [1954] 1 Q.B. 170; [1953] 3 W.L.R. 895   p.85

R. v Pagett (1983) 76 Cr. App. R. 279; [1983] Crim. L.R. 393 CA   pp.26, 27

R. v Park (1987) Cr. App. R. 164   p.263

R. v Parker [1977] 1 W.L.R. 600; [1977] 2 All E.R. 37 CA   p.62

R. v Parker [1993] Crim. L.R. 856 CA   pp.300, 310

R. v Parkes [1973] Crim. L.R. 358   p.261

R. v Parsons [2009] EWCA Crim 64   pp.355, 361

R. v Patel [2004] EWCA Crim 3284; [2005] 1 Cr. App. R. 27; (2005) 169 J.P. 93   pp.156, 157

R. v Pattni [2001] Crim. L.R. 570   p.236

R. v Pearson [1992] Crim. L.R. 193 CA   pp.99, 111, 382

R. v Pembliton (1874) L.R. 2 C.C.R. 119   p.67

R. v Perkins (1946) 36 J. Cr. L. & Cr 393   p.27

R. v Petters and Parfitt [1995] Crim. L.R. 501   p.352

R. v Pitchley (1973) 57 Cr. App. R. 30; [1972] Crim. L.R. 705 CA   p.265

R. v Pitham (1976) 65 Cr. App. R. 45; [1977] Crim. L.R. 285 CA   p.212

R. v Pittwood (1902) 19 T.L.R. 37   p.16

R. v Pommell [1995] 2 Cr. App. R. 607; (1995) 92(27) L.S.G. 32 CA   pp.441, 444, 449, 458

R. v Pooley Unreported January 16, 2007   p.416

R. v Pordage [1975] Crim. L.R. 575 CA   p.393

R. v Poulton (1832) 5 Car. & P. 329   p.85

R. v Powell and English [1999] 1 A.C. 1; [1997] 3 W.L.R. 959 HL   pp.348, 349, 352, 353, 354, 355, 357, 358, 361, 382, 383

R. v Preddy [1996] A.C. 815; [1996] 3 W.L.R. 255 HL   p.220

R. v Prentice and Sullman [1995] 1 A.C. 171; [1994] 3 W.L.R. 288 HL   p.116

R. v Price, *The Times*, December 22, 1971   p.93

R. v Prince (1875) L.R. 2 C.C.R. 154   p.71

R. v Purdy (1945) 10 J.C.L. 182   p.449

R. v Qadir [1997] C.L.Y. 1200; [1997] 9 Arch. News 1 CA   p.315

R. v Quayle [2005] EWCA Crim 1415; [2005] 1 W.L.R. 3642; [2006] 1 All E.R. 988 CA   pp.442, 455, 456

R. v Quick [1973] Q.B. 910; [1973] 3 W.L.R. 26 CA   pp.410, 411, 412, 415, 417, 426, 427

R. v R [2010] EWCA Crim 194; [2010] 2 Cr. App. R. 3   p.94

R. v R (Rape: Marital Exemption) [1992] 1 A.C. 599; [1991] 3 W.L.R. 767 HL   pp.4, 5, 363

R. v Rafferty [2007] EWCA Crim 1846; [2008] Crim. L.R. 218 CA   p.355

R. v Rahman [2008] UKHL 45; [2009] 1 A.C. 129; [2008] 3 W.L.R. 264   pp.349, 352, 354, 356, 357, 358, 359, 383

R. v Raphael [2008] EWCA Crim 1014; [2008] Crim. L.R. 995   p.240

R. v Rashford [2005] EWCA Crim 3377; [2006] Crim. L.R. 547   p.436

R. v Reader (1978) 66 Cr. App. R. 33 CA   p.271

R. v Reardon [1999] Crim. L.R. 392   p.352

R. v Reynolds [1988] Crim. L.R. 679 CA   p.93

R. v Richardson (1834) 6 Car. & P. 335   p.262

R. v Richardson [1999] Q.B. 444; [1998] 3 W.L.R. 1292 CA   p.165

R. v Richardson and Irwin [1999] 1 Cr. App. R. 392; [1999] Crim L.R. 494 CA   pp.387, 398, 400, 404, 405, 426

R. v Richens [1993] 4 All E.R. 877; (1994) 98 Cr. App. R. 43 CA   p.100

R. v Roberts (1972) 56 Cr. App. R. 95; [1972] Crim. L.R. 27 CA   pp.32, 145, 146, 171

R. v Roberts [1997] R.T.R. 462; [1997] Crim. L.R. 209 CA (Crim Div)   p.348

R. v Robinson [1915] 2 K.B. 342   p.316

R. v Robinson [1977] Crim. L.R. 173 CA   p.232

R. v Robinson [2000] 5 Arch. News 2   p.366
R. v Rodger and Rose [1998] 1 Cr. App. R. 143 CA   p.443
R. v Rogers [2003] EWCA Crim 945; [2003] 1 W.L.R. 1374; [2003] 2 Cr. App. R. 10   pp.33, 34, 123
R. v Rogers [2007] UKHL 8; [2007] 2 A.C. 62; [2007] 2 W.L.R. 280   p.153
R. v Rook [1993] 1 W.L.R. 1005; [1993] 2 All E.R. 955 CA   pp.365, 382
R. v Rossiter [1994] 2 All E.R. 752; (1992) 95 Cr. App. R. 326 CA   p.99
R. v Rostron [2003] EWCA Crim 2206   p.273
R. v Ruffell [2003] EWCA Crim 122; [2003] 2 Cr App.R. (S.) 53   pp.20, 35, 118, 126
R. v Ryan (1996) 160 J.P. 610; [1996] Crim. L.R. 320 CA   p.252
R. v S (Vageesan) [2008] EWCA Crim 346   p.188
R. v Safi [2003] EWCA Crim 1809; [2004] 1 Cr. App. R. 14; [2003] Crim. L.R. 721   p.445
R. v Saik [2006] UKHL 18; [2007] 1 A.C. 18; [2006] 2 W.L.R. 993   pp.326, 327
R. v Sanders (1982) 75 Cr. App. R. 84; [1982] Crim. L.R. 695 CA   p.265
R. v Sanderson (1993) 98 Cr. App. R. 325 CA   p.94
R. v Sandhu [1998] 1 P.L.R. 17; [1997] J.P.L. 853 CA   pp.76, 77
R. v Satnam and Kewal (1984) 78 Cr. App. R. 149; [1985] Crim. L.R. 236 CA   p.63
R. v Saunders [1985] Crim. L.R. 230; (1985) 82 L.S.G. 1005 CA   p.148
R. v Savage and Parmenter [1992] 1 A.C. 699; [1991] 3 W.L.R. 914 HL   pp.44, 146, 147, 148, 149, 170
R. v Scarlett [1993] 4 All E.R. 629; (1994) 98 Cr. App. R. 290 CA   p.432
R. v Scott (1979) 68 Cr. App. R. 164; [1979] Crim. L.R. 456 CA   p.324
R. v Seers (1984) 79 Cr. App. R. 261; (1985) 149 J.P. 124 CA   p.93
R. v Seymour [1983] 2 A.C. 493; [1983] 3 W.L.R. 349 HL   pp.63, 116
R. v Shadrokh-Cigari [1988] Crim. L.R. 465 CA   p.230
R. v Sharp [1987] Q.B. 853; [1987] 3 W.L.R. 1 CA   p.447
R. v Shayler [2002] UKHL 11; [2003] 1 A.C. 247; [2002] 2 W.L.R. 754   pp.449, 451
R. v Sheehan [1975] 1 W.L.R. 739; [1975] 2 All E.R. 960 CA   p.393
R. v Shepherd (1987) 86 Cr. App. R. 47; [1987] Crim. L.R. 686   p.447
R. v Shivpuri [1987] A.C. 1; [1986] 2 W.L.R. 988 HL   p.321
R. v Shorty [1950] S.R. 280   p.38
R. v Simcox [1964] Crim. L.R. 402 CA   p.94
R. v Siracusa (1990) 90 Cr. App. R. 340; [1989] Crim. L.R. 712 CA   p.327
R. v Slater [1996] Crim. L.R. 300   p.265
R. v Slingsby [1995] Crim. L.R. 570   pp.163, 164
R. v Small (1987) 86 Cr. App. R. 170; [1988] R.T.R. 32 CA   pp.231, 232
R. v Smith (1826) 172 E.R. 449   p.18
R. v Smith [1959] 2 Q.B. 35; [1959] 2 W.L.R. 623   pp.26, 29, 36
R. v Smith [1974] Q.B. 354; [1974] 2 W.L.R. 20 CA   pp.297, 385
R. v Smith [1979] Crim. L.R. 251   p.18
R. v Smith [2001] 1 A.C. 146; [2000] 3 W.L.R. 654 HL   pp.5, 104, 105, 106, 107, 112, 135, 171

R. v Smythe (1980) 72 Cr. App. R. 8 CA   p.262

R. v Speck [1977] 2 All E.R. 859; (1977) 65 Cr. App. R. 161 CA   p.16

R. v Spratt [1990] 1 W.L.R. 1073; [1991] 2 All E.R. 210 CA   p.63

R. v Spriggs [1958] 1 Q.B. 270; [1958] 2 W.L.R. 162 CA   p.93

R. v Steane [1947] K.B. 997; [1947] 1 All E.R. 813 CA   pp.48, 449

R. v Steer [1988] A.C. 111; [1987] 3 W.L.R. 205 HL   p.300

R. v Stephens (1866) L.R. 1 Q.B. 702   p.68

R. v Stephenson [1979] Q.B. 695; [1979] 3 W.L.R. 193 CA   pp.61, 298

R. v Stewart [2009] EWCA Crim 593; [2009] 1 W.L.R. 2507; [2010] 1 All E.R. 260   p.95

R. v Stone and Robinson [1977] Q.B. 354; [1977] 2 W.L.R. 169 CA   pp.19, 122

R. v Stringer (1992) 94 Cr. App. R. 13; [1991] Crim. L.R. 639 CA   p.341

R. v Strudwick (1994) 99 Cr. App. R. 326 CA   p.341

R. v Stubbs (1989) 88 Cr. App. R. 53; (1988) 10 Cr. App. R. (S.) 97 CA   p.389

R. v Sullivan [1981] Crim. L.R. 46 CA   p.149

R. v Sullivan [1984] A.C. 156; [1983] 3 W.L.R. 123 HL   pp.414, 416, 417

R. v T [1990] Crim. L.R. 256   p.417

R. v Tabassum [2000] 2 Cr. App. R. 328; [2000] Lloyd's Rep. Med. 404 CA   pp.165, 166, 202

R. v Tamm [1973] Crim. L.R. 115   p.266

R. v Tandy [1989] 1 W.L.R. 350; [1989] 1 All E.R. 267 CA   pp.94, 95

R. v Taran [2006] EWCA Crim 1498   p.176

R. v Taylor (1869) L.R. 1 C.C.R. 194   p.148

R. v Taylor [2001] EWCA Crim 1044; [2002] Crim. L.R. 205   p.324

R. v Taylor [2009] EWCA Crim 544   pp.150, 171

R. v Terry [1984] A.C. 374; [1984] 2 W.L.R. 23 HL   p.281

R. v Thomas (1985) 81 Cr. App. R. 331; [1985] Crim. L.R. 677 CA   pp.143, 180

R. v Thornton (No.1) [1992] 1 All E.R. 306; (1993) 96 Cr. App. R. 112 CA   p.101

R. v Thornton (No.2) [1996] 1 W.L.R. 1174; [1996] 2 All E.R. 1023 CA   p.100, 104

R. v Tolson (1889) 23 Q.B.D. 168; (1889) L.R. 23 Q.B.D. 168   pp.70, 387

R. v Toothill [1998] Crim. L.R. 876   p.315

R. v Tosti [1997] Crim. L.R. 746   pp.317, 319

R. v Turner (No.2) [1971] 1 W.L.R. 901; [1971] 2 All E.R. 441 CA   pp.224, 225

R. v Tyrell [1894] 1 Q.B. 710   p.367

R. v Uddin [1999] Q.B. 431; [1998] 3 W.L.R. 1000 CA   pp.357, 359

R. v Valderrama-Vega [1985] Crim. L.R. 220 CA   p.442

R. v Velumyl [1989] Crim. L.R. 299 CA   p.242

R. v Venna [1976] Q.B. 421; [1975] 3 W.L.R. 737 CA   p.142

R. v Vickers [1957] 2 Q.B. 664; [1957] 3 W.L.R. 326 CA   p.87

R. v Vincent [2001] EWCA Crim 295; [2001] 1 W.L.R. 1172   p.275

R. v Wacker [2002] EWCA Crim 1944; [2003] Q.B. 1207; [2003] 2 W.L.R. 374   pp.117, 118

R. v Wain [1995] 2 Cr. App. R. 660 CA   p.228

R. v Walker (1992) 13 Cr. App. R. (S.) 474 CA   p.89

R. v Walker [2006] All E.R. (D) 08   p.191

R. v Walker and Hayles (1990) 90 Cr. App. R. 226; [1990] Crim. L.R. 44 CA   p.57

R. v Walkington [1979] 1 W.L.R. 1169; [1979] 2 All E.R. 716 CA   p.255

R. v Waltham (1849) 3 Cox C.C. 148   p.148

R. v Watson [1989] 1 W.L.R. 684   pp.123, 124

R. v Webb [2006] EWCA Crim 2496   p.358

R. v Webster [2006] EWCA Crim 2894   p.230

R. v Webster [2006] EWCA Crim 415; [2006] 2 Cr. App. R. 6; [2006] R.T.R. 19   p.347

R. v Webster and Warwick [1995] 2 All E.R. 168; [1995] 1 Cr. App. R. 492 CA   p.300

R. v Weller [2003] EWCA Crim 815; [2004] 1 Cr. App. R. 1   p.105

R. v Wheeler (1991) 92 Cr. App. R. 279 CA   p.219

R. v White [1910] 2 K.B. 124; (1910) 4 Cr. App. R. 257 CA   pp.25, 31

R. v White [2001] EWCA Crim 216; [2001] 1 W.L.R. 1352; [2001] Crim. L.R. 576   pp.135, 153

R. v Whitehouse [1941] 1 W.R.R. 112   p.365

R. v Whiteley (1991) 93 Cr. App. R. 25; (1991) 155 J.P. 917 CA   p.294

R. v Whitta [2006] EWCA Crim 2626; [2007] 1 Cr. App. R. (S.) 122   p.176

R. v Whybrow (1951) 35 Cr. App. R. 141; (1951) 95 S.J. 745   p.320

R. v Wiley, 169 E.R. 408; (1850) 2 Den. 37   p.266

R. v Willer (1986) 83 Cr. App. R. 225; [1987] R.T.R. 22 CA   p.440

R. v Williams [1923] 1 K.B. 340; (1924) 17 Cr. App. R. 56 CA   pp.201, 202

R. v Williams [1987] 3 All E.R. 411; (1984) 78 Cr. App. R. 276 CA   pp.385, 386, 434, 436, 437

R. v Williams [1992] 1 W.L.R. 380; [1992] 2 All E.R. 183 CA   p.32

R. v Williams [2001] 1 Cr. App. R. 23; [2001] Crim. L.R. 253   pp.212, 220

R. v Willoughby [2004] EWCA Crim 3365; [2005] 1 W.L.R. 1880; [2005] 1 Cr. App. R. 29   pp.117, 123

R. v Wills (1991) 92 Cr. App. R. 297 CA   p.228

R. v Wilson [1997] Q.B. 47; [1996] 3 W.L.R. 125 CA   pp.162, 163, 165

R. v Windle [1952] 2 Q.B. 826; [1952] 2 All E.R. 1 CA   p.418

R. v Wood [2002] EWCA Crim 832   p.237

R. v Wood [2008] EWCA Crim 1305; [2009] 1 W.L.R. 496; [2008] 3 All E.R. 898   p.94

R. v Woodman [1974] Q.B. 754; [1974] 2 W.L.R. 821 CA   p.225

R. v Woods (1981) 74 Cr. App. R. 312; [1982] Crim. L.R. 42 CA   p.398

R. v Woollin [1999] 1 A.C. 82; [1998] 3 W.L.R. 382 HL   pp.49, 53, 55, 56, 57, 59, 87, 115, 330

R. v Wright [2000] Crim. L.R. 510 CA   p.444

R. v Yemoh [2009] EWCA Crim 930; [2009] Crim. L.R. 888   pp.354, 358, 359, 383

R. v Yuthiwattana (1985) 80 Cr. App. R. 55; (1984) 16 H.L.R. 49 CA   p.16

R. (on the application of Jones) v Bedfordshire and Mid Bedfordshire Magistrates Court [2010] EWHC 523 (Admin); (2010) 174 J.P. 278   p.154

R. (on the application of Purdy) v DPP [2009] UKHL 45; [2010] 1 A.C. 345; [2009] 3 W.L.R. 403   p.17

Read v Coker (1853) 138 E.R. 1437   p.141

Richmond upon Thames LBC v Pinn and Wheeler Ltd [1989] R.T.R. 354; 87 L.G.R. 659 DC   p.372

Roe v Kingerlee [1986] Crim. L.R. 735 DC   pp.293, 310

Roper v Knott [1898] 1 Q.B. 868 QBD   p.294

Roy Bowles Ltd, *The Times*, December 11, 1999   p.130

S (Adult Patient: Sterilisation: Patient's Best Interests), Re [2001] Fam. 15; [2000] 3 W.L.R. 1288 CA   p.452

SW v United Kingdom [1996] 1 F.L.R. 434; (1996) 21 E.H.R.R. 363 ECtHR   p.4

Salabiaku v France (1998) 13 E.H.R.R. 379 ECtHR   p.76

Salomon v Salomon and Co Ltd [1897] A.C. 22 HL   p.374

Scott v Commissioner of Police of the Metropolis [1975] A.C. 819; [1974] 3 W.L.R. 741 HL   p.280

Smith v Leech Brain and Co [1962] 2 Q.B. 405; [1962] 2 W.L.R. 148 QBD   pp.35, 35

Smith v Chief Superintendent of Woking Police Station (1983) 76 Cr. App. R. 234; [1983] Crim. L.R. 323 QBD   p.141

Sopp v Long [1970] 1 Q.B. 518; [1969] 2 W.L.R. 587 QBD   p.372

Southwark LBC v Williams [1971] Ch. 734; [1971] 2 W.L.R. 467 CA   pp.452, 455

Stansbie v Troman [1948] 2 K.B. 48; [1948] 1 All E.R. 599 CA   p.29

State v Kinchen (1910) 52 So. 185   p.365

Sunday Times v United Kingdom (1979–80) 2 E.H.R.R. 245; (1979) 76 L.S.G. 328 ECtHR   p.120

Sweet v Parsley [1970] A.C. 132; [1969] 2 W.L.R. 470 HL   pp.69, 79

T v DPP   pp.146, 171

Teglgaard Hardwood Ltd Unreported 2003   p.130

Tesco Supermarkets Ltd v Nattrass [1972] A.C. 153; [1971] 2 W.L.R. 1166 HL   pp.375, 376

Thorne v Motor Trade Association [1937] A.C. 797; (1938) 26 Cr. App. R. 51 HL   p.258

Thornton v Mitchell [1940] 1 All E.R. 339   p.345

Treacy v DPP [1971] A.C. 537; [1971] 1 All E.R. 110 HL   pp.210, 258

Troughton v Metropolitan Police [1987] Crim. L.R. 138 QBD   p.276

Turberville v Savage, 86 E.R. 684; (1669) 1 Mod. 3 KB   p.140

Tuck v Robson [1970] 1 W.L.R. 741; [1970] 1 All E.R. 1171 DC   p.347

Vane v Vane [1965] A.C. 486; [1964] 3 W.L.R. 1218 HL   pp.372, 373

Vehicle Inspectorate v Nuttall [1999] 1 W.L.R. 629; [1999] 3 All E.R. 833 HL   p.73

Wai Yu-Tsang v R [1992] 1 A.C. 269; [1991] 3 W.L.R. 1006 PC (HK)   p.280

Walters v Lunt [1951] 2 All E.R. 645; (1951) 35 Cr. App. R. 94 DC   p.268

Warner v Commissioner of Police of the Metropolis [1969] 2 A.C. 256; [1968] 2 W.L.R. 1303 HL   p.71

Welham v DPP [1961] A.C. 103; [1960] 2 W.L.R. 669 HL   p.280

Wheatley v Commissioner of Police of the British Virgin Islands [2006] UKPC 24; [2006] 1 W.L.R. 1683; [2006] 2 Cr. App. R. 21 PC (BVI)   p.233

Wilcox v Jeffery [1951] 1 All E.R. 464; [1951] 1 T.L.R. 706 DC   pp.343, 344

Williams v Phillips (1957) 41 Cr. App. R. 5; (1957) 121 J.P. 163 DC   p.226

Winzar v Chief Constable of Kent, *The Times*, March 28, 1983 DC   pp.22, 68

Woolmington v DPP [1935] A.C. 462; (1936) 25 Cr. App. R. 72 HL   pp.8, 79, 91, 413, 419

Worthy v Gordon Plant (Services) Ltd [1989] R.T.R. 7 DC   p.376

X NHS Trust v T (Adult Patient: Refusal of Medical Treatment) [2004] EWHC 1279 (Fam); [2005] 1 All E.R. 387; [2004] 3 F.C.R. 297   p.452

Table of Statutes

1839 Metropolitan Police Act (2 & 3
  Vict. c.47)
  s.44 p.372
1861 Accessories and Abettors Act (24 & 25
  Vict. c.94)
  s.8 pp.332, 342, 344, 345, 367
  Offences against the Person Act (24 &
  25 Vict. c.100) pp.138, 149, 156, 158,
  159, 442
  s.9 p.84
  s.10 p.84
  s.18 pp.15, 45, 46, 80, 138, 144, 146, 147,
  148, 150, 151, 153, 159, 168, 169, 170, 171,
  318, 364, 394, 396, 412, 426, 427
  s.19 p.84
  s.20 pp.15, 44, 64, 80, 138, 144, 146, 147,
  148, 149, 150, 152, 153, 159, 160, 163,
  164, 166, 167, 168, 169, 170, 171, 202,
  255, 298, 364, 394, 396, 412, 416,
  426, 427
  s.23 pp.33, 61
  s.39 p.139
  s.47 pp.44, 73, 138, 139, 141, 144, 145, 146,
  147, 149, 152, 153, 158, 159, 160, 162,
  164, 166, 168, 169, 170, 171, 348, 391,
  394, 426, 427
  s.55 p.71
  s.57 p.387
  s.58 p.85
  s.59 p.85
1872 Licensing Act (35 & 36 Vict. c.94)
  s.12 p.23

1883 Explosive Substances Act (46 & 47
  Vict. c.3)
  s.3(a) p.350
  s.4(1) p.435
  1885 Criminal Law Amendment
  Act (48 & 49 Vict. c.69)
  s.5 p.367
1887 Merchandise Marks Act (50 & 51 Vict.
  c.28) p.371
1893 Sale of Goods Act (56 & 57 Vict.
  c.71) p.227
1929 Infant Life (Preservation) Act (19 & 20
  Geo. 5 c.34)
  s.1 p.85
1933 Children and Young Persons Act (22 &
  23 Geo. 5 c.12)
  s.1 p.122
  s.50 p.423
1938 Infanticide Act (1 & 2 Geo. 6 c.36)
  s.1 p.126
1951 Rivers (Prevention of Pollutions) Act
  (14 & 15 Geo. 6 c.64)
  s.2(1) p.73
1956 Sexual Offences Act (4 & 5 Eliz.
  2 c.69)
  s.14 p.72
    (2) p.72
    (3) p.72
  s.44 p.175
1957 Homicide Act (5 & 6 Eliz. 2
  c.11) pp.91, 97
  s.2 p.90, 91, 92, 93, 94, 97, 105, 107, 132

(1) p.96
(2) pp.9, 91, 98
(4) p.364
s.3 pp.90, 98, 99, 100, 104, 105, 107, 113, 132, 445
s.4 p.90, 114, 133
1960 Indecency with Children Act (8 & 9 Eliz. 2 c.33)
s.1 pp.16, 72
(1) p.71
1961 Suicide Act (9 & 10 Eliz. 2 c.60)
s.1 p.114
s.2 pp.17, 114
1964 Criminal Procedure (Insanity) Act (c.84) p.423
s.1 p.413
s.5(3) p.413
1965 Dangerous Drugs Act (c.15)
s.5(b) p.69
Murder (Abolition of Death Penalty) Act (c.71)
s.1(1) p.86
1967 Criminal Law Act (c.58)
s.3 pp.404, 431, 432, 434, 458
(2) p.432
s.4 pp.341, 368, 378
s.5 pp.369, 378
Sexual Offences Act (c.60) pp.2, 7
Criminal Justice Act (c.80) p.150
s.8 pp.45, 46, 392
1968 Firearms Act (c.27)
s.5 p.441
Trade Descriptions Act (c.29) p.371
s.24(1) p.73
Theft Act (c.60) pp.12, 210, 223, 231, 235, 239, 244, 252, 253, 260, 262, 277, 278, 281, 295
s.1 pp.210, 213, 243, 244, 268, 275
s.2 pp.231, 237, 244
(1) pp.217, 231, 233
(a) p.232
(c) pp.226, 232

(d) p.237
(2) p.232
(3) p.237
ss.2–6 p.210
s.3 pp.211, 227, 243, 382
(1) pp.218, 219, 232
(2) pp.218, 219, 243, 264
s.4 pp.220, 221, 243, 244
(1) pp.220, 284
(2) p.221
(a) p.221
(b) pp.221, 222
(c) p.222
(3) p.222
(4) p.222
s.5 pp.224, 225, 244, 296
(1) pp.224, 226, 229, 230, 244
(2) pp.226, 296
(3) pp.227, 228, 229, 244
(4) pp.227, 229, 230, 244
(5) p.296
s.6 pp.239, 240, 244
(1) pp.239, 240, 241, 242, 243
(2) pp.242, 243
s.8 pp.248, 287
(2) pp.250, 287
s.9 p.251
(1)(a) pp.188, 251, 252, 255, 256, 257, 287, 382
(b) pp.251, 252, 254, 255, 256, 257, 287, 382
(2) p.188
(4) p.254
s.10 pp.256, 287
s.12 p.272
s.13 p.223
s.15 pp.213, 216, 274, 277, 288
s.15A pp.278, 288
s.16 pp.278, 288
s.20(2) pp.278, 288
s.21 pp.257, 260, 287
(1) p.259

(2) p.258
s.22 pp.261, 287
s.24(2) pp.269, 270
  (3) p.268
  (4) p.267
s.24A p.268
s.25 pp.272, 273, 274, 288
  (1) p.272
s.34 p.276
  (2)(a) p.260
    (b) p.267
  Medicines Act (c.67)
s.58(2)(a) p.73
s.121 p.73
1969 Genocide Act (c.12) p.84
1971 Misuse of Drugs Act (c.38) p.455
s.5 p.33
  Criminal Damage Act (c.48) pp.64,
  223, 292, 293, 295, 305, 310,403
s.1 pp.46, 302, 303, 304, 305
  (1) pp.292, 297, 299, 301, 302, 305,
    309, 310
  (2) pp.299, 300, 301, 302, 305,
    309, 310
  (3) pp.301, 302
s.2 pp.302, 303, 308, 309, 310
  (1)(a) pp.303, 305
    (b) pp.303, 305
s.3 pp.303, 304, 309, 310
  (1)(a) pp.304, 305
    (b) pp.304, 305
s.5 pp.301, 302, 303, 304, 305, 309, 408
  (2) pp.308, 309, 403
    (a) pp.306, 307, 308, 309
    (b) pp.307, 308, 311
  (3) pp.309, 403
  (5) p.305
s.10 pp.295, 296, 310
  (2) p.296
  (3) p.296
  (4) p.296
  (5) p.294

1974 Health and Safety at Work etc.
  Act (c.37) p.370
1977 Criminal Law Act (c.45) pp.278, 279,
  281, 285, 288, 324
s.1(1) pp.324, 336
  (b) p.327
  (2) p.326
s.2(2) pp.325, 337
s.5(2) p.278
  (8) p.325
1978 Theft Act (c.31) pp.231, 277, 278,
  281, 285
s.1 pp.276, 278, 285, 286, 288
s.2 pp.278, 283, 288
s.3 pp.274, 275, 276, 288
  (2) p.275
  (3) p.276
1979 Customs and Excise Management
  Act (c.2)
s.170(2) p.386
1980 Magistrates' Courts Act (c.43)
s.44 p.345
  (1) p.367
1981 Criminal Attempts Act (c.47) pp.316,
  319
s.1 pp.13, 336
  (1) p.314
  (2) pp.321, 336
  (3) p.321
  (4) p.314
s.4(3) p.315
  Contempt of Court Act (c.49)
ss.1–7 p.68
1986 Insolvency Act (c.45) p.72
s.362(1)(a) pp.71, 76
  Public Order Act (c.64) p.199
1988 Criminal Justice Act (c.33)
s.39 pp.138, 139
  Road Traffic Act (c.52)
s.1 p.84
s.3A p.84
▼ **1989 Official Secrets Act (c.6)** p.451

1990 Computer Misuse Act (c.18) pp.223, 294

1991 Criminal Procedure (Insanity and Unfitness to Plead) Act (c.25) pp.413, 415, 423
s.1 p.414
Property Misdescriptions Act (c.29)
s.1 p.370
Water Resources Act (c.57)
s.85 p.372
(1) pp.24, 29

1996 Law Reform (Year and a Day Rule) Act (c.19)
s.1 p.86
s.2 p.86

1997 Protection from Harassment Act (c.40) pp.138, 155, 158
s.1 pp.155, 171
(1) p.157
(3) p.158
s.2 pp.152, 155, 157, 159, 168, 170
s.4 pp.152, 156, 157, 159, 168, 170, 171
(1) pp.157, 159
(3) p.158
(c) p.158
(5) p.157
s.7(2) p.156
(3) p.156
(4) p.156

1998 Crime and Disorder Act (c.37) p.152
s.1(1) p.304
s.28 p.153
(1)(a) pp.153, 154
(b) pp.153, 154
(4) p.153
(5) p.154
s.29 p.152
s.30 pp.292, 305, 309
s.32 p.152
s.34 p.424
Human Rights Act (c.42) pp.4, 5
s.2 pp.5, 6

s.3 p.6
s.6 p.6
Sch.1 p.120

2001 Anti-terrorism, Crime and Security Act (c.24) p.152
s.39 p.305

2003 Sexual Offences Act (c.42) pp.74, 174, 182, 183, 187, 188, 197, 198, 202, 204, 253, 385, 395
s.1 pp.174, 190, 204, 207
(1) p.174
(2) p.176
ss.1–4 pp.189, 205, 385, 395
s.2 pp.176, 178, 181, 182, 191, 207, 395, 396
(1) p.181
(2) p.176
ss.2–4 p.205
s.3 pp.176, 177, 178, 190, 207, 395, 396
(1) p.177
(2) p.176
s.4 pp.176, 178, 183, 184, 191, 395, 396
(1) p.183
(2) p.176
s.5 pp.189, 190
ss.5–8 p.189
s.6 p.190
s.7 pp.190, 191
(1) p.192
s.8 p.191
s.9 pp.191, 192, 195, 367
(1) p.192
(c) p.192
ss.9–13 p.194
s.10 pp.191, 192, 195, 196
(1)(c) p.192
s.14 pp.194, 195
s.15 p.194
s.16 pp.192, 193, 194
(2) p.193
s.17 pp.192, 193, 194
(1) p.193
(2) p.193

s.21 p.193
s.23 p.193
s.25 pp.184, 195, 196, 197
    (1) p.195
s.26 pp.184, 195, 196, 197
    (1) p.196
s.27 pp.196, 197
    (2) p.196
s.28 p.196
s.29 p.196
s.61 pp.186, 200, 207
ss.61–63 pp.186, 205
s.62 pp.186, 188
s.63 pp.188, 189, 315
s.64 pp.184, 185, 205
    (2) p.185
s.65 pp.184, 185, 186, 205
s.74 pp.176, 197, 201, 202, 205, 207
s.75 pp.176, 177, 180, 181, 182, 184, 197,
    pp.199, 205, 206
    (2) pp.199, 200
        (d) p.202
        (f) pp.200, 202, 207
s.76 pp.176, 177, 180, 181, 182, 184, 197,
    200, 205, 206
    (2) p.200
        (a) pp.200, 202
s.78 pp.178, 180
s.79(2) p.175
    (3) p.175
    (8) p.178
    Criminal Justice Act (c.44) p.8
s.58 p.7
s.75 pp.7, 8
s.76 p.7
**2004 Domestic Violence, Crime and
    Victims Act (c.28)** pp.413, 423
s.5 pp.22, 127, 128, 133, 341
    (1) p.20
2006 Fraud Act (c.35) pp.216, 231, 239,
    268, 272, 274, 275, 277, 278, 279, 280,
    281, 283, 285, 286, 287, 288, 324

s.1 pp.281, 286, 288, 289
s.2 pp.281, 282, 283, 285, 289
    (5) pp.282, 283
ss.2–4 p.281
s.3 pp.282, 283, 285, 289
s.4 pp.283, 284, 285, 289
    (2) p.284
s.5 p.284
    (3) p.284
    (4) p.284
s.6 pp.274, 288
s.8 p.274
s.11 pp.221, 285, 286, 289
    **Police and Justice Act
    (c.48)** p.294
**2007 Corporate Manslaughter and
    Corporate Homicide Act (c.19)** pp.130,
    131, 134, 376
s.1 p.131
    (4)(c) p.131
s.8 p.131
s.17 p.132
s.18 p.131
    Serious Crime Act (c.27) pp.337,
    364, 367
Pt 2 pp.328, 329, 330, 331, 332, 333, 336,
    337, 408
s.44 pp.329, 332, 335, 337
    (1) p.330
    (2) p.330
ss.44–46 p.329
s.45 pp.329, 330, 332, 335, 337
    (2) p.330
s.46 pp.329, 330, 332, 335, 337
s.47 pp.330, 331, 332
    (5) pp.331, 332
        (a) p.333
    (8) p.331
s.49 pp.330, 331, 332
s.50 p.333
s.51 p.334
s.65 p.330

**2008 Criminal Justice and Immigration
  Act (c.4)** pp.68, 434
  s.73 p.194
  s.76 pp.387, 432, 434, 437, 458
    (2) p.434
    (3) p.434
    (4) pp.386, 436
    (5) pp.404, 405, 436
    (6) p.438
    (7) p.434
**2009 Coroners and Justice
  Act (c.25)** pp.89, 91, 96, 97,
  109, 112, 115, 121, 126, 133,
  436, 437

s.52 pp.91, 96
s.54 pp.109, 112, 113
    (1)(c) p.112
    (2) p.111
    (3) p.112
    (4) p.111
    (5) p.113
    (6) p.113
    (8) p.364
s.55 pp.109, 111, 113
    (3) p.111
    (4) p.111
    (6) p.112
s.56 p.109

Guided Tour

Chapter Overview
Each chapter opens with a bulleted outline of the main concepts and ideas to be covered.

Defences II—Defences which
Justify or Excuse the Offence **13**

CHAPTER OVERVIEW

In this chapter we:

- analyse the defences of consent (briefly), self-defence and the prevention of crime, duress and necessity
- explore the concept of justificatory and excusatory defences
- consider the effect of a mistake on each of the defences
- consider whether necessity exists as a defence at all or is, where it is available, another form of duress.

Summary

End of Chapter Question

Key Extracts
Key extracts are boxed throughout to make them easily identifiable.

VOLUNTARY ASSOCIATION WITH VIOLENT CRIMINALS

A person may bring the duress upon himself and, where he does, the defence fails. This is called self-induced duress. For example, in **Fitzpatrick [1977] N.I. 20**, an IRA case, the Court of Criminal Appeal in Northern Ireland held:

"A person may become associated with a sinister group of men with criminal objectives and coercive methods of ensuring that their lawless enterprises are carried out and thereby voluntarily expose himself to illegal compulsion … If a person voluntarily exposes and submits himself … to illegal compulsion, he cannot rely on the duress to which he has voluntarily exposed himself as an excuse either in respect of the crimes he commits against his will or in respect of his continued but unwilling association with those capable of exercising upon him the duress which he calls in aid."

Some of the issues involved here include:

Key Cases
All cases are highlighted making your research of the subject easier.

THE EFFECT OF THE DEFENCE

If the defence succeeds, whether common law or statutory, D's conduct is regarded as lawful and he is completely acquitted. It can be a defence to any crime including murder. If the defence fails, D is guilty.

An unsuccessful argument of self-defence can have a bearing on sentence where it is regarded as a mitigating factor. Of course, this cannot affect the life sentence on a murder charge. If D is charged with murder, and the defence has failed because the amount of force used was excessive, the offence is not reduced to manslaughter (**Clegg [1995] 1 All E.R. 334**). Many students make the error of thinking self-defence operates in the same way as the partial defences to murder (provocation/loss of self-control or diminished responsibility), and the Nathan Committee (House of Lords, 1989) proposed that excessive force self-defence should reduce murder

Over to you boxes
A tool to help you develop your critical thinking abilities, Over to you boxes challenge you to engage with and question the subject.

Over to you...

Duress is a complex defence and there is much to revise. You should learn the elements (you might think of them as hurdles that D must jump successfully in order for the defence to succeed) but at all times keep your eye on the burden of proof. D must adduce evidence of duress (enough to meet the evidential burden, see Ch.1) and the prosecution bears the proof burden; i.e. that, for example, D was not subjected to the "right" sort of threat, or the situation lacked immediacy, or he associated with the "wrong" people and so on. Try to revise at least one authority for each "hurdle".

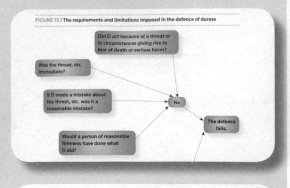

FIGURE 13.1 **The requirements and limitations imposed in the defence of duress**

Did D act because of a threat or in circumstances giving rise to fear of death or serious harm?

Was the threat, etc. immediate?

If D made a mistake about the threat, etc. was it a reasonable mistake?

 No

Would a person of reasonable firmness have done what D did?

The defence fails.

According to obiter in **Clegg [1995] 1 All E.R. 334**, there is no defence of superior orders, i.e. D cannot rely on the defence that he was merely following the orders of someone with authority over him, either in civilian life or in the military.

Summary

1. **Consent.** Many offences against the person, including the non-fatal assaults and sexual offences, cannot be committed where V consents, see Ch. 5.

 ## End of Chapter Question

Question

"The courts seem unable to decide whether the defence of necessity does exist as a form of duress, or does not exist at all."

Consider the truth of the above statement.

Further Reading

I. Dennis, "A Pointless Exercise" [2008] Crim. L.R. 507; "Defending self-defence" [2010] Crim.
   L.R. 167 and "Duress, Murder and Criminal Responsibility" (1980) 96 L.Q.R. 208.
S. Gardner, "Direct Action and the Defence of Necessity" [2005] Crim. L.R. 371.
D. Lanham, "Offensive Weapons and Self Defence" [2005] Crim. L.R. 85.
D. Ormerod, "Necessity of circumstance" [2006] Crim. L.R. 148.
P. Reed, "Rashford—Self-defence and Motive for Revenge" (2006) 166 Crim. Law. 1.

Self Test Questions

To test your knowledge gained from this section go online to *http://www.sweetandmaxwell. co.uk* and take our online self test questions. Here you will also find key updates to ensure that you are only ever one click away from an instant update.

Diagrams, charts, etc.
Included throughout, diagrams, charts and grids enable you to grasp complex legal principles with ease.

Summary
Each chapter closes with a summary to recap the main points and ensure you haven't missed anything crucial.

Q&A
Hone your essay answering skills with the end of chapter questions. Each question comes with guidance on what you should have included in your answer.

Further Reading
To help you broaden your perspective we provide selected further reading at the end of each chapter.

Self Test Questions
You can further test your knowledge with our online multiple choice questions located at sweetandmaxwell.co.uk.

Introduction to Criminal Law

1

CHAPTER OVERVIEW

In this chapter we:

- consider what the criminal law is and what it is for, i.e. its function or nature

- introduce the subjectivist and objectivist standpoints in the criminal law

- explain the allocation of the burden and standard of proof in criminal cases

- review the sources of the criminal law

- summarise the appeals' system

- discuss the reform of the criminal law

Summary

Introduction

This book is concerned with the substantive criminal law as taught on standard Criminal Law courses. We concentrate, therefore, on the rules of criminal liability rather than, for example, the reasons why people commit crimes or on other aspects of the criminal process such as criminal procedure, evidence and sentencing. The aim of the book is to enable students to achieve a clear, detailed and deep understanding of the criminal law. This is done by focusing on the general principles of criminal liability, the main criminal offences and defences and the theoretical basis of liability, as well as providing critical commentary wherever possible.

The study of the criminal law is a study of *liability* (guilt) or lack of liability. This involves an examination of what has to be proved (the elements or ingredients of the crime), by whom (usually, but not always, the prosecution) leading to a conclusion on what the law *is*, and from there to a debate, where appropriate, on whether the law is as it *should be*.

In this first chapter, we deal with some of the vital background matters, as well as introducing some themes which will run throughout this book, those of the conflict between a subjectivist and an objectivist approach to the criminal law and the issue of reform.

Nature and Function of the Criminal Law

What is a crime or, put another way, what is the nature of a crime, necessarily involves a consideration of what should be a crime, i.e. a consideration of the function of the criminal law. Hence the nature and function of the criminal law are interrelated and hard to separate. What is a crime and what should be a crime are actually difficult questions to answer and any answers may change over time. What is considered criminal in one age becomes lawful in another, for example consensual sex between homosexual adults was an offence until the Sexual Offences Act 1967 was passed and what was once lawful, for example driving without wearing a seat belt, is now unlawful.

Many would define a crime as something which results in harm to a victim such as murder or assault but there are many victimless crimes such as speeding, insider dealing and attempt offences. Further, even if harm has been caused, this does not necessarily mean that a crime has been committed; someone who harms in self-defence rather than, for example, an unprovoked attack does not commit a criminal offence. Normally, a crime will also require some blameworthy state of mind to impose liability, what we call the mens rea, but this is not always necessary; there are many regulatory offences, known as crimes of strict liability, which do not require proof of mens rea.

It is not possible to provide a definition of a crime, even in respect of where it prohibits behaviour which society considers universally morally wrong. For example, abortion is not unlawful when carried out in certain proscribed circumstances. There is not even a general consensus as to what should be criminal: many believe that taking "soft drugs" should be legal, others that the use of all drugs should be prohibited. Some people take the view of "live and let live" and if people want to act in a certain way that does not harm others then they should be allowed to do so, whereas others consider that the public interest requires people to be protected from themselves. This is particularly highlighted by the criminal law's approach to consensual acts of sado-masochism which, following the case of **Brown [1994] 1 A.C. 212 HL**, are unlawful even if no significant harm results.

Added to this is the difficulty of distinguishing a crime from a civil wrong. The civil law is concerned with compensating the victims of wrongs rather than with the punishment of the wrongdoers, so the aim of civil proceedings is different from that of criminal proceedings. However, there is no clear distinction between the nature of the conduct required for each, and it is not always possible to predict whether certain conduct will be governed by the civil law or the criminal law. As Clarkson and Keating, *Criminal Law: Text and Materials*, 6th edn observe, telling lies about someone which damages their reputation is treated as a civil wrong but a person who tells lies which result in someone transferring their property to him commits an offence of fraud. There is also, occasionally, an overlap between the criminal law and the civil law, for example an assault can be both a tort and a crime. Given the lack of any key ingredient in all crimes, it is not then surprising that no completely satisfactory definition has ever been given. The distinguished academic Professor Glanville Williams searched in vain for a clear definition and eventually settled upon the following: "in short, a crime is an act capable of being followed by criminal proceedings having a criminal outcome" ("The Definition of a Crime" [1955] C.L.P. 107). This definition does not really take us any further. It means that the only way to determine whether something is a crime is to look to the sources of the criminal law, cases and statutes, to find out whether commission of the activity in question will result in the institution of criminal proceedings, and if conviction is followed by criminal sanctions.

Subjectivism and Objectivism in the Criminal Law

A debate has been running over many years as to whether the criminal law should adopt a subjective or an objective approach to criminal liability. Those who take a subjectivist line assert that a defendant should be liable only for those consequences of his actions which he himself intended or foresaw, even if such consequences differ from the actual consequences because the latter may well be beyond his control. Objectivists focus not on the defendant's state of mind but on the actual consequences of his actions; they assert that, as well as consequences which are intended or foreseen, a defendant should also be liable for any consequences which he has not foreseen but which a reasonable person in that situation would have foreseen. Imposing liability where a defendant has given no thought to a risk of certain consequences is difficult to reconcile with the traditional approach that there can be no liability unless the defendant has formed the mens rea for the crime of which he has committed the actus reus (see Ch.2) and this is the main criticism of the objectivist approach.

The highpoint for objectivists was the decision in **Metropolitan Police Commissioner v Caldwell [1982] A.C. 341** (see p.62–63) which introduced an objective form of recklessness into the criminal law. However, in recent years, the subjectivist approach has found favour with the courts. The landmark ruling in **G [2004] 1 A.C. 1034 HL**, (see p.61), for example, saw the abolition of *Caldwell* recklessness and a return to a subjective assessment of recklessness. Lord Bingham stated:

> "It is clearly blameworthy to take an obvious and significant risk of causing injury to another. But it is not clearly blameworthy to do something involving a risk of injury to another if … one genuinely does not perceive the risk. Such a person may fairly be accused of stupidity or lack of imagination, but neither of those failings should expose him to conviction of serious crime or the risk of punishment … It is neither moral nor just to convict a defendant … on the strength of what someone else would have apprehended if the defendant himself had no such apprehension."

Sources of Criminal Law

English criminal law is a combination of both statute and common law (judge-made law which has developed in a piecemeal fashion over centuries). Most crimes have now been put onto a statutory footing, with new offences created by Parliament every year, but some still remain common law offences such as murder and manslaughter. The role of the courts is, however, no longer the creation of new offences, merely the interpretation of existing offences. In **Knuller (Publishing, Printing and Promotions) Ltd v DPP [1973] A.C. 435**, the House of Lords renounced its power to create new criminal offences. Nevertheless, in **R. v R [1991] 2 All E.R. 257**, the House of Lords upheld the judgment of the Court of Appeal which had removed the marital exemption from liability for rape and, in doing so, effectively created the offence of rape in marriage.

The implementation of the Human Rights Act 1998 (see p.5 below) must now effectively preclude the creation of new offences by the judiciary as art.7 of the European Convention on Human Rights prevents retrospective criminalisation; conduct which was not criminal at the time it was committed cannot become so because a court later decides it should be. However, it is interesting to note that *R. v R* was taken on appeal to the European Court of Human Rights (**CR v United Kingdom [1996] 1 F.L.R. 434**) which held that there was no violation of art.7 in that instance. This was on the basis that the decision that it was criminally wrong for a man to have non-consensual sex with any woman, even his wife, advanced the intended aims of the Convention of promoting human dignity and freedom and further, that art.7 does not prohibit the gradual evolution of the common law and *R. v R* was merely the culmination of a judicial trend towards removing the marital exemption.

Whilst the majority of offences are statutory, general principles of liability are, in the main, still derived from the common law, for example, the concepts of actus reus and mens rea (the elements of criminal liability); many defences such as necessity, intoxication, automatism and insanity; and the principles governing liability for participation in a criminal offence.

The Doctrine of Precedent

Until October 2009, the highest appeals court in England and Wales was the Appellate Committee of the House of Lords. On October 1, 2009, the Supreme Court of the United Kingdom replaced the Appellate Committee of the House of Lords, but previous decisions of the House continue to bind the Supreme Court (unless it departs from them), and decisions of both the House of Lords and the Supreme Court bind all inferior courts unless there is a conflicting decision of the European Court of Human Rights or European Court of Justice which will then take precedence. Where there is no Supreme Court or House of Lords' precedent, a decision of the Court of Appeal will be binding on all lower courts but decisions of the Court of Appeal may subsequently be overruled by the Supreme Court. Where there is no Supreme Court, House of Lords' or Court of Appeal precedent, a decision of the High Court is binding on the courts below it, i.e. the Crown Court and the magistrates' court. Decisions of the Crown Court and magistrates' court are not binding and are usually unreported.

Decisions of the Privy Council are not binding on the English courts but are strongly persuasive. However, in **James and Karimi [2006] 1 All E.R. 759**, the Court of Appeal stated that a decision of the Privy Council can, in exceptional circumstances, overrule a previous decision of the House of Lords (and presumably in similar exceptional circumstances, the Supreme Court) and that, as exceptional circumstances existed in that case, the House of Lords' decision in **Smith [2001] 1 A.C. 146** had been overruled by the Privy Council in **Attorney General for Jersey v Holley [2005] 3 All E.R. 371**. The exceptional circumstances were: nine Law Lords had heard the case in the Privy Council and the decision of the majority was to the effect that they were clarifying definitively the relevant law; the majority who decided in this way made up half of the total number of Law Lords and, consequently, any appeal to the House of Lords would be decided in line with the Privy Council decision.

The Human Rights Act 1998

Section 2 of the Human Rights Act 1998 (HRA) directs judges when determining an issue arising in connection with a Convention right to take into account the jurisprudence of the

European Court on Human Rights (ECtHR). Though it has not done so yet, it is likely that this will gradually begin to affect English Criminal law. Section 2 might also require a lower court to ignore the precedent of a higher court where the higher court's decision (even pre-HRA) conflicts with the ECHR.

Section 3 of the HRA requires judges to interpret legislation so far as possible in line with the Convention. Where a statute cannot be so construed the court must make a declaration of incompatibility. The declaration does not render the relevant statute invalid but does require Parliament to consider the need for reforming it. This power has not yet been exercised by the courts in a case involving the substantive criminal law.

The impact of the Act on the common law is unclear. Section 6 of the Act provides that it is unlawful for a public authority to act in a way which is incompatible with a Convention Right. Both the Crown Prosecution Service (CPS) and the courts are public bodies. Hence, it is possible that where a defendant is charged with a common law offence or raises a defence which is incompatible with the Convention, s.6 may require the CPS or court to interpret the common law in line with the Convention. There is, as yet, no authority on this point.

Structure of the Courts and Appeals Against Conviction or Acquittal

In criminal cases, the courts of first instance are the magistrates' court (summary trial) and the Crown Court where the trial is before a judge and jury (trial on indictment). Most prosecutions are brought by the CPS in the name of the Crown against the defendant (also referred to as the accused). A defendant convicted in the magistrates' court may appeal against his conviction to the Crown Court on a point of fact or law. A less commonly used appeals procedure, available to both the defendant and the prosecution, is to appeal from the magistrates' court to the Administrative Court of the High Court by way of case stated either on a point of law or on the basis that the magistrates' court exceeded its jurisdiction. The High Court may either acquit or, where the prosecution successfully appeal against an acquittal, remit the matter back to the magistrates with a direction to convict. Appeal is permitted on a point of law by either side from the High Court to the Supreme Court, provided the High Court considers the matter is one of general public importance and has granted leave to appeal or the Supreme Court has granted leave.

Appeals against conviction in the Crown Court are normally heard by the Criminal Division of the Court of Appeal although appeal (by either side) by way of case stated to the High Court is also possible (though not often used) on a point of law. The sole basis of appeal to the Court of Appeal is that the conviction was unsafe though the appeal may be based on fact, law or both.

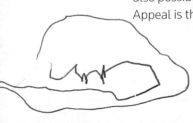

The prosecution may appeal to the Court of Appeal under s.58 of the Criminal Justice Act 2003 (CJA) where the judge has erred in law in making a ruling effectively terminating the prosecution's case so that the case as a whole collapses before the jury delivers its verdict. This may occur where, for example, the trial judge agrees with a defence submission at the close of the prosecution case that there is not enough evidence against the defendant and makes a finding of "no case to answer".

The Attorney General may also refer a matter to the Court of Appeal for clarification of a point of law (known as an Attorney General's Reference). This does not affect a defendant's acquittal.

A long standing rule existed at common law which prevented a defendant being prosecuted for a second time after having been acquitted. This was known as the rule against "double jeopardy". Sections 75 and 76 of the CJA introduced changes to the rule against double jeopardy in respect of "qualifying offences", of which there are 30 including murder, attempted murder, manslaughter, kidnapping, rape, attempted rape, various sexual offences under the Sexual Offences Act 2003, offences concerning class A drugs, serious criminal damage and arson offences, war crimes and terrorism offences. Section 76 makes it possible, in certain limited

FIGURE 1 Illustration of the hierarchy of the criminal courts and the appeals process

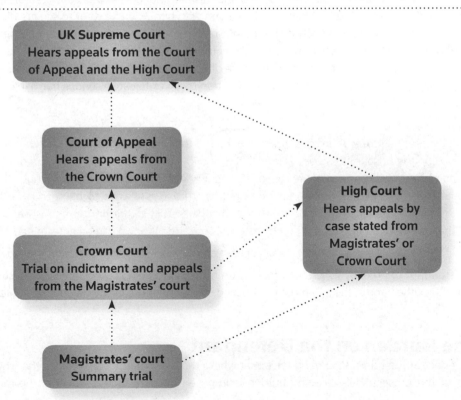

circumstances, for a retrial to take place despite an earlier acquittal. This may occur if there is new, compelling evidence of the guilt of the defendant and a retrial is in the public interest. Under s.75, the prosecution may apply for a retrial after an acquittal even where the acquittal occurred before the CJA 2003 came into force.

Appeal from the Court of Appeal is to the Supreme Court. Either side may use this appeals procedure but solely on a matter of law which the Court of Appeal has certified is of general public importance and, provided the Court of Appeal or the Supreme Court has granted leave to appeal. The Attorney General may also refer a matter of law to the Supreme Court from the Court of Appeal.

Burden and Standard of Proof

What the Prosecution must Prove

It is a basic principle of English criminal law that a person is innocent until proven guilty. In evidential terms, this means that the prosecution bears the "legal burden" of proving the defendant committed the offence with which he is charged (**Woolmington v DPP [1935] A.C. 462 HL**). The defendant in this case (D) had shot his estranged wife, was convicted of murder and appealed. He claimed that he had taken a gun with him when he went to see his wife with the intention of shooting himself if she did not return to him, but that the gun had gone off accidentally. The trial judge had directed the jury that it was up to D to prove to the jury that the killing was an accident; not murder. The House of Lords held this to have been a misdirection; the prosecution had to prove D killed with intention to kill or to cause serious harm in order to establish guilt. Viscount Sankey L.C. stated:

> "… while the prosecution must prove the guilt of the prisoner, there is no such burden laid on the prisoner to prove his innocence, and it is sufficient for him to raise a doubt as to his guilt; he is not bound to satisfy the jury of his innocence … Throughout the web of the English Criminal Law one golden thread is always to be seen, that is the duty of the prosecution to prove the prisoner's guilt … the principle … is part of the common law of England and no attempt to whittle it down can be entertained."

The standard of proof by which the prosecution must prove guilt is proof "beyond reasonable doubt"; in other words, the jury must be satisfied so that it is sure of the defendant's guilt.

The Burden on the Defendant

The effect of the rule in *Woolmington* is that where the defendant merely denies the whole or part of the prosecution's case, no burden is imposed on him. Where, however, he raises a defence, he bears an "evidential burden" of adducing sufficient evidence (evidence upon which a properly directed jury would be entitled to find that his defence was made out) to persuade the judge to leave the defence to the jury.

For example, if a defendant raises the defence of duress, he will have to adduce evidence that he acted under duress before the judge will allow the defence to go before the jury. Once the defendant has satisfied this evidential burden, the prosecution bears the legal burden of disproving the defence.

Certain defences go beyond the imposition of an evidential burden and actually impose a burden of proof on the defendant. There are many of these so-called reverse proof burdens in the criminal law, but two main defences which you will encounter in this textbook which impose a "reverse onus" are the common law defence of insanity and the statutory defence of diminished responsibility (Homicide Act s.2(2)). Where the defendant bears the legal burden of proving a defence, the standard of proof is the civil standard of proof, i.e. proof "on the balance of probability".

It is possible to argue that placing the legal burden on the defendant violates art.6(2) of the European Convention on Human Rights (the presumption of innocence). However, in **H v UK, Application No 15023/89, April 4, 1990**, the European Commission on Human Rights held that requiring the defendant to prove the defence of insanity did not violate art.6(2). Similarly, in the consolidated appeals of **Lambert; Ali; Jordan [2001] 1 All E.R. 1014**, the Court of Appeal held that the legal burden of proving the defence of diminished responsibility imposed by s.2(2) of the Homicide Act 1957 did not contravene art.6(2).

Reform of the Criminal Law

As we saw above, the criminal law is an amalgam of common law, which has developed in a piecemeal fashion over many centuries, and numerous statutes, many of which are also extremely old. This can sometimes make the law unclear and difficult to find. As Buxton J. stated in the Criminal Law Review ([2000] Crim. L.R. 331),

> "... the present jumble of ancient statutes, more modern accretions to them, and the acres of judicial pronouncements should be replaced by a criminal code that would set out the criminal law in rational, accessible and modern language."

The Law Commission, which was set up in 1965, has as one of its aims the codification of the criminal law. It produced a Draft Criminal Code in 1989: *Criminal Code for England and Wales* (Law Com. No. 177) which would have codified much of the existing law on offences against the person, property and public order and general principles of liability. The Draft Criminal Code mainly restated the law but parts of it were intended to resolve areas of inconsistency or uncertainty and to introduce reform. However, the Draft Code was not enacted, principally because it was too enormous a task for Parliament and the political will was lacking. Since then the Law Commission has concentrated on reform proposals for discrete areas of law such as non-fatal offences against the person, intoxication, fraud and deception, accessorial liability and homicide. These proposals are considered in this textbook in the relevant chapters.

Summary

1. The study of the criminal law is the study of liability, i.e. of guilt or innocence.

2. It is notoriously difficult to define the criminal law, but conduct is criminal if criminal consequences flow from a finding of guilt, e.g. imprisonment.

3. A debate rages in the criminal law about whether liability should be judged subjectively or objectively. On the whole, the subjective approach prevails in respect of most crimes examined in this book.

4. The courts of criminal first instance are the magistrates' court and the Crown Court. The appellate courts are the High Court, Court of Appeal and the Supreme Court.

5. The golden thread of English criminal law is that the prosecution bears the burden of proving the accused is guilty beyond reasonable doubt. A defendant may bear a burden of proof (a reverse proof burden) in respect of a defence, although in this book, these are limited to insanity and diminished responsibility, which the accused must prove on a balance of probabilities.

6. It is always good practice to be aware of any proposals for reform published by the Law Commission.

Actus Reus

2

CHAPTER OVERVIEW

In this chapter we:

● assess the meaning of the term actus reus, and consider what amounts to conduct, circumstances and consequences

● analyse what conduct (by act or omission) may amount to actus reus

● consider which crimes may be committed by omission and when duties to act arise at common law and under statute

● emphasise the importance of causation in result crimes, and consider how causation is proven

● identify when and how the chain of causation may be broken

● analyse the rules governing the coincidence in time of actus reus and mens rea.

Summary

End of Chapter Question

Further Reading

Self Test Questions

Introduction

Liability for most criminal offences arises only if the prosecution can prove that the defendant carried out an act or failed to act in circumstances prohibited by the law; and that at the same time, his state of mind was prohibited, and he had no defence. The basis of this liability is the Latin phrase: actus non facit reum nisi mens sit rea. This translates as "the act is not guilty unless the mind is guilty"; therefore actus reus means guilty act and mens rea means guilty mind. Clearly, there is a difference between an accident which causes injury and a deliberate act which injures another. The difference may not be in the act, but in the state of mind of the actor. Chapter 3 explores the various prohibited states of mind, the mens rea, in detail. This chapter focuses on the acts, omissions, circumstances and consequences which are prohibited in law.

The Latin terms actus reus and mens rea, although strange and confusing at first, will quickly become familiar to any student of the criminal law. Despite criticism of the terms from the highest quarters, they are a useful way of referring to the elements of each crime that have to be proved (usually by the prosecution). Criticism of the terms actus reus or guilty act, and mens rea or guilty mind, arises over the obscurity of the terms. For example, in **Miller [1983] 1 All E.R. 978 HL,** Lord Diplock said:

> "My Lords, it would I think be conducive to clarity of analysis of the ingredient of a crime that is created by statute, as are the great majority of criminal offences today, if we were to avoid bad Latin and instead to think and speak … about the *conduct* of the accused and the *state of mind* at the time of that conduct, instead of speaking of actus reus and mens rea." (emphasis added)

It is certainly misleading to think of actus reus as encompassing only an act, as the phrase is broad enough to cover acts, omissions, circumstances and results. It is for this reason that the Law Commission in its draft Criminal Code Bill (Law Com. No. 177, 1989) prefers the terms "external elements" for the actus reus (denoting external as outside the mens rea or mind of the defendant) and "fault element" for mens rea.

Definition of Actus Reus

The actus reus of each crime is specific to that crime. For example, the actus reus of theft is the appropriation of property belonging to another. The actus reus of so-called "joy-riding" is taking a conveyance for one's own or another's use, without the consent of the owner or other lawful authority. These two offences are defined in the Theft Act 1968.

A useful and practical method of determining the actus reus of a crime is to analyse the definition of the crime in order to identify the mens rea (see Ch.3), and remove that from the definition, then whatever is left is actus reus. A more technically acceptable approach, however, is to identify that part of the crime that is defined in terms of:

1. an act or an omission to act; and/or
2. occurring in specified surrounding circumstances; and/or
3. causing any requisite prohibited consequence.

Each of these, whether it is an act or omission, a circumstance and/or a consequence, is a part of the actus reus of the crime. It is important to note that not all crimes will have all of these elements and a crime can be phrased in terms of an act, or in terms of a result, only. Most commonly, crimes are stated in terms of conduct. For example, under s.1 of the Criminal Attempts Act 1981, the actus reus of an attempted crime is "do[ing] *an act* which is more than merely preparatory to the commission of an offence" (emphasis added). Some crimes are defined by a prohibited result, for example murder, the actus reus of which is causing the death of another. Exceptionally, the actus reus may not require any conduct by the defendant at all. This is where the offence simply requires proof of a defined state of affairs, e.g. being in possession of a controlled drug.

Acts and Omissions

Conduct Crimes

It is sometimes useful to identify certain crimes as conduct crimes. This means the actus reus is phrased in terms of an act or omission, as opposed, for example, to a result or consequence. As seen above, attempted crimes are phrased in terms of acts only, so it is impossible to commit an attempted offence by omission. In some other crimes, the conduct can consist of a failure or omission to act by the defendant, such as failure to report a road traffic accident, or the wilful neglect of a child. Whether by act or omission, there is a fundamental requirement that the conduct is voluntary.

Voluntary Conduct

Voluntary in this context does not mean wanted or desired (which in fact denotes mens rea more than actus reus), but that the defendant's muscular movements are under the control and direction of his conscious mind. If they are not, they are regarded as involuntary and, even though the defendant has carried out the act or omission, he cannot be said to have performed the actus reus. It is common to see this requirement phrased as the defence of automatism but, as you will see, it is not a defence so much as a failure by the prosecution to be able to prove an element of the crime; the actus reus.

It is automatism: if D suffers:

> "a spasm, a reflex action or a convulsion; or an act done by a person who is not conscious of what he is doing, such as an act done whilst suffering from concussion or whilst sleep walking" (Lord Denning in **Bratty v Attorney General for Northern Ireland [1961] 3 All E.R. 523 HL**).

Other examples given by Goff L.J. in **Bell [1984] 3 All E.R. 842 CA,** include:

1. where D loses control whilst driving his car, due to a swarm of bees or an attack by a malevolent passenger; or
2. by a sudden blinding pain; or
3. becoming suddenly unconscious by reason of a blackout; or
4. suffering some vehicle failure, such as a blow-out or through the brakes failing.

Automatism is not a catch-all defence for unconscious or semi-conscious conduct, however, so if D fell asleep whilst driving, he could be convicted of careless driving, even though he was not conscious when the car went out of control as he was clearly at fault in failing to pull over when he realised he was tired.

The two requirements for the defence of automatism are:

1. a total loss of voluntary control;
2. caused by an external factor.

External factors, in addition to those mentioned above, include a blow to the head, medication for conditions such as epilepsy, diabetes and arteriosclerosis, and external influences such as hypnotism and some drugs. The defence of automatism is explored in detail in Ch.12.

Omissions

The Exception not the Rule

Crimes are more often expressed in terms of acts than omissions, but it is possible to be criminally liable for a failure to act. Unlike in other jurisdictions, such as France, the law in England and Wales imposes no general wide-sweeping obligation on citizens to act to save another, or prevent physical harm to others. The general principle is that the English criminal law does not require people to do good; it merely prevents them from behaving badly. There are several reasons for making liability for omissions the exception, rather than the rule. First, imposing liability for an offence of failing to act would be hard if not impossible to enforce, as:

> "If there is an act, someone acts; but if there is an omission, everyone (in a sense) omits. We omit to do everything in the world that is not done. Only those of us omit in law who are under a duty to act." (*Textbook of Criminal Law*, 2nd edn, Williams).

Consequently, whilst it may be morally repugnant to watch a child drowning in a few inches of water without rescuing it, criminal liability does not arise, unless the observer owes the child a duty to save it, for example, because he is the child's father.

Second, proof of causation might be impossible. The stranger watching the child drowning in the puddle above might successfully argue that the child would have died anyway, so his omission did not cause the death (see further **Dytham (1979) 69 Cr. App. R. 387** at pp.17–18 below). Nevertheless, as we shall see, the courts do impose liability despite the causation difficulties where there is a legal duty to act.

Third, an offence of failing to act would conflict with the notion of individual responsibility. For example, suppose D held a dinner party at which a guest, X, became very inebriated, after which X drove home. If X had a crash and killed someone on the way home, would D be liable for failing to stop X from driving? It is considered to be unfair to impose a duty on D to prevent X from driving whilst he was intoxicated. If X is an adult and autonomous, he can decide whether to break the law, and that decision is not one for which D should also take responsibility because he may not have a say in X's decision. He might be under such a duty under French law, but not English law. One of the reasons why English law takes this stance is because through the taxation system, public funds are used to pay for professional rescuers. So, why should an ordinary member of the public put himself at risk in carrying out a rescue that could be better carried out by professionals? Given that funds are allocated, and that a well-meaning rescuer could himself get into trouble and need to be rescued; and also that criminal or civil liability may arise where a person assumes responsibility to save but actually makes the situation worse, the approach of the criminal law is that no liability arises where D does nothing at all.

However, the English criminal law *does* fix liability for an omission if two conditions are satisfied:

1. the offence is capable of being committed by omission;
2. the defendant was under a legal duty to act, either at common law or under statute.

Offences Capable of Being Committed by Omission

Sometimes, as we saw above with attempts, the definition of the offence makes clear that it cannot be committed by omission. In the absence of such clear words in the definition, there are no general principles to apply to determine whether a particular offence can be committed by omission. It is, therefore, necessary to consider the decisions of the courts in respect of a specific offence. In relation to offences against the person, for example, it is well established that murder and manslaughter (by gross negligence or recklessness) and wounding and grievous bodily harm (GBH) offences contrary to ss.18 and 20 of the Offences Against the Person Act 1861 can be committed by omission; but rape cannot, and assault and battery can only in limited circumstances (see p.144). As for property offences, criminal damage can be committed by omission but burglary and robbery cannot.

In **Speck [1977] 2 All E.R. 859**, the defendant was convicted of gross indecency contrary to s.1 of the (now repealed) Indecency with Children Act 1960 which provided that "Any person who commits an act of gross indecency with or towards a child under the age of fourteen … shall be liable …". The defendant had allowed a girl to place her hand on his trousers, putting pressure on his penis, and he had an erection. He had not asked her to do so, or encouraged her to keep her hand there. However the Court of Appeal dismissed his appeal against conviction holding that his *inactivity* was capable of amounting to an invitation to the child to undertake the act done. So, although the offence states "an act", his inactivity, according to the appeal court, amounted to sufficient activity to justify a conviction.

Whilst in **Ahmad (1987) 84 Cr. App. R. 64**, a landlord was not guilty of "doing *acts*" calculated to interfere with the peace or comfort of a residential occupier where he failed to complete works that were necessary to make the premises habitable (finishing the bathroom to make it useable), in **Yuthiwattana (1985) 80 Cr. App. R. 55** the defendant landlord did do an *act* calculated to interfere with the peace or comfort of the tenant when he *failed* to replace the front door key the tenant had lost.

Common Law Duties

CONTRACTUAL DUTIES

Contracts are private agreements that do not have legal effect outside the terms of the contract. They apply to the parties inter se or between themselves only. The criminal law has always been reluctant to rely on a contract to impose liability. However, exceptionally, it has done so where the breach of contract endangers the public. For example, in **Pittwood (1902) 19 T.L.R. 37**, although the defendant's contractual duties as a level crossing operator were owed to his employer, he was convicted of manslaughter when he failed to shut the gate before a train was due, resulting in the death of the victim. Were the same situation to arise today, liability could alternatively be imposed under the *Miller* principal, as explained on pp.21–22 below, rather than under the contract.

Doctors are under a duty to their patients. The duty arises either because of their contracts of employment or under the law of Torts. The leading case discussing the responsibility of doctors towards their patients is **Airedale NHS Trust v Bland [1993] A.C. 789**. Bland had attended the Hillsborough football stadium and was very seriously injured when overcrowding in the stand led to many fans being crushed. His cortex (that part of the brain which governs higher functions at the conscious level) was destroyed, but his brain stem (which controls reflexive functions at an unconscious level) enabled his heart and lungs to work unaided. He had been in a persistent vegetative state for over three years when the hospital authority applied for a declaration that it was lawful for the doctors to discontinue treatment and artificial feeding by nasal tube. All agreed there was no hope of his recovery at all. Without treatment and feeding, Bland would die within a relatively short time.

It is part of the original terms of the doctor's Hippocratic Oath "never [to] do harm to anyone" and, this translates in legal terms to being under a positive (tortious or contractual) duty to act to treat and care for his patients. The House of Lords held, however, that as "responsible and competent medical opinion" took the view that it was not in the patient's "best interests" to continue the treatment and care, the declaration sought by the hospital authority would be granted. This is a civil case, but has application to the criminal law as well. This is not just because civil cases are persuasive on criminal courts; nor that House of Lords' cases are more persuasive than those of inferior courts, but where the highest court in any jurisdiction makes a judgment about life and death, such a decision is of great influence should a criminal court have to decide on the liability of a party in such a case in the future.

So, if it is in the best interests of the patient, it cannot be unlawful to omit to continue treatment, but:

> "the termination of artificial feeding and hydration for patients in a persistent vegetative state will in virtually all cases require the prior sanction of a High Court judge" (Practice Note issued by the Official Solicitor ([1994] 2 All E.R. 413).

Prior sanction is not, however, needed in an emergency (**Frenchay Healthcare NHS Trust v S [1994] 1 W.L.R. 601**). It is important not to overstate the effect of these judgments. They allow only the discontinuation of treatment, and it would be a criminal offence to take active steps to kill (e.g. by way of an overdose) someone in a persistent vegetative case, even if it was in the patient's "best interests". Even where such steps are taken to assist another's suicide, that is an offence contrary to s.2 of the Suicide Act 1961. Charges may not necessarily be brought though, depending on the facts. At the time of writing, the Director of Public Prosecutions has issued a new policy for prosecutors specifying the factors that should be taken into account when deciding if charges should be brought for assisted suicide following the House of Lords' decision in **R. (on the application of Purdy) v DPP [2009] 3 W.L.R. 403**. See further *http://www.cps.gov. uk/publications/prosecution/assisted_suicide_policy.html* (last accessed February 26, 2010).

DUTY ARISING OUT OF A PUBLIC OFFICE

In *Dytham*, D, a uniformed police officer who was about to go off duty, watched and did nothing to intervene when a man was thrown out of a night club and then kicked and beaten to death in the gutter. D was convicted of the common law offence of misconduct in a public office. His appeal against conviction was dismissed because his omission had been wilful, unreasonable and so contrary to the public interest so as to call for condemnation and punishment. Interestingly, D was not charged with manslaughter, despite the fact that he was under a contractual duty to protect V, and failed to do so. As discussed on p.15 above, the prosecution may have decided it would be impossible to prove that D had caused V's death.

RELATIONSHIP

It is trite law that a parent or guardian owes a moral and legal duty to its minor child; so, it was murder in **Gibbins and Proctor (1918) 13 Cr. App. R. 134 CCA**, where a father deliberately failed to feed his child; his life partner was also convicted as she had assumed de facto parental responsibility. It is not clear in law how far other familial operate to impose a duty to care for another. In **Smith (1826) 172 ER 203**, for example, it was held that there was no legal obligation on one brother to feed the other, who was an adult but also helpless. In the same case, it was considered that a spouse has a duty of care to the other, but in the more recent case of **Smith [1979] Crim. L.R. 251**, this was supplemented with a requirement of the victim's incapacity and dependency on the other. D's wife died after giving birth to a still-born child at home. She had adamantly refused to allow her husband to call medical help because of her acute phobia about doctors. Although she did finally relent, she died before medical assistance could save her. D was charged with manslaughter of his wife. The jury could not agree and was discharged, but the trial judge suggested that what is relevant in this situation is the wife's:

> "capacity to make rational decisions. If she does not appear too ill it may be reasonable to abide by her wishes. On the other hand, if she appeared desperately ill then whatever she may say it may be right to override".

More recently in **Hood [2004] 1 Cr. App. R. (S.) 73**, the husband was convicted of the gross negligence manslaughter of his wife because he delayed calling for medical assistance for her, he being her sole carer, for three weeks after a fall which contributed to her weakened state and her ultimate death from pneumonia.

It would seem to be a logical extension of this principle of a duty between spouses to one between civil partners in a situation of incapacity and dependency, although in the US case of **People v Beardsley (1907) 113 N.W. 1128**, a man did not owe a duty to his lover who had taken an overdose of morphine.

What is less clear, and there is no case law to assist us, is whether the duty extends, for example, to children who are independent adults, but who may rely on their parents for assistance every now and again. Consider, for example, an adult child who lives independently, but goes to the parental home if illness strikes. The family relationship per se does not appear to be sufficient to impose a duty, as shown by the cases examined below.

ASSUMPTION OF RESPONSIBILITY

If a person voluntarily undertakes the responsibility to care for another who is dependent on them, whether a member of his family or not, then he is under a duty to continue to act. In **Stone and Dobinson [1977] 2 All E.R. 341**, the Court of Appeal upheld the convictions of the defendants for manslaughter when they failed to summon help for Stone's sister who had died whilst under their, rather pathetic, care. The sister, Fanny, was anorexic and had refused to accept their food. The first defendant, Stone, was 67, partially deaf, nearly blind and of low intelligence. His partner, Dobinson, was described by the court as ineffectual and inadequate. Sometime before her death, the defendants had attempted to summon medical assistance, but when Fanny later refused to communicate or eat, they did nothing, not even alerting the social worker who occasionally visited Stone's son. A duty was owed by the defendants to Fanny; and the reasons for imposing a duty seem to be cumulative:

1. Fanny was a blood relation to Stone;
2. she was living in his house; and
3. the defendants had voluntarily assumed a duty to act by their attempts to care for her.

The decision to uphold the convictions attracted much criticism. Had the defendants turned Fanny away when she arrived on their doorstep, no crime would have been committed. Is it better, therefore, to refuse to help, than to try, but fail? Also, is it fair of the law to impose liability on a person who is incapable of doing "normal" acts, such as asking for help? On the other hand, the defendants were not totally blameless; they had tried to get a doctor to see her at an earlier date, but there were complications because Fanny was not registered with a local GP, and they had given up. Had they told the social worker, another doctor, or any other authority, it is widely accepted that they would have discharged their duty to the best of their (limited) ability.

Less controversial cases include **Nicholls (1874) 13 Cox C.C. 75**, where a grandmother was guilty of manslaughter for neglecting her grandchild after its mother died, and **Instan [1893] 1 Q.B. 450**. D lived with her 73-year-old aunt to whom, while she was healthy, D owed no duty. The aunt then contracted gangrene in her leg which rendered her totally helpless. D bought food with her aunt's money, but gave none to her, did not seek medical assistance, and told no-one of this condition. D was convicted of manslaughter on the basis that she was under, and breached, a duty of care. The exact nature of the duty was not identified by the Court for Crown Cases Reserved. Lord Coleridge C.J. held that the only way in which the aunt could be fed was by the acts of the defendant, but he did not specify whether the legal duty arose because of an assumption of responsibility, through a contractual obligation by taking her money, or for some other reason.

In the more recent case of **Khan (Uzma) [2009] 1 W.L.R. 2036**, the deceased had been murdered by her husband, but this appeal concerned the convictions of three members of the same house-hold, namely the sisters and brother-in-law of the husband, for allowing the death of a vulnerable adult, contrary to s.5(1) of the Domestic Violence, Crime and Victims Act 2004. The prosecution case against each defendant was that the deceased's condition during the three weeks before the final attack on her was such that it was and must have been apparent to each of them that she had been and was being subjected to serious physical violence. The Court of Appeal dismissed their appeals, holding that the defendants were aware or *ought to have been aware* of the deceased's physical condition. The words in italics impose a duty on an objective basis; not what D knew (subjective) but also what he *should have known*. This is expanded in the case of **Evans [2009] 1 W.L.R. 1999** discussed below.

So, is it possible to assume responsibility, and thus be under a duty, outside family relation-ships? The Court of Appeal was certainly willing to consider extending the law in **Khan and Khan [1998] Crim. L.R. 830** to a drug dealer who supplied heroin snorted by the victim in the dealer's flat. The duty, as a minimum, would be to summon medical assistance when the victim lapsed into a coma. In **Ruffell [2003] 2 Cr. App. R. (S.) 53**, the defendant and deceased had each self-injected with drugs, but when the deceased showed signs of overdose, the defendant first tried to revive him and then left the deceased outside his house. He telephoned the deceased's mother asking her to collect her son. The deceased later died of hypothermia and opiate intoxication. The trial judge rejected D's submission that he did not owe a duty of care to the deceased: the deceased was a guest of D in his family home and he was a friend and D had taken upon himself the duty of trying to revive him after what had happened; that created a sufficient nexus to give rise to a duty of care.

Although *Ruffell* is an appeal against sentence rather than conviction, the Court Appeal approved the trial judge's reasoning. The defendant had assumed a duty when he tried to revive the deceased, and breached it when he left him outside in the cold.

In *Evans*, the defendant supplied her sister with heroin, which the sister self-administered. The Court of Appeal held that a duty did not arise simply from the fact of supply, but because the defendant realised her sister had overdosed and did not summon medical help. In fact, the Court went further, and held:

> "when a person has created or contributed to the creation of a state of affairs which he knows, *or ought reasonably to know*, has become life threatening, a consequent duty on him to act by taking reasonable steps to save the other's life will normally arise." (emphasis added).

The italicised words again denote an objective basis for finding liability. It may be said that whenever a drug dealer supplies drugs to a user who self-injects or self-administers the drug, even if the drug dealer does not *know* the situation is potentially life-threatening (say, he leaves before he realises the drug user has overdosed), it could be said he *ought reasonably to know*.

Over to you...

The exact boundaries of when a person owes a duty in the criminal law are not set. You may be assessed on the "grey" areas where there are no decided cases, as outlined above. Your task involves reviewing the decided cases and reaching an informed conclusion, depending on the facts.

In *Evans*, the reference to the "state of affairs" is adopted from the case of **Miller [1983] 2 A.C. 161** which we consider now.

CREATION OF A DANGEROUS SITUATION (SUPERVENING FAULT)

Miller was a squatter who fell asleep smoking a cigarette, whilst resting on a mattress in a house. He awoke to find the mattress smouldering, but instead of putting the fire out, he merely moved to another room and went back to sleep. Convicted of criminal damage, he appealed on the basis that it is impossible to commit criminal damage by omission and/or he was not under a duty to act. However, the House of Lords held that even though D had inadvertently and without fault created a dangerous situation, he had a duty to take steps reasonably available to him on becoming aware of the danger to prevent further damage. D was therefore guilty of arson (i.e. causing criminal damage by fire). Steps which would have relieved D of his duty would, for example, have been for D to raise the alarm, or call the fire brigade. It is for the court to decide what steps are reasonable for D to take in any given situation but they would certainly not include any actions putting himself at significant risk.

On the facts, the defendant in **Fagan v Metropolitan Police Commissioner [1968] 3 All E.R. 442 DC** could have been convicted using the *Miller* principle where the fault-free creation of a dangerous situation was followed by deliberate (or even reckless) failure to rectify the situation. D was told by a police officer not to park his car in a particular place but to park it elsewhere. He parked it on the officer's foot! When the officer told D to move the car, D rudely refused. D was convicted of battery even though it was accepted that the initial parking on the foot was accidental, but the court had doubts over whether it was possible to assault or batter someone by an omission. Instead, the court adopted a "continuous" act analysis; that driving the car onto the foot and leaving it there was a continuous act. The continuous act theory attracted support from the Court of Appeal in *Miller*, but the House of Lords regarded the failure to act as distinct from the inadvertent initial act.

The principle in *Miller* extends to a duty to warn another of the risk of injury where D creates the danger and thereby exposes another to a reasonably foreseeable risk of injury which subsequently materialises. Hence, D committed the actus reus of an assault in **DPP v Santa-Bermudez [2004]**

Crim. L.R. 471, when, prior to a body search, he failed to inform a police officer of the presence of exposed hypodermic needles in his pocket.

Who Decides if There is a Duty?

Case law has not been clear, until recently, on whether the existence of a duty was for the judge alone, for the jury alone or for both to decide. This was addressed in *Evans* (above) and Ormerod summarises the situation thus:

> "As to responsibility for determining the existence of a duty, inconsistent authorities had generated considerable academic debate whether the duty question was to be determined by the judge or the jury and whether it was a pure question of fact ... The court provides welcome clarification that whether D owes a duty of care remains a question of law. The jury should be directed on what the law is, for example whether a duty existed if they find certain facts to be established." ([2009] 9 Crim. L.R. 661, Case Commentary to *Evans*).

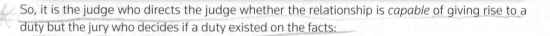

So, it is the judge who directs the judge whether the relationship is *capable* of giving rise to a duty but the jury who decides if a duty existed on the facts:

> "In any cases where the issue is in dispute ... and assuming that the judge has found that it would be open to the jury to find that there was a duty of care, or a duty to act, the jury should be directed that if facts a + b and/or c or d are established, then in law a duty will arise, but if facts x or y or z were present, the duty would be negatived." (per Lord Judge C.J. in *Evans*).

Statutory Duties

There are hundreds of statutory offences which impose liability for omissions. For example, consider the offence under s.5 of the Domestic Violence, Crime and Victims Act 2004 mentioned in respect of *Khan (Uzma)* above. Many of the motoring offences of which you have heard such as failing to display a vehicle tax disc, failing to stop after or report an accident and failing to conform to a traffic signal also fix criminal liability for failing to act.

State of Affairs Offences

In **Winzar v Chief Constable of Kent (1983), The Times, March 28**, the police were called to remove D, who was drunk, from a hospital. D was put in a police car and was then charged with being found drunk on the highway—the highway being where the police car was parked! It seems bizarre that D could be convicted of an offence where he had no choice at all about his location, but the offence under s.12 of the Licensing Act 1872 is complete if a person is perceived to be drunk on the highway. This is the state of affairs prohibited by the law and it is irrelevant that D's presence is not of his own volition. It is wrong to say that the offence has no actus reus; the actus reus is completed by the state of affairs, and D's act or omission is irrelevant (i.e. it is not a conduct crime). It is worth noting, however, that the offence under s.12 above has no mens rea requirement. This is actually an offence of absolute liability, and we shall be considering this concept again on p.68 in relation to strict liability offences.

Circumstances

We have noted that crimes may be defined in terms of a result (consequence) or some form of conduct (act or omission), or both. A further common element of the actus reus is the presence of some defined surrounding circumstances. The particular circumstances which are required are governed by the definition of the particular crime in issue. For example, the actus reus of theft is satisfied if D appropriates (conduct) property which belongs to another. It is the circumstance that the property belongs to another. If the property has been abandoned, it does not belong to another and the actus reus of the crime is not complete.

Any element of the crime which refers to the *victim's* state of mind is also an element of the actus reus. For example, rape requires the penetration of a person who does not consent. The lack of consent of the victim is part of the actus reus of the offence. Failure by the prosecution to prove lack of consent must result in an acquittal.

Causation

Result Crimes

Result crimes are those crimes where the actus reus requires a result or consequence. Both murder and manslaughter are result crimes; that is that D's conduct results in another's death. Obviously, conduct is needed; the death must be brought about by D by some form of conduct such as stabbing, poisoning, strangling, deliberate neglect, etc. but as long as the consequence is achieved, the law does not proscribe the method in a result crime. Rather, the critical feature of a result crime is the proof that D caused the result. This is expressed in the following terms: there must be a chain of causation between the defendant's conduct and the result.

In most cases, there will be no complexity or controversy; if D stabs the victim seven times, and the victim dies immediately, we can safely conclude D caused the death. Confusion can arise, however, where there are multiple concurrent or consecutive events, all of which could be said to have contributed to the result. For example, consider the facts of one of the key cases; Cheshire [1991] 1 W.L.R. 844. D shot the victim in the stomach and leg in a fish and chip shop. V was placed in intensive care in hospital. When he developed breathing difficulties, he was fitted with a tracheotomy to help him breathe. More than two months later, when the original injuries were no longer life threatening, V died as a result of windpipe constriction associated with the tracheotomy. D was charged with V's murder. A consultant surgeon gave evidence at trial that death had been caused by negligent medical treatment; had the windpipe constriction been correctly identified and treated, V would not have died. The negligence could be viewed as a subsequent or consecutive event which might have broken the chain of causation. We will return to this case below to examine whether the negligence did relieve the defendant of liability.

Before we discuss the relevant legal principles, it is vital to understand that the question of causation is not necessarily what the lay person thinks it is. The lay person might think that the question for the court is, "What (or who) caused the result?" but instead it is, "Did the defendant charged with this offence cause the result prohibited in the definition of the crime charged?" The facts of **Empress Car Co (Abertillery) Ltd v National Rivers Authority [1998] 1 All E.R. 481** serve to illustrate this point. The defendant company had on its land a storage tank which was filled with oil. The tank was surrounded by a protective bund or embankment. D had fitted a pipe to the tank with a tap on the pipe, and an unknown third party opened the tap, which was unlocked, causing the oil to escape outside the area protected by the bund. The escaped oil drained into a nearby river and D was charged with the offence of "causing … polluting matter … to enter … controlled waters" contrary to s.85(1) of the Water Resources Act 1991. If we ask "Who caused the result?" the answer is the unknown third party. Clearly, the defendant company would then have to be acquitted; but if we ask "Did the defendant cause the result?" we can better apply the relevant law and attribute responsibility (or not) to the party who has been charged, here it is the company.

That said, neither legal principle nor clearly enunciated legal rules are especially easy to discover within this topic. Many commentators justify this lacuna by saying the cases are decided on grounds of "policy", but as Ormerod (Smith and Hogan, *Criminal Law*, 12 edn) comments:

> "an analysis of causation cannot proceed independently of the criterion of blameworthiness and, going further, is dependent on it. Causation cannot be judged in purely objective physical terms."

puts the inconsistencies down to the "diversity of factual circumstances" and the "rather loose language" adopted by the courts. So, "the best that can be offered by way of guidance is a series of principles, some of which are openly in conflict".

Establishing the Chain of Causation

Our task is to assess whether D caused the result and this requires us to consider the link between D's act and its consequence(s). What the prosecution has to prove is that there is a chain of causation between the defendant's act and the consequence. The test to establish the chain of causation has two limbs. First, D's conduct must *in fact* cause the prohibited consequence; and, second, D's conduct must *in law* cause that consequence.

Factual Causation

The first element consists of asking whether or not D in fact caused the result. It is a matter of simple logistics and the answer is normally very obvious. In relation to murder or manslaughter, since everyone dies sooner or later, the question is "would the victim have died then?" The defendant must be said to have caused an acceleration of death. For an example of how this works we can consider the case of **White [1910] 2 K.B. 124**, although on the facts, causation was not established. D put potassium cyanide into his mother's drink intending her to drink it and die. However, she suffered a heart attack and died having drunk only a quarter of the liquid. Medical evidence established that her death resulted from heart failure and not from poisoning. D did not in fact cause his mother's death. As causation was not established, there was no actus reus, but he was convicted of attempted murder.

A result that would have occurred anyway and that D could not have prevented is not caused by D; but if D could have prevented it, it may be said to have been caused by him. According to Ormerod (Smith and Hogan, *Criminal Law*, 12th edn, the "culpable element" must be attributable to D's act or omission. In **R. v Dalloway (1847) 2 Cox 273**, D was driving a horse and cart without holding the reins. A child suddenly jumped into the road, and was run over and killed. The jury could convict of manslaughter only if it was satisfied that D could have stopped if he was using the reins and driving properly. If the jury felt D could not have stopped even if driving carefully, he did not in fact cause the death (see also **Longbottom (1849) 3 Cox C 439**).

There are two other ways the "in fact" test can be phrased: But for D's acts, would the result have occurred? Or, was D the causa sine qua non (without which cause) of the result? However the test is phrased, though, it is the same. If the answer to the test is that D did not in fact cause the result, then that is the end of the matter. However, if D was the factual cause of the result, a further, legal test of causation must be employed.

Legal Causation

As Professor Williams explained (*Textbook of Criminal Law*, 2nd edn):

"When one has settled the question of but-for causation, the further test to be applied to the but-for cause in order to qualify it for legal recognition is not a test of causation but a moral reaction. The question is whether the result can fairly be said to be imputable to the defendant … If the term 'cause' must be used, it can best be distinguished in this meaning as the 'imputable' or 'responsible' or 'blameable' cause, to indicate the value-judgment involved."

It is not just a case, however, of having a moral reaction or making a value-judgment. There are legal rules involved, and misdirection on this point could lead to a successful appeal. The reason for there being two stages to the test of causation (fact and law) is that we are not all legally responsible for every consequence of each of our acts. Every act has an infinite number of possible consequences and we cannot be found to be legally responsible for them all. At some stage, consequences which may be unforeseen or even unforeseeable cannot be attributed to the original actor; even if we might find a factual causal link between them.

A defendant is said to have been the legal cause of the result if his contribution to that result was an "operating and substantial cause" (**Smith [1959] 2 All E.R. 193 CMAC**) although it has been held that just "substantial" or even "more than negligible" are acceptable directions to the jury. Where there are a number of possible contributory causes, provided D's conduct was "more than a slight or a trifling link", D's conduct does not have to be the only cause or even the most important cause of it (**Kimsey [1996] Crim. L.R. 35**). As Goff L.J. stated in **R. v Pagett (1983) 76 Cr. App. R. 279:**

"in law the accused's act need not be the sole cause, or even the main cause … it being enough that his act contributed significantly to the result".

It is usually not difficult to find that D made a "more than negligible" contribution to the outcome. In **Benge (1865) 4 F. & F. 504**, a train crash occurred when the train driver failed to spot that part of the track had been lifted for repair. A signalman had been sent down the track to flag the danger, but he had not been sent far enough down the line when the train arrived. It was the foreman platelayer, D, who was convicted of manslaughter. He had misread the timetable and authorised the track being lifted. The simultaneous or consecutive contributions to the resulting deaths by the signalman and train driver did not absolve D from criminal responsibility.

Breaking the Chain of Causation

Once the chain is established, usually a simple matter, it is possible for an intervening event, or novus actus interveniens, to break the chain. It is important to recall that if the chain of causation is broken, D is relieved of liability. The outcome in some of the cases below is inconsistent, but there are "policy" considerations, moral reactions, issues of blameworthiness involved, and sometimes, the appeal courts seem to perpetuate the confusion by failing to clarify the law; possibly to secure the conviction of a "clearly" guilty party.

Events which may break the chain of causation include:

1. naturally occurring events;
2. the conduct of a third party;
3. negligent medical treatment; and/or
4. actions or reactions of the victim.

NATURALLY OCCURRING EVENTS

Natural events which are reasonably foreseeable do not break the chain of causation, but extraordinary, unforeseeable or abnormal events, sometimes called "Acts of God" do. For example, per **Perkins (1946) 36 J Cr L & Cr 393**, if D knocks V unconscious and leaves him on the beach below the high water mark so that V is drowned by the incoming tide, D has legally caused V's death. The event of the tide coming in is natural, foreseeable and it does not break the chain of causation. If, on the other hand, V dies whilst lying unconscious on the beach when he is hit by rocks falling from the cliff above during an earthquake, the courts might well say that this was extraordinary and D's conduct would no longer be the legal cause of death. The reason for the distinction is considered below.

THE CONDUCT OF A THIRD PARTY

Where the intervening event between D's conduct and the result is the act of a third party, the test is whether the conduct of that third party was "free, deliberate and informed". If it was, the chain of causation is broken; and this is true whether or not the third party's conduct was foreseeable.

In **Latif [1996] 1 W.L.R. 104**, D arranged to export heroin from Pakistan to the UK. The delivery was intercepted by a British customs officer. On appeal against conviction for being knowingly concerned in the fraudulent evasion of the prohibition on importation of a controlled drug, the House of Lords held that the free, deliberate and informed intervention of the customs officer broke the chain of causation and D had not caused the crime. He was, however, guilty of an attempt.

In *Pagett*, D was surrounded by police officers who were trying to arrest him. D was armed with a loaded shotgun and he shot at the police. He used his 16-year-old pregnant girlfriend as a human shield in the event that the officers returned fire, which of course they did when he fired on them, and the girlfriend was killed. D appealed against his conviction for manslaughter on the basis that it should have been left to the jury to consider that his was not the "imputable" cause of his girlfriend's death. The Court of Appeal, dismissing his appeal, accepted that occasionally the intervention of a third person might be regarded as a new intervening act (a novus actus interveniens), but a reasonable act performed for the purpose of self-preservation, including a reasonable act of self-defence, is not one. So, while the officers' actions were certainly deliberate and informed, they could not be said to be a free reaction to the situation.

In the *Empress Car Co* case (above), it was the act of the unknown third party who opened the tap which "caused" the oil to flow into the river. This person clearly did an act which was free, deliberate and informed; and probably malicious. Adopting the principles explained above, the defendant company could clearly argue the chain of causation (from storing the oil in a tank with an unlocked tap to the oil draining into the water) was broken by the act of the third party. However, staggeringly, the company's appeal against conviction was dismissed. For the House of Lords, the principle was not whether the third party's act was free, deliberate and informed, but rather whether it:

> "... should be regarded as a normal fact of life or something extraordinary. If it was in the general run of things a matter of ordinary occurrence, it will not negative the causal effect of the defendant's acts, even if it was not foreseeable that it would happen to that particular defendant or take that particular form. If it can be regarded as something extraordinary, it will be open to the justices to hold that the defendant did not cause the pollution ... The distinction between ordinary and extraordinary is one of fact and degree to which the justices must apply their common sense and knowledge of what happens in the area."

It is submitted that Lord Hoffman, who delivered the leading speech of a unanimous House, confused the two tests explained above. Naturally occurring interventions are judged by the measure of reasonable foreseeability, but the same is not true for acts of a third party. The foreseeability of a free, deliberate and informed act of a third party has never been relevant. There is a very good reason for this. Natural events are, on the whole, unstoppable. Therefore, if they are foreseeable, they should not relieve D of liability. On the other hand, human beings are autonomous. We are free to make decisions about our actions. We are therefore also responsible for the consequences of our actions, as is a third party whose intervention interrupts the consequences of our acts. They take over in terms of responsibility in a way that could not be paralleled by a natural event. If the *Empress Cars* test is adopted as the general rule for causation, the danger is that:

> "... D's criminal liability for causing an actus reus would not be under his own control, but would instead be subject to the autonomous choice of someone else." (Simester and Sullivan, *Criminal Law: Theory and Doctrine*, 2nd edn)

The ratio decidendi of *Empress* is limited however and the decision is restricted to the operation of s.85(1) of the Water Resources Act 1991. It is acknowledged that there is scope for the decision to govern the causal test for all regulatory (strict liability) offences, but it should not be adopted further afield. Ormerod (Smith and Hogan, *Criminal Law*, 12th edn) traces the cause of Lord Hoffmann's confusion to his reliance on a Torts case (**Stansbie v Troman [1948] 2 K.B. 48**), the result of which is that *Empress* is an "aberrant authority" and "ought not to be followed".

NEGLIGENT MEDICAL TREATMENT

It is a common consequence of a criminal act that medical treatment is required. Such treatment might be capable of constituting the free, deliberate and informed conduct discussed above; and may therefore break the chain of causation. Two points must be made. The first is that sound medical practice will not break the chain of causation: a doctor who switches off a life support machine is not the cause of the death where V was originally and criminally injured by D (**Malcherek and Steel [1981] 1 W.L.R. 690**). The second point is that even poor medical treatment which itself contributes to death will not break the chain of causation as long as the wound itself is still playing a significant (i.e. more than minimal) role in bringing about the death.

In **Smith [1959] 2 Q.B. 423**, D, a soldier, was charged with murder after a barrack-room brawl. V had received two bayonet wounds, one of which pierced the lung and caused haemorrhaging. While being carried to the medical reception station for treatment he was dropped twice. The medical officer then failed to realise the seriousness of the wound and gave the wrong treatment, described by the court as "thoroughly bad". However, D was found to have been the cause of the death. According to Lord Parker C.J.:

> "Only if it can be said that the original wounding is merely the setting in which another cause operates can it be said that the death does not result from the wound. Putting it in another way, only if the second cause is so overwhelming as to make the original wound merely part of the history can it be said that the death does not flow from the wound."

An example of medical treatment amounting to an overwhelming cause could have arisen in **Jordan (1956) 40 Cr. App. R. 152 CA** (in fact, the issue did not arise at trial and the Court of Appeal allowed the appeal because the jury had not been directed to consider the question of causation). The original wound caused by D had almost healed when V died because the hospital had continued to administer an antibiotic to V to which he had already shown himself intolerant. The medical treatment was described by the court as "palpably wrong".

windpipe

Jordan should now be read in light of *Cheshire* (above) where medical experts similarly testified to the negligence of the medical treatment; and still the chain was not broken. The Court of Appeal rephrased the "so overwhelming" test from *Smith*, above, in the following terms:

> "when the victim of a criminal attack is treated for wounds or injuries by doctors or other medical staff attempting to repair the harm done, it will only be in the most extraordinary and unusual case that such treatment can be said to be so independent of the acts of the defendant that it could be regarded in law as the cause of the victim's death to the exclusion of the defendant's acts."

And further,

> "... the accused's acts did not need to be the sole or even the main cause of the death, it being sufficient that his acts contributed significantly to that result, and that even though negligence in the treatment of the victim was the immediate cause of his death, [the jury] should not regard it as excluding the responsibility of the accused unless the negligent treatment was *so independent of his acts and in itself so potent in causing death that they regarded the contribution made by his acts as insignificant.*" (emphasis added)

The Court of Appeal quoted Professors Hart and Honore, authors of one of the authoritative writings on causation:

> "treatment which falls short of the standard expected of the competent medical practitioner is unfortunately *only too frequent* in human experience for it to be considered *abnormal* in the sense of extraordinary" (emphasis added).

It is sobering that medical negligence is almost to be expected:

> "Whilst medical treatment unsuccessfully given to prevent the death of a victim with the care and skill of a competent medical practitioner will not amount to an intervening cause, it does not follow that treatment which falls below that standard of care and skill will amount to such a cause" (per Beldam L.J.).

References to the italicised terms indicate that the true test adopted is one of foreseeability, and that negligent medical treatment is within a range of foreseeable risks. Whilst it is all a matter of degree (so potent, so independent, etc.), it is a logical consequence that only outrageously (grossly) negligent treatment will break the chain of causation.

Even if medical treatment, administered correctly and in a timely manner, could save the victim, the chain of causation may still not be broken. In **Mellor [1996] 2 Cr. App. R. 245**, D stabbed an elderly victim causing broncho-pneumonia from which V died. However, expert testimony was given to the effect that if oxygen had been administered to V in sufficient time, it was likely the broncho-pneumonia would not have been fatal. Despite this, D's conviction was upheld by the Court of Appeal as the stabbing by D contributed significantly to V's death. Schiemann L.J. stated:

> "In homicide cases, where [V] does not die immediately, supervening events will occur which are likely to have some causative effect leading to [V's] death; for example, a delay in the arrival of the ambulance, a delay in resuscitation, [V's] individual response to medical or surgical treatment, and the quality of medical, surgical and nursing care. Sometimes such an event may be the result of negligence or mistake or bad luck. It is a question of fact and degree in each case for the jury to decide, having regard to the gravity of the supervening event, however caused, whether the injuries inflicted by the defendant were a significant cause of death".

Where the defendant injures a victim who has a pre-existing condition which is not discovered until he is treated, the law is that only an extraordinary and unusual medical decision that life saving treatment is not possible will break the chain of causation. In **McKechnie (1992) 94 Cr. App. R. 51**, D assaulted V causing him severe brain damage. When he arrived at the hospital, it was discovered that V had a duodenal ulcer. The doctors decided not to operate on the ulcer, however, because they thought V might die under the anaesthetic as a result of the head injuries suffered in D's attack. The ulcer burst five weeks later and V died. D was held liable for V's death. D's appeal against conviction was dismissed. The case has aroused some academic comment as one could opine that "but for" the duodenal ulcer, V might not have died, so D was not the factual cause of death, (cf. *White* on p.25 above). However, "but for" the head injuries sustained in the attack, the ulcer could have been operated upon successfully (presuming it would have been discovered had V not been attacked, of course).

ACTIONS OR REACTIONS OF THE VICTIM

Where the event between the last act of the defendant and the ultimate result is an action or reaction of the victim, the law is a confusing mix of the "free, deliberate and informed" and the "reasonably foreseeable" tests considered above.

■ The "flight" cases

Suppose that D has threatened V with physical harm and V feels he has to escape the threat, V's reaction to "flight" is likely to be viewed as reasonably foreseeable rather than unusual or extraordinary. The same conclusion is reached if the situation is considered from the alternative legal stance, i.e. whether it is "free, deliberate and informed" because, as D has threatened V, V's reaction is not truly "free". It does not, therefore, break the chain of causation.

In **Roberts (1971) 56 Cr. App. R. 95**, D made unwanted sexual advances to V, a young girl who was a passenger in his car. D boasted of his sexual exploits and of how he had used force on women in the past. He attempted to remove her clothing and V, being terrified, jumped from the moving car. She was injured as a result. The question was who caused the injuries: D or V herself? In the words of Stephenson L.J., dismissing D's appeal:

> "The test is: Was it the natural result of what the alleged assailant said and did, in the sense that it was something that could reasonably have been foreseen as the consequence of what he was saying or doing?"

When considering whether a reaction could reasonably have been foreseen, the question is not a subjective one (could D reasonably have foreseen it?) but wholly objective (might a reasonable person "finding himself in the circumstances in which the accused was" have foreseen the victim's reaction? (**Marjoram [2000] Crim. L.R. 372 CA**)).

A disproportionate response, or over-reaction, is likely to absolve D of liability. On similar facts to *Roberts*, but in the absence of proof of any threat made by D to V, in **Williams [1992] 2 All E.R. 183 CA**, the question was:

> "whether the deceased's reaction in jumping from the moving car was within the range of responses which might be expected from a victim placed in the situation in which he was".

The same test was used here as was used in *Roberts*; was the victim's reaction "daft"?

■ Neglect by V

Cases examined here are situations in which V neglects to treat his injuries or makes them worse, and the issue is whether D is absolved from liability in this event. This part should to be read in light of the operation of the thin skull rule considered on p.35 below.

In **Holland (1841) 2 Mood. & R. 351**, D cut V's finger very badly. The wound became infected but V refused to comply with the medical advice, which was to have his finger amputated or risk his life. V developed lockjaw as a result of the wound and died. The court found D liable for V's death. The judge told the jury that it made no difference whether the wound was in its own nature instantly mortal or whether it became the cause of death because V did not use the best treatment.

In **Dear [1996] Crim. L.R. 595**, D attacked V with a knife after being told V had sexually assaulted D's 12-year-old daughter. V had been found by a neighbour but he refused all assistance and was adamant that an ambulance should not be called. V had reopened the knife wounds or, at least, had not staunched the blood flow following the reopening of the wounds. He died two days after the initial assault. A note found by the victim's body was referred to by police as a suicide note. Medical evidence was given that the victim would have survived the attack had the injuries been properly treated. D appealed against conviction for murder on the ground, inter alia, that V's actions had broken the chain of causation, but the Court of Appeal dismissed his appeal because the jury had been correctly directed that they were entitled to find that D's conduct was an operating and substantial cause of death. In his Commentary to the case in the Criminal Law Review, Professor John Smith queried whether the case would have been rightly decided, if the original knife wounds inflicted by D had been almost healed when V reopened them:

"It is not so clear that the wounds were an operating and substantial physical cause of death. Arguably, it was then the same as if he had cut his throat or blown his brains out—acts which would have killed him whether he was wounded or not ... If this reaction (whether by blowing his brains out or doing what he actually did) was (in the words used by the defendant in *Roberts* (1971) 55 Cr. App. R. 95) so 'daft as to make it [V's] own voluntary act', the chain of causation is broken. It seems that, pace *Blaue*, D does not have to take a 'daft' victim as he finds him."

■ The drugs cases

If the conduct of the victim can be an issue when it comes to assessing whether or not D caused the result, consider this: V is a drug addict, and D is a drug dealer. If D supplies V with the drugs he requires, and if V overdoses and dies, would D have caused V's death? Or did V cause his own death?

The courts were unwilling to acquit D where he was a drug dealer charged with manslaughter by unlawful act until the decision of the House of Lords in **Kennedy [2008] 1 A.C. 269**. In essence, manslaughter by unlawful act requires proof of a deliberate, dangerous and criminal act which causes death. The nature of the role taken by D can influence the outcome. For example, in **Cato [1976] 1 W.L.R. 110**, V made up a syringe with drugs supplied by D, but then D injected V. D caused the death. On the other hand, in **Dalby [1982] 1 W.L.R. 425**, D was not liable because V self-injected the drug. In **Rogers [2003] 1 W.L.R. 1374**, D provided the drugs and although he did not inject V, he did hold a tourniquet around V's arm as V self-injected. The problem with *Rogers* is that D neither administered nor, common sense would suggest, caused the drug to be administered (the Offences Against the Person Act 1861 s.23 prohibits the administration of, or the causing to be administered, or the causing to be taken any poison or other destructive or noxious thing). The deceased was an independent adult with freedom of choice and he chose to inject himself with drugs. As we have seen, the free, deliberate and informed choice of a party, even a victim, breaks the chain of causation. It is trite to say D should not have supplied the drugs; but there is an offence governing that conduct under s.5 of the Misuse of Drugs Act 1971.

Nevertheless, the Court of Appeal in *Rogers* held D's conduct amounted to "active participation in the injection process"; akin to being an accomplice perhaps? This produces an additional problem in that self-injection of a drug is not per se a crime, and one cannot be criminally liable, even as an accomplice, to conduct which is not criminal.

The most offending case was **Finlay [2003] EWCA Crim 3868**. D prepared a syringe and handed it to V for self-injection. V then self-injected. D's conviction for manslaughter was upheld. Here, the Court of Appeal rejected liability based on accessorial liability, which is a relief; but then held the parties were joint principals (even where the victim was not guilty of a crime; so joint principals in what?) and further, rejected the argument that all free and deliberate acts break the chain of causation.

Both *Rogers* and *Finlay* have been overruled by *Kennedy*. D gave V a syringe of heroin ready for injection. V self-injected and later died. The Court of Appeal, following the previous authorities, dismissed D's appeal against conviction but certified a point of law for the House of Lords:

> "When is it appropriate to find someone guilty of manslaughter where that person has been involved in the supply of a class A controlled drug, which is then freely and voluntarily self-administered by the person to whom it was supplied, and the administration of the drug then causes his death?"

The House of Lords allowed D's appeal and answered the certified question: "In the case of a fully informed and responsible adult, never".

It was found in this case that V had freely and voluntarily administered the injection to himself, knowing what it was. This meant it could not be said D had caused the heroin to be administered to V or taken by him. Informed adults of sound mind were treated as autonomous beings able to make their own decisions on how to act. This is free will. It may be of interest to note that the Scottish High Court of Justiciary held in **Kane and MacAngus v HM Advocate [2009] HCJAC 8** that it was open to a jury, on facts such as *Kennedy*, to convict D of culpable homicide, a crime founded on reckless conduct rather than an act which causes death.

The House's decision in *Kennedy* did not apply in English law to manslaughter by way of gross negligence (*Evans*, above) where, even if V does self-inject, a conviction may be secured *if* there is a duty of care between D and V. In *Evans* discussed on p.20 above, the appellant owed a duty to her 16-year-old half sister, which in giving her heroin for the victim to self inject and subsequently not seeking medical assistance when it was clear V had overdosed, was breached. The complications considered above in proving causation did not arise; liability arose because D was under a legal duty by her creation of or contribution to a dangerous situation, and it was the breach of duty which caused V's death. This is a clear extension of the *Miller* principle to include not just inadvertent acts which create a dangerous situation, but advertent or intentional acts.

In *Ruffell* (also above), the deceased died of hypothermia and opiate intoxication; the former was caused by D leaving V outside in the cold, but the latter was caused by V's self-injection. These were concurrent causes of death and, as we have seen, provided the defendant's cause was a significant cause (not necessarily the sole cause or a more significant cause than any other) and the jury is directed properly, it is open to the jury to find D's breach of duty caused the death.

Over to you...

To summarise:

If D supplied V with drugs and V self-injected, where V is an informed adult, and V dies, D is not guilty of unlawful act manslaughter.

BUT

If D supplied V with drugs and became aware (or should have done) that the situation was or had become life-threatening, a duty of care arises which is breached if D fails to help/summon help. If the jury finds D's breach of duty to be "gross" D can be convicted of gross negligence manslaughter. (Ch.4)

THIN SKULL RULE

The law of tort recognises the rule that a defendant must take his victim as he finds him, so that where a claimant suffers a latent, or hidden, physical or psychological defect of some sort, the defendant is liable where his act causes more serious damage that might otherwise have been suffered (see, e.g. **Smith v Leech Brain and Co [1962] 2 Q.B. 405**). This is a doctrine firmly rooted in policy and, provided the type of harm was foreseeable, the defendant is liable even if the extent of the harm was not.

The criminal law has also adopted this doctrine. In **Hayward (1908) 21 Cox C.C. 692**, D had an argument with his wife and he chased her into the street. She suddenly collapsed and died due to a combination of the exertion and a pre-existing thyroid condition, of which D was unaware. The thyroid condition was both unforeseen and unforeseeable, but D had caused her death. The law is that D has to take the victim's condition as he found it. So, if V has a thin skull (sometimes called an eggshell skull) or is a haemophiliac so that blows which even a reasonable person would foresee as causing no more than moderate injury, actually results in death, D will legally have caused that death.

How far can this principle be taken? The problem is this: When considering the reaction of the victim, the rule as described on p.31 above is one of reasonable foreseeability (**Corbett [1996] Crim. L.R. 594**). However, where the thin skull rule applies, the issue of foreseeability is totally irrelevant. In **Blaue [1975] 1 W.L.R. 1411**, D attacked a young girl with a knife, causing a serious stab wound which pierced her lung. V was taken to hospital and was told by the surgical registrar that a blood transfusion was necessary. The girl was a Jehovah's Witness and she refused the transfusion because it was contrary to her religious beliefs. She was told that if she did not have the transfusion she would die. She persisted in her refusal and died the following day. D appealed against his conviction for manslaughter on the grounds that her refusal was unreasonable, and unforeseeable. His appeal was dismissed and the Court of Appeal extended the eggshell skull rule to include not only physical peculiarities of the victim, but also the mental outlook and beliefs of the victim. Notwithstanding the reasonableness, or foreseeability, or lack of, in her refusal to have a blood transfusion, she did not die from that refusal:

> "It has long been the policy of the law that those who use violence on other people must take their victims as they find them. This in our judgment means the whole man, not just the physical man. It does not lie in the mouth of the assailant to say that his victim's religious beliefs which inhibited him from accepting certain kinds of treatment were unreasonable. The question for decision is what caused her death. The answer is the stab wound. The fact that the victim refused to stop this end coming about did not break the causal connection between the act and death."

We might therefore conclude that *Blaue* is no more than an application of the rule from *Smith* (p.25–28), the initial injury was still a substantial and operating cause of death, and her religious beliefs were not an intervening act.

Reform of Causation

The Law Commission's Draft Criminal Code Bill 1989 cl.17 reads:

(a) Subject to subsections (2) and (3), a person causes a result which is an element of an offence when

   (i) he does an act which makes a more than negligible contribution to its occurrence; or

   (ii) he omits to do an act which might prevent its occurrence and which he is under a duty to do according to the law relating to the offence.

(b) A person does not cause a result where, after he does such an act or makes such an omission, an act or event occurs

   (i) which is the immediate and sufficient cause of the result;

   (ii) which he did not foresee; and

   (iii) which could not in the circumstances reasonably have been foreseen.

The same vague concepts and phrases arise (more than negligible, immediate and sufficient, reasonably … foreseen) and many of the decisions which need attention (*Empress Cars* for example) are not tackled.

Coincidence in Time of Mens Rea and Actus Reus

Suppose D received an urgent phone call at work telling him that his wife had been injured in a car crash. He drove to the hospital and on arrival he ran into the reception area, accidentally colliding with another person, V, causing V severe injuries. Suppose that later, D discovered that V was in fact the driver of the other car who had been drunk when he crashed into D's wife's car. When D found this out, he wanted to kill V. The fact that D formed a state of mind to hurt, injure or even kill V later, cannot render the accidental collision in the hospital reception into an assault. Another way of saying this is that actus reus and mens rea must coincide in time.

Coincidence in time is, however, an elastic concept and the judges have stretched it as far as possible to secure the conviction of "guilty" defendants. In each of the three cases below, it could have been a straightforward matter of dismissing the appeals against conviction on the basis that the chains of causation were not broken. As we shall see, however, it is not that simple.

In **Thabo Meli v The Queen [1954] 1 All E.R. 373 PC**, the two defendants, in execution of a pre-conceived plot to kill V, took him to a hut. They hit him over the head intending to kill him. Then, believing him to be dead, they took him out and rolled him over a cliff. The plan was to make it all look like an accident, but medical evidence established that the injuries received in the hut were not sufficient to cause the death, which was in fact due to exposure when he was left at the foot of the cliff. The defendants appealed against their convictions on the basis that, while the first act (hitting V) was accompanied by mens rea, it was not the cause of death; and the second act (rolling him over the cliff and leaving him to die of exposure), was the cause of death, but it was not accompanied by mens rea. Rather than dismiss the appeal on the basis of normal principles of causation, the Privy Council responded to the appellants' submissions by holding that:

> "It was impossible to divide up what was really one series of acts in this way. There is no doubt that the accused set out to do all these acts in order to achieve their plan, and as parts of their plan."

The concept of a series of acts, or a continuing transaction, was adopted by the Court of Appeal in *Fagan* (p.21 above) and again, in the absence of a preconceived plan, in **Church [1965] 2 All E.R. 72 CCA**. D had a fight with V, thought he had killed her, and threw her in the river. The

Court of Appeal adopted the "continuing transaction" theory, because of "a series of acts designed to cause death ..." But the "series of acts" were not pre-arranged or preconceived and were in fact thought of in a state of panic after the initial attack.

The Court of Appeal in **Le Brun [1991] 4 All E.R. 673** openly admitted that in certain cases the "coincidence" rule has an exception. D hit his wife knocking her unconscious. While he was trying to drag her body along the street to avoid detection, he lost his grip. Her head hit the pavement, fracturing her skull and causing her death. The court held that that where the assault and the eventual act causing death are part of the same sequence of events, the act which causes death and the necessary mental state to constitute manslaughter need not coincide in point of time. In this case, not only was there no pre-arranged plan but D knew that V was still alive at the time he dropped her. The theory advanced above, that the cases can be explained on the basis of causation, was also recognised as the court held:

> "The actions of the appellant in dragging the victim away with the intention of evading liability [did not break] the chain which linked the initial blow with the death".

The problems with the continuing transaction theory are, first, that mens rea and actus reus clearly do not coincide, but the law has been stretched unnecessarily to accommodate them in such a way that the jury could equally find the defendant in *Le Brun* guilty had he in fact been dragging his wife to the car to take her to hospital. Secondly, the vagueness of the approach to "a series of events" which are not pre-planned or preconceived, works unfairly against defendants. Where the actus reus of the crime occurs over time, provided the mens rea is satisfied at some time during the actus reus, the defendant is guilty. This approach has been rejected elsewhere in the Commonwealth (**Shorty [1950] S.R. 280**, a case from Southern Rhodesia, now Zimbabwe).

Summary

1.   Actus non facit reum nisi mens sit rea translates as "the act is not guilty unless the mind is guilty" and means that criminal liability is usually dependent on proof of:

     (a) actus reus;

     (b) mens rea; and

     (c) no defence.

2. The actus reus is defined as all/some of:

   (a) an act or omission to act;

   (b) a state of affairs;

   (c) specified surrounding circumstances; and

   (d) any consequences of D's act/omission prescribed by the offence definition.

3. Voluntary conduct—D's conduct, i.e. muscular movements, must be performed under the control and direction of D's conscious mind. This is usually referred to as the defence of automatism.

4. Omissions—D is liable only where he fails to act when the common law imposes a duty to act or under statute. A duty can arise through:

   (a) contract;

   (b) blood or other close relationship, e.g. parent and dependant child, but if a "dependant" of full capacity instructs D to cease caring this may absolve D;

   (c) assumption of responsibility to care; and

   (d) by the creation of a dangerous situation—if D creates danger by his conduct he is under a duty to take reasonable steps to nullify the danger when he becomes aware of it.

5. Causation—see Figure 2 (p.40).

6. Coincidence of actus reus and mens rea—D must possess the requisite mens rea at the moment he performs the actus reus. But if D's conduct is a series of acts forming one transaction mens rea at any time in the sequence will suffice whether or not they form part of a pre-arranged plan.

FIGURE 2 Causation—Summary:

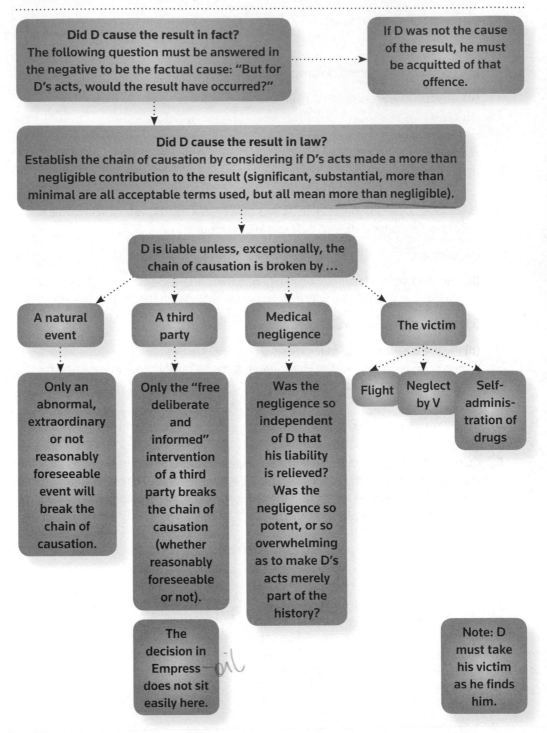

End of Chapter Question

Question
"The criminal law recognises a person has the right to choose whether or not to act."

Assess the truth of the statement above in the context of criminal liability for an omission.

Points of Answer
♦ Students would be expected to comment that the title is true insofar as liability cannot arise where there is no duty, but failure to act where there is a duty can give rise to a crime.

♦ A person cannot choose to be under a duty or not.

♦ Duties can arise, for example:
- in a relationship (*Gibbins and Proctor*);
- where the defendant assumes responsibility for another (*Stone and Dobinson*, *Nicholls*, *Instan* cf. *Khan and Khan*);
- where D creates a dangerous situation (also called the supervening fault principle, *Miller*, *Santa-Bermudez*, *Evans*);
- where there is a contractual duty (*Pittwood*); or
- where the duty arises out of a public office (*Dytham*).

♦ Students would also be expected to explain that duties are the exception rather than the rule in the criminal law for the reasons mentioned on pp.14–15.

Further Reading

A. Ashworth, "The Scope of Criminal Liability for Omissions" (1989) 105 L.Q.R. 424.

J. Chalmers, "Fireraising by Omission" (2004) 10 S.L.T. 59.

G. Dingwall and A. A. Gillespie, "Reconsidering the good Samaritan: a duty to rescue?" [2008] 39 Cambrian L.R. 26–39

T. Elliott and D. Ormerod, "Acts and omissions—a distinction without a difference?" [2008] 39 Cambrian L.R. 40–59.

A. Leavens, "A causation approach to criminal omissions" (1988) 76 Cal L.R. 547.

G. Meade, "Contracting into Crime: A Theory of Criminal Omissions" (1991) 11 O.J.L.S. 147.

D. Ormerod, "Case Comment. R. v Evans (Gemma): manslaughter—gross negligence—deceased supplied by defendant with heroin which proved fatal" [2009] 9 Crim. L.R. 661.

A. Reed, "Supervening Fault and Gross Negligence Manslaughter". (2009) C.L. & J. 173 (44) 693.

J. Rogers, "Death, Drugs and Duties" [2009] Arch. News (6) 6–9.

J.C. Smith, "Liability for Omissions in Criminal Law" (1984) 4 Legal Studies 88.

G. Williams, "Criminal Omissions—The Conventional View" (1991) 107 L.Q.R. 86 and "Gross negligence manslaughter and duty of care in "drugs" cases: R v Evans" [2009] 9 Crim. L.R. 631.

Self Test Questions

To test your knowledge gained from this section go online to *http://www.sweetandmaxwell.co.uk* and take our online self test questions. Here you will also find key updates to ensure that you are only ever one click away from an instant update.

Mens Rea

3

CHAPTER OVERVIEW

In this chapter we:

- assess the meaning of the term mens rea

- consider how to determine the mens rea for a particular offence

- consider how to prove mens rea

- explore the meaning of the common mens rea terms of intention, recklessness and negligence

- consider the principle of transferred malice—what it is and how it operates

- consider crimes which have no mens rea at all (absolute liability) or no mens rea in relation to at least one element of the actus reus (strict liability)

- consider the judicial task in deciding if an offence is one of strict liability

- discuss the justification for strict liability.

Summary

End of Chapter Question

Further Reading

Self Test Questions

Introduction

As explained in Ch.2, most offences require that when the defendant committed the actus reus of the offence he did so with the appropriate state of mind. This mental element of an offence is known as the mens rea (though the term favoured by the Law Commission is "fault element"). In this chapter, we will consider in more detail the concept of mens rea and look at the most common mens rea terms of intention, recklessness and negligence. We will also consider the doctrine of transferred malice and, finally, crimes of strict liability—those crimes where mens rea is not required in respect of at least one element of the actus reus.

Determining the Mens Rea

Mens rea is the mental state expressly or impliedly referred to in the definition of the crime in question. As with the actus reus, the mens rea will, therefore, vary from crime to crime.

The starting point when determining the mens rea for a crime is the definition of that crime. Thus, for example, in the offence of murder (defined as the unlawful killing of a human being by a human being during the Queen's Peace with malice aforethought (Coke 3 Co Inst 47)), the mens rea is malice aforethought (meaning intention to kill or to cause grievous bodily harm).

The crime of murder requires proof of only one element of mens rea but some offences require proof of more than one element of mens rea. For example, theft (defined as the dishonest appropriation of property belonging to another with the intention permanently to deprive) requires proof of both dishonesty and intention permanently to deprive.

Sometimes, a mens rea term is not included in the definition of the crime but this does not necessarily mean that mens rea is not required; it may mean that the mens rea is implied and has been left to the courts to define. For example, the assault offence under s.47 of the Offences Against the Person Act 1861 of assault occasioning actual bodily harm contains no mens rea term in its definition. However, at common law, the mens rea has been held to be the same as that for the offence of assault (**Savage and Parmenter [1992] 1 A.C. 699 HL**). In some offences, the mens rea does not correspond with the actus reus. For example, in the offence of unlawful and malicious wounding contrary to s.20 of the Offences Against the Person Act 1861, the actus reus involves wounding whereas the mens rea is defined as "maliciously" which has been interpreted by case law to mean with intention or recklessness as to whether *some harm* might occur (*Savage and Parmenter*). In this example, the requisite mens rea (maliciously) falls short of what is required for commission of the actus reus (wounding). In some offences, known as crimes of ulterior intent, the mens rea goes beyond that which is required for the actus reus. For example, in the offence of unlawful and malicious wounding with intention to cause grievous bodily harm contrary to s.18 of the Offences Against the Person Act 1861, the actus reus involves wounding whereas the mens rea requires proof of an intention to cause grievous bodily harm, rather than intention merely to wound.

Motive

Mens rea should not be confused with motive, i.e. the reason why the defendant committed the offence. The defendant's motive is generally irrelevant to his mens rea, though it may be relevant:

1. to an offence which requires an element of racial or religious motivation (see pp.152–154);
2. to a defence, for example necessity;
3. in demonstrating what the defendant wished to achieve; or
4. to punishment.

Even good motives are irrelevant to mens rea; the mercy killer intends to kill just as much as the cold-blooded killer. Hence, in **Chiu-Cheung v Queen, The [1995] 1 A.C. 111**, an undercover police officer pretending to be a drug dealer was held by the Privy Council to have formed the mens rea for conspiracy to import drugs when he agreed with a drug trafficker to import illegal drugs, despite his worthy motives.

Very occasionally, the mens rea of an offence may be so defined as to take account of the defendant's motive for acting as he did. For example, the ardent anti-vivisectionist who liberates animals from an animal-testing laboratory may successfully argue that he is not liable for theft because he is not dishonest (under the *Ghosh* test for dishonesty) in that he considered that ordinary people would agree that his actions were morally justified, not dishonest (see further pp.236–237).

Proof of Mens Rea

An issue closely related to mens rea is the question of proof: how can the prosecution prove what was going on in the defendant's mind when he performed the actus reus? At one time, it was presumed that a defendant foresaw and intended the natural consequences of his actions (**DPP v Smith [1961] A.C. 290**). However, the presumption was abolished by s.8 of the Criminal Justice Act 1967 which directs the court or jury to consider all the evidence in the case in order to determine the defendant's intention or level of foresight.

Section 8 provides:

> A court or jury in determining whether a person has committed an offence,
>
> **(a)** shall not be bound in law to infer that he intended or foresaw a result of his actions by reason only of its being a natural and probable consequence of those actions; but
> **(b)** shall decide whether he did intend or foresee that result by reference to all the evidence drawing such inferences from the evidence as appear proper in the circumstances.

Section 8 applies only to those offences which require one of the two most common forms of mens rea: intention and recklessness (foresight). It does not, therefore, apply to crimes of negligence, considered at p.65 below.

Common Forms of Mens Rea

The mens rea terms used most often in criminal offences are intention, recklessness and, to a lesser extent, negligence. Intention is perceived as being the most serious form of mens rea, presumably because it involves a defendant *deliberately* choosing to act in such a way as to bring about a certain consequence. A defendant who acts with intention is considered to be more culpable than someone who merely foresees the consequence (recklessness) or acts carelessly (negligence). It is for this reason that intention is reserved for the most serious offences such as murder. Some less serious offences are phrased in terms of intention or recklessness, or recklessness only or, occasionally, negligence.

It is important to note that these terms do not exist in isolation; one must intend or be reckless as to the particular consequence required by the offence in question. Hence, in murder for example, one must intend to kill or to cause grievous bodily harm and, for an offence under s.1 of the Criminal Damage Act 1971, one must intend or foresee the damage or destruction of property belonging to another.

Intention

"How to define intention?" has been a question which has vexed the minds of judges, academics and law students alike for many years. It ought not to be so; the mens rea of such serious crimes as murder and wounding or causing grievous bodily harm with intent contrary to s.18 of the Offences Against the Person Act 1861, which carry a maximum life sentence, ought to be clear and readily understood. Unfortunately, it has not been possible to produce an authorita-tive definition for which there is universal support and the history of the meaning of the word intention in the criminal law has been beset by the struggle between two conflicting interpreta-tions of how widely intention should be construed.

In this topic, we will consider the primary meaning of intention-so-called direct intention—and the secondary meaning of intention, which has been attributed to it by criminal lawyers, of oblique intention. However, before doing so, it is useful to begin with an explanation of what intention is not. According to **Moloney [1985] A.C. 905**, "Intention is something quite different from motive or desire." Hence, one can intend a consequence without necessarily desiring its occurrence; one may act out of duty or necessity rather than desire for a certain outcome. For example, a defendant who kills in self-defence intends to kill as the only means to save himself but he may not have wished for, or desired, the victim's death. Lord Bridge (in *Moloney*) pro-vided a further example of the distinction:

> "A man who, at London Airport, boards a plane which he knows to be bound for Manchester, clearly intends to travel to Manchester, even though Manchester is the last place he wants to be and his motive for boarding the plane is simply to escape pursuit. The possibility that the plane may have engine trouble and be diverted to Luton does not affect the matter. By boarding the Manchester plane, the man conclusively demonstrates his intention to go there, because it is a moral certainty that that is where he will arrive."

DIRECT INTENTION

This is the primary or ordinary meaning of intention: one intends a consequence if it is one's aim or purpose to achieve it. Thus, for example, if D stabs V in the heart with his knife he acts with direct intention to kill; it is his aim to kill. Similarly, if D decides to kill V and sets fire to a house knowing V is inside, D has direct intention to kill or to cause grievous bodily harm.

A test for determining whether a consequence was the defendant's purpose is R.A. Duff's "test of failure" which he suggested in "Intention, Agency and Criminal Liability: Philosophy of Action and the Criminal Law" (1990). The test is: would the defendant consider his actions a failure if the result did not ensue? Duff applied his test to the facts of **Hyam v DPP [1975] A.C. 55.** D had put lighted newspaper through V's letter box, causing the deaths of V's two children. D was tried for murder and claimed that she had not meant to kill, merely to frighten V, her love rival. Applying the "test of fail-ure" D could not be said to have directly intended to kill or cause grievous bodily harm because she would not have viewed what she did as a failure if the victims had not been injured or killed.

Unfortunately, the test of failure is not fool-proof; it falls down where a result is a means to achieve a desired outcome. J. Herring, *Criminal Law Text, Cases and Materials*, 3rd edn, uses the following example to illustrate this: M kills his relative, A. His purpose in doing so is to get his inheritance from A. Applying the test of failure, would mean that A's death was not D's purpose as he would not have viewed his actions as a failure if he had managed to inherit without causing A's death. However, D would most likely be held to have directly intended A's death because the desired result of inheriting is achieved through killing A. Similarly, if D shoots at V who is standing behind a window and breaks the window glass, D has direct intent to do criminal damage to the glass as well as to kill even though he would not have considered his actions a failure if he had killed without breaking the glass; he has to break the glass in order to kill V.

Occasionally, the courts will hold that what seems obviously to be a case of direct intent is in fact not. **Steane [1947] 1 All E.R. 813** was just such a case. D was charged with intentionally aiding the King's enemies in that he had broadcast propaganda for Germany during the Second World War. D claimed his reason for doing so was to save himself and his family from a concentration camp. The court held that D's purpose was to save his family rather than to assist the enemy even though he knew his desired outcome of saving his family could only be attained by assisting the enemy. The decision seems to have been based purely on sympathy for the defendant's predicament rather than basic principles of intention and is likely to be confined to its facts.

OBLIQUE INTENTION

This is the secondary meaning attributed to intention and is relevant where the actual outcome of his actions was not the defendant's aim or purpose but was foreseen by him as a potential consequence of his actions. According to G. Williams, "Oblique Intention" (1987) 46 C.L.J. 417:

> "Oblique intention is something you see clearly, but out of the corner of your eye. The consequence is (figuratively speaking) not in the straight line of your purpose, but a side-effect that you accept as an inevitable or 'certain' accompaniment of your direct intent … There are twin consequences of the act, x and y; the doer wants x, and is prepared to accept its unwanted twin y. Oblique intent is, in other words, a kind of knowledge or realisation. Oblique intent is, perhaps, best explained by this oft-cited example: D plants a bomb on a plane in order to recover the insurance money for the cargo (his direct intent). He does not wish for the crew and passengers to die but foresees this outcome as being virtually certain. As the present test for oblique intent is whether the specified consequence was a virtual certain consequence of D's actions and D foresaw it as a virtual certain consequence, a jury could in such circumstances find that D intended to kill those on board the plane."

■ The case for oblique intent

Having considered briefly what is meant by oblique intent, it is worth considering whether the criminal law should, in fact, accommodate both forms of intention, direct and oblique, or whether intention should be confined to its ordinary meaning so that only those consequences which were the defendant's purpose would be intended. Most commentators argue that intention ought to encompass both direct and oblique intent but not all do so. J. Finnis, "Intention and Side-Effects" in Frey and Morris (eds), *Liability and Responsibility,* argues, quite convincingly, that a defendant is morally responsible for foreseen-but-unintended consequences (which he refers to as "side-effects") but ought not to be as responsible as he would for those consequences which were intended. He writes,

> "It is well to recall how foreign to the commonsense concept of intention is the academics' notion that what is foreseen as certain is intended … One who hangs curtains knowing that the sunlight will make them fade does not thereby intend that they shall fade. Those who wear shoes don't intend to wear them out. Those who fly the Atlantic foreseeing certain jetlag don't do so with the intention to get jetlag; those who drink too heavily rarely intend the hangover they know is certain … Indeed, we might call the academics' extended notion of intent the Pseudo-Masochistic Theory of Intention—for it holds that those who foresee that their actions will have painful effects upon themselves *intend* those effects."

One further criticism of the extended meaning of intention concerns the potential overlap created between intention and recklessness. The difficulties this can create can be seen by comparing the offences of murder and reckless manslaughter. Under the extended meaning of intention, the jury may now find a defendant liable for murder where he foresaw death or grievous bodily harm as a virtually certain consequence of his actions (**Woollin [1999] 1 A.C. 82**). However, they could find him liable for only (reckless) manslaughter if they determined that he foresaw death or grievous bodily harm as being a highly probable consequence of those actions (**Lidar (2000) 4 Arch. News 3**, see further Ch.4). Should the difference between a murder conviction and one for manslaughter hinge on the fractional difference between foresight of virtual certainty and foresight of high probability and, further, how easy will it be for a jury to appreciate the difference?

These criticisms are, however, outweighed by the strong moral argument in favour of oblique intent: that a person who aims to kill (most cases of oblique intent have arisen in the context of murder) is as morally culpable as the person who merely foresees death as virtually certain. If one considers the example on oblique intent cited above involving the bomb on the plane, the defendant in such a case is viewed as being as morally culpable as if he had wanted the people on board to die because he has shown no regard for human life. Such a person should not be considered reckless and merely liable for manslaughter. Hence, oblique intent conveniently allows such killings to be murder.

The conflict begins

It is the oblique form of intention which has caused the most difficulties of interpretation. Two distinct issues have arisen:

1. The relationship between intention and foresight; if one merely foresees a consequence of one's actions (to the proscribed degree of probability) does one, therefore, intend that consequence or is this merely evidence from which an inference of intent may be drawn?
2. The exact degree of foresight required for a finding of oblique intent.

These two issues will be explored here briefly and then, in further depth, via an analysis of the leading cases on intention in murder over the last 25 years.

The relationship between intention and foresight

Over the years, foresight of a consequence (to the proscribed degree of probability) has been viewed at times as being intention and, at other times, as merely evidence from which the jury *may* infer intent but has discretion not to do so. The former approach was neatly described by C. Kaveny, "Inferring Intention from Foresight" (2004) 120 L.Q.R. 81 as the "Identity View" of intention; the latter is conveniently described as the "Inference View" of intention but sometimes these two views are referred to, respectively, as treating oblique intention as a question of law or fact. As we shall see later, it is the inference, or question of fact, view which has so far prevailed.

The degree of foresight

Several possibilities exist for the degree of foresight required for oblique intent. These range from, at one end of the spectrum, foresight of a consequence as merely probable through highly probable then virtually certain to actual certainty. The test adopted by the courts has changed over time but is now settled as being one of foresight of a virtual certainty.

Is a direction on oblique intent always necessary?

In *Moloney*, the House of Lords held that a trial judge should avoid giving the jury guidance on the meaning of intention except in exceptional circumstances:

"The golden rule should be that ... the judge should avoid any elaboration or paraphrase of what is meant by intent, and leave it to the jury's good sense to decide whether the accused acted with the necessary intent unless the judge is convinced that, on the facts and having regard to the way that the case has been presented, ... some further explanation or elaboration is strictly necessary to avoid misunderstanding." (per Lord Bridge)

That this is still the case was confirmed recently in **McNamara and Bennett [2009] EWCA Crim 2530**. Therefore, where the defendant's actions consisted of a direct attack on the victim, for example shooting V in the chest, which the prosecution alleges was done with intention to kill, the trial judge should direct the jury in terms of direct intention only. This is often referred to as giving the simple direction on intention. Exceptional circumstances would seem to be those where the defendant claims he acted with a purpose other than to kill or cause grievous bodily harm, for example merely to frighten, or to damage the plane's cargo in the example given above.

■ The changing approach of the courts

Having discussed the issues which arise in the context of oblique intent, it is now appropriate to consider how the courts have grappled with these issues. This will take us on a journey spanning almost 20 years from the House of Lords in *Moloney* through to the most recent pronouncement of the Court of Appeal in **Matthews [2003] 2 Cr. App. R. 30**.

Moloney

D was charged with the murder of V, his step-father, with whom he had been drinking heavily one evening, when they disagreed about who was the quickest at loading and firing a shotgun. D had gone to get two shotguns and was the first to load his. V said he could, "outshoot," "outload" and "outdraw" D and "I didn't think you'd got the guts, but if you have, pull the trigger." D said later, "I did not aim the gun. I just pulled the trigger and he was dead." He claimed to have no idea that in discharging the gun it would injure V: "It was just a lark." The House allowed D's appeal and, in doing so, addressed both the status of foresight in intention and the appropriate direction on oblique intent. With regard to the former issue, they stated that foresight on the defendant's part of a consequence occurring is merely evidence from which an inference of intent may be drawn by the jury; it is not equivalent to intent. Hence, the inference (question of fact) view of oblique intention was adopted. The court further held that intent could be inferred where the relevant consequence was foreseeable as a natural consequence of the defendant's act and the defendant himself foresaw it as a natural consequence. According to Lord Bridge, natural consequence meant, "in the ordinary course of events a certain act will lead to a certain consequence unless something unexpected supervenes to prevent it." Thus, rather than seek to define intention, the court had set out guidelines to assist a jury in determining when they could infer intention. This would be the approach adopted by the judiciary in subsequent cases.

It was only a year later that their Lordships were called upon to reconsider these issues in **Hancock and Shankland [1986] A.C. 455**.

Hancock and Shankland

The defendants were striking miners during the miners' strike of the 1980s. They pushed a concrete post and block from a bridge onto the road below. The block smashed through the windscreen of a taxi, in which the miner was travelling, and killed the taxi driver. The defendants claimed they had not intended to injure anyone; only to prevent a strike breaker getting to work. Their appeals against their convictions for murder were allowed by the House of Lords. Lord Scarman, who gave the leading speech, re-affirmed that foresight of a consequence is merely evidence of intent. However, he also stated that the *Moloney* direction on oblique intent was defective in that it failed to refer to the probability of a consequence occurring and also required

> "an explanation that the greater the probability of a consequence the more likely it is that the consequence was foreseen and that if that consequence was foreseen the greater the probability is that that consequence was also intended."

Later in the same year that *Hancock and Shankland* was decided, the Court of Appeal revisited the exact same issues as their Lordships had done in the case of **Nedrick (1986) 83 Cr. App. R. 267**.

Nedrick

The defendant, who had a grudge against V, poured paraffin through the letterbox of V's house and set light to it. The house caught fire and a child inside died. D claimed his intention was merely to frighten V, not to kill or cause grievous bodily harm to anyone. D's appeal against his conviction for murder was successful; he lacked the mens rea for murder because he lacked the requisite intent. In the leading judgment, Lord Lane C.J. set out the following guidelines for juries in cases involving oblique intent:

> "Where the charge is murder and in the rare cases where the simple direction is not enough, the jury should be directed that they are not entitled to infer the necessary intention unless they feel sure that death or serious bodily harm was a virtual certainty (barring some unforeseen intervention) as a result of the defendant's actions and that the defendant appreciated that such was the case."

Thus, the test for oblique intent became one of foresight of a virtual certainty and, in Lord Lane's view, where the defendant did foresee the required consequence as being virtually certain:

> "The inference may be *irresistible* that he intended that result, however little he may have desired or wished it to happen [though] [t]he decision [would be] one for the jury to be reached upon a consideration of all the evidence" (emphasis added).

In phrasing his judgment in such terms, Lord Lane C.J. appeared to go as near as he could towards adopting an identity view of intention (treating oblique intention as a question of law) but just stopped short of doing so, presumably because of the clear House of Lords' judgments to the contrary in *Moloney* and *Hancock and Shankland*.

The House of Lords returned to the issue of oblique intent three years later in *Woollin*.

Woollin

D lost his temper and threw his three-month-old son onto a hard surface. The baby sustained a fractured skull from which he died. D appealed against his conviction for murder, ultimately to the House of Lords, on the basis that he lacked the requisite intent because, as the prosecution had accepted at his trial, he had neither desired to kill his son nor to cause him grievous bodily harm.

Lord Steyn, giving the leading speech in the House, stated that the simple direction on intention (see p.51) was not appropriate on the facts of the case and that guidance on intention was necessary. However, he rejected the approach, taken by the trial judge and the Court of Appeal, that it would be appropriate for a jury to infer intention from a substantial risk of grievous bodily harm:

> "... the phrase 'substantial risk' blurred the line between intention and recklessness, and hence between murder and manslaughter. The misdirection enlarged the scope of the mental element required for murder. It was a material misdirection."

On the basis of this misdirection, their Lordships quashed D's conviction for murder and substituted one for manslaughter.

Lord Steyn also stated that, where appropriate, trial judges should give the *Nedrick* direction on intention save that they should use the words "not entitled to find ... unless" rather than "entitled to infer ... unless." He did not explain why he preferred find to infer but it is probable that it was because "find" can be better understood by a jury. Lord Steyn then seemed to go even further and to equate foresight of virtual certainty with intention when he stated that, "Moloney adopted a test of what may constitute intention which is similar to the 'virtual certainty test' in Nedrick" and later, when he said, "a result foreseen as virtually certain is an intended result." Thus, as Lord Lane C.J. had done in *Nedrick*, Lord Steyn went as far as possible towards treating foresight of virtual certainty as intention. However, he specifically stated that a jury should not be directed that a finding of intention would be "irresistable" where there was such foresight.

Following *Woollin*, there was some doubt as to its exact effect in light of Lord Steyn's statements above. Had the decision held that foresight of a virtually certain consequence is intention, i.e. that oblique intent is intention, just the same as direct intent is intention, or had the status quo been maintained and oblique intent (foresight of a consequence as virtually certain) was merely evidence of intent? The former view gained support from the judgment of the Court of Appeal two years later in the civil case of **A, Re [2001] Fam. 147**.

A, Re

The Court of Appeal (Civil Division) was required to consider whether a surgeon who carried out an operation to separate conjoined twins, knowing that saving the life of one was virtually certain to result in the death of the other, weaker twin, would intend the death of the weaker twin. The Lords Justices of Appeal stated that if the doctor foresaw that the death of the weaker twin was virtually certain, the doctor intended to kill (rather than that a jury would be entitled to find the doctor intended to kill). Hence, foresight of a consequence as virtually certain was actually treated by the court as intention.

The most recent pronouncement on the matter came from the Court of Appeal in **Matthews [2003] 2 Cr. App. R. 30**.

Matthews

The defendants threw V off a bridge into a river despite having been told by V that he could not swim. V drowned and the defendants were charged with his murder; the prosecution alleging that the defendants had intended to kill V as the death of a non-swimmer thrown off a bridge into a wide river was a virtual certainty. The defendants were convicted of murder and appealed on the basis that the trial judge had misdirected the jury on intention.

The Court of Appeal, without referring to *A, Re* agreed that the trial judge had misdirected the jury when he directed them to find that intention to kill was proved if they were satisfied that death was a virtually certain consequence of the defendants' actions and that they had appreciated there was a virtual certainty of death. Foresight of a virtual certainty was, in the court's view, merely evidence from which the jury may find intention. The court did, however, acknowledge that there is very little difference between a rule of evidence and one of substantive law. Indeed, the court upheld the defendants' convictions on the basis that a properly directed jury would inevitably have decided that death was virtually certain, that the defendants would have foreseen this and would have found, therefore, that the defendants intended to kill.

Over to you...

Why, do you think, have the courts been so reluctant to say that oblique intent is intent if there is so little difference between a rule of evidence and one of substantive law?

The following grid summarises the development of the law on oblique intent.

FIGURE 3 **Grid summarising the development of the law on oblique intent**

Case	Court	Charge	Salient points
Moloney (1985)	House of Lords	Murder	Foresight of a consequence is not intent; it is merely evidence from which the jury can make an inference of intent. Set out guidelines for juries to follow. Test of: was the consequence foreseen as a natural consequence?
Hancock and Shankland (1986)	House of Lords	Murder	Confirmed foresight of a consequence is merely evidence from which the jury can make an inference of intent. *Moloney* direction on degree of foresight was defective.
Nedrick (1986)	Court of Appeal	Murder	Confirmed foresight of a consequence is merely evidence from which the jury can make an inference of intent. Test of: was the consequence foreseen as a virtually certain consequence?
Woollin (1999)	House of Lords	Murder	Lord Steyn: (i) Judges should give the *Nedrick* direction on intent save that they should use the words "not entitled to find ... unless" rather than "entitled to infer ... unless." (ii) "A result foreseen as virtually certain is an intended result."
A, Re (2001)	Court of Appeal (Civil Division)	N/A	If D foresaw the death of V was virtually certain, he intended to kill.
Matthews (2003)	Court of Appeal	Murder	Foresight of a consequence is merely evidence from which the jury can make an inference of intent but there is very little difference between a rule of evidence and one of substantive law.

Over to you...

We have been through a complex area of law here. In an essay question it may be appropriate for you to provide the assessor with a detailed analysis of all the cases covered. However, in a problem question, you should always try to apply the current law. To assist you, this is the current state of the law:

1. A defendant intends a consequence if it his aim or purpose.
2. Even if it was not his aim or purpose, the jury is entitled to find that he intended it if the consequence was (objectively) virtually certain and he, himself, foresaw it as virtually certain.
3. Foresight of a consequence as virtually certain is not itself intention but merely evidence of intention.

■ Unresolved Issues

Even after *Woollin* and *Matthews*, some matters are still unresolved:

1. If a jury is "not entitled to find the necessary intent unless" the defendant foresaw the consequence as being virtually certain, in which circumstances will they do so and in which will they not? Given that oblique intent is predominantly an issue in the offence of murder, the choice for the jury will be between convicting the defendant of murder or for the less serious crime of manslaughter. Unfortunately, there is no guidance to be found in the case law on how the jury should exercise this discretion, leading to the possibility of inconsistency in approach. A. Norrie, "After Woollin" [1999] Crim. L.R. 532, suggests that the jury would not find intention where there was a "moral threshold" such that even though the accused could foresee a result as virtually certain, it is so at odds with his moral conception of what he was doing that it could not be conceived as a result that he intended. He suggests that this might be the approach a jury would adopt, for example, where the defendant kills out of necessity (it is not settled whether necessity is available as a defence to murder). He also applies his test to some of the leading murder cases, such as *Moloney* and *Woollin*, in which he argues that the moral threshold was not crossed. *Moloney* liked his step-father and *Woollin* had not previously harmed his baby; in neither was the defendant morally deserving of the label "murderer." Conversely, the defendant in *Hyam* (see p.47) might have crossed the moral threshold. Norrie suggests that there was "manifest wrongdoing," a level of hate in the defendant's actions, and no redeeming aspect to the moral relationship between the defendant and her victims.

   Norrie's test of "moral threshold" provides a possible answer but, until there is some judicial pronouncement on this matter the nature of the "plug" that fills the gap between foreseeing a consequence as virtually certain but not intending it and foreseeing the consequence as virtually certain and therefore intending it, remains disappointingly elusive.

2. The test for oblique intent has traditionally been viewed as in two parts:
   (a) was the consequence (objectively) a virtual certain consequence of the defendant's actions; and
   (b) did the defendant himself foresee it as a virtually certain consequence?

But is a two-stage test necessary? Must a consequence be objectively virtually certain if the defendant himself has foreseen it as virtually certain? A two-stage test may work unfairly in the defendant's favour where he has particular knowledge or expertise relevant to the situation which the objective bystander would not share or where the defendant mistakenly believes the consequence is virtually certain but the objective bystander would conclude that it was not. Is it right that a defendant in these situations be acquitted?

3. Does oblique intent apply in all offences involving intention, or just in murder? According to Lord Bridge in *Moloney*, it applies to all offences of specific intent (which is meant to be those satisfied by intention only). However, their Lordships in *Woollin* stated that intention would not inevitably carry "precisely the same meaning in every context in the criminal law." Despite such dicta in *Woollin*, the current formulation of oblique intent has been applied in several offences other than murder, for example, to the offences under s.18 of the Offences Against the Person Act 1861 (**Bryson [1985] Crim L.R. 669**), under s.16 of the Firearms Act 1968 (**Jones [1997] Crim. L.R. 510**) and attempted murder (**Walker and Hayles (1990) 90 Cr. App. R. 226**). It is unclear, however, whether it would apply to attempts generally.

4. The situation of the terrorist and the time bomb. In *Moloney*, Lord Bridge considered the situation involving:

> "… the terrorist who plants a time bomb in a public building and gives timely warning to enable the public to be evacuated … [who] knows that, following evacuation, it is virtually certain that a bomb disposal squad will attempt to defuse the bomb. In the event the bomb explodes and kills a bomb disposal expert …"

His Lordship's speech seemed to assume that the terrorist would be guilty of the murder of the disposal expert. But is this likely? Does the terrorist actually foresee death or grievous bodily harm as virtually certain if he has given advance warning of the bomb? He might foresee as virtually certain that the bomb squad will attempt to defuse the bomb but does he foresee it as virtually certain that one of them will be killed or sustain grievous bodily harm in doing so? The issue was revisited by Lord Steyn in *Woollin* where he considered that the defendant might not be guilty of murder, only manslaughter, in such circumstances. For a more detailed analysis of these issues, see A. Pedain, "Intention and the Terrorist Example" [2003] Crim. L.R. 579.

5. Are the good motives of the defendant relevant, i.e. if a defendant acts in order to achieve a good purpose but foresees that an undesired, bad consequence is also virtually certain to occur, might he be found to have intended that undesired consequence? For example, might a doctor, who prescribes to a dying patient painkillers which have the side-effect of shortening the victim's life, escape liability for murder? In the civil case of **Airedale NHS Trust v Bland [1993] A.C. 789 HL**, Lord Goff considered that because the treatment is in the patient's best interests, a doctor in such circumstances would not be liable for murder; death would be attributable to the existing disease or injury. The principle applied in such situations is known as the doctrine of double effect. The doctrine formed the basis of the trial judge's summing up in **Moor, Newcastle Crown Court, May 11, 1999** where, on facts similar to those referred to by Lord Goff in *Airedale*, the trial judge emphasised to the jury the importance of the doctor's primary purpose in administering the drugs. The jury acquitted the doctor of murder.

A slightly different situation arose in **A, Re [2001] Fam. 147.** As explained above at p.54, the Court of Appeal was required to consider whether a surgeon who carried out an operation to separate conjoined twins, knowing that saving the life of one was virtually certain to result in the death of the other, weaker twin, would intend the death of the weaker twin. The difference between this case and those involving double effect is that, in this case, the treatment was not in the best interests of the victim (the twin who would inevitably die as a result of the operation). The court did not, therefore, rely on the doctrine of double effect to justify their decision that the surgeon would not be

FIGURE 3.1 **The relationship between intention and foresight in homicide**

D's state of mind	Type of mens rea	Offence
Death or GBH is D's aim or purpose.	Direct intent	Murder
Death or GBH is not D's aim or purpose but is: (a) viewed as a virtual certain consequence by the jury and foreseen by D as such.	Oblique intent	Murder if the jury finds intent, otherwise involuntary manslaughter
(b) foreseen by D as a highly probable consequence of his actions.	Recklessness	Involuntary manslaughter

liable for murder. The court stated that if the doctor foresaw that the death of the weaker twin was virtually certain, the doctor intended to kill but could rely on the defence of necessity (see further Ch.13).

REFORM OF INTENTION

In the winter of 2005, the Law Commission produced Consultation Paper No.177: "A New Homicide Act for England and Wales?" Whilst making proposals for reform of the law governing homicide (see p.88 for the final proposals), the paper also made suggestions for the reform of intention. The Commission made two suggestions for consultation: (i) providing a new statutory definition of intention primarily based on previous Commission attempts at a definition and (ii) codification of the present common law position. Both suggestions are considered here as both have merit but only the proposal to codify the law was adopted in the Commission's final report, "Murder, Manslaughter and Infanticide" (Law Com No.304, 2006).

■ A new definition

The new definition would define intention as either direct or indirect. Hence, oblique intent would become indirect intent and, more significantly, would be upgraded from mere evidence of intent to a species of intent itself. Direct intent was defined in the proposals as acting "in order to bring a result about" and indirect intention as, "knowing that it will be virtually certain to occur" or "knowing that it would be virtually certain to occur if he or she were to succeed in his or her purpose of causing some other result." A proviso was also proposed: "a person is not to be deemed to have intended any result which it was his or her specific purpose to avoid." The Commission gave the following example of when the proviso might apply: A father jumps with his child from a burning building, and also throws a second child out. While he and the first child are badly injured, the second child dies. The father knows that death is a virtual certainty for the second child, but that it is an absolute certainty if they remain in the building. He hopes against hope that the child will be caught, or otherwise saved, but it is not. The proviso has the effect that the father does not intend to kill his child because his specific purpose is to avoid the actual result, the child's death.

As the Law Commission recognised, the new definition approach would have the attraction of certainty. However, it would also have the disadvantage of being inflexible. The view of many consultees was that it would also complicate the law and confuse juries. This proposal was, therefore, rejected in the final report.

■ Codification of the common law

The Commission's alternative suggestion to a new all-encompassing definition was to define direct intent as in the definitional model above and, in respect of oblique intent, to codify the common law approach in the cases from *Moloney* through to *Woollin*. These cases, you will recall, sought not to define intention but merely to lay down a set of guidelines to assist a jury in determining when it is entitled to find intention. As the Law Commission recognised, this approach allows for flexibility and "moral elbow room" (similar to the "moral threshold" suggested by Norrie—see p.56 above) but has the disadvantage of a lack of certainty. Codification of the law was the proposal favoured by the Commission in its final report. Under these proposals, a jury would not be entitled to find intention unless the defendant thought that the result was a virtually certain consequence of his or her actions.

Recklessness

Recklessness is the second most serious form of mens rea. It is sometimes used on its own as mens rea, for example in manslaughter but, more commonly, as an alternative to intention, for example, in criminal damage and assault offences. Recklessness, as with intention, is not defined in any statute. It has, therefore, been left to the common law to interpret the term. It will be seen that the meaning attributed to recklessness has changed over time but has now been settled as involving subjective foresight of a risk of particular consequences or circumstances and the decision, nevertheless, to take that risk in circumstances where it is unreasonable or unjustified to do so.

UNJUSTIFIED RISK

Whether a risk is unjustified is determined objectively, by weighing the social utility of the conduct undertaken against the likelihood and severity of any harm or damage that might thereby be occasioned and assessing, in light of this, whether a reasonable person would have taken such a risk. The Law Commission, "Working Paper on the Mental Element in Crime" (Law Com. No.89, 1978) gave the following examples to explain where a risk might be justified:

> "The operation of public transport ... is inevitably accompanied by risk of accident beyond the control of the operator, yet it is socially necessary that these risks be taken. Dangerous surgical operations must be carried out in the interests of the life and health of the patient, yet the taking of these risks is socially justifiable."

Where there is such a high social utility in the activity, only a very high risk or harm may render the conduct unreasonable. Where there is no social utility in the activity but a high risk of harm such as by playing Russian roulette, the risk would inevitably be considered unreasonable. Between these extremes, there will be more difficult cases where there is moderate social utility in the activity and moderate risk of harm. It will always be for the jury to decide whether, on the facts, the risk was justifiable.

A SUBJECTIVE OR OBJECTIVE ASSESSMENT OF THE RISK?

Once a risk has been judged to have been (objectively) unjustifiable, the next question to consider is the perspective from which we judge foresight of the risk. If we assess the risk from the defendant's viewpoint and ask whether *he* foresaw the risk, we adopt a subjective test for recklessness. However, if we assess the risk according to whether a *reasonable person* would have foreseen it, we adopt an objective test for recklessness. As will be seen below, it is the subjective test which has prevailed.

There is, however, one state of mind not covered by either subjective or objective recklessness: that of the defendant who takes an unjustified risk because he wrongly concludes that there is no such risk or that he has taken sufficient precautions to eliminate the risk. As such a defendant is neither subjectively nor objectively reckless, he ought to be acquitted of an offence requiring recklessness.

THE CURRENT LAW

In **G [2004] 1 A.C. 1034**, the House of Lords held that a defendant is reckless (for the purposes of criminal damage) with respect to:

1. a circumstance if he is aware of a risk that it exists or will exist;
2. a result if he is aware of a risk that it will occur;

and, nevertheless, takes that risk where, in the circumstances known to him, it was unjustifiable to do so.

Although their Lordships expressly limited their test of recklessness to offences involving criminal damage, it is submitted that this subjective test will be applied throughout the criminal law. This type of recklessness, where the defendant himself must have appreciated the relevant risk, is termed subjective or *"Cunningham"* recklessness (**Cunningham [1957] 2 Q.B. 396** being the case in which it was first developed). The facts of *Cunningham* illustrate the operation of the test. D pulled a gas meter from the wall of a cellar of an empty house in order to steal the money from it. He left the gas pipe leading to the meter broken and with gas leaking out of it (something which he had not considered might happen). The gas seeped through into the neighbouring house and thereby endangered the life of the occupier (his future mother-in-law!) who breathed it in. D was charged with maliciously administering a noxious substance so as to endanger life, contrary to s.23 of the Offences Against the Person Act 1861. The Court of Appeal quashed D's conviction, holding that "maliciously" required intention or foresight by the defendant of a risk of gas escaping and being inhaled, and D had not foreseen such a risk.

A person is not subjectively reckless if he has not foreseen a risk even if, had he stopped to think about it, he would have appreciated such a risk or if the risk would have been obvious to others. Consequently, in **Stephenson [1979] 2 All E.R. 1198**, D, who had crept into a hollow in a large haystack and lit a fire to keep warm was not liable for arson when the haystack caught fire and was destroyed. A reasonable person might have appreciated the risk of the haystack burning down but there was no evidence that the defendant, who suffered from schizophrenia, had.

Subjective recklessness does, however, encompass deliberately closing one's mind to the obvious (**Parker [1977] 2 All E.R. 37**) presumably because, as Lord Bingham observed in *G*, a person must first realise that there is a risk in order to then close their mind to it. Hence, on the facts of *Parker*, D was reckless for the purposes of criminal damage when, having flown into a rage because a public telephone was not working, he slammed down the handset on the phone thereby damaging the telephone receiver. D said that it had not occurred to him that he might damage the receiver. The Court of Appeal held that a defendant cannot escape the consequences of his actions by saying "I never directed my mind to the obvious consequences because I was in a self-induced state of temper." The correct direction in such circumstances would be:

> "A man is reckless in the sense required when he carries out a deliberate act knowing or closing his mind to the obvious fact that there is some risk of damage resulting from that act but nevertheless continuing in the performance of that act."

Over to you...

D, a very quick-tempered person, flies into a blind rage with V over an imagined insult and, without thinking about what he is doing, smashes his fist down on V's glass topped coffee table causing a large crack.

1. **Does D intend damage?**
2. **Is D reckless as to doing damage and do you think he should be considered reckless?**

THE JOURNEY FROM CUNNINGHAM TO G VIA CALDWELL

Two years after the court in *Stephenson* applied "*Cunningham*" (subjective) recklessness in criminal damage, the House of Lords was required to revisit the meaning of recklessness in this context in the case of **Metropolitan Police Commissioner v Caldwell [1982] A.C. 341**. Lord Diplock, with whom the majority agreed, stated that:

> "A person charged with an offence is 'reckless as to whether or not any such property be destroyed or damaged' if (1) he does an act which in fact creates an obvious risk that property will be destroyed or damaged and (2) when he does the act he [i] either has not given any thought to the possibility of there being any such risk or [ii] has recognised that there was some risk involved and has nonetheless gone on to do it."

This judgment widened the scope of recklessness beyond advertant risk taking (covered in (2) [ii] above) to also include inadvertent risk taking (at (2)[i] above), what became known as objective or "*Caldwell*" recklessness.

Shortly after *Caldwell*, in **Lawrence [1982] A.C. 510**, Lord Diplock's formulation was amended to refer to "an obvious and serious" risk. The effect of these decisions was that a defendant would be reckless not only where he appreciated the relevant risk (subjective recklessness) but, also, even if he did not appreciate it, if the risk was one which would have been obvious (objective recklessness). The term "obvious" was interpreted in subsequent case law to require the risk to be obvious to the reasonable man, not to the defendant.

The significance of *Lawrence* was that their Lordships applied this new formulation of recklessness not in the context of criminal damage but to the offence of causing death by reckless driving. The following year, in **Seymour [1983] 2 A.C. 493**, *Caldwell* recklessness was applied again outside the offence of criminal damage, this time to the offence of manslaughter. Indeed, dicta in *Seymour* suggested that *Caldwell* recklessness ought to be applied in all offences involving recklessness unless Parliament had stated otherwise. It seemed at the time that objective, *Caldwell* recklessness was on the ascendancy. However, in subsequent cases involving assault offences (for example **Spratt [1990] 1 W.L.R. 1073**) and rape (**Satnam and Kewal (1984) 78 Cr. App. R. 149**), the courts chose not to follow this dicta (presumably because of the harshness of *Caldwell* recklessness, an issue explored below on p.64). The offence of causing death by reckless driving was subsequently abolished and, in **Adomako [1995] 1 A.C. 171**, *Caldwell* recklessness was finally confined to criminal damage offences only when the House of Lords overruled *Seymour* and abolished objective recklessness in manslaughter. The champions of a subjectivist approach to recklessness had only one battle left: its abolition in crimes of criminal damage. This came in the momentous decision of the House of Lords in *G*.

THE DECISION IN G

G concerned two defendants aged 11 and 12 who set light to some newspapers in the back yard of a shop and then threw the newspapers under a dustbin. They left the scene without putting out the fire. The fire spread to the shop and caused considerable damage. The defendants were charged with arson (criminal damage by fire) in respect of the shop on the basis that they had been reckless as to causing damage by fire. The defendants contended that they had not appreciated that the fire would spread; they had thought it would burn itself out on the concrete floor of the yard. They were convicted following a direction based on *Caldwell*; they were reckless if they failed to appreciate a risk of damage which would have been obvious to the reasonable man. As the risk of damage would have been obvious to any adult, they were reckless because they had failed to appreciate it, notwithstanding the fact that their youth probably prevented them from being able to appreciate such a risk. The harshness of the decision led to an appeal, ultimately to the House of Lords. In quashing their convictions, the House reviewed the development of *Caldwell* recklessness and chose, unanimously, to overrule *Caldwell* which they described as "neither just nor moral." Thus, the test for recklessness in criminal damage offences was brought into line with that in other offences; subjective recklessness had prevailed.

■ Why was Caldwell overruled?

Although their Lordships sought to justify their decision, inter alia, on a misinterpretation in *Caldwell* of Parliament's intent in relation to mens rea when it passed the Criminal Damage Act 1971, their main reason for overruling *Caldwell* was that *Caldwell* recklessness was too harsh a form of recklessness (and had been criticised by academics, the judiciary and practitioners alike). As explained above, the term "obvious" had been interpreted by the courts so that the question was not whether the risk was one which would have been obvious to the defendant had he thought about it but, rather, whether it was one which would have been obvious to the hypothetical reasonable adult—a person who was not endowed with any characteristic of the defendant which might have affected his perception of the risk. The harshness of this interpretation can be seen in the decision at first instance in *G* and also in **Elliot v C (A minor) [1983] 2 All E.R. 1005**. D was a 14-year-old child with learning difficulties. She had been out all night without sleep when she entered a garden shed in which she found some white spirit which she poured onto an old carpet and then lit in order to keep warm. This caused a fire which destroyed the shed. D was charged with criminal damage and acquitted. The prosecution appealed to the High Court by way of case stated on the ground that the magistrates had erred in taking into account that the risk would not have been obvious to D even if she had thought about it. The High Court allowed the appeal and ordered the magistrates to convict on remitting the case, on the basis that it was only necessary that the risk be obvious to the reasonably prudent adult, irrespective of the fact that, due to her age and low intelligence, the risk would not have been obvious to D had she stopped to think about it.

Their Lordships in *G* did consider whether to keep the *Caldwell* direction on recklessness and merely refine it so that the risk would have to be one which would have been obvious to the defendant if he had given any thought to the matter. However, they determined that to do so would overcomplicate the task of the jury or magistrates:

> "It is one thing to decide whether a defendant can be believed when he says that the thought of a given risk never crossed his mind. It is another, and much more speculative, task to decide whether the risk would have been obvious to him if the thought had crossed his mind. The simpler the jury's task, the more likely is its verdict to be reliable."
>
> (per Lord Bingham of Cornhill)

More recently, in **Brady [2006] EWCA Crim 2413**, the Court of Appeal rejected a submission that recklessness for the purposes of s.20 assault required foresight of "an obvious and significant" risk of harm. Thus, recklessness remains purely subjective in nature and a clear line exists between recklessness and the final form of mens rea we consider, negligence, which continues to be assessed objectively.

Negligence

A person is negligent if he fails to appreciate a risk which he ought to have appreciated because a reasonable person would have appreciated it or, where he does consider the possibility of such a risk but wrongly decides either that there is no risk or that the risk is negligible and worth taking. You will usually see this referred to as the defendant "falling below the standards of the reasonable man." A defendant can be liable in negligence where he has not even thought about the possibility of a certain consequence occurring, simply because a reasonable person with D's level of experience and in his position would not have acted as D did. For this reason, negligence is considered a harsh fault element. (It is perhaps best to refer to negligence as a "fault element" as the Law Commission does, rather than as mens rea, because negligence does not require a specific state of mind; merely that the defendant acted in a certain way). In this respect, negligence is very similar to the now-abolished objective form of recklessness in *Caldwell*.

The absence of mens rea in its strict sense in negligence is possibly the reason why negligence is seldom used as the basis of criminal liability for serious crimes; it is more commonly a basis of civil liability. It does, however, form the basis of liability for such offences as manslaughter by gross negligence (see p.115), the new offence of causing or allowing the death of a child or vulnerable adult (see p.127), driving without due care and attention, and public nuisance.

Other Forms of Mens Rea

There are many forms of mens rea beyond those explored above, for example, knowledge, wilful blindness, maliciously and dishonesty. These are explored in detail in later chapters in the context of the relevant offences.

A new mens rea term of "awareness of risk" was suggested by the Law Commission in its report, "Murder, Manslaughter and Infanticide" (Law Com. No.304, 2006), to be used in the new homicide offences of first and second degree murder which they proposed (see Ch.4). "Awareness," would involve "conscious advertence to the risk". It is the Law Commission's view that the term is:

> "... expressed in perfectly ordinary language and is meant to be understood according to such usage. We expect the Appeal Courts to affirm that this is the case and say that the understanding of the phrase is a matter for the jury with common sense guidance from the trial judge. We would not expect the Appeal Courts to subject the phrase to any gloss. Nor do we expect the Appeal Courts to embark upon a refined analysis of the phrase from case-to-case with a view to constructing a precise legal meaning of it."

Watch this space!

The Doctrine of Transferred Malice

It is a basic rule of the criminal law that if the defendant, with the mens rea of a particular crime, does an act which causes the actus reus of the same crime, he will be guilty of that crime even though the end result is unintended in that, for example, a different victim is harmed or different property is damaged or stolen to that which was intended. This is due to the operation of the principle of transferred malice whereby the defendant's mens rea is transferred from the intended victim or property to the unintended victim or property. There is no authority as to whether the doctrine applies only to the transfer of intention or whether it extends to the transfer of recklessness. However, academic opinion, for example Ormerod (Smith and Hogan, *Criminal Law*, 12th edn) tends to the view that the doctrine does allow for the transfer of recklessness.

The following example illustrates the operation of the doctrine: D intends to kill X and shoots at X but misses and kills V who is standing unnoticed nearby; D is liable for the murder of V. Transferred malice was applied to convict the defendant in **Latimer (1886) 17 Q.B.D. 359**. D was involved in a quarrel with X in a pub. He removed his belt and swung it towards X. The belt glanced off X and severely injured V. D was found guilty of the unlawful and malicious wounding of V.

One might have thought that the doctrine was unnecessary because offences against the person and against property do not include in their definitions a requirement that the particular person harmed was the intended victim or that the property damaged or stolen was that intended to be damaged or stolen. For example, the actus reus of murder is the unlawful killing of a human being during the Queen's Peace; the mens rea (malice aforethought) is the intention to kill or to cause grievous bodily harm. If the requisite intent is merely in relation to someone, not necessarily the victim, the defendant is liable if he intends to kill anyone. Taking this approach, if D intended to kill A, but killed V by mistake, he has still killed a person with the intention to kill a person and should be liable for murder. However, in **Attorney General's Reference (No.3 of 1994) [1997] 3 W.L.R. 421**, the House of Lords rejected this view. The court stated that the mens rea for murder is the intention to kill or cause grievous bodily harm to the *actual victim*. On this basis, the doctrine of transferred malice is necessary as, without it, a defendant would escape liability in respect of the unintended victim. On the facts of the case, however, the defendant was not liable for the murder of a baby whose mother D stabbed whilst the baby was still in her womb and who, although born alive, died later from injuries sustained in the stabbing. The court refused to apply transferred malice to make D liable for murder for the following reasons:

1. the baby had not been born at the time of the stabbing and, in the court's view, mens rea can only be transferred to someone in existence at the time the mens rea is formed; and
2. mens rea cannot be transferred twice, i.e. from the mother to the foetus and from the foetus to the child it would become.

Limitations on Transferred Malice

The doctrine of transferred malice only applies where the actus reus committed by the defendant, and the mens rea with which he acts, are for the same offence. Thus, if D, with the mens rea for offence A, commits the actus reus of offence B, D is not liable for either offence A or B. This can be illustrated by the facts of **Pembliton (1874) L.R. 2 C.C.R. 119**. D threw a stone at V, intending to harm V, but missed and broke a window instead. D was not guilty of malicious damage as he lacked the mens rea for such an offence.

Over to you...

Might D be liable for criminal damage in such circumstances if V was standing in front of the window at the relevant time on the basis that D was reckless as to doing damage?

Transferred Malice and Defences

The doctrine allows for the transfer of defences as well as liability (**Gross (1913) 23 Cox CC 455**). This means that any defence which the defendant would have been able to plead had the outcome been as he had actually intended will still be available. Thus, for example, if D attacks A in self-defence but misses and injures V, he can plead self-defence in respect of any liability in relation to V.

Offences of Strict Liability

An offence of strict liability is one without mens rea, or without mens rea as to at least one element of the actus reus. This means a person can be convicted of an offence in the absence of proof of fault or blameworthiness (i.e. no intention, recklessness or even negligence). For example, in **Callow v Tillstone (1900) 64 JP 823**, a butcher asked a veterinary surgeon to check whether a carcass was fit for human consumption. The vet did not check the meat, but did certify that it was sound. The butcher, relying on the certificate, offered the meat for sale, but was then convicted of the strict liability offence of exposing unsound meat for sale. The butcher could not have done more to assure himself of the fitness of the meat, but he was guilty as the offence was satisfied on proof of the offer for sale of meat which, whether known to the seller or not, was unfit.

Absolute and Strict Liability

Often used interchangeably, the terms absolute and strict liability do have different meanings. An absolute crime is one which requires no mens rea for any element of the actus reus. Often referred to as "state of affairs offences", in terms of actus reus, absolute liability crimes require no conduct or result, and they are very rare.

The following two cases provide examples of such offences. In **Larsonneur (1933) 24 Cr. App. R. 74**, D was an illegal alien who was held to have been "found" in the UK, though she was in the UK on that day only because she had been arrested and brought to the UK, against her will. In **Winzar v Chief Constable of Kent (1983), The Times, March 28**, D was perceived to be drunk on a highway, but the highway on which he was "found" was the road to which the police had taken him (see p.22) after having removed him from a nearby hospital.

Ormerod (Smith and Hogan, *Criminal Law*, 12th edn) asserts that:

> "[o]ffences of this type are to be treated with great caution. They are commonly associated with tyrannical regimes. Larsonneur and Winzar were convicted of offences the commission of which was in fact procured by the police, and this seems particularly offensive ... situational offences are rightly condemned when they do not allow the accused to adjust his behaviour to remain within the law."

Strict Liability at Common Law

Vicarious liability for public nuisance is technically a common law strict liability offence (**Stephens (1866) L.R. 1 Q.B. 702 CCR**). However, it should no longer be prosecuted under the common law (Home Office, 2005) but under a raft of statutory provisions for which there is no space in this text for a review. Publication of a defamatory libel is a crime of strict liability, as is the publication of material which interferes with the course of justice, but the latter activities are now governed by the Contempt of Court Act 1981, ss.1–7. Blasphemous libel, the publication of material likely to outrage and insult the Christian religion, was also an offence of strict liability but was abolished under the provisions of the Criminal Justice and Immigration Act 2008. Ultimately therefore, there is very little strict liability remaining at common law.

Strict Liability Under Statute

HOW THE COURTS DETERMINE WHETHER AN OFFENCE IS ONE OF STRICT LIABILITY

Most modern Acts of Parliament specify the mens rea requirement of the offence in question, but some do not, and some do not clearly direct that such an omission is deliberate, i.e. that the offence is intended to be strict. The task has thus fallen to the judiciary to decide, wherever a statutory provision is silent as to mens rea, whether the crime has a mens rea requirement (notwithstanding the absence of a verb such as intend or know), or is strict.

In **Gammon (Hong Kong) Ltd v Attorney General of Hong Kong [1985] A.C. 1**, the defendants were the contractor, project manager and site agent all involved in the construction of a building in Hong Kong. The building collapsed and they were charged under a Hong Kong Ordinance (the equivalent of an Act of Parliament) with having deviated in a material way from the plans which had been submitted and approved. There was no evidence that they realised the deviation they made was "material". Dismissing their appeals against conviction, the Privy Council suggested that the following reasoning should be adopted to determine if a crime imposes strict liability which, on the facts of this case, it did:

1. there is a presumption of law that mens rea is required before a person can be held guilty of a criminal offence;
2. the presumption is particularly strong where the offence is "truly criminal" in character;
3. the presumption applies to statutory offences, and can be displaced only if this is clearly or by necessary implication the effect of the statute;
4. the only situation in which the presumption can be displaced is where the statute is concerned with an issue of social concern, and public safety is such an issue; and
5. even where a statute is concerned with such an issue, the presumption of mens rea stands unless it can also be shown that the creation of strict liability will be effective to promote the objects of the statute by encouraging greater vigilance to prevent the commission of the prohibited act.

The following discussion applies only where the offence in issue is a statutory crime, and there is no mens rea word present. If there is a mens rea word, obviously the crime is not strict. The same is not necessarily true the other way around, however, and it is worth noting from the outset that the starting point is that where the offence is silent as to mens rea, there is a mens rea requirement in that crime which must be proven before D can be convicted.

■ Presumption of mens rea

In **Sweet v Parsley [1970] A.C. 132**, D had been convicted of being "concerned in the management of certain premises which were used for the purpose of smoking cannabis", contrary to s.5(b) of the Dangerous Drugs Act 1965. D was a teacher who sublet a house to tenants and, although she kept one room in the house for her own use, she did not live there. It was agreed she had not known the tenants had been smoking cannabis but the magistrates treated the offence as one of strict liability. Her appeal was allowed by the House of Lords. As Lord Reid noted:

"Sometimes the words of the section which creates a particular offence make it clear that mens rea is required in one form or another. Such cases are quite frequent. But in a very large number of cases there is no clear indication either way. In such cases there has for centuries been a presumption that Parliament did not intend to make criminals of persons who were in no way blameworthy in what they did. That means that whenever a section is silent as to mens rea there is a presumption that, in order to give effect to the will of Parliament, we must read in words appropriate to require mens rea."

A presumption is a rule of law that holds a thing to be true. It is an assumption that a state of affairs is so. Presumptions can be rebuttable or irrebuttable. A rebuttable presumption is one which may be contradicted. An irrebuttable one cannot. The presumption in favour of mens rea is rebuttable. For example, the presumption of mens rea was rebutted in *Gammon* (above).

As the starting point is that even where the statute is silent as to mens rea, it is nevertheless required, what mens rea is needed? The judges, through the normal process of statutory interpretation must imply, or "read in", the mens rea where the statute is silent. In **Tolson (1889) L. R. 23 Q.B.D. 168**, Cave J. suggested that what would be required was an honest and reasonable belief in respect of the element of the actus reus in issue. Recent case law has moved more convincingly towards an entirely subjective mens rea (**B v DPP [2000] 2 A.C. 428**, see below), and it is likely that an honest belief is required, whether or not it is reasonable.

Negligence is not a suitable mens rea to be read in (**Gray's Haulage Co Ltd v Arnold [1966] 1 All E.R. 896**), and in most statutory provisions it is not possible to imply a mens rea of negligence (see pp.77–78 below).

◼ True crimes

The presumption in favour of mens rea is particularly strong where the offence is truly criminal. This means that the judge must categorise the crime in the case as either a "true" crime or not. This is not a distinction made by Parliament. Once the legislature criminalises conduct, it is truly a crime. Where the legislature has failed to specify the mens rea, the judiciary must then decide whether the crime is a "true" crime or, on the other hand, a regulatory or "quasi-crime". The distinction is merely a device, a tool to be used as part of the reasoning to reach a conclusion as to whether an offence is of strict liability. Essentially, what it means is that offences which are not "true" crimes are more likely to be strict.

It is often said that one can identify a true crime and a regulatory crime on sight. For example, murder is a true crime, but offering for sale unfit meat is regulatory. This distinction is often found according to instinct, gut-feeling, rather than being based on any coherent legal principle. Regulatory offences tend to be regarded as having no social stigma, but a cursory glance at the crimes covered in this part of the text shows a broad range of "types" of conduct, and strict liability is found in crimes involving:

1. driving;
2. the environment;
3. public health;

4. the sale of food;
5. trades descriptions; and
6. drugs (see **Warner v Commissioner of Police of the Metropolis [1969] 2 A.C. 256.**)

Crimes involving victims of a particular age, especially minors, were historically regarded as regulatory. The leading case was **Prince (1875) L.R. 2 C.C.R. 154**. D was charged with taking an unmarried girl under the age of 16 out of the possession of her father against his will, contrary to s.55 of the Offences Against the Person Act 1861. D knew the girl was under the possession of her father, but reasonably believed she was 18. She was in fact under 16. The Court for Crown Cases reserved held that the offence required mens rea as to the possession of the father, but the offence was strict as to age. Accordingly, D's mistake as to her age was irrelevant, despite the fact that it was reasonable. Making liability strict was felt necessary in order to protect victims as it prevented mistake being available as a defence.

Although not specifically overruled, *Prince* is no longer good law. The importance of the presumption in favour of mens rea was shown in *B v DPP*. B, a boy aged 15, repeatedly requested a 13-year-old girl to perform oral sex during a bus journey. He was convicted of inciting a girl under the age of 14 to commit an act of gross indecency, contrary to s.1(1) of the Indecency with Children Act 1960 (since abolished). B said he honestly believed that the girl was over 14 and, on appeal to the House of Lords, it was argued that, as the Act was silent as to the mens rea of the offence, the common law presumption that mens rea was necessary should apply. Many predicted the appeal would be dismissed, *Prince* having established that liability was strict as to the age element of such crimes. However, the House of Lords allowed the appeal and restated the strength of the presumption of mens rea. Unlike the Divisional Court, the House could not find within the Act any clear pattern of offences where mens rea would be required and offences where it would not. The House of Lords also noted that the presumption can be displaced only where it is considered necessary to do so, and here it was not necessary, nor was it "compellingly clear" that Parliament intended liability to be strict (per Lord Steyn). The mens rea, which was for the prosecution to prove, was lack of an honest belief that the complainant was aged 14 or over and it was not necessary that D's belief had to be based on reasonable grounds.

It is easy to overstate the effect of the decision in *B v DPP*. It did not abolish strict liability, nor did it direct that regulatory offences are not be construed as strict, but it did emphasise the presumption in favour of mens rea is very strong for a true crime.

Relevance of offence seriousness

The Court of Appeal in **Muhamad [2003] 2 W.L.R. 1050** acknowledged that the distinction between true and regulatory crimes has resulted in "classificatory difficulties" and held that the presumption of mens rea can be more readily displaced where the offence is not serious. Rather than consider whether the offence under s.362(1)(a) of the Insolvency Act 1986 (materially contributing to one's insolvency by gambling) was regulatory or truly criminal, Dyson L.J. instead directed that the starting point is to determine the seriousness of the offence and then, how much weight, if any, should be attached to the presumption. This appears to be an important change in emphasis from the presumption of mens rea, which is then even stronger for "true" crimes, to an initial decision on the severity of the crimes leading to the presumption, or not as the case may be. In line with *B v DPP* and *K* (below):

> "the more serious the offence, the greater the weight to be attached to the presumption, and conversely, the less serious the offence, the less weight to be attached."

One of the factors influencing the seriousness of the crime is the maximum sentence available, but it is not conclusive per se. For example, in **Howells [1977] Q.B. 614**, the offence of possessing a firearm without holding a firearm certificate was one of strict liability, notwithstanding the maximum sentence of five years' imprisonment. This was a very harsh decision which meant that even an honest and reasonable belief that a firearm was an antique replica was no defence to a charge, but the Court of Appeal said the wording of the Act was clear and the purpose of the legislation could not be achieved if the prosecution had to prove mens rea.

■ Necessary implication to displace the presumption

The presumption can be displaced only if this is clearly, or by necessary implication, the effect of the statute. In *Muhamad* (above), the Court of Appeal was persuaded that, because the other offences in the Insolvency Act 1986 carried a ten-year sentence, and the offence with which *Muhamad* was charged carried only a two-year maximum sentence, the presumption that mens rea had to be proved against D was negated by necessary implication.

The House of Lords in *B v DPP*, however, did not find it to be a necessary implication to displace the presumption of mens rea in s.1 of the Indecency with Children Act 1960, and the same approach was adopted in **K [2002] 1 A.C. 462**, under s.14 of the Sexual Offences Act 1956 (now repealed). The offence was the indecent assault of a child. Under s.14(2), a girl under the age of 16 could not give consent to an indecent assault. Under s.14(3), a defective could also not give consent, but there was a reverse proof burden which allowed D to prove he did not know, and had no reason to believe, her to be a defective. A similar reverse proof burden applied in s.14(3) to a defendant who had "married" a victim who was under the age of 16, which allowed D to prove a reasonable belief that she was his wife. There was, however, no parallel defence that D believed the girl to be 16 or over. The prosecution submitted that this omission of a statutory defence in relation to the belief of the girl's age, and the inclusion elsewhere of such a defence, suggested that Parliament had not intended for a defendant to escape liability on that basis. However, the House of Lords recognised that this would mean a defendant who had married a minor had more protection in law than one who had not. Therefore, it was necessary for the Crown to prove the absence of a genuine belief that the girl was 16 or over when the offence was committed. Unless excluded by express words or necessary implication, guilty knowledge would be a required element of a statutory offence.

Relevance of the wording of the statute and surrounding sections

In order to displace the presumption of mens rea, a careful analysis of the words used is needed. For example, in **James & Son v Smee [1955] 1 Q.B. 78**, the offence under the Motor Vehicles

(Construction and Use) Regulations 1951 was phrased in terms of either using or permitting a vehicle with a defective braking system to be used. D was charged with the latter which, it was held on appeal, imported a state of mind. One cannot permit without knowing that one is doing so. However, there would not have been a defence if charged with using the vehicle, which would have been interpreted strictly (cf. **Vehicle Inspectorate v Nuttall [1999] 1 W.L.R. 629 HL**).

The statute must always be read as a whole. In **Pharmaceutical Society of Great Britain v Storkwain Ltd [1986] 1 W.L.R. 903**, D supplied prescription medication on receipt of prescriptions which looked genuine but which were forgeries. D did not know the prescriptions to be forged, nor was there any evidence of dishonesty, but the House of Lords upheld the conviction. Section 58(2)(a) of the Medicines Act 1968 provided that "no person shall sell by retail ... a medicinal product ... except in accordance with a prescription given by an appropriate practitioner". The House of Lords considered the other offences in the Act, and s.121 in particular, which provided defences to certain crimes but not others based on a lack of knowledge and stated (per Lord Goff):

> "It is very difficult to avoid the conclusion that, by omitting section 58 from those sections to which section 121 is expressly made applicable, Parliament intended that there should be no implication of a requirement of mens rea in section 58(2)(a)."

Where the offence is phrased in terms of causing a result, the courts have invariably held that "causing" imports strict liability. For example, there is no mens rea as to the elements of occasioning (causing) actual bodily harm under s.47 of the Offences Against the Person Act 1861. In **Alphacell v Woodward [1972] A.C. 824**, D was the owner of paper making mills. The waste-product from the paper making process was pumped into two tanks on the banks of a river. Pumps were used to remove the waste from the tanks but, if the pumps failed, the waste would enter the river and pollute it. Foliage blocked the pump inlets and such an overflow occurred. D was convicted of "causing" polluting matter to enter the river contrary to s.2(1) of the Rivers (Prevention of Pollutions) Act 1951. D had not been in any way negligent, but liability was strict and the appeal against conviction was dismissed.

Relevance of inclusion of a defence
Where a defence of no-negligence/due diligence is included (see below), this is a good indicator that the offence is one of strict liability. An example of such a defence is provided by s.24(1) of the Trades Descriptions Act 1968. This provides D with a defence if he can prove that he committed the offence due to a mistake, or in reliance of information supplied to him or due to the act or default of another or an accident or some other cause beyond his control and he exercised due diligence to avoid commission of the offence.

Judicial rationale for displacing the presumption
Judges often reason that when they do or do not displace the presumption of mens rea, they are simply giving effect to the intention of Parliament. This is a fiction, probably designed to

appease critics of the judges making the law. But it is a convention that where statutory provisions are silent as to mens rea, the judiciary will presume a mens rea requirement. Parliament knows this, and the judges know this, but they phrase it in terms of seeking out and giving effect to the intention of Parliament. As Lord Devlin noted in *Samples of Lawmaking* (1962):

> "The fact is that Parliament has no intention whatever of troubling itself about mens rea. If it had, the thing would have been settled long ago. All that Parliament would have to do would be to use express words that left no room for implication. One is driven to the conclusion that the reason why Parliament has never done that is that it prefers to leave the point to the judges and does not want to legislate about it."

Where Parliament is particularly concerned about mens rea, it seems to find no trouble at all in specifying the state of mind required (see, for example, the complex legal situation under the Sexual Offences Act 2003 including the evidential presumptions dealing with proof of the defendant's state of mind, discussed in Ch.6).

■ Social concern and public safety

The only situation in which the presumption can be displaced is where the statute is concerned with an issue of social concern. However, this is not particularly helpful guidance as it would be difficult to conclude that any criminal act is not concerned, somehow, with issues of social concern.

For example, despite a maximum sentence of two years' imprisonment, the crime of selling a lottery ticket to a person under the age of 16 was one of strict liability because gambling, especially under-age gambling, was a matter of social concern (**Harrow LBC v Shah [1999] 2 Cr. App. R. 457**). The severity of the sentence was noted, but considered to be "very far from conclusive … where the offence was plainly not truly criminal in character".

■ Encouraging vigilance and compliance

Even where a statute deals with an issue of social concern, the presumption of mens rea stands unless it can also be shown that the creation of strict liability will be effective to promote the object of the statute by encouraging greater vigilance to prevent the commission of the prohibited act. Lord Salmon warned in *Alphacell Ltd v Woodward* (above):

> "It is of the utmost public importance that our rivers should not be polluted. The risk of pollution, particularly from the vast and increasing number of riparian industries, is very great. … If this appeal succeeded and it were held to be the law that no conviction could be obtained … unless the prosecution could discharge the often impossible onus of proving that the pollution was caused intentionally or negligently, a great deal of pollution would go unpunished and undeterred to the relief of many riparian factory owners. As a result, many rivers which are now filthy would become filthier still and

> many rivers which are now clean would lose their cleanliness. The legislature no doubt recognised that as a matter of public policy this would be most unfortunate."

In *Shah* (above), Mitchell J. said that the statutory provisions should attract strict liability in order to encourage greater vigilance in preventing the commission of the prohibited act. Newsagents and shopkeepers may not be able to enunciate that the offence is one of strict liability, but they do know that the sale of a lottery ticket to a person under 16, or alcohol to a person under 18, or cigarettes, or knives, and so on, to an underage purchaser, even where the mistake as to age is made in honest good faith, is a crime.

In **Blake [1997] 1 W.L.R. 1167**, D was convicted of broadcasting on a pirate radio station under the Wireless Telegraphy Act 1949. His defence was that he believed that he was making demonstration tapes and did not know that he was transmitting. The Court of Appeal dismissed his appeal. The Court acknowledged that the crime was "truly" criminal, which is usually conclusive that mens rea is required, but the strong presumption was nevertheless displaced by two very important factors:

1. the risk of interference by the unauthorised broadcasts with the emergency service communication systems; and
2. (per Hirst L.J.) "the imposition of an absolute offence must surely encourage greater vigilance on the part of those establishing or using a station, or installing or using the apparatus, to avoid committing the offence, e.g. in the case of users by carefully checking whether they are on air; it must also operate as a deterrent".

Over to you...

What we are discussing here is what happens when a judge has to decide if a statutory offence which is silent to mens rea is one of strict liability or not. The starting point is that it is not (i.e. the presumption of mens rea) but thereafter the judge must weigh other factors, not one of which is usually conclusive in itself, including;

1. **The nature of the crime.**
2. **The seriousness of the crime.**
3. **The wording of the provision itself.**
4. **The wording of other provisions in the same Act.**
5. **The wording of similar provisions in other Acts.**
6. **Previous case law.**
7. **The existence of a defence.**
8. **Matters of social concern and public safety, and**
9. **The deterrent effect.**

European Convention on Human Rights' Challenges

Article 6(2) of the European Convention on Human Rights provides for the presumption of innocence. Crimes of strict liability were mooted to violate this presumption because, once the prosecution proves the actus reus, D is presumed guilty and his state of mind is not only irrelevant, it cannot be admitted into evidence, even if it establishes a lack of fault on D's part (**Sandhu [1997] Crim. L.R. 288**, see below).

The European Court of Human Rights held, however, that presumptions can operate within a legal system without breaching art.6, provided the presumptions remain within reasonable limits which take into account the importance of what is at stake and respect the rights of the defence (**Salabiaku (1998) 13 E.H.R.R. 379**). However, in **Barnfather v Islington LBC [2003] 1 W.L.R. 2318**, the Divisional Court held that art.6(2) merely provided criteria against which procedural and evidential matters could be scrutinised but did not extend to consideration of the substance of a domestic offence. This means that strict liability offences cannot be challenged as being contrary to art.6.

However, a very interesting challenge was made to strict liability under art.7 of the Convention in *Muhamad*. Article 7(1) of the European Convention on Human Rights provides that no one shall be held guilty of any criminal offence on account of any act or omission which did not constitute a criminal offence under national or international law at the time when it was committed. It has been held that this provision requires signatory states to ensure standards of clarity in the criminal law, so that citizens can reliably predict whether the particular form of conduct at issue will contravene the criminal law (**Kokkinakis v Greece (1994) 17 E.H.R.R. 397**). In *Muhamad*, the defence argued that if liability under s.362(1)(a) of the Insolvency Act 1986 was strict, first, it would be objectionably uncertain because a gambler would not know, when he placed his bet, whether he ran a real risk of prosecution if he lost. Second, the defence submitted that making the crime one of strict liability was neither necessary in a democratic society, nor proportional to any legitimate aim. There was no pressing social need to criminalise bankrupts, and to penalise them without the requisite mens rea would be disproportionate. The Court of Appeal was not persuaded but a challenge may succeed in future under art.7 against the imposition of strict liability in respect of other offences.

Can the Imposition of Strict Liability be Justified?

We return to the Latin phrase first mentioned at p.12 above; actus non facit reum nisi mens sit rea. Whenever strict liability is found, the guilty act (actus reus) is not accompanied by a guilty mind (mens rea) and therefore, at a fundamental level, legal principle is offended.

As noted above, the presence or absence of a guilty or innocent state of mind is irrelevant to liability and, therefore, cannot be adduced (*Sandhu*). It is required, however, for the judge to set the correct sentence, and

> "[t]hat the sentence should be imposed by the judge on a basis of fact different from that on which [D is] convicted is deplorable" (Ormerod, Smith and Hogan, *Criminal Law*, 12th edn).

Card, (Card, Cross and Jones, *Criminal Law*, 18th edn) calls *Sandhu* a quite inexplicable case.

Strict liability is harsh; it allows a defendant to be convicted even though there was nothing at all he could have done to comply with the law. Consider the butcher in *Callow v Tillstone* (above). His conviction was desperately unfair. He behaved impeccably and, given the chance to do it all over again, he probably would not have changed his conduct, but it was felt acceptable to convict him in order to ensure, as far as possible, the safety of food offered for sale to the public. Reasonable errors, even those made in good faith and without negligence, do not relieve D of liability (unless there is a no-negligence/due diligence defence, see above and below). For example, in *Shah* (above), however well-trained and attentive the sales assistant was to his task, liability could not be avoided. The criminal law has gone further than deterring careless behaviour and now penalises fault-free conduct.

At p.74 above, we noted that strict liability is imposed where the judge feels that to do so will encourage vigilance and compliance. This, in turn, will protect the public and public protection is the argument most frequently given for the imposition of strict liability. Roscoe Pound, in an oft-cited passage in The Spirit of the Common Law, gave his support to this argument when he stated:

> "The good sense of the courts has introduced a doctrine of acting at one's peril with respect to statutory crimes which express the needs of society. Such statutes are not meant to punish the vicious but to put pressure upon the thoughtless and inefficient to do their whole duty in the interest of public health or safety or morals."

However, there is no evidence to suggest that strict liability improves standards of public health and safety. Strict liability may even have the opposite effect to that intended in that, if liability is strict, there is no incentive to take any precautions at all. Further, a mens rea of negligence would surely suffice instead of strict liability. It is, though, almost impossible to use the rules of statutory construction to imply a standard of reasonableness to a statute which does not itself already do so. It is far easier to imply a mens rea of knowledge as to circumstances or intention as to conduct. For example, consider the facts of *James v Smee* (above) where the Court of Appeal held that "permitting" imports knowledge, but "using" does not. When a judge decides that the presumption in favour of mens rea is not displaced, he must work within the existing words of the section to imply the mens rea. The aim of the legislation in *James v Smee* was to deter the owner of vehicles from neglecting the brakes, and then allowing the vehicles to be used. The problem was that importing a requirement of negligence would have been impossible. The only way the offence could be "read" would be to say:

1. it is an offence negligently to use, or permit to be used, a vehicle with defective brakes; or
2. it is an offence to use, or permit to be used, a vehicle with negligently defective brakes,

but neither fits what the crime is designed to do. It is not the use of the vehicle which is negligent but the neglect regarding the state of the brakes. There is, therefore, one choice—strict liability or not. There is no half-way house of negligence possible.

Another common argument put forward to justify strict liability is that it is difficult or even impossible to pursue offenders if mens rea has to be proven, so many guilty people would escape liability (consider *Alphacell v Woodward*, above); strict liability is easier to enforce and thereby saves court time and leads to more guilty pleas. Whilst that might be true, the argument is fatuous. It is always difficult to prove mens rea, full stop. Crimes such as murder and rape are notoriously difficult to prove, that does not mean there is a good reason to make them strict liability.

Despite a plethora of criticism from academics, strict liability does have its supporters. The social scientist Lady Wootton, for example, (writing in *Crime and the Criminal Law*, 2nd edn) focused on the primary function of the courts as being prevention of forbidden acts and saw crimes of strict liability as fulfilling that function:

> "If ... the primary function of the court is conceived as the prevention of forbidden acts, there is little cause to be disturbed by the multiplication of offences of strict liability. If the law says that certain things are not to be done, it is illogical to confine this prohibition to occasions on which they are done from malice aforethought; for at least the material consequences of an action, and the reasons for prohibiting it are the same whether it is the result of sinister malicious plotting, of negligence or of sheer accident."

She considered that any unfairness created by equating all levels of blameworthiness when considering liability could be mitigated in sentencing:

> "The question of motivation is in the first instance irrelevant. But only in the first instance. At a later stage, that is to say, after ... conviction, the presence or absence of guilty intention is all-important for its effect on the appropriate measures to be taken to prevent a recurrence of the forbidden act."

The Alternatives

Two alternatives to strict liability were suggested in *Sweet v Parsley*. The first is often described as a "half-way house" between strict liability and the requirement of mens rea. This would require the prosecution to prove the actus reus of the offence and the defence to then prove lack of fault. This is condemned for conflicting with the golden thread of *Woolmington*, explained in Ch.1. The second alternative is to require a mens rea of negligence, see above.

A third possibility is to mitigate the harshness of strict liability with a defence of due diligence as some statutes now do. However, such defences are not uniformly available, and certainly cannot be "read in" by the judiciary wishing to avoid the unfairness of strict liability. Again, such defences can be criticised as they normally require the defendant to prove lack of mens rea and that he took all reasonable precautions and exercised all due diligence.

Summary

Mens Rea

1.   The mens rea is the mental state expressly or impliedly referred to in the definition of the crime in question.

2.   Mens rea is distinct from motive.

3.   Intention has two meanings in the criminal law: (a) direct intent whereby a consequence was the defendant's aim or purpose and (b) oblique intent where the actual outcome of D's actions was not his aim or purpose but was merely foreseen by him as a possible consequence of his actions.

4.   Direct intent is intent whereas oblique intent is not actual intent; it is merely evidence from which a jury is entitled to find intent.

5.   A jury is not entitled to find intent unless the consequence was virtually certain to occur and D foresaw the consequence as virtually certain.

6.   A person is reckless if he himself recognises the relevant risk and decides to take it in circumstances where it is unjustified to do so. This is often referred to as subjective recklessness.

7.   Negligence is rarely used as the basis of criminal liability for serious crimes. It involves inadvertent risk taking or incorrectly concluding that there is no risk involved.

8.   Under the principle of transferred malice, the mens rea in relation to an intended victim can be transferred to make the defendant liable where it is an unintended victim who is actually harmed. The principle applies also to offences against property and permits the transfer of defences as well as liability.

Strict liability

1. An offence of strict liability is one without mens rea, or without mens rea as to at least one element of the actus reus.

2. Very rare at common law, strict liability is often used for statutory "regulatory" crimes of social concern and public safety, notwithstanding the rebuttable presumption in favour of mens rea.

3. The judges may dispose of the presumption only where it is a necessary implication of the Act, and to do so would ensure greater vigilance to prevent the commission of the actus reus.

4. Generally regarded as contrary to legal principle, strict liability cannot be challenged under art.6 ECHR, but may be subject to a challenge under art.7.

End of Chapter Question

Question
Although of crucial importance in the criminal law, the term "intention" is still without a satisfactory definition, despite the best efforts of the courts.

Discuss

Points of Answer

♦ Introduction—refer to the quote in the question. The courts have had to interpret the term as it is so important in the criminal law; it is the sole mens rea of many serious offences such as murder and s.18 or the alternative to recklessness for others such as s.20 but is not defined by statute. The difficulties have arisen in determining how widely intention should be defined.

♦ Explain that there are two types of intent, direct and oblique intent, and what each means.

♦ Identify the problem the courts have faced: whether to define intention narrowly, in terms of direct intent only, or broadly, encompassing both direct and oblique intent and, if the latter approach, whether oblique intent is actual intent or merely evidence of intent.

♦ Explore by reference to the leading cases from *Moloney* through to *Woollin* and *Matthews* the various attempts to grapple with this issue.

♦ Consider the current position. Is the status quo satisfactory? Identify any problems left unresolved.

♦ Discuss reform proposals.

Further Reading

Mens Rea

R.A. Duff, "The Obscure Intentions of the House of Lords" [1986] Crim. L.R. 771 and "Intention, Agency and Criminal Liability: Philosophy of Action and the Criminal Law" (1990)

J. Finnis, *Intention and Side-Effects* in Frey and Morris (eds), *Liability and Responsibility* (Oxford University Press, 1991)

Lord Goff, "The Mental Element in the Crime of Murder" (1988) 104 L.Q.R. 30.

J. Horder, "Transferred Malice and the Remoteness of Unexpected Outcomes from Intentions" [2006] Crim. L.R. 383.

C. Kaveny, "Inferring Intention from Foresight" (2004) 120 L.Q.R. 81.

I. Kugler, "Conditional Oblique Intention" [2004] Crim. L.R. 284.

A. Norrie, "After Woollin" [1999] Crim. L.R. 532 and "Between Orthodox Subjectivism and Moral Contextualism: Intention and the Consultation Paper" [2006] Crim. L.R. 486.

A. Pedain, "Intention and the Terrorist Example" [2003] Crim. L.R. 579.

A. P. Simester, "Murder, Mens Rea and the House of Lords Again" (1999) L.Q.R. 115 17.

G. Williams, "Oblique Intention" (1987) 46 C.L.J. 417 and "The Mens Rea for Murder: Leave it Alone" (1989) 105 L.Q.R. 387.

W. Wilson, "Doctrinal Rationality after Woollin" (1999) 62 M.L.R. 448.

Strict Liability

L.H. Leigh, "Strict and Vicarious Liability" (1982).

P. Brett, "Strict Liability: Possible Solutions" (1974) 37 M.L.R. 417.

Doegar, "Strict Liability in Criminal Law and Larsonneur Reassessed" [1998] Crim. L.R. 791.

J. Horder, "Strict Liability, Statutory Construction and the Spirit of Liberty" (2002) 118 L.Q.R. 458.

A.P. Simester (ed.), "Appraising Strict Liability" Oxford University Press 2005

M. Smith and A. Pearson, "The Value of Strict Liability" [1969] Crim. L.R. 5.

J. Stanton-Ife, "Strict liability: stigma and regret" [2007] 27 O.J.L.S. 151

Self Test Questions

To test your knowledge gained from this section go online to *http://www.sweetandmaxwell.co.uk* and take our online self test questions. Here you will also find key updates to ensure that you are only ever one click away from an instant update.

Homicide

4

CHAPTER OVERVIEW

In this chapter we:

● **examine the offences of unlawful homicide**

● **identify the actus reus of unlawful homicide as causing the death of a human being under the Queen's Peace**

● **distinguish the offences of voluntary and involuntary manslaughter, from each other and from murder**

● **explore the partial defences to murder, under both common law and the Homicide Act 1957, and under the Coroners and Justice Act 2009**

● **investigate the component elements of the offences of reckless, unlawful act and gross negligence manslaughter**

● **analyse the offence of manslaughter as committed by a company and liability under the Corporate Manslaughter and Corporate Homicide Act 2007**

Summary

End of Chapter Question

Further Reading

Self Test Questions

Introduction

A homicide occurs when one human being causes the death of another human being. Not all homicides are unlawful. An example of a lawful homicide would be where D kills an aggressor who is threatening to kill him, and D responds in self-defence. It is also lawful homicide if the driver of a motor car crashes into and kills a pedestrian who wanders into the road without looking; provided of course the driver is driving in a competent and lawful manner.

It is unlawful homicide if the actus reus of homicide is proven, along with the mens rea relevant to the specific offence charged. Our study focuses primarily on murder and manslaughter but other homicide offences, with which we have no space to deal, include:

1. genocide (Genocide Act 1969);
2. causing death by dangerous driving (Road Traffic Act 1988 s.1, as amended); and
3. causing death by careless driving when under the influence of drink or drugs (Road Traffic Act 1988 s.3A, as amended).

The Actus Reus of Homicide

Whether the offence is murder or manslaughter, the actus reus is the same. Derived from the writings of Coke (Coke's Institutes, 3 Co. Inst. 47), the actus reus of homicide is: "when a [person] ... unlawfully killeth ... any reasonable creature in rerum natura under the [Queen's] peace."

In modern language, this means the actus reus of homicide is the unlawful killing of a human being by a human being at peacetime. As we shall see, the death used to have to occur within a year and a day, but that is no longer the case.

Jurisdiction

Any person who commits murder or manslaughter in any other country can be tried in the courts of England and Wales if he is a British citizen (Offences Against the Person Act 1861 s.9). If the fatal blow is struck within England, but death occurs elsewhere, a similar provision provides for the jurisdiction of the English courts under s.10.

VICTIM

Coke's definition above refers to any reasonable creature in *rerum natura*, but this can be shortened to a more understandable term—human being. This means that only a human being can be the victim of murder or manslaughter.

LIFE AND DEATH

■ Life

A foetus is not a human being and, therefore, cannot be the victim of murder or manslaughter. A foetus does not become a human being until it has been wholly expelled from, and has an existence independent of, its mother. This is usually signified by it taking a breath (**Poulton (1832) 5 Car. & P. 329** and **Enoch (1833) 5 Car. & P. 539**). "Independent of its mother" does not, however, exclude a conjoined twin who is wholly dependent on its twin for oxygenated blood (**A (Children)(Conjoined twins: surgical separation), Re [2001] Fam. 147**).

According to the House of Lords in **Attorney General's Reference (No. 3 of 1994) [1998] A.C. 245**, D can be guilty of murder or manslaughter if a child is born alive but subsequently dies from the ante-natal injuries inflicted by D. If the injuries were inflicted only to the mother and the child is later born alive and then dies, this is not murder, as the doctrine of transferred malice does not apply; see p.66. It may, however, be manslaughter of the child under the unlawful and dangerous act doctrine (see pp.121–126 below).

A foetus is subject to some protection under the criminal law even if it cannot be the victim of murder or manslaughter. There are a number of abortion-related crimes under ss.58 and 59 of the Offences Against the Person Act 1861, as amended, and there is an offence of child destruction in respect of foetuses "capable of being born alive" (presumed at 28 weeks (The Infant Life (Preservation) Act 1929 s.1)).

■ Death

There is no legal definition of death. The nearest the law has come to a definition is the obiter dictum in **Malcherek and Steel [1981] 2 All E.R. 422**, where the Court of Appeal mooted the idea that a person whose brain stem had ceased to function would be legally dead, notwithstanding that their heart and lungs were kept working by mechanical means. Brain stem death, however, is not to be confused with a victim such as Antony Bland (see p.16) A persistent vegetative state is not "brain-death" (**Airedale NHS Trust v Bland [1993] 1 All E.R. 821 HL**).

QUEEN'S PEACE

It is not unlawful to kill an alien enemy during the course of military operations, or during battle, or possibly even rebellion (**Page [1954] 1 Q.B. 170**).

THE YEAR AND A DAY RULE

It used to be the law for all homicide offences that death had to occur within a year and a day of D's act which caused death. This was to recognise that if a victim survived for that long, in ancient times and in the absence of modern medical treatment, the subsequent death could not be said to attributable to D. This arbitrary deadline of 365+1 days was abolished by s.1 of the Law Reform (Year and a Day Rule) Act 1996. Section 2 of the Act provides that the Attorney General must consent to any homicide prosecution where:

1. the injury alleged to have caused the death was sustained more than three years before the death occurred, or
2. the person has previously been convicted of an offence [such as an assault] committed in circumstances alleged to be connected with the death.

CAUSATION
All unlawful homicides are result crimes. It must be proven that D caused the death, see Ch.2.

UNLAWFUL
As was noted above, not all homicides are unlawful; but for the actus reus of murder and manslaughter to be satisfied, the killing must be unlawful. Killing in self-defence is not unlawful (**Beckford v Queen [1988] A.C. 130**). The defence of necessity may also render a killing justified, and so lawful (*A (Children) Re*, above, and see Ch.13).

Murder

Murder is a common law offence. It is defined as the unlawful killing of a human being during the Queen's Peace with malice aforethought.

An offender aged 21 and over who is convicted of murder must be sentenced to imprisonment for life under s.1(1) of the Murder (Abolition of Death Penalty) Act 1965. There is no room here to debate the mechanisms, and controversy, surrounding early release from prison after serving the minimum term imposed by the judge. What needs to be acknowledged is that murder is still subject to a mandatory sentence of life imprisonment. Manslaughter, on the other hand, carries a maximum life sentence, not a mandatory one.

The difference in the seriousness between the offences of murder and manslaughter must be reflected in the definitions and, as murder and manslaughter have the same actus reus, logically what distinguishes them is the mens rea.

. . . .

The Mens Rea of Murder
The traditional term used to describe the mens rea of murder is "malice aforethought" according to Coke (Coke's Institutes, 3 Co. Inst. 47).

MALICE AFORETHOUGHT

Malice aforethought is an unfortunate phrase. If translated into modern language, it implies the defendant must have borne the victim ill-will (malice) and planned the killing (afore-thought). This is not the law. According to Lord Hailsham in **Hyam v DPP [1975] A.C.55**:

> "the sooner the phrase is consigned to the limbo of legal history the better for precision and lucidity in the interpretation of our criminal law".

The House of Lords in **Moloney [1985] 1 All E.R. 1025**, described "malice aforethought" as an "anachronistic and now wholly inappropriate phrase which still lingers on in the definition of murder to denote the necessary mental element". Their Lordships held that the "necessary mental element" is:

1. an intention to kill; or
2. an intention to cause grievous bodily harm.

According to the House of Lords in **Woollin [1999] 1 A.C. 82**, we can state that D intends death or grievous bodily harm (GBH) if it is his aim, objective or purpose to bring either of them about. If it is not his aim or purpose, the jury is not entitled to find intention unless death or GBH was a virtually certain consequence of his conduct and D foresaw death or GBH as virtually certain to result from his conduct (see further Ch.3).

IMPLIED MALICE

Implied malice is the term given to the lesser form of mens rea for murder; that is, the mens rea of intention to do GBH, rather than the more serious mens rea of intention to kill. If "grievous bodily harm" meant injuries which are life-threatening, there would be no controversy. However, although GBH means "really serious" harm (**DPP v Smith [1960] 3 All E.R. 161 HL**) a broken jaw, arm or leg can amount to GBH. If D aims to break his victim's jaw, he intends to cause grievous bodily harm. If V then dies from unforeseen medical complications (as we discussed in Ch.2), D can be convicted of murder (**Vickers [1957] 2 Q.B. 664, Cunningham [1981] 2 All E.R. 863**).

In light of the mandatory life sentence noted above, it is considered to be harsh that an intention to cause GBH, i.e. harm amounting to less than a life-threatening injury, suffices for the mens rea of murder. In *Hyam*, two of their Lordships (Lords Diplock and Kilbrandon) urged their fellow Lords to agree to change the law so that implied malice would be satisfied only by an intention to cause injury likely to endanger life, but they were outvoted by the majority.

Reform of Murder

In November 2006, the Law Commission published a report, "Murder, Manslaughter and Infanticide" (Law Com. No.304, 2006) which proposed a "ladder" of offences with first degree murder at the top of the ladder (i.e. the most serious crime) carrying a mandatory life sentence where D killed with direct or oblique intent to kill, or where D killed with an intent to do serious injury with an awareness of a serious risk of causing death. It would be second degree murder, which would carry a discretionary life sentence, where:

1. D killed with intent to do serious injury (without an awareness of a serious risk of causing death);
   or
2. D killed where he intended to cause some injury or a fear of injury or a risk of injury, and was aware of a serious risk of causing death;
   or
3. it would be first degree murder but for a defence of provocation, diminished responsibility or killing pursuant to a suicide pact.

What is clear, however, is that for the foreseeable future, the ladder of offences will not be enacted. A later Government Consultation Paper (19/08 in July, 2008) proceeded on the basis that murder will remain a single offence and only two of the partial defences (considered on pp.96 and 109 below) have been amended.

Manslaughter

There are two main types of manslaughter, known as voluntary and involuntary respectively. The terms "voluntary" and "involuntary" are misleading and they do not mean literally what they say, but rather they indicate whether the mens rea for murder is present.

In cases of voluntary manslaughter, D has satisfied the actus reus of homicide and has the mens rea for murder. He has been charged with murder. However, he is convicted of manslaughter because of the success of a specific defence. There are currently three such defences: diminished responsibility; provocation (to be replaced by loss of self-control) and suicide pact.

On the other hand, if D has satisfied the actus reus of homicide but did not have the mens rea for murder, he is guilty of involuntary manslaughter if he satisfies the mens rea requirements of that offence. The offence of involuntary manslaughter covers a huge range of activities and states of mind. It covers offenders charged with murder who foresaw death, say, as highly probable, but not as a virtual certainty. At the other end of the scale in terms of seriousness, it is involuntary manslaughter to cause a death where D is merely reckless as to a battery, but which causes death (see constructive manslaughter on pp.121–126 below). In **Walker (1992) 13 Cr. App. R. (S.) 474**, Lord Lane C.J. described the breadth of the offence as, "rang[ing] in gravity from the borders of murder right down to those of accidental death".

The Home Office Response to the Law Commission's 1996 (No.237) Report comments that the different types of conduct, all of which amount to manslaughter:

> "... [have] led to problems for judges who have difficulty in determining the appropriate sentence for an offence which is so wide and who are unable to receive the jury's guidance on matters that are crucial to the severity of the penalty deserved, such as the accused's foresight of the risk of causing death. It can also lead to problems for the public in understanding why the judge in any given case has awarded the particular sentence." (Home Office, 2000)

The figure on p.90 indicates the various forms of manslaughter.

Voluntary Manslaughter

Despite the actus reus and mens rea of murder being satisfied where the offence is voluntary manslaughter, the special defences allow the judge discretion when sentencing. The maximum sentence for manslaughter (voluntary and involuntary) is life imprisonment, but it is not a mandatory sentence.

Diminished responsibility, provocation (which is to be replaced by a defence of loss of self-control, see below) and suicide pact are referred to as "special defences" to murder. This is because they apply only to murder and not to any other crimes (provocation may be a factor in sentencing for other offences, but does not affect liability). They are also called "partial" defences because they do not result in an acquittal, but reduced liability.

Over to you...

The partial defences have received considerable attention in the past few years; by the Law Commission, Government and Parliament. This attention has resulted in:

1. amendments to the defence of diminished responsibility, and
2. abolition of the defence of provocation

in the Coroners and Justice Act 2009 (C&JA 2009).

(continued on p.91)

FIGURE 4 **The types of manslaughter**

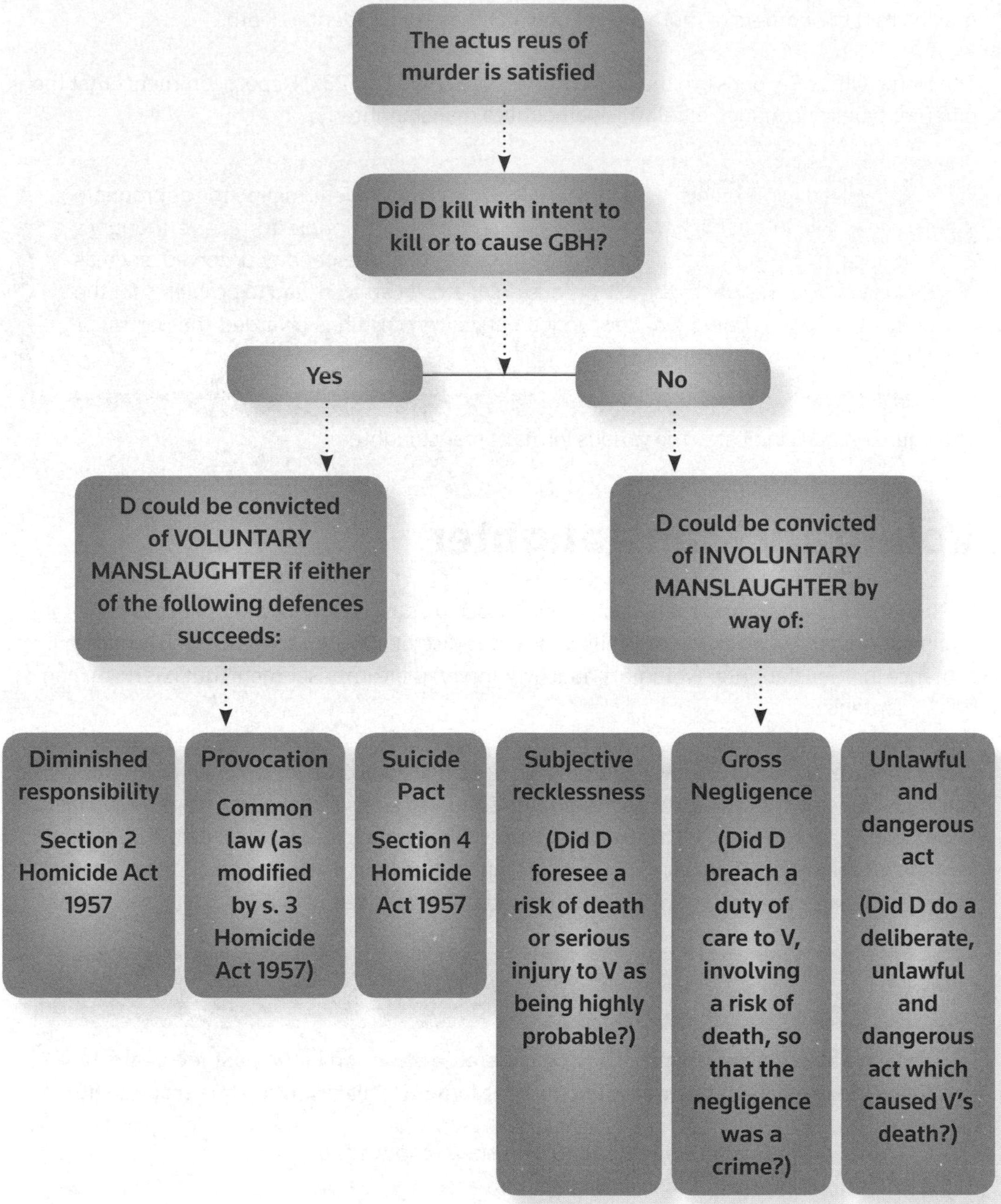

The actus reus of murder is satisfied

Did D kill with intent to kill or to cause GBH?

Yes — No

Yes: D could be convicted of VOLUNTARY MANSLAUGHTER if either of the following defences succeeds:

No: D could be convicted of INVOLUNTARY MANSLAUGHTER by way of:

Diminished responsibility	Provocation	Suicide Pact	Subjective recklessness	Gross Negligence	Unlawful and dangerous act
Section 2 Homicide Act 1957	Common law (as modified by s. 3 Homicide Act 1957)	Section 4 Homicide Act 1957	(Did D foresee a risk of death or serious injury to V as being highly probable?)	(Did D breach a duty of care to V, involving a risk of death, so that the negligence was a crime?)	(Did D do a deliberate, unlawful and dangerous act which caused V's death?)

At the time of writing, March 2010, we have been waiting for announcement of when the provisions in question will come into force, but none has been forthcoming. Therefore, we will:

1. explain the law as it stands under the common law and the Homicide Act 1957 first, and in the present tense, and
2. explain the law as it is on the statute book (the C&JA 2009) thereafter, and in the future tense. The law in the C&JA may of course be in force by the time you read and use this book, so you should then use the past and the present tense respectively in your explanations.

Diminished Responsibility

This special defence was introduced in England and Wales in the Homicide Act 1957 but was adopted from Scottish law. It was historically viewed as a type of temporary insanity although, as we shall see, the defence is far broader than that of insanity, and the sentence for voluntary manslaughter, even by way of diminished responsibility, is imprisonment. Defendants who successfully plead not guilty by reason of insanity to murder may be (though not necessarily) institutionalised indefinitely in a secure mental hospital (see further Ch.12). It is, therefore, clear why a defendant would prefer to plead the defence under s.2 of the Homicide Act 1957 (HA 1957).

The special defence is, on the whole, quite straightforward. In fact, it is not often considered by a jury because it is not uncommon for the prosecution to accept a plea of diminished responsibility on a murder charge. If the judge agrees, there is no need for a trial (the same cannot be said for the defence of provocation, below, which should be considered by the jury).

Diminished responsibility does not operate to reduce attempted murder to attempted manslaughter (**Campbell [1997] Crim. L.R. 227**).

BURDEN OF PROOF

As we discussed in Ch.1, it is for the prosecution to prove the case against the defendant beyond reasonable doubt, and this generally includes disproving his defence(s) too. However, if the defence of diminished responsibility goes to trial (if the plea has not been accepted by either the prosecution or the judge, say) then s.2(2) of the HA 1957 places the burden of proof on the defendant to prove the defence on the balance of probability (**Dunbar [1958] 1 Q.B. 1**).

This reversal of the normal proof burden is in line with the defence of insanity (**M'Naghten (1843) 4 St. Tr. NS 847**), but is out of step with the "golden rule" of *Woolmington* (see Ch.1, p.8). A challenge was made to the reverse proof burden contained in s.2(2) HA 1957 in the consolidated appeals of **Lambert; Ali; Jordan [2001] 1 All E.R. 1014**, but the Court of Appeal held the section did not contravene the presumption of innocence in art.6(2) of the European Convention on Human Rights. Had the reversal been of an element of a crime itself, the matter would be different, but, according to Lord Woolf C.J., s.2 HA 1957 simply allows D to establish a special defence or exception to liability and the prosecution must prove all of the elements of the crime itself. On reflection, this is no justification at all. The prosecution has the burden of disproving provocation, which is also a special defence or exception to liability, so it is nonsense to suggest that where a defence permits an exception to liability, it is ever appropriate for the defendant to have to prove it. To argue further, as some do, that where the defendant puts his mind in doubt, he must prove it, is similarly irrational. Denial of mens rea puts the defendant's state of mind in issue, but it does not involve him having a burden of proof on that matter.

SECTION 2 HOMICIDE ACT 1957

Section 2 of the Homicide Act 1957 provides:

> **(1)** Where a person kills or is a party to the killing of another, he shall not be convicted of murder if he was suffering from such abnormality of mind (whether arising from a condition of arrested or retarded development of mind or any inherent causes or induced by disease or injury) as substantially impaired his mental responsibility for his acts and omissions in doing or being a party to the killing.
> **(2)** On a charge of murder, it shall be for the defence to prove that the person charged is by virtue of this section not liable to be convicted of murder.
> **(3)** A person who but for this section would be liable, whether as principal or as accessory, to be convicted of murder shall be liable instead to be convicted of manslaughter.

Section 2 has been amended by s.52 of the Coroners and Justice Act 2009, which we consider on p.96 below)

▥ Abnormality of mind

The leading case on the meaning of abnormality of mind is **Byrne [1960] 2 Q.B. 396**. D was charged with the murder of a young girl whom he had strangled and whose dead body he had mutilated in response to a sexual impulse or urge which was so strong that he found it difficult or impossible to resist. His appeal against conviction for murder was allowed by the Court of Criminal Appeal, and a conviction for manslaughter (voluntary) was substituted. Lord Parker C.J. said that:

> "Abnormality of the mind … means a state of mind so different from that of ordinary human beings that the reasonable man would term it abnormal. It appears to us to be wide enough to cover the mind's activities in all its aspects, not only the perception of

physical acts and matters and the ability to form a rational judgement as to whether an act is right or wrong, but also the ability to exercise will-power to control physical acts in accordance with that rational judgement."

Clearly, an irresistible sexual urge or impulse is "abnormal", and the definition given by Lord Parker C.J. is broad enough to cover Byrne's psychosis. In **Jama [2004] EWCA Crim 960**, the Court of Appeal noted that "Asperger's Syndrome is an abnormality of mind [even though it] may be suffered by persons of perfectly normal intelligence."

The *Byrne* definition is very wide, and it is the breadth of the definition that should be contrasted with the very narrow term "disease of mind" in the defence of insanity. For example, a disassociative illness in **Price (1971), The Times, December 22**, which would not have been classed as insanity, was within the defence of diminished responsibility. In a similar vein, **Reynolds [1988] Crim. L.R. 679** holds that pre-menstrual tension is an "abnormality of mind", but it would not be a "disease" under the insanity rules (see Ch.12). On the other hand, states of mind which are "diseases" for the purposes of insanity will always amount to abnormal states of mind for diminished responsibility.

Perhaps this limited overlap explains why there is confusion between the two defences, and the defence under s.2 HA 1957 is often referred to as "partial" or "borderline insanity" (**Spriggs [1958] 1 Q.B. 270**). The Court of Appeal in **Seers (1984) 79 Cr. App. R. 261** held, however, that such a parallel should not be drawn, as many states of mind which amount to abnormal states are not diseases for the purposes of insanity, and to state or imply otherwise could confuse juries.

The cause of the abnormality
The cause of the abnormality must:

1. arise from a condition of arrested or retarded development of mind or
2. any inherent causes or
3. induced by disease or injury.

This list is finite. Any abnormality of mind not arising from a cause listed above does not fall within the defence. That said, the causes (or aetiologies) have not been interpreted narrowly. For example, arrested or retarded development, disease or injury, would all cover congenital defects and illnesses or, for example, brain injury. Where the source of the defendant's condition is not so easily identified, the term "any inherent cause" has been construed widely. For example, in **Ahluwahlia (1993) 96 Cr. App. R. 133**, the court extended the scope for relying on depression as an abnormality of mind beyond chronic reactive depression (as was held in *Seers*) to include endogenous depression (depression without any identifiable external cause). Other examples of inherent cause accepted by the courts include Battered Woman Syndrome (**Hobson [1998] 1 Cr. App. R. 31**), paranoia (**Simcox [1964] Crim. L.R. 402**) and functional mental illness (**Sanderson (1993) 98 Cr. App. R. 325**).

Whether mere emotions can come within specified causes is unclear. Section 2 was intended to exclude emotions such as bad temper, rage and jealousy. However, rage was allowed as a specified cause in **Coles (1980) 144 J.P.N. 528** and jealousy in **Miller (1972), The Times, 16 May**.

■ Substantial impairment

Nowhere in s.2 is the word "diminished" used. Rather, the phrase is "substantially impaired his mental responsibility". In determining this issue, the jury does have the benefit of hearing expert medical evidence on the defendant's abnormality of mind and its cause and such evidence is, in practice, essential (**Dix (1981) 74 Cr. App. R. 306**) but the question as to whether there has been a substantial impairment is a question of fact. The Court of Appeal recognised in *Byrne* that it is a matter of degree for the jury to decide and, in **Lloyd [1967] 1 All E.R. 107**, stated that for it to be substantial, "the impairment need not be total but it must be more than trivial or minimal". However, it is an ordinary English word and in **Mitchell [1995] Crim. L.R. 506**, the Court of Appeal held that it was not necessary for the judge to explain the meaning of "substantial". This was recently confirmed in **R. v R [2010] EWCA Crim 194**.

■ Impairment and the effects of alcohol

Alcohol and drugs are not acceptable causes of abnormality of mind (**Fenton (1975) 61 Cr. App. R. 261**). If intoxication is one of two or more causes of the abnormality of mind, the jury must be directed that they should ignore the effect of the drink or drugs and that they have to be satisfied that the abnormality from one of the permitted "specified causes" in s.2 substantially impaired D's mental responsibility for the fatal acts (**Gittens [1984] 3 All E.R. 252**). In **Dietschmann [2003] 1 A.C. 1209 HL**, the court held that there is no requirement under s.2 that the abnormality be the sole cause of the fatal act. Hence, a defendant who is intoxicated and suffering from a permitted cause such as, for example, depression does not have to establish that, had he been sober, he probably would not have killed. In such circumstances, a jury would have to consider whether, despite the intoxication, D's (allowed) abnormality of mind substantially impaired his mental responsibility for the killing.

Alcoholism (as opposed to intoxication per se) may afford a defence of diminished responsibility. Until recently, chronic alcoholism (or alcohol dependency syndrome as it is often referred to) could have fallen into the defence if the jury was satisfied (a) that alcoholism had injured his brain, i.e. caused gross impairment of judgement and emotional responses or (b) that the intoxication was involuntary in the sense that D could not resist the impulse to have the first drink of the day (**Tandy (1988) 87 Cr. App. R. 45**). However, the Court of Appeal in **Wood [2009] 1 W.L.R. 496** acknowledged that there were problems with the "involuntary" test from *Tandy* because an alcoholic who drinks because of an irresistible craving for alcohol might nevertheless appear to be drinking voluntarily. The court cited an academic, Julia Tolmie, who, in her article "Alcoholism and Criminal Liability" (2001) M.L.R. 688 observed that the *Tandy* test appeared:

"to have required that the defendant, to benefit from the defence, conform to a model of alcoholism that even the most hardened alcoholic would find ... difficult to meet ... even if the alcoholic in question does not have choice about whether or not they will drink, they will often have an apparent choice about when and where they commence drinking."

Thus, Lord Judge C.J. held that when assessing whether D's mental responsibility for his actions at the time of the killing was substantially impaired as a result of the syndrome, the jury should focus only on the effect of alcohol D drank as a direct result of his illness or disease and ignore the effect of any alcohol consumed voluntarily. Unfortunately, the judgment fails to provide assistance to a jury in determining the very difficult question of whether D's decision of when and what to drink was indeed "voluntary" or arose from the alcohol dependency itself.

The issue was revisited again in **Stewart [2009] EWCA Crim 593**. Lord Judge C.J. (again) gave the judgment of the court. He set out the following approach to be adopted in cases where diminished responsibility is pleaded on the basis of alcohol dependency syndrome:

1. The jury determines whether D was indeed suffering from an abnormality of mind at the time of the killing. The judge is likely to direct the jury that it does not necessarily follow from the fact that D suffers from alcohol dependency syndrome that he has established the necessary abnormality of mind. This depends on the jury's findings about the nature and extent of the syndrome and whether, looking at the matter broadly, D's consumption of alcohol before the killing is fairly to be regarded as the involuntary result of an irresistible craving for, or compulsion to, drink.

2. If D proves the necessary abnormality of mind, the next question is whether this was caused by disease or illness. The answer to this question will normally follow from whatever answer is appropriate to the first question.

3. If both 1. and 2. above are satisfied, then the direction about whether D's mental responsibility for what he did was substantially impaired should be addressed in conventional terms. The jury should be assisted with the concept of substantial impairment, and may properly be invited to reflect on the difference between a failure by D to resist his impulses to behave as he actually did, and an inability consequent on it to resist them.

4. In answering their questions, the jury should be directed to consider all the evidence, including the opinions of the medical experts. The issues likely to arise in this kind of case include (a) the extent and seriousness of D's dependency, if any, on alcohol (b) the extent to which his ability to control his drinking or to choose whether to drink or not, was reduced, (c) whether he was capable of abstinence from alcohol, and if so, (d) for how long, and (e) whether he was choosing for some particular reason, such as a birthday celebration, to decide to get drunk, or to drink even more than usual. D's pattern of drinking in the days leading to the day of the killing, and on the day of the killing itself, and notwithstanding his consumption of alcohol, his ability, if any, to make apparently sensible and rational decisions about ordinary day to day matters at the relevant time might all be relevant.

The guidance on the directions to the jury is helpful but does not go far enough; it is, as Professor Ashworth pointed out in his commentary on the case ([2009] Crim. L.R. 807):

> "afflicted with the same problem [as *Wood*] of determining whether D's apparent choices of when and what to drink were real choices, or actions stemming chiefly from his alcohol dependency".

Diminished Responsibility under the Coroners and Justice Act 2009

Section 52 of the C&JA has amended s.2(1) of the Homicide Act 1957, substituting the original wording with;

(1) A person ("D") who kills or is a party to the killing of another is not to be convicted of murder if D was suffering from an abnormality of mental functioning which—
(a) arose from a recognised medical condition,
(b) substantially impaired D's ability to do one or more of the things mentioned in subsection (1A), and
(c) provides an explanation for D's acts and omissions in doing or being a party to the killing.

(1A) Those things are—
(a) to understand the nature of D's conduct;
(b) to form a rational judgment;
(c) to exercise self-control.

(1B) For the purposes of subsection (1)(c), an abnormality of mental functioning provides an explanation for D's conduct if it causes, or is a significant contributory factor in causing, D to carry out that conduct.

The main changes will therefore be as follows.

ABNORMALITY OF MIND WILL BECOME ABNORMALITY OF MENTAL FUNCTIONING

Although the term "mental functioning" is not defined in the Act, it is anticipated that the new test will be more specific in respect of the work to be done by the expert witnesses (doctors, psychiatrists, etc.). The current *Byrne* test is seen as being too wide and too vague, see p.92 above and the 2006 Law Commission Report "Murder, Manslaughter and Infanticide" (Law Com. No.304, 2006), Pt.5 from para.5.83 onwards.

THE ABNORMALITY WILL HAVE TO ARISE FROM A RECOGNISED MEDICAL CONDITION

The aetiologies (see p.93 above) will be replaced with a requirement that the abnormality must arise simply from a "recognised medical condition". This change is designed to broaden the causes generally available, but without permitting intoxication to be a valid cause because drunkenness cannot be a recognised medical condition. That said, alcoholism is. The current finite list in the Homicide Act 1957 has been subject to extensive judicial tinkering (pp.93–94 above) and is widely regarded as containing out-of-date terms unsuitable in a modern medical setting. "Recognised medical condition" will also be wide enough to cover physical, psychiatric and psychological conditions, whether currently recognised, or recognisable in the future as medical advances and diagnoses change. See the Ministry of Justice 2008 Consultation Paper "Murder, manslaughter and infanticide: proposals for reform of the law" (available on the Ministry's website), para.49.

Over to you...

Is this change of wording necessary? Review the case law on the aetiologies examined above. Are there any reported cases that could not be said to have arisen from a "recognised medical condition" anyway? Are there cases where D did not have a cause from an aetiology in s.2 which he would have in future under the C&JA 2009?

SUBSTANTIAL IMPAIRMENT WILL STAY, BUT ...

There will still be a requirement that D proves a substantial impairment (the *Lloyd* test will probably still be used for this, p.94 above) but instead of an impairment of mental responsibility, which is a very vague phrase (Law Com. 304, para.5.110), in future the impairment will have to be proven to affect;

1. D's understanding of the nature of his conduct,
2. D's ability to form rational judgment or
3. D's ability to exercise self-control (for factual examples, see Law Com. 304 para.5.121).

This question will probably one of fact for the jury.

A NEW ELEMENT

A new element will be introduced. The mental impairment will have to be proved to have caused *or was a significant contributory factor in causing D* to act as he did (in killing). It is not clear what impact this new requirement will have or what the rationale for it is.

THE BURDEN OF PROOF

The burden of proof in respect of the defence will remain on D because s.2(2) has not been amended. see p.91 above.

Provocation

Essentially, provocation is where D has killed in the heat of the moment, having lost his self-control where the reasonable person would have reacted in the same way in the same situation. It is murder, with a partial defence, which results in a conviction for voluntary manslaughter.

Provocation is a common law defence which has been modified by statute (the Homicide Act s.3). The classic direction on provocation was given by Lord Devlin in **Duffy [1949] 1 All E.R. 932** as:

> "… some act or series of acts (done by the dead man to the accused) which would cause in any reasonable man, and actually causes in the accused, a sudden and temporary loss of self-control, rendering the accused so subject to passion as to make him or her for the moment not master of his mind."

SECTION 3 HOMICIDE ACT 1957

Section 3 of the Homicide Act 1957 provides:

> Where on a charge of murder there is evidence on which the jury can find that the person charged was provoked (whether by things done or by things said or by both together) to lose his self-control, the question whether the provocation was enough to make a reasonable man do as he did shall be left to be determined by the jury, and in determining that question the jury shall take into account everything both done and said according to the effect which in their opinion, it would have on a reasonable man.

The success or failure of the defence is a matter of fact for the jury ("evidence on which the jury can find … shall be left to be determined by the jury"). In **Acott [1997] 1 All E.R. 706 HL**, at his trial for the murder of his mother, D's defence was total denial of the actus reus, but it was the prosecution's case that he had lost his temper and killed her in a rage. Appealing against his conviction for murder, D argued that the prosecution's suggestions to him in cross-examination amounted to evidence of provocation; and the judge should have left the defence to be determined by the jury. The House of Lords dismissed his appeal, holding that the trial judge can leave the issue to the jury only where there is some actual evidence as to what had been said or done which allegedly caused D to lose his self-control. This had to be more than just speculation based on questions asked during cross-examination. Interestingly, whether there is sufficient evidence of provocation is a question of *fact* to be decided by the *judge*, taking into account all the circumstances of the case.

If the judge finds sufficient evidence of provocation, however, the defence must then be left to the jury, whether or not the defendant relies on it (**Rossiter [1994] 2 All E.R. 752**). A judge should not allow himself to be persuaded by defence counsel not to direct the jury to consider provocation, merely because the defence team wish to obtain a complete acquittal on the charge of murder rather than a conviction for voluntary manslaughter (**Burgess and McLean [1995] Crim L.R.425**).

The elements of the defence under s.3 are;

1. provocative conduct;
2. actual loss of self-control; and
3. the reasonable man.

■ Provocative conduct

The parenthetical phrase in s.3 is that the provocative conduct must be "by things done or by things said or by both together". This modifies the common law governing provocation which provided that words alone were incapable of amounting to provocative conduct for the purposes of the defence (**Holmes v DPP [1946] 2 All E.R. 124 HL**).

So, what conduct amounts to "things said or done" for the purposes of s.3? The answer is any conduct. Even whether the constant crying of a young baby could constitute provocation should have been left to be determined by the jury (**Doughty (1986) 83 Cr. App. R. 319**), although obviously the defence would have failed given that the reasonable person would never have reacted as the defendant did in killing the child.

Misdirected retaliation

At common law, only "acts done by the dead man to the accused" could be considered (**Duffy [1949] 1 All E.R. 932**). This rule has been abolished by s.3. In **Davies [1975] 1 All E.R. 890**, D's wife had left him for another man. D killed his wife when he became angry after he saw her lover waiting for her to leave work. The Court of Appeal held that it was not necessary to show that D was provoked to lose his self-control by the deceased. Words or acts emanating from another person are capable of amounting to provocative conduct. In **Pearson [1992] Crim. L.R. 193**, D killed his father in reaction to the father's violent abuse of D's younger brother. The Court of Appeal held that provocative conduct by the deceased to someone other than the defendant may be considered by the jury, and that loss of self-control can arise due to fear of violence to another.

Cumulative provocation

Provocation need not be an isolated incident or one taunt; a defendant may have been provoked over a period of time. Such provocation is called cumulative provocation and a defendant may seek to rely on such provocation to explain why, perhaps, some trivial remark or incident was the "final straw" which caused him to snap and kill. Thus, the final provocation is considered not in isolation but, instead, in the context of all that has gone before it. A defendant may only rely on cumulative provocation, however, where he does actually suffer a sudden and temporary loss of self-control in response to the final taunt—the subjective test (below) must still be satisfied (**Thornton (No.2) [1996] 2 All E.R. 1023**).

Self-induced provocation

In **Edwards v The Queen [1973] A.C. 648**, D attempted to blackmail V and V reacted by threatening D with a knife. D's response was to stab V 27 times. The Privy Council held that criminal conduct on the part of D led to the provocative conduct by V and therefore could not form the basis of a plea of provocation. However, such a hard-and-fast rule conflicts with s.3 and the Court of Appeal in **Johnson [1989] 1 W.L.R. 740**, has clarified that self-induced provocation must be left for the jury's consideration, and it is simply one factor for the jury to consider in deciding whether a reasonable man would have done as D did.

■ Actual loss of self-control

If D did not lose his self-control, even if the reasonable person would have done, it is murder, not manslaughter. The test, which is one of fact for the jury, is entirely subjective: did the defendant actually lose his self-control? It involves more than being angry, or a loss of temper, but is less that a total loss of self-control. According to *Duffy*, D must:

> "suffer a sudden and temporary loss of self-control, rendering him so subject to passion as to make him or her for the moment not master of his mind".

It is not, however, necessary that D did not know what he was doing though he must be "unable to restrain himself from doing what he did" (Lord Taylor C.J. in **Richens [1993] 4 All E.R. 877**).

Sudden and temporary

"Temporary" is not particularly relevant; a defendant may still rely upon the defence even if his loss of self-control lasts some time. However, in practice, most instances of lost self-control are temporary.

Over to you...

The comment in *Duffy* that the actual loss of self-control be "sudden" raises two issues. First, if there has been a time gap between the provocation and the killing will the defence always fail? Second, must D's reaction, the loss of self-control, immediately follow the provocation? Consider your views on these questions before we address them in law.

The answer to the first question is that if D has calmed down after the provocative conduct, then the defence is likely to fail on the grounds that he is no longer "out of control." Reason has had time to resume its seat (**Hayward (1833) 6 Car. & P. 157**). Hence, in **Ibrams (1981) 74 Cr. App. R. 154**, where the last act of provocation occurred five days before D's fatal response, this was not a case of provocation, but premeditated murder. The defence also failed on this ground in **Ahluwalia [1992] 4 All E.R. 889**. D's husband had abused her for many years. One evening, he told her that he would hurt her the following day unless she paid a bill. D waited until her husband was asleep then took some paraffin upstairs, poured it over her sleeping husband and set fire to him, killing him.

More recently, the courts have taken a more generous approach to "cooling off periods" so that they will not necessarily preclude the defence, though the longer the time gap and the stronger the evidence of deliberation, the less likely the defence is to succeed. In **Thornton [1992] 1 All E.R. 306**, for example, the defence was left to the jury (though they rejected it) where D, following provocation from her abusive husband, went to the kitchen for a carving knife, sharpened the knife and then went to another room where she stabbed her husband. Similarly, in **Baillie [1995] 2 Cr. App. R. 31**, the Court of Appeal stated that the defence ought to have been left to the jury where D, following the provocation, had gone to the attic to fetch a gun and then driven his car for two miles, filling up with petrol on the way, before shooting his victim.

The answer to the second question is that a delayed response will not necessarily mean that the defence fails. "Sudden" does not mean "immediate;" it simply means that there must be no premeditation. In some circumstances (particularly in cases involving domestic violence), a defendant has a "slow burn" to anger, rather than an explosive and immediate violent reaction, i.e. the provocation is followed by a time gap after which the defendant suddenly snaps. This was recognised in *Ahluwalia*:

> "The subjective element ... would not as a matter of law be negatived simply because of the delayed reaction ... provided that there was at the time of the killing a 'sudden and temporary loss of self-control' caused by the alleged provocation."

The reasonable man

Clearly, it is never reasonable to kill in reaction to provocation, however serious. The reasonable reaction is to walk away and ignore the taunts or the conduct. The law, however, despite reference to the reasonable man (person), does not require a reasonable reaction. Neither does it permit an excessively angry or volatile defendant to be afforded a defence solely on the grounds of his temper. In reality, the "reasonable man" test exists to inject a level of objectivity to the defence to prevent bad-tempered defendants relying on the defence where they have made no effort to control their reactions. In **Morhall [1996] A.C. 90**, Lord Goff explained it thus:

> "The function of the test is only to introduce, as a matter of policy, a standard of self-control which has to be complied with if provocation is to be established in law."

Suppose that V taunts a very tall person about his height; or a person with acne about his skin condition; or a redhead about the colour of his hair, and so on. We identify such taunts which are directed at a particular "characteristic" of the defendant as affecting the gravity of the provocation. Such characteristics may be distinguished from other characteristics that affect D's general ability to control his response; his self-control characteristics. Another way of phrasing this distinction is between D's provocativeness (where the taunt is directed at or affects or is affected by a particular characteristic, also known as a gravity characteristic) and his provocability (where D is more easily provoked than another person might be).

Over to you...

It is very important you grasp the difference between provocativeness (or gravity characteristics) and provocability (or self-control characteristics) if you are to master the cases which follow.

Clearly, a defendant will wish the reasonable person to be endowed with as many of his own characteristics as possible because the more the reasonable person is like the defendant, the more likely it is that the jury will conclude that the reasonable person would have killed in the defendant's situation. But, with which, if any, of D's characteristics can the reasonable person be endowed? Will it be none, only those which affect the gravity of the provocation to him, only those which affect his powers of self-control or will it be all his characteristics?

Historically, neither provocativeness nor provocability characteristics were relevant to the objective test. At common law, the reasonable person did not possess any special characteristics of the defendant even if they would have affected the gravity of the provocation. For example, in **Bedder v DPP [1954] 1 W.L.R. 1119**, the reasonable man was not imbued with the defendant's impotence, despite V's taunting of D about that very characteristic. This was a very harsh decision; a man not suffering from impotence would not react to a taunt about it in the same way as a man who was impotent. Yet the House of Lords saw no reason to depart from its previous decision in **Mancini v DPP [1942] A.C. 1**, that the reasonable man could not be invested with the "unusually excitable or pugnacious temperament" of D. Accordingly, Lord Simonds rejected the submission of the appellant, that the question should be what would be the reaction of the impotent reasonable man in the circumstances:

"... for that proposition I know of no authority; nor can I see any reason in it. It would be plainly illogical not to recognise an unusually excitable or pugnacious temperament in the accused as a matter to be taken into account, but yet to recognize (sic) for that purpose some unusual physical characteristic, be it impotence or another."

Lord Simonds had not considered, however, the difference between provocativeness and pro-vocability. In **DPP v Camplin [1978] 2 All E.R. 168**, the House of Lords acknowledged some of D's characteristics would be relevant to the gravity of the provocation. Camplin was a boy of 15, who had been forcibly buggered by V, a man in his 50s. V had then taunted and laughed at D. D had lost his self-control and killed V by hitting him over the head with a chapatti pan. The House of Lords held that the trial judge had misdirected the jury in instructing them to regard the reasonable man as a normal adult and not to invest him with D's youth. The reasonable person was someone:

> "having the power of self-control to be expected of an ordinary person of the sex and age of the accused but in other respects sharing such of the accused's characteristics as ... would *affect the gravity of the provocation to him* ..." (emphasis added)

The decision in *Camplin* overruled *Bedder*, but it did not result in the total acceptance of all of the defendant's characteristics for the purpose of the objective test. The jury could consider the age, sex and other characteristics of D affecting the gravity of the provocation, but not those characteristics only affecting D's self-control such as exceptional excitability, pugnacity or ill temper.

How can the characteristic affect the gravity of the provocation? Consider the facts of *Morhall*. D was a glue-sniffing addict. The victim nagged him about his addiction and his inability to kick the habit. Obviously, a glue-sniffing non-addict would have found it easy to ignore the taunts, but Morhall was an addict and this characteristic increased the effect of the provocation on him. It was, therefore, a relevant characteristic, to be taken into account despite the fact that it was discreditable. (Presumably, other discreditable characteristics could also be taken into account, such as D's paedophilia, if relevant). What might not have been relevant, however, would have been characteristics that were not the subject of the taunt, such as his height, weight or sexual orientation. However, in **Gregson [2006] EWCA Crim 3364**, the Court of Appeal held that the jury was obliged to consider D as he was "warts and all". This includes characteristics such as illness which affect the gravity of the provocation even if not the subject of the taunts. On the facts of *Gregson*, D's depression and epilepsy were relevant characteristics for the jury's consideration even though the taunt was about being jobless, because D blamed his illnesses for not having a job.

Intoxication by drink or drugs is always to be ignored, however. As a matter of policy, the reasonable person is always sober (*Morhall*).

So, could characteristics be taken into account if they did not increase the provocativeness of the conduct of the victim, but merely made D more prone to be provoked in general? They should not have been, but the Court of Appeal during the 1980s and early 1990s began to accept that self-control characteristics might be considered by the jury. As we shall see, this caused a conflict between the Court of Appeal and the Privy Council in the first instance and between the House of Lords and the Privy Council later.

In **Humphreys [1995] 4 All E.R. 1008**, D killed her partner, a man who was violent to towards her and lived off her earnings as a prostitute. According to expert evidence, D had an abnormal mentality with immature attention seeking traits. When V taunted D about her failed suicide attempt, she stabbed and killed him. Her peculiar characteristics affected her self-control so the judge, following *Camplin*, precluded the jury from taking them into account. Her appeal was allowed by the Court of Appeal.

It was in light of this decision that the appeal in **Thornton No.2 [1996] 1 W.L.R. 1174** was allowed. The Home Secretary had referred the case, which had received a huge amount of media attention, back to the Court of Appeal, which heard fresh medical evidence relating to D's personality disorder as a result of suffering from battered woman syndrome. The Court of Appeal held that such characteristics could be relevant to how the notional reasonable person would have reacted to the trigger incident.

The Privy Council rejected this development in **Luc Thiet Thuan v The Queen [1997] A.C. 131**. Luc stated he had lost self-control and killed his ex-girlfriend when she taunted him about his lack of sexual prowess and compared him unfavourably with her new lover. Expert evidence was accepted that D suffered brain damage which made him easily provoked and prone to outbursts of violence. Appealing against his conviction for murder, the Privy Council took the opportunity to review the English Court of Appeal cases, and concluded that individual peculiarities which did not affect the gravity of the provocation could not be taken into account. It was no defence under s.3 to plead that D was simply more provocable than the average person. *Morhall* was approved because, in that case, the characteristics were relevant to the taunt itself. So, if the taunts by the victim in *Luc* had been about his brain damage and inability to control himself, these would have been relevant to the defence. However, they were not relevant when considering whether the reasonable person would have acted as D did to taunts unrelated to the characteristics. Indeed, there was a defence for such defend-ants in such circumstances; diminished responsibility. The appellant's submission that mental infirmity should be relevant to the defence of provocation, "would, in their Lordships' opinion, be to incorporate the concept of diminished responsibility indirectly into the law of provocation".

Lord Goff delivered the leading speeches in both *Morhall* and *Luc*, but it is of note that Lord Steyn delivered a powerful dissent in *Luc*. He cited the battered women syndrome cases as examples of what he saw as logically inconsistent rules; that the syndrome was relevant in assessing actual loss of self-control (the subjective test), but not when considering whether the reasonable woman would have done the same thing (the objective test). It was his dissent which was followed by the House of Lords in **Smith (Morgan James) [2001] 1 A.C. 146**.

D had stabbed his friend following an argument after a great deal of alcohol had been consumed. There was evidence that D was suffering from serious clinical depression which would have "disinhibited" him and lowered his powers of self-control. The House of Lords had to decide between the conflicting decisions of the Privy Council and the Court of Appeal, and Lord Hoffmann, in the bare majority, came down on the side of the English authorities. The question for the jury on the objective test was whether they thought "the behaviour of the accused had measured up to the standard of self-control which ought reasonably to have been expected of him". Section 3 of the 1957 Act had, according to the majority, modified the common law position as stated in *Camplin*. An objective standard of behaviour continued to be expected ("reasonably to have been expected of him") but, quite remarkably, the jury did not have to be directed along the lines of the reasonable person at all.

The breadth of the majority decision amazed many legal academics, and was widely criticised for blurring the distinction between the subjective and objective tests. You will recall that Lord Goff in *Morhall* had described the "reasonable person test" as providing a policy-driven and objective standard of self-control to be complied with by all offenders. The majority opinions in *Smith* allowed for a great deal of flexibility in the objective test; a test which would now vary enormously from defendant to defendant. The minority opinions of Lords Hobhouse and Millet, which were in line with the decision in *Luc*, were to the effect that there should only be one, constant and objectively defined test in s.3 HA 1957.

The majority decision also called into question the overlap between the two partial defences. Where there was evidence of provocative conduct, the same characteristics could now be taken into account for the purpose of both abnormality of mind under s.2 and the objective test under s.3. The effect of this led to an illogical distinction in the allocation of the proof burdens (if pleading both defences, a defendant would have to prove abnormality of mind, but the prosecution would have to disprove provocation, on the same evidence).

The one limit placed on the new objective standard in *Smith* was that the jury should be directed to ignore emotional traits "such as jealousy and obsession ... [or a] tendency to violent rages or childish tantrums". However, in **Weller [2003] EWCA Crim 815 CA**, the Court of Appeal stated, to the contrary, that:

> "the jury must *not* be directed that they should take no account of ... [characteristics such as D's excessive jealousy and possessiveness] and it is essential that it is made clear that such matters may form part of their deliberations" (emphasis added).

Smith is no longer good law. The matter was revisited by the Privy Council in **Attorney General for Jersey v Holley [2005] 3 W.L.R. 29**. D and the deceased were both violent alcoholics with a history of mutual abuse. On the day of V's death, they had been drinking heavily and arguing. D had been chopping wood with an axe. V then told D she had been sleeping with another man and taunted D that he did not have the "guts" to strike her with the axe. She was wrong; he struck her seven or eight times, killing her. The crucial issue on appeal against his conviction for murder was whether his alcoholism was a relevant characteristic for the jury's consideration of the objective test given that it did not affect the gravity of the provocation to him; merely his powers of self-control.

The Privy Council held (by six to three) that it was not:

> "Under the statute [the Homicide Act 1957, s.3] the sufficiency of the provocation ('whether the provocation was enough to make a reasonable man do as [the defendant] did') is to be judged by one standard, not a standard which varies from defendant to defendant. Whether the provocative act or words and the defendant's response met the 'ordinary person' standard prescribed by the statute is the question the jury must consider, not the altogether looser question of whether, having regard to all the circumstances, the jury consider the loss of self-control was sufficiently excusable. The statute does not leave each jury free to set whatever standard they consider appropriate in the circumstances by which to judge whether the defendant's conduct is 'excusable'."

The Privy Council considered that Parliament had set an objective standard against which to measure a defendant's loss of self-control and the courts were not free to apply a more flexible standard which took account of a defendant's particular abnormalities. The court accepted that it was:

> "inherent in the use of this prescribed standard as a uniform standard applicable to all defendants ... the possibility that an individual defendant may be temperamentally unable to achieve this standard."

Accordingly, D's alcoholism could not be taken into account on the objective test.

The judgment follows *Luc* and not *Smith*, but what power does the Privy Council have to affect the authority of a House of Lords' decision? The answer, according to the traditional rules of stare decisis, is none. Unlike a judgment of the House of Lords, the advice of the Privy Council is not binding. On the other hand, nine members of the House of Lords presided in *Holley*, so the decision could not have had more authority in terms of judicial seniority.

A five-strong Court of Appeal then held in **James and Karimi [2006] 1 All E.R. 759** that, because in *Holley* all nine members of the Privy Council were Lords of Appeal in Ordinary, six of whom agreed (and those six constituted half of the Law Lords at the time), and all nine agreed that the decision had definitively clarified the law (notwithstanding the dissents on what the law should be), the inferior courts were bound to prefer the Privy Council decision over an earlier conflicting decision of the House of Lords. In effect, the Court of Appeal has held that the Privy Council in *Holley* has overruled the House of Lords in *Smith*.

Over to you...

In a problem question on provocation, you will commonly be provided with particular information about the defendant's personality. Try to deal with any factors which are non-contentious first. So, D's age and sex will be relevant to the reasonable man test, and so too will any characteristics at which the taunt in aimed (adopting a broad brush approach, see *Gregson*) so work out what the "thing(s) done or said" were and what they related to, then show that those characteristics are admissible.

Next, look at D's general personality traits including his ability to control himself/ any addictions to, say, drugs or alcohol, that form a history to the events but do not form part of the taunt. These are the characteristics that were discussed in *Smith (Morgan)* and *Holley*. Explain that *Holley* does not permit such characteristics to be admissible under s.3. Bear in mind that they might, however, be relevant to a defence of diminished responsibility under s.2.

■ Other factors

Circumstances

Aside from particular identifiable characteristics which affect the gravity of the provocation (*Holley*), the jury must consider the wider context of the provocation. In *Morhall*, the court stated that the defendant's circumstances such as history and lifestyle, as well as characteristics, may be taken into account if relevant. So should the defendant's past relationship with, or experience of, the victim (**Horrex [1999] Crim. L.R. 500**). In *Horrex*, the provocative conduct consisted of violence and threats by V, not against D but against G. This had to be viewed in the light of D's very close relationship to G whom he regarded as a mother figure. The gravity of the provocation could be considered only in this light.

Proportionality

It is curious that the common law denied the defence where the reaction was seriously disproportionate to the provocation offered (**Mancini v DPP [1941] 3 All E.R. 272**) because the very nature of the defence is that it is an over-reaction. However, even though words alone can now amount to provocative conduct under s.3, proportionality is a factor which the jury must take into account in deciding if the reasonable man would have done as D did. An over-reaction does not prevent the success of the defence, but the more disproportionate the retaliation, the less likely the jury is to say that a reasonable man would have done as D did (**Brown [1972] 2 Q.B. 229**).

Provocation as a consequence of a mistake of fact

Where a defendant is provoked as a result of a mistake of fact, he should be treated as if the facts had been as he assumed them to be (**Brown (1776) 168 E.R. 177**). This is so even if that mistake was an intoxicated mistake (**Letenock (1917) 12 Cr. App. R. 221**), although this decision seems dubious in light of the decision of the Court of Appeal in **O'Grady [1987] Q.B. 995** on intoxicated mistaken belief in self-defence (see Ch.12).

The availability of the defence to women

Provocation has been the subject of much criticism on the grounds that it is discriminatory against women. One of the subjects of the criticism is the "sudden and temporary" requirement (p.100 above). It is suggested that men have more of a tendency to react immediately and violently to provocation than women do, and this is especially true where the female defendant has finally "snapped" and killed her long-term abusive male partner or husband. Case law has made some steps towards recognition of the perceived unfairness of this apparent gender bias in the subjective test. First, obiter dictum in *Ahluwalia* recognised the possibility of a slow burn to anger rather than an immediate impulsive reaction.

Second, the Court of Appeal held in *Humphreys* that even relatively trivial provocative conduct can be considered by the jury when assessing actual loss of self-control where the cumulative effect (see pp.99–100 above) of the victim's conduct could be viewed as the "final straw." D and V had a tempestuous relationship and V had subjected D to physical violence and sexual abuse over a long period of time. The "final straw" act of provocation by V was a comparatively minor taunt about D's attention seeking suicide attempts—she had slashed her wrists on the night in question. The Court of Appeal held the jury should have been directed to consider the wider context of V's taunts and their volatile relationship.

As regards the objective test, during the 1990s the courts began to accept battered woman syndrome as a characteristic which could be taken into account on the objective test even if its only relevance was that it reduced the woman's powers of self-control. Following the decision in *Holley*, however, battered woman syndrome can no longer be taken into account on the objective test except in so far as it would affect the gravity of the provocation to her. Thus, the question for the jury now is whether, in their opinion:

> "having regard to the actual provocation and their view of its gravity for the defendant, a woman of her age having ordinary powers of self-control might have done what the defendant did."

In her article, "Justice Devlin's legacy: Duffy—a battered woman 'caught' in time" [2009] Crim. L.R. 851, Susan Edwards analyses the decision in *Duffy* and follows the development of the law from that case, in 1949, to the present day, concluding it has been catastrophic for battered women who kill, not only for the requirement of a sudden loss of self-control, but also because:

"It would appear that on a strict reading of *Holley* no longer will it be possible for a battered woman to argue that her capacity for self-control is lowered because of the effects of abuse. Her capacity for self-control must be standard. This will mean bizarrely that she will have to react as if she has no knowledge of his past violence or likelihood of future violence. She will have to present her loss of self-control as reasonable, relying only on the gravity to her of the provocation."

Provocation and the Coroners and Justice Act 2009

Concerns that the current defence is too wide in some respects and too narrow in others led for calls for the defence to be abolished, and s.56 of the CJ&A 2009 will do just that. Provocation will be replaced with a new defence where D loses self-control.

Sections 54 and 55 of the C&JA 2009, which must be read together, provide:

54 (1)   Where a person ("D") kills or is a party to the killing of another ("V"), D is not to be convicted of murder if—

(a) D's acts and omissions in doing or being a party to the killing resulted from D's loss of self-control,

(b) the loss of self-control had a qualifying trigger, and

(c) a person of D's sex and age, with a normal degree of tolerance and self restraint and in the circumstances of D, might have reacted in the same or in a similar way to D.

(2) For the purposes of subsection (1)(a), it does not matter whether or not the loss of control was sudden.

(3) In subsection (1)(c) the reference to "the circumstances of D" is a reference to all of D's circumstances other than those whose only relevance to D's conduct is that they bear on D's general capacity for tolerance or self-restraint.

(4) Subsection (1) does not apply if, in doing or being a party to the killing, D acted in a considered desire for revenge.

(5) On a charge of murder, if sufficient evidence is adduced to raise an issue with respect to the defence under subsection (1), the jury must assume that the defence is satisfied unless the prosecution proves beyond reasonable doubt that it is not.

(6) For the purposes of subsection (5), sufficient evidence is adduced to raise an issue with respect to the defence if evidence is adduced on which, in the opinion of the trial judge, a jury, properly directed, could reasonably conclude that the defence might apply.

(7) A person who, but for this section, would be liable to be convicted of murder is liable instead to be convicted of manslaughter.

55 ... (2) A loss of self-control had a qualifying trigger if subsection (3), (4) or (5) applies.

(3) This subsection applies if D's loss of self-control was attributable to D's fear of serious violence from V against D or another identified person.

(4) This subsection applies if D's loss of self-control was attributable to a thing or things done or said (or both) which—

(a) constituted circumstances of an extremely grave character, and

(b) caused D to have a justifiable sense of being seriously wronged.

(5) This subsection applies if D's loss of self-control was attributable to a combination of the matters mentioned in subsections (3) and (4).

(6) In determining whether a loss of self-control had a qualifying trigger—

(a) D's fear of serious violence is to be disregarded to the extent that it was caused by a thing which D incited to be done or said for the purpose of providing an excuse to use violence;

(b) a sense of being seriously wronged by a thing done or said is not justifiable if D incited the thing to be done or said for the purpose of providing an excuse to use violence;

(c) the fact that a thing done or said constituted sexual infidelity is to be disregarded.

Therefore, the new defence will consist of;

1. a loss of self-control,
2. attributed to a qualifying trigger, and
3. an objective test.

Not all current case law will cease to have effect when the new law comes into force, but it is not always clear which cases continue to apply and which will not. We highlight this as we assess the possible impact of the provisions.

LOSS OF SELF-CONTROL

D will still have to lose his self-control though there is no requirement that he or she does so suddenly. The Law Commission advised that the loss of self-control requirement was "unnecessary and undesirable" (Law Com. 304, para.5.17 onwards). The Government disagreed, however, and at para.36 of the Ministry of Justice Consultation Paper (above), explained they wanted to retain the requirement because of the:

"... risk of the partial defence being used inappropriately, for example in cold-blooded, gang-related or 'honour' killings. Even in cases which are less obviously unsympathetic, there is still a fundamental problem about providing a partial defence in situations where a defendant has killed while basically in full possession of his or her senses, even if he or she is frightened, other than in a situation which is complete self-defence."

So, there will have to be a loss of self-control, but not necessarily immediately following the qualifying trigger, provided the loss of self-control is attributed to that trigger(s) (s.54(2)). The Government in its Consultation Paper said that "This would allow for situations where the defendant's reaction has been delayed or builds gradually." This is clearly an attempt to appease the critics of this requirement, given the effect it has on battered women who kill, but it is far from clear how a person can *actually* lose self-control other than suddenly. In addition, and perhaps it is a tautology to require it specifically, there cannot be a loss of self-control where D acted in a considered desire for revenge (s.54(4)).

We saw on p.101 that provocation might still be available in the situation where D is provoked to lose his self-control but there is a delay between the provocation and the killing. However, case law suggested that the longer the delay the chances of the defence succeeding decreased because it became less likely that D was *still* "out of control" at the time of the killing. The Explanatory Notes to the 2009 Act, whilst accepting that there is now no requirement that the loss of self-control be sudden, recognise that:

"it will remain open, as at present, for the judge (in deciding whether to leave the defence to the jury) and the jury (in determining whether the killing did in fact result from a loss of self-control and whether the other aspects of the partial defence are satisfied) to take into account any delay between a relevant incident and the killing."

QUALIFYING TRIGGER

There will have to be a qualifying trigger for the loss of self-control (s.55) or the defence will fail. There will be a qualifying trigger only if;

1. D had a fear of serious violence from V against D or another person (s.55(3)). This subsection will include, for example, cases such as *Pearson* (p.99 above) and is clearly capable of encompassing the battered spouse cases, or
2. there was a thing or were things either said or done or both which constituted circumstances of an extremely grave character and caused D to have a justifiable sense of being seriously wronged (s.55(4)). This is a parallel to the current defence of provocation (for example it would encompass the facts of *Camplin*), but new terms are introduced to

limit the defence, for example the circumstances must be extremely grave, D's sense of being wronged must be justifiable, and he cannot simply be wronged but must be seriously wronged, or

3. both; *unless*

4. D has incited the trigger as an excuse to use violence, and/or

5. the trigger for the loss of self-control is sexual infidelity (s.55(6)), see *Davies* on p.99 above. It is unclear whether sexual infidelity could be admissible as relevant to the history to the case if there is another acceptable qualifying trigger which causes the loss of self-control. It seems odd that honour killings are not expressly excluded as qualifying triggers if there was a need to state sexual infidelity is.

Over to you...

Consider the facts of *Baillie* on p.101 above. Apply the facts to the law as it will be if the provisions of the C&JA 2009 come into force. Do you foresee any problems with the new defence covering those facts?

THE OBJECTIVE TEST

A person of D's age and sex (reflecting the common law from *Camplin*), with a normal degree of tolerance and self-restraint (codifying the *Holley* test) and in the circumstances of D will have to react in the same or in a similar way to D (s.54). The word "characteristics" is not used in the sections and it is hoped this may, therefore, mean the provocability/provocativeness distinction will be confined to the pages of legal history, but what is unclear is the scope of "circumstances" in cases such as *Morhall* or *Luc Thiet Thuan*. The phrase "in the circumstances of D" in s.54(1)(c) sounds wide enough to include personality traits which are relevant to what is said or done to D to cause the loss of self-control, but then in s.54(3) the jury must disregard circumstances "whose only relevance to D's conduct is that they bear on D's general capacity for tolerance or self-restraint" which seems to exclude them. There will, no doubt, be case law clarifying the apparent ambiguity in due course.

Over to you...

Would a person who killed on similar facts to *Smith (Morgan James)* (pp.104–105 above) be able to plead the loss of self-control defence? If not, would his particular characteristics amount to a "recognised mental condition" and therefore fall into the amended defence of diminished responsibility?

BURDEN OF PROOF

The burden of proof will remain on the prosecution but the judge will have to be satisfied there is sufficient evidence of the defence for the legal burden on the prosecution to engage (this is the evidential burden on D to adduce evidence to "pass the judge" and leave the matter to the jury; the prosecution must disprove the defence). This will give the trial judge more control over whether to leave the defence to the jury or not than under the current law (p.98 above).

FIGURE 4.1 A comparison of provocation and the loss of self-control defence

Source of law	Common law and s.3 of the Homicide Act 1957	Sections 54 and 55 of the Coroners and Justice Act 2009
Elements of the defence	Things said or done or both, for example *Doughty*.	This element applies only in respect of the second qualifying trigger below.
	Actual (sudden and temporary, *Duffy*) loss of self control, but with the possibility of a slow-burn reaction, *Ahluwahlia, Baillie*.	Loss of self-control (unless D acted in a considered desire for revenge) attributed to a qualifying trigger 1. D had a fear of serious violence from V against D or another person, and/or 2. things were said or done or both which constituted circumstances of an extremely grave character and caused D to have a justifiable sense of being seriously wronged (might this exclude facts such as *Baillie*?)
	The "reasonable" man test, taking into account D's age and sex (*Camplin*) and those characteristics affecting the gravity of the provocation (*Morhall*) but in other respects having an ordinary power of self-control (*Holley*).	Objective test; a person of D's sex and age (*Camplin*), with a normal degree of tolerance and self restraint (*Holley*) and in the circumstances of D (would this include facts such as *Morhall or Gregson?*), might have reacted in the same or in a similar way to D.
Burden of proof	On the prosecution, but where there is evidence of the defence, even if the defence is not relying on it, it must be left to the jury.	On the prosecution (s.54(5) and (6)) where the judge is satisfied there is sufficient evidence adduced to raise the issue.

Suicide Pact

A suicide pact is an agreement between parties which has as its object the death of both or all of them, irrespective of whether each is to take their own life. Where D has entered a pact, and killed V with the intention of killing himself afterwards, but then has not committed suicide, it is voluntary manslaughter and not murder (HA 1957 s.4). The reason why D subsequently failed to kill himself is irrelevant, so long as he can prove that at the time of entering into the pact it was his genuine intention to commit suicide.

There is a very slim line between voluntary manslaughter by way of suicide pact, and the separate offence of assisting or encouraging suicide under s.2 of the Suicide Act 1961. The difference between the two is in either killing V or helping V to die. The first is voluntary manslaughter which carries a maximum life sentence. The second is assisting suicide, which has a maximum sentence of 14 years' imprisonment. The victim in a suicide pact or the person who is assisted does not commit a crime; it is no longer an offence to commit or attempt to commit suicide (The Suicide Act 1961 s.1).

REFORM OF SUICIDE PACT

The Law Commission proposed retention of the defence in "Murder, Manslaughter and Infanticide" which would have reduced first degree murder to second degree murder. These proposals have not been taken forward to the Coroners and Justice Act 2009 and are therefore unlikely to be adopted in the foreseeable future.

Involuntary Manslaughter

There are three types of involuntary manslaughter:

1. (subjective) reckless manslaughter;
2. gross negligence manslaughter; and
3. constructive, also called unlawful act, manslaughter.

Where a defendant is charged with manslaughter, the indictment does not have to specify the type of manslaughter. D will be convicted if the prosecution can prove the elements of one (or more) of the offences detailed below.

Reckless Manslaughter

Where a defendant who has been charged with murder is acquitted, or his conviction quashed on appeal, it is possible for the murder conviction to be substituted with a conviction for manslaughter. This might happen where the mens rea for murder was not satisfied, but D did foresee the risk of serious harm or even death as a high probability, but not as a virtual certainty. This is what happened in the leading case of *Woollin*. Of course, D may be charged with manslaughter and the prosecution may be able to establish that D was reckless.

In **Lidar (1999) 4 Arch. News 3**, the Court of Appeal developed the current test for reckless manslaughter. D had driven away from the scene of a fight with one of the antagonists hanging inside his car, continuing to fight with D's front passenger. V fell and was crushed under the car's wheels. The court stated that a defendant would be liable for manslaughter where he foresaw (recklessness is subjective) death or serious harm as being highly probable. The existence of this type of manslaughter, doubted in some academic quarters, was explicitly recognised by the Law Commission in 2006 (below) and more recently again by the Court of Appeal in **Dudley [2006] 2 Cr. App. R. (S) 77**.

REFORM

The Law Commission recommended in its 2006 report, "Murder, Manslaughter and Infanticide" that some instances of what are now reckless manslaughter are too serious to be manslaughter and should become second degree murder. It is highly unlikely these proposals will be enacted in the foreseeable future given the absence of such reform in the Coroners and Justice Act 2009. It was the recommendation of the Law Commission that it would be second degree murder if D kills with intent to cause some injury or a fear of injury or a risk of injury, and with awareness of a serious risk of causing death. The Law Commission considered that reckless manslaughter would then no longer be required as a separate fault element as the remaining killings which currently fall under the umbrella of reckless manslaughter would fall within gross negligence manslaughter; if D realises there is a risk of death but unjustifiably carries on with his conduct that is gross negligence. In the view of the Law Commission, therefore, cases such as *Lidar* could be prosecuted under a reformed gross negligence manslaughter.

Gross Negligence Manslaughter

DEVELOPMENT OF THE LAW

Negligence is a cause of action in the law of Tort. The criminal law has borrowed the concept, but criminal liability for a negligent homicide arises only where the negligence is gross. The difference between ordinary, tortious negligence and criminal, gross negligence has taxed the courts for almost a century.

In **Bateman (1925) 19 Cr. App. R. 8**, V died as a result of a negligently performed medical operation. Lord Hewart's famous statement required that criminal negligence …

"went beyond a mere matter of compensation between subjects, and showed such a disregard for the life and safety of others as to amount to a crime against the state, and conduct deserving punishment."

Clearly this is a question of degree (went beyond ... such a disregard) but no attempt was made to identify, even approximately, when civil negligence became criminal. The House of Lords in **Andrews v DPP [1937] A.C. 576** suggested that the line between civil and criminal negligence would be crossed when the behaviour of the defendant was reckless. As we have seen, however, the word reckless has a very specific meaning in the criminal law (beyond what lay people might refer to as culpable carelessness). So, when Lord Diplock extended the meaning to encompass an objective mens rea in *Caldwell*, it became possible for an offender to commit manslaughter without having given any thought to the possibility of there being a risk of harm (**Seymour [1983] 2 A.C. 493**).

THE CURRENT LAW

In light of the objectivity of the test, and before their Lordships overruled *Caldwell* in *G*, they had already overruled *Seymour* in **Adomako [1995] 1 A.C. 171**, and taken the law back to the tests in *Bateman* and *Andrews*.

In *Adomako*, D was an anaesthetist whose job it was to ensure that patients undergoing operations were able to breathe whilst under anaesthetic. One patient died after the tube supplying the oxygen became disconnected. The connection point was hidden beneath a cover over the patient. It took D four-and-a-half minutes to notice the problem, and then he misdiagnosed the situation. An expert witness stated the problem would have been obvious to any competent anaesthetist within 15 seconds. D was convicted following the trial judge's direction along the lines of *Bateman*. He appealed and the Court of Appeal heard the appeals in the cases of **Prentice and Sullman [1994] Q.B. 302** and **Holloway [1993] 4 All E.R. 935** at the same time.

In *Prentice and Sullman*, the defendants were junior doctors who erroneously injected a drug into the spine of a patient who then died. Neither defendant had checked the labels on the box of syringes nor on the syringe itself before injecting, either of which would have revealed that the drug was lethal if spinally injected. In *Holloway*, D was an electrician who installed the electrics on a new central heating system. He misconnected some of the terminals causing the death by electrocution of the householder when he touched the kitchen sink. The trial judges in both *Holloway* and *Prentice and Sullman* had directed the juries in accordance with the House of Lords' authority at the time, *Seymour*. On consolidated appeal with *Adomako*, their convictions were quashed. *Adomako* was the only appellant whose conviction was upheld, so he alone appealed to the House of Lords. Lord Mackay, in a unanimous judgment dismissing the appeal, held:

"The ordinary principles of the law of negligence apply to ascertain whether or not the defendant has been in breach of a duty of care towards the victim who has died. If such breach of duty is established the next question is whether that breach of duty caused the death of the victim. If so, the jury must go on to consider whether that breach of duty should be characterised as gross negligence and therefore as a crime. This will depend on the seriousness of the breach of duty committed by the defendant in all the circumstances in which the defendant was placed when it occurred. The jury will have to consider whether the extent to which the defendant's conduct departed from the proper standard of care incumbent upon him, involving as it must have done a risk of death to the patient, was such that it should be judged criminal."

Therefore, in cases involving manslaughter by breach of a duty of care, the relevant questions are whether:

1. a duty of care existed;
2. that duty had been breached;
3. the breach involved a risk of death;
4. the breach had caused the death; and, if so,
5. the breach should be characterised as gross negligence and a crime.

▉ D owes V a duty of care

In *Adomako*, Lord Mackay stated:

"The ordinary principles of the law of negligence apply to ascertain whether or not the defendant has been in breach of a duty of care towards the victim who has died."

This means the law of tort determines if a duty is owed to the victim. Hence, a duty exists, for example, between a doctor and patient, between a driver and other road users and also their own passengers, between employer and an employee acting in the course of his employment and a landlord to his tenant. Where the defendant and his victim do not fall within such a recognised relationship, the position in tort is complex but it is submitted that a criminal court would ask whether it was reasonably foreseeable that D's actions would cause V's death. For a detailed analysis of the nature of the duty in this context, see J. Herring and E. Palser, "The duty of care in gross negligence manslaughter" [2007] Crim. L.R. 24.

The role of the judge and jury here is that the judge must first determine whether there is sufficient evidence to establish a duty; whether such a duty actually exists is then to be determined by the jury. However, where there is clearly a duty of care as, for example, between a doctor and his patient, the judge can direct the jury that a duty exists (**Willoughby [2005] 1 W.L.R. 1880**).

The relationship between tortious duties and the criminal law was explored in **Wacker [2003] Crim. L.R. 108**. D was a Dutch lorry driver who had hidden 60 illegal Chinese immigrants in an airtight container on his lorry. He had closed the ventilator to the container. The lorry was searched at Dover where it was discovered that 58 of the immigrants had died from suffocation. The law of tort has a maxim known as ex turpi causa non oritur actio, which negates any duty where the parties were engaged in a joint unlawful enterprise. The illegality prevents civil liability arising. The Court of Appeal, Criminal Division, rejected the appellant's submission that this maxim applies on a charge of gross negligence manslaughter. The criminal law is happy to rely on the civil law governing duty of care to define the relationships where criminal liability can arise for this type of manslaughter, but when Lord Mackay said in *Adomako* that the normal principles of the law of tort apply to the crime of manslaughter, he cannot have had in mind a rule preventing the conviction of a grossly negligent defendant merely because the victim would not have had a civil right of action.

Where the defendant's omission to act has led to the victim's death, liability for gross negligence manslaughter can only arise if D was under a duty to act such as a contractual, assumed, special relationship or statutory duty or because he had created a dangerous situation (see further Ch.2). Where a duty to act exists, so does a duty of care. The situation involving a duty in the context of an omission was considered in **Khan and Khan [1998] Crim. L.R. 830**. The defendants were drug dealers who supplied the victim with heroin. She was probably a first time user and, after snorting a quantity of heroin which was double that which an experienced user might have taken, began to cough and went into a coma. The defendants knew she was in a coma, and in need of assistance, but left her in their flat and when they came back she was dead. The prosecution had argued that the defendants breached a duty to summon medical assistance. The trial judge failed to direct the jury on whether, in law, a duty could arise in such a situation and it is for this reason that their appeals were allowed. However, the Court of Appeal was prepared to envisage a duty might arise, but without deciding the matter. There would be no such duty in the civil law. The criminal law might then be prepared to extend the categories where duties are owed, or may merely be content to extend the *Miller* principle (creation of a dangerous situation and failing to rectify it). One could also view *Wacker* in the same light: D created the dangerous situation by shutting the ventilator and was under a duty to rectify it.

Previous cases restricted the rule to the inadvertent creation of a danger, but recently this has been extended to the advertent or even intentional creation of a danger, see **Ruffell [2003] 2 Cr. App. R. (S.) 53** and **Evans [2009] 1 W.L.R. 1999** in Ch.2.

Over to you...

Consider the HIV transmission cases in Ch.5 such as *Dica* and *Konzani*. If, knowing he was HIV positive, D had unprotected sexual intercourse with V without disclosing his HIV status, and V subsequently died of an AIDS related illness (factually it is not contended D was the cause of the HIV transmission), do you think D could be convicted of gross negligence manslaughter? Your answer will in part depend on whether you think he owed a duty of care in the criminal law to disclose his medical condition to V.

D breaches that duty of care

The defendant may breach his duty of care by his positive act or an omission. Again, basic principles of the tort of negligence apply. Thus, the jury will determine whether D has breached his duty, i.e. whether he has fallen below the standard to be expected of the reasonable man or, where D holds himself out as possessing certain skills, the reasonably competent surgeon, electrician, etc.

On an application for leave to appeal, the Court of Appeal in **Mark [2004] EWCA Crim. 2490** held that actual foresight of a risk was not essential for this type of manslaughter. D was the manager of a cleaning company and he wished to appeal against his conviction for gross negligence manslaughter after the death of an employee from an explosion caused by cleaning fluids. D contended he had been ignorant of the risk, but the Court of Appeal held the breach of duty was to be assessed objectively and lack of foresight was, therefore, irrelevant.

The breach involves a risk of death

In *Adomako*, Lord Mackay stated:

> "The jury will have to consider whether the extent to which the defendant's conduct departed from the proper standard of care incumbent upon him, *involving as it must have done a risk of death to the patient*, was such that it should be judged criminal." (emphasis added).

Thus, a reasonably prudent person (or doctor, electrician, driver, etc. depending on the circumstances) would have to have foreseen a risk of death in D's actions or omission. In **Misra and Srivastava [2004] EWCA 2375**, two doctors were convicted of manslaughter by gross negligence after their patient died from toxic shock syndrome where a simple course of antibiotics would have saved his life. The Court of Appeal again confirmed that the risk to which the victim must be exposed is a risk of death, not merely of bodily injury or injury to health. In **Brown (Uriah) [2005] 2 W.L.R. 1558**, the Privy Council went further and suggested that only a very high risk of death would suffice.

Over to you...

Consider again the HIV transmission hypothetical posed above. If you think D did owe a duty to disclose, do you also think on those facts there was a high risk or even a very high risk of death? Your answer may dictate whether or not you would convict D of this offence.

■ The breach causes the death of the victim

The causation requirement is dealt with in accordance with principles explained in Ch.2.

■ The breach is sufficiently serious to constitute gross negligence

This element has proved controversial. The question is whether D's conduct is bad enough to be regarded as grossly negligent. If it is grossly negligent, it is a crime, and only criminal conduct is grossly negligent. Lord Mackay could not be drawn on to provide more guidance on when ordinary negligence becomes criminal; he said it would be "unwise to attempt to categorize or detail specimen directions". Although foresight on D's part is not required for gross negligence manslaughter, the defendant's state of mind may be relevant in assessing the grossness and criminality of his conduct (**Attorney General's Reference (No.2 of 1999) [2000] Q.B. 796**). This may allow a jury to acquit a defendant who might objectively have acted very dangerously but did so in the context of, for example, inexperience, stress, mistake or confusion which allows the jury to conclude that the conduct was not "bad enough" to justify punishment.

Over to you...

A final question on the HIV transmission case. In your view, as a question of fact, do you think this is a gross negligence situation, i.e. "bad enough" to convict?

THE PROBLEMS WITH GROSS NEGLIGENCE MANSLAUGHTER

The main problem with the current test for gross negligence manslaughter is its vagueness and inherent circularity. It is vague because no guidance is given on where the line between negligence and criminality is drawn, and it is circular because it states that D's negligence is criminal if it is, in the jury's eyes, criminal. The circularity of the test was expressly acknowledged by Lord Mackay in *Adomako*, but he felt that:

> "in this branch of the law I do not believe that is fatal to its being correct as a test of how far conduct must depart from accepted standards to be characterised as criminal. This is necessarily a question of degree …"

Article 7(1) of the European Convention of Human Rights (Human Rights Act 1998 Sch.1) provides that no one shall be held guilty of any criminal offence on account of any act or omission which did not constitute a criminal offence under national or international law at the time when it was committed. It has been held that this provision requires signatory states to ensure standards of clarity in the criminal law, so that citizens can reliably predict whether the particular form of conduct at issue will contravene the criminal law (**Kokkinakis v Greece (1994) 17 E.H.R.R. 397**).

According to the European Court of Human Rights in **Sunday Times v UK (1979–1980) 2 E.H.R.R. 245**:

"... the law must be adequately accessible ... [and] formulated with sufficient precision to enable the citizen to regulate his conduct: he must be able – if need be with appropriate advice—to foresee, to a degree that is reasonable in the circumstances, the consequences which a given action may entail. Those consequences need not be foreseeable with absolute certainty ... many laws are inevitably couched in terms which, to a greater or lesser extent, are vague and whose interpretation and application are questions of practice."

Because the "grossness" of the negligence under *Adomako* is for the jury to decide in the absence of a clear definition, the appellants in *Misra and Srivastava* challenged the vagueness and circularity of the test, and alleged it leaves a question of law to be decided by the jury. What may be "so bad" for one jury, may not be for another. The challenge failed. However, the reasoning on this point is no clearer than the test for grossness in *Adomako*. The Court of Appeal held that "grossness" is an issue of fact. If the jury makes a finding that the negligence was so bad it is a crime, a verdict of guilty would follow consequentially on the basis of the finding; the verdict of guilt was not something additional to the finding. Just because one jury panel may convict and another acquit is not reason enough, on its own, to find the crime to be uncertain.

A further criticism which can be levelled at this type of manslaughter is that, because a defendant does not have to have foreseen the risk of death to V, he is liable in homicide whereas, were his victim to survive but in, say, a persistent vegetative state, he would not even have been liable for an offence against the person due to his lack of mens rea.

REFORM
The 2006 Law Commission Report (Law Com No.304) built on proposals already contained in the 1996 Report (Law Com No.237). It was proposed that there would continue to be a form of manslaughter phrased in terms of gross negligence (conduct falling far below what can reasonably be expected) as to a risk of causing death where the risk that D's conduct will cause death would have been obvious to the reasonable person in D's position. However, the pure objectivity of the test would be amended to become relative to D's capacity to appreciate the nature and degree of risks, which may be affected by youth or disability. These proposals are not contained in the Coroners and Justice Act 2009.

Constructive Manslaughter
This type of manslaughter is called constructive or unlawful act manslaughter. Either term is acceptable. Because liability for this type of manslaughter is built up from a baseline of another crime, we say that liability has been constructed from a lesser crime into a much more serious crime; hence constructive manslaughter. It is also unlawful act manslaughter because proof of

a criminally unlawful and dangerous act is a prerequisite to proof of the offence of manslaughter itself.

For example, the defendants in **DPP v Newbury [1977] A.C. 500** stood on a railway bridge and pushed a large stone off the bridge and into the path of an approaching train. The stone broke through the glass of the train cab and struck and killed the guard. The defendants did an act (pushing the slab), it was criminally unlawful (although the exact crime was not specified, it would have amounted to criminal damage, battery or a statutory assault, such as inflicting GBH), it was clearly dangerous and it caused death. The House of Lords confirmed that there are four elements to the offence of unlawful act manslaughter:

1. D intentionally did an act;
2. which was criminally unlawful;
3. which was dangerous; and
4. which caused the victim's death.

INTENTIONALLY DOING AN ACT

It is best to think of this element as a deliberate act, rather than intentional. This is because when lawyers see a test phrased in terms of intention, they are tempted to think it is the consequence which must be intended. That is not true for this element of this offence. Provided the prosecution can prove to the jury's satisfaction that D did a deliberate act, there is no need to prove D foresaw or intended the result (death, or even harm) of the act. So, in *Newbury*, all the prosecution had to prove was that the defendants intended to push the block off the bridge.

This element is satisfied by an act only, and omissions are excluded (**Lowe [1973] Q.B. 702**). If D commits manslaughter by omission, the prosecution must prove either recklessness (*Stone and Dobinson*) or gross negligence (*Adomako*). In *Lowe*, the Court of Appeal held the charge of wilful neglect of a child under s.1 of the Children and Young Persons Act 1933 could not form the basis of liability for unlawful act manslaughter and, in the absence of proof of recklessness or gross negligence, D's conviction was quashed.

THE ACT IS UNLAWFUL

It is no defence for D to say he did not think his act was unlawful as ignorance of the law is not a defence. However, only criminal acts and not civil wrongs, can form the basis of this type of manslaughter (**Franklin (1883) 15 Cox C.C. 163**). Not all criminal offences suffice either. In *Andrews v DPP*, the House of Lords held that negligently committed crimes (see *Lowe* above) are excluded from the offence. In other words where the basis of the criminality of D's conduct is that he committed an omission and/or was negligent, he can be convicted of manslaughter only if he falls within either of the other heads of recklessness or gross negligence manslaughter.

For example, driving is a lawful activity, but if it is performed negligently it becomes criminal. Driving without due care and attention, or careless driving, cannot then form the unlawful act for constructive manslaughter.

The Court of Appeal put this (House of Lords') dicta in doubt in *Willoughby*. Rose L.J. held that the same set of facts could give rise to liability under either gross negligence or unlawful act manslaughter, and accordingly these two heads of manslaughter are not mutually exclusive. Whilst that may be correct for positive acts which kill, careless acts, or omissions, which kill are prosecutable under gross negligence manslaughter only. Any alternative is in direct contradiction of the House of Lords' opinion in *Andrews v DPP*. See, further, David Ormerod's commentary in the Criminal Law Review at [2005] Crim. L.R. 389.

The criminal act may be any crime. A manslaughter prosecution has, for example, been based on arson (**Goodfellow (1986) 83 Cr. App. R. 23**), robbery (**Dawson (1985) 81 Cr. App. R. 150**), burglary (**Watson [1989] 1 W.L.R. 684**), maliciously administering a noxious substance (**Rogers [2003] 1 W.L.R. 1374**, see below on p.33) and even something as minor as a technical assault (**Hayward (1908 21 Cox C.C. 530**). Whichever offence is relied on by the prosecution as the base crime for constructive manslaughter, all elements of the offence must be established and this includes the actus reus and any mens rea. In **Lamb [1967] 2 Q.B. 981**, D killed his friend by shooting him with a revolver in tragic circumstances where his ignorance of how the gun worked led to death. Not realising that a revolver's mechanism revolves one chamber before the firing pin is struck, D checked that there was no bullet in the chamber opposite the firing pin but not the next chamber. He then fired it at V. The actus reus of a battery was satisfied, but the mens rea, which is intention to apply force to the victim or foresight that force might be applied, was not. D was found not liable for manslaughter.

THE ACT IS DANGEROUS

In **Church [1966] Q.B. 59**, D had a fight with V, and thinking he had killed her, threw her in the river where she died by drowning. He appealed against his conviction for manslaughter on the ground, inter alia, that the judge had misdirected the jury when he told them it was irrelevant that D thought V was dead when he threw her in the river. His appeal was dismissed. Edmund-Davies J. held that:

> "the unlawful act must be such as all sober and reasonable people would inevitably recognise must subject the other person to, at least, the risk of some harm resulting therefrom albeit not serious harm."

This formulation was approved in *Newbury* where the House of Lords stressed that the test for "dangerous" was entirely objective and that it did not matter whether the defendant appreciated that his unlawful act was dangerous.

It was further held by the Court of Appeal in *Dawson* that the "harm" that must be recognised by the "sober and reasonable person" means physical harm. A risk of emotional upset is not enough. To this, we must add the caveat from **Carey [2006] EWCA Crim 17**, that the harm caused to the victim must cause the death for an unlawful act manslaughter charge to be satisfied. The victim had been punched by the defendants and had run away. Unfortunately, V had a severely diseased heart, which had been unknown to her, her family and her doctors. She collapsed and died after running away, and medical evidence suggested she might not have died had she not been running. The Court of Appeal held that the manslaughter charge should have been withdrawn from the jury as the only physical harm to the victim did not cause her death.

For this type of manslaughter, therefore, D need not foresee any harm at all, provided his act was objectively dangerous in that a sober and reasonable person would recognise the risk of some physical harm to V. Where the unlawful act relied on by the prosecution does not require foresight of harm, for example criminal damage (see *Newbury* above), D can be convicted of an unlawful homicide where he did not foresee any injury or harm whatsoever.

The dangerousness element is objective and judged against what a reasonable man would regard as dangerous. This may cause an apparent conflict with the issue of causation. For example, in *Dawson*, the defendants robbed a petrol station cashier using a replica gun and a mask. The cashier had a weak heart and the fright of the incident caused him to have a heart attack. The Court of Appeal held that:

1. shock produced by terror or fright was insufficient as harm under the *Church* test;
2. harm had to be physical; and
3. the knowledge that could be ascribed to the "sober and reasonable man" did not include the knowledge that V had a weak heart, i.e. the reasonable person would only be endowed with the knowledge which the defendant possessed at the time of the offence.

This case is often cited as an exception to the rule that D must take V as he finds him, weaknesses and all. However, it is not a case about causation (under the thin skull rule), but is about whether D's act was *Church* dangerous, i.e. that all sober and reasonable people would inevitably recognise must subject V to some harm.

An obvious risk that D has ignored almost certainly would be dangerous. In *Watson*, D committed a burglary of the home of an 87-year-old man. When D became aware of the presence and frailty of the man, then at that stage the sober and reasonable bystander would have realised D's act was dangerous, even if D did not. Similarly, the reasonable observer would not make an unreasonable mistake. In **Ball [1989] Crim. L.R. 730**, D kept a mixture of live and blank bullets in his pocket. He loaded the gun with what he thought were blanks, but he had not checked. He then fired at V, and killed her with a live round. This was dangerous as a reasonable observer would have checked.

Over to you...

If a burglar broke into a house late at night and disturbed the householder so much they suffered a heart attack and died, would the prosecution be able to establish an unlawful and dangerous act was committed on these facts? What other information might you need to form a conclusion?

THE ACT CAUSES DEATH

It is the unlawful act that must cause the death. This is determined in accordance with normal principles of causation (see Ch.2).

MUST THE ACT BE DIRECTED AT ANOTHER?

Not surprisingly, given that this is a serious fatal offence against another which can be satisfied in the absence of any foresight of harm, the Court of Appeal in **Dalby [1982] 1 All E.R. 916**, held that there was a fifth element to the offence, that the unlawful act must be "directed at another". Therefore, on the facts of the case, the unlawful supply of heroin to V could not be an unlawful act. However, *Dalby* was in this respect inconsistent with *Newbury*, so the Court of Appeal in *Goodfellow* explained *Dalby* as requiring no more than that the death should be a direct result of D's unlawful act with "no fresh intervening cause" (per Lord Lane C.J.). In *Goodfellow*, D set fire to his council house in an extreme attempt to be re-housed by the local authority. His wife, girlfriend and son were all killed. He appealed against conviction on the basis that the act of arson was not directed at any person, so he could not be convicted of unlawful act manslaughter. His appeal failed, and the House of Lords in **Attorney General's Reference (No.3 of 1994) [1998] A.C. 245** confirmed that there is no such requirement in constructive manslaughter.

■ Manslaughter by supplying drugs

Unfortunately, it is all too common for a drug user, or addict, to die from taking illegal drugs. The questions that the court has had real difficulty in dealing with (no pun intended) are:

1. whether the person who supplied the drugs committed an unlawful act in the act of supply or in administering or causing V to administer the drug; and
2. whether the supply caused the death of the victim.

We saw in Ch.2 that the House of Lords answered both these questions in the negative in **Kennedy No.2 [2008] 1 A.C. 269:**

1. It is an unlawful act to supply drugs BUT where V self-administers the drug, D does not CAUSE V to administer the drug (where V is a fully informed adult) and therefore

2. V's self-administration breaks the chain of causation. D's act does not cause V's death for the purposes of unlawful act manslaughter.

However, we also considered in Ch.2 whether D can be liable on similar facts for manslaughter by gross negligence, and using the authorities of **Miller [1983] 1 All E.R. 978, Ruffell [2003] 2 Cr. App. R. (S) 53** and **Evans [2009] 1 W.L.R. 1999**, we saw that D may be convicted of gross negligence where:

1. He owed V a duty of care (for example by the creation of or contribution towards a dangerous situation; we suggest in this context the situation must be potentially life-threatening (**Misra [2004] EWCA 2375**, above), and
2. he breached that duty (commonly by not informing the authorities or seeking assistance), and
3. the breach of duty caused (contributed to) V's death [NB *Kennedy No.2* does not apply to manslaughter by gross negligence where it is the breach which must cause death, not the unlawful act], and
4. the jury finds the breach to be grossly negligent.

REFORM OF CONSTRUCTIVE MANSLAUGHTER

In response to the 1996 Law Commission Report "Legislating the Criminal Code: Involuntary Manslaughter", the Home Office published its response in "Reforming the Law on Involuntary Manslaughter: The Government's Proposals" (2000). Rather than abolish the offence completely, which was the original proposal of the Law Commission, the Government suggested it should be replaced with a narrower crime. Almost identical proposals were adopted in the Law Commission's Report in 2006 which recommended constructive manslaughter be replaced by an offence of criminal act manslaughter which would be committed where D kills V through the commission of a criminal act:

1. which was intended by D to cause injury; or
2. which D was aware involved a serious risk of causing some injury.

These proposals are not contained in the Coroners and Justice Act 2009.

. . . .

Infanticide

A defendant can be charged with infanticide or, where charged initially with murder or manslaughter, a jury can return a verdict of not guilty to murder but guilty of infanticide. Infanticide is governed by s.1 of the Infanticide Act 1938 and applies to the killing, by any wilful act or omission, by a woman of her child under the age of 12 months whilst the balance of her mind was disturbed due to the effects of the birth or consequent lactation. A very minor reform to the wording of the defence is contained in the Coroners and Justice Act 2009.

Causing or Allowing the Death of a Child or Vulnerable Adult

Section 5 of the Domestic Violence, Crime and Victims Act 2004 created the offence of causing or allowing the death of a child or vulnerable adult who is a member of the same household. The offence was introduced to cover the situation where a child or vulnerable adult has died and it is clear that one of their carers caused the death (either by a positive act or an omission) but it is not clear which of them it was and nor is it clear which of them was an accessory. The mens rea of the offence is negligence, though less than that required for gross negligence manslaughter. The obvious example of where such problems might arise is where a child has died whilst at home with his parents and siblings and one of them must have caused the child's death but it is impossible to prove which one.

Section 5 provides:

> **(1)** A person ("D") is guilty of an offence if
>   **(a)** a child or vulnerable adult ("V") dies as a result of the unlawful act of a person who
>   **(i)** was a member of the same household as V, and
>   **(ii)** had frequent contact with him,
>   **(b)** D was such a person at the time of that act,
>   **(c)** at that time there was a significant risk of serious physical harm being caused to V by the unlawful act of such a person, and
>   **(d)** either D was the person whose act caused V's death or
>   **(i)** D was, or ought to have been, aware of the risk mentioned in paragraph (c),
>   **(ii)** D failed to take such steps as he could reasonably have been expected to take to protect V from the risk, and
>   **(iii)** the act occurred in circumstances of the kind that D foresaw or ought to have foreseen.
>
> **(2)** The prosecution does not have to prove whether it is the first alternative in subsection (1)(d) or the second (subparas (i) to (iii)) that applies.
> **(3)** If D was not the mother or father of V
>   **(a)** D may not be charged with an offence under this section if he was under the age of 16 at the time of the act that caused V's death;
>   **(b)** for the purposes of subs. (1)(d)(ii) D could not have been expected to take any such step as is referred to there before attaining that age.
>
> **(4)** For the purposes of this section
>   **(a)** a person is to be regarded as a "member" of a particular household, even if he does not live in that household, if he visits it so often and for such periods of time that it is reasonable to regard him as a member of it;

(b) where V lived in different households at different times, "the same household as V" refers to the household in which V was living at the time of the act that caused V's death.

The offence carries a maximum period of imprisonment of 14 years.

The offence clearly has an ambit extending beyond the carer to members of the same household. In **Khan (Uzma) [2009] 1 W.L.R. 2036**, the defendants had shared a house with the deceased who was murdered by her husband, a member of their family. Their appeals against conviction for offences under s.5 were dismissed, and the Court of Appeal held that the s.5 offence was based on a positive duty on members of the same household to protect children or vulnerable adults whose ability to protect themselves from violence, abuse or neglect was significantly impaired. If there was sufficient frequency of contact between D and the eventual victim, and it was proved D was aware of the risk of serious physical harm, or ought to have been aware of it, and foresaw, or ought to have foreseen, the occurrence of the unlawful act or course of conduct which resulted in death, D could be convicted only if D had failed to take the steps which could reasonably have been expected. However, had the householders also been beaten by the husband who had been convicted of murder, the jury might have felt it was not reasonable for the defendants to have taken protective steps for the eventual victim.

Corporate Manslaughter

THE COMMON LAW

There are certain crimes a company cannot commit. One such crime is murder. This is because the only sentence available is imprisonment, and a fine (generally regarded as the only possible punishment that can be imposed on a company) is not an alternative.

However, a company (or a corporation; there is a difference in law between the two, but we use the terms interchangeably here as the difference is not relevant to this topic) can commit manslaughter (**Attorney General's Reference (No.2 of 1999) [2000] Q.B. 796**).

The common law provided that where a corporation was charged with manslaughter (under the head of gross negligence as a company could not and cannot commit unlawful act manslaughter and has never been indicted for reckless manslaughter), an individual director or senior manager must first have been convicted of the crime before the corporation could be. This was because of the identification doctrine, which is explored in Ch.11.

In 1987, the roll-on roll-off ferry, the Herald of Free Enterprise, sank after leaving the port of Zeebrugge in Belgium with its bow doors open. 192 people died. The assistant bosun, who had responsibility for shutting the doors, was asleep in his cabin. The first officer would normally have double checked the doors were closed but, due to staff shortages, he was on the bridge and could not check as there were no warning lights on the bridge for this simple task. Previous requests for warning lights to indicate whether the doors were open had been made to the board of directors of the company (P&O, formerly Townsend Thoresen) but had been greeted with the response: "Nice, but don't we already pay someone?", and "Do they need indicator lights to tell them whether the assistant boatswain is awake and sober?" Prosecutions for manslaughter were brought against the assistant bosun, the bosun, the first officer, both captains and two members of the board of directors, and the company. All failed. Someone who could be "identified" with the company would first have to be guilty of manslaughter. As there was insufficient evidence to convict any of those individual defendants, the case against the company had to fail.

There was a public outcry and the Government set up an inquiry into the matter. That enquiry led to the Sheen Report in 1988. This concluded that the company had failed to operate a safe system of work:

> "The underlying or cardinal faults lay higher up in the company. The Board of Directors did not appreciate their responsibility for the safe management of their ships ... All concerned in management ... were guilty of fault ... From top to bottom the body corporate was infected with the disease of sloppiness."

The identification doctrine was not fit for purpose. In a large corporation with a complex senior management structure and widespread delegation of operational matters (including health and safety), the process of identification became impossible. Nor was it possible to group together as a quantitative task a number of managers and employees to make the requisite fault.

This doctrine, referred to as the aggregation principle, was specifically rejected by the Court of Appeal in *Attorney General's Reference (No.2 of 1999)*. This was the appeal brought after the collapse of the trial which arose out of the train crash at Southall in September 1997, which killed seven and injured 151. The cause of the crash was the defendant train company's negligent manner of operating the High Speed Train from Swansea to London Paddington. However, the only worker charged was the driver and it was accepted he was not a controlling mind of the company. The judge ruled that it was a condition precedent to a conviction for manslaughter by gross negligence for a guilty mind to be proved and that where a non-human defendant was prosecuted, it might only be convicted via the guilty mind of a human being with whom it might be identified. Following that ruling, verdicts of not guilty were entered in relation to those seven counts but the Attorney General appealed against the acquittal asking the appeal court to consider, inter alia, whether a non-human defendant could be convicted of the crime of manslaughter by gross negligence in the absence of evidence establishing the guilt of an identified human individual for the same crime. The Court of Appeal answered with a very definite "no". The court stated:

> "A corporation's liability for manslaughter is based solely on the principle of identification, which was just as relevant to actus reus as to mens rea. Unless an identified individual's conduct, characterisable as gross criminal negligence, could be attributed to the corporation, the corporation was not in the present state of the common law liable for manslaughter."

There was only a handful of successful prosecutions, but only against small companies. The first was against Peter Kite and his company OLL Ltd. Several sixth-form students had died after their canoes capsized when the weather took a turn for the worse as they were canoeing across Lyme Bay. The company which ran the adventure centre had a single managing director, and he had been warned on several occasions of the risk his negligent handling of the company might have by former instructors at the centre. One of them had written to him saying "otherwise you might find yourself trying to explain why someone's son or daughter will not be coming home". Both the managing director of the company and the company itself were convicted of the manslaughter of the victims (**Kite and OLL Ltd [1994] 144 N.L.J. 1735**). Since this case, there have been successful prosecutions in **Jackson Transport (Ossett) Ltd (1996) (November) Health and Safety at Work 4**; **Roy Bowles Ltd (1999), The Times, December 11**; **Teglgaard Hardwood Ltd (2003)** unreported and **Dennis Clothier and Sons Ltd (2003)** unreported.

THE CORPORATE MANSLAUGHTER AND CORPORATE HOMICIDE ACT 2007

In 1996, the Law Commission's report, "Legislating the Criminal Code: Involuntary Manslaughter" (Law Com. 237) included a proposal for a brand new and separate offence of corporate killing based on the failure of management of the corporation to provide a safe system of conducting the company's activities. In 1997, the enactment of a new offence of corporate killing was one of the Labour party's manifesto pledges. The Law Commission proposal formed the basis for the Government's subsequent consultation paper in 2000, "Reforming the Law on Involuntary Manslaughter: the Government's Proposals" which eventually led to the draft Corporate Manslaughter Bill (Cm 6497), published in March 2005. This was finally introduced into the House of Commons in July 2006 and was carried forward into the 2006–2007 Parliamentary session. The law is now found in the Corporate Manslaughter and Corporate Homicide Act 2007.

Under s.1, an organisation is guilty of an offence if the way in which any of its activities are managed or organised by its senior management (so-called management failure) is a substantial element in the breach of duty which causes a person's death. This means liability is based on a serious breach of a duty of care owed by the company to the deceased, and not, as previously, by making liability contingent on the guilt of a particular individual. The identification doctrine has been abolished in respect of manslaughter.

Under s.1(4)(c), "senior management" means the persons who play significant roles in the making of decisions about how the whole or a substantial part of its activities are to be managed or organised, or the actual managing or organising of the whole or a substantial part of those activities. The activities of the senior managers can be considered collectively as well as individually, but what amounts to a substantial part of a very large and diverse company's activities is not clearly identified. For example, it is not clear whether a UK site manager of an international food and drink corporation would be a senior manager if he had executive responsibility for his site, amounting to say, one per cent of the global turnover of the company, if he had no responsibility at all for decisions at a higher level. This continues to present a problem in huge multi-national companies where delegation of operations is the only realistic method of business organisation.

The breach of the duty is "gross" if it falls far below what can reasonably be expected of the organisation in the circumstances. This is very similar to the current circular test from *Adomako*, it is entirely a matter of fact for the jury to determine and attracts the same criticisms for these two elements as were made above. Under s.8, the jury must consider whether the organisation failed to comply with any health and safety legislation that relates to the alleged breach and, if so, how serious that failure was and how much of a risk of death it posed. They jury may also take into account any matters it feels are relevant including, but not limited to, the attitudes, policies, systems or accepted or even tolerated practices within the organisation and any health and safety rules.

Controversially, s.18 prohibits any individual liability arising. It states:

> **(a)** An individual cannot be guilty of aiding, abetting, counselling or procuring the commission of an offence of corporate manslaughter.

Academic opinion was split on whether individual directorial responsibility should sit alongside, or even replace, corporate responsibility for criminal offences. On the one hand, a company does not commit the crime, the human agent does, so the human agent should be (individually or jointly) criminally liable. It is thought that if an individual director was under the threat of prosecution, (not under the identification doctrine, but as an accessory to the company's crime) this may operate as an effective deterrent. Opposing views argued that corporate liability needs to be viewed afresh, and the common law method of attributing anthropomorphic form to a company, that is trying to fit corporations into the existing law on individuals, did not work. Now we have moved to the position in the Act of examining corporations as entities in their own right rather than as a conglomeration of individuals, no individual accessorial liability is either needed, or wanted. Chris Clarkson has been persuaded that when companies kill it is a qualitatively (and often quantitatively) different form of homicide to when individuals kill each other. Corporate manslaughter bears a closer qualitative analogy to motor (vehicular) manslaughter and thus deserved its own, correctly labelled, offence (C. Clarkson, *Understanding Criminal Law*,

5th edn, Sweet and Maxwell, London). Celia Wells in her book: *Corporations and Criminal Responsibility,* 2nd edn, Clarendon, forcefully argued that human beings behave very differently collectively—in a board of directors, say—than individually.

Of course, whether a corporation is successfully prosecuted for corporate manslaughter, an individual director, or worker, may himself face prosecution under the common law heads of gross negligence, reckless or even unlawful act manslaughter.

Section 17 provides that a prosecution for corporate manslaughter may not be brought without the consent of the Director of Public Prosecutions.

Summary

1. **Homicide**—A homicide occurs when one human being causes the death of another human being. It is unlawful homicide if the actus reus of homicide is proven, along with the mens rea relevant to the specific offence charged. The actus reus of homicide is the unlawful killing of a human being by a human being during the Queen's Peace.

2. **Murder**—a common law offence, subject to a mandatory sentence of life. The mens rea is malice aforethought, satisfied by proof of either intent to kill or intent to do grievous bodily harm (implied malice).

3. **Voluntary Manslaughter**—D has actus reus and mens rea for murder but the offence is reduced to manslaughter by one of three partial defences under the Homicide Act 1957:

    (a) Section 2; diminished responsibility●

    D is charged with murder. D must prove:

    (i) abnormality of mind;

    (ii) due to arrested or retarded development of mind, inherent cause, disease or injury;

    (iii) leading to substantial impairment of responsibility.

    (b) The common law, as amended by s.3; provocation●

    D is charged with murder. P must disprove:

    (i) things done or said or both together; causing

    (ii) D to lose his self-control;

    (iii) where a reasonable person would have done as D did.

If the provisions of the Coroners and Justice Act 2009 come into force, diminished responsibility will be amended and provocation will be abolished, replaced with a new defence based on loss of self-control.

(c) Section 4; suicide pact •

D is charged with murder. D must prove he entered an agreement with V with the aim of the death of each of them. D has killed V, but then has not committed suicide.

4. Involuntary manslaughter—the actus reus for homicide is satisfied, but without malice aforethought. There are three forms:

(a) subjective recklessness

D kills foreseeing serious injury as being highly probable.

(b) gross negligence

(i) D owes V a duty of care,

(ii) the duty had been breached,

(iii) the breach involves a risk of death,

(iv) the breach had caused the death and, if so,

(v) the breach is grossly negligent and therefore a crime.

(c) unlawful act (constructive) manslaughter

(i) D intentionally did an act,

(ii) which was criminally unlawful,

(iii) which was dangerous,

(iv) which caused the victim's death.

5. Infanticide—D can be charged with murder, manslaughter, or with infanticide. The offence is the killing, by any wilful act or omission, by a woman of her child under the age of 12 months whilst the balance of her mind was disturbed due to the effects of the birth or consequent lactation.

6. It is an offence for a person to cause or allow the death of a child or vulnerable adult who is a member of the same household (The Domestic Violence, Crime and Victims Act 2004 s.5)

7. Corporate Manslaughter—A corporation's liability for manslaughter was based at common law solely on the identification doctrine. An identified individual had to be first convicted of manslaughter by gross negligence and only then could that criminality be attributed to the corporation. The Corporate Manslaughter and Corporate Homicide Act 2007 now governs corporate manslaughter where a person's death is caused by an organisational managerial failure.

End of Chapter Question

Question

During a criminal law tutorial, an argument erupted between two students, Andrew and Mark, about the defence of insanity. Andrew picked up one of his textbooks and threw it at Mark with intent to cause him serious harm. Mark ducked, and the book's spine struck Sheila, another student, on her temple. Sheila fell unconscious.

Jane, the law lecturer, who was a trained first aider, panicked when she saw that Sheila was unconscious. Two other students, Jo and Samantha, picked Sheila up to take her to the reception area and phone for an ambulance. Unfortunately, they banged Sheila's head against the door frame as they left, exacerbating Sheila's injuries.

When the ambulance arrived, Sheila was taken immediately to the hospital. She had a brain scan. A junior doctor misread the scan and wrongly decided Sheila needed urgent brain surgery.

Sheila lapsed into a coma during the operation and doctors subsequently indicated there was no chance of recovery. With Sheila's family's agreement, they turned off the machines keeping Sheila alive. Sheila died.

Andrew is charged with the murder of Sheila. Discuss his criminal liability, if any.

Points of Answer

♦ The charge is murder. Define offence. The actus reus is causing the death of a human being. The only issue was whether A was the cause of S's death. To be a cause, both the "but for" and the legal test must be used. But for A's act, S would not have died (cf. *White*) so A is the factual cause of death. In legal terms, provided his act was a more than nominal cause, it need not be the sole cause (*Kimsey*). This is established as the book spine hitting S on the head was a more than nominal contribution to death. Causation is then dependent on whether anything broke the chain. You may need to refer to Ch.2 for full understanding of this answer outline.

♦ First, was the tutor's inability to help a free, deliberate and informed act? *Latif* and *Paggett* suggest it might not be (she is a trained not a professional first aider) and even *Empress Cars* (recently of course restricted to its facts, see *Kennedy* HL) would suggest it is not unusual for a first-aid trained teacher to panic. This, therefore, would probably not break the chain of causation.

♦ The acts of Jo and Samantha should be considered in light of the facts and decision in *Smith*, and clearly would not be sufficient to break the chain, but the doctor's negligence in misreading the scan might be viewed as so potent, independent, etc. per *Cheshire, Jordan* that the chain of causation would be broken. Provided the law is well explained, it does not matter whether you conclude it does or does not break the chain—as this is a matter of fact, it therefore cannot be wrong if based on accurate authorities.

♦ On these facts, turning off the life-support machines is not a break in the chain of causation (*Malcherek*).

♦ The mens rea of murder is malice aforethought which is satisfied by intent to kill or intent to cause GBH (*Moloney*). GBH is defined as really serious harm. We are told that A intended to cause serious harm, so all you must then deal with is the fact that A intended to cause M that harm, but the charge is murder of S. It is possible to transfer his mens rea from Mark to Sheila using *Latimer*.

♦ There is no question of oblique intent here.

Avoid common errors:

One major error here would be to discuss manslaughter rather than murder. The question specifies the charge. Ignore it at your peril! Another would be to ignore the medical negligence causation cases (above). Three points must be emphasised:

1. Do not use *Adomako* as an authority on causation; it is the authority for gross negligence manslaughter and no-one is charged with that offence here.
2. Medical negligence may break the chain of causation, but it does not have to be *Adomako* negligence.
3. The doctor's liability is not asked for.

Further Reading

A. Ashworth and B. Mitchell, "Rethinking English Homicide Law" (2000, OUP).

B. Barrett, "Liability for safety offences: is the law still fatally flawed?" [2008] I.L.J. 100.

C. Barsby and D. Ormerod, "Manslaughter though gross negligence—whether sufficient certainty as to ingredients" [2005] Crim. L.R. 234.

G. Bastable, "Making a Killing" [2008] Euro Law 15.

S. Boileau and G. Burn, "Corporate manslaughter: A new test of liability" E.G. (2006) No.0650 p.76.

I. Dennis (ed.), "The Law Commission's Report on Homicide" [2007] Crim. L.R. 107.

S. Edwards, "Justice Devlin's legacy: Duffy—a battered woman 'caught' in time" [2009] Crim. L.R. 851.

M.W.H. Hsaio, "Abandonment of the doctrine of attribution in favour of gross negligence test in the Corporate Manslaughter and Corporate Homicide Act 2007" [2009] Comp. Law 110.

J. Herring and E. Palser, "The duty of care in gross negligence manslaughter" [2007] Crim. L.R. 24.

L.H. Leigh, "Two New Partial Defences to Murder" (2010) 174 (5) CL&JW 53.

R.D. Mackay, "The Coroners and Justice Act 2009—partial defences to murder (2) The new diminished responsibility plea" [2010] Crim. L.R. 290.

J. Miles, "The Coroners and Justice Act 2009: a 'dog's breakfast' of homicide reform" [2009] Arch. News 6.

A. Norrie, "The Coroners and Justice Act 2009—partial defences to murder (1) Loss of control" [2010] Crim. L.R. 275

S. Ramage, "Corporate Manslaughter and Corporate Homicide Act 2007 explained" [2007] Crim. Law. 5.

O. Quick and C. Wells, "Getting Tough With Defences" [2006] Crim. L.R. 514.

C. Wells, "Battered Women Syndrome and Defences to Homicide: Where Now?" (1994) 14 Legal Studies 266 and *Corporations and Criminal Responsibility*, 2nd edn (Clarendon, 2001).

W. Wilson, "The Structure of Criminal Defences" [2005] Crim. L.R. 108.

Key Papers on corporate manslaughter include: Law Commission Report, "Legislating the Criminal Code: Involuntary Manslaughter", (LC237) 1996; Home Office, "Reforming the Law on Involuntary Manslaughter: The Government's Proposals", 2000; Law Commission Report, "Partial Defences to Murder", (LC290) 2004; Law Commission Consultation Paper "A New Homicide Act for England and Wales?" (LCCP177) 2005.

Self Test Questions

To test your knowledge gained from this section go online to *http://www.sweetandmaxwell. co.uk* and take our online self test questions. Here you will also find key updates to ensure that you are only ever one click away from an instant update.

Non-fatal Offences Against the Person

5

CHAPTER OVERVIEW

In this chapter we:

- provide the definition and analyse the actus reus and mens rea requirements of the offences of assault and battery and the offences contrary to ss.47, 20 and 18 of the Offences Against the Person Act 1861

- consider what constitutes a racially or religiously aggravated assault

- consider what constitutes an offence of harassment under the Protection from Harassment Act 1997

- provide critical commentary where appropriate of the offences mentioned

- analyse and comment on the extent to which a person may give valid consent to harm or injury to him or herself.

Summary

End of Chapter Question

Further Reading

Self Test Questions

Introduction

There are numerous offences against the person involving non-fatal, non-sexual injury to the victim, most of which are contrary to the Offences Against the Person Act 1861 (OAPA 1861). Some offences, such as impeding a person endeavouring to save himself from a shipwreck and obstructing or assaulting a clergyman or other minister in the discharge of his duties, are now seldom prosecuted and are also unlikely to appear on a conventional Criminal law syllabus. For these reasons, they will not be covered further in this chapter. Instead, the main focus of this chapter will be the principal non-fatal offences against the person, namely assault and battery and the aggravated assaults under ss.47, 20 and 18 OAPA 1861. Racially and religiously aggravated assaults, offences under the Protection from Harassment Act 1997 and the defence of consent are also considered. Sexual offences are examined in Ch.6.

Non-fatal offences against the person increase in seriousness according to the severity of the injury caused and the mens rea with which it was caused. For this reason, they are sometimes described as a "ladder" of offences with the least serious, assault, on the bottom rung and the most serious, wounding or causing grievous bodily harm with intent, at the top.

The Offences of Assault and Battery

Assault and battery are separate offences and should be charged separately in an indictment (**DPP v Little (1992) 95 Cr. App. R. 28**). They are both summary only offences and are punishable by a maximum of six months' imprisonment or a fine. The definition of each offence is examined fully below but, in essence, an assault merely requires V to expect harm to ensue from D's actions whereas a battery requires non-consensual contact between D and V's body or clothes. Thus, D may commit an assault without a battery (where, for example, he waves a dagger at V) and a battery without an assault (where, for example, he pokes the dagger into V's back). D may, however, be liable for both offences arising out of the same set of circumstances. Thus, in the example above, if D was first to wave the dagger at V and then to poke it against V's body, he would commit both an assault and a battery.

Assault and battery were not included in the OAPA 1861, are defined only at common law and were traditionally viewed as common law offences. However, the position is now less clear. There is authority (*Little*, above) that the offences are statutory and have, indeed, been so since the enactment of the OAPA 1861. If this view is correct, under which section should the offences be charged? As the 1861 Act does not specifically include either offence, the only possibility is s.39 of the Criminal Justice Act 1988 which provides that assault and battery are summary offences and details the penalties for both. However, this section does not specifically state that a person who commits an assault or a battery does so contrary to the provision. To further complicate matters, a statement in support of the common law status of the offences was subsequently expressed by the Divisional Court in **Haystead v Chief Constable of Derbyshire [2000] 3 All E.R. 890**. The statement was, though, only obiter and without reference to the decision in *Little*.

Assault

The term "assault" is used in two different senses in non-fatal offences against the person. First, there is the actual offence of assault. This is often described by commentators as a "technical" or "psychic" assault, in order to distinguish it from "common assault." The term common assault is used in the context of s.47 to embrace both a technical or psychic assault and a battery but, confusingly, is also used in s.39 to refer to a technical or psychic assault only! It is a technical or psychic assault which is considered in this part of the chapter.

Assault was defined in **Fagan v Metropolitan Police Commissioner [1968] 3 All E.R. 442**, as an act by which the defendant intentionally or recklessly causes another person to apprehend the application to his body of immediate, unlawful force. Examples of assault would, therefore, include D threatening to harm V, shaking his fist at V or pointing a weapon at him.

THE ACTUS REUS OF ASSAULT

This involves:

1. an act;
2. which causes the victim to apprehend the application of immediate and unlawful force.

■ Apprehension of unlawful force

There is no assault unless the victim (V) apprehends, i.e. expects the application of unlawful force to his body. Thus, for example, there is no assault where the intended victim does not see his assailant wielding his weapon or does not think that the weapon will be used. Further, where D makes a threat but there is no apprehension of harm on V's part because, for example, he believes the gun being pointed at him is not loaded, there is no assault (**Lamb [1967] 2 Q.B. 981**). Conversely, in **Logdon v DPP [1976] Crim. L.R. 121**, the actus reus of assault was satisfied where D threatened V with an imitation firearm as V believed the gun to be real and that it was about to be fired. Although in most instances of assault the victim will fear harm, actual fear is not required; it is merely the expectation of an attack which must be established. In **Ireland and Burstow [1998] A.C. 147**, Lord Steyn went further and suggested that it is not even necessary that the victim is certain that the defendant will use violence against him; that he might do so is sufficient.

As the threat posed must be of *unlawful* force (as is the case with all offences against the person), a defence rendering the force lawful, for example, self-defence or prevention of crime (see Ch.13) or consent (see p.160 below) would mean that no assault was committed.

The requirement that force is threatened would suggest that the victim must expect to be harmed but this is not the case. A threat to touch unlawfully, i.e. to commit a battery, is sufficient.

■ An act

The actus reus is phrased in terms of an "act." This means that an assault cannot be committed by an omission (*Fagan*)—though see below—but, can it be committed by words?

Assault by words alone

The position with regard to assault by words was unclear until the decision of the Court of Appeal in **Constanza [1997] 2 Cr. App. R. 492**, in which the court accepted that threatening letters sent by the defendant to the woman he had been stalking constituted an assault. Thus, it would seem that words in written form can be an assault so that emails, faxes and texts could also. Further, if the written word can contain an assault so, surely, must the spoken word. That this is so was confirmed by their Lordships in *Ireland* where it was held that not only could words amount to an assault but so could, in certain circumstances, a silent phone call (see further p.142 below).

Words accompanying an assault

Whilst it was not always clear whether a defendant could assault by words alone, it has been established for many years that words accompanying a threatening gesture might be relevant in that they negate liability because the defendant, by his choice of words, is making clear that he has no intention to carry out the threat. Conversely, where it is evident from the words used by the defendant that he does intend to carry out the threat unless the victim complies with a certain specified condition, the words will reinforce the assault. The latter is often called a conditional assault. The following two examples illustrate the point.

Example 1

D shakes his fist at V and says, "I would hurt you if it wasn't for the fact that we have known each other such a long time ..."

Example 2

D shakes his fist at V and says, "I will hurt you unless you get out of my sight right now ..."

In both examples, there is a threatening gesture (D shaking his fist at V) which on its own could be an assault. However, liability for assault could only ensue from Example 2, where D's words actually strengthen the threat posed by the fist because, unless V complies with the specified condition, he will be hurt. There is no assault in Example 1 because D's words make clear that, for the specified reason, he will not do anything to V.

An example of words negating an assault is the old case of **Turberville v Savage (1669) 1 Mod. 3**. Here, it was held that there was no assault where D made a threatening gesture by placing his hand on his sword and said, "If it were not assize-time, I would not take such language from you." D's words indicated that as the judges were in town he would not use force. A case in which the words used reinforced the assault is **Read v Coker (1853) 138 E.R. 1437**. D and his servants surrounded V, rolled up their sleeves (an assault) and threatened to break V's neck if he did not leave the premises. V was able successfully to sue D for assault (assault is a tort as well as a criminal offence). Both these cases were decided before it was established that words alone may amount to an assault. Presumably, the decisions in these two cases would be the same today whether or not there was an accompanying threatening gesture as it could be determined from D's words alone whether or not he intended to harm V.

■ Immediate

Immediate refers to the harm apprehended rather than to the apprehension itself. So, it is correct to say that V apprehends immediate harm, not that V immediately apprehends some future harm. Consequently, it is not an assault if the defendant merely causes the victim an immediate apprehension of unlawful force if such harm will not actually occur until some considerable time later. However, the courts' approach to the immediacy requirement is still quite flexible. According to Watkins L.J. in **R. v Horseferry Road Metropolitan Stipendiary Magistrate, Ex p. Siadatan [1991] 1 Q.B. 260**:

> "It seems to us that the word 'immediate' does not mean 'instantaneous'; that a relatively short time interval may elapse between the act which is threatening, abusive or insulting and the unlawful violence. 'Immediate' connotes proximity in time and proximity in causation; that it is likely that violence will result within a relatively short period of time and without any other intervening occurrence."

It may not even be necessary for the defendant and his victim to be together when the threat is made. In **Smith v Superintendent of Woking Police Station (1983) 76 Cr. App. R. 234**, D was liable for assault where he terrified a woman by looking at her through her ground floor bedroom window late at night. The court held that he had committed an assault although he could not use force immediately, had not tried to enter and even though the victim might have fled before he was able to enter because D was "immediately adjacent, albeit on the other side of a window."

The court considered the issue of immediacy again in *Constanza* (above). D had stalked V for more than two years, followed her home from work, made many phone calls to her home, some of which were silent, sent in excess of 800 letters to her, often drove past her home, visited her against her wishes and wrote offensive comments on her front door. D was convicted under s.47 OAPA 1861 (which requires an assault or battery) in respect of the last letter sent, which had made V afraid. On dismissing D's appeal against conviction, the court stressed the point that V knew D, who lived near her, and that she thought that he might turn up at any time. In accepting the requirement of immediacy was satisfied, the court further stated, somewhat confusingly, that it was sufficient that the threat be of harm "at some time not excluding the immediate future." This must mean that it is sufficient that V apprehends the use of force in the immediate future but a more specific statement of the law on how far into the future "immediate" lasts would have been welcome.

The most recent pronouncement on the issue was in *Ireland*. Their Lordships had to consider whether an assault could be committed by a silent phone call and, if it could, whether the immediacy requirement might be satisfied in relation to such a phone call. Lord Steyn stated that;

> "as there is no reason why a telephone caller who says to a woman in a menacing way 'I will be at your door in a minute or two' may not be guilty of an assault where he causes his victim to apprehend immediate personal violence"

there was no reason why a silent phone call could not have the same effect. Whether it would do so would, he considered, depend on the facts of the case and the impact of the call on the victim—does she fear the imminent arrival of the defendant? The extension of the meaning of immediate to imminent, which means to happen soon, suggests a less rigid test may be applied in future. Unfortunately, though, their Lordships gave no guidance as to exactly how much further a requirement of imminent harm takes us.

THE MENS REA OF ASSAULT

This involves:

1. intention; or
2. subjective recklessness (**Venna [1975] 3 All E.R. 788**)

as to causing another to apprehend immediate and unlawful force.

Accordingly, if D causes V to apprehend unlawful force but does so without intending or foreseeing such apprehension, he will not be liable for assault. Thus, for example, if D, a very shy and nervous character, without any thought that V might be made upset or fearful, makes a silent phone call to V which causes V distress, D's lack of foresight of the risk will mean that he lacks the mens rea for assault and is not liable.

Over to you...

D finds out that his friend, Z, has been seeing his girlfriend, Sharon, behind his back. D sends Z a text saying, "If you don't stop seeing Sharon, I'll kick your face in!" Does D commit an assault?

Battery

There have been several definitions of a battery suggested by the courts. One of the clearest comes from **Collins v Wilcock [1984] 3 All E.R. 374** where it was described as "the actual infliction of unlawful force on another person [with the appropriate mens rea]." Other, equally valid, definitions use the word "apply" rather than "inflict" and "violence" or "harm" rather than "force."

THE ACTUS REUS OF BATTERY

This involves the infliction of unlawful force.

◼ Unlawful Force

Battery, as with all non-fatal offence against the person, requires the use of unlawful force. Force is a slightly misleading term in that it implies some violence behind the contact. In many instances some violence will have been used by the defendant, but this is not essential as any unlawful touching can constitute a battery.

No harm need result from the force but, where very minor harm occurs which is not sufficient to amount to actual bodily harm, a battery will be the appropriate charge. The Crown Prosecution Service has drafted a set of Charging Standards providing guidelines to prosecutors on charging in borderline cases. They can be viewed online at: *http://www.cps.gov.uk/legal/l_to_o/ offences_against_the_person/*. The guidelines, which have no legal force, suggest that the correct charge would be for a battery where the injury involves any of the following: grazes; scratches; abrasions; minor bruising; swellings; reddening of the skin; superficial cuts and a black eye.

Contact with the victim is required (*Ireland*) (although, as seen below, it may be indirect). The defendant does not necessarily have to make contact with the victim's body; contact with their clothes will suffice (**Day (1845) 1 Cox C.C. 207**) even if the victim does not feel such contact (**Thomas (1985) 81 Cr. App. R. 33**).

It has sometimes been asserted (e.g. by the majority of their Lordships in **Brown [1994] 1 A.C. 212**) that the contact must be hostile. Other cases, e.g. **F v West Berkshire HA [1990] 2 A.C. 1** have taken a contrary view. A better, and more straightforward approach, is to ask whether the contact was unlawful, in the sense that the defendant acted without a defence which would have rendered the force lawful.

◼ Indirect force

A battery is most frequently committed by direct physical contact between the defendant and his victim. However, battery is not limited to such situations. The offence can be committed by the use of a weapon or other implement, even a car, as in the case of *Fagan*. Further, a battery may be committed by the indirect use of force. The following cases illustrate the point. In **Martin (1881) 8 Q.B.D. 54**, D was found liable for battery where he had called out "Fire" in a theatre leading to several people being crushed against an iron bar when they fled to the exit. In **DPP v K (1990) 1 All E.R. 331**, D, a schoolboy, took with him to the toilets a test tube of sulphuric acid which he had removed from the school laboratory without permission. Whilst in the toilets he heard footsteps and panicked. He poured the acid into the hot air dryer. V, the next pupil to use the dryer, was scarred by acid which squirted out of the dryer when he used it. The Divisional Court convicted D under s.47 OAPA 1861 on the basis that D's battery had occasioned V actual bodily harm. The most recent example is **Haystead v Chief Constable of Derbyshire [2000] 3 All E.R. 890**. D punched V who was holding a baby. This caused V to drop X, the baby she had been holding, onto the floor. The Divisional Court dismissed D's appeal against conviction for battery on X.

■ Omissions

The Divisional Court held in *Fagan* that a mere omission to act would not amount to an "assault" (meaning a common assault in the s.47 OAPA sense of assault or battery). This seems a strange decision given that the offences under ss.20 and 18 and also fatal offences against the person such as murder and manslaughter may be committed by omission. In *Fagan* (see Ch.2), you will recall that D unintentionally drove on to a police officer's foot and failed to drive off when he realised what he had done. Rather than base liability on a battery by omission, the court applied the continuing act principle and stated that all D's actions were part of one transaction. The decision in *Fagan* preceded that in **Miller [1983] 2 A.C. 161** to the effect the defendant is liable for the consequences resulting from his failure to take reasonable steps to rectify a dangerous situation which he had, even inadvertently, created. In **DPP v Santa-Bermudez [2004] Crim. L.R. 471**, the Divisional Court held that D was liable for an assault occasioning actual bodily harm based on this principle. He had placed hypodermic needles in his pockets and, when later asked by a police officer who was going to search him if he had on him any sharp objects, he said "no". The police officer was then injured by a needle when she carried out the search. Liability was imposed because, by failing to warn her about the needles in his pockets, D had exposed the police officer to a reasonably foreseeable risk of injury. Thus, it seems that D may now commit an assault or battery by omission in the limited circumstances where he has created a dangerous situation and then failed to take reasonable steps to rectify it, such failure resulting in V apprehending or sustaining unlawful force.

Over to you...

Why do you think the court in *Fagan* was unwilling to say that D had committed a battery by omission?

THE MENS REA OF BATTERY
This involves:

1. intention; or
2. subjective recklessness (*Venna*)

as to inflicting unlawful force.

Assault Occasioning Actual Bodily Harm

The s.47 Offence
Section 47 OAPA 1861 provides:

> Whosoever shall be convicted on indictment of any assault occasioning actual bodily harm shall be liable to imprisonment for not more than 5 years.

The Actus Reus of the s.47 Offence
This involves:

1. assault;
2. occasioning;
3. actual bodily harm (ABH).

ASSAULT
Assault is used in s.47 to encompass both the offences of assault and battery. It is not necessary that both an assault and a battery are committed as, otherwise, it would not be possible to commit the offence against, for example, a sleeping or blind victim. Although actual bodily harm will most frequently be occasioned by a battery, it is possible to commit the offence by an assault as, for example, in **Roberts (1971) 56 Cr. App. R. 95**, in which D had given a young girl a lift in his car and tried to pull her tights off. She resisted and he told her he would beat her up if she did not take them off. He then tried to remove her coat. Such actions on D's part amounted to an assault as they caused V to fear D would hurt her. V jumped out of the moving car and was injured. D was convicted under s.47.

The term assault will be used in the rest of this section to imply an assault or a battery.

OCCASIONING

Occasioning means the same as causing (*Roberts*), see further Ch.2. Thus, it must be established that there was an assault, and ABH, and that such harm was caused by the assault. In *Roberts*, applying the normal principles of causation, the Court of Appeal held that D was the cause of V's actual bodily harm because such harm was a reasonably foreseeable consequence of D's assault. The court stated that only if V's reaction was totally unreasonable or "daft" would the chain be broken so that D would be liable for assault only.

Where the ABH is occasioned by a battery, it must be caused by the act of D which produced the force, rather than by the force which D intended or foresaw (**Savage and Parmenter [1992] 1 A.C. 699**). The facts of *Savage and Parmenter* illustrate the point. D threw a pint of beer over V. V was soaked by the beer but also cut by a fragment of flying glass from the beer glass which had hit a table and shattered when D let go of it. D asserted that he was not liable for s.47 assault because he had not foreseen V being hit by a piece of glass. The House of Lords held that the deliberate drenching with beer was a battery and the act which constituted the battery also caused the glass to shatter and cut V. Thus, the battery had occasioned the ABH.

ACTUAL BODILY HARM

The nature of the injury or the "harm" under the terms of this section need not be really serious. In **Miller [1954] 2 Q.B. 282**, actual bodily harm was defined as "any hurt or injury calculated to interfere with the health or comfort of V". However, in **Chan-Fook [1994] 2 ALL E.R. 552**, the Court of Appeal stated that "harm" requires injury and, consequently, the phrase "interfere with the health or comfort of V" should no longer be used as a direction to juries because it might lead jurors to conclude that injury is not required. According to the court, harm would be "actual" where it was not so trivial as to be wholly insignificant and whether this was so was a question of fact and degree to be determined by the jury. The effect of these two cases, therefore, is that ABH can be defined as any hurt or injury which is not so trivial as to be wholly insignificant.

Actual bodily harm need not be permanent, but must be more than merely transient or trifling (*Chan-Fook*). It can involve a momentary loss of consciousness (**T v DPP [2003] Crim. L.R. 662**), cutting off a woman's ponytail ((**DPP v Smith [2006] 2 ALL E.R. 116**) as hair is part of the body) and psychiatric injury (*Ireland*). However, the term "bodily harm" (as used in s.47 and also ss.18 and 20, see below) does not encompass mere emotions such as fear, distress or panic (*Chan-Fook*) or even psychological harm falling short of psychiatric illness (**R. v D [2006] 2 Cr. App. R. 24**). Hence, if the prosecution wish to assert that V's injury amounts to a psychiatric illness and this is not admitted by the defence, expert evidence must be called by the prosecution (*Chan-Fook*).

The Crown Prosecution Service Charging Standards also suggest that s.47 is the appropriate charge where V has sustained temporary loss of sensory function, minor cuts, severe bruising, a broken nose, loss or breaking of a tooth, minor fractures and minor cuts which require stitches.

The Mens Rea of the s.47 Offence

Only the mens rea for assault (or battery) need be proven (*Savage and Parmenter*). It is not necessary, therefore, to prove that D foresaw actual bodily harm, only that he intended or was subjectively reckless as to inflicting, or creating the apprehension of, unlawful force.

Offences Involving Wounding or Grievous Bodily Harm

There are two statutory provisions creating offences involving wounding and grievous bodily harm: s.20 and s.18. As with the other non-fatal offences considered, the wound or grievous bodily harm must be unlawful. Consequently, a defence rendering the injury lawful, for example, self-defence, prevention of crime or consent would mean that no offence was committed.

The s.20 Offence

Section 20 OAPA 1861 provides:

> Whosoever shall unlawfully and maliciously wound or inflict any grievous bodily harm upon any other person, either with or without any weapon or instrument shall be guilty of an offence and being convicted thereof shall be liable to imprisonment for five years.

Section 20 may be committed by:

1. unlawful and malicious wounding;
2. unlawfully and maliciously inflicting grievous bodily harm.

The Actus Reus of the s.20 Offence

This involves either:

1. unlawful wounding; or
2. unlawfully inflicting grievous bodily harm (GBH).

The prosecution need only prove that a wound or GBH occurred, not both. Hence, a wound, which in basic terms requires a break in the skin, does not have to be serious enough to constitute GBH (although it may do) and, similarly, GBH does not require the skin to be broken (although it may be).

WOUND

The defendant's act must wound; the normal principles of causation apply (see Ch.2). It was once thought that a wound must result from a battery (see, for example, **Taylor (1869) L.R. 1 C.C.R. 194**) but this view was rejected in *Savage and Parmenter*, although their Lordships acknowledged that the circumstances in which a wound would occur in the absence of a battery would be quite rare.

A wound involves a break in both the layers of the skin, dermis and epidermis (**JJC (A minor) v Eisenhower (1984) 78 Cr. App. R. 48**). Thus, it is the depth of the injury which is crucial, not its width; a large scratch which only breaks the outer layer of the skin will not constitute a wound but a small deep gash will. Nor is the presence of blood a deciding factor: in *Eisenhower*, ruptured blood vessels in V's eye caused by pellets from an air gun did not constitute a wound because both layers of skin were not broken. The skin is given a broad meaning to include the membrane lining the cheek or urethra (**Waltham (1849) 3 Cox. C.C. 442**).

GRIEVOUS BODILY HARM

Grievous bodily harm was defined in **DPP v Smith [1961] A.C. 290** as really serious harm, though it is not a misdirection for a trial judge to direct merely in terms of serious harm, omitting the word "really" (**Saunders [1985] Crim. L.R. 230**). Whether an injury is serious is determined objectively, rather than from the victim's perspective (**Brown [1998] Crim. L.R. 485**). The court can, however, take into consideration individual characteristics of the victim and the impact of the injury on that particular individual. Thus, in **Bollom [2004] 2 Cr. App. R. 6**, in assessing the severity of the injuries, the court took into account the fact that the victim was a 17-month-old baby who was likely to be more badly affected by extensive bruising than, for example, a six foot healthy adult. Where more than one injury is occasioned, each in itself not amounting to GBH, the injuries taken as a whole may amount to GBH (**Grundy [1977] Crim. L.R. 543**).

As well as physical injury, GBH can encompass biological harm such as infection with the HIV virus (*Dica* **[2004] 3 W.L.R. 213**) and a serious psychiatric injury (*Burstow*, whose appeal was heard by the House of Lords together with that of *Ireland*). As with ABH, appropriate expert evidence is essential to prove psychiatric injury. The Crown Prosecution Service Charging Standards also suggest that an injury would constitute GBH where it results in: substantial loss of blood, usually necessitating a transfusion; lengthy treatment or incapacity; permanent disability or permanent loss of sensory function; permanent, visible disfigurement; broken or displaced limbs or bones, including fractured skull; broken cheek bone, jaw, ribs, etc.

"INFLICT" GRIEVOUS BODILY HARM

Section 20 requires GBH to be "inflicted" whereas the corresponding offence in s.18 is phrased in terms of GBH being "caused". This led to conflicting case law concerning whether inflict should be interpreted more narrowly than cause so as to require an assault and the application to the body of direct or indirect force. The matter was finally settled by the House of Lords in *Ireland and Burstow* in relation to the appeal of Burstow. D, refusing to accept that his girlfriend no longer wished to see him, made silent phone calls to her home, followed her to work, sent hate mail, visited her home, stole clothing from her washing line and left condoms in her garden. As a result, V suffered from serious depression. D appealed against his conviction under s.20, contending inter alia, that GBH had not been "inflicted." Their Lordships held that it had; psychiatric harm can be inflicted for the purposes of s.20. In the leading speech, Lord Steyn rejected the argument that there was a need to establish an assault under s.20 and also rejected as "absurd" the argument that there must be a direct or indirect application of force to the body. Although he did not accept that inflict and cause are exactly synonymous (he did not, unfortunately, explain when their meanings would differ) he considered that there is no "radical divergence" between the meanings of both words as used in the 1861 Act.

Ireland and Burstow was followed in *Dica*, in which the Court of Appeal held that D had inflicted GBH contrary to s.20 OAPA 1861 when he had unprotected sexual intercourse with his victims thereby infecting them with the HIV virus; D's actions had caused GBH therefore he had inflicted GBH. Similarly, in **Brady [2006] EWCA Crim. 2413**, the defendant was held to have inflicted GBH on V when he had lost his balance and fallen from a perching position on a low railing above a crowded dance floor onto V below. The court was of the opinion that even If D's actions might have been accidental, GBH would still have been inflicted as there is no requirement for liability under s.20 that D assault V. (D was not, however, liable under s.20 due to deficiencies in the trial judge's summing up.)

The Mens Rea of the s.20 Offence

The mens rea for a s.20 offence is maliciously. This has been interpreted as meaning with intention or subjective recklessness as to some harm (*Savage and Parmenter*). It is not necessary for the defendant to foresee a wound or GBH; proof that he foresaw some harm might occur (not would occur (**DPP v DA [2001] Crim. L.R. 140**)) is sufficient. An intention solely to frighten is not sufficient for liability under s.20, only for s.47 (**Sullivan [1981] Crim. L.R. 46**). In *Brady*, the Court of Appeal rejected the submission that recklessness in s.20 requires foresight of an "obvious and serious" risk of injury; foresight is purely subjective, see Ch.3.

Over to you...

Do you think the prosecution would have an easy task establishing the mens rea for a s.20 offence where D has sent V a series of suggestive emails resulting in her developing a serious psychiatric disorder?

The s.18 Offence

Section 18 OAPA 1861 provides:

> Whosoever shall unlawfully and maliciously by any means whatsoever wound or cause any grievous bodily harm to any person with intent to do some grievous bodily harm to any person or with intent to resist or prevent the lawful apprehension or detainer of any person, shall be guilty of an offence, and shall be liable to imprisonment for life.

Section 18 may be committed by:

1. unlawful and malicious wounding with intent to do grievous bodily harm or resist, etc.
2. unlawfully and maliciously causing grievous bodily harm with intent to do grievous bodily harm or resist, etc.

The Actus Reus of the s.18 Offence

The actus reus of s.18 is satisfied by a wound or GBH. The meanings of these terms were discussed in respect of s.20 above. As explained above, the difference in the actus reus between s.20 and s.18 is that s.20 refers to *inflict* GBH, whereas s.18 refers to *cause* GBH. The impact, if any, of this difference was examined above. The normal principles of causation apply to causing GBH (see Ch.2).

The Mens Rea of the s.18 Offence

The mens rea for s.18 is "maliciously" and "with intent to do some grievous bodily harm or with intent to resist etc ..." It is worth noting that although s.18 creates a wounding offence, the mens rea of s.18 does not include an intention to wound. Consequently, the Court of Appeal held that the trial judge had misdirected the jury in a trial for s.18 wounding when he stated that the prosecution must prove that the defendant had intended to cause GBH or to wound (**Taylor [2009] EWCA Crim 544**). Intent to do GBH and intent to resist the lawful apprehension or detainer of any person (i.e. intent to resist arrest of D or another) are alternative forms of the mens rea for s.18; they do not create separate offences.

It was stated obiter in **Mowatt [1968] 1 Q.B. 421**, that where an offence under s.18 is alleged to have been committed with intent to do GBH, maliciously adds nothing. This would appear to be on the basis that if the defendant intended GBH he must have been malicious. Where, however, the defendant acts with intent to resist arrest, maliciousness (as defined above) does have to be proven because an intent to resist arrest does not necessarily involve an intent or recklessness as to doing some harm. In **Morrison (1989) 89 Cr. App. R. 17**, the police entered a house to evict squatters. D dragged a woman police officer to a closed window which he jumped through. The officer suffered permanent facial scarring from the broken glass and D was charged with unlawful and malicious wounding with intent to resist arrest. The Court of Appeal held that it was necessary to establish not only D's intention to resist arrest but also that he foresaw that he might do some harm.

It is irrelevant whether the defendant knew that the harm he intended was serious. What is important is whether the harm which the defendant intended was, objectively viewed, serious harm.

Mere foresight of GBH will not suffice for a conviction; s.18 is a crime of intention only (**Belfon [1976] 3 All E.R. 46**). The meaning of intention is the same as that for murder, (see Chs 3 and 4) so it encompasses both direct and oblique intention (**Bryson [1985] Crim. L.R. 669**).

FIGURE 5 Illustration of the different ways in which s.18 may be committed

Actus Reus	Mens Rea
Wound	Malicious and intent to resist, etc.
Wound	Intent to cause grievous bodily harm
Cause grievous bodily harm	Malicious and intent to resist, etc.
Cause grievous bodily harm	Intent to cause grievous bodily harm

Reform

In his forward to the draft Offences Against the Person Bill 1998, the then Home Secretary, Jack Straw, summed up the problems with the existing law, the need for reform and the aims of the proposed reform:

"The criminal law that applies to violence against the person derives from both common and statute law, but the unrepealed parts of the Offences Against the Person Act 1861 provide the bulk of the statutory offences. That Act was itself not a coherent restatement of the law, but a consolidation of much older law. It is therefore not surprising that the law has been widely criticised as archaic and unclear and that it is now in urgent need of reform. Reforming the law on violence against the person is not just an academic exercise—criminal cases involving non-fatal offences against the person make up a large part of the work of the courts and cost a great deal of taxpayers money … It is therefore particularly important that the law governing such behaviour should be robust, clear and well understood. Unclear or uncertain criminal law risks creating injustice and unfairness to individuals as well as making the work of the police and courts far more difficult and time-consuming. The Government's aim is that the proposed new offences should enable violence to be dealt with effectively by the courts and that the law should be set out in clear terms and in plain, modern language."

Despite this statement concerning the importance of reform, it is now several years since the Bill was published and, with no steps towards enactment in the meantime, it seems unlikely that this Bill will ever reach the statute books. The Bill proposes replacing the existing assault offences with the following:

1(1) A person is guilty of an offence if he intentionally causes serious injury to another. (maximum of life imprisonment)

2(1) A person is guilty of an offence if he recklessly causes serious injury to another. (maximum of 7 years on indictment, 6 months and/or a fine summarily)

3(1) A person is guilty of an offence if he intentionally or recklessly causes injury to another. (maximum of 5 years on indictment, 6 months and/or a fine summarily)

4(1) A person is guilty of an offence if—

    (a) he intentionally or recklessly applies force to or causes an impact on the body of another, or

    (b) he intentionally or recklessly causes the other to believe that any such force or impact is imminent.

(2) No such offence is committed if the force or impact, not being intended or likely to cause injury, is in the circumstances such as is generally acceptable in the ordinary conduct of daily life and the defendant does not know or believe that it is in fact unacceptable to the other person. (maximum of 6 months and/or a fine)

Racially and Religiously Aggravated Assaults

Racially aggravated assaults were introduced by the Crime and Disorder Act 1998 which was later amended by the Anti-terrorism, Crime and Security Act 2001 to include religiously aggravated assaults. Section 29 of the 1998 Act (as amended) provides that it is an offence if a person commits a common assault, s.47 or s.20 offence which is racially or religiously aggravated. Section 32 extends this to an offence under s.2 or s.4 of the Protection from Harassment Act 1997 (below). Where an offence is committed under either provision, the maximum penalties which can be imposed are higher than for the equivalent non-racially or religiously aggravated crime. Thus, for example, five years is the maximum penalty for a s.47 or s.20 offence whereas the maximum penalty for the racially or religiously aggravated versions of these offences is seven years. In respect of common assault, the maximum penalty increases from six months to two years. Offences under s.18 OAPA 1861 are not included in the statute, presumably because the maximum penalty for such offences is already life imprisonment, which cannot be increased.

Meaning of Racially or Religiously Aggravated

Section 28 of the 1998 Act provides that there are two ways in which an offence may be racially or religiously aggravated:

1. if at the time of committing the offence, or immediately before or after doing so, hostility was demonstrated towards the victim based on the victim's membership (or presumed membership) of a racial or religious group (s.28(1)(a));
2. if the offence is motivated (wholly or partly) by hostility towards members of a racial or religious group based on their membership of that group (s.28(1)(b)).

RACIAL GROUP

A racial group means a group of persons defined by reference to race, colour, nationality (including citizenship) or ethnic or national origins (s.28(4)). In **White [2001] 1 W.L.R. 1352**, the Court of Appeal held that racial group should be given a broad, non-technical, meaning as generally used in common parlance. On the facts, the word "African" did describe a "racial group" defined by reference to race as:

> "[i]n ordinary speech, the word 'African' denotes a limited group of people regarded as of common stock and regarded as one of the major divisions of humankind having in common distinct physical features. It denotes a personal characteristic of the blacks of Africa."

The court also held that a racially aggravated offence may be committed by one member of a racial group against another member of the same racial group.

In **Rogers [2007] 2 A.C. 62**, D had shouted "bloody foreigners" and "go back to your own country" at three Spanish women. He was convicted of a racially aggravated public order offence and appealed. His submission that his offence was not racially aggravated because he had not shown hostility to a particular group (he had not said "bloody Spaniards"), merely to foreigners as a whole, was rejected by the House of Lords. Baroness Hale, giving the leading judgment, emphasised the need for a flexible non-technical approach to the meaning of "racial group", stating that it is "[t]he context which will illuminate what the conduct shows." Adopting this approach led the court to conclude that those who are not of British origin constitute a racial group for the purposes of the statute.

RELIGIOUS GROUP

A religious group means a group of persons defined by reference to religious belief or lack of religious belief (s.28(5)). Religious belief is not defined in the statute.

The Act extends to *presumed* membership of a racial or religious group so that were the defendant to attack his victim in the mistaken belief that the victim belonged to a particular racial or religious group, the offence would still be made out.

"BASED ON"

There is no requirement that the prosecution establish that D's sole reason for the alleged hostility was V's race or religion. Therefore, the offence can be made out even where there are additional grounds for D's hostility.

HOSTILITY DEMONSTRATED TOWARDS THE VICTIM OR WHOLLY OR PARTLY MOTIVATED BY HOSTILITY, ETC.

It is only necessary to establish *either* the demonstration of hostility (28(1)(a)) or that the offence was motivated by hostility, etc. (28(1)(b)); not both (**DPP v Green (2004), The Times, July 7**).

Section 28(1)(a) imposes an objective test and the prosecution need only prove the behaviour; no motive is required (**R. on the application of Jones) v Bedfordshire and Mid Bedfordshire Magistrates' Court (LTL February 19, 2010)**. Whether the words used actually demonstrated racial hostility is a question of fact for the jury (**DPP v Howard [2008] EWHC 608 (Admin)**). The demonstration of hostility may occur in the absence of the victim of the substantive offence (**Parry v DPP [2004] EWHC 3112**) but must have occurred either at the time of the offence, immediately before or immediately after the substantive offence (*Parry v DPP*). The most obvious example of demonstrating hostility would be a racial or religious insult directed against the victim.

Under section 28(1)(b), the motivation behind the defendant's behaviour must be proved. Unlike an offence based on the demonstration of hostility, one based on motivation by hostility can be based on evidence of what the defendant has said or done on previous occasions (**G v DPP (2004) 148 S.J.L.B. 149**).

Stalking and the Protection from Harassment Act 1997

Stalking and harassment have become particular problems in recent years. Perhaps one of the reasons is an increase in the availability of indirect methods of communication, such as emailing and text messaging. A long campaign of anonymous intimidation can cause fear, anxiety, depression and worse. The phenomenon was recognised in the case of *Ireland and Burstow*, which was examined above, in which Lord Steyn commented:

> "My Lords, it is easy to understand the terrifying effect of a campaign of telephone calls at night by a silent caller to a woman living on her own. It would be natural for the victim to regard the calls as menacing. What may heighten her fear is that she will not know what the caller may do next ... Harassment of women by repeated silent telephone calls, accompanied on occasions by heavy breathing, is apparently a significant social problem. That the criminal law should be able to deal with this problem, and so far as is practicable, afford effective protection to victims is self-evident."

Harassment

Section 2 of the Protection from Harassment Act 1997 makes it an offence to pursue a course of conduct of harassment under s.1:

1(1) A person must not pursue a course of conduct—
(a) which amounts to harassment of another, and
(b) which he knows or ought to know amounts to harassment of the other.

(1A) A person must not pursue a course of conduct—
(a) which involves harassment of two or more persons, and
(b) which he knows or ought to know involves harassment of those persons, and
(c) by which he intends to persuade any person (whether or not one of those mentioned above)—
   (i) not to do something that he is entitled or required to do, or
   (ii) to do something that he is not under any obligation to do.

1(2) For the purposes of this section, the person whose course of conduct is in question ought to know that it amounts to or involves harassment of another if a reasonable person in possession of the same information would think the course of conduct amounted to or involved harassment of the other.

Under s.7(3), a "course of conduct" must generally involve conduct on at least two occasions against one person, or conduct on at least one occasion against two or more persons. Under subs.(2), harassment includes alarming the person or causing the person distress, but not necessarily both (**DPP v Ramsdale [2001] EWHC Admin 106**). According to the High Court in **Hipgrave v Jones [2004] EWHC 2901**, harassment can cover a very wide range of conduct. It may involve actions alone, or words alone (s.7(4)), or both. Examples given include actions which may be so grave as to amount to criminal offences against public order, or against the person under the 1861 Act. Acts of harassment may cause serious alarm or they may be little more than insensitive behaviour, so long as they cause distress. Words may be, at one extreme, incitements to, or threats of, violence that cause alarm, or at the other, unwelcome text messages sent, for example, to a woman wrongly thought of by D to be his girlfriend.

Whilst there must be conduct against one person on two occasions, the court must remember that the two occasions in question must be part of a "course" of activity. For example, in **Kelly v DPP [2002] EWHC 1428**, it was decided that listening to three telephone messages made in five minutes but heard at the same time, did amount to a course of conduct. In **Lau v DPP [2000] Crim. L.R. 580**, the Divisional Court held that whilst a minimum of two incidents are necessary the fewer the number of incidents and the further apart they are, the less likely that there will be a finding of harassment. However, there is no rule and it will depend upon the facts of each individual case. In **Baron v Crown Prosecution Service (June 13, 2000)**, two letters sent four-and-a-half months apart could be a course of conduct amounting to harassment. On the other hand, in **Curtis [2010] EWCA Crim 123**, a series of six incidents (most of them assaults), over the course of nine months during a volatile relationship where there had been aggression on both sides, did not constitute a course of conduct. In **Patel (Nitin) [2005] 1 Cr. App. R. 27**, the Court of Appeal directed that the issue is whether or not the incidents, however many there might have been, can properly be said to be so connected in type and in context as to justify the conclusion that they can amount to a course of conduct.

A further, and more serious offence, is provided in s.4.

Putting People in Fear of Violence

Section 4 of the Act makes it an offence where:

4(1) A person whose course of conduct causes another to fear, on at least two occasions, that violence will be used against him is guilty of an offence if he knows or ought to know that his course of conduct will cause the other so to fear on each of those occasions.

4(2) For the purposes of this section, the person whose course of conduct is in question ought to know that it will cause another to fear that violence will be used against him on any occasion if a reasonable person in possession of the same information would think the course of conduct would cause the other so to fear on that occasion.

There can be cases where the requirements of s.4 are met in relation to two persons, provided the course of conduct causes one complainant to fear, on at least two occasions, that violence will be used against him, as opposed to another. In **Caurti v DPP [2002] Crim. L.R. 131**, D had not committed offences under s.4 when he caused a wife to fear violence would be used against her husband, nor when the husband feared violence was to be used against his wife.

The offence under s.2 (above) is triable summarily only, but the more serious offence under s.4 is triable either way. Where a s.4 offence is tried at the Crown Court, it is open for the judge to direct the jury that if it finds D not guilty of the s.4 offence, it may find him guilty of an offence under s.2 (this is by virtue of the provisions in s.4(5)). However a judge must be careful to direct the jury correctly on each count where this is done. In **Patel (Nitin) [2005] 1 Cr. App. R. 27**, the Court of Appeal allowed D's appeal following conviction for a s.2 offence (having been acquitted of the s.4 offence) as the trial judge's direction was deficient. All the judge had said was that a "course of conduct" meant conduct on at least two occasions. The issue for the jury should have been whether or not the incidents, however many there might have been, could properly be said to be so connected in type and in context as to conclude that they amounted to a course of conduct (*Lau v DPP* (above)).

The Mens Rea of the Harassment Offences

The mens rea under both ss.1(1) and 4(1) involve both subjective (the defendant "knows") and objective (he "ought to know") tests. It is no defence for D to say he did not realise the victim would find the conduct distressing where it would have been obvious to the reasonable person that D's conduct amounted to harassment. Further, D will still be liable if he knows it is harassment but the reasonable person would not consider it to be so.

The leading case here is **R. v C (Sean Peter) [2001] EWCA Crim 1251**. The defendant, a paranoid schizophrenic, sent letters to his Member of Parliament on a number of occasions which included some threats of violence and death. D appealed against conviction on the grounds that the judge should have directed the jury to consider his mental disorder as a relevant condition of the reasonable man. However, the appeal was dismissed. The Divisional

Court reviewed the purpose of the 1997 Act and found that "stalking" was particularly likely to be committed by offenders with obsessive or unusual psychological makeup. If the statute were to be construed as defence counsel submitted, the result would be to remove the protection afforded to a large number of victims, which could not have been the intention of Parliament.

Specific Defences to Harassment

Under ss.1(3) and 4(3), no offence is committed if a defendant can show that the course of conduct was pursued for the purpose of preventing or detecting crime, or under any other statute or rule of law or that in the particular circumstances the pursuit of the course of conduct was reasonable (under subs.4(3)(c) it must have been reasonable for the protection of himself or another or for the protection of his or another's property.)

Over to you...

Consider the prolific use of internet-based social networking sites, such as Facebook. In your view, would bullying amount to an offence or offences under the Protection from Harassment Act 1997? Do you think it is appropriate to criminalise such behaviour?

STALKING; OFFENCES AGAINST THE PERSON ACT 1861 OR PROTECTION FROM HARASSMENT ACT 1997?

Because of the rule against duplicity, an offender cannot be charged under both the 1861 and the 1997 Acts for conduct amounting to harassment, but the prosecution can pursue him under one or the other, bearing in mind some of the issues raised in the figure below.

FIGURE 5.1 **Illustration of issues which arise when prosecuting stalking cases under the 1861 and 1997 Acts**

Offence	Where the harassment includes threats of violence	Where the harassment is by silence, such as in *Ireland*
Section 47 OAPA	A threat alone is an assault but is insufficient to form the basis of s.47 unless there is actual bodily harm in the form of psychological/psychiatric harm. There are also issues	V must fear the application of force, harm or violence (for the assault). It may take time for V to have such a fear (usually victims of silent phone calls go through confusion, denial, anger and frustration before fear). As with threats, V must suffer psychological/ psychiatric harm

	of the immediacy of the threatened harm, but the prosecution should be able to prove intent or at least recklessness as to causing V to apprehend harm.	and there is the issue of immediacy. The prosecution must also be able to prove that D intended or foresaw that V would apprehend force, harm or violence. This is an entirely subjective test and, say, D foresaw that V might be confused but not afraid then strictly, D must be acquitted.
Section 20 or 18 OAPA	The threat itself is not an infliction/causing harm. Section 20/18 can be made out only if the effect of the threat is to cause V to suffer serious psychological/psychiatric harm. For the mens rea of s.20, the prosecution must prove D foresaw V might suffer some psychological/ psychiatric harm. The mens rea of s.18, i.e. intention to cause GBH in the sense of serious psychological/ psychiatric harm will be harder to establish.	Silence is not an infliction/causing of GBH per se, but if the effect of silent phone calls is to cause serious psychological/psychiatric harm, then the actus reus is established. For s.20 the prosecution must prove D foresaw V might suffer some psychological/psychiatric harm. For s.18, the mens rea of intention to cause GBH in the sense of serious psychological/psychiatric harm will be harder to establish.
Sections 2 or 4 PHA	The maximum sentence under s.2 is only six months and the prosecution may feel that is insufficient to reflect the gravity of D's actions. The sentence under s.4 is five years (the same maximum as for both ss.47 and 20 above) but under s.4(1), V must fear that violence will be used against him, not might nor could. The prosecution may feel unable to meet its proof burden on that matter.	The mens rea for both ss.2 and 4 offences are both subjective and objective; note that D can be convicted even if he did not realise the effect of his conduct if a reasonable person would think the course of conduct amounted to harassment (s.2) or would cause V to have fear of violence (s.4).

Consent

Assaults such as those mentioned above are criminal only if done without the valid consent of the person affected; that is, the person who would otherwise be the "victim" if he had not consented. Although consent is often referred to as a "defence", it is not for the defendant to prove. Instead, it is an assertion by the defendant that the prosecution cannot satisfy its burden of proof with respect to the crime as charged.

Is Consent a True Defence?

An important but rather complex distinction can be made at this stage. Some defences are genuine defences; that is, the prosecution can establish that the defendant performed the actus reus with the mens rea, but nonetheless, the defendant is not guilty because he has an excuse in the form of a defence. The defence of duress is an example of an excusatory defence (see Ch.13). On the other hand, what is referred to as a "defence" may in fact operate to negative an ingredient of the definition of the offence itself. Instead of excusing the conduct, it justifies the conduct so that there is, in fact, no actus reus. Prevailing wisdom has it that consent is such a defence. In the definition of each of the non-fatal offences above, the force applied to V had to be unlawful force. Any force applied by the defendant to another with the other's consent, cannot be *unlawful* force. This means that valid consent negates the actus reus of the crime; there is no actus reus. This view prevailed in **Kimber [1983] 1 W.L.R. 1118 CA**, approved by the House of Lords in **B v DPP [2000] 2 A.C. 428**.

By contrast however, the majority's obiter view in **Brown [1994] 1 A.C. 212 HL**, was that the absence of consent was not a "definitional" element of the crime so that the presence of consent would not negate the actus reus. Rather, consent was simply a defence which operated in a similar way as duress. Normally this makes no difference to the end result, but there is one area where it seems to be a critical distinction and that is where D makes a mistake that the victim is consenting. We return to mistake in Ch.12.

Valid Consent

We have seen already in this chapter that the slightest touching of someone can constitute a battery. However, it would be impossible to carry on normal day-to-day activities if, say, every time a person was nudged in a queue, jostled in a busy shop or street or shook someone's hand without first asking their permission, criminal liability ensued. Consequently, the criminal law holds that such conduct is impliedly consented to and no battery is committed, see dicta of Robert Goff L.J. in **Collins v Wilcock [1984] 3 All E.R. 374**.

A victim may appear to have consented but the consent is invalid and the defendant is liable. For example, in certain circumstances consent obtained by fraud is invalid (see pp.165–166) and, at times, a person is prevented from giving consent in law even where they may have apparently consented in fact (see pp.161–165). If the victim is not capable of giving consent, or is too young to understand the nature of the act, his apparent consent will be legally invalid. For example, a person cannot give consent;

1. to their own murder or
2. to sexual intercourse if he or she is a child or
3. where they are too young to understand the nature of the act. In **Burrell v Harmer [1967] Crim. L.R. 169**, the apparent consent of two boys aged 12 and 13 to being tattooed was invalid.

The Public Interest and Valid Consent

Lord Lane C.J. in **Attorney General's Reference (No.6 of 1980) [1981] Q.B. 715** said that:

> "it is not in the public interest that people should try to cause or should cause each other actual bodily harm for no good reason ... it is an assault if actual bodily harm is intended and/or caused."

The facts of the case involved two young men who had a quarrel and then agreed to have a fist fight, which resulted in actual bodily harm being caused to one of them. Fighting is not in the public interest so their apparent consent was legally invalid.

It is, however, implicit from the statement above that even where actual bodily harm or worse is caused, if there is a good reason for an activity then consent may operate as a defence. The House of Lords also recognised this in **Brown [1994] 1 A.C. 212**, widely regarded as the leading case on consent (see p.164 below). On the facts, the apparent consent of the participants to acts of sadomasochism was not in the public interest. Lord Templeman held that:

> "Society is entitled and bound to protect itself against a cult of violence. Pleasure derived from the infliction of pain is an evil thing. Cruelty is uncivilised."

On the other hand, a good reason for an activity will exist where the public interest requires consent to operate. Clearly, then, as the public's view of an activity changes, so will the courts' approach as to whether there is a good reason for it. For example, it was once not possible for a man to consent to a vasectomy operation merely to avoid pregnancy (**Bravery v Bravery [1954] 3 All E.R. 59**) but this procedure is now lawful.

Medical surgery for therapeutic reasons (and possibly also for cosmetic purposes or organ transplantation) is considered in the public interest as is participation in a "dangerous exhibition", i.e. a circus act or stunt show (**Attorney General's Reference (No.6 of 1980)**). So also, in certain circumstances, is participation in sport and even rough horseplay (considered below). In *Brown*, their Lordships recognised that ear piercing, ritual circumcision of males and religious flagellation would be "good reasons" as would tattooing. This was also the stance taken in relation to branding the victim in **Wilson [1996] 2 Cr. App. R. 241.** D, at his wife's request, branded his initials on her buttocks with a hot knife. The wounds became infected and D was convicted of assault occasioning actual bodily harm contrary to s.47 of the Offences against the Person Act 1861. His appeal against conviction was allowed because:

1. his desire was to assist his wife "in what she regarded as the acquisition of a desirable piece of personal adornment, perhaps in this day and age no less understandable than the piercing of nostrils or even tongues for the purposes of inserting decorative jewellery", and
2. there was no aggressive intent on the part of the husband (see further below at p.163), and
3. it was not in the public interest that such consensual activity between husband and wife in the privacy of the matrimonial home should be a matter for criminal prosecution.

CONSENT IN SPORTS

A person can consent to the risk of an accidental injury occurring during a properly conducted contact sport such as football or rugby (**Barnes [2005] 2 All E.R. 113**). With regards to boxing, a person can consent to the deliberate infliction of harm by his opponent where the bout takes place under the governing bodies' rules (see obiter statements in *Brown*). The position must also be the same where a person takes part in a properly conducted martial art. We know from *Attorney General's Reference (No.6 of 1980)* above, that where D deliberately injures V outside a "field" of play, this is not tolerated on grounds of public policy. This begs the question: What is the position where harm occurs on the field of play but outside the rules of play? The Court of Appeal in **Barnes [2005] 2 ALL E.R.113** reviewed the previous case law and we can extract the following general rules from the decision:

1. Most organised sports have their own disciplinary procedures for enforcing their particular rules and standards of conduct. Criminal prosecution should therefore be reserved for those situations where the conduct is sufficiently grave properly to be categorised as criminal.
2. Whether the conduct reached the objective threshold level for it to be criminal depends on all the circumstances; and the type of sport, the level at which it was played, the nature of the act, the degree of force used, the extent of the risk of injury and the state of mind of the defendant are all likely to be relevant in that regard. The fact that play was within the rules and practice of the game and did not go beyond it is a firm indication that what had occurred was not criminal. Further, it must be borne in mind that, in highly competitive sports, conduct outside of the rules might be expected

to occur in the heat of the moment, and even if the conduct justified not only being penalised but also a warning or even a sending off, the threshold level required for it to be criminal might not be reached.

CONSENT TO HORSEPLAY

A person can give valid consent to the risk of harm occasioned during rough and undisciplined horseplay, provided there is no intention to harm (**Jones (1986) 83 Cr. App. R. 375**, in which teenagers seriously injured other teenage boys when they tossed them in the air during "the bumps" but accidentally failed to catch them). The Courts-Martial Appeal Court also accepted the existence of the "horseplay" exception in **Aitken [1992] 1 W.L.R. 1006**. RAF officers at a mess party set fire to the fire-resistant clothing of a fellow officer who treated it as a joke. V sustained severe burns but the Appeal Court ruled that a finding by the lower court that the defence of consent was not available was incorrect.

SEXUAL ACTIVITY

Where injury is caused during non-sadomasochistic sexual activity but there is no "aggressive intent," there is no liability. In **Slingsby [1995] Crim. L.R. 570**, for example, the defendant was not liable where the victim died as a result of an injury which was accidentally caused during consensual sexual activity. D, with V's consent, had penetrated V's vagina and rectum with his hand. V suffered cuts caused by the D's signet ring, but she did not realise the serious nature of the injuries. When she later died of septicaemia as a result of the cuts D was charged with manslaughter based on an unlawful and dangerous act. Proof of manslaughter in this case depended on proof of an assault which caused death, but the judge at the Crown Court in Nottingham held that the sexual activity to which both parties had agreed had not involved the deliberate infliction of injury or harm and, but for the fact that D was wearing a signet ring, no injury at all would have been caused or could have been contemplated. V had sustained her unfortunate injuries as an accidental consequence of the sexual activity which had taken place with her consent. *Brown* was distinguished because there was no aggressive intent on the part of the defendant. A similar approach was taken in *Wilson*, considered above at p.162) and in **Meachen [2006] EWCA Crim 2414**. In the latter case, the Court of Appeal held that the prosecution must show that D intended to cause some bodily harm or caused such harm reck-lessly. The case against D was that he had administered drugs to the victim, had anal inter-course with her and inserted a large object into her anus while she was unconscious, causing her very serious injuries. The defence case was that the victim had consented to taking drugs with D, that D had, with the victim's consent, used his fingers to penetrate her anus and she had moved vigorously up and down on them. On appeal, the Court of Appeal agreed with D's submission that, in the absence of any acceptance by him that he intended some injury to the victim or foresaw the risk of injury, the judge could not have ruled that there was no defence in law to the s.20 offence or the indecent assault.

The Public Interest and Invalid Consent

The dicta in *Attorney General's Reference (No.6 of 1980)* (see p.161 above) and its approval by the House in *Brown*, has not received universal support. It is the phrase "intended and/or caused" which is controversial; it has created two problems of interpretation. First, the reference by the court to "intended and/or caused" suggests that even if actual bodily harm is not caused, but is intended, V's consent is invalid and D is liable for a battery. Dicta in **Boyea (1992) 156 J.P. 505**, is also to this effect. However, in *Barnes*, the Court of Appeal stated that there would be no liability in such circumstances. Secondly, the phrase also seems to imply that where actual bodily harm is *caused*, the intention or foresight of the defendant as to actual bodily harm is irrelevant. That said, more recent cases have approached the matter as if the phrase read intended *and* caused, omitting the "or". That was the situation in both *Slingsby* and *Meachen* above. It now seems consent will only be invalid where there is the deliberate (or possibly even reckless, as in *Emmett* below) infliction of injury plus the conduct is not in the public interest.

SADOMASOCHISM

In *Brown*, the appellants were a group of sadomasochists, who had willingly and enthusiastically participated in the commission of acts of violence against each other for the sexual pleasure it engendered in the giving and receiving of pain. They were convicted of various offences under ss.20 and 47 of the Offences against the Person Act 1861 relating to the infliction of wounds or actual bodily harm on genital and other areas of the body of the consenting victim. They appealed against conviction on the ground that consent prevented the prosecution from proving an essential element of the offence. Their convictions were upheld, the majority of their Lordships holding that, as actual bodily harm was intended and caused, consent was irrelevant, there being no public interest in causing harm during sadomasochistic activity. Lord Templeman in the majority said:

> "In some circumstances violence is not punishable under the criminal law. When no actual bodily harm is caused, the consent of the person affected precludes him from complaining. There can be no conviction for the ... offence of common assault if the victim has consented ... Even when violence is intentionally inflicted and results in ... wounding or serious bodily harm the accused is entitled to be acquitted if the injury was a foreseeable incident of a lawful activity in which the person injured was participating. The violence of sadomasochistic encounters involves the indulgence of cruelty by sadists and the degradation of victims. Such violence is injurious to the participants and unpredictably dangerous. I am not prepared to invent a defence of consent for sadomasochistic encounters which breed and glorify cruelty and result in offences under sections 47 and 20 of the Act of 1861."

A later appeal to the European Court of Human Rights was also unsuccessful (**Laskey v United Kingdom (1997) 24 E.H.R.R. 39**) as it was held that State interference in this aspect of private life could be justified on the basis of "protection of health".

The decision in *Brown* was followed in **Emmett (1999), The Times, October 15**. V had suffered very serious injuries as a result of (consensual) sadomasochistic sexual practices with her partner. The injuries were caused as a result of asphyxiation and her breasts being burnt by lighter fluid. D's conviction for recklessly occasioning actual bodily harm was upheld by the Court of Appeal. The court accepted that *Brown* was not authority in all circumstances where consent was a contentious issue, but *Wilson* (above) would be distinguished as that case involved consensual behaviour between husband and wife and there was no evidence of significant harm. In the instant case, the potential damage was far greater, a fact of which D was aware. Where the realistic risk went beyond transient injury, the issue of consent became immaterial. The emphasis of the Court of Appeal on the spousal relationship in *Wilson* (which could be distinguished here) is surely a relic of the last century. On the other hand, this case clarified that the law makes no distinction between homosexual and heterosexual sadomasochism; neither is in the public interest.

FRAUD

Not all frauds, lies or failures to tell the whole truth will negate consent. It all depends on the precise issue or matter to which the fraud relates, as illustrated below.

■ Fraud as to identity

The issue of identity fraud arose in **Richardson [1998] 3 W.L.R. 1292**, when patients were unaware that their dentist had been suspended by the General Dental Council. The Court of Appeal held that in these circumstances an assault could occur only where consent was given in the mistaken belief that the dentist was someone other than she truly was. In the instant case, whilst the complainants had been unaware that D was no longer qualified to practise, they were fully aware of her identity and their consent negated any assault.

■ Fraud as to the nature and quality of the act

In **Tabassum [2000] 2 Cr. App. R. 328**, the defendant was convicted of three counts of indecent assault against three different complainants. He had asked several women to take part in a breast cancer survey he was carrying out in order to prepare a software package to sell to doctors. The women consented to D showing them how to carry out a breast self-examination which involved them undressing and allowing D to feel their breasts. Each complainant said she had only consented because she thought D had medical qualifications or relevant training. He had no such medical training, but there was no evidence of sexual motive. The Court of Appeal dismissed D's appeal, agreeing with the trial judge that consent had been given only because the complainants had mistakenly believed that D was medically qualified or had had relevant training and, therefore, the consent was for medical purposes only. In the circumstances, there was no true consent since the complainants were consenting to touching for medical purposes, not to indecent behaviour. There was, accordingly, consent to the nature of the act but not to its quality.

The same conclusion might have been drawn from the facts in **Clarence (1888) 22 Q.B. 23**, but in this case the defendant's appeals against conviction under ss.47 and 20 OAPA 1861 were allowed despite the fact that he had infected his wife with gonorrhoea. It appeared that, knowing he was infected, he had sexual intercourse with his wife, without telling her of the infection, with the result that the disease was communicated to her. It was clear from evidence at trial that, had she been aware of his condition, she would not have submitted to the intercourse. Using the reasoning from *Tabassum*, we might conclude that the wife had consented to the nature of the act (sexual intercourse) but not the quality (infection with a disease). However, the distinction between the nature and quality of the act was not considered in *Clarence*, where Wills J. gave the following analogy:

> "[For the Crown it was argued] that the husband was guilty of a fraud in concealing the fact of his illness; that her consent was therefore obtained by fraud, and was, therefore, no consent at all … This reasoning seems to me eminently unsatisfactory. That consent obtained by fraud is no consent at all is not true as a general proposition either in fact or in law. If a man meets a woman in the street and knowingly gives her bad money in order to procure her consent to intercourse with him, he obtains her consent by fraud, but it would be childish to say that she did not consent …"

Clarence is, however, no longer good law. The criminal law has imported the concept of informed consent form the civil law in the significant case of *Dica*, below.

INFORMED CONSENT

In **Dica [2004] 3 W.L.R. 213**, the defendant, who knew he was HIV positive, had unprotected sexual intercourse with two women on a number of occasions. They both became infected with the virus. D was convicted by a jury of recklessly inflicting grievous bodily harm contrary to s.20 OAPA 1861, following the trial judge's decision that the women's consent was irrelevant. D appealed against his conviction and was later convicted on retrial in 2005. On the first appeal, Judge L.J. stated:

> "These victims consented to sexual intercourse. Accordingly, the appellant was not guilty of rape. Given the long-term nature of the relationships, if the appellant concealed the truth about his condition from them, and therefore kept them in ignorance of it, there was no reason for them to think that they were running any risk of infection, and they were not consenting to it. On this basis, there would be no consent sufficient in law to provide the appellant with a defence to the charge under [the OAPA 1861] s.20."

The victim's knowledge of the defendant's condition at the time of intercourse is therefore crucial on a charge under s.20. Accordingly, if the victim gives consent knowing of the defendant's condition there is no liability, but if the victim consents in ignorance of the defendant's condition, guilt results. Knowledge of the risk is a prerequisite of consent to it. This sensible and logical decision overrules *Clarence* which is now recognised as contrary to principle (consent to sexual intercourse is no longer regarded as the same thing as consent to the risk of disease or injury).

The Court of Appeal in *Dica* also appeared to draw the distinction between consent under s.20 and consent where the harm was intended (in light of the decision in *Brown*, above):

> "... [T]he Crown did not allege, and we therefore are not considering the deliberate infection, or spreading of HIV with intent to cause grievous bodily harm. In such circumstances, the application of what we may describe as the principle in Brown [1994] 1 AC 212 means that the agreement of the participants would provide no defence to a charge under section 18 of the 1861 Act."

In **Konzani [2005] EWCA Crim 706**, D, knowing he was HIV positive, had unprotected sexual intercourse with three women without telling any of them that he was HIV positive. All three of the women contracted the HIV virus. Following conviction for offences contrary to s.20, it was D's argument before the Court of Appeal that by consenting to unprotected sexual intercourse with him, the complainants had impliedly consented to all the risks associated with sexual intercourse. He argued that as infection with the HIV virus is only one possible consequence of unprotected sexual intercourse, the complainants had consented to the risk of contracting the HIV virus from him. The Court of Appeal dismissed his appeal. It was clear following *Dica* that, as D had not disclosed his condition to the complainants, their consent to sexual intercourse could not prevent liability. For a complainant's consent to relevant risks to provide a defence, her consent had to be an informed consent.

Konzani had also argued on appeal that his honest belief in the complainants' consent should negate his liability. The Court of Appeal was not convinced, holding that on facts such as these any such honest belief must be concomitant with the consent. A complainant could not give an informed consent to something of which she was ignorant and, in such circumstances, silence was incompatible with honesty, or with a genuine belief that there was an informed consent. Accordingly, a defence of honest belief in consent would not be available where consent itself would not provide a defence.

Summary

1. Assault and battery are common law offences. An assault requires D to intentionally or recklessly cause V to apprehend immediate and unlawful force. An assault can be committed by words alone and even by a silent phone call. Words accompanying a threatening gesture may cancel out the assault or reinforce it depending on the words used. A battery requires the intentional or reckless infliction (either direct or indirect) of unlawful force.

2. Assault occasioning actual bodily harm is a statutory offence, contrary to s.47 OAPA 1861. Actual bodily harm is any hurt or injury calculated to interfere with the health or comfort of the victim. It need not be permanent but must be more than trifling. It can include psychiatric injury. The mens rea is that for an assault or battery.

3. Section 20 may be committed by maliciously wounding or inflicting grievous bodily harm. Section 18 may be committed by maliciously wounding or causing grievous bodily harm with intent. A wound requires a break in both the layers of the skin. Grievous bodily harm is serious harm. There is no practical difference between "inflict" in s.20 and "cause" in s.18. The factor distinguishing the two sections is the mens rea. The mens rea for s.20 is maliciously which means intention or recklessness as to doing some physical harm; the mens rea for s.18 is intention to do grievous bodily harm or to resist or prevent the lawful apprehension or detainer of any person.

4. Summary of liability, see figure 5.2

FIGURE 5.2 **Summary of liability**

Injury (Actus Reus)	Mens Rea	Offence
Serious harm or a wound	+ Intention to do serious harm or to resist, etc.	= s.18
Serious harm or a wound	+ Intention or recklessness as to doing some physical harm	= s.20
Serious harm or a wound	+ Intention or recklessness as to inflicting, or causing the apprehension of, unlawful force	= s.47
Actual bodily harm	+ Intention or recklessness as to inflicting, or causing the apprehension of, unlawful force	= s.47
The apprehension or infliction of unlawful force	+ Intention or recklessness as to inflicting, or causing the apprehension of, unlawful force	= Assault or Battery

5. The Protection from Harassment Act 1997 prohibits harassment (s.2) and putting people in fear of violence (s.4) on the basis of a course of conduct which D knows or ought to know amounts to harassment or will cause such fear.

6. A person who commits an assault or battery or an offence under s.47 or s.20 OAPA 1861 or ss.2 or 4 PHA 1997 which is racially or religiously motivated may receive a penalty which is more severe than that available for the offence under normal circumstances.

7. Consent

Where a "victim" gives a valid consent to harm, there is no liability. Consent may be rendered invalid by fraud as to identity or the nature or quality of the act. Consent involving the transmission of infectious diseases focuses liability on whether V knew and consented to the risk of infection. Informed consent may be valid to ABH or even GBH, but never to intentional harm. Otherwise, the availability of the defence depends on some or all of:

(a) the degree of harm;

(b) whether the harm was caused intentionally, recklessly, or even accidentally; and

(c) public policy.

....

FIGURE 5.3 **Summary of the effect of consent**
....

Assault or battery	**+ valid consent**	**= no liability**
Actual bodily harm or more serious injury	**+ valid consent**	**= liability**
Actual bodily harm or more serious injury	**+ valid consent + a public interest in the activity**	**= no liability**

◄..

End of Chapter Question

Question

Several months ago, Vera went on a blind date with Dean who lived locally and with whom she had been in telephone contact, having been introduced via an internet dating site. Vera was not attracted to Dean and refused to see him again. Dean, however, wanted to pursue a relationship. He began sending Vera emails requesting another date. When she did not reply, he started phoning her and sending numerous emails threatening to "hurt her" for treating him so badly. Vera began to suffer depression. One night, in an effort to cheer her up, Vera's friends, Sally and Linda, take her to a nightclub but Dean is already there. Sally sees Dean on the dance floor and begs him to leave Vera alone. Dean does not welcome this interference. He smashes the bottle he is carrying against a table at the side of the dance floor and lashes out at Sally with it but slips on some beer that has been spilt on the floor, loses his balance and hits Vera who is standing next to Sally. The bottle hits Vera's face, causing a deep cut to her cheek. Sally jumps backwards out of the way of the glass and falls onto Linda. The impact causes them both to tumble awkwardly to the ground. Linda breaks her arm and Sally suffers temporary concussion.

1. Consider the criminal liability of Dean.

Note; parts 2. and 3. of this question are at the end of Ch.12

Points of Answer

Dean may be liable for various non-fatal offences against the person and harassment.

♦ Threatening emails and phone calls, etc.

• This could be GBH or ABH depending on the severity of the depression and his mens rea (MR). The depression must be a recognised psychiatric illness, not merely distress, if it is to be ABH or GBH; otherwise it is only an assault. If not admitted by the defence, expert evidence will be required (*Chan-Fook*). If the depression is serious harm, it could be s.18/20 depending on MR. Define offences. Does he intend to cause her GBH by his emails and calls (MR for s.18) or does he just intend or foresee some harm (the MR for s.20; *Savage and Parmenter*)?

• If the injury is not GBH or he lacks MR for 18/20, it could be ABH under s.47. Define. An assault is required. An assault can be committed by both written and verbal words (*Constanza*). There is an issue of immediacy as he would not do anything straight away but, as he lives locally, she may think he could turn up at any time (*Constanza*). The assault occasions the ABH. Only the MR for the assault is required (*Savage and Parmenter*). Does he intend her to apprehend immediate and unlawful force?

• Liability could arise under ss.2 and 4 of the Protection from Harassment Act. Define offences. He may commit an offence under s.2 (a course of conduct amounting to harassment in breach of s.1) in respect of sending her emails asking for a date. MR satisfied if he ought to have known his conduct involved harassment as he did intend to persuade her to go out with him. He may commit an offence under s.4 in respect of the phone and email threats to "hurt her". Unlike the assault, there is no requirement that Vera fear "immediate" violence. MR satisfied as he will have known that his course of conduct would cause Vera to fear violence would be used against her.

- ◆ Deep cut to Vera's cheek
    - • This could be s.18/20 wounding depending on MR—whether he intended GBH (an intention to wound is insufficient for s.18; *Taylor*) or only some harm. Define offences. Section 18 is the more likely offence as he smashed the bottle and lashed out with it. A deep cut would constitute a wound (*Eisenhower*). He does not intend GBH/some harm to Vera but, applying the doctrine of transferred malice (*Latimer*), MR is transferred from the intended victim (Sally) to the unintended victim (Vera).
- ◆ Linda's broken arm
    - • This could be s.18/20 GBH depending on Dean's MR re Sally. There is an issue of causation as the injury is indirectly caused by Sally jumping out of the way and falling onto Linda. He is both the factual (but-for) and legal (operating and substantial; *Smith*) cause of her injury. "Inflict" in s.20 does not require the application of force by D; it means essentially the same as cause (*Ireland and Burstow*). So, if Dean only possessed the MR for s.20, he could be liable for inflicting GBH.
- ◆ Sally's concussion
    - • Temporary concussion is ABH (*T v DPP*) so this could be a s.47. There is an issue of causation as Sally is hurt indirectly when she falls jumping out of the way. Occasioning means cause (*Roberts*) and Dean is clearly both the factual and legal cause of Sally's injury—jumping out of the way is not a novus actus interveniens (*Roberts*). MR is that for assault or battery (*Savage and Parmenter*). This can be satisfied as he had at least the MR for an assault.

Further Reading

C.M.V. Clarkson, "Law Commission Report on Offences against the Person and General Principles: (1) Violence and the Law Commission" [1994] Crim. L.R. 324.

N. Geach, "Regulating Harassment: Is the Law Fit for the Social Networking Age?" (2009) J.C.L. 73 (241)

J. Horder, "Reconsidering Psychic Assault" [1998] Crim. L.R. 392.

S. Leake and D. Ormerod, "Case Commentary on R v Dica" [2004] Crim. L.R. 944.

S. Ryan, "Reckless transmission of HIV: knowledge and culpability" [2006] Crim. L.R. 981

M. Weait, "Criminal Law and the Sexual Transmission of HIV: R v Dica" (2005) M.L.R. 121 and "Knowledge, Autonomy and Consent: R v Konzani" [2005] Crim. L.R. 763.

http://www.cps.gov.uk/legal/l_to_o/offences_against_the_person/

Self Test Questions

To test your knowledge gained from this section go online to *http://www.sweetandmaxwell.co.uk* and take our online self test questions. Here you will also find key updates to ensure that you are only ever one click away from an instant update.

Sexual Offences

6

In this chapter we:

- provide the definition and analyse the actus reus and mens rea requirements of the most serious sexual offences against adults contrary to the Sexual Offences Act 2003

- provide the definition and analyse the actus reus and mens rea requirements of a range of sexual offences against children contrary to the Sexual Offences Act 2003

- explore the concept of consent under the Sexual Offences Act 2003

Summary

End of Chapter Question

Further Reading

Self Test Questions

Introduction

There are many offences involving sexual misconduct; some are long established and some have been newly created by the Sexual Offences Act 2003 to criminalise activity which has been made possible only by the introduction of new technology and means of communication such as the internet (for example, the offence of sexual grooming).

The law relating to sexual offences was codified by the Sexual Offences Act 2003. The legislation did not just bring all sexual offences under one statutory umbrella; it changed the definitions of some offences (most notably rape), changed the titles of others and created new offences. These changes were deemed necessary by the Government because the existing law was seen as "archaic, incoherent and discriminatory" and did not reflect "changes in society and social attitudes" (per Lord Falconer L.C. in a speech to the House of Lords in 2003).

In this chapter we consider the main sexual offences involving adults (including rape, sexual assault, assault by penetration and causing another to engage in sexual activity) and we also mention the key elements of some of the other sexual crimes, such as family offences and the three preparatory offences. We then consider the sexual offences against children, noting the different elements from the adult crimes (notably an age requirement but no requirement of absence of consent) and then we analyse in full the concept of consent, which features both as part of the actus reus and the mens rea of most sexual offences against adults.

Rape

. . . .

The Offence of Rape

Section 1 of the 2003 Act provides a new definition of rape; the former definition being narrower in scope in that it only involved vaginal or anal sexual intercourse with a non-consenting complainant (who may also be referred to as the victim) where the defendant knew or was reckless as to whether his victim consented. The new offence includes oral, penile penetration and there is a change to the mens rea to involve a lack of a reasonable belief in consent. Section 1(1) provides:

> A person (A) commits an offence if—
> **(a)** he intentionally penetrates the vagina, anus or mouth of another person (B) with his penis,
> **(b)** B does not consent to the penetration, and
> **(c)** A does not reasonably believe that B consents.

The maximum sentence for rape is life imprisonment. The penalty is the same whether the penetration is of the mouth, anus or vagina; all three forms of rape are regarded as of equal gravity (**Ismail [2005] 2 Cr. App. R. 88**).

The Actus Reus of Rape

This involves:

1. a person;
2. who penetrates with his penis;
3. the vagina, anus or mouth of the complainant (who may be a man or a woman);
4. who does not consent to the penetration.

PERSON

Although the statute refers to "a person", this offence may only be committed by a man as principal because of the requirement of penile penetration. As the Act permits parts of the body to include those which have been surgically reconstructed, the offence may also be committed by a transsexual who has been given a surgically constructed penis.

PENETRATION

Penile penetration of the complainant's vagina (includes the vulva (s.79(3) and a surgically constructed vagina), anus or mouth is required. Prior to the 2003 Act, the prosecution could establish penetration of the vagina merely by proof that there was entry, however slight; it was not necessary to further prove that the hymen was ruptured (**Hughes (1841) 9 Car. & P. 752**) or that seed was emitted (Sexual Offences Act 1956 s.44). The 2003 Act does not provide any guidance on the degree of penetration required so one must assume that the common law position still applies and that it extends to cover those situations where the anus or mouth is penetrated.

The Act states that penetration is a continuing act from entry to withdrawal (s.79(2)). Hence, if the defendant continues to penetrate after consent has been withdrawn and he knows consent has been withdrawn, he is guilty of rape. How much time a man has to withdraw before his failure to do so will constitute rape is unclear but it was the Government's view when the Act was proceeding through Parliament that he would be allowed a "reasonable time" in which to withdraw; what is "reasonable" is to be determined by the jury, which will inevitably lead to inconsistent decisions.

ABSENCE OF CONSENT

It is rape if the complainant does not consent to penetration. Consent in the context of sexual offences is such a broad topic and, as consent is relevant not just to rape but also to the offences of sexual assault, assault by penetration and causing a person to engage in sexual activity, it is considered separately at the end of this chapter. For present purposes, it is sufficient to note that there is a definition of consent for the purposes of offences under the Act in s.74 and there are two presumptions concerning the complainant's lack of consent, the first evidential and the second conclusive, which arise under ss.75 and 76 respectively if certain specified circumstances apply.

The Mens Rea of Rape

The defendant must:

1. intend to penetrate the complainant; and
2. not reasonably believe that the complainant consents to the penetration.

The reference to reasonable belief in consent overrules **DPP v Morgan [1976] A.C. 182** (see Ch.12) in the context of rape so that D can no longer assert he lacked mens rea because he honestly, albeit unreasonably, believed his victim consented. A direction on lack of reasonable belief in consent is not required in every case; only those where there is evidence from which a jury might conclude that V did not consent but D thought she was consenting (**Taran [2006] EWCA Crim 1498**).

Section 1(2) (this provision is repeated in ss.2(2), 3(2) and 4(2) as the mens rea of a lack of reasonable belief applies to the ss.2, 3 and 4 offences also) provides:

> Whether a belief is reasonable is to be determined having regard to all the circumstances, including any steps [the defendant] has taken to ascertain whether [the complainant] consents.

When the 2003 Act was proceeding through Parliament, Government ministers suggested that the reference to "all the circumstances" would allow the jury to take into account the defendant's personal characteristics, i.e. to ask was it reasonable for *this* defendant to hold the belief he claims? If such a test were adopted, it might allow, for example, evidence of a defendant's learning difficulties or of a previous sexual relationship between D and V to be taken into account in assessing the reasonableness of D's belief. However, at the time of writing, there is still no case law on this.

In **Whitta [2006] EWCA Crim 2626**, D pleaded guilty to assault by penetration under s.2 of the 2003 Act following the trial judge's ruling that "all the circumstances" in s.2(2) did not include mistaken identity. D had attended a party at V's house and had stayed over afterwards. During the night he climbed into V's bed and penetrated her vagina with his fingers. V told him to "fuck off" and he immediately apologised and left the room. D claimed that he had mistakenly believed S was sleeping in the bed and that it was S that he had penetrated. He had been flirting with S at the party and asserted that she had indicated she wished to continue matters after the party as she was also staying at the same house. The Court of Appeal disagreed with the trial judge's analysis that a mistake, however reasonable, as to the identity of the person to whom the sexual activity is directed is irrelevant to the mens rea of reasonable belief in consent.

The presumptions under ss.75 and 76 concerning consent which are considered at the end of this chapter (pp.198–202) apply also to the defendant's reasonable belief in consent. Consequently, the prosecution may rely on an evidential presumption (s.75) that the defendant did not reasonably believe that the complainant consented, or a conclusive presumption (s.76) to that effect.

Sexual Assault

The Offence of Sexual Assault

Section 3 creates the offence of sexual assault which replaces the old offence of indecent assault. It is a broad offence which can encompass at one end of the spectrum mere kissing, if considered sexual, and at the other end of the spectrum, touching a person's private parts. Section 3(1) provides:

> A person (A) commits an offence if—
> **(a)** he intentionally touches another person (B),
> **(b)** the touching is sexual,
> **(c)** B does not consent to the touching, and
> **(d)** A does not reasonably believe that B consents.

The maximum sentence for sexual assault is 10 years on indictment; six months if tried summarily.

The Actus Reus of Sexual Assault

This involves:

1. a person (a man or a woman);
2. who touches the complainant (a man or a woman);

3. sexually; and

4. the complainant does not consent to the touching.

TOUCHING

Although the s.3 offence is called sexual assault, it is not an assault in the technical sense but "touching" which must be established. Section 79(8) provides that touching includes touching with any part of the body, with anything else, through anything and touching amounting to penetration. Touching can also involve contact with V's clothing (**R. v H [2005] Crim. L.R. 735**).

Over to you...

Why do you think the s.3 offence requires touching rather then merely proof of an assault?

What does the "touching" requirement exclude from the ambit of the offence?

SEXUAL

The touching must be sexual, an issue to be decided by the jury. The term "sexual" also forms part of the actus reus of the offences of assault by penetration (s.2) and intentionally causing someone to engage in sexual activity (s.4). So, all comments made about this term in the context of sexual assault apply equally to these offences.

"Sexual" is explained in s.78 which provides:

... penetration, touching or any other activity is sexual if a reasonable person would consider that—

(a) whatever its circumstances or any person's purpose in relation to it, it is because of its nature sexual, or

(b) because of its nature it may be sexual and because of its circumstances or the purpose of any person in relation to it (or both) it is sexual.

This means that, as with the term "indecent" which preceded it, there are three possibilities concerning whether the touching, etc. (penetration or activity) is sexual. It may be:

1. sexual by nature;

2. capable of being sexual; or

3. objectively not sexual.

■ Sexual by nature

The touching, (etc.) is sexual by nature where a reasonable person would always consider it sexual, for example touching the complainant's private parts. In such circumstances, the touching, etc. is sexual regardless of the defendant's purpose.

■ Capable of being sexual

Where a reasonable person would consider that, because of its nature, the touching, etc. is ambiguous, i.e. it may or may not be sexual, but is capable of being sexual, the circumstances and/or the defendant's purpose can render the touching, etc. sexual.

A similar approach was taken by previous case law for the offence of indecent assault. In **Court [1989] A.C. 28**, D, a shop assistant, put a 12-year-old girl across his knee and spanked her bottom outside her shorts. When he was later asked by the police why he had done so, D replied "I don't know, buttock fetish." Spanking the girl's bottom was considered by the House of Lords to be an ambiguous action because, on the one hand, the buttocks are an intimate part of the body, though he had not spanked her bare bottom and, on the other hand, the buttocks are also a part of the body which can be spanked for chastisement. D's motives for spanking the girl—his buttock fetish—were, therefore, crucial in determining that the battery was indecent.

This situation, as it applies under the 2003 Act, was considered by the Court of Appeal in **R. v H [2005] Crim. L.R. 735.** V, who was walking her dog at about 22.00, encountered a young man, D, who asked her "Do you fancy a shag?" V ignored him and continued on her way. D followed her, grabbed her tracksuit bottoms by the fabric in the area of the right pocket, attempted to pull her towards him and, unsuccessfully, to cover her mouth with his hand. V managed to break free and ran home. D was convicted of sexual assault and his conviction was upheld on appeal. The Court of Appeal suggested the following two-stage test which would apply in cases such as this where the touching is not sexual by nature:

1. Because of its nature might the touching be sexual? (The circumstances before or after the touching or the defendant's purpose in relation to the touching are irrelevant in answering this question.) If the answer is yes,
2. Whether, because of its circumstances or the defendant's purpose in relation to it, or both, it was sexual.

Over to you...

Anne visits her gynaecologist, Darren, for a necessary intimate medical examination. Darren performs the examination in accordance with the correct procedure but is secretly sexually excited by doing so as he finds Anne very attractive.

Does Darren commit a sexual assault?

■ Objectively not sexual

Where a reasonable person would view the touching, etc. as incapable of being sexual, it will not be so, regardless of the defendant's purpose. This means that if the touching is objectively viewed as not being sexual, it will not be so even if the defendant obtains sexual gratification from it. Consequently, certain bizarre sexual fetishes may not fall within the definition of the offence. A similar approach was taken under the previous offence of indecent assault. In **Thomas (1985) 81 Cr. App. R. 331**, the court held that touching the hem of a girl's skirt did not constitute an indecent assault, despite any indecent purpose on the defendant's part, as the act was not in itself indecent. Similarly, in **George [1956] Crim. L.R. 52**, D was not liable for indecent assault where, on a number of occasions, he removed a girl's shoe from her foot for sexual gratification because removing a shoe was not in itself indecent. However, in *H*, the Court of Appeal expressed reservations as to whether or not it would now be possible for the removal of a shoe in such circumstances to be sexual as defined in s.78 and that it ought to be for the jury to decide. It seems, therefore, that the position concerning strange sexual fetishes is not completely clear, but the less obviously sexual the fetish, the less likely the jury will consider it to be sexual.

Over to you...

In the hit American legal drama of the late 1990s, Ally McBeal, one of the characters had a fetish for touching a woman's "wattle"—the fleshy fold of skin hanging from the neck or throat.

Do you think a jury in this country would find that doing so constituted a sexual assault if done without consent?

ABSENCE OF CONSENT

It is sexual assault if the complainant does not consent to the sexual touching. The issue of consent is explored on pp.196–204.

The Mens Rea of Sexual Assault

The defendant must:

1. intend to touch the complainant; and
2. not reasonably believe that the complainant consents to the touching.

The presumptions under ss.75 and 76 concerning consent which are considered at the end of this chapter (pp.198–203) apply also to the defendant's reasonable belief in consent. Consequently, the prosecution may rely on an evidential presumption (s.75) that the defendant did not reasonably believe that the complainant consented, or a conclusive presumption (s.76) to that effect.

Assault by Penetration

The Offence of Assault by Penetration

Section 2 creates the offence of assault by penetration. Section 2(1) provides:

> A person (A) commits an offence if—   *Mouth?*
> **(a)** he intentionally penetrates the vagina or anus of another person (B), with a part of his body or anything else,
> **(b)** the penetration is sexual,
> **(c)** B does not consent to the penetration, and
> **(d)** A does not reasonably believe that B consents.

The maximum sentence for assault by penetration is life imprisonment.

The Actus Reus of Assault by Penetration

This involves:

1. a person (a man or a woman);
2. who penetrates the vagina or anus of the complainant (a man or a woman) with a part of his body or anything else;
3. sexually; and
4. the complainant does not consent to the penetration.

PENETRATION

Penetration in this context bears the same meaning as in rape (see p.175). The s.2 offence may be committed where the defendant penetrates the complainant's vagina or anus with a part of his/her body, for example a finger, or anything else such as a bottle or weapon. Where the penetration is penile penetration of the complainant's vagina, anus or mouth, the appropriate charge is rape rather than assault by penetration. However, if there is doubt as to the source of the penetration, for example because V cannot remember, does not know or lacks mental capacity (as in **Lyddaman [2006] EWCA 383**) the defendant ought to be charged under s.2.

Where the penetration is non-penile penetration of V's mouth, the appropriate charge would be sexual assault.

Over to you...

Why do you think this offence only encompasses penetration of the complainant's vagina or anus whereas rape also encompasses penetration of the complainant's mouth?

SEXUAL

The penetration must be sexual. This term is considered in detail on pp.178–180. Given the meaning attributed to "sexual" under the 2003 Act, penetration may be sexual by nature, capable of being sexual or objectively not sexual at all. Penetration may be sexual by nature where, for example, D penetrates V's vagina with a broken bottle; it may be merely capable of being sexual where, for example, D penetrates V's vagina with his finger—this has the potential to be sexual but will not be so if carried out in a doctor's surgery (circumstances) on medical grounds (purpose). If the penetration is objectively viewed as not being sexual, it will not be so even if the defendant obtains sexual gratification from doing it. It may, however, constitute a non-fatal offence against the person.

ABSENCE OF CONSENT

It is assault by penetration if the complainant does not consent to the penetration. The issue of consent is explored on pp.196–204.

The Mens Rea of Assault by Penetration

The defendant must:

1. intend to penetrate the complainant; and
2. not reasonably believe that the complainant consents to the penetration.

The presumptions under ss.75 and 76 concerning consent which are considered at the end of this chapter (pp.198–203) apply also to the defendant's reasonable belief in consent. Consequently, the prosecution may rely on an evidential presumption (s.75) that the defendant did not reasonably believe that the complainant consented, or a conclusive presumption (s.76) to that effect.

Causing a Person to Engage in Sexual Activity

The Offence Under s.4 (Causing Another, etc.)

Section 4 creates the offence of causing another to engage in sexual activity without consent. Section 4(1) provides:

> A person (A) commits an offence if—
> **(a)** he intentionally causes another person (B) to engage in an activity,
> **(b)** the activity is sexual,
> **(c)** B does not consent to engaging in the activity, and
> **(d)** A does not reasonably believe that B consents.

The maximum sentence for causing a person to engage in sexual activity is 10 years on indictment and six months if tried summarily, although certain forms of activity involving penetration can be punished by a sentence of life imprisonment (s.4(1)).

The Actus Reus of an Offence Under s.4 (Causing Another, etc.)

This involves:

1. a person (a man or a woman);
2. who causes the complainant to engage in sexual activity; and
3. the complainant does not consent to the activity.

SEXUAL ACTIVITY

Activity is a broad concept; at one end of the spectrum it can involve words alone and at the other it can involve penetration. "Sexual" is considered in detail on pp.178–180. Given the meaning attributed to "sexual" under the 2003 Act, an activity may be sexual by nature, capable of being sexual or objectively not sexual at all. Some examples of the situations s.4 is intended to cover would be where:

1. D compels V to penetrate her;
2. D forces V to masturbate himself;
3. D forces V to masturbate X.

Section 4 has also been successfully prosecuted where the defendant has sent the complainant text messages trying to persuade her to perform a sexual act on him, as in **Hinton-Smith [2005] EWCA Crim 2575**.

ABSENCE OF CONSENT

It is the offence of causing a person to engage in sexual activity if the complainant does not consent to the sexual activity. The issue of consent is explored on pp.196–204.

The Mens Rea of an Offence Under s.4 (Causing Another, etc.)

The defendant must:

1. intend to cause the complainant to engage in sexual activity; and
2. not reasonably believe that the complainant consents to the sexual activity.

The presumptions under ss.75 and 76 concerning consent which are considered at the end of this chapter (pp.198–203) apply also to the defendant's reasonable belief in consent. Consequently, the prosecution may rely on an evidential presumption (s.75) that the defendant did not reasonably believe that the complainant consented, or a conclusive presumption (s.76) to that effect.

Sex With an Adult Relative: Penetration

The Offences Involving Sex with an Adult Relative

Incest, the offence of having sexual intercourse with a close relative, has been replaced under the 2003 Act by a number of family offences. Sections 25 and 26 concern certain sexual activity involving children, and are considered below. Sections 64 and 65 deal with family sexual offences involving *consenting* adult relatives. Section 64 creates an offence in respect of the relative who performs the penetration (A); s.65 creates an offence in respect of the relative who is penetrated (B).

Both offences are punishable by a maximum of two years' imprisonment if tried on indictment; six months if tried summarily.

The Actus Reus of the s.64 Offence

The actus reus of the s.64 offence (committed by A) involves:

1. A (who must be aged 16 or over);
2. who penetrates B's vagina or anus with a part of his body or anything else or penetrates B's mouth with his penis;
3. the penetration is sexual;
4. B is aged 18 or over; and
5. A and B are related in a specified manner (see below).

RELATIVE

Subsection 2 of ss.64 and 65 provides that A and B are relatives for the purposes of these offences if they are related as parent, grandparent, child, grandchild, brother, sister, half-brother, half-sister, aunt, uncle, niece or nephew. Adoptive relatives are excluded from both offences. Thus, for example, it will not be an offence under either section for an adoptive brother and sister aged over 18 to have sexual intercourse.

The Mens Rea of the s.64 Offence

This is satisfied where:

1. the penetration is intentional; and
2. A knows or could reasonably have been expected to know that he is related to B in the manner specified.

An evidential burden is placed on A so that, unless he can adduce sufficient evidence that there is an arguable case as to whether or not he knew or could reasonably have been expected to know that B was a relative, it is presumed that he did know or could reasonably have been expected to know.

The Actus Reus of the s.65 Offence

The actus reus of the s.65 offence (committed by B) involves:

1. A penetrates B's vagina or anus with a part of A's body or anything else, or penetrates B's mouth with his penis;
2. B consents to the penetration;
3. the penetration is sexual;
4. A is aged 18 or over; and

5. B is aged 16 or over;
6. A and B are related in a specified manner (see p.185 above).

The Mens Rea of the s.65 Offence

B must know, or could reasonably have been expected to know, that he is related to A in the manner specified.

An evidential burden is placed on B so that, unless he can adduce sufficient evidence that there is an arguable case as to whether or not he knew or could reasonably have been expected to know that A was a relative, it is presumed that he did know or could reasonably have been expected to know.

The Preparatory Offences

Sections 61 to 63 create three preparatory offences of:

1. administering a substance with intent;
2. committing an offence with intent to commit a sexual offence; and
3. trespassing with intent to commit a sexual offence.

None of these offences require the defendant to have actually gone on to commit a sexual offence or attempted to do so. However, if the defendant does commit the intended offence, he can be convicted of the substantive sexual offence in addition to the preparatory offence.

All three offences are punishable by a maximum of 10 years' imprisonment (except where the offence is one under s.62 of kidnap or false imprisonment with intent to commit a sexual offence, for which the maximum penalty is life imprisonment).

Administering a Substance with Intent

In an effort to combat the increasing use of so-called "date rape" drugs administered without the victim's knowledge, the s.61 offence of administering a substance with intent was introduced. It is an offence under s.61 to intentionally administer a substance to, or cause a substance to be taken by, another person (V), where the defendant knows that V does not consent to taking that substance and intends to stupefy or overpower V so that any person can engage in sexual activity involving V.

THE ACTUS REUS OF ADMINISTERING A SUBSTANCE, ETC.

This involves:

1. a person (a man or a woman);
2. administering or causing to be taken by V;
3. any substance; and
4. V does not consent to taking the substance.

■ Administration

The actus reus is complete upon administration or causing the substance to be taken. The substance may be administered to V in any way, for example, in a drink, by injection or by covering V's face with a cloth impregnated with the substance. Under a similar provision in previous legislation, administration did not occur where a drug was left in the victim's food or drink but V did not consume it; it was merely an attempt. It is likely that this view will continue to be taken under the 2003 Act.

The offence applies both where the defendant himself administers the substance to V and where D causes the substance to be taken by V. D might cause the substance to be taken where, for example, D persuades A to administer a substance to V so that D can have sex with V because A knows V socially and can more easily slip the substance into V's drink than D can.

■ Substance

Although the offence was aimed at the use of "date rape drugs" such as Rohypnol, it will also apply to the use of other (even legal) substances with the relevant intention. Hence, in **Coomber [2005] EWCA Crim 1113**, the "substance" administered for the purposes of s.61 was sleeping tablets. Section 61 encompasses D spiking V's drink with alcohol provided V did not know that she/he was drinking alcohol, but it would not encompass D encouraging V to get drunk so that D could have sex with V, where V knew that she/he was drinking alcohol.

■ Absence of consent

This is self-explanatory.

THE MENS REA OF ADMINISTERING A SUBSTANCE, ETC.

The defendant must:

1. intend to administer the substance/cause it to be administered or taken;
2. know that V does not consent to taking the substance; and
3. intend to stupefy or overpower V so that any person can engage in sexual activity involving him/her.

Committing an Offence with Intent to Commit a Sexual Offence

Under s.62 it is an offence to commit a criminal offence with intent to commit a relevant sexual offence. The offence covers the situation where the defendant commits a criminal offence with the intention of committing a subsequent sexual offence. It would apply, for example, where D assaults V to subdue her so that he can more easily rape her, or stalks or kidnaps V so that he can later rape her.

THE ACTUS REUS OF THE s.62 OFFENCE

This involves the commission of the preparatory offence.

THE MENS REA OF THE s.62 OFFENCE

This is the mens rea required for the preparatory offence and the intention to commit a relevant sexual offence. A "relevant sexual offence" is a sexual offence under the Act and includes aiding, abetting, counselling or procuring such an offence.

The defendant was acquitted on appeal for this offence in **R. v S (Vageesan) [2008] EWCA 346** as he lacked mens rea. The complainant (V) was married to D who she alleged had dragged her from their sofa, punched her and demanded that she go upstairs. D then struck his own father when he tried to intervene, causing him to fall to the floor. V asserted that once upstairs she was raped repeatedly by D. D was charged with several counts of rape and attempted rape and with committing common assault (the altercation) with intent to commit a sexual offence. At trial, D was acquitted on all counts save that for the s.62 offence but this conviction was overturned on appeal as there was no evidence that the common assault was committed with intent to commit a sexual offence.

Trespass with Intent to Commit a Sexual Offence

Prior to the enactment of the Sexual Offences Act 2003, the offence of burglary under s.9(1)(a) of the Theft Act 1968 included, under subs.2, entering a building or part thereof as a trespasser with intent to rape. The 2003 Act removed rape from the list of relevant offences in s.9(2) and s.63 created an offence of trespass with intent to commit a sexual offence.

Section 63 provides:

> A person commits an offence if—
> **(a)** he is a trespasser on any premises,
> **(b)** he intends to commit a relevant sexual offence on the premises and
> **(c)** he knows that, or is reckless as to whether, he is a trespasser.

THE ACTUS REUS OF TRESPASS WITH INTENT, ETC.

This involves trespass on any premises. "Premises" is defined as including a structure or part of a structure. "Structure" is itself defined as including a tent, vehicle or vessel or other temporary or moveable structure.

THE MENS REA OF TRESPASS WITH INTENT, ETC.

The defendant must:

1. intend to commit a relevant sexual offence on the premises; and
2. know or be reckless as to whether he is a trespasser.

"Relevant sexual offence" is defined above on p.188 above.

Sexual Offences Involving Children

Sexual Offences Involving Children Under the Age of 13

Sections 5–8 create offences which mirror the offences under ss.1–4 above, except liability is strict as to the age of the child (**R. v G [2008] 1 W.L.R. 1379**), and there is no need to prove the child complainant's lack of consent (he/she simply cannot consent) and therefore no need to prove the defendant's lack of reasonable belief in consent.

THE OFFENCE OF RAPE OF A CHILD UNDER 13

Section 5 creates the offence of rape of a child under 13, and it provides:

> **(1)** A person commits an offence if—
> **(a)** he intentionally penetrates the vagina, anus or mouth of another person with his penis, and
> **(b)** the other person is under 13.

The maximum sentence for this offence is life imprisonment.

The offence shares certain actus reus elements with the offence under s.1 and where they do, they carry the same meaning (see p.175 above). Note the mens rea for s.5 is limited to an intention to penetrate and there is no actus reus or mens rea element in respect of consent.

THE OFFENCE OF ASSAULT BY PENETRATION OF A CHILD UNDER 13

Section 6 creates the offence of assault of a child under 13 by penetration, and it provides:

> **(1)** A person commits an offence if—
> **(a)** he intentionally penetrates the vagina or anus of another person with a part of his body or anything else,
> **(b)** the penetration is sexual, and
> **(c)** the other person is under 13.

The maximum sentence for this offence is life imprisonment.

Where the offence under s.6 shares the same actus reus requirements as the offences already examined (ss.1 and 3 above in particular) they carry the same meaning. Note also the lack of actus reus and mens rea in respect of consent.

THE OFFENCE OF SEXUAL ASSAULT OF A CHILD UNDER 13

Section 7 creates an offence of sexual assault of a child under 13 and it provides:

> **(1)** A person commits an offence if—
> **(a)** he intentionally touches another person,
> **(b)** the touching is sexual, and
> **(c)** the other person is under 13.

The maximum sentence for sexual assault of a child under 13 is 14 years on indictment; six months if tried summarily.

This offence mirrors that in s.2 examined above, but note again the lack of actus reus and mens rea in respect of consent.

THE OFFENCES OF CAUSING OR INCITING ANOTHER TO ENGAGE IN SEXUAL ACTIVITY WITH A CHILD UNDER 13

Section 8, which corresponds to the s.4 offence, creates two offences **Walker [2006] All E.R. (D) 08**:

1. intentionally causing a child under 13 to engage in sexual activity;
2. intentionally inciting a child under 13 to engage in sexual activity.

Note again the absence of actus reus and mens rea requirements as to consent. Section 8 provides:

> **(1)** A person commits an offence if—
> **(a)** he intentionally causes or incites another person (B) to engage in an activity,
> **(b)** the activity is sexual, and
> **(c)** B is under 13.

The maximum sentence for an offence involving causing or inciting:

1. penetration of B's anus or vagina,
2. penetration of B's mouth with a person's penis,
3. penetration of a person's anus or vagina with a part of B's body or by B with anything else, or
4. penetration of a person's mouth with B's penis,

is life imprisonment. Otherwise, the maximum sentence is 14 years on indictment; six months if tried summarily. Inciting under s.8 includes inciting the world in general, as well as any identifiable person (**Jones [2007] 2 Cr. App. R. 21**).

SEXUAL OFFENCES INVOLVING CHILDREN UNDER THE AGE OF 16

Sections 9 and 10 create offences which are mostly repetitive of (and therefore add nothing to) the crimes under ss.7 and 8 where the child is under 13 (i.e. liability as to age where the complainant is under 13 is strict). However, there is an additional element where the child is under 16 but the defendant reasonably believes the child is 16 or over (subs.(c) in each).

THE OFFENCE OF SEXUAL ACTIVITY WITH A CHILD

Section 9 provides:

> **(1)** A person aged 18 or over (A) commits an offence if—
> **(a)** he intentionally touches another person (B),
> **(b)** the touching is sexual, and
> **(c)** either—
>   **(i)** B is under 16 and A does not reasonably believe that B is 16 or over, or
>   **(ii)** B is under 13.

The maximum sentence is 14 years imprisonment.

The effect of subs.(c)(1) is that the defendant cannot be convicted where, although the complainant was in fact under 16, the defendant reasonably believed he/she was aged at least 16.

Over to you...

Given the overlap between ss.7(1) and 9(1) where the child complainant is under 13, the preferred charge is s.7(1).

THE OFFENCE OF CAUSING OR INCITING A CHILD TO ENGAGE IN SEXUAL ACTIVITY

Section 10 provides:

(1) A person aged 18 or over (A) commits an offence if—
(a) he intentionally causes or incites another person (B) to engage in an activity,
(b) the activity is sexual, and
(c) either—
  (i) B is under 16 and A does not reasonably believe that B is 16 or over, or
  (ii) B is under 13.

The maximum sentence for an offence involving causing or inciting:

1. penetration of B's anus or vagina,
2. penetration of B's mouth with a person's penis,
3. penetration of a person's anus or vagina with a part of B's body or by B with anything else, or
4. penetration of a person's mouth with B's penis,

is 14 years' imprisonment. Otherwise, the maximum sentence is 14 years on indictment; six months if tried summarily. Under s.10 (1)(c)(i), D cannot be convicted where, although the complainant was in fact under 16, D reasonably believed he/she was aged at least 16.

Abuse of a Position of Trust

Sections 16 and 17 create new offences where the defendant is in a position of trust in relation to the complainant, where the relevant age for the reasonable belief in consent requirement is 18 rather than 16.

Section 16 deals with the offence of sexual assault where there is a position of trust. It provides:

> **(1)** A person aged 18 or over (A) commits an offence if—
> **(a)** he intentionally touches another person (B),
> **(b)** the touching is sexual,
> **(c)** A is in a position of trust in relation to B,
> **(d)** where subsection (2) applies, A knows or could reasonably be expected to know of the circumstances by virtue of which he is in a position of trust in relation to B, and
> **(e)** either—
>> **(i)** B is under 18 and A does not reasonably believe that B is 18 or over, or
>> **(ii)** B is under 13.

Section 17 deals with the offence of causing or inciting another to engage in sexual activity where there is a position of trust. Section 17(1) provides:

> **(1)** A person aged 18 or over (A) commits an offence if—
> **(a)** he intentionally causes or incites another person (B) to engage in an activity,
> **(b)** the activity is sexual,
> **(c)** A is in a position of trust in relation to B,
> **(d)** where subsection (2) applies, A knows or could reasonably be expected to know of the circumstances by virtue of which he is in a position of trust in relation to B, and
> **(e)** either—
>> **(i)** B is under 18 and A does not reasonably believe that B is 18 or over, or
>> **(ii)** B is under 13.

The maximum sentence for offence under ss.16 and 17 is five years on indictment; six months if tried summarily.

Section 21 provides a non-exhaustive list of where a person is in a position of trust, and it includes, for example, where the defendant looks after persons under 18 who are detained by law in an institution, and the complainant is detained in that institution; where the complainant is resident in a home where the defendant is a carer; the same for a hospital, a children's home, etc. or where the defendant is the complainant's teacher.

ABUSE OF POSITION OF TRUST—THE MARRIAGE EXCEPTION
Section 23 provides a defence to a charge against A under ss.16 or 17 where A and B are lawfully married and B is aged over 16. The burden is on A to prove that he and B were lawfully married at the relevant time.

Over to you...

Why do you think the age of consent in respect of the abuse of position of trust sexual offences is 18 rather than 16?

Offences Involving Sexual Grooming

Grooming is a term used to describe the actions of an adult taken to befriend a child in order for the child's inhibitions to be lowered so the child enters a sexual relationship with the adult (or even becomes a prostitute or involved in child pornography). English law now criminalises conduct by the adult ahead of the meeting (which could take place online; but the offence is not limited to internet grooming), it criminalises the meeting itself, and any assaults which take place at the meeting or afterwards, most of which we have already examined above.

ARRANGING OR FACILITATING COMMISSION OF A CHILD SEX OFFENCE

Section 14 provides it is an offence if a person:

> **(1)** ... intentionally arranges or facilitates something that he intends to do, intends another person to do, or believes that another person will do, in any part of the world, and
> **(b)** doing it will involve the commission of an offence under any of sections 9 to 13.

The maximum sentence for an offence under s.14 is 14 years on indictment; six months if tried summarily.

MEETING A CHILD FOLLOWING SEXUAL GROOMING, ETC.

Section 15 (as amended by the Criminal Justice and Immigration Act 2008 s.73) provides that:

> **(1)** A person aged 18 or over (A) commits an offence if—
> **(a)** A has met or communicated with another person (B) on at least two occasions and subsequently—
> **(i)** A intentionally meets B,
> **(ii)** A travels with the intention of meeting B in any part of the world or arranges to meet B in any part of the world, or
> **(iii)** B travels with the intention of meeting A in any part of the world,

(b) A intends to do anything to or in respect of B, during or after the meeting mentioned in paragraph (a)(i) to (iii) and in any part of the world, which if done will involve the commission by A of a relevant offence,

(c) B is under 16, and

(d) A does not reasonably believe that B is 16 or over.

The maximum sentence for an offence under s.14 is 10 years on indictment; six months if tried summarily.

Sex with a Child Relative

THE OFFENCES

Sections 25 and 26 deal with familial sexual offences, effectively replacing the old common law crimes of incest with a child under 18. The offence in s.25 mirrors that of s.9 (above) plus it has the additional element of familial relationship. The offence under s.26 is loosely based on that in s.10 but is significantly narrower. This is because it applies to the "incitement" of certain activity, but not "causing" such activity.

Section 25 creates the offence of sexual activity with a child family member. Section 25(1) provides:

(1) A person (A) commits an offence if—

(a) he intentionally touches another person (B),

(b) the touching is sexual,

(c) the relation of A to B is within section 27,

(d) A knows or could reasonably be expected to know that his relation to B is of a description falling within that section, and

(e) either—

(i) B is under 18 and A does not reasonably believe that B is 18 or over, or

(ii) B is under 13.

Where the offence involves:

1. penetration of B's anus or vagina with a part of A's body or anything else,
2. penetration of B's mouth with A's penis,
3. penetration of A's anus or vagina with a part of B's body, or
4. penetration of A's mouth with B's penis,

the maximum sentence is 14 years' imprisonment. Otherwise, it is a maximum of five years if on indictment; six months if tried summarily.

Section 26 creates the offence of inciting (but not causing) a child family member to engage in sexual activity. Section 26(1) provides:

> **(1)** A person (A) commits an offence if—
> **(a)** he intentionally incites another person (B) to touch, or allow himself to be touched by, A,
> **(b)** the touching is sexual,
> **(c)** the relation of A to B is within section 27,
> **(d)** A knows or could reasonably be expected to know that his relation to B is of a description falling within that section, and
> **(e)** either—
>> **(i)** B is under 18 and A does not reasonably believe that B is 18 or over, or
>> **(ii)** B is under 13.

The maximum sentence is the same as for the s.26 offence.

Section 27 provides that A and B are relatives for the purposes of ss.25 and 26 (and this list is not exhaustive) if they are related by blood or adoption as: parent; grandparent; brother; sister; half-brother or half-sister; stepbrother or stepsister; cousins; aunt or uncle; or A is or has been B's foster parent; or they are, or have been, members of the same household.

DEFENCES

Section 28 provides a defence to a charge against A under ss.25 or 26 where A and B are lawfully married and B is aged over 16. The burden is on A to prove that he and B were lawfully married at the relevant time. Section 29 provides a defence to a charge against A under ss.25 or 26 where the relationship between A and B did not fall within s.27(2), either by blood or adoption. Hence, the defence is precluded where A and B are related as parent, grandparent, brother, sister, half-brother, half-sister, aunt or uncle or where A was the foster parent of B. The defence arises if immediately before A and B became related so as to fall within ss.25 and 26, a sexual relationship already existed between A and B which was not then unlawful. The burden is on A to prove that the relationship with B did not fall within s.27(2) and that the sexual relationship already existed before A and B became related.

Consent

The offences involving an adult complainant of: rape; sexual assault; assault by penetration; and causing a person to engage in sexual activity, discussed earlier in this chapter, all require that the complainant did not consent. Here, we explore the concept of consent as it apples to these offences.

Background to the Provisions in the 2003 Act

A significant number of rape cases are committed by someone known to the complainant, with often no independent evidence available. As a consequence, the case will often turn on the issue of whether the complainant consented. However, no precise definition of consent for the purposes of sexual activity existed prior to the commencement of the Sexual offences Act 2003. What was clear, though, was that there was no requirement that the complainant, V, actually communicate her lack of consent to the defendant or that she demonstrate it by physical resistance (**Malone [1998] 2 Cr. App. R. 447**). (This continues to be the case under the statute, see discussion of s.74 below and **R. v H [2007] EWCA Crim 2056**). Beyond this basic premise, consent at common law was a rather confusing concept. One particular difficulty was how to deal with the situation where the complainant *appeared* to have consented but did not *truly* consent. A complainant's "apparent" consent might be due to any number of reasons such as, for example, fear, deception or intoxication. The effect, if any, of these factors on consent, both at common law and now under the 2003 Act, is discussed below.

One of the major changes brought by the 2003 Act is the attempt to clarify the whole issue of consent, first by providing a statutory definition of the term (s.74) and then by creating presumptions concerning consent (ss.75 and 76). Where there is an issue of consent and one of the presumptions applies, the prosecution will seek to rely on the presumption but in a case where neither presumption applies, it will rely on the fall-back position in s.74.

The Meaning of Consent—s.74

Section 74 defines consent as follows:

> "... a person consents if he agrees by choice, and has the freedom and capacity to make that choice."

The term "capacity" is not defined in the Act but, presumably, an adult ought to be able to consent provided he or she possesses the mental capacity to consent, i.e. has sufficient knowledge of the sexual character of the act to be able to give an informed consent to it (**R. v C [2009] 1 Cr. App. R. 15**). The effect of intoxication on capacity to agree by choice is considered on pp.202–203.

The reference to "freedom" is intended to provide statutory acceptance that the absence of resistance does not indicate consent as V may still have lacked the freedom to choose. She may, for example, have been too scared to resist. There is no consent where D threatens V with the use of force unless V acquiesces to the sexual act, as in such circumstances V clearly lacks the freedom to consent (and a s.75 presumption may well apply, see below). But, how will a court determine whether V had freedom to choose in a situation where there were no such threats but V still felt she had no choice and so reluctantly submitted to sexual activity?

At common law, the courts grappled with the difficult issue of differentiating real consent from mere submission. In **Olugboja (1981) 73 Cr. App. R. 344**, for example, V was terrified because D's friend had just committed a rape and so offered no resistance while D had sexual intercourse with her. Although D's rape conviction was overturned, the Court of Appeal did acknowledge that there was a difference between consent and submission but did not clarify what that difference was. Similarly, in **Marston [2007] EWCA Crim 2477**, a case decided under the 2003 Act, the Court of Appeal confirmed that there is a difference between consent and compliance, a term which, it is submitted, can substitute for submission in this context. In *Olugboja*, Dunn L.J. opined that whether there was consent or mere submission was to be determined by the jury on the facts of each case. This is likely to continue to be the approach under the statute. Hence, the jury may take into account the individual circumstances and character of the complainant in assessing whether there was consent. This may, however, lead to juries having to make difficult factual distinctions between seemingly similar cases. Where, for example, V is threatened by D with dismissal from employment or with financial ruin unless he/she engages in sexual activity with D or cultural pressure is placed on V to do so, the jury will have to consider V's individual circumstances and strength of character and the strength and source of the pressure in assessing whether V submitted or still had the freedom to choose and, therefore, consented. It is generally thought that where V is not threatened but, rather, is promised a benefit, this is less likely to invalidate consent. The casting couch is the classic example—the young, ambitious actress submits to sex with the film director because he promises her a role in his new film. It is possible to argue that in such circumstances V still had the freedom to choose. However, if V was struggling financially and desperately needed the money the role would bring in order to pay her bills, a jury might decide otherwise. This illustrates the need to consider each case individually.

The Presumptions About Consent

The statute creates both conclusive (the presumption cannot be rebutted) and evidential (rebuttable) presumptions concerning consent and belief in consent which apply to the sexual offences of rape, sexual assault, assault by penetration and causing a person to engage in sexual activity without consent.

SECTION 75—THE EVIDENTIAL PRESUMPTIONS ABOUT CONSENT

Where the prosecution proves that the defendant did the relevant act required by the actus reus (e.g. intentional penetration for rape), and can also prove that one of a list of circumstances specified in s.75(2) existed and that the defendant knew one of those circumstances existed, the complainant is taken not to have consented to the act and the defendant is presumed not to have reasonably believed that the complainant consented. The prosecution is not, however, required to further prove that the relevant circumstance caused the lack of consent. In order to rebut the presumption, the defendant will need to adduce sufficient evidence to persuade the judge that there is an issue about consent which ought to go before a jury. This may come from examination in chief of the defendant or defence witnesses or by cross-examination of prosecution witnesses. If the defendant succeeds in persuading the judge of this, it is the task of the prosecution to prove beyond reasonable doubt that the complainant did not consent and that the defendant did not reasonably believe that the complainant consented.

Specified circumstances

The s.75 presumptions arise where one of the following, largely self-explanatory, circumstances in subs.2 can be established:

> **(a)** any person was, at the time of the relevant act or immediately before it began, using violence against the complainant or causing the complainant to fear that immediate violence would be used against her/him;
> **(b)** any person was, at the time of the relevant act or immediately before it began, causing the complainant to fear that violence was being used, or that immediate violence would be used, against another person;

It is worth noting that for both (a) and (b) the source of the violence need not be the defendant but that (a) and (b) differ in that (a) relates to violence or threats against the complainant and (b) relates to violence or threats against a third party. It is, as yet, unclear how flexibly the courts will interpret "immediately before" in this context. It is possible that it will be interpreted in a similar manner as under the Public Order Act 1986 [1991] 1 Q.B. 260, i.e.:

> "not ... instantaneous ... violence but ... [suggesting] proximity in time and proximity in causation; that it is likely that violence will result within a relatively short period of time and without any other intervening occurrence" **(Horseferry Road Magistrates' Court Ex.p Siadatan [1991] 1 Q.B. 260).**

> **(c)** the complainant was, and the defendant was not, unlawfully detained at the time of the relevant act;
> **(d)** the complainant was asleep or unconscious at the time of the relevant act;

(e) because of the complainant's physical disability, the complainant would not have been able at the time of the relevant act to communicate to the defendant whether the complainant consented;

(f) any person had administered to or caused to be taken by the complainant, without the complainant's consent, a substance which, having regard to when it was administered or taken, was capable of causing or enabling the complainant to be stupefied or overpowered at the time of the relevant act.

Provision (f) encompasses not just the use of date-rape drugs and alcohol—the classic example would be D spiking V's soft drink—but any substance capable of overpowering the complainant. The reference to "capable of" ensures that the prosecution is not required to establish that the substance actually stupefied or overpowered V, only that it had the potential to do so. Where s.75(2)(f) applies, D may also commit an offence under s.61 of administering a substance with intent, see p.186.

SECTION 76—THE CONCLUSIVE PRESUMPTIONS ABOUT CONSENT

Where the prosecution proves that the defendant did the relevant act required by the actus reus (e.g. intentional penetration for rape) and can also prove that one of two circumstances specified in s.76(2) existed and that the defendant knew one of those circumstances existed, the complainant is conclusively presumed not to have consented to the act and the defendant is conclusively presumed not to have reasonably believed that the complainant consented. Both situations require intentional deception so will not apply where the complainant is mistaken but was not intentionally deceived.

■ Specified circumstances

The s.76(2) circumstances are:

(a) the defendant intentionally deceived the complainant as to the nature or purpose of the relevant act;

(b) the defendant intentionally induced the complainant to consent to the relevant act by impersonating a person known personally to the complainant.

The conclusive nature of the s.76 presumptions has led to the provision being interpreted quite narrowly, see for example, **Jheeta [2007] EWCA Crim 1699**, in which the court stressed that the conclusive presumptions, "require the most strict scrutiny." Hence, the s.76(2)(a) presumption does not arise where the complainant is merely deceived by D's lies into engaging in sexual activity with him, as occurred in *Jheeta*. V was involved in a sexual relationship with D when she began to receive threatening text messages and phone calls which, unbeknown to her, came from D. V consulted D about the messages and calls and he informed her that he would contact the police on her behalf. V tried to end the relationship with D but started to receive text messages, allegedly from the police, advising her, inter alia, that unless she slept with D she would be fined. V continued the sexual relationship but, whenever she attempted to end it, she received further text messages in the same vein. D was eventually charged with rape and admitted what he had done and that his scheme had persuaded V to have sex with him more often than she would otherwise have done. The Court of Appeal held that in such circumstances the prosecution would not be able to rely on s.76 as D's lies, although very persuasive, did not deceive V as to the nature or purpose of inter-course, merely the situation in which she found herself. However, as V had not exercised a free choice in having sex with D, there was no consent within the meaning given in s.74.

The defendant intentionally deceived the complainant as to the nature of the relevant act

At common law, a mistake as to the nature of the act negated consent (for rape) but such mistakes were uncommon and are likely to continue to be so under the statute. Two notable examples at common law were **Flattery (1877) 2 Q.B.D. 410** and **Williams [1923] 1 K.B. 340**.

In *Flattery,* D deceived V as to the nature of the act when he had sexual intercourse with her, having persuaded her that he was performing a surgical procedure. In *Williams*, D, a singing teacher, had sexual intercourse with a female pupil by pretending that it was a method of voice training. The girl believed him, did not realise he was having sexual intercourse with her, and so did not resist. In both cases, D was liable for rape on the basis that his deception vitiated V's consent. A conclusive presumption of lack of consent would now exist in such circumstances.

In **Linekar [1995] 2 Cr. App. R. 49**, the deception was not sufficient to vitiate consent. The complainant (V) was a prostitute who agreed to have intercourse with D for £25. After inter-course had taken place, D left without paying V and the jury at D's trial for rape concluded that D had never intended to pay. D's appeal against conviction for rape was successful as V had consented to sexual intercourse and D's deception as to his willingness to pay was not suffi-cient to vitiate that consent; there was no mistake as to the nature of the act, i.e. sexual inter-course. (The Court of Appeal in *Jheeta* concluded that there would have been no deception as to purpose—sexual gratification—either.)

Failure to disclose one's HIV status before engaging in unprotected sexual intercourse does not constitute a deception as to the nature of the act, merely as to the risk of infection so D is not liable for rape (**R. v B [2007] 1 W.L.R. 1567**) but may be liable for inflicting grievous bodily harm, contrary to s.20 of the Offences Against the Person Act 1861 if V is infected, see Ch.5.

The defendant intentionally deceived the complainant as to the purpose of the relevant act

At common law, a deception as to quality was capable of vitiating consent, see, for example, **Tabassum [2000] 2 Cr. App. R. 328**, discussed on p.165. D had asked several women to take part in a breast cancer survey he was carrying out in order to prepare a software package to sell to doctors. The women consented to D showing them how to carry out a breast self-examination which involved them undressing and allowing D to feel their breasts. Each complainant said she had only consented because she thought D had medical qualifications so that their consent was for medical purposes only. D had no medical training. D was convicted of indecent assault because the complainants' consent was vitiated by their mistake as to the quality of his act.

The 2003 Act refers to a deception as to purpose rather than quality but it is submitted that "purpose" is intended to cover the same situations as quality did at common law. A post-Act example of such a deception is provided by **Devonald [2008] EWCA 527.** D, believing A had treated his daughter badly when they were in a relationship, set out to embarrass A. Purporting to be X, a 16 year old girl, D began an internet correspondence with V. In the course of this correspondence, he persuaded V to masturbate in front of a webcam. V did so in the belief that he was masturbating for the sexual gratification of X. On appeal against D's conviction for causing a person to engage in sexual activity without consent, the defence submitted that the prosecution could not rely on s.76(2)(a) because the provision was concerned with deception as to the relevant act—and V knew he was engaged in a sexual act-rather than as to the surrounding circumstances. This submission failed as V had been deceived as to the purpose of the masturbation.

The defendant intentionally induced the complainant to consent to the relevant act by impersonating a person known personally to the complainant

Where the defendant pretends to be the complainant's partner so that the complainant consents to the relevant act, the complainant is conclusively presumed not to have consented. The Act does not specify what degree of intimacy is required for a person to be "known personally" to the complainant. The presumption applies only to fraud as to the defendant's identity; it does not apply to deception as to attributes, for example medical qualifications.

The Intoxicated Complainant

If the complainant is so drunk that she/he has fallen asleep or become unconscious when the specified activity commences, the evidential presumption under s.75(2)(d) would apply. Alternatively, where the intoxication is a result of the administration of alcohol to the complainant without the complainant's consent (for example by spiking the complainant's drink), the evidential presumption under s.75(2)(f) would apply. Where neither presumption applies and the complainant appeared to consent but later avers that she/he did not as she/he was too drunk to consent, the question for the jury will be whether the intoxicated complainant had the freedom and capacity to choose to engage in the activity (i.e. s.74 applies).

The effect of intoxication on the complainant's capacity to consent to sexual activity was first considered in November 2005 by Swansea Crown Court in the case of *Dougal*. At D's trial for rape V, the complainant, admitted she had been drunk at the time she had sex with D but said that she could not remember giving her consent. The prosecution accepted that "a drunken consent is still a consent" and considered V's inability to remember whether she had consented fatal to their case. They decided to offer no further evidence and, as a consequence, the trial judge directed an acquittal. The decision to withdraw the case from the jury attracted much public criticism and even led the Government to consult on the merits of a statutory definition of capacity (see 2006 Consultation Paper—Protecting Victims—Justice for victims of rape) although, ultimately, no action was taken.

The issue of intoxicated consent was subsequently revisited by the Court of Appeal in **Bree [2007] EWCA Crim 804**. D and the complainant, V, had spent the evening drinking together before returning to V's flat and engaging in sexual intercourse. At D's trial for rape, V admitted her recollection of events was "very patchy." She claimed that, although she did not say "no" to sexual intercourse, recalled saying "no" when D asked her if she had a condom, and could not say whether she had responded to D's advances or given him encouragement, she did not consent to sexual activity with D. D's submission was that V was conscious throughout, even removed her own pyjamas and had consented to sex. D's appeal against his conviction for rape was allowed by the Court of Appeal. The court held that if, through intoxication, the complainant had temporarily lost her capacity to choose whether to have sexual intercourse, she was not consenting and, subject to the defendant's state of mind, if intercourse took place that would be rape but, if the complainant nevertheless remained capable of choosing whether to have intercourse, and agreed to do so, that would not be rape. The court referred to the statement of prosecuting counsel in *Dougal* that "a drunken consent is still consent" and stated that:

> "In the context of consent to intercourse, the phrase lacks delicacy, but, properly understood, it provides a useful shorthand accurately encapsulating the legal position."

The court considered that what would not be relevant in determining the issue of consent was:

> "whether the alcohol made either or both less inhibited than they would have been if sober, nor whether either or both might afterwards have regretted what had happened, and indeed wished that it had not ... [or] whether either or both may have had very poor recollection of precisely what had happened."

Sir Igor Judge observed that:

> "as a matter of practical reality, capacity to consent may evaporate well before a complainant becomes unconscious [but] [w]hether this [was] so ... depends on the actual state of mind of the individuals involved on the particular occasion."

He also considered it unrealistic to create a grid system relating to some prescribed level of alcohol consumption as:

> "[e]xperience shows that different individuals have a greater or lesser capacity to cope with alcohol than others, and indeed the ability of a single individual to do so may vary from day to day."

In *R. v H*, the complainant, V, was again intoxicated at the time sexual intercourse took place with D and again claimed that she did not consent. V was a 16 year old girl who had drank a litre of vodka and smoked cannabis during New Year celebrations. She became separated from her friends and ended up in a car with three strangers. One of these men, D, was later charged with raping V in the car. V claimed that D had asked her for sex, pulled her clothes up over her face and had sexual intercourse with her. She said that she could not remember what her response to D's request had been as she was drunk but that she had not wanted to have sex with him, did not think that she had done so willingly and did not think that she would have consented. D argued that V clearly had capacity to consent as she had rejected advances from the other two men and that, as V could not remember what she had said to D, the prosecution could not exclude the possibility that she had actually said "yes". The trial judge withdrew the case from the jury on the basis of no case to answer. The prosecution successfully appealed against this decision. The Court of Appeal held that the issue of consent ought to have been left to the jury:

> "It would be a rare case indeed where it would be appropriate for a judge to stop a case in which, on one view, a 16 year old girl, alone at night and vulnerable through drink, is picked up by a stranger who has sex with her within minutes of meeting her and she says repeatedly she would not have consented to sex in these circumstances." (per Hallett L.J.).

The court also stated that *Bree* had "expressly disavowed" the premise that V's failure to remember whether she had consented is fatal to a prosecution.

Summary

1. All sexual offences now fall under the Sexual Offences Act 2003.

2. Rape, contrary to s.1, involves the intentional, non-consensual penetration of the victim's vagina, anus or mouth by the defendant's penis where the defendant does not reasonably believe that the victim consents to the penetration.

3. The term sexual is used in the offences under ss.2–4 which involve, respectively, sexual penetration; sexual assault (requires touching); and causing a person to engage in sexual activity. Touching, penetration or an activity may be sexual by nature, capable of being sexual depending on the defendant's motives and the circumstances or objectively not sexual.

4. The offence of incest has been replaced with a range of offences. Sections 64 and 65 create offences involving consensual sexual penetration between adult relatives.

5. Sections 61–63 create preparatory offences involving administering a substance with intent; committing an offence with intent to commit a sexual offence; and trespass with intent to commit a sexual offence.

6. Many of the sexual offences involving children replicate the offences involving adults, but where the offence is committed against a child under the age of 13, liability in respect of the age is strict. Consent is irrelevant. Where the offence is committed against a child under the age of 16 (but 13 or over), the defendant may have a defence where he reasonably believed the complainant was 16 or over. Where the defendant is in a position of trust, the relevant age of the complaint is 18. Other sexual offences against children include familial sexual crimes. The Sexual Offences Act also created new offences relating to grooming.

7. The 2003 Act creates two types of presumptions concerning consent: evidential presumptions (s.75) and conclusive presumptions (s.76) which apply to the offences under ss.1–4 of the Act. Consent is defined in s.74 of the Act as being where a person agrees by choice and has the freedom and capacity to make that choice. An intoxicated complainant can still consent to sexual activity.

FIGURE 6 Summary of consent issues in offence of rape

Intentional penetration of vagina, anus or mouth	+ consent			**= D not liable**
Penetration of vagina, anus or mouth	+ no consent	+ MR of rape		**= D liable**
Intentional penetration of vagina, anus or mouth	+ a s.75 factor existed	+ D knew s.75 factor existed	+ D fails to rebut presumption	**= D liable**
Intentional penetration of vagina, anus or mouth	+ a s.76 factor existed	+ D knew s.76 factor existed		**= D liable**

End of Chapter Question

Question

Stacey meets Nigel at his house party. When she flirts with him and asks whether he has brought any condoms with him, he thinks she is interested in a sexual encounter. He decides to make things easier for himself by slipping some sedatives into her orange juice. He drinks only water all evening. Towards the end of the party, Stacey feels very drowsy and Nigel offers to carry her to the spare room to lie down and she agrees. As he is doing so, he feels her breasts through her top. He lays her on the bed and penetrates her anus with his penis. She does not protest. She falls asleep and he penetrates her vagina with the bottle he brought with him. At this point, Stacey's friend Rachel who has been drinking vodka all night staggers into the room to see how her friend is. Nigel asks if she wants to join her friend in a "three-some." Rachel does not reply but falls onto the bed and does not try to stop Nigel when he has vaginal sexual intercourse with her. Stacey wakes up at this point and realises what is happening. She shouts at Nigel to leave them both alone and he leaves the room. Stacey and Rachel report Nigel to the police. Stacey says that she felt too tired to resist Nigel when he penetrated her anus. Rachel asserts that she was very drunk and cannot remember whether she consented to sex but does not think that she would have.

Consider Nigel's liability under the Sexual Offences Act 2003.

Points of Answer

Nigel may be liable for various sexual offences under the Act.

♦ Slips some sedatives into Stacey's juice
  • This could be the offence under s.61 of administering a substance with intent. Define. The substance is the sedative as it need not be an unlawful substance (*Coomber*). Mens rea (MR)—The administration is intentional. He thinks she wants a sexual encounter and wants to make things easier for himself. Does that suggest he also intends to stupefy or overpower her so that he can engage in sexual activity?

♦ Feels Stacey's breasts through her top
  • This could be s.3 sexual assault. Define. This can be committed through clothing (*H*). Touching her breasts is likely to be sexual by its nature. Does she consent? She is likely to say not. The s.75(2)(f) evidential presumption applies as he put the sedatives in her drink. The presumption applies to MR also. He may try to rebut the presumption by pointing to what she had said at the party but it will be difficult to do so.

♦ Anal sex with Stacey
  • This could be s.1 rape. Define. As regards consent and MR re lack of reasonable belief in consent, presumption 75(2)(f). still applies. She did not resist but was under no obligation to do so (*Malone; H*).

- ◆ Penetration of Stacey's vagina with the bottle
  - • This could be s.2 assault by penetration. Define. The penetration is sexual by its nature. As regards consent and MR re lack of reasonable belief in consent, presumption 75(2)(f) still applies as does 75(2)(d) as she is now asleep. The presumptions will be difficult to rebut on the facts.
- ◆ Vaginal sex with Rachel
  - • This could be s.1 rape if Rachel did not consent. No presumptions regarding consent apply. The prosecution must prove lack of consent, relying on the meaning of consent in s.74. Is there any relevance in her being drunk? Drunken consent is still consent (*Bree*). If this is a drunken consent by Rachel, Nigel will not be liable but the fact that Rachel does not do anything does not necessarily mean that she is consenting. Her failure to remember whether she had consented is not fatal to a prosecution (*Bree; H*).

Further Reading

A. Ashworth, "Case Comment. Rape: rape of a child under 13—mental element—consent" [2006] Crim. L.R. 930

I. Bantekas, "Can Touching Always Be Sexual When There Is No Sexual Intent" (2008) 73 J.C.L. 251

M. Bohlander, "Mistaken Consent to Sex, Political Correctness & Correct Policy" (2008) J.C.L. 412.

C. Elliott and C. de Than, "The case for a rational reconstruction of consent in criminal law" [2007] 70 M.L.R. 225.

J. Elvin, "The Concept of Consent under the Sexual Offences Act 2003" (2008) J.C.L. 519.

E. Finch and V. Munro, "Intoxicated Consent and the Boundaries of Drug assisted Rape" [2003] Crim. L.R. 773 and "The Sexual Offences Act 2003: Intoxicated Consent and Drug Assisted Rape Revisited" [2004] Crim. L.R. 789.

A. Gillespie, "Prostitution or abuse? The Sexual Offences Act 2003" [2005] Crim. L.R. 285 and "Indecent Images, Grooming and the Law" [2006] Crim. L.R. 412

H. Gross, "Rape, moralism and human rights" [2007] Crim. L.R. 220

J. Herring, "Mistaken Sex" [2005] Crim. L.R. 311.

S. McLaughlin, "Online sexual grooming of children and the law" (2009) 14(1) Comms. L.8

P. Rumney & R. Fenton, "Intoxicated Consent in Rape: Bree and Juror Decision-making" (2008) 71 M.L.R. 279.

P. Rook and R. Ward, "Sexual Offences: Law and Practice" (2004) and (2007) supplement.

D. Selfe, "Sexual Assault and the Sexual Offences Act 2003—A Touch Too Far" (2006) 165 Crim. Law. 3.

J. Temkin and B. Krahė, "Sexual Assault and the Justice Gap: A question of Attitude" (Hart 2008)

S. Wallerstein, "A drunken consent is still consent—or is it? A Critical Analysis of the Law on Drunken Consent to sex following Bree" [2009] J.C.L. 318.

D. Warburton, "Rape: Consent and Capacity" (2007) 71 J.C.L. 394.

R. Williams, "Deception, Mistake, and Vitiation of the Victim's Consent" (2008) 124 L.Q.R. 132 "Setting the Boundaries: Reforming the Law on Sex Offences" (HO 2000).

"Sexual Offences Act 2003: A Stocktake of the Effectiveness of the Act since its implementation" London: Home Office 2006 para.46.

Self Test Questions

To test your knowledge gained from this section go online to *http://www.sweetandmaxwell. co.uk* and take our online self test questions. Here you will also find key updates to ensure that you are only ever one click away from an instant update.

Offences Against Property I—Theft

7

CHAPTER OVERVIEW

In this chapter we:

- explore the aims of the Theft Act 1968

- provide the definition of the offence of theft

- analyse the actus reus requirements of appropriation; property; and belonging to another

- analyse the mens rea requirements of dishonesty and intention permanently to deprive

- provide critical commentary where appropriate of the elements above.

Summary

End of Chapter Question

Further Reading

Self Test Questions

Introduction

Offences against property are wide-ranging and deserving of a thorough and detailed analysis. For this reason, the following three chapters are devoted to property offences. The subject matter of this chapter is the single offence of theft. In the following two chapters, the related offences of robbery, burglary, blackmail, handling, going equipped and fraud will also be considered, as will criminal damage.

The law governing theft is found in the Theft Act 1968. The 1968 Act resulted from the Eighth Report of the Criminal Law Revision Committee (Cmnd 2977, 1966). The aims of the statute were primarily to codify the law relating to the most significant of the offences against property (other than criminal damage), to replace the old complex offence of larceny with the offence of theft, to move the emphasis away from taking property to the infringement of a person's rights in property and to do so by drafting the legislation in:

> "... simple language, as used and understood by ordinary literate men and women [and to avoid] as far as possible those terms of art which have acquired a special meaning understood only by lawyers in which many of the penal enactments were couched" (per Lord Diplock in **Treacy v DPP [1971] 1 All E.R. 110).**

Unfortunately, the aim of simplifying the law has not been achieved, as evidenced by the complex body of case law that has developed since enactment, particularly in respect of key concepts such as appropriation and property belonging to another. Major difficulties have arisen because theft-type offences involve infringement of property rights and property rights are governed not by the criminal law but by the civil law of property and contract. For example, property may only be stolen if it belongs to another but whether it does so is largely governed by the civil law and any changes in the civil law of ownership will necessarily also affect the criminal law. Further difficulties have arisen in practice because words used in the 1968 Act which would seem not to be particularly complex or "terms of art" such as dishonesty are not defined in the statute and have been left to juries to determine. This has led to problems of interpretation and inconsistency of decisions. It is for these reasons that there have been calls for reform (see, for example, the dicta of Beldam L.J. in **Hallam [1994] Crim. L.R. 323** who described the law as being "in urgent need of simplification and modernisation") though no reform proposals have, as yet, been suggested by the Law Commission.

The Offence of Theft

Theft is the main offence created by the Theft Act 1968. The offence is defined in s.1, and ss.2–6 expand upon the key concepts included in the definition. Section 1 provides:

A person is guilty of theft if he dishonestly appropriates property belonging to another with the intention of permanently depriving the other of it.

The offence is punishable by a maximum of seven years' imprisonment.

The Actus Reus of Theft

This involves:

1. appropriation (of);
2. property;
3. belonging to another.

Appropriation

Appropriation is defined in s.3, which provides:

(1) Any assumption by a person of the rights of an owner amounts to an appropriation, and this includes, where he has come by the property (innocently or not) without stealing it, any later assumption of a right to it by keeping or dealing with it as owner.

ASSUMPTION OF THE RIGHTS OF AN OWNER

The s.3 definition of appropriation involves an assumption by the defendant of the rights conferred by ownership of the property. The rights of an owner are very wide-ranging and include the right to touch, eat, sell, use, possess, hire, lend or destroy the property (though assuming such a right will not be theft unless done with the appropriate mens rea). One might have thought that the wording "*the* rights of an owner" would mean that the defendant would have to assume *all* rights of ownership to the property but this is not how appropriation has been interpreted by the House of Lords. In **Morris [1983] 3 All E.R. 288**, their Lordships held that appropriation merely requires an assumption of any of the rights of an owner, not all of the owner's rights. The defendant had switched price labels on items in a supermarket, gone to the cash desk where he paid for the goods at the lower price and was then arrested. The court held that he had appropriated the goods by assuming a right of an owner to fix their sale price. It did not matter that, in being willing to pay for them, he had not assumed the owner's right to be paid.

A significant implication of the decision in *Morris* is that theft can occur at a much earlier stage than is obvious merely by observing the defendant's actions because an appropriation does not require the defendant actually to take the property but merely to assume a right of an owner to it. Consequently, what might appear to be merely an attempted theft because the defendant has simply touched the property may be theft itself. Thus, in **Corcoran v Anderton (1980) Cr. App. R. 104**, D appropriated property and was liable for robbery (which requires theft accompanied by force) rather than attempted robbery when he tried to grab a woman's handbag from her hand, causing it to fall to the ground.

APPROPRIATION WITHOUT TAKING POSSESSION

As explained above, one may appropriate goods merely by touching them as this is an assumption of a right of an owner. However, it is not necessary to touch goods or even to possess them in order to appropriate. In **Pitham and Hehl (1976) 65 Cr. App. R. 45**, whilst P, the owner of a house was in prison, D, who was not living in the property, offered P's furniture for sale to Pitham. Pitham was aware that D did not own the furniture. D was held to have appropriated the furniture as soon as he offered to sell to Pitham because, in doing so, he had assumed a right of an owner to sell it. Although the principle that one can appropriate without actually possessing is sound, the actual decision in *Pitham* is open to criticism and the point is well put in *Smith's Law of Theft*, Ormerod and Williams, 9th edn:

> "Pitham, the buyer, knew very well that D had no authority to sell P's property; and D knew that the buyer knew that. D did not purport to be the owner or to be acting with his authority. It was not really an offer to sell at all but a proposal for a joint theft of the goods ... To invite another to steal is not to assume or exercise any right of the owner. If it were otherwise, all those conspiring to steal specific property would already be guilty of theft."

CHEQUES AND BANK CREDITS

As will be seen below (on p.220) a credit on a bank account is property. It is a "thing in action"; the contractual right of the owner of the account to have the bank pay him the sum (debt) it owes him. Where a defendant presents P's cheque or requests that money be transferred from P's bank account to his own, he appropriates a thing in action belonging to P—an assumption of a right of P to have that request met or cheque cashed (**Governor of Pentonville Prison, Ex. p. Osman [1989] 3 All E.R. 701** in which the appropriation took the form of a telex request to a bank to transfer funds). The appropriation occurs where and when the request is made (in the case of telexes, where and when it is sent) or the cheque is presented (*Osman* and approved in **Ngan [1998] 1 Cr. App. R. 331**) (as this is the act which amounts to assuming a right of the owner to reduce their bank account (**Williams (Roy) [2001] 1 Cr. App. R. 362**)). It is irrelevant whether the bank then cashes the cheque or complies with the requested transfer of funds, an appropriation has still occurred (*Osman*).

However, if P's account is overdrawn and has no overdraft facility, the presentation of P's cheque by D or D's request that money be transferred from P's bank account to his own is not theft (though it could be an attempt to steal) because no *property* is appropriated as P has no right to have the bank pay him the money. Similarly, where D, the owner of a bank account, uses his own cheque card to back a cheque for a sum which he knows is greater than that in his account (and he has no overdraft facility or will exceed it), there is no theft from the bank (**Navvabi [1986] 3 All E.R. 102**). Again, although the bank will be obliged to meet the cheque, it is not possible to identify any specific property stolen from it. This is because there was no money in the account in the first place and so no corresponding right to sue. Therefore, there was no thing in action to be appropriated. The appropriate charge in such circumstances would be one of fraud (see Ch.8).

APPROPRIATION, CONSENT AND UNAUTHORISED ACTS

Until the issue was settled in **Gomez [1993] A.C. 442 HL**, a vexed question concerning appropriation was whether it necessarily involved an unauthorised act on the defendant's part or whether there could be an appropriation even if the owner consented to the defendant's actions in respect of the property. In *Morris*, the House of Lords had stated obiter that:

> "In the context of s.3(1), the concept of appropriation involves not an act expressly or impliedly authorised by the owner but an act by way of adverse interference with or usurpation of those rights."

On this basis, D would not appropriate goods in a supermarket merely by picking them up off the shelf as this was an act which the shop owner would have impliedly consented to. Rather, the appropriation would occur only when D did something not consented to, for example, switching the price labels.

Morris was in conflict on this point with the earlier decision of their Lordships in **Lawrence [1972] A.C. 626** where it was decided that s.1 of the Theft Act 1968 was not to be construed in such a way as to include the words "without the consent of the owner", i.e. theft did not require an unauthorised act. Lawrence (D) was a taxi driver who indicated to his Italian passenger that the £1 he had given him for a ride was insufficient and, with V's permission, took another £6 from V's open wallet. The correct fare for the journey was 52p. D was tried for theft (rather than the more appropriate charge of obtaining property by deception contrary to Theft Act 1968 s.15 (now abolished)). D's argument on appeal against conviction that there was no theft because V had consented to him taking his money was rejected by the House of Lords.

The uncertainty in this area was resolved by their Lordships in **Gomez [1993] 1 All E.R. 1**. D was the assistant manager of an electrical goods shop who was asked by an acquaintance to supply goods in exchange for two building society cheques which D knew to be stolen. D supplied the goods after first obtaining the shop manager's authority to do so in exchange for the cheques by telling him that the cheques were as good as cash. D was charged and convicted of theft but the conviction was quashed on appeal by the Court of Appeal. The Crown then appealed to the House of Lords. The certified question for their consideration was:

> "When theft is alleged and that which is alleged to be stolen passes to the defendant with the consent of the owner, but that has been obtained by false representation, has (a) an appropriation within the meaning of section 1(1) of the Theft Act 1968 taken place, or (b) must such a passing of property necessarily involve an element of adverse interference with or usurpation of some right of the owner?"

By a majority of 4:1 their Lordships restored the defendant's conviction and, in so doing, answered the certified question "yes" to (a) and "no" to (b). Thus, the court chose to follow *Lawrence*. They did so on the basis that the decision in *Lawrence* was ratio whereas what had been said in *Morris* concerning consent was merely obiter. The House acknowledged that an appropriation may involve an unauthorised act but stated that it could equally involve an authorised act. A strong dissenting judgment was given by Lowry L.J. The majority of their Lordships had considered it would "serve no useful purpose" to interpret appropriation, as used in the Theft Act, by reference to the Criminal Law Revision Committee (CLRC) Report on which the Act was based. Lord Lowry disagreed with this view and argued that to have referred to the Report would have shown that it was the dictum in *Morris* which represented the intention of Parliament.

The decision of the majority in *Gomez* raises several important issues, namely whether the decision applies only to cases of consent induced by deception; the scope of appropriation; and the overlap created between theft and obtaining property by deception.

▪ Does Gomez apply only to cases of consent induced by deception?

The certified question for their Lordships in *Gomez* referred to consent obtained "by false representation". However, the court did not limit its decision to this situation. Lord Keith of Kinkel accepted that where D switches price labels in a supermarket he appropriates them because, in so doing, he assumes a right of an owner to them. In such circumstances, no deception has, as yet, occurred but an appropriation has. The point is also inherent in the judgment of Lord Browne-Wilkinson:

> "For myself ... I regard the word 'appropriation' in isolation as being an objective description of the act done irrespective of the mental state of either the owner or the accused."

If D's mental state is, therefore, irrelevant to appropriation, it must be irrelevant that he intends to deceive. In **Hinks [2001] 2 A.C. 241** (see p.216 below), the issue was settled beyond doubt by Lord Steyn who stated:

"It is true of course that the certified question in Gomez referred to the situation where consent has been obtained by fraud. But the majority judgments do not differentiate between cases of consent induced by fraud and consent given in any other circumstances. The ratio involves a proposition of general application."

■ The scope of appropriation

The effect of allowing appropriation to include an act which is done with the consent of the owner is a considerable widening of the scope of appropriation. According to *Smith's Law of Theft*, 9th edn by Ormerod and Williams, an appropriation may now be committed by "Anyone doing anything whatever to property belonging to another, with or without the authority or consent of the owner." As a consequence, what appears to be a lawful act may, in fact, be the offence of theft. Appropriation is now a neutral concept and it is the defendant's mens rea, rather than any "manifest criminality" (see Giles and Uglow "Appropriation and Manifest Criminality in Theft" (1992) 56 J.C.L. 179), which determines liability. This is well illustrated by the example of a defendant in a supermarket. As D appropriates goods as soon as he assumes a right of an owner to them, he appropriates an item as soon as he picks it up from the shelf or even merely by touching it. Following *Gomez*, the implied consent of the shop owner to D doing this is irrelevant. This does not, however, make every customer in a shop who picks up an item liable for theft. The crucial factor is the defendant's mens rea. It is only the dishonest shopper who does not intend to pay the full price for the goods who is liable for theft. The honest shopper may appropriate but he does not steal. This means that a theft can occur as soon as the dishonest shopper touches the goods, rather than at a later stage when he does something which he is obviously not permitted to do (such as put them in his own pocket).

Over to you...

- **Why do you think theft is not usually prosecuted if D, a dishonest shopper, merely touches the goods? What do you think D would have to do for a prosecution to proceed?**
- **D picks up a mini camcorder in an electrical store and puts it in his pocket intending to keep it. He then notices that there is a CCTV camera watching him and he puts the camcorder back on the shelf and leaves the shop. Has D committed theft?**

Two weeks after the decision of the House of Lords in *Gomez*, the Court of Appeal in **Gallasso (1992) [1993] Crim. L.R. 459** held that appropriation required a "taking". This is clearly inconsistent with *Gomez* and must be considered to have been per incuriam and, consequently, not binding.

The scope of appropriation was considered, more recently, in **Briggs [2004] 1 Cr. App. R. 34**. D deceived her elderly relatives into transferring a credit balance (the proceeds of sale of their property) into a bank account in her name. D was convicted of theft and appealed. The court held, relying on **Naviede [1997] Crim. L.R. 662**, that D had not appropriated the credit balance belonging to her relatives: D had done nothing which could be described as an assumption of a right of the owner over that credit balance; D's relatives were the only ones exercising rights over the account. Hence, an appropriation requires a physical act on the part of the defendant himself and merely deceiving the victim into transferring his property to D will not suffice.

Briggs appears difficult to reconcile with *Gomez* and, indeed, *Gomez* was not referred to in the judgment of the court. Had the case been drawn to the court's attention, Silber J. may not have stated as he did that:

> "It is not easy to see why an act of deceiving an owner to do something would fall within the meaning of 'appropriation' ".

■ The overlap between theft and obtaining property by deception

One of the effects of the decision in *Gomez* that an appropriation can occur where there has been consent, even one which has been given as a result of a deception, was that many instances of obtaining property by deception under s.15 were also theft. Section 15 has now been repealed, and a new offence of fraud introduced by the Fraud Act 2006 (see Ch.8). However, it would be impossible for the courts to interpret the new offence in a way that creates no such overlap between fraud and theft.

APPROPRIATION AND GIFTS

Where the defendant becomes the owner of property as a result of a gift which is valid under the civil law, might he nevertheless have appropriated the property and be potentially liable for theft? This was the issue which faced their Lordships in *Hinks*. In this case, D befriended V, a 53-year-old man of limited intelligence. D was charged with the theft of a substantial sum of money from V, the prosecution alleging that D had influenced V to give D the money. D claimed that the sums of money were either loans or gifts and there was evidence that V was capable of making a valid gift. By a majority of 3:2 the House of Lords dismissed D's appeal against conviction for theft. Their Lordships, following *Gomez*, held that, as an appropriation does not require the absence of consent, a person could appropriate property belonging to another where the other person made him an indefeasible gift of property, retaining no proprietary interest or any right to resume or recover any proprietary interest in the property. Presumably, this principle will apply not only to gifts but also to the situation where D, under the terms of a contract, acquires an indefeasible right to property. This does not mean that every gift (or acquisition of property under contract) involves a theft; only a person who dishonestly obtains a gift of property (or transfer of property under a contract) may be liable for theft. According to Lord Steyn, therefore, "In practice the mental requirements of theft are an adequate protection against injustice."

Over to you...

Lord Hutton gave a dissenting judgment. He said, "... it appears contrary to common sense that a person who receives money or property as a gift could be said to act dishonestly, no matter how much ordinary and decent people would think it morally reprehensible for that person to accept the gift."

Do you agree with this sentiment? In any event, where a valid gift is made, even if D exerts some undue influence on V, might he not be dishonest because he believes he is legally entitled to the property or has the owner's consent to the appropriation under s.2(1) (see p.231 below)?

As with *Gomez*, the decision of their Lordships in *Hinks* raises several important issues, namely its impact on the scope of appropriation; the potential conflict with the civil law it creates; and the court's reasons for deciding as it did.

■ A further expansion of the scope of appropriation

Their Lordships in *Hinks* could have taken the opportunity to impose a limitation on the scope of appropriation effected by *Gomez* by distinguishing between cases of consent induced by fraud and consent given in any other circumstances. As explained above, however, their Lordships chose not to do draw such a distinction. Thus, *Hinks* widens the scope of appropriation and, in doing so, thereby places even further emphasis on the element of dishonesty in theft.

■ Conflict with the civil law

The judgment creates a potential conflict between the criminal and civil law as conduct which is not wrongful in a civil sense may now be theft. This conflict was recognised by their Lordships but was not considered sufficient reason to depart from the decision in *Gomez*. Indeed, Lord Steyn was of the opinion that a conflict did not mean that it was necessarily the criminal law rather than the civil law which was defective. In his opinion, following *Gomez* also had the advantage of eliminating the need to explain to a jury civil law concepts in respect of appropriation (presumably such concepts as void and voidable contracts) in "an overly complex corner of the law." The implications of this conflict may, however, be far-reaching. Counsel for the defendant cited the following example from Smith and Hogan, Criminal Law as illustrative of the possible implications of relying on the mens rea of theft to filter out certain appropriations from the ambit of theft:

> "P sees D's painting and, thinking he is getting a bargain, offers £100,000 for it. D realises that P thinks the painting is a Constable, but knows that it was painted by his sister and is worth no more than £100. He accepts P's offer. D has made an enforceable contract and is entitled to recover and retain the purchase price."

Lord Steyn accepted that a jury might find D in this example to be guilty of theft if he was deemed dishonest even though he had committed no civil wrong but considered that justice would prevail because a prosecution in such circumstances would be unlikely. However, with respect to Lord Steyn, it is surely inappropriate for the substantive criminal law to have such loopholes which can be plugged only by relying on prosecutorial discretion.

■ The court's justification for its decision

Given the potential difficulties, what was the court's justification for deciding as they did? The reason given was that they were applying *Gomez* and, also, that to decide that a gift was not capable of amounting to an appropriation would be "likely to place beyond the reach of the criminal law dishonest persons who should be found guilty of theft." So there it is: their Lordships decided as they did because it was in the interests of justice to do so.

LATER ASSUMPTION OF A RIGHT

The latter part of s.3(1) extends the meaning of appropriation to include the situation where a defendant who initially appropriates property without stealing it (for example because he was not dishonest) later assumes a right to it by keeping or dealing with it as owner. Where this later appropriation is done with the appropriate mens rea, D may be liable for theft. Thus, D would appropriate, and might be liable for theft, in the following examples:

1. D borrows V's property and later dishonestly decides to keep it.
2. D finds a gold watch and, not knowing who the owner is, decides to keep it. He later finds out that the watch belongs to V but decides to keep the watch anyway.
3. D is unknowingly given too much change by a shopkeeper and, when he realises the mistake, dishonestly decides to keep the overpayment.

The latter part of s.3(1) relates to the situation where the earlier appropriation was not theft. However, where the earlier appropriation does amount to theft, any later keeping or dealing with the property will not be an appropriation (**Atakpu [1994] Crim. L.R. 693**). Consequently, once goods have been stolen, they cannot be stolen again by the same thief exercising further rights over them.

THE BONA FIDE PURCHASER

Section 3(2) provides:

> Where property or a right or interest in property purports to be transferred for value to a person acting in good faith, no later assumption by him of rights which he believed himself to be acquiring shall, by reason of any defect in the transferor's title, amount to theft of the property.

The aim of this section is to prevent a defendant being liable for theft by virtue of the latter part of s.3(1) (see p.218 above) where he purchases goods in good faith and for value and subsequently finds out that the goods were stolen but decides to keep them anyway or to sell them on. Section 3(2) only protects purchasers for value in good faith so that a defendant who merely receives the property as a gift or purchases the property knowing it to be stolen would not be protected. Section 3(2) was applied in **Wheeler (1991) 92 Cr. App. R. 279**. D purchased some antiques, not knowing that they were stolen. When he was later informed by the police that they were stolen property, he sold one of them. He was found not liable for theft as, although he had appropriated by keeping or dealing with the property as an owner, he was protected by s.3(2).

It should be noted that s.3(2) only protects the purchaser from liability for theft. Thus, a purchaser of stolen property who subsequently sells the property may not be liable for theft by virtue of s.3(2) but might still be liable for fraud (see Ch.8).

IS APPROPRIATION AN INSTANTANEOUS OR CONTINUING ACT?

Cases prior to *Gomez* had taken the view that an appropriation does not have to be an instantaneous action; depending on the circumstances, it might be a continuing act. This may be significant in robbery where force must occur immediately before or at the time of the theft and it is important to determine whether the theft is complete when the force is used (see further Ch.8). In *Atakpu*, the court stated obiter that, although *Gomez* did not leave much leeway for treating an appropriation as capable of continuing, the law was, in fact, unchanged by that decision. Thus, an appropriation can be continuous, but for how long does it last? In *Atakpu*, the court stated that it would be for the jury to determine in each case when the appropriation ended and that an appropriation may last as long as the thief can sensibly be regarded as in the act of stealing, or is "on the job."

Property

Where a defendant is charged with theft, the exact property stolen must be specified in the indictment. Generally, there will be no difficulty in saying that what was appropriated was property. However, in those cases where property is a contentious issue, the defendant may seek to argue that he did not appropriate *property* because what was appropriated is excluded from the definition of property either by statutory exception or at common law. In such cases, it is necessary to consider the precise meaning attributed to property.

Property is defined in s.4 of the Theft Act 1968. Section 4(1) provides:

> "Property" includes money and all other property, real or personal, including things in action and other intangible property.

Thus, property has a very wide meaning which includes not only personal property such as money (coins and notes), jewellery, vehicles, etc. but also land (with certain exceptions considered below), things in action and other intangible property.

THINGS IN ACTION

The definition of property encompasses a "thing in action" (traditionally known as a "chose in action", this is the right to bring an action in law) such as a debt. A credit balance in a bank account is a thing in action because it represents the contractual right of the owner of the account (P), whilst the account is in credit, to have the bank pay him the sum (debt) it owes him (**Davenport [1954] 1 All E.R. 602**). Dishonestly causing the debiting of P's account is, therefore, theft of P's thing in action, rather than theft of P's money (**Kohn (1979) 69 Cr. App. R. 395**).

Where D obtains a cheque from P in D's favour (i.e. written out to D), in addition to the cheque itself, he also obtains a thing in action: *his own* right to have P's bank pay him to the value of the cheque. This should be distinguished from P's thing in action—the credit balance in his account for the amount of that cheque. So, if D, by deception, persuades P to issue a cheque in D's favour, D obtains his own thing in action but this is not property which previously belonged to P before he wrote the cheque (**Preddy [1996] A.C. 815**). D may not, therefore, be liable for theft of the cheque, of property *belonging to another*, when he pays it into his account as the increase in his bank credit never belonged to anyone but him. (The same position would apply where D has control of P's account and causes funds to be transferred electronically from P's account to his own, for example through the "CHAPS" system.) D may, however, be liable if charged with theft of *P's credit balance*, as this is a different thing in action, and cashing the cheque involves a reduction of that credit balance (**Williams (Roy) [2001] 1 Cr. App. R. 362**).

As for the cheque itself, can it, as a piece of paper, be stolen? The defendant may contend that he does not intend permanently to deprive of the piece of paper as it will ultimately be returned to P, via P's bank, with all its virtue as a piece of paper intact (see below at p.241).

Obiter statements in *Preddy* to the effect that there was no such intention were treated as ratio in **Graham [1997] 1 Cr. App. R.** and subsequently followed in **Clark [2001] 1 Cr. App. R. 14**, which felt bound by *Graham*. Hence, cheques cannot, as pieces of paper, be stolen. An agreed overdraft facility is also property, a thing in action, and so can be stolen (*Kohn*). As was seen above, however, there is no theft of property where D cashes a cheque on P's account which is overdrawn without prior approval because P has no right to have the bank pay him the money. Further examples of things in action which constitute property include an insurance policy and copyright (though breach of copyright is unlikely to be theft due to the absence of an intention permanently to deprive).

OTHER INTANGIBLE PROPERTY

Other intangible property includes gas, an export quota (**Attorney General of Hong Kong v Chan Nai-Keung [1987] 1 W.L.R. 1339 PC**) and patents. Services do not come within the definition of property so it is not possible, for example, to steal a taxi ride or a haircut. Services are covered by s.11 of the Fraud Act 2006 which deals with dishonestly obtaining services (see p.285).

Both under s.4 and at common law, restrictions are imposed on what may constitute property and may, therefore, be stolen.

EXCLUSION BY S.4
■ Land

Section 4(2) provides that, subject to exceptions (a)–(c) below, land (real property) or things forming part of land and severed from it cannot be stolen.

Where D is a trustee, etc.
Section 4(2)(a) provides that D may steal land:

> when he is a trustee or personal representative, or is authorised by power of liquidator of a company, or otherwise, to sell or dispose of land belonging to another, and he appropriates the land or anything forming part of it by dealing with it in breach of the confidence reposed in him; ...

Thus, a trustee would steal land subject to the trust if he sells it for his own purposes rather than the purpose specified in the trust.

Where D is not in possession of land
Section 4(2)(b) provides that D may steal land:

> when he is not in possession of the land and appropriates anything forming part of the land by severing it or causing it to be severed, or after it has been severed; ...

Thus, for example, D who is not in possession of V's land might commit theft if he allowed his cattle to graze on V's grassy field or dug up V's plants or soil. If D picked fruit or mushrooms from V's land he would fall within s.4(2)(b) but might be protected by s.4(3), see below.

Where D is a tenant who appropriates fixtures

Section 4(2)(c) provides that D may steal:

> when, being in possession of the land under a tenancy, he appropriates the whole or part of any fixture or structure let to be used with the land.

Thus, for example, D, a tenant, may commit theft if he removes a fixture such as a fireplace from the property he has rented.

■ Mushrooms, fruit, etc.

Section 4(3) provides:

> A person who picks mushrooms growing wild on any land, or who picks flowers, fruit or foliage from a plant growing wild on any land, does not (although not in possession of the land) steal what he picks, unless he does it for reward or for sale or other commercial purpose.
>
> For purposes of this subsection "mushroom" includes any fungus, and "plant" includes any shrub or tree.

The subsection therefore exempts from liability for theft a person who picks wild mushrooms or flowers, fruit or foliage from a plant growing wild. Due to the inclusion of the words "picks … from a plant", it will be theft if (except in the case of a mushroom) the whole plant is removed. Further, the exemption does not apply if the wild mushroom, flower, etc. is picked for reward, sale or other commercial purpose.

■ Wild creatures

Domestic animals such as cats and dogs are property and may be stolen. Section 4(4) deals with wild animals and provides:

> Wild creatures, tamed or untamed, shall be regarded as property; but a person cannot steal a wild creature not tamed nor ordinarily kept in captivity, or the carcass of any such creature, unless either it has been reduced into possession by or on behalf of another person and possession of it has not since been lost or abandoned, or another person is in the course of reducing it into possession.

Thus, it is possible to steal a wild animal which has been tamed or is kept in captivity, for example a lion kept in a zoo. The term, "reduce into possession" was considered in **Cresswell v DPP [2006] EWHC 3379 (Admin)**. The Divisional Court held that merely enticing badgers into traps from time to time using food did not amount to reducing the badgers into possession so as to render them property (for the purposes of the Criminal Damage Act 1971, which bears a similar meaning to property under the Theft Act 1968). A wild animal which is not tamed nor ordinarily kept in captivity (or its carcass) may not be stolen unless it has been reduced into possession *by another* (or is in the process of being so reduced) for example, by being caught or killed, provided possession has not been lost or abandoned. Thus, poaching is not theft because the poacher, and not another, reduces the animal into his possession.

EXCLUSION UNDER THE COMMON LAW

■ Electricity
Gas and water may be stolen but electricity cannot (**Low v Blease [1975] Crim. L.R. 513**).

However, it is possible to commit an offence under s.13 of abstracting electricity. The offence, which is punishable on indictment by a maximum of five years' imprisonment, is committed where the defendant dishonestly and without due authority uses electricity or dishonestly causes electricity to be diverted or wasted.

■ Confidential Information
Confidential information, such as a trade secret or the contents of a prospective exam paper, was excluded from the scope of theft in **Oxford v Moss (1978) 68 Cr. App. R. 183**. In this case, a student unlawfully took possession of a copy of an exam paper he was due to sit and returned it after he had read the contents. The court held that the student was not guilty of theft even though the exam paper was now useless, because information is not property and cannot, therefore, be stolen.

> ## Over to you...
>
> - **Is it a satisfactory position that trade secrets cannot be stolen?**
> - **Professor J.C. Smith in his commentary on *Oxford* ([1978] Crim. L.R. 119) argued that D could have been liable for theft from the University of the piece of paper itself. On what basis could this be theft? Read pp.241–242 below to help you decide.**

Although there is no liability for theft of confidential information, there are offences under the Computer Misuse Act 1990 concerning unauthorised accessing of confidential information held on a computer.

■ A corpse

Neither a corpse nor part of it is property. Thus, where a brain was removed, preserved in paraffin at post mortem and then stored in a hospital, the relatives of the deceased had no right in property to the brain and so no action in conversion when it was not returned to them with the rest of the deceased's body (**Dobson v North Tyneside HA [1997] 1 W.L.R. 596**). If, however, a corpse, or a part of it, is altered for the purposes of medical or scientific research or exhibit, it thereby acquires value and becomes property which can be stolen, as in the case of **Kelly and Lindsay [1999] Q.B. 621**. Kelly, a sculptor, and Lindsay, a laboratory technician, took body parts from the Royal College of Surgeons for use by Kelly to make plaster casts. They were both convicted of theft of the body parts which had acquired value by "the application of skill, such as dissection or preservation techniques, for exhibition or teaching purposes."

Belonging to Another

Property must belong to someone other than the defendant at the moment it is appropriated although it is not necessary to specify who that person was. As with property, there will generally be no difficulty in saying that what was appropriated belonged to another but issues may sometimes arise concerning this aspect of the actus reus because s.5 allows property to be seen as belonging to a wider range of persons than the actual owner. This means that it is possible to steal from more than one person.

"Belonging to another" is first explored in s.5(1) which provides:

> Property shall be regarded as belonging to any person having possession or control of it, or having in it any proprietary right or interest (not being an equitable interest arising only from an agreement to transfer or grant an interest).

OWNERSHIP, POSSESSION AND CONTROL

The owner of property may not necessarily be the person in possession or control of it when it is appropriated. One significant effect of s.5(1) is, therefore, that property may be stolen from someone who does not actually own the property nor has any proprietary interest in it but merely has possession or control of the property at the relevant time. Taken to its logical conclusion, this means that it must be possible to steal one's own property from someone in possession or with control over it. This is precisely what occurred in **Turner (No.2) [1971] 2 All E.R. 441**. D took his car to a garage for repair. The repairs were completed and the car was left outside the garage overnight prior to being collected the next day by D. V, the garage-owner, did not know that D had a spare set of keys to the car. Without first obtaining V's consent, D used the keys to get into the car that night and took it home without paying for the repairs. The trial judge directed the jury to ignore V's lien over the car for the unpaid work and to base its decision on the fact that V was in possession and control of the car. D was found guilty of stealing his own car and the Court of Appeal, which felt bound to ignore the lien issue also, upheld the conviction.

Over to you...

Do you think it sensible that a person can be liable for theft of their own property?

A different decision was, however, reached in **Meredith [1973] Crim. L.R. 253** where D, without paying the removal charge, took his car from a police pound where it was being lawfully stored having been towed away for causing an obstruction. The trial judge directed that D could not be liable for theft of his car because the police, although entitled to payment of the removal charge, had no right as against the owner to retain the car. This seems the only basis on which the two cases are distinguishable; in *Turner*, V did have a right to possess the car as against the owner until his bill was paid.

It is worth at this point exploring what is meant by "possession" and "control." There is considerable overlap between both terms and, as either possession or control will suffice, it is not necessary to explore any differences in detail. Possession will often bring with it physical control but this is not required. For example, when you are a guest at someone's house for a drink you have control of the glass you use to drink from but the host still has possession of the glass. Possession and control do not have to be lawful. Thus, it is possible to steal property from someone who himself stole the property in the first place (*Kelly and Lindsay*). It is generally accepted that possession requires knowledge of possession but control does not. Thus, in **Woodman [1974] Q.B. 754**, V was found to be in control of property on his land, the presence of which he was unaware. V, the owner of a disused factory had sold off all the scrap metal on the site but retained control of the site. Unknown to V, the purchaser of the scrap had left some behind. D took some of this metal and was held to have been correctly convicted of theft from V.

PROPRIETARY RIGHT OR INTEREST

Section 5 extends the meaning of "belonging to another" to include those with a proprietary interest in the property. The ambit of proprietary interests is too broad a topic for a textbook on Criminal law so we will concentrate on issues which will most commonly incur liability for theft.

■ Co-ownership and partnerships

The legal owner of property has a proprietary interest in it. Where there is co-ownership of property or a partnership, each of the joint owners will have a proprietary interest and can, therefore, steal the property from the other. Thus, in **Bonner [1970] 2 All E.R. 97**, a partner was liable for theft when he dishonestly sold partnership property without his partner's consent.

A company is considered a separate legal entity from the directors and shareholders. Accordingly, directors, even those in sole control of the company, may steal from the company if they appropriate the company's assets dishonestly (**Attorney General's Reference (No.2 of 1982) [1984] Q.B. 624**).

■ Equitable proprietary interest

Although equitable interests arising only from an agreement to transfer or grant an interest are excluded from s.5(1), other equitable interests are not. Thus, a trustee (who has a legal interest in the trust property) may steal trust property from the beneficiaries of the trust as they have an equitable proprietary interest in it. Constructive trusts were excluded from the ambit of s.5(1) in **Attorney General's Reference (No.1 of 1985) [1986] Q.B. 491** but they do come within s.5(2), see below.

Where the beneficiaries are not identifiable, for example in the case of charitable trusts, difficulties may occur in relying on s.5(1) to determine whether property belongs to another. Section 5(2) prevents such problems. It provides:

> Where property is subject to a trust, the persons to whom it belongs shall be regarded as including any person having a right to enforce the trust, and an intention to defeat the trust shall be regarded accordingly as an intention to deprive of the property any person having that right.

Thus, s.5(2) allows trust property to belong to anyone with a right to enforce the trust, such as the Attorney General in the case of charitable trusts.

ABANDONED PROPERTY

If property is merely lost, it still belongs to the owner and can be stolen. Where, however, the owner abandons his property it no longer belongs to anyone and cannot be stolen.

Abandonment will not readily be inferred by the courts. It occurs where the owner has given up all rights to the property without conferring an interest in the property on someone else. The difficulty in establishing that property has been abandoned is illustrated by **Williams v Phillips (1957) 41 Cr. App. R. 5** in which the court held that property which had been thrown in a dustbin had not been abandoned: it remained in the owner's possession until collection by the local authority refuse collectors at which point it became the local authority's property by possession. Accordingly, the dustman who kept something he found in V's bin could be liable for theft.

It must be noted, that a defendant who believes property to have been abandoned when it has not may commit the actus reus of theft but will not necessarily be liable for theft because he may not be regarded as dishonest within s.2(1)(c), see pp.231–232 below).

CASES WHERE OWNERSHIP HAS ALREADY PASSED WHEN THE DEFENDANT FORMS THE MENS REA

Property must belong to another at the time of the appropriation. It is self evident that property will cease to belong to another once the owner's entire interest in the property has passed to D. As explained above (p.215), appropriation may occur at an early stage in events but it is not always easy to prove dishonesty when someone does that which they are permitted to do. Unfortunately, by the time the defendant does something not authorised, and thereby demonstrates his dishonesty, the property may have ceased under the civil law to belong to the original owner, for example, because it has been consumed by the defendant, and so cannot be stolen. Thus, in **Edwards v Ddin [1976] 1 W.L.R. 942**, D was not liable for theft from a garage when he drove off after filling up his car with petrol without paying for it. It was not possible to prove dishonesty until D drove off but, by that stage, the property belonged to D (under the Sale of Goods Act 1893) so there was no coincidence of actus reus and mens rea.

Similarly, where D consumes a meal in a restaurant and then leaves without paying for it, he does not commit theft (**Corcoran v Whent [1977] Crim. L.R. 52**). In both instances, however, D may be liable for an offence under s.3 of the Theft Act 1978 of making off without payment (see p.274).

SPECIAL CASES WHERE PROPERTY WOULD OTHERWISE BELONG TO THE DEFENDANT AT THE TIME OF THE DISHONEST APPROPRIATION

Sections 5(3) and 5(4) deal with situations where, under the civil law, ownership of property has passed to the defendant prior to the dishonest appropriation so that, but for such provisions, the property could not be stolen by the defendant.

■ Property received for a particular purpose

Section 5(3) provides:

> Where a person receives property from or on account of another, and is under an obligation to the other to retain and deal with that property or its proceeds in a particular way, the property or proceeds shall be regarded (as against him) as belonging to the other.

Section 5(3) applies where D has received property (usually money) from, or on account of O, on condition that the property is to be used for a particular purpose. Where the condition creates an obligation on D to retain and deal with the property only in the way specified, the effect of the provision is that, although ownership of the property passes under the civil law to D when he receives it, the property is still treated as belonging to O under the criminal law. Thus, D can steal the property if he does not comply with the obligation. Section 5(3) applies not only to the original property but also its proceeds, i.e. property which represents that which D originally received from O.

Section 5(3) was designed to cover the situation which arose in **Davidge v Bunnett [1984] Crim. L.R. 297**. D was given money by her flatmates to pay the joint gas bill but spent it on Christmas presents. D was found liable for theft as she was under an obligation to use the money only to pay the gas bill.

The obligation

Section 5(3) only applies where there is a *legal* obligation under the civil law owed to the victim, rather than a mere moral or social obligation (**Mainwaring (1982) 74 Cr. App. R. 99**). In *Davidge v Bunnett* above, there was a legal obligation under contract law. It may be otherwise where the parties are members of the same family as domestic arrangements are not normally intended to create legal relations. D must also know that he is under an obligation; knowledge on the part of D's agent is insufficient (**Wills (1991) 92 Cr. App. R. 297**).

Property received for a particular purpose

Where D is not under an obligation to deal with property *in a particular way*, s.5(3) does not apply. A mere contractual obligation *to do something* is not sufficient; in such circumstances the remedy for non-compliance is to sue for breach of contract. Thus, for example, where O contracts with D, a handyman, to erect a fence in his garden and pays D a £100 deposit, if D fails to erect the fence O's remedy is to sue for the return of his £100. Section 5(3) does not apply because D was under no obligation to use the £100 in a particular way. If the £100 had been given to D in order to buy fencing, however, the relevant obligation would arise and the £100 would still belong to O. The point is illustrated by **Hall [1973] Q.B. 126**. D was a travel agent who received deposits from customers for their holidays. The money was paid into D's general trading account. D's business collapsed before he arranged the clients' holidays and he was unable to repay their money. D was held not liable for theft (although he may have been liable for breach of contract) as there was no special arrangement to give rise to the obligation required by s.5(3). D was not under a duty to use the money received from clients to pay for their particular holidays. The position may have been different had D not paid the money into the business' general trading account but into a separate account from which money was to be used to purchase the tickets.

On account of another

Section 5(3) extends to the situation where D receives money from O "on account of X", i.e. where D is expected to pay the money over to X. This commonly occurs in cases involving charity collectors who receive money from sponsors but then fail to hand over their collections to the charity. Will s.5(3) apply in such circumstances? In **Lewis v Lethbridge [1987] Crim. L.R. 59**, D was sponsored to run for a charity in the London Marathon but, having completed the run, failed to hand over the sponsorship money to his designated charity. D's conviction for theft was quashed on the basis that there was no s.5(3) obligation on D to account for the money to the charity. The decision was disapproved in **Wain [1985] 2 Cr. App. R. 660** in which D organised events which raised money for charity. He then paid the money into his account and made drawings from the account. The court held that s.5(3) applied; the sponsors intended to give the money to the charity and this imposed a trust obligation on the collector to give the money to the charity. Consequently, the money belonged to the beneficiaries of the trust, i.e. the charity and D was liable for theft from the charity. It was irrelevant that the charity did not require its collectors to hand over the specific notes and coins which they collected.

Overlap with s.5(1)

In many instances the court could rely on s.5(1) rather than s.5(3) because someone other than the defendant will have a proprietary interest in the property and the property will, therefore, be treated as belonging to them. However, it is easier to rely on s.5(3) rather than become involved in analysing complicated civil law concepts such as equitable proprietary interests.

■ Property got by another's mistake

Section 5(4) provides:

> Where a person gets property by another's mistake, and is under an obligation to make restoration (in whole or in part) of the property or its proceeds or of the value thereof, then to the extent of that obligation the property or proceeds shall be regarded (as against him) as belonging to the person entitled to restoration, and an intention not to make restoration shall be regarded accordingly as an intention to deprive that person of the property or proceeds.

Section 5(4) covers the situation in which the original owner, O, transfers property to D under a mistake which is not sufficient to prevent ownership of the property passing to D under the civil law. Although ownership has passed, the property is still treated as belonging to the original owner under the criminal law. Thus, if D then realises there has been a mistake and is legally obliged to make restitution but fails to do so (appropriation by keeping or dealing as owner), intending permanently to deprive, he can be liable for theft. The provision applies not only to the original property but also to its proceeds or the value thereof (so that it is not necessary that D cannot return the exact coins or notes received).

Section 5(4) was introduced to cover the type of situation which later arose in **Attorney General's Reference (No.1 of 1983) [1985] Q.B. 182**. D failed to make restitution to her employer in respect of wages which had been mistakenly overpaid to her by direct debit from her employer's bank account to her own. D was held to be liable for theft as she was under an obligation to make payment to her employers to the value of the overpayment once she discovered the mistake.

The obligation

As with s.5(3), the obligation to make restitution must be a legal one not a moral or social one (**Gilks [1972] 1 W.L.R. 1341** in which a mistake which led to overpayment on a gambling win was held not to fall within s.5(4) as gambling debts are legally unenforceable).

The circumstances in which an obligation to make restitution will arise are governed by the civil law of restitution and are beyond the scope of this book. Most examples will, however, concern the overpayment of money situation which arose in the *Attorney General's Reference* above.

Overlap with s.5(1)

It is not always necessary to rely on s.5(4) as there is a common law rule that, where money or other property is transferred under a mistake of fact, the person who transfers it retains an equitable proprietary interest in it or its proceeds which means it belongs to another for the purposes of s.5(1). In **Shadrokh-Cigari [1988] Crim. L.R. 465**, a large sum of money (£286,000 instead of £286) was mistakenly transferred into an American bank account and then to an English bank account of X, a boy. X's guardian, Y, procured X to authorise the English bank to issue banker's drafts drawn in favour of Y for most of the sum transferred. Y then used the drafts for his own purposes. Although the Court of Appeal recognised that the application of s.5(4) would have led to the same result, they based their decision on s.5(1) and held that there had been a theft from the English bank. Y had appropriated the drafts which belonged to the English bank for the purposes of s.5(1) because, having transferred them to Y under a mistaken belief that Y could properly deal with the funds in the account, the bank, despite having transferred ownership, had retained an equitable proprietary interest in the drafts.

The same approach was taken in **Webster [2006] EWCA Crim 2894**. X was a soldier to whom a medal was sent in error (he had already received one) for service in Iraq. X gave the medal to D who sold it on an internet auction site. At D's trial for theft, an issue arose as to whether the medal still belonged to the Crown. The court held that the medal had been sent to X in fundamental error which meant that the Crown retained an equitable proprietary interest in it. Therefore, the medal still belonged to the Crown under s.5(1) of the Theft Act 1968 and could be stolen.

Over to you...

D is visiting friends in a nearby town. She buys some food at the supermarket before setting off back home. Her shopping costs £4.50. She pays at the checkout with a £5 note but the cashier gives her change for £10 in error. D is preoccupied and does not notice the mistake until she gets home some time later. When she realises she decides not to return to the shop with the overpayment as it is too far to make the journey back and will cost her more than the overpayment in bus fares. She thinks that she will pay the money back when she is next visiting her friends.

Does D commit the actus reus of theft?

Once you have read about the mens rea of theft, consider also whether she has the requisite mens rea.

The Mens Rea of Theft

This involves:

1. dishonesty; and
2. intention permanently to deprive.

- -

Dishonesty

This element of theft requires consideration of the partial definition contained in s.2 of the Act and of the meaning attributed to dishonesty at common law.

SECTION 2(1)

Given the increased significance placed on dishonesty in theft following the decisions in *Gomez* and *Hinks* and the fact that dishonesty is part of the mens rea not just of theft but also of other offences under the Theft Acts 1968 and 1978 and the Fraud Act 2006 (see Ch.8), it would be helpful if there were a simple, clear definition of dishonesty in the Theft Act. Alas, this is not the case. Dishonesty is not defined in the statute. This was a deliberate omission by the CLRC because "dishonesty is something which laymen can easily recognise when they see it". Some guidance is given on dishonesty in s.2 but the section merely provides three specific instances in which a person's conduct will *not* be regarded as dishonest for the purposes of theft; it says nothing about what will be regarded as dishonest. Section 2(1) provides:

> A person's appropriation of property belonging to another is not to be regarded as dishonest—
> **(a)** if he appropriates the property *in the belief that he has in law the right to deprive the other of it*, on behalf of himself, or of a third person; or
> **(b)** if he appropriates the property *in the belief that he would have the other's consent* if the other knew of the appropriation and circumstances of it; or
> **(c)** (except where the property came to him as trustee or personal representative), if he appropriates the property *in the belief that the person to whom the property belongs cannot be discovered by taking reasonable steps*. (emphasis added)

Section 2(1) is phrased in subjective terms, based on the defendant's actual belief, rather than whether he reasonably believed one of the three grounds existed. Thus, in **Small (1987) 86 Cr. App. R. 170**, where the defendant was charged with stealing a car he had genuinely thought to be abandoned, the Court of Appeal held that the trial judge had misdirected the jury by referring to whether or not the defendant reasonably believed the car had been abandoned.

■ Belief in a legal right to deprive

A defendant will not be regarded as dishonest where he appropriates property believing that he has a legal right to do so either on behalf of himself or another. A belief in a moral right is insufficient for the purposes of s.2(1)(a) although a defendant who holds such a belief may not be found dishonest under the common law, see p.234). As long as the defendant believes he has such a right, it is irrelevant whether he believes he is entitled to appropriate in the manner he does. Consequently, in **Robinson [1977] Crim. L.R. 173**, the trial judge was held to have misdirected the jury when he told them D must have *honestly believed he was entitled to use force* to take the money to which he believed he was legally entitled. Section 2(1)(a) may also protect a defendant who finds property and, although he knows the identity of the owner, believes it is now his by finding, as in *Small* above. Hence, the defendant who seeks to rely on the old maxim "Finders keepers" will fail under the civil law but may not be dishonest under the criminal law.

■ Belief in consent

A defendant will not be regarded as dishonest where he appropriates property believing the owner would have consented to his doing so had he known of the appropriation and the particular circumstances of it. Thus, although actual consent of the owner does not preclude appropriation (*Gomez*), belief that the owner would consent will preclude dishonesty. It is the *belief* as to how the appropriation would be viewed by the owner which is relevant to dishonesty, not how the owner would have actually viewed the appropriation. The provision is intended to cover those situations where D believes the owner would not mind him taking his property, for example where D borrows his neighbour's tools from his garage or takes some of a fellow student's milk from the fridge in a student house.

■ Belief that the owner cannot be located

Where property has been lost (but not abandoned) it remains property belonging to the original owner and can be stolen. However, a defendant who finds such property will not be dishonest if he believes he cannot find the owner by taking reasonable steps. Due to the effect of the latter part of s.3(1) (see p.218 above), a defendant who finds property and later discovers the identity of the owner may be liable for theft, however, if he then decides to keep the property as he would no longer be able to rely on s.2(1)(c).

WILLINGNESS TO PAY

Section 2(2) provides:

> A person's appropriation of property belonging to another may be dishonest notwithstanding that he is willing to pay for the property.

Thus, willingness to pay does not preclude dishonesty. Consequently a defendant might still be considered dishonest where, knowing that the owner does not wish to sell his property, he takes it and leaves the purchase price. In **Wheatley v Commissioner of Police of the British Virgin Islands [2006] 1 W.L.R. 1683 PC**, the Privy Council stated that, although most cases of theft would involve an original owner becoming poorer because of the defendant's actions, the prospect of loss was not determinative of dishonesty. Hence, there could be dishonesty on the facts of the case where a contract had been made by D with V and services rendered to V for an appropriate price in circumstances where D was legally disqualified from entering into such a contract. Whether such a defendant is actually dishonest, however, will be determined by the jury applying the *Ghosh* test for dishonesty, see p.234 below.

SITUATIONS NOT COVERED BY S.2(1)

Just because s.2(1) provides for three specific cases in which a person's conduct will not be regarded as dishonest, this does not mean that conduct must be regarded as automatically dishonest because it does not fall within the scope of s.2(1). But how, then, is dishonesty beyond the s.2(1) cases to be determined in any given case and who should decide whether the defendant was dishonest, the judge or the jury? It is these issues which has given rise to considerable difficulty and difference of opinion amongst the judiciary and commentators alike.

■ Dishonesty: a question of fact or law?

Until the matter was settled in **Feely [1973] Q.B. 530**, it was unclear whether dishonesty ought to be determined as a matter of law by the judge or should be treated as a question of fact for the jury. Some commentators, such as Professor J.C. Smith, were of the view that once a jury had determined the defendant's state of mind, the issue of whether this amounted to dishonesty should be a question of law for the judge to determine since it involves the interpretation of a word in a statute. The merits of this approach would be greater certainty and more consistent verdicts. The Court of Appeal decided, however, in *Feely* that the issue of dishonesty is *entirely* one of fact for the jury: it is for the jury to decide both what the defendant's state of mind was *and* whether such a state of mind was dishonest. *Feely* was the manager of a betting shop who had, against the express prohibition of doing so, taken £30 from his employer's safe. He was charged with theft and claimed that he had only borrowed the money and had intended to put the £30 back. He was also owed by his employer more than twice the amount he took from the till. Feely's conviction for theft was quashed by the Court of Appeal as the trial judge had erred in not leaving the question of dishonesty to the jury. In the court's view:

> "Jurors, when deciding whether an appropriation was dishonest can reasonably be expected to, and should, apply the current standards of ordinary decent people. In their own lives they have to decide what is and what is not dishonest. We can see no reason why, when in a jury box, they should require the help of a judge to tell them what amounts to dishonesty."

Such an approach is in line with the CLRC who had chosen the word dishonesty in preference to "fraudulently" because they considered it to be a word which juries would more easily understand. There are difficulties, though, with such an approach. It can lead to uncertainty and inconsistent verdicts because there is no shared common standard of dishonesty and individual jurors may well reach different conclusions on similar facts. This issue is explored in more detail below.

■ The common law test of dishonesty

Although the question of whether the defendant was dishonest is a jury question, the courts have provided guidelines for a jury to follow in deciding the issue. Over the years, these guidelines have changed from the purely objective in *Feely* (applying the current standards of ordinary decent people) to a purely subjective test in **Boggeln v Williams [1978] 1 W.L.R. 873** (did D himself believe what he did was dishonest?) to finally the current test, a hybrid of the two, in **Ghosh [1982] 2 All E.R. 689.** The *Ghosh* test is a two-stage test:

> **1.** Was what D did dishonest according to the ordinary standards of reasonable and honest people?

If it was not dishonest by those standards, that is the end of the matter and the prosecution fails. If it was dishonest by those standards, then the jury must consider the second question.

> **2.** Did D realise that what he did was by those standards dishonest?

If the answer to the second question is also "yes", then D was dishonest.

The first part of the *Ghosh* test has its roots in the *Feely* objective test. The second part has a subjective element but does not entirely permit the defendant to be his own arbiter of dishonesty: the question is not whether D considered his conduct dishonest but whether he considered ordinary reasonable and honest people would consider it to be so.

■ Reasons for a hybrid test

According to Lord Lane C.J. in *Ghosh*, the issue at the heart of dishonesty is whether it is intended to characterise a course of conduct which can be established quite independently of the defendant's state of mind or whether it is intended to describe a state of mind. In the court's view, the defendant's knowledge and belief must be relevant to dishonesty. Lord Lane gave the following example to illustrate why dishonesty cannot be judged purely by an objective standard:

> "... a man ... comes from a country where public transport is free. On his first day here he travels on a bus. He gets off without paying. He never had any intention of paying. His mind is clearly honest; but his conduct, judged objectively by what he has done, is

> dishonest. It seems to us that in using the word 'dishonestly' in the Theft Act 1968, Parliament cannot have intended to catch dishonest conduct in that sense, that is to say conduct to which no moral obloquy could possibly attach.

He continued,

> If we are right that dishonesty is something in the mind of the accused ... then if the mind of the accused is honest, it cannot be deemed dishonest merely because members of the jury would have regarded it as dishonest to embark on that course of conduct."

Thus, in the court's view, dishonesty must also involve a subjective element; hence a test requiring both an objective and subjective assessment of dishonesty.

■ Criticisms of the Ghosh test

As was seen above, the Court of Appeal in *Ghosh* chose to adopt neither a purely objective nor a purely subjective test but, instead, a hybrid of the two. In doing so they created a test which is itself not without criticism. It is considered too complicated and over-sophisticated for juries. It was criticised by Professor Griew, "Dishonesty: the objections to Feely and Ghosh" [1985] Crim. L.R. 341 because it has at its root the *Feely* test. In his view, *Feely* is defective in several respects. First, there is no shared common standard of dishonesty, which can lead to inconsistency in verdicts. Recent research by E. Finch and S. Fafinski of Brunel University (summarised online at *http://business.timesonline.co.uk/tol/business/law/article6823915.ece*) supports Professor Griew's contention. It shows that there is no universal standard of honesty with people's views as to what is dishonest being affected by age, gender and whether the individual has committed the relevant act themselves. The researchers were not even able to obtain a consensus of those canvassed on what one would have thought clear-cut examples of dishonesty such as whether it is dishonest to take a DVD from a shop without paying!

The first limb of the *Ghosh* test requires a finding of fact by the jury/magistrates which explains why, despite the lack of agreement on dishonesty, there have been few appeals based on the first limb but it did give rise to an appeal in **DPP v Gohill and Walsh [2007] EWHC 239 (Admin)**. The DPP appealed by way of case stated against a decision by the magistrates to acquit the respondents of charges of theft and false accounting. The respondents worked for a tool and plant hire company that hired equipment to members of the public for a fee. The company had a policy that if hired equipment was returned to the store within two hours of being hired because it was faulty or incorrect equipment had been chosen, no fee was charged. On a number of occasions, the respondents allowed working and correctly-chosen equipment to be returned within two hours and, on such occasions, the customers normally tipped them £5 or £10. The respondents altered the computer records to show that the equipment had simply been reserved or was faulty so that no hire charge was applicable. They accepted that they had acted contrary to company procedure but asserted that they had acted to promote the business and in the interests of customer care so that the company benefited "in the long run". The magistrates' court acquitted on the basis that by the standards of reasonable and honest people the respondents had not acted dishonestly. The High Court considered this decision perverse. According to Leveson L.J., it was "quite impossible to justify the proposition that [by] the ordinary standards of reasonable and honest people what they did was not dishonest." The court remitted the case to a different magistrates' bench to determine whether the second stage of the *Ghosh* test was satisfied, i.e. whether the respondents knew that what they were doing was dishonest according to the standards of reasonable and honest people.

Professor Griew also criticised the *Feely* element of the *Ghosh* test because it can complicate and lengthen contested trials as any evidence of the defendant's state of mind and motives will be relevant at trial. Further, he viewed it as unsuitable where the case involves intricate financial dealings or those in a specialised market because juries will not have the relevant experience to appreciate the context in which the appropriation took place.

The House of Lords has not yet been asked to rule on the suitability of the *Ghosh* test and until they are asked to do so it remains good law. In **Pattni and others [2001] Crim. L.R. 570**, the Crown Court rejected an argument that the test was too vague and, therefore, contravened art.7 of the European Convention on Human Rights.

■ The Robin Hood defence
According to Lord Lane C.J. in *Ghosh*:

> "It is dishonest for a defendant to act in a way which he knows ordinary people consider to be dishonest, even if he asserts or genuinely believes that he is morally justified in acting as he did."

Thus, he considered the *Ghosh* test would not allow a defendant to plead the so-called "Robin Hood defence", i.e. to argue, as Robin Hood might have done when he stole from the rich to give to the poor, that his conduct was morally right so he did not consider ordinary people would view it as dishonest. Lord Lane gave the example of the modern-day Robin Hood or the ardent anti-vivisectionist who removes animals from testing laboratories. Although such a person might consider himself morally justified in his actions, he would still be dishonest in Lord Lane's view because he would know that ordinary people would consider his actions dishonest. But was Lord Lane C.J. correct in this assumption? Elliott, "Dishonesty in theft: A Dispensable Concept" [1982] Crim. L.R. 395 and Professors Griew and Smith, amongst others, have argued that the *Ghosh* test still allows for the Robin Hood defence: a defendant who believes so strongly that what he is doing is morally just may also believe that ordinary people would agree with him and would not, provided the jury believed him in this, be dishonest under *Ghosh*.

But is allowing the modern Robin Hood to escape liability for theft such a bad thing? Professor Smith (*Smith's Law of Theft*, 9th edn by Ormerod and Williams) argued that it is. He asserted that the anti-vivisectionist in the example should be liable for theft because:

> "One who deliberately deprives another of his property should not be able to escape liability because of *his* disapproval, however profound and morally justified, of the lawful use to which that property was being put by its owner. In deciding whether a state of mind should be regarded as dishonest it is not irrelevant to consider how the matter will be regarded ... by the victim. ... The law fails in one of its purposes if it does not afford protection to a person against what he quite reasonably regards as a straightforward case of theft."

According to Griew, the *Ghosh* test will assist not only a defendant who believes his actions morally justified but also someone who moves in a circle where it is considered acceptable behaviour to take advantage of certain groups in society, for example bookmakers or employers. Such a defendant may claim, successfully if believed, that he did not consider ordinary people would consider his actions dishonest were he to take property from a victim belonging to such a group.

■ Is the full Ghosh direction always necessary?

It is not always necessary for a trial judge to direct on both limbs of the *Ghosh* test; it must only be given in full where the defendant argues that whatever anyone else might think, he did not think he was dishonest. It was not, therefore, necessary in **Wood [2002] EWCA Crim 832**, where the sole question was as to the genuineness of the defendant's belief as to the situation he was in (he thought the property he took had been abandoned), not as to the ordinary person's notion of dishonesty.

REFORM OF DISHONESTY

Given the plethora of criticism of the current test for dishonesty, it is not surprising that there have been many suggested reform proposals. These include making dishonesty a question of law for the judge instead of one of fact for the jury (Griew). This could be done by rephrasing s.2 so as to provide an exhaustive definition of dishonesty. One such suggestion by Ormerod, (Smith and Hogan, *Criminal Law*, 12th edn) is to do so but with the addition of a further provision: (d) "he intends to replace the property with an equivalent and believes that no detriment whatever will be caused to the owner by the appropriation." Ormerod argues that s.2(1)(d) would exempt, for example, the person who takes money from his employer's till against his employer's instructions but intending to replace it before the employer notices it is missing.

A much more fundamental reform, suggested by Elliott, is to dispense with the concept of dishonesty entirely. He suggests inserting into the Theft Act a new s.2(3) to the effect that:

FIGURE 7 **Summary of dishonesty**

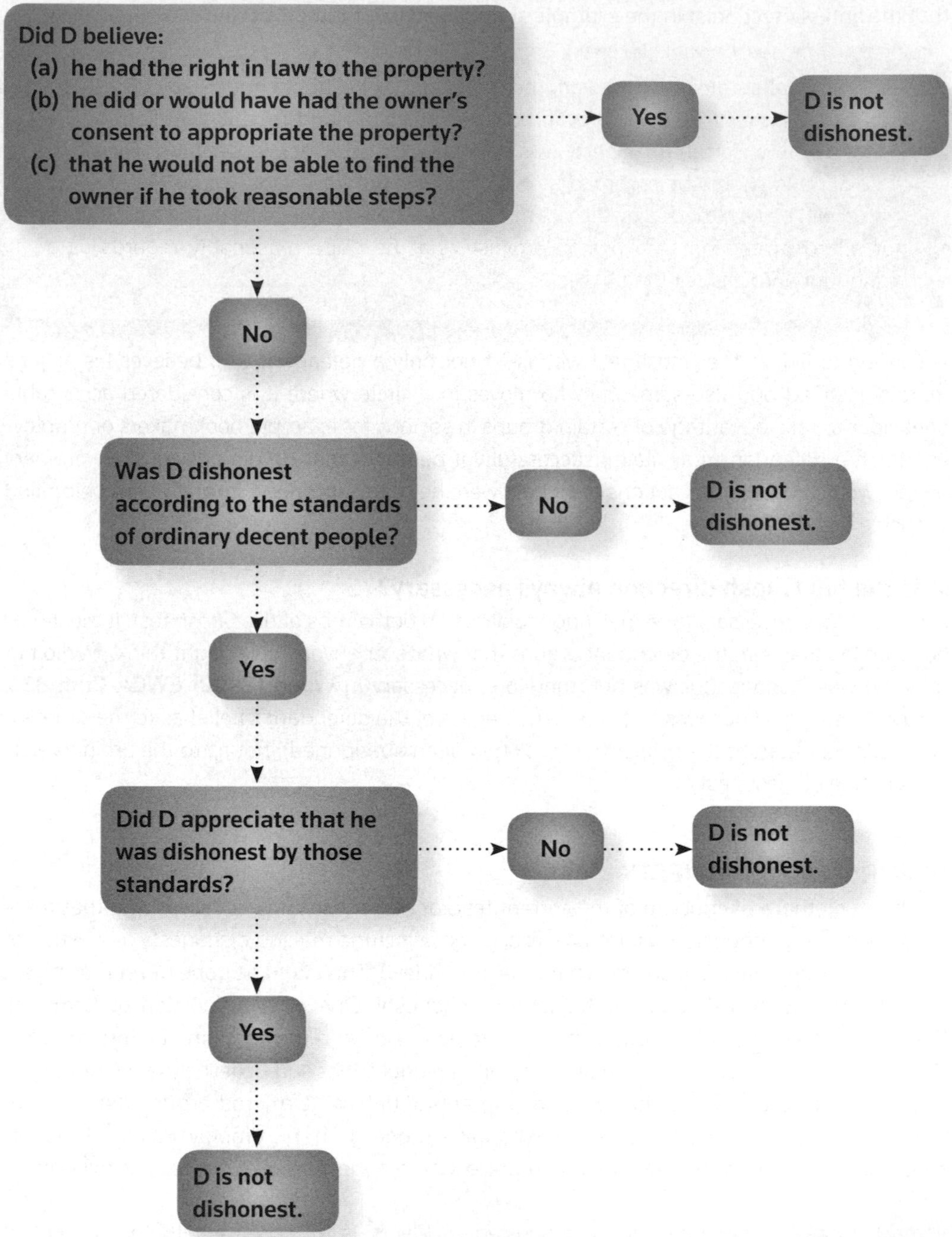

Did D believe:
(a) he had the right in law to the property?
(b) he did or would have had the owner's consent to appropriate the property?
(c) that he would not be able to find the owner if he took reasonable steps?

Yes → D is not dishonest.

No

Was D dishonest according to the standards of ordinary decent people?

No → D is not dishonest.

Yes

Did D appreciate that he was dishonest by those standards?

No → D is not dishonest.

Yes

D is not dishonest.

> "No appropriation of property belonging to another which is not detrimental to the interests of another in a significant way shall amount to theft of the property."

This, it is submitted, would not be entirely problem-free or any improvement on *Ghosh*. Would, for instance, petty pilfering no longer be considered theft? Would it be impossible to steal from the very wealthy? Whatever the merits of the aforementioned reform proposals, it is unlikely that any statutory reform will take place until after the reform of the law on deception instituted by the Fraud Act 2006 (see Ch.8) has been fully felt.

Intention Permanently to Deprive

The defendant must "intend permanently to deprive" (although there is no requirement that the defendant actually deprives permanently) so that if D intends to return property he has appropriated at some time in the future, mens rea cannot be established. There is no authority to suggest it is necessary to establish that the defendant intended permanently to deprive *by* the act which constitutes the appropriation; the law only requires that D appropriates the property and at that time he intends permanently to deprive O of it some time in the future.

Over to you...

D, a supervisor at a clothes factory, deliberately drops a pile of perfect quality clothes into the bin kept on the premises for faulted clothes so that she can empty it later after her boss has left the premises and take the clothes home for herself.

Does D commit theft? If so, is it when she drops the clothes into the bin or not until later when she empties the bin or not until she actually leaves the premises with the clothes?

Although the phrase, "intention permanently to deprive" is not defined in the Theft Act 1968, establishing such an intention on the part of the defendant will, in most cases, cause no difficulties. Where, for example, the defendant has sold another's property to a third-party or has consumed or destroyed another's property there is little doubt about his intentions. Nevertheless, situations may sometimes arise in which there is doubt whether the defendant intended permanently to deprive, for example where D did intend to return O's property but only once O had paid him for it or D pawned O's property and sent O the pawn ticket for O to redeem his property himself. Section 6 of the 1968 Act, though not defining "intention permanently to deprive," does address such problems by giving the term a broad scope. Section 6(1) provides:

> A person appropriating property belonging to another without meaning the other permanently to lose the thing itself is nevertheless to be regarded as having the intention of permanently depriving the other of it if his intention is to treat the thing as his own to dispose of regardless of the other's rights: and a borrowing or lending of it may amount to so treating it if, but only if, the borrowing or lending is for period and in circumstances making it equivalent to an outright taking or disposal.

There are two aspects to s.6(1):

1. Where it is the defendant's intention to treat the thing as his own to dispose of regardless of the other's rights.
2. A borrowing or lending equivalent to an outright taking or disposal.

INTENTION TO TREAT THE THING AS HIS OWN TO DISPOSE OF REGARDLESS OF THE OTHER'S RIGHTS

The phrase "intention permanently to deprive" featured in the old offence of larceny, the precursor to theft. Under the old law, the phrase was interpreted as encompassing, inter alia, the following situations:

1. D takes O's property intending to sell it back to O;
2. D takes O's property intending to return it only on performance of a specified condition (the "ransom" cases);
3. D pawns O's property intending to send O the pawn ticket someday.

Such situations also now fall within s.6. So, for example, in **Raphael & Johnson [2008] Crim. L.R. 995**, the defendants intended permanently to deprive when they took V's car with the aim of contacting him later to give him the opportunity to buy it back. Section 6 is, however, broader in scope than the old law and is not limited to the situations listed above (**Fernandes [1996] Cr. App. R. 175**, in which D, a solicitor, who invested client's money in a risky business venture where it was lost, did intend to treat the thing as his own to dispose of regardless of the other's rights because he dealt with the property in such a way that he risked loss.)

■ "To dispose of"

As Professor Smith recognised (in his commentary on **Cahill [1983] Crim. L.R. 142**), in order to prove an intention permanently to deprive, it is important that meaning is attributed to the phrase "dispose of regardless of the other's rights" in s.6(1) because the phrase "treat the thing as his own" means no more than that D appropriates the property. The need to ascribe meaning to "dispose of regardless of the other's rights" was acknowledged in *Cahill* where the court said it should be given its dictionary meaning, i.e.:

"To deal with definitely: to get rid of; to get done with, finish. To make over by way of sale or bargain ..."

Regrettably, the Divisional Court did not refer to *Cahill* when they reached their curious decision in **DPP v Lavender [1994] Crim. L.R. 297** in which greater emphasis was placed on the defendant's intention "to treat the thing as his own" than on "dispose of regardless of the other's rights". D took two doors from a council property undergoing repair and used them to replace damaged doors at another council property of which his girlfriend was the tenant. He was charged with theft of the two doors and argued that he had not had the intention permanently to deprive the council of the doors. The Divisional Court held that D had stolen the doors even though they remained in the possession of the council. The court considered the dictionary meaning of "dispose of" to be too narrow and that it could include "dealing with" the property (the doors). In the court's view, the appropriate question to ask was whether D intended to treat the doors as his own, regardless of the council's rights. The answer was yes as D had dealt with the doors regardless of the council's rights not to have them removed and in so doing had manifested an intention to treat the doors as his own.

Meaning was attributed to both the phrase "to treat the thing as his own" and to "dispose of regardless of the other's rights" in **Marshall [1998] 2 Cr. App. R. 282.** D had acquired London Underground tickets and travel cards which had not expired from passengers who had completed their journeys. He then sold them on to passengers who were about to start their journey. D was convicted of theft and appealed on the basis that he had lacked the intention of permanently depriving London Underground of the tickets because once the tickets expired they would be retained by the London Underground ticket machines. The Court of Appeal rejected this argument stating that D had the requisite intention since he intended to treat the tickets as his own to dispose of regardless of London Underground's rights as sole vendor of tickets and even though they would ultimately be returned to London Underground.

BORROWING

■ Intending to return property when it no longer has value
Generally, instances of borrowing another's property will not be theft due to the lack of an intention permanently to deprive the other of the property. However, certain borrowing will amount to theft due to the terms of the second limb of s.6(1). In **Lloyd [1985] Q.B. 829**, the court held that a mere borrowing is:

"never enough to constitute the necessary guilty mind unless the intention is to return the thing in such a changed state that it can truly be said that all its goodness or virtue was gone."

D had removed films from a cinema for a couple of hours at a time so that he could make pirate copies of them. His conviction for theft was quashed as there was no intention of permanently depriving. Even though D would have caused the copyright owner severe financial loss by the scam, the goodness and virtue of the films would not have been lost when they were returned as they could still be shown in cinemas. Although Lloyd was not guilty of theft on the facts, Lord Lane did give the following examples of circumstances in which a borrowing would amount to an intention permanently to deprive because it would involve returning an item when all its "goodness" had gone:

1. D borrows O's railway ticket, uses it to get a free ride and then returns it to O;
2. D borrows O's football or theatre season ticket, uses it to see the season's games or performances and then returns the ticket to O;
3. D borrows O's non-rechargeable batteries, uses them until they are flat and then returns them to O.

Over to you...

An issue left unclear following *Lloyd* is the position where D intends to return the property when it still has some value, albeit reduced value. Is there intention permanently to deprive in such circumstances? If there isn't, might it still be possible, provided the facts permit, to charge theft of a thing in action? So, for example, if D used O's season ticket for only some of the season's matches before returning it, could he be charged with theft? If so, of what?

■ Borrowing money

If the defendant appropriates money intending to spend it but to repay the owner with different coins or notes, he still has an intention to permanently deprive of the particular coins or notes which he took (**Velumyl [1989] Crim. L.R. 299**). The defendant will, of course, not be liable for theft unless he is also dishonest. As was seen above (p.232), a willingness to pay does not preclude dishonesty though a jury might not necessarily consider such a defendant to be dishonest.

LENDING

The reference to borrowing or lending in s.6(1) suggests that a lending by someone in lawful possession of O's property will be treated the same as a borrowing, for which, see above.

PARTING WITH ANOTHER'S PROPERTY UNDER A CONDITION AS TO ITS RETURN

Section 6(2) of the 1968 Act creates the possibility of theft arising where the defendant parts with another's property under a condition as to its return which he may not be able to perform. It provides that:

> Without prejudice to the generality of subsection (1) above, where a person, having possession or control (lawfully or not) of property belonging to another, parts with the property under a condition as to its return which he may not be able to perform this (if done for purpose of his own and without the other's authority) amounts to treating the property as his own to dispose of regardless of the others rights.

Section 6(2) would apply, for example, where D, without O's knowledge, borrows O's gold watch. He then pawns it. He intends to redeem the watch and return it to O but cannot be certain that he will be able to do so. This would amount to an intention permanently to deprive.

CONDITIONAL INTENTION

Does D intend permanently to deprive where he only intends to take property if, once he has examined it, he considers it worth stealing? In **Easom [1971] 2 Q.B. 315**, the court held that such a "conditional" intention is not sufficient for the purposes of theft. The defendant in this case took a woman's handbag and searched through it looking for anything worth keeping. He found nothing he wanted and discarded the bag and its contents. His conviction for stealing the handbag and its contents was quashed on appeal as he did not intend permanently to deprive of the handbag and its actual contents. The defendant could now be liable for attempting to steal *from* the handbag as he did intend to steal anything in it worth having, such as money, and impossibility does not prevent a conviction for an attempt, see further p.320

◄ ···

Summary

1. A person is guilty of theft, contrary to s.1 of the Theft Act 1968, if he dishonestly appropriates property belonging to another with the intention of permanently depriving the other of it.

2. The actus reus of theft is the appropriation of property belonging to another.

3. An appropriation is defined in s.3 as any assumption of the rights of an owner. It is only necessary to establish that D assumed a right, not all the rights of an owner. An appropriation can occur even where the owner consents to the act by which D assumes such a right and can, therefore, include the situation where V makes D a valid gift. Appropriation does not require physical possession of the property and can involve a continuing act. A bona fide purchaser of stolen property is protected from theft liability by s.3(2).

4. Property is defined in s.4 as including money, other personal property and things in action. Land and wild animals may only be stolen in limited circumstances. Confidential information, electricity and a corpse are not property and cannot be stolen.

5. Belonging to another is explored in s.5. The extended meaning given to the term by s.5(1), which includes having possession or control of property, means that it is possible to steal one's own property. Property which has been abandoned cannot be stolen. Where D receives property for a particular purpose and is legally obliged to use it for that purpose, the property is still treated as belonging to the original owner (s.5(3)) and can be stolen. Where property is transferred to D by another's mistake and D is legally obliged to return it, the property is still treated as belonging to the original owner (s.5(4)) and can be stolen.

6. The mens rea of theft is dishonesty and intention permanently to deprive.

7. A partial definition of dishonesty in terms of what will not be dishonest is given in s.2. What will be considered dishonest is a question for the jury applying the test in *Ghosh*.

8. Section 6 extends the scope of intention permanently to deprive to include an intention to treat the thing as one's own to dispose of regardless of the owner's rights and certain borrowing and lending. A conditional intention is not sufficient for theft.

End of Chapter Question

Question

Franco was a law student who had run out of money. He was very hungry but could not afford to buy food. He went to a local restaurant and told the manager he had been robbed and all his money had been taken. The manager felt very sorry for Franco and gave him a meal for free.

Franco then got on a tram to go to his local college for a tutorial. Payment for travel on the tram was due by the passenger to the conductors on the trams, not in advance. Franco saw where the conductor was, and boarded the tram at the other end. He then left the tram at the next stop when he saw the conductor come into his carriage.

Franco walked the rest of the way to college. When he arrived, he realised he had forgotten his pens. He went into the campus stationery shop and picked up a pen and put it in his pocket. He then noticed there was Closed Circuit Television (CCTV) in the shop and he thought he might have been recorded putting the pen in his pocket, so he took the pen out and replaced it on the shelf. Franco left the shop and went to his tutorial.

Discuss Franco's criminal liability, if any, for theft under the Theft Act 1968.

Note; the same factual scenario is also addressed in Ch.8 in respect of fraud offences.

Points of Answer

- ◆ Start with a clear definition of the offence of theft under s.1 of the Theft Act 1968.
- ◆ Deal with the elements of the offence by assessing each "event" in turn and by explaining and applying the actus reus first then mens rea.
- ◆ The meal
  - • It is an appropriation to assume a single right of the owner and this applies even if there is apparent consent of the owner (*Gomez; Hinks*). The food is property (s.4) and it belongs to another (s.5). Franco is also dishonest (he cannot fall under s.2; if he thought the owner would consent he would not have lied; so apply *Ghosh*; you are likely to reach the same conclusion) and had intention permanently to deprive, so the actus reus and mens rea coincide in time and are satisfied (*Edwards v Ddin*). At the end of Ch.8 we also consider whether the events give rise to a fraud offence.
- ◆ Tram
  - • There cannot be a theft because there is no property. At the end of Ch.8 we consider instead whether the events give rise to a fraud offence.
- ◆ Pen in the shop
  - • Theft is fairly straightforward—there is an appropriation whether using *Morris* or *Lawrence* or *Gomez*, the pen is property, it belongs to another and Franco is *Ghosh* dishonest (or else why did he put it back?) and at the time of the appropriation, he had intention permanently to deprive, even though he ultimately did not deprive (intention is mens rea, not actus reus). Theft has technically been committed, but the facts are unlikely to give rise to a charge because there is no overt "theft".

◄ ....

Further Reading

A.L. Bogg and J. Stanton-Ife, "Theft as Exploitation" (2003) Legal Studies 402.

A.L. Christie, "Should the law of Theft Extend to Information?," (2005) J.C.L. 347.

R. Cross, "Protecting Confidential Information under the Criminal Law of Theft and Fraud" (1991) 11 Ox. J.L.S. 264.

D.W. Elliott, "Dishonesty in Theft: A Dispensable Concept" [1982] Crim. L.R. 395.

S. Gardner, "Property and Theft" [1998] Crim. L.R. 35.

M. Giles and S. Uglow, "Appropriation and Manifest Criminality in Theft" (1992) 56 J.C.L. 179.

R. Glover, "Can Dishonesty Be Salvaged? Theft and the Grounding of the MSC Napoli" (2010) 74 J.C.L. 53.

E.J. Griew, "Dishonesty: The Objections to Feely and Ghosh" [1985] Crim. L.R. 341.

A. Halpin, "The Test for Dishonesty" [1996] Crim. L.R. 283.

R. Heaton, "Cheques and Balances" [2005] Crim. L.R. 747.

E. Melissaris, "The Concept of Appropriation and the Offence of Theft" (2007) M.L.R. 581.

S. O'Doherty, "Appropriation and Dishonesty" J.P. 2001, 165(6), 97.

S. Parsons, "Theft liability in business and other civil law relationships" Bus. L.R. 2005, 26(6), 141 and, "Dishonest appropriation after Gomez and Hinks" J.C.L. 2004, 68(6), 520.

S. Shute, "Appropriation and the Law of Theft" [2002] Crim. L.R. 450.

A.T.H. Smith, "Theft as sharp practice: who cares now?" [2001] C.L.J. 21

J.C. Smith, "Reforming the Theft Acts" Bracton L.J. 1996, 28, 27.

J.C. Smith, "Stealing Tickets" [1998] Crim. L.R. 723.

http://business.timesonline.co.uk/tol/business/law/article6823915.ece

Self Test Questions

To test your knowledge gained from this section go online to *http://www.sweetandmaxwell.co.uk* and take our online self test questions. Here you will also find key updates to ensure that you are only ever one click away from an instant update.

Offences Against Property II

8

CHAPTER OVERVIEW

In this chapter we:

- provide the definitions of the offences of robbery, burglary, blackmail, handling, going equipped, making off without payment and fraud

- analyse the actus reus and mens rea requirements for each offence

- provide critical commentary where appropriate of the offences mentioned.

Summary

End of Chapter Question

Further Reading

Self Test Questions

Introduction

In this chapter we continue our consideration of offences involving property. It is impossible to provide an introduction to the offences here by a theme or a common approach because the offences do not have much in common other than, on the whole, they do not involve offences against the person (note however robbery, although regarded as a property offence because it is based on the existence of a theft, also involves force or the threat of force to a person). These crimes tend to be grouped together, then, as general non-theft property crimes. We leave the offence of criminal damage to Ch.9 only because it is a complex offence which requires detailed examination.

Robbery

The Offence

Robbery is an offence contrary to s.8 of the Theft Act 1968. It is essentially an aggravated form of theft. It involves stealing accomplished by force or threats of force. Section 8 provides:

> **(1)** A person is guilty of robbery if he steals, and immediately before or at the time of doing so, and in order to do so, he uses force on any person or puts or seeks to put any person in fear of being then and there subjected to force.

The maximum sentence for the offence is life imprisonment.

The Actus Reus of Robbery

This involves:

1. theft;
2. use of force on any person;
3. immediately before or at the time of the theft;
4. in order to steal.

THE REQUIREMENT OF THEFT

There is no liability for robbery if there is no theft. So, if one of the elements of theft is missing, for example the defendant was not dishonest, there can be no robbery. Similarly, if there is no attempted theft, there is no attempted robbery. The robbery is complete when the theft is complete, i.e. once the dishonest appropriation of property belonging to another with the intention permanently to deprive has occurred. Given the broad meaning attributed to appropriation by **Morris [1983] 3 All E.R. 288** and **Gomez [1993] A.C. 442 HL**, the defendant can be liable for robbery (rather than merely attempted robbery) simply by using force to take hold of property with the intention of stealing it. It is not necessary that the defendant actually take the property (see *Corcoran v Anderton* at p.211).

USE OR THREAT OF FORCE ON ANY PERSON

The meaning of force in this context is a question of fact for the jury to determine (**Dawson (1976) 64 Cr. App. R. 170**) in which the court rejected an argument that nudging someone so that he lost his balance could not constitute force). It is unlikely, however, that a pickpocket would be liable for robbery, only for theft, because he uses stealth, not force, in order to appropriate the property.

Express or implied threats of force will also suffice for robbery. The threat may be verbal or by gesture, for example a raised fist or a knife to the victim's throat. In **Bentham [2005] UKHL 18**, the threat consisted of D pointing his fingers inside his jacket pocket to give the appearance of holding a gun whilst threatening to shoot V unless he handed over money and jewellery.

It is not necessary that the intended victim actually fears force; the offence requires only that the defendant seeks to put his victim in fear of force as "otherwise, the bravery of the victim would determine the guilt of the assailant" (per Gross J. in **B & R. v DPP [2007] EWHC 739 (Admin)**).

The force must be *on any person*. However, in the snatching situation where force is applied to the *property* in order to wrench it from the victim's grasp the defendant may still be convicted of robbery, presumably on the basis that where force is applied to property it is also applied to the person holding that property. Thus, in **Clouden (1987) Crim. L.R. 56**, where D pulled on a woman's shopping bag to force it from her hand, the Court of Appeal stated that it was for the jury to decide whether this was robbery. Moreover, the reference to "any" person means that the force (or threat thereof) does not have to be directed at the actual owner or person in possession of the property; it could be directed, for example, at a security guard attempting to restrain the thief.

IMMEDIATELY BEFORE OR AT THE TIME OF THE STEALING

The force or threats must occur immediately before or at the time of the theft. Consequently, force or threats thereof which occur long before the theft takes place will not constitute robbery (though it could still be blackmail, see p.257). The use of force or threats of force after the theft is complete will, similarly, only give rise to liability for theft and a non-fatal offence against the person, not robbery. It may, therefore, sometimes be crucial to determine whether a theft is complete when the force is used.

We saw on p.219 that an appropriation may be instantaneous or, depending on the circumstances, may be treated as a continuing act and that this remains the position even after *Gomez* **(Atakpu [1994] Crim. L.R. 693)**. This means that an appropriation can continue until the point at which the force is used, thereby making the offence robbery rather than simply theft. Consequently, in **Hale [1978] Crim. L.R. 596**, where the defendants went into V's home and took her jewellery box, the court held that the theft was still ongoing when, a few seconds later, they used force tying her up. In *Atakpu*, the court stated that it would be for the jury to determine in each case when the appropriation ended and that an appropriation may last as long as the thief can sensibly be regarded as in the act of stealing, or is "on the job."

Over to you...

D, a thief, uses force on V, a householder, who confronts him when he is escaping out the back door of V's home.

Is this robbery? If so, might it be robbery if V had not confronted D but had chased him down the street and was then attacked by D?

IN ORDER TO STEAL

The force or threats thereof must be in order to steal. It is simply a non-fatal offence against the person plus a theft, rather than robbery, where D, having attacked V, takes his property on the spur of the moment.

The Mens Rea of Robbery

The mens rea of robbery requires proof not only that the defendant intended to steal but also that he intended to use force on a person or to put a person in fear of force in order to steal.

Assault with Intent to Rob

Under s.8(2) of the Theft Act 1968, a defendant may commit the offence of assault with intent to rob where he commits an assault or battery on his victim, intending to steal, but is unsuccessful in appropriating the property. As with robbery, the offence is punishable by a maximum of life imprisonment.

Burglary

The Offences

There are two offences of burglary, contrary to s.9(1)(a) or 9(1)(b) of the Theft Act 1968. Section 9 provides:

> **(1)** A person is guilty of burglary if—
> **(a)** he enters any building or part of a building as a trespasser and with intent to commit any such offence as is mentioned in subsection (2) below; or
> **(b)** having entered any building or part of a building as a trespasser he steals or attempts to steal anything in the building or that part of it
> or inflicts or attempts to inflict on any person therein any grievous bodily harm.
>
> **(2)** The offences referred to in subsection (1)(a) above are offences of stealing anything in the building or part of a building in question, of inflicting on any person therein any grievous bodily harm and of doing unlawful damage to the building or anything therein.

Burglary is punishable by a maximum period of 14 years' imprisonment if the building in question was a dwelling and 10 years in any other case.

SECTION 9(1)(a)

Section 9(1)(a) creates an offence where the defendant, on entry to a building or part of a building as a trespasser, has the intent to steal, inflict grievous bodily harm (GBH) or damage the building or anything therein. It is the intention with which the defendant enters that is important under s.9(1)(a). Hence, the defendant would not be liable under s.9(1)(a) if he entered as a trespasser and, only once inside, decided to steal (**Bennett [2007] EWCA Crim 2815**). It is not necessary to prove that, having entered, the defendant did actually commit one of the specified offences.

SECTION 9(1)(b)

Section 9(1)(b) creates an offence where the defendant, having entered the building or part thereof as a trespasser, steals, inflicts GBH or attempts to do either. This offence may, therefore, be committed where the defendant had no particular unlawful intent when he entered but, once inside, commits one of the specified offences. Unlike s.9(1)(a), the specified offences under s.9(1)(b) do not include criminal damage.

The Actus Reus of Burglary

Although the two offences differ in some respects, certain elements of the actus reus are common, namely:

1. entry;
2. into a building or part of a building;
3. as a trespasser.

ENTRY

In most instances, it will be clear that the defendant has entered the building but difficulties may arise in two situations:

1. where only part of the defendant's body is inside the building, for example where D has merely inserted his arm inside an open window in order to snatch something from inside, or
2. where the defendant is outside the building but inserts an instrument inside in order, for example, to gain entry to the building in order to steal.

Unfortunately, there is no indication in the 1968 Act as to what will amount to an "entry" for the purposes of burglary and the term has been left to be defined by case law.

■ Entry by part of the body

Prior to the 1968 Act, the old common law rule was that entry by any part of the body was sufficient but the court cast doubt on the validity of this test in **Collins [1973] Q.B. 100** where it was stated that entry must be "effective and substantial." In **Brown [1985] Crim. L.R. 212**, the Court of Appeal held that D had entered a shop when, with his feet still on the ground, he leaned into it via a broken window in order to remove articles on display there. The court stated that the issue of whether there has been an entry is one for the jury and that a jury could decide that the defendant had entered if entry was merely *effective*. Although "effective" was not defined, the modification from "effective and substantial" to "effective" and the actual decision in the case indicate that there is no need for the whole or even most of the defendant's body to be inside the building.

One might have thought that effective would mean that enough of the defendant's body is inside the building to enable him to commit the relevant offence but this is not the case. In **Ryan [1996] Crim. L.R. 320**, D was found in the early hours of the morning stuck in a downstairs window of a house with his head and right arm inside the window, which was resting on his neck, and the rest of his body outside the window. The court held that there was evidence on which a jury could find that D had entered the building; entry could involve only part of D's body and did not depend on whether enough of his body was actually inside the building to allow him to commit the relevant crime.

Over to you...

Do you think that the court would decide that D had entered a building via an open window if he was caught standing on a ladder as he was just about to haul himself up into a bedroom window from outside with only his fingertips on the inside of the window ledge?

■ Entry via an instrument

The position regarding entry where the defendant inserts an instrument inside the building but not a part of his body, is unclear. Prior to the enactment of the Theft Act 1968, there was an entry where the insertion was for the purpose of committing a relevant offence (for example a gun inserted in order to shoot someone inside the building) but not where it was simply in order to gain access to the building. Unfortunately, there has been no case law on the point since the Act came into force. In *Collins*, the court stated that it was unnecessary to consider the old common law rules on entry so the law may have changed but the position is unclear.

AS A TRESPASSER

Trespass is not defined in the Theft Act 1968 and reliance must be placed on the meaning of the term under the civil law. Under tort law, trespass requires that the defendant does not have the consent of the owner to be there. For liability under the criminal law, mens rea as to trespass will also be required (*Collins*) so that the defendant must know or be (subjectively) reckless as to whether he enters without the owner's consent. It was on this basis that the defendant in *Collins* was not a trespasser. Wearing only his socks, D had climbed up a ladder onto a bedroom window-sill, intending to rape V (this could be burglary under the law prior to the Sexual Offences Act 2003) who invited him in for sex, mistakenly believing him to be her boyfriend. D was not a trespasser when he entered because his belief that he had V's permission to do so negated the mens rea for trespass.

The defendant must enter the building or part of it *as a trespasser* so it will not be burglary if the defendant becomes a trespasser after he has entered, for example if D remains in the building after permission to be there has been withdrawn. It would be burglary, however, if, once permission is withdrawn, D enters another part of the building to commit (or actually commits) a relevant offence.

Consent to be in a building may be express or implied (for example customers have implied permission to enter the public parts of a shop); it may be general or only given for a specific purpose; it may relate to the whole building or only part of it. Consent obtained by fraud, as for example where D pretends to be there to read the electricity meter, is not a valid consent and D would be a trespasser in such circumstances. The consent may be given by the owner of the relevant building or part of it or by someone lawfully in possession of it or even by members of the household, as in *Collins* where it was the owner's daughter who gave permission to the defendant to enter.

■ Trespass and exceeding one's permission to enter

A person may have permission to enter a building or a part of it but exceeds that permission by entering with an unlawful purpose, thereby becoming a trespasser. This was the view taken in **Jones and Smith [1976] 3 All E.R. 54**. The defendants entered the house of Smith's father and stole two TVs. They were convicted of burglary under s.9(1)(b) and appealed. Smith argued that this was only theft not burglary; he had not trespassed because his father had given him a general permission to go into his house whenever he wanted. This argument was rejected. The court held that a person enters as a trespasser if he enters knowing that he is entering in excess of the permission that has been given to him or is reckless in that regard; Smith had a general permission to enter the house but not in order to steal.

Over to you...

A defendant enters a shop having made his mind up before entering that he will steal once inside.

Could this be burglary on the basis that he has entered in excess of his implied permission to be there? What do you think are the practical difficulties in proving a burglary has been committed in such circumstances? If burglary is not charged, what might the prosecution charge instead?

ANY BUILDING OR PART OF A BUILDING

■ Building

There is no definition of building in the Act but it seems that the premises must be reasonably permanent to qualify as such. Thus, a tent is not a building. The term includes dwellings, shops, factories and offices. "Building" is construed widely and includes the outbuildings of a dwelling, for example a detached garage, a tool shed, a greenhouse or a barn. All such premises are buildings, whether or not they are inhabited. Section 9(4) extends the ambit of building to include "inhabited vehicle or vessel" whether or not the occupant is there at the time. Consequently, building also includes caravans, houseboats, and campervans but only whilst they are being used as a habitation.

> ## Over to you...
>
> During the week, V works away from home and during that time he lives on a houseboat moored on a river. He returns to his house at weekends. D breaks into the houseboat on a Saturday, while V is at his house, and steals the TV.
>
> Could this be burglary?

Occasionally, difficulties may arise in deciding where to draw the line in determining whether a certain structure constitutes a building. For example, in **B and S v Leathley [1979] Crim. L.R. 314**, it was held that a three tonne freezer container some 25ft by 7ft 7in size which had been in position for three years and was likely to remain there, had doors and was connected to the electricity supply was a building. However, in **Norfolk Constabulary v Seekings [1986] Crim. L.R. 167**, the court held that an articulated trailer which had been used as a temporary store for a year, had electricity, steps and lockable shutters was not a building.

■ Part of a building

A defendant may be a lawful entrant in one part of a building and a trespasser in another; supermarket customers, for example, have permission to enter the shop but not to enter the area marked "staff only". Each individual room in a building is a separate part of the building hence a defendant may lawfully enter one room but trespass into the next. Part of a building is widely construed so that in **Walkington [1979] 2 All E.R. 716**, D, a customer, became a trespasser when he went behind a moveable three-sided rectangular counter in a shop as the area behind the counter was out of bounds to customers.

. . . .

The Mens Rea of Burglary

The mens rea for trespass must be established for both offences. Also, where the defendant is charged under s.9(1)(a), he must have entered with the ulterior intent to steal something in the building, do GBH to someone in there or do damage whilst in there. D's ulterior intent may be conditional—an intention to steal only if there is anything worth taking or to injure or damage anyone or anything that happens to be inside the building. Provided it is not alleged in such circumstances that D intended to steal a particular item, injure a particular person or damage particular property, D can still be liable for burglary (**Attorney General's References (Nos 1 and 2 of 1979) [1979] 3 All E.R. 143**). This is so even if there is actually no property or person in the building at all (the impossibility of effecting the ulterior intent is irrelevant).

Where the defendant is charged under s.9(1)(b), it must be established that he did actually steal or inflict GBH (contrary to the Offences Against the Persons Act 1861 s.20) or attempt either offence. Thus, the mens rea for such an offence must be proved.

FIGURE 8 **Illustration of the different ways in which burglary may be committed**

Actus Reus	Mens Rea	Offence
Entry into building/part of building as a trespasser.	Mens rea for trespass and intent to steal.	Burglary under s.9(1)(a)
Entry into building/part of building as a trespasser.	Mens rea for trespass and intent to inflict GBH.	Burglary under s.9(1)(a)
Entry into building/part of building as a trespasser.	Mens rea for trespass and intent to do criminal damage.	Burglary under s.9(1)(a)
Having entered building/part of building as a trespasser, steals.	Mens rea for trespass and mens rea for theft.	Burglary under s.9(1)(b)
Having entered building/part of building as a trespasser, attempts to steal.	Mens rea for trespass and intent to steal.	Burglary under s.9(1)(b)
Having entered building/part of building as a trespasser, commits GBH.	Mens rea for trespass and malicious.	Burglary under s.9(1)(b)
Having entered building/part of building as a trespasser, attempts GBH.	Mens rea for trespass and intent to inflict GBH.	Burglary under s.9(1)(b)

Aggravated Burglary

Section 10 of the Theft Act 1968 provides that it is aggravated burglary, an offence punishable by a maximum of life imprisonment, where a person commits a burglary and has with him at the time a firearm (includes an air gun or air pistol) or imitation firearm, any weapon of offence or explosive. In *Bentham* (considered on p.249), the House of Lords stated that D did not have "with him" an "imitation firearm" when he pointed his fingers inside his jacket pocket to give the appearance of holding a gun; D could not possess his hand or fingers as they were part of him. "Weapon of offence" is defined as:

"any article made or adapted for use for causing injury to or incapacitating a person, or intended by the person having it with him for such use." The reference to "intended by the person having it with him for such use" extends the definition to include articles which are not normally considered weapons, such as a baseball bat, rope, screwdriver or tape, which the defendant intends to use in injuring or incapacitating his victim (or intends so to use should the need arise (**Kelly (1992) 97 Cr. App. R. 245**)).

The defendant must have the firearm, weapon, etc. *with him* at the relevant time. The phrase was interpreted in **Klass [1998] 1 Cr. App. R. 453** as requiring D to be armed with the relevant device; ready access to it is insufficient. D must be armed with the device at the time he commits the burglary; this means:

1. at the time he enters with the relevant intent where burglary is committed under s.9(1)(a); or
2. when he commits, or attempts to commit, theft or GBH where burglary is committed under s.9(1)(b).

Consequently, in **Francis [1982] Crim. L.R. 363**, D was liable for burglary but not aggravated burglary when he had put down the sticks he had used to gain entry prior to committing a theft from the building. There was no evidence that he intended to steal when he entered holding the sticks and, when he did steal, he no longer had the sticks with him. On the other hand, a defendant who enters without a weapon but picks one up once inside the building and has it with him when he commits the specified offence may be liable for aggravated burglary as in **O'Leary (1986) 82 Cr. App. R. 341**, where D armed himself with a knife he found in the kitchen after he had entered the building and used it to threaten the householder during the subsequent theft.

Blackmail

The Offence
Blackmail is an offence contrary to s.21 of the Theft Act 1968. Section 21 provides:

> **(1)** A person is guilty of blackmail if, with view to gain for himself or another or with intent to cause loss to another, he makes any unwarranted demand with menaces …

The maximum sentence for blackmail is 14 years' imprisonment.

The Actus Reus of Blackmail
This involves:

1. making a demand;
2. with menaces.

DEMAND

A demand can take any form—verbal, in writing or by conduct. It can be express or implied so that there was a demand in **Collister v Warhurst (1955) 39 Cr. App. R. 100** in which two police-men told V, falsely, that he would be prosecuted for an offence but that this could be avoided if V was to pay them. The court held that this was an implied demand as:

> "the demeanour of the accused and the circumstances of the case were such that an ordinary reasonable man would understand that a demand … was being made …"

According to s.21(2), the nature of the act or omission demanded is immaterial, and it is also immaterial whether the menaces relate to action to be taken by the person making the demand. This means that blackmail is not limited to a demand for the transfer of money (though the defendant must intend to cause gain or loss of something of economic value, see p.260 or to action that the defendant intends to take himself. It would still be blackmail where, for example, D was to threaten V that his men would beat V up if he did not do as D demanded.

A verbal demand is made at the time it is spoken whether or not the intended victim actually hears it. A demand contained in a letter is made where and when it is posted and it is irrelevant whether the intended victim read or even received the letter (**Treacy v DPP [1971] A.C. 537**). (Presumably, the same rule will apply to faxes and to sending an email or text message.) How-ever, where a letter is posted abroad to a victim in England or Wales, the demand is made when the letter is delivered and the offence will come within the jurisdiction of the English courts (*Treacy*).

MENACES

There is no statutory definition of "menaces" and the term is, therefore, to be given its common law meaning which includes not only threats of violence but also threats of anything detrimental or unpleasant (**Thorne v Motor Trade Association [1937] A.C. 797**). In **Clear [1968] 1 All E.R. 74**, the court stated that what was required was that the threat was of:

> "such a nature and extent that the mind of an ordinary person of normal stability and courage might be influenced or made apprehensive so as to accede unwillingly to the demand."

This test was applied in **Harry [1974] Crim. L.R. 32** in which letters from a college "Rag Week" treasurer asking 115 local shopkeepers to buy indemnity posters to protect them from "Rag Activity" which would cause inconvenience did not constitute blackmail; there were no menaces as only a few of the shopkeepers had complained, most were unconcerned about the alleged threat.

■ The timorous victim

The *Clear* test is an objective one, based on whether an ordinary person of normal stability and courage would feel they had no choice but to give in to the demand. It is, therefore, irrelevant that the victim is not affected by the threats if the ordinary person of normal stability would be. Conversely, where the victim is affected by the threats because, for example, he is exceptionally timorous, but the ordinary person would not be so affected, menaces can still be made out provided the defendant was aware of the likely effect of his actions on the victim (**Garwood [1987] 1 All E.R. 1032**).

The Mens Rea of Blackmail

The mens rea of blackmail requires that the demand is:

1. unwarranted; and
2. made with a view to gain or intent to cause loss.

UNWARRANTED

Section 21(1) provides:

> … a demand with menaces is unwarranted unless the person making it does so in the belief—
>
> **(a)** that there are reasonable grounds for making the demand; and
> **(b)** that the use of the menaces is a proper means of reinforcing the demand.

The effect of s.21(1) is that a demand is "unwarranted" unless the defendant *believed* not only that he was justified in making the demand, because he believed he was legally or morally entitled to make it (even a mistaken belief will suffice, see *Harvey* below), but also that the means he adopted were a proper means of enforcing that demand.

The focus on the defendant's belief means that unwarranted is assessed subjectively and not on the basis of whether reasonable grounds actually existed for making the demand or whether menaces were, in fact, a proper means of enforcing it. However, an entirely subjective test would result in the defendant being his own judge of what is proper and this would unfairly assist the defendant with low moral standards. Consequently, "unwarranted" has been interpreted so that a defendant who believed his demand was justified but knew what he was threatening to do is a crime cannot assert that he believed the menaces to be a proper means of enforcing the demand (**Harvey (1981) 72 Cr. App. R. 139**). Harvey (D) paid V a substantial sum for a consignment of cannabis which V failed to supply. Angered, D kidnapped V's wife and child and threatened to rape, maim and kill them unless he got his money back. D honestly believed he had reasonable grounds for making the demand, even though legally he did not have reasonable grounds, as the contract was legally unenforceable. However, his demand was unwarranted because he knew what he threatened to do was unlawful and not, therefore, proper.

Even where the defendant threatens action which is not criminal or action which he does not know to be criminal, the menaces may still be unwarranted if he did not believe the harm threatened would generally be regarded as proper, i.e. (in the view of the Criminal Law Revision Committee upon whose 8th Report the Theft Act 1968 was based) morally and socially acceptable behaviour.

VIEW TO GAIN OR INTENT TO CAUSE LOSS

The defendant must make the demand with a view to gain for himself or another or with the intention to cause loss to another. Section 34(2)(a) provides:

> "gain" and "loss" are to be construed as extending only to gain or loss in money or other property, but as extending to any such gain or loss whether temporary or permanent; and
>
> **(i)** "gain" includes a gain by keeping what one has, as well as a gain by getting what one has not; and
> **(ii)** "loss" includes a loss by not getting what one might get, as well as a loss by parting with what one has.

■ Money or property

Blackmail is essentially concerned with the protection of economic interests. This is emphasised by the fact that the defendant must intend to cause loss or gain of money or other property. This means that a threat, for example, that D would expose V's affair unless she had sex with him would not constitute blackmail as there would be no view to gain or to cause loss of property. A wide meaning is given to property, as illustrated by **Bevans (1988) 87 Cr. App. R. 64**, in which a threat by a person suffering from osteoarthritis to a doctor that he would shoot him unless he gave him a painkilling injection was blackmail. Further, a demand with menaces that V give D a job may constitute blackmail because the job will bring with it payment in money.

■ Gain or loss

A wide meaning is attributed to "gain" and "loss" by s.21. A gain or loss may be temporary, for example where D causes V to make a loan of property. It is not a requirement that the demand relates to the transfer of property. So, blackmail can involve a demand that V abandon his claim against V in respect of certain property (D has a view to gain by keeping what he has).

■ Demanding repayment of a debt

Can a demand be made with a view to gain where the defendant merely demands repayment of a debt? The answer is yes. In **Lawrence and Pomroy [1971] Crim. L.R. 645**, the Court of Appeal assumed that there may be a view to gain even where the defendant is seeking to recover that to which he is legally entitled. Similarly, in **Parkes [1973] Crim. L.R. 358**, the court stated there is a view to gain in such circumstances because, "getting hard cash as opposed to a mere right of action is getting more than one already has." However, if the defendant does no more than merely threaten legal proceedings it is unlikely that blackmail can be made out because the demand will not be "unwarranted".

Over to you...

D threatens to expose V, a local, married councillor, to the press for associating with rent boys unless V pays him the money he owed him. At his trial for blackmail, he asserts that his demand was not unwarranted and not made with a view to gain.

Is D likely to succeed with these assertions?

Handling Stolen Goods

The Offence

Handling is an offence contrary to s.22 of the Theft Act 1968 in respect of assisting a thief to dispose of stolen goods. Section 22 provides:

A person handles stolen goods if (otherwise than in the course of stealing) knowing or believing them to be stolen he dishonestly receives the goods, or dishonestly undertakes or assists in their retention, removal, disposal or realisation by or for the benefit of another, or if he arranges to do so.

Handling is punishable by a maximum period of imprisonment of 14 years.

There is only one offence of handling (**Nicklin [1977] 2 All E.R. 444**) but there are two limbs to the offence and so two possible counts of handling. The prosecution should state in the indictment within which limb the alleged handling falls. The two limbs are:

1. Dishonestly receiving stolen goods.
2. Dishonestly undertaking or assisting in the retention, removal, disposal or realisation of stolen goods by or for the benefit of another.

The Actus Reus of Handling Stolen Goods

This involves:

1. handling;
2. otherwise than in the course of stealing;
3. stolen goods.

HANDLING

Although there is only one offence of handling, it may be committed in a number of different ways:

1. Receiving the stolen goods.
2. Undertaking the retention, removal, disposal or realisation of the stolen goods for the benefit of another person.
3. Assisting in the retention, removal, disposal or realisation of the stolen goods by another person.
4. Arranging to do any of the above.

The different combinations involving undertaking and assisting the retention, removal disposal and realisation of stolen goods and arranging to do any of these, mean that handling may be committed in a total of 18 different ways!

■ Receiving

Receiving is the only form of handling which does not require that it was done "for the benefit of another" (see p.264). Receiving is not defined in the Theft Act 1968 but case law decided under similar provisions in earlier legislation defined receiving as the taking of possession or control of property, either jointly or exclusively, and this is likely to remain so under the Theft Act 1968. Consequently, it would not be receiving where D merely inspects the goods in the thief's presence during negotiations or, as in **Hobson v Impett (1957) 41 Cr. App. R. 138**, helps a thief to remove stolen goods from a lorry. If the thief retains exclusive control, there is no receiving (**Richardson (1834) 6 Car. & P. 335**). Nor is there receiving where the defendant is unaware that he has possession or control of the goods (*Hobson v Impett*). Possession does not require physical handling so, for example, things in action, such as the proceeds of a stolen cheque credited to a bank account, may be received. Property may be received for a temporary purpose only, for example concealing the goods from the police (*Richardson*). Receiving is a finite act of taking into one's possession or control (**Smythe (1980) 72 Cr. App. R. 8**). It involves a receipt from someone else. Thus, where the defendant finds stolen goods and then takes possession of them, he does not receive them (**Haider (1985) CA unreported**).

Can a thief receive?

A thief will generally only be liable for handling by receiving where he has aided and abetted the receipt by another because he is already in possession or control and cannot, therefore, receive as principal. However, the thief may receive as principal in certain circumstances. For example, if D steals goods and, in the course of the theft, delivers them to E. Days later, E returns the goods to D. D has become a handler by receiving.

Arranging to Receive

This occurs where the defendant's preparations to receive the goods fall short of an attempt to receive but a concluded agreement has been reached that the defendant will receive the goods. It is not necessary that the agreement is made with the thief as an arrangement made with a person innocently in possession of stolen goods would be sufficient if the defendant knew that the goods were stolen.

The goods must have already been stolen at the time of the agreement; an agreement to handle goods which are to be stolen in the future will not constitute handling but may amount to a conspiracy to handle (**Park (1987) Cr. App. R. 164**, see further Ch.10). If no agreement is reached, an offer by the defendant to receive the goods may still amount to an attempt to handle.

As the offence of arranging to receive is committed by reaching the agreement, the defendant will still be liable for the offence even if it later becomes impossible to handle the goods or he subsequently changes his mind or takes no steps to execute the agreement.

■ Undertaking or assisting in the retention, removal, disposal or realisation of the goods by or for the benefit of another person

A defendant may commit handling by the retention, removal, disposal or realisation of stolen goods in the following two ways:

1. D may *undertake* the activity *for the benefit of another person*.
2. The activity may be undertaken *by another person* and D may assist him.

Undertaking

This covers the situation where the defendant sets out to retain, remove, dispose of or realise stolen goods (hereinafter referred to as the *specified activities*) on his own initiative.

Assisting

This applies where the defendant joins the thief or another handler in one of the specified activities. Simply refusing to answer police questions rather than deliberately lying to the police does not constitute assisting.

Over to you...

- The police visit D's house enquiring about goods found in X's possession which match those goods which were recently stolen from Y. D knows that the goods in question were stolen by X but tells the police that the goods belong to him and that he lent them to X.

Does D commit handling?

- The police visit D's house enquiring about goods which have been stolen from Y. D knows the whereabouts of the stolen goods and refuses to say where they are.

Does D commit handling?

If the original thief or original receiver and D act together in one of the specified activities, D may commit the offence in both ways—by undertaking and assisting.

By or for the benefit of another

Handling, other than by receiving, requires that the specified activity is "by or for the benefit of another". This means that where it is alleged that the defendant *undertook* the specified activity it must have been *for the benefit of another* and, where it is alleged he *assisted* in a specified activity, he must have assisted a specified activity which was carried out "*by another person*" (**Bloxham [1983] 1 A.C. 109**). Further, "another" has the same meaning whether it is alleged that the defendant undertook or assisted in one of the four specified activities (*Bloxham*).

If the defendant undertakes one of the four activities solely for his own benefit, he cannot be convicted of handling unless he has received the goods with the relevant mens rea as only receiving can be for one's own benefit. Thus, if D innocently receives the stolen goods and then merely retains them for his own benefit, he cannot be convicted of handling (although he might be liable for theft (subject to Theft Act 1968 s.3(2)), see Ch.7). As most thieves will retain, remove, dispose of or realise the stolen goods, this requirement prevents them also being handlers. However, a thief could become a handler if, following the theft, he then undertakes one of the specified activities for the benefit of another person.

Sellers usually sell for their own benefit and the buyer benefits only from the purchase, not from the realisation. This means that a person who sells stolen goods does *not* undertake their realisation *for the benefit of another* (*Bloxham*). The defendant in this case purchased a car for £1,300, not knowing that it was stolen. He subsequently began to suspect that the car was stolen and sold it almost a year later for only £200. The purchaser willingly bought the car without any documentation. The defendant was convicted of handling by undertaking or assisting in the realisation of the car for the benefit of the buyer but his conviction was quashed by the House of Lords as the sale was not for the benefit of the buyer.

If D1 and D2 are jointly charged in one count of doing one of the four specified activities "by or for the benefit of another", the "other" must be someone other than D1 and D2 as "another" does not include a person who is a co-accused on the same charge of handling (**Gingell [2000] 1 Cr. App. R. 88**). Despite this, an agreement between D1 and D2 that D1 would do one of the specified activities for the benefit of D2 is a conspiracy to handle (**Slater [1996] Crim. L.R. 300**).

Retention

Retention was defined in **Pitchley (1973) 57 Cr. App. R. 30** as to "keep possession of, not lose, continue to have." Retention is a continuing act so that if the defendant comes by property innocently and then discovers it was stolen, he retains if he continues to keep possession of it. A defendant might, for example, undertake the retention of stolen goods where he stores the goods for the thief or another handler in his lock up garage.

Assisting in the retention requires that "something must be done by the offender, and done intentionally and dishonestly, for the purpose of enabling the goods to be retained" (**Kanwar [1982] 2 All E.R. 528**). On the facts of *Kanwar*, D had assisted in the retention of stolen goods when she told lies to protect her husband who had dishonestly brought stolen goods into the home; D knew that if the deception was successful, her husband would be able to retain the goods. In **Burroughes (CA, November 29, 2000, unreported)**, the court held that assisting in the retention of goods by housing them requires proof that the defendant concealed them or made them more difficult to identify or held them pending their ultimate disposal or by some other act that was part of the chain of the dishonest handling. In the absence of such conduct, a mere failure to inform the police, knowing that the goods are stolen, is not assisting in their retention.

The requirement that the defendant's actions must be for the purpose of enabling the goods to be retained means that it is not assisting merely to use them, knowing them to be stolen. D did not, therefore, assist in the retention of stolen goods where he used a stolen heater and battery charger in his father's garage (**Sanders (1982) 75 Cr. App. R. 84**).

Some examples of assisting, taken from the old cases, suggest that the defendant would assist in the retention of stolen goods where, for example, he:

1. puts the thief in contact with the owner of a warehouse where the goods may be stored; or
2. provides tarpaulins to cover the goods which are in the possession of the thief or the handler or covers them himself in order to hide them.

Removal

This refers to the movement of stolen goods from one place to another. Thus, for example, the defendant undertakes or assists in the removal of stolen goods by or for the benefit of another in the following situations:

1. D undertakes the removal of stolen goods where he transports them for X's benefit.
2. D assists in the removal of stolen goods where he helps X to unload stolen goods from a van.
3. D assists in the removal of stolen goods where he lights the way for X to carry the goods from a house to a barn so that X may negotiate their sale (**Wiley (1850) 2 Den. 37**).
4. D assists in the removal of stolen goods if he lends the thief a lorry for their removal.

Disposal

This covers dumping, destroying, giving away or transforming stolen goods. So, for example, D undertakes or assists in the disposal of stolen goods by or for the benefit of another in the following situations:

1. D undertakes the disposal of stolen goods where he melts down (transforms) stolen gold candlesticks for the benefit of another.
2. D assists in the disposal of stolen goods by another if he advises the thief how to get rid of the stolen goods.

Assisting in the disposal of stolen goods requires some act of assistance or encouragement; the mere fact that the defendant benefits from the disposal does not amount to assistance. Thus, the defendant in **Coleman [1986] Crim. L.R. 56** did not assist in the disposal of stolen goods where he knew that his wife was using money which she had stolen to pay the conveyancing fees on the purchase of a property in their joint names; assistance would require D to have urged his wife to use the stolen money or to have agreed that she should.

Realisation

This involves the exchange of stolen goods for money or other property. For example, D undertakes or assists in the realisation of stolen goods by or for the benefit of another in the following situations:

1. D undertakes the realisation of stolen goods for the benefit of another where he sells stolen goods as agent for a third party (e.g. the thief).
2. D assists in the realisation of stolen goods by another if he puts a dealer in stolen goods in contact with the thief.
3. D assists in the realisation of stolen goods when he pays a sub-contractor for goods he has employed the sub-contractor to make and which are then delivered to the purchaser, if D knows or believes that the materials used to make the goods are stolen (**Tamm [1973] Crim. L.R. 115**).

Arranging to undertake or assist in one of the specified activities

A mere arrangement to do any of the acts which amount to undertaking or assisting is sufficient. For example, the defendant arranges to undertake or assist in the following situations:

1. D arranges to undertake the realisation of stolen goods when he agrees to negotiate their sale.
2. D arranges to assist in the removal of stolen goods by another when he sends a van to collect the thief and the stolen goods.

OTHERWISE THAN IN THE COURSE OF STEALING

All forms of handling must occur "otherwise than in the course of stealing." The "stealing" is the theft of the goods in the first place, before the alleged handling. This requirement prevents a thief becoming a handler whilst he is still taking part in the original theft. Without this stipulation, almost every incident involving a theft by two or more people would also be handling by at least one of them.

EFFECT OF THE CONTINUING NATURE OF THEFT

As was seen in Ch.7, an appropriation, and therefore a theft, may be a continuing act. As handling only begins when the theft is complete, it may be necessary in some cases to determine whether the theft is complete or still ongoing when the defendant receives or does one of the four specified activities. This will be a question for the jury to determine (*Atakpu*). Unless there is an issue on the evidence that the defendant was the thief or that the handling was in the course of the stealing, the prosecution does not have to prove that the handling was otherwise than in the course of the stealing (**Cash [1985] Q.B. 801**).

STOLEN GOODS

■ Goods

Goods are defined in s.34(2)(b) as:

> ... includ[ing] money and every other description of property except land, and includ[ing] things severed from the land by stealing.

■ The meaning of stolen

The goods must already have been stolen at the time of the handling. Section 24(4) of the Theft Act 1968 gives a wide meaning to "stolen" for the purposes of handling. The effect of the provision is that goods are stolen if they:

1. have been stolen contrary to s.1 of the Theft Act 1968;
2. have been obtained by blackmail or by fraud (contrary to the Fraud Act 2006);
3. consist of money dishonestly withdrawn from an account to which a wrongful credit has been made (Theft Act 1968 s.24A);
4. have been the subject of an act done in a foreign country which was:

   (a) a crime by the law of that country; and which
   (b) had it been done in England, would have been theft, blackmail or fraud.

■ There must have been a theft

The goods must actually be stolen. Thus, if the goods are not stolen, the defendant cannot be liable for handling even if he believes them to be stolen (**Haughton v Smith [1975] A.C. 476**). D might, however, be guilty of attempted handling in this situation.

Goods may appear to be stolen but, actually, are not because the person who originally appropriated them is not liable for theft. This may be because, for example, the alleged thief lacked mens rea or because he was doli incapax, as in **Walters v Lunt [1951] 2 All E.R. 645**.

Over to you...

D negotiates with Y for the sale of a load of copper piping taken from a builder's yard by X. X is arrested by the police with the piping in his possession but when questioned reveals that he is only 9 years of age. D is charged with handling. D thought X was 13 as he looks a lot older than his age.

Can D be liable for handling? If not, could he be liable for any other offence?

■ When might goods cease to be stolen?

The goods must remain stolen at the time of the handling but what happens if the goods have already been returned to their owner? Section 24(3) deals with this situation. It provides:

But no goods shall be regarded as having continued to be stolen goods after they have been restored to the person from whom they were stolen or to other lawful possession or custody, or after that person and any other person claiming through him have otherwise ceased as regards those goods to have any right to restitution in respect of the theft.

Restoration of the goods to their owner or to other lawful possession or custody

Once goods have been returned to their owner (or his agent) or to the person from whom they were stolen, they cease to be stolen goods. Goods also cease to be stolen once they have been, taken into possession by the police (**Attorney General's Reference (No.1 of 1974), Re [1974] 2 All E.R. 899**).

Sometimes it is difficult to determine whether, on the facts, goods which have been located by the police have been "restored". Whether goods have been restored will hinge upon whether they have been taken into possession and this, in turn, depends upon the intentions of the police officer concerned. In *Attorney General's Reference (No.1 of 1974), Re,* a police officer found an unattended car which he could see contained packages of new clothing which he suspected were stolen and which subsequently proved to be the case. He removed the rotor arm from the car to immobilise it and kept the car under observation. After about 10 minutes, D appeared, got into the car and tried to start the engine. When questioned by the police officer, D gave an implausible explanation and was arrested and charged with handling stolen goods. The Court of Appeal held that the question of whether the police officer's conduct in examining the goods, removing the rotor arm of the car and keeping the goods under observation amounted to taking possession of the goods depended primarily on the police officer's intention: had the officer made up his mind to take possession of the goods so that they could be removed and he would have disposal of them or, at that stage, did he still have an open mind whether to take possession of them or not and was merely concerned to ensure that the driver did not get away without being questioned?

A similar approach was taken in **Greater London Metropolitan Police Commissioner v Streeter (1980) 71 Cr. App. R. 113** in which the Divisional Court held that goods had not ceased to be stolen where a security guard, an employee of the owner, merely marked them for the purpose of identifying them later and the police kept them under observation. The security guard had not taken possession merely by writing on them and neither he nor the police intended to exercise possession or control over the goods.

Where a person ceases to have any right to restitution

The issue of whether a person ceases to have any right to restitution involves consideration of the civil law of restitution. The position is quite complex but may be illustrated by the following example. D deceives O into agreeing to sell goods to him. The deception renders the contract voidable. If O discovers the deception but chooses to ratify the contract by delivering the goods to D, the goods cease to be stolen.

■ Goods representing those originally stolen

Section 24(2) extends the ambit of stolen goods beyond the original goods, or parts of them, to also include the proceeds of those goods. Section 24(2) provides:

> For purposes of these provisions reference to stolen goods shall include, in addition to the goods originally stolen and parts of them (whether in their original state or not),—

(a) any other goods which directly or indirectly represent or have at any time represented the stolen goods in the hands of the thief as being the proceeds of any disposal or realisation of the whole or part of the goods stolen or of goods so representing the stolen goods; and

(b) any other goods which directly or indirectly represent or have at any time represented the stolen goods in the hands of the handler of the stolen goods or any part of them as being the proceeds of any disposal or realisation of the whole or part of the stolen goods handled by him or of goods so representing them.

The following example illustrates the operation of s.24(2). D sells a stolen motorbike to A for £50. The money is now also stolen goods, as would anything D bought with the money. Proceeds of stolen goods become themselves stolen goods under s.24 (2) where:

1. they are in the hands of the thief or handler; and
2. they represent directly or indirectly the stolen goods.

In the hands of the thief or the handler

The proceeds of stolen goods must have, at some time, been "in the hands of the thief or the handler." The phrase was interpreted in **Forsyth [1997] 2 Cr. App. R. 299**, as meaning "in the possession or under the control of the thief or handler." Consequently, goods which have passed though the hands of an innocent person (someone who does not know they are stolen) are not stolen goods.

The effect of s.24(2) is best explained by the following examples:

1. D sells a stolen motorbike to A for £50 and receives the money in cash. The motorbike and the cash are both now stolen goods. The cash is stolen goods as it directly represents the original stolen goods (motorbike) in the hands of the thief (D) as being the proceeds of the sale of the motorbike.
2. If D then gives £20 of the £50 to B who knows that it represents part of the original stolen goods, B can be convicted of handling.
3. If B buys a CD with the £20, the CD becomes stolen goods once it is in B's hands as it indirectly represents the original stolen goods in the hands of the handler as the proceeds of sale of part of goods representing the original stolen goods.
4. If C receives the CD from B, knowing that it has represented part of the stolen goods in the hands of B, C can be convicted of handling.
5. If E receives the CD from C, not knowing that it represents the original stolen goods, and then sells it for £10, the £10 which E receives is not stolen goods—E is not a handler because he lacks mens rea—so the cash does not represent the original stolen goods in the hands of a handler.

The Mens Rea of Handling Stolen Goods

The defendant must handle the goods:

1. knowing or believing them to be stolen; and
2. dishonestly.

KNOWING OR BELIEVING THE GOODS TO BE STOLEN

In **Reader (1978) 66 Cr. App. R. 33**, the court held that the words knowledge and belief are ordinary words whose meaning should be left up to the common sense of the jury. Nevertheless, the courts have endeavoured to provide guidance on both terms. Knowledge and belief are both to be assessed subjectively, i.e. it must be proved that the defendant knew or believed that the goods were stolen rather than that he ought to have known or believed that the goods were stolen (**Atwal v Massey [1971] 3 All E.R. 881**). A person knows that goods are stolen if he has actual, not constructive, knowledge of this (**Hall (1985) 81 Cr. App. R. 260**).

Belief is something short of knowledge and might be said to be the state of mind of a person who said to himself:

> "I cannot say for certain that those goods are stolen, but there can be no other reasonable conclusion in the light of all the circumstances, in the light of all that I have heard and seen."

This is sufficient for belief even if the defendant said to himself:

> "Despite all that I have seen and all that I have heard, I refuse to believe what my brain tells me is obvious" (*Hall*).

However, in *Forsyth*, the court held that what was said in *Hall* was potentially confusing as a jury might conclude the defendant was guilty if there were circumstances of great suspicion from which the only reasonable conclusion was that the goods were stolen but which the defendant could not bring himself to believe. There is, therefore, no adequate definition of belief.

■ Suspicion and wilful blindness

Suspicion, however strong, that goods are stolen does not constitute a belief that they are stolen (**Moys (1984) 79 Cr. App. R. 72**)). Wilful blindness, where the defendant has a suspicion that something is so and consciously decides not to take steps to confirm or deny the fact, is not sufficient either (**Griffiths (1974) 60 Cr. App. R. 14**). Hence, the judge had misdirected the jury when he stated that it was enough that the defendant, "suspecting that the goods were stolen deliberately shut his eyes to the consequences." Strangely, however, knowledge or belief may be inferred from wilful blindness (*Griffiths*).

DISHONESTY

Dishonesty is determined according to the *Ghosh* test (see p.234). The inclusion of this element in the definition means that the defendant ought not to be liable for handling where, for example, he receives stolen goods knowing them to be such but intending to return them to the true owner or the police.

Going Equipped for Stealing

The Offence

Section 25(1) of the Theft Act 1968 (as amended by the Fraud Act 2006) provides:

> A person shall be guilty of an offence if, when not at his place of abode, he has with him any article for use in the course of or in connection with any burglary or theft.

For the purposes of s.25, "theft" includes the offence of taking a conveyance, contrary to s.12 of the Theft Act 1968. The side note to s.25 refers to the offence as going equipped for stealing and this is the title which will be used in this book. The offence is punishable by a maximum period of imprisonment of three years.

The Actus Reus of Going Equipped

This involves:

1. the defendant has with him;
2. any article;
3. for use in the course of or in connection with a burglary or theft;
4. the defendant was not at his place of abode.

THE DEFENDANT HAS WITH HIM

The phrase "has with him" has not, as yet, been interpreted by the courts. Clearly, though, the defendant has "with him" an article if he has it on his person but the term has an extended meaning which includes having an article in one's possession or control. It is generally thought this covers articles which are readily accessible (c.f. aggravated burglary). This shows that, despite the shorthand title of the offence, the defendant does not have to be "going equipped" to commit the offence under s.25. Even brief possession of the article will suffice, as in **Minor v DPP (1987) Cr. App. R. 378**, in which the defendant and his accomplice were convicted under s.25 having been arrested when they were preparing to siphon off petrol from a car. The defendants had had "with them" two empty petrol cans and a tube but there was no evidence that they had taken these items with them from their homes. The decision has been criticised by Smith and Hogan, *Criminal Law*, 12th edn, by Ormerod, because it would permit the conviction under s.25 of a burglar who merely picks up a nearby stone to break a window. In the author's view, "has with him" requires more than that the defendant obtains the article prior to a theft.

ANY ARTICLE

An article for the purposes of s.25 is one which the defendant intended to use (or permit another to use) in furtherance of a burglary or theft. Such an article could be virtually anything, for example a diving suit which would allow D to dive in a lake for golf balls (**Rostron (2003) All E.R. (D) 269**) or bottles of wine which D, a hotel waiter, intended to sell to the hotel diners for his own profit (**Doukas [1978] 1 All E.R. 1061**).

FOR USE IN THE COURSE OF OR IN CONNECTION WITH A BURGLARY OR THEFT

Although the article must be for use in the course of or in connection with a burglary or theft, it is not necessary to establish that it was in connection with a particular burglary or theft (**Ellames (1974) 60 Cr. App. R. 7**) or even one to be committed by the defendant himself. "For use" is limited to present or future use; the offence is not committed where the defendant is found with articles on him which he had used in connection with an offence and is busy trying to dispose of them (*Ellames*).

THE DEFENDANT WAS NOT AT HIS HIS PLACE ABODE

The defendant must have the article with him when he is not at his place of abode. There is no statutory definition of place of abode but it has been interpreted as meaning a site where the occupier intends to abide and can include a car (and presumably also a caravan) if the defendant is homeless and living in it (**Bundy [1977] 2 All E.R. 382**). This meant that, on the facts of *Bundy*, D was not at his place of abode because, when he was arrested, he was not where he normally parked up his car—he was driving it.

The Mens Rea of Going Equipped

Although no mens rea is specified in s.25, we would suggest that what is required is:

1. knowledge on the defendant's part that he has the article with him; and
2. intention to use the article in the course of or in connection with a burglary or theft.

Possession of Articles for use in Frauds

The Fraud Act 2006 removed the word "cheat" from the list of offences in s.25 of the Theft Act 1968 for which a person might "go equipped" as "cheat" related to an offence of obtaining property by deception under s.15, which the 2006 Act also abolished. The removal of the word "cheat" from s.25 created a gap in the law which was filled by the creation of a new offence, under s.6 of the Fraud Act 2006, of possession of articles for use in frauds.

Section 6 makes it an offence for a person to possess or have under his control any article for use in the course of or in connection with any fraud. The wording is similar to s.25 of the Theft Act 1968, although this offence is wider as it is not limited to the situation where the defendant is away from his place of abode. It was Parliament's intention that a general intention to commit fraud would suffice and that the new offence should attract the case law on s.25 which, as we saw above, established that proof is required that the defendant had the article for the purpose, or with the intention, that it be used in the course of, or in connection with, the offence.

The maximum penalty for this offence is five years' imprisonment.

"ARTICLE"

Section 8 provides that, for the purposes of s.6, "article" includes any program or data held in electronic form. The Explanatory Notes to the 2006 Act give the following examples of cases where electronic programs or data could be used in fraud: a computer program can generate credit card numbers; computer templates can be used for producing blank utility bills; computer files can contain lists of other peoples' credit card details and draft letters can be used in connection with "advance fee" frauds.

Making Off Without Payment

The Offence

Section 3 of the Theft Act 1978 provides:

> A person who, knowing that payment on the spot for any goods supplied or service done is required or expected from him, dishonestly makes off without having paid as required or expected and with intent to avoid payment of the amount due shall be guilty of an offence.

Making off is punishable by a maximum period of imprisonment of two years.

The crime is commonly known as bilking and was originally designed to do two main things:

1. criminalise the activities of a defendant where the prosecution can prove the appropriation of property belonging to another under s.1 of the Theft Act 1968, but cannot necessarily establish the mens rea of theft occurred at the same time (see Ch.7, p.227) such as driving off from a self-service petrol station without paying for the petrol; and

2. criminalise the obtaining of services in the absence of a deception, or where the services were obtained honestly in the first place, and once obtained, D dishonestly decided not to pay. For example, D booked into a hotel intending to pay, but left at the end of the stay and decided not to pay. This second point was important because the old deception offences were defined in terms of the deception *causing* the obtaining; as we will see however, the Fraud Act offences are far wider, there is no causation requirement between the fraud and anything obtained as a result, and accordingly this second point may now be redundant (see in particular p.285 below).

The Actus Reus of Making Off

The actus reus of "making off" involves:

1. D making off;
2. from the spot where payment is required or expected;
3. without having paid as required or expected;
4. for goods supplied or for service done.

D MUST MAKE OFF

In making off, D need not run, sneak out or stealthily disappear. The term "making off" means simply what it says, leaving, and the jury does not need direction to understand it (**Brooks and Brooks (1982) 76 Cr. App. R. 66**). If D is stopped at the exit he will usually have committed only an attempt (**McDavitt [1981] Crim. L.R. 843**), but this is a question of fact.

However, if V has given D permission to leave because D has lied to him, or made a false representation to the effect, say, that he will pay later, or his company will be paying for him, then D has not committed an offence under s.3 (**Vincent [2001] 1 W.L.R. 1172**). Charges of dishonestly obtaining services or fraud could be brought, however.

FROM THE SPOT WHERE PAYMENT IS REQUIRED OR EXPECTED

Section 3(2) of the Theft Act 1978 provides that "payment on the spot" includes payment at the time of collecting goods on which work has been done, or in respect of which service has been provided. Normally, therefore, the spot will be the exit of the shop, or, say, the check-out or till area (think of a supermarket). Until that "spot" is left, there is no crime, even if D is dishonestly intending not to pay.

Services may not have an easily identifiable "spot" for payment though. In **Aziz [1993] Crim. L.R. 708**, D refused to pay for a taxi ride. The Court of Appeal held that the normal "spot" for payment is at the end of the ride but, on these facts, D made off when he got out of the car and ran off en route to a local police station. This is to be contrasted with **Troughton v Metropolitan Police [1987] Crim. L.R. 138 DC.** D was drunk and hailed a taxi home. The driver was unable to get D to give his precise address because of D's intoxication, so the driver drove D to a police station. The court held that no offence had yet occurred. No payment was required or expected at any particular spot (yet) because there was no agreed destination.

WITHOUT HAVING PAID AS REQUIRED OR EXPECTED

As stated above, if D has deceived V into believing payment is not due at the spot, there is no offence. The required payment must be one which is legally enforceable (s.3(3)).

FOR GOODS SUPPLIED OR FOR SERVICE DONE

The definition of "goods" for the purposes of s.3 is found in s.34 of the Theft Act 1968:

> "goods", except in so far as the context otherwise requires, includes money and every other description of property except land, and includes things severed from the land by stealing.

Although not expressly stated, it was thought that "service" bore the same meaning as in s.1 of the 1978 Act, but as that definition has been abolished and none has replaced it, we must await a case to decide the matter.

The Mens Rea of Making Off

The mens rea involves D:

1. acting dishonestly;
2. with knowledge that payment on the spot is required or expected; and
3. intention to avoid payment of the amount due.

D MUST ACT DISHONESTLY

Dishonesty is assessed under the *Ghosh* test (see Ch.7 p.234).

D MUST KNOW THAT PAYMENT ON THE SPOT IS REQUIRED OR EXPECTED FROM HIM

This is self-explanatory.

D MUST INTENT TO AVOID PAYMENT OF THE AMOUNT DUE

The House of Lords in **Allen [1985] A.C. 1029**, held that the prosecution must prove that D intended to make permanent default, i.e. never to pay. If D made off, but intended to pay later, or knew he would have to do so (because the person to whom payment was due knew his address), he would not be guilty.

Over to you...

D says he walked out of a restaurant without paying in protest at the poor service and poor food. He says he thinks he acted reasonably and honestly, and thinks that ordinary honest people would agree.

Is the actus reus of making off satisfied? Is the mens rea?

Fraud

Before the enactment of the Fraud Act 2006, there was no such thing as an offence of "fraud". Instead there were a number of crimes under common law and the Theft Acts 1968 and 1978 which involved deception. There was, and still is, a common law offence of conspiracy to defraud.

The Old Deception Offences

The offences involving deception under the two Theft Acts were very technical, very specific and resulted in excessively complicated case law, most of which is now irrelevant. There were eight main offences involving deception under the Theft Acts 1968 and 1978:

FIGURE 8.1 **The abolished deception offences**

Section 15 of the Theft Act 1968	Dishonestly obtaining property belonging to another by deception with the intention of permanently depriving the other of it.

Section 15A of the Theft Act 1968	Dishonestly to obtain for oneself, or another, a money transfer by any deception.
Section 16 of the Theft Act 1968	Obtaining a "pecuniary advantage" by dishonest deception
Section 20(2) of the Theft Act 1968	This made it an offence dishonestly to procure the execution of a valuable security by deception.
Section 1 of the Theft Act 1978	Dishonestly to obtain services by deception
Section 2 of the Theft Act 1978	There were three crimes of dishonestly obtaining the "evasion of a liability" by deception

THE COMMON ELEMENTS OF THE DECEPTION OFFENCES UNDER THE THEFT ACTS 1968 AND 1978

All eight of the Theft Act crimes could be committed only where:

1. there was a deception;
2. the deception *caused* the obtaining of the relevant thing under each section; and
3. it was done dishonestly.

As we will see, the first and second elements have been abolished by the new Fraud Act 2006. However, before we consider that Act in any detail, we must acknowledge the continued existence of the common law offence of conspiracy to defraud.

Conspiracy to Defraud

The law governing conspiracy is hugely, and unnecessarily, complex. There were numerous common law offences of conspiracy which were partially reformed by the Criminal Law Act 1977, but the common law offence of conspiracy to defraud was specifically retained (s.5(2)).

The intention in 1977 was to keep the law under review, and abolish the common law crime as soon as possible. Nothing happened. The Law Commission again called for the abolition of the offence in 2002 (Law Commission, "Fraud" Law Com. No.276) and it was hopefully anticipated that the Fraud Act 2006 would see the end of the crime, but yet again, Parliament did not do so for fear of leaving a gap in the law. The Explanatory Notes of the Fraud Act 2006 explain this lack of activity:

> "[due to] serious practical concerns about the ability to prosecute multiple offences in the largest and most serious cases of fraud and a desire to see how the new statutory offences worked in practice before abolishing conspiracy to defraud ... the Government concluded that immediate abolition of conspiracy to defraud would create considerable risks for the effective prosecution of fraud cases. The Government proposed to reassess whether there is a continuing need to retain conspiracy to defraud in the light of the operation of the new offences and the Law Commission's impending report on encouraging and assisting crime. The Law Commission has now published its report on Inchoate Liability for Assisting and Encouraging Crime (Law Com. No.300, Cm. 6878, 2006 para.6)."

So, what is wrong with the offence?

The first criticism relates to the width of the offence. It is a crime to conspire to defraud, whether or not the fraud itself amounts to a crime or even a tort. Therefore, the offence can be committed by two people who agree to do something which, if they were acting alone, would not be unlawful. This situation has been described by the Law Commission as an "indefensible anomaly" (Law Commission, "Fraud", 2002, Law Com. 276, para.1.4).

Second, there is considerable, confusing and unnecessary overlap between the common law rules and the Criminal Law Act 1977. The concurrent operation of the common law and statutory offence was only ever intended to be a temporary measure, yet it prevails almost 30 years later. The 2002 Report acknowledged that:

> "... [i]n a capitalist society, commercial life revolves around the pursuit of gain for oneself and, as a corollary, others may lose out, whether directly or indirectly. Such behaviour is perfectly legitimate" (para.3.6).

> Yet, "the conduct in question would undoubtedly fall within the definition of the offence, leaving prosecutors with an uncommonly broad discretion when ... deciding whether to pursue a conspiracy to defraud case" (para.3.8).

The statutory crime is, essentially, an agreement to pursue a course of conduct which, if carried out in accordance with the intentions of the parties, will necessarily amount to or involve a crime. The common law offence, on the other hand, does not even have to amount to an agreement to commit a crime.

In essence, the common law offence only requires proof of an agreement between two or more conspirators dishonestly and with intention to deprive another or others of something which is his or would or might have been his, but for D's conduct (**Welham v DPP [1961] A.C. 103 HL**). The crime cannot be committed by an individual. So, we can see that where an individual commits a "fraud" offence, liability could arise only under the substantive offences of the Theft Acts or, now, under the Fraud Act 2006, considered below.

The leading case on conspiracy to defraud is **Scott v Metropolitan Police Commissioner [1974] 3 All E.R. 1032**. D agreed with the employees of a cinema to lend him the films so that he could copy them and sell the pirate copies. He would then return the films, with the cinema owners none the wiser. The House of Lords acknowledged that this activity did not involve the commission of any substantive criminal offence. There was no theft because intention to return the films intact meant that there was no intention permanently to deprive (see Ch.7). Further, there was no "property" under the Theft Acts so there was neither theft nor any obtaining of property by deception and, indeed, there was not even a deception of the owners as they were completely unaware of what was happening. Nevertheless, their Lordships held this was no bar to conviction for conspiracy to defraud.

The offence of conspiracy to defraud, according to the House of Lords, includes a dishonest agreement:

1. to deprive a person of something which is his or to which he is or would be or might be entitled (here, the owners would be deprived of profits from the cinema-goers who would not go to the cinema because they had pirate copies of the films); or
2. to injure some proprietary right of his (such as an agreement among disgruntled employees to pocket an employer's profit, see **Adams v R [1995] 1 W.L.R. 52**).

In fact, provided there is an agreement, there is no need to prove:

1. any deception or fraud,
2. actual economic loss through the carrying out of the agreement (**Wai Yu-tsang v R [1992] 1 A.C. 269 PC**),
3. any risk of economic loss (**Welham v DPP [1961] A.C. 103 HL**), so it could include for example, an agreement dishonestly to make a public official act contrary to his public duty, or even
4. that it is the conspirators' primary purpose to defraud (it is enough if they are aware that their agreement might result in a defraud (**Attorney General's Reference (No.1 of 1982) [1983] Q.B. 751**)).

Therefore, the offence is wide enough to include conduct such as agreeing to commit theft, robbery and burglary; and there is even an intention to defraud by the dishonest failure to display a vehicle excise licence (tax disc), even where D intends to pay for a new one (**Terry [1984] A.C. 374**). At the very least, this means the offence falls foul of the principle of fair-labelling; that is, a crime should reflect the conduct intended to be covered by it, but no less and no more. The crime of conspiracy to defraud is so wide it fails to specify when a fraud is being committed and when it is not. This could result in charges being brought which should not be, and vice versa. Ormerod says of the offence that it is:

> "one of the most controversial in English criminal law ... [i]t is excessively broad ... offends against the principles of legality, certainty and fair warning, and results in an offence which is commonly defined by reference only to the concept of dishonesty – a concept that is ill-suited to shoulder that responsibility." (Ormerod, Smith and Hogan, *Criminal Law*, 12th edn).

Conspiracy to defraud has not been abolished by the Fraud Act 2006, and more's the pity. If the common law offence had been abolished following the Law Commission's recommendation (Law Com. 300), any agreement to commit a fraud could be prosecuted as a statutory conspiracy under the Criminal Law Act 1977 as an agreement to carry out any fraud under the Fraud Act 2006. This would mean it would no longer be a crime to agree to conduct which is not criminal per se.

The Fraud Act 2006

There is one offence of fraud under s.1 of the Fraud Act 2006, with three ways of committing it, under ss.2–4. These are by false representation, by failing to disclose information and by abuse of position. The concept of deception from the Theft Acts 1968 and 1978 is abolished.

Fraud is punishable by a maximum period of imprisonment of 10 years.

SECTION 2

> **(1)** A person is in breach of this section if he—
>   **(a)** dishonestly makes a false representation, and
>   **(b)** intends, by making the representation—
>   **(i)** to make a gain for himself or another, or
>   **(ii)** to cause loss to another or to expose another to a risk of loss.

(2) A representation is false if—
  (a) it is untrue or misleading, and
  (b) the person making it knows that it is, or might be, untrue or misleading.

(3) "Representation" means any representation as to fact or law, including a representation as to the state of mind of—
  (a) the person making the representation, or
  (b) any other person.

(4) A representation may be express or implied.
(5) For the purposes of this section a representation may be regarded as made if it (or anything implying it) is submitted in any form to any system or device designed to receive, convey or respond to communications (with or without human intervention).

Under s.2, a representation may be an express statement (e.g. "I will pay for my hotel room") or it may be implied by conduct. Pre-Fraud Act 2006 examples of representations implied by conduct include:

1. when we book into a hotel, we impliedly represent that we will pay for the room (**Harris (1975) 62 Cr. App. R. 28**);
2. when we order a meal in a restaurant we impliedly represent that we will pay for the meal (**DPP v Ray [1974] A.C. 370**);
3. when we pay by cheque, that there will be enough funds for the cheque to clear (**Gilmartin [1983] Q.B. 953**);
4. when we use a cheque guarantee card (or a credit card (**Lambie [1982] A.C. 449**) that we have the issuer's authorisation to use the card (**Metropolitan Police Commissioner v Charles [1977] A.C. 177**).

These continue to be valid examples of representations under s.2 of the Fraud Act. It is unclear whether a representation may be made by silence alone (unless D is under a duty to disclose under s.3 below). It is a fraud only if the representation is false, which it is if it is either untrue or is merely misleading. How "misleading" it has to be will be an area for judicial debate. There is no need to prove that the false representation caused the obtaining of the thing. The purpose of s.2(5) is to reverse the common law position where there was no deception without a human being's mind (i.e. the deception had to con V, or V had to be taken in by the deception). That meant deception could not be operated on a machine including a computer. Section 2(5) provides that the new crimes encompass fraud on a machine.

As to mens rea, the representation must be made knowing it is, or knowing it might be, untrue or misleading; it must be made dishonestly (the *Ghosh* test survives the enactment of these new crimes); and it must be made with a view to produce a gain to D or another or loss or the risk of loss to the victim. Actual gain or loss is not, however, needed. The definitions of gain and loss are considered below.

SECTION 3

A person is in breach of this section if he—

(a) dishonestly fails to disclose to another person information which he is under a legal duty to disclose, and

(b) intends, by failing to disclose the information—

(i) to make a gain for himself or another, or

(ii) to cause loss to another or to expose another to a risk of loss.

The Law Commission ("Fraud" 2002) gave some examples of the types of conduct which might fall within s.3 (paras 7.28–7.29):

1. False information provided in company prospectuses in order to attract investment,

2. False information provided on an application for a contract of insurance,

3. Failure of a solicitor to share vital information with a client in order to perpetrate a fraud against the client (this final example is also conduct prohibited by s.4).

The pre-Fraud Act 2006 case of **Firth (1990) 91 Cr App R 217** illustrates this section. *Firth* was a hospital surgeon who dishonestly failed to disclose that some of his clients were private rather than funded out of national (taxpayers') funds. He therefore was able to keep the private fees for himself. He was guilty of an offence under s.2 Theft Act 1978 (evasion of liability by deception). On the same facts, this would also be a fraud under the Fraud Act 2006. There is a slim possibility that his conduct could amount to an implied false representation under s.2 (by omission), but it is certainly a failure to disclose under s.3 which more obviously encompasses his conduct. However, it is at least arguable that his conduct might also be covered by s.4 of the Act. It is rather concerning that the breadth of the new forms of fraud creates such an overlap.

SECTION 4

(1) A person is in breach of this section if he—

    (a) occupies a position in which he is expected to safeguard, or not to act against, the financial interests of another person,

    (b) dishonestly abuses that position, and

    (c) intends, by means of the abuse of that position—

        (i) to make a gain for himself or another, or

        (ii) to cause loss to another or to expose another to a risk of loss.

(2) A person may be regarded as having abused his position even though his conduct consisted of an omission rather than an act.

This is essentially an abuse of financial position crime, but the key terms "position", "safeguard", "financial interests" and "abuse" are not defined. This form of fraud may be committed by act or omission (subs.(2)). In relation to the *Firth* case above, this section is breached if it was the defendant's professional duty to protect the financial interests of the hospital, which it probably was.

Section 4 is designed to cover fraudsters such as bankers, investment advisers or solicitors who are under a financial duty to another and fail to perform that duty, dishonestly, with a view to gain or cause loss. A trustee might similarly be caught, even in the absence of any operative deception, if he perpetrated a fraud on trust money, but this type of fraud could equally apply to financial dealings within a family in the absence of a formal contractual or other relationship.

THE MENS REA OF FRAUD

Each way of committing fraud involves mens rea as to gain and/or loss, although the prosecution does not need to prove an actual gain or loss. Fraud has thus been made a conduct crime. The Theft Acts offences were all result crimes (something had to be obtained by the deception). The new offences broadly cover conduct such as lying with a view to economic advantage. The terms "gain" and "loss" are given a restricted meaning under s.5 and extend only to gain or loss in money or other property (defined in exactly the same terms as the Theft Act 1968 s.4(1)) but do include temporary or permanent gains and/or losses. Under subss.(3) and (4), gain includes a gain by keeping what one has, as well as a gain by getting what one does not have, and loss includes a loss by not getting what one might get, as well as a loss by parting with what one has.

Over to you...

B is the assistant manager in a shop and he asks C, the manager, if C would agree to sell some goods to a third party, D, If D pays by cheque. B assures C that D is credit worthy. B knows C is not, and that the cheque will not clear.

Even if C turns down B's request, has B committed a fraud offence and if so, which type of fraud (ss.2, 3 or 4?) has been committed?

If C agrees to B's request and the cheque subsequently does not clear, what offence(s) might now have been committed (you might consider both fraud and theft here)?

INCHOATE LIABILITY

The new fraud offence can be an inchoate crime. Therefore, a person can be convicted of an attempt to commit a fraud, incitement to commit fraud or, under the Criminal Law Act 1977, a statutory conspiracy to commit a fraud under the Fraud Act 2006. The continued existence of the common law offence (conspiracy to defraud, above on p.278) causes us to speculate what purpose it can possibly serve in light of both the well-founded criticisms mentioned above and the breadth of the new fraud crime. Rather than attempt to clarify this before enactment, Parliament has left it to the judiciary to resolve. When, exactly, is a statutory conspiracy to commit a fraud to be preferred over a common law conspiracy to defraud?

. . . .

Dishonestly Obtaining Services

Section 1 of the Theft Act 1978 provided that it was an offence dishonestly to obtain services by deception. Examples of such services include obtaining a taxi ride, a haircut or a repair of one's central heating boiler, and so on, when there was no intention of paying. The offence has been replaced with a new offence under s.11 of the Fraud Act 2006 of obtaining services dishonestly. In the new crime, there is no need to prove a deception or false representation. Unlike the fraud offence above, it is a result, rather than a conduct, crime. On the whole, it replicates some of the old Theft Act 1978 offence.

Section 11 of the Fraud Act 2006 provides:

(1) A person is guilty of an offence under this section if he obtains services for himself or another—

> **(a)** by a dishonest act, and
> **(b)** in breach of subsection (2).
>
> **(2)** A person obtains services in breach of this subsection if—
> **(a)** they are made available on the basis that payment has been, is being or will be made for or in respect of them,
> **(b)** he obtains them without any payment having been made for or in respect of them or without payment having been made in full, and
> **(c)** when he obtains them, he knows—
> **(i)** that they are being made available on the basis described in paragraph **(a)**,
>
> or
>
> **(ii)** that they might be,
> but intends that payment will not be made, or will not be made in full.

The maximum sentence under s.11 is five years' imprisonment.

It is an offence to obtain services (neither term is defined in the Act) for which a payment has been, is being or will be expected. The crime cannot be committed for gratuitous services, which is the same as under the old law.

Unlike the previous offence, however, the new one can be committed only if D intends to avoid payment or payment in full. So, if a parent lies about the religion of their child to secure a place at a fee-paying religious school, always intending to pay the fees in full, no offence under s.11 of the Fraud Act 2006 is committed (however, an offence under s.1 of the Fraud Act 2006 has been committed, which you may recall is a conduct crime, and there is no need to prove that a specific thing (or a service) was obtained.). The old s.1 of the Theft Act 1978 crime could be committed even if D fully intended to pay, and did in fact pay, but had made a deception.

Unlike the old offence, this offence is not an inchoate crime so no charge can be laid for conspiracy to commit, incitement to commit or an attempt to commit the offence of dishonestly obtaining services. Of course, if such an agreement were made between two or more people, there is little doubt that would satisfy the common law offence of conspiracy to defraud.

Over to you...

It is possible to commit the new s.11 offence via a machine, such as downloading software or giving false credit card details to an automated booking system for a concert or train journey?

Summary

1. Robbery, contrary to s.8 of the Theft Act 1968, involves: (a) theft (b) use or threat of force on any person (c) immediately before or at the time of the theft (d) in order to steal. The issues of whether: (a) there was force and (b) it was used on a person are for the jury to determine. If D assaults V after committing the theft, there are two offences—theft and a separate offence of assault.

2. D may be liable for the offence of assault with intent to rob, contrary to s.8(2) of the Theft Act 1968, where he commits an assault or battery on his victim, intending to steal, but is unsuccessful in appropriating the property.

3. There are two offences of burglary, contrary to s.9(1)(a) and 9(1)(b) of the Theft Act 1968. Both offences require: (a) entry (b) into a building or part of a building (c) as a trespasser. An entry must be effective. A trespasser is someone who does not have permission to be in the building and knows this to be the case (or is reckless). Premises must be reasonably permanent to qualify as a building. The s.9(1)(a) offence also requires the intent on entry to steal, do gbh or criminal damage. The s.9(1)(b) offence requires that, once in the building, D steals, inflicts gbh or attempts either.

4. D may be liable for aggravated burglary, contrary to s.10 of the Theft Act 1968, where he commits a burglary and has with him at the time a firearm or imitation firearm, any weapon of offence or explosive.

5. Blackmail, contrary to s.21 of the Theft Act 1968, is committed where D: (a) makes a demand (b) with menaces which is (c) unwarranted and (d) with a view to gain for himself or another or with intent to cause loss to another. A demand may be in any form: verbal, in writing or by conduct and can be implied from the circumstances. "Menaces" includes not only threats of violence but also threats of anything detrimental or unpleasant. A demand is unwarranted unless made in the belief that there are reasonable grounds for making the demand and that the use of the menaces is a proper means of reinforcing the demand. D must make the demand with a view to gain/cause loss of money or other property.

6. Handling, contrary to s.22 of the Theft Act 1968, is committed where D: (a) handles (b) stolen goods (c) otherwise than in the course of stealing (d) knowing or believing them to be stolen (e) and D is dishonest. Handling may be committed by: (i) receiving the stolen goods (ii) undertaking the retention, removal, disposal or realisation of the stolen goods for the benefit of another person (iii) assisting in the retention, removal, disposal or realisation of the stolen goods by another person or (iv) arranging to do any of these. Stolen goods are those which: (a) have been stolen (b) have been obtained by blackmail or fraud (c) consist of money dishonestly

withdrawn from an account to which a wrongful credit has been made or (d) represent those originally stolen. Goods cease to be stolen once they have been restored to the person from whom they were stolen or into police custody or where the owner ceases to have a right to restitution. A person knows that goods are stolen if he has actual, not constructive, knowledge of this. Belief is something short of knowledge but is not satisfied by either suspicion or wilful blindness as to whether the goods are stolen. Dishonesty is determined according to the *Ghosh* test.

7. Going equipped, contrary to s.25 of the Theft Act 1968, involves D: (a) having with him (b) any article (c) for use in the course of or in connection with a burglary or theft whilst not at his place of abode. There is also an offence under s.6 of the fraud Act 2006 of possession of articles for use in frauds.

8. Making Off Without Payment, contrary to s.3 of the Theft Act 1978 requires that: (a) D must make off (b) from the spot where payment is required or expected (c) for goods supplied or services done and (d) D acts dishonestly and (e) D knows that payment on the spot is required or expected from him and (f) D intends to avoid payment of the amount due.

9. The main offences pre-Fraud Act 2006 were

   - Section 15 TA 1968—dishonestly obtaining property by deception with the intention of permanently depriving the other of it.
   - Section 15A TA 1968—dishonestly obtaining a money transfer by deception.
   - Section 16 TA 1968—dishonestly obtaining a pecuniary advantage by deception.
   - Section 20(2) TA 1968—dishonestly procuring the execution of a valuable security by deception.
   - Section 1 TA 1978—dishonestly obtaining services by deception.
   - Section 2 TA 1978—three crimes of dishonestly obtaining the evasion of a liability by deception.

The Theft Acts deception offences have been replaced with offences under the Fraud Act 2006. It is fraud under s.1 if D (a) makes a false representation, (b) fails to disclose or (c) abuses his position, where D intends to make a gain or avoid a loss. There is another offence of dishonestly obtaining services.

10. Conspiracy to defraud. The abolition of this crime was proposed before enactment of the Criminal Law Act 1977, and again in 2002, but it continues to exist. A very wide and complex offence, it consists of an agreement between two or more conspirators dishonestly and with intention to deprive another or others of something which is his or would or might have been his, but for D's conduct. There is no need for the conspiracy to relate to a crime.

End of Chapter Question

Question

Franco was a law student who had run out of money. He was very hungry but could not afford to buy food. He went to a local restaurant and told the manager he had been robbed and all his money had been taken. The manager felt very sorry for Franco and gave him a meal for free.

Franco then got on a tram to go to his local college for a tutorial. Payment for travel on the tram was due by the passenger to the conductors on the trams, not in advance. Franco saw where the conductor was, and boarded the tram at the other end. He then left the tram at the next stop when he saw the conductor come into his carriage.

Franco walked the rest of the way to college. When he arrived, he realised he had forgotten his pens. He went into the campus stationery shop and picked up a pen and put it in his pocket. He then noticed there was Closed Circuit Television (CCTV) in the shop and he thought he might have been recorded putting the pen in his pocket, so he took the pen out and replaced it on the shelf. Franco left the shop and went to his tutorial.

Discuss Franco's criminal liability, if any, for offences under the Fraud Act 2006.

Note; the same factual scenario is also addressed in Ch.7 in respect of fraud offences.

Points of Answer

♦ Start by explaining that fraud is an offence contrary to s. 1 of the Fraud Act 2006 (FA), but only if D has breached ss.2, 3 or 4.

♦ Take each event in turn (note the structure recommended at the end of Ch.7 for the offence of theft).

♦ Meal
  • As well as the offence of theft, consider also an offence under s.1 FA by breach of s.2 (false representation; he lies) and possibly even s.11 (the services are the waiting staff in the restaurant). Dishonesty has already been considered. Franco does this with a view to make a gain so the mens rea is satisfied.

♦ Tram
  • An offence under s.1 FA has been committed only if Franco's conduct is a false representation (s.2) which, using pre-Fraud Act cases, such as *Harris and Ray*, it is. Consider dishonesty again. You may also draw the same conclusion as above re s.11 services.

♦ Pen in the shop
  • Here, there is no fraud or services so the Fraud Act is not applicable. Theft was considered at the end of Ch.7.

Further Reading

P. Aldridge, "Attempted Murder of the Soul: Blackmail, Piracy and Secrets" (1993) 13 OJLS 368.

I. Dennis, "The Fraud Act 2006" [2007] Crim. L.R. 1.

M. Griffiths, "Internet corporate blackmail: a growing problem" J.P. 2004, 168(33), 632–633.

D. Ormerod, "The Fraud Act 2006—Criminalising Lying" [2007] Crim. L.R. 193.

J.R. Spencer, "The Mishandling of Handling" [1981] Crim. L.R. 682 and "Handling, Theft and the Mala Fide Purchaser" [1985] Crim. L.R. 92 and 440.

The Explanatory Notes to the Fraud Act 2006.

Self Test Questions

To test your knowledge gained from this section go online to http://*www.sweetandmaxwell.co.uk* and take our online self test questions. Here you will also find key updates to ensure that you are only ever one click away from an instant update.

Offences Involving Property III—Criminal Damage

9

CHAPTER OVERVIEW

In this chapter we:

- provide the definitions and analyse the actus reus and mens rea requirements of the simple and aggravated offences of criminal damage

- examine the offences of arson and aggravated arson

- examine the simple and aggravated offences involving threatening to destroy or damage property and of possessing anything with intent to destroy or damage property

- provide critical commentary where appropriate of the offences mentioned

- explore the concept of recklessness under the Criminal Damage Act 1971

- consider what constitutes racially or religiously aggravated criminal damage

- analyse the lawful excuses to criminal damage offences under s.5 of the Criminal Damage Act 1971.

Summary

End of Chapter Question

Further Reading

Self Test Questions

Introduction

In this chapter we complete our consideration of offences involving property with an analysis of offences under the Criminal Damage Act 1971.

The Criminal Damage Act 1971

The Criminal Damage Act 1971 creates several offences relating to damage or destruction of property, namely:

1. A simple offence relating to the destroying or damaging of property belonging to another.
2. An aggravated offence, relating to the destroying or damaging of any property by someone intending thereby to endanger the life of another, or being reckless in that regard.
3. Arson, involving destroying or damaging property by fire.
4. An offence of threatening to destroy or damage property.
5. An offence of possessing anything with intent to destroy or damage property.

Additionally, s.30 of the Crime and Disorder Act 1998 (as amended) creates an offence of racially or religiously aggravated criminal damage.

The Simple (or Basic) Offence of Criminal Damage

Section 1(1) of the 1971 Act provides:

> A person who without lawful excuse destroys or damages any property belonging to another intending to destroy or damage any such property or being reckless as to whether any such property would be destroyed or damaged shall be guilty of an offence.

Criminal damage is punishable by a maximum period of 10 years' imprisonment.

The Actus Reus of Criminal Damage

This involves:

1. damaging or destroying;
2. property;
3. belonging to another.

DAMAGE

There is no definition of damage in the 1971 Act and the term has been left to be interpreted by case law. It is a question of fact and degree in each case for the jury (or magistrates), applying their own common sense (**Roe v Kingerlee [1986] Crim. L.R. 735 DC**). Although there is no precise legal definition of damage and each case is decided on its facts, the following have proven to be relevant considerations in determining whether damage has occurred.

■ Effort and expense

The fact that harm is only temporary and can be rectified does not prevent it being damage. In such circumstances, the cost and effort involved in the rectification required will be relevant. In *Roe v Kingerlee*, graffiti smeared in mud on a cell wall was capable of being damage where expense (£7) was incurred in washing it off. Similarly, in **Hardman v Chief Constable of Avon and Somerset [1986] Crim. L.R. 330**, drawing on a pavement using water soluble paints and chalks was held to constitute damage as the local authority was involved in expense in using high pressure water jets to clean the pavement. This was despite the fact that rain would eventually have washed the chalk away.

Conversely, in **A (a juvenile) [1978] Crim. L.R. 689**, where D spat onto the back of a police officer's overcoat, he was not liable for criminal damage to the coat as the spittle could have been removed by a damp cloth. The decision might have been different if a stain had been caused which required washing or dry cleaning to remove.

Damage often involves physical harm to property but this is not essential provided effort and expense is involved in restoration (or there has been impairment of usefulness, see below). Thus, in **Henderson and Battley (CA, 24 November 1984, unreported)**, there was damage to land where the landowner was put to expense in removing rubbish which had been dumped on it, even though the land itself was not physically damaged.

■ Impairment of the value or usefulness of the property

Damage may be caused where there has been permanent or temporary impairment of the value or usefulness of the property (**Morphitis v Salmon [1990] Crim. L.R. 48 DC**, see below). It was on this basis that the Court of Appeal in **Fiak [2005] EWCA Crim 2381** held that damage had occurred when a prisoner in a police station cell flushed his blanket down the toilet, causing the toilet to overflow and flood his and two adjoining cells. There was damage both to the blanket which was wet, though not visibly soiled, as it was unusable until it was cleaned and dry; and to the cells, as they remained out of action until they were cleaned out.

Where there has been impairment of value or usefulness, the property may still be damaged even though it looks exactly as it did before. Thus, in **Cox v Riley (1986) 83 Cr. App. R. 54)**, erasure of programs on a printed circuit card used to control a computerised saw was held to constitute damage to the card which, though unchanged in appearance, had lost its usefulness to its owner. Similarly, in **Whiteley (1991) 93 Cr. App. R. 25**, damage was held to have been caused by D when he hacked into a computer network and altered some data stored on disks. *Cox v Riley* and *Whiteley* both pre-dated the coming into force of the Computer Misuse Act 1990 which was subsequently amended by the Police and Justice Act 2006 which substituted a new s.10(5) into the Criminal Damage Act 1971.

Section 10(5) provides that a modification of the contents of a computer or computer storage medium is not criminal damage unless it physically impairs the computer or computer storage medium. However, the principle that impairment of the value or usefulness of property can constitute damage without the need for any change in the physical appearance of the property remains good law. Consequently, erasure of, for example, information stored in electro-magnetic form, such as an audiotape, could be damage to the tape.

It is *not* a requirement that there has been *both* impairment of usefulness and a reduction in value; only one is required. Thus, there was damage in **Roper v Knott [1898] 1 Q.B. 868** where beer was watered down; it was not useless but was less valuable than before.

■ The nature of the property

The nature of the property harmed is also significant. In *Morphitis v Salmon*, a scratch on a scaffold bar did not constitute damage as scratches were a normal occurrence with scaffolding and did not impair its usefulness. A scratch on a car's paintwork would, however, constitute damage; it would require effort and expense in repainting it.

Can removal of parts from a machine constitute damage?

Though there have been no cases under the Act, it is likely that the pre-Act cases would be followed. In **Fisher (1865) LR 1 CCR 7 DC**, the court held that removal of parts necessary for a machine to work constituted damage to the machine.

Can clamping a car constitute damage to the car?

Mere denial of use of property will not necessarily amount to damage to the property; in **Drake v DPP [1994] R.T.R. 411 DC**, the court held that clamping a car did not constitute damage to the car as it did not involve any "intrusion into the integrity of the object".

Over to you...

D takes V's house keys. As well as liability for theft of the keys, does D commit criminal damage to V's house because V cannot enter?

DESTROY

There is no definition of "destroy" in the 1971 Act but it clearly goes beyond damage and would include, for example, killing another's pet cat or dog or demolishing a building or dismantling a car.

PROPERTY

Generally, there will be no difficulty in saying that what was damaged was property. However, in those cases where property is a contentious issue, the defendant may seek to argue that he did not damage *property* because what was damaged is excluded from the definition of property by the Criminal Damage Act 1971. In such cases, it is necessary to consider the precise meaning attributed to property.

Property is defined in s.10 of the Act which provides:

> In this Act "property" means property of a tangible nature, whether real or personal, including money and
>
> **(a)** including wild creatures which have been tamed or are ordinarily kept in captivity, and any other wild creatures or their carcasses if, but only if, they have been reduced into possession which has not been lost or abandoned or are in the course of being reduced into possession; but
> **(b)** not including mushrooms growing wild on any land or flowers, fruit or foliage of a plant growing wild on any land. For the purpose of this subsection "mushroom" includes any fungus and "plant" includes any shrub or tree.

This definition of property is similar to that under the Theft Act 1968 (see p.219) and you should refer back to that definition for a detailed discussion of what constitutes property. However, there are some notable differences:

1. Land may be damaged, though only exceptionally may it be stolen.
2. Intangible property cannot be damaged but may be stolen.
3. Wild mushrooms and flowers, fruit and foliage growing wild may not be damaged but can, in certain circumstances, be stolen.

BELONGING TO ANOTHER

In order to be liable for the simple offence of criminal damage, the defendant must damage or destroy property belonging to another. There will generally be no difficulty in saying that what was damaged belonged to another but issues may sometimes arise concerning this aspect of the actus reus because s.10(2), just like s.5 of the Theft Act 1968 (see p.224), allows property to be seen as belonging to a wider range of persons than the actual owner.

Section 10(2) of the 1971 Act provides that property shall be treated as belonging to any person:

(a) having the custody or control of it;

(b) having in it any proprietary right or interest (not being an equitable interest arising only from an agreement to transfer or grant an interest); or

(c) having a charge on it.

A defendant may damage property belonging to another where he damages his own property if that property also belongs to someone else by virtue of s.10(2), for example because it is co-owned or in V's custody when D damages it.

Over to you...

D finds out that her husband has been having an affair and as an act of revenge she badly scratches the paintwork on their jointly owned sports car which her husband loves but she hates.

Does D commit the actus reus of criminal damage?

Once you have read about the mens rea of criminal damage and lawful excuses to it, consider whether she has the mens rea and also whether she has a lawful excuse.

In terms broadly similar to s.5(2) and s.5(5) of the Theft Act 1968, s.10(3) and 10(4) of the 1971 Act make special provision for damage to certain trust property (notably, that subject to charitable trusts which are enforceable by the Attorney General) and the property of a Corporation Sole (for example, the Public Trustee, the Treasury Solicitor, parsons and bishops of the Church of England) which could possibly become vacant due to, for example, the death of the incumbent.

Section 10 ensures that damage to such property can amount to an offence under the 1971 Act in providing that:

(3) Where property is subject to a trust, the persons to whom it belongs shall be so treated as including any person having a right to enforce the trust.

(4) Property of a corporation sole shall be treated as belonging to the corporation notwithstanding a vacancy in the corporation.

The Mens Rea of Criminal Damage

The mens rea of criminal damage is:

1. intention; or
2. recklessness

as to damage or destruction of property belonging to another.

INTENTION

Where it is alleged that the damage or destruction was intentional, the prosecution must prove that the defendant not only intended the act which caused the damage but also that the act should cause *damage to property belonging to another*. If the defendant merely intends to do the act which in fact causes the damage, for example firing a gun, but does not intend that his act will actually do damage to property belonging to another, but it does cause such damage, for example because the bullet ricochets and breaks a neighbour's car window, the defendant will lack the relevant intent (though he may be reckless, see below). As to the meaning of intention in the criminal law, see Ch.3.

If the defendant mistakenly believes he is damaging his own property, he will also lack the relevant intent as in **Smith [1974] Q.B. 354.** D, the tenant, was permitted by his landlord to install some stereo equipment and wiring. He also put in roofing materials, wall panels and floorboards to hide the wiring which, once installed, became fixtures and, therefore, the property of the landlord. When the tenant came to leave the property, he removed the wiring for his stereo equipment and in doing so, substantially damaged the wall panels, etc. which he had installed. He was charged with criminal damage contrary to s.1(1) of the 1971 Act. He successfully argued that he lacked intent as, not knowing property law, he honestly believed he had damaged his own property.

Over to you...

Do you think a graffiti artist intends to do damage when he paints what he considers a work of art on someone else's building?

RECKLESSNESS

Recklessness is subjective only (**G [2004] A.C. 1034**, overruling **Metropolitan Police Commissioner v Caldwell [1982] A.C. 341** which had applied objective recklessness in criminal damage offences, see Ch.3). Subjective recklessness in the context of criminal damage offences can be illustrated by the facts of **Stephenson [1979] 2 All E.R. 1198**, a pre-*Caldwell* case which actually represents the current position in law. D, who suffered from schizophrenia, crept into a hollow in a large haystack and lit a fire to keep warm. The haystack caught fire and was destroyed. The Court of Appeal, in quashing D's conviction for arson, held that recklessness was to be assessed not on the basis of whether a reasonable man would have appreciated the risk of damage but whether D had appreciated it which, because of his schizophrenia, there was no evidence he had (see also p.61).

In **Cooper [2004] EWCA Crim 1382**, a case decided shortly after G, the defendant, D, who had learning difficulties, used lighter fuel to set light to the underside of the mattress in his room in a hostel, causing the mattress to become scorched. He was convicted of arson being reckless as to whether life was endangered. The Court of Appeal, which quashed his conviction as the trial judge had given the *Caldwell* direction on recklessness to the jury, stated that the risk (of endangering life as the charge related to the aggravated offence, see p.299) must be both "obvious and significant to the defendant" and:

> "if [D] realised there was a risk, but dismissed it as negligible, it cannot be said he realised he was taking an obvious and significant risk."

The reference to "obvious and significant" is rather puzzling both because it has never been part of the standard direction on subjective recklessness and because "obvious" risk was always associated with *Caldwell* recklessness. Subsequently, in **Brady [2006] EWCA Crim 2413**, the Court of Appeal stated (per Hallett L.J.) that:

> "it is, in our view, simply unarguable that, as a matter of law, since G a trial judge is bound to qualify the word 'risk' by the words 'obvious and significant.' "

Although the case concerned s.20 assault, the reference to G suggests that the court considered the direction on recklessness in criminal damage offences would be the same as that in non-fatal offences against the person. We would suggest, therefore, that the risk need be neither obvious nor significant to the defendant in criminal damage offences and that the appropriate direction is that D is reckless with respect to criminal damage (or endangering life) where, aware that he has created a risk of doing damage to property belonging to another (or of endangering life), he decides to take that risk and it is, in the circumstances known to him, unreasonable to take that risk.

Lawful Excuse

The defendant is only liable for the simple offence if he committed it without lawful excuse. Lawful excuse is considered on p.305.

The Aggravated Offence

Section 1(2) of the 1971 Act creates the aggravated offence of criminal damage. It provides:

> A person who without lawful excuse destroys or damages any property, whether belonging to himself or another—
>
> **(a)** intending to destroy or damage any property or being reckless as to whether any property would be destroyed or damaged; and
> **(b)** intending by the destruction or damage to endanger the life of another or being reckless as to whether the life of another would be thereby endangered; shall be guilty of an offence.

Aggravated criminal damage is punishable by a maximum period of life imprisonment.

The Differences Between the Simple Offence and The Aggravated Offence

There are two differences between the offences:

1. Under s.1(2) one may be liable for damaging one's own property, whereas the s.1(1) offence may only be committed in respect of property belonging to another.
2. Under s.1(2) there is an aggravating feature of intention or recklessness as to endangering life.

The Actus Reus of Aggravated Criminal Damage

All that needs to be established for the actus reus of aggravated criminal damage is that the defendant damaged or destroyed any property.

MUST LIFE BE ENDANGERED FOR LIABILITY UNDER S.1(2)?

It is not necessary for the prosecution to prove that anyone's life was in fact endangered as life endangerment is not an aspect of the actus reus, only the mens rea. This was confirmed in **Parker [1993] Crim. L.R. 856**. D lodged with a council house tenant in a semi-detached house. One evening, when both D's and the adjoining property were otherwise unoccupied, D started a fire inside his residence, in the hope that this would assist his landlady to persuade the council to re-house her. D was convicted of the aggravated offence on the basis that he had been reckless as to endangering life. It was irrelevant that, as his neighbours had been out when he started the fire, their lives were never at risk.

The Mens Rea of Aggravated Criminal Damage

As well as the intention or recklessness as to damaging or destroying property, the defendant must also intend or be reckless as to endangering life by the damage or destruction. The meaning of both intention and recklessness was discussed on pp.297–298.

"BY THE DESTRUCTION OR DAMAGE"

A defendant is not liable for aggravated criminal damage if he merely intends or is reckless as to endangering life by his actions; the defendant must actually intend or be reckless as to endangering life *by the damage* (**Steer [1988] A.C. 111 HL**). *Steer* was not liable under s.1(2) where he fired a gun from outside a house at a person standing behind a window. He may have recognised the risk to life from shooting the bullets (the act) but not from the damage to the window or property in the bedroom (the damage).

In the consolidated appeals of **Webster and Warwick [1995] 1 Cr. App. R. 492**, the Court of Appeal went further than it had done so in *Steer*. In *Webster*, D pushed a heavy copingstone from the parapet of a railway bridge onto a passenger train passing below. The stone landed on the rear bulkhead of a carriage and a corner of the stone penetrated the roof. The passengers were showered with material from the roof but received no physical injury. D was convicted under s.1(2) and appealed. The Court of Appeal held that if D merely intended (or was reckless) that the stone itself would crash through the roof of the train, thereby directly injuring passengers, s.1(2) would not apply. However, if D intended (or was reckless) that the stone would smash the roof so that material from it (the damage) might descend upon passengers, thereby creating a risk of endangering life, he would be guilty of the aggravated offence. In *Warwick*, D drove a stolen car from which a passenger threw bricks at a pursuing police car. One of the bricks smashed a window of the police car, showering the officers in the car with broken glass. D was also convicted under s.1(2) and appealed. The Court of Appeal held that where D threw a brick at a window of a moving vehicle causing it to shatter, the question whether he committed an offence under s.1(2) depended not on whether V might be hit by the brick but on whether D intended to hit the window (or was reckless) and intended (or was reckless) as to whether any resulting damage (the falling pieces of glass or an obscured windscreen) would endanger life.

The defendant is liable for the aggravated offence where he intends or is reckless as to endangering life by the damage he *intended or was reckless as to causing*, not by the damage he actually caused (**Dudley [1989] Crim. L.R. 57**). Thus, the defendant in *Dudley* was liable under s.1(2) where he threw a petrol bomb into a house intending to endanger life. D was liable notwithstanding the fact that the resulting fire (the actual damage) was soon put out with little real damage done.

FIGURE 9 **Illustration of the ways in which the simple and aggravated offences of criminal damage may be committed**

Actus Reus	Mens Rea	Offence
Damage or destruction of property belonging to another.	Intention or recklessness as to damage or destruction of property belonging to another.	s.1(1)
Damage or destruction of property belonging to another.	Intention or recklessness as to damage or destruction of property belonging to another and intention or recklessness as to endangering life thereby.	s.1(2)
Damage or destruction of one's own property.	Intention or recklessness as to damage or destruction of such property.	No offence
Damage or destruction of one's own property.	Intention or recklessness as to damage or destruction of property and intention or recklessness as to endangering life thereby.	s.1(2)

Lawful Excuse

The lawful excuses provided by s.5 of the 1971 Act do not apply to the aggravated offence. However, all other general defences, for example duress and prevention of crime, do apply.

Arson

Section 1(3) creates the offence of arson, an offence committed by destroying or damaging property by fire. Section 1(3) provides:

An offence committed under this section by destroying or damaging property by fire shall be charged as arson.

Arson is punishable by a maximum period of life imprisonment.

The Charge

Where the defendant destroys or damages property by fire the correct course is to charge him with an offence under s.1(1) and 1(3), or an offence under s.1(2) and 1(3), as appropriate. It is preferable, but not mandatory, in the context of a charge brought in the magistrates' court, to refer specifically to arson in the charge, rather than to damage to property by fire (**Drayton [2005] EWCA Crim. 2013**).

The Actus Reus of Arson

This is the damage or destruction of property (belonging to another, if the simple offence is charged) by fire.

WHAT TYPE OF FIRE DAMAGE WILL CONSTITUTE ARSON?

The damage required for arson does not have to be significant—it could, for example, simply involve charring of wood. It is, however, not sufficient that property is merely blackened by smoke, although this could constitute attempted arson.

The Mens Rea of Arson

The mens rea of arson requires that the defendant intended or was reckless as to damaging property belonging to another by fire. The mens rea of aggravated arson requires that the defendant intended or was reckless as to damaging property by fire and intended or was reckless as to whether life would thereby be endangered.

Lawful Excuse

The lawful excuses provided by s.5 (see p.305) apply to the simple offence of arson but not to the aggravated offence. All general defences apply to both the simple and the aggravated offence.

Threatening to Destroy or Damage Property

Section 2 of the 1971 Act creates an offence in respect of threatening to destroy or damage property (i.e. threatening to commit a s.1 offence).

Section 2 provides:

> A person who without lawful excuse makes to another a threat, intending that that other would fear it would be carried out,—
>
> **(a)** to destroy or damage any property belonging to that other or a third person;
>
> or
>
> **(b)** to destroy or damage his own property in a way which he knows is likely to endanger the life of that other or a third person;
>
> shall be guilty of an offence.

The offence is punishable by a maximum period of 10 years' imprisonment. A defendant may commit an offence under s.2 in one of two ways:

1. By threatening to destroy or damage property belonging to another.
2. By threatening to destroy or damage his own property in a way in which he knows is likely to endanger someone else's life.

Whether a threat has been made is determined objectively, as is the question of whether the threat was one to destroy or damage property (**Cakmak [2002] 2 Cr. App. R. 10**). Both forms of the offence require that the defendant makes the threat intending that the person to whom it is made will fear the threat will be carried out; recklessness in this regard is insufficient. Further, where there is such intent, it is immaterial that the intended victim does not actually fear that the threat will be carried out (*Cakmak*).

Lawful Excuse

The lawful excuses provided by s.5 (see p.305) apply where the defendant is charged merely with threatening to destroy or damage property under s.2(1)(a) but not where it is alleged the defendant made the threat knowing that it was likely to endanger life under s.2(1)(b). All general defences apply to both forms of the offence.

Possessing Anything with Intent to Destroy or Damage Property

Section 3 of the 1971 Act creates an offence in respect of having in one's custody or under one's control something to be used to destroy or damage property (i.e. to be used to commit a s.1 offence). Although the terms custody and control are used in s.3, for convenience, the offence is usually referred to as *possessing* something with intent.

Section 3 provides:

> A person who has anything in his custody or under his control intending without lawful excuse to use it or cause or permit another to use it—
>
> **(a)** to destroy or damage any property belonging to some other person; or
> **(b)** to destroy or damage his own or the user's property in a way which he knows is likely to endanger the life of some other person;
>
> shall be guilty of an offence.

The offence is punishable by a maximum period of 10 years' imprisonment. A defendant may commit an offence under s.3 in one of two ways:

1. By having in his custody or under his control something which he intends to use, or cause another to use, in order to destroy or damage property belonging to another.
2. By having in his custody or under his control something which he intends to use or cause another to use to destroy or damage his own or the user's property in a way in which he knows is likely to endanger someone else's life.

Possession of an item will only bring the defendant within the scope of s.3 if the defendant intended to use the item in order to damage or destroy property. The intent required may be conditional in that the defendant intends to use the item only if necessary.

. . . .

Lawful Excuse

The lawful excuses provided by s.5 (see p.305) apply where the defendant is charged under s.3(1)(a) but not where the charge is under s.3(1)(b). All general defences apply to both forms of the offence.

Racially or Religiously Aggravated Criminal Damage

Section 30 of the Crime and Disorder Act 1998 (as amended by the Antiterrorism, Crime and Security Act 2001 s.39) provides that a person is guilty of an offence if he commits an offence under s.1(1) (the simple offence of criminal damage) which is racially or religiously aggravated. The offence is punishable by a maximum period of 14 years' imprisonment (as opposed to 10 years for the non-racially or religiously aggravated offence).

An offence is racially or religiously aggravated if:

1. at the time of committing it, or immediately before or after doing so, the defendant demonstrated hostility to the person to whom the property belongs, based on that person's membership or presumed membership of, or association with members of a racial or religious group; or
2. the offence is motivated wholly or partly by hostility towards members of a racial or religious group based on their membership of, or association with, members of that group.

A prosecution for racially aggravated criminal damage was successful in **DPP v M [2004] 1 W.L.R. 2758** in which D said, "Bloody foreigners" immediately prior to breaking the window of a kebab shop. The Court of Appeal held that D's words were capable of being construed as expressing hostility based on the victim's personal membership of a racial group. For a more detailed analysis of racially and religiously aggravated offences, see Ch.5.

Lawful Excuse

The 1971 Act provides that each offence must be committed *without lawful excuse*. The Act provides two specific lawful excuses—complete defences—to an offence under s.1(1) and to an offence charged under s.2(1)(a) or 3(1)(a); these lawful excuses do not apply to the aggravated offence under s.1(2) or to an offence charged under s.2(1)(b) or 3(1)(b). The lawful excuses may apply in addition to any other general defence available under statute or common law (s.5(5)).

Section 5 provides:

> **(2)** A person charged with an offence to which this section applies shall, whether or not he would be treated for the purposes of this Act as having a lawful excuse

apart from this subsection, be treated for those purposes as having a lawful excuse—

(a) if at the time of the act or acts alleged to constitute the offence he believed that the person or persons whom he believed to be entitled to consent to the destruction of or damage to the property in question had so consented, or would have so consented to it if he or they had known of the destruction or damage and its circumstances; or

(b) if he destroyed or damaged or threatened to destroy or damage the property in question or, in the case of a charge of an offence under section 3 above, intended to use or cause or permit the use of something to destroy or damage it, in order to protect property belonging to himself or another or a right or interest in property which was or which he believed to be vested in himself or another, and at the time of the act or acts alleged to constitute the offence he believed-

(i) that the property, right or interest was in immediate need of protection; and

(ii) that the means of protection adopted or proposed to be adopted were or would be reasonable having regard to all the circumstances.

(3) For the purposes of this section it is immaterial whether a belief is justified or not if it is honestly held.

(4) For the purposes of subsection (2) above a right or interest in property includes any right or privilege in or over land, whether created by grant, licence or otherwise.

Belief in Consent

Section 5(2)(a) provides a lawful excuse where the defendant damaged property in the honest belief that the person or persons he *believed* entitled to consent to the damage had consented to the damage or would so consent. The defendant may have held such a belief because, for example, he has always been allowed to treat V's property as his own and mistakenly believed V would have agreed to the damage or D has damaged V's property believing it to be Y's property for which he has consent to do damage or D misinterpreted a remark made by the owner of the property and mistakenly thought the owner wished the property to be damaged.

The section 5(2)(a) lawful excuse was pleaded successfully in **Denton [1982] 1 All E.R. 65**. D set fire to his employer's property as he thought his employer had asked him to do so to enable him to make an insurance claim because the business was in financial difficulties. The Court of Appeal accepted that the employer was entitled to consent to the damage and that D had honestly believed he had consent. The court held that D was entitled to rely on s.5(2)(a) notwithstanding the fact that the reason he destroyed the property was so that his employer could perpetrate a fraud against the insurance company. This illustrates that where there is belief in consent, the actual reason for carrying out the damage is immaterial.

The defendant's claim of lawful excuse was unsuccessful in **Blake v DPP [1993] Crim. L.R. 586 DC.** D, a vicar, was one of a group of demonstrators protesting against the use of military force by the allies in Iraq and Kuwait. Using a marker pen he wrote a Biblical quotation on a concrete pillar outside the Houses of Parliament and was arrested for criminal damage. He claimed that he had a lawful excuse under s.5(2)(a) in that he believed he had acted in accordance with God's wishes and that God was entitled to consent to the damage. The court dismissed D's appeal against conviction ruling, inter alia, that a belief, however powerful, genuine and honestly held that God owned the property and that God had consented to damage the pillar did not raise or amount to a lawful excuse under the domestic law of England.

Belief in Protection of Property

Section 5(2)(b) provides a lawful excuse where the defendant damaged property in order to protect property (his own or another's) which he believed was in immediate need of protection provided he also believed that the means of protection adopted were reasonable in the circumstances.

THE DEFENDANT'S PURPOSE

The defendant's purpose must be to protect *property*; the lawful excuse does not apply where the purpose was to protect a person (**Baker [1997] Crim. L.R. 497**).

Where the defendant's purpose is the protection of property, it is irrelevant whether the defendant acted to prevent unlawful damage; acting to prevent lawful damage is also permitted (**Jones [2005] Q.B. 259**). However, if the defendant's purpose is anything other than the protection of property, he cannot rely on the s.5(2)(b) lawful excuse (**Hunt (1978) 66 Cr. App. R. 105**). The defendant in this case assisted his wife in her job as warden of a block of old people's flats. He set fire to some bedding in order, he alleged, to demonstrate that the fire alarm was not working so that that the fault would be rectified, thereby protecting the flats from fire damage. He was charged with arson and pleaded the s.5(2)(b) lawful excuse. The court decided that the damage was carried out to draw attention to the problem with the fire alarm; it was not done in order to protect property.

The lawful excuse also failed on this ground in **Kelleher [2004] EWCA Crim. 561**. D had decapitated a statue of Baroness Thatcher and argued that he did so because he held her to blame for developments in world politics which he believed made the world a more dangerous place and caused him to fear for his son's future. The court held that D could not rely on the s.5(2)(b) lawful excuse because he had not acted to protect property.

Unlike the property damaged, the property to be protected may be intangible, for example, a right of way over land, as in **Chamberlain v Lindon [1998] 2 All E.R. 538 DC** (see below).

THE TWO-STAGE TEST

Where property is damaged in order to protect other property, the lawful excuse will only succeed if the defendant satisfies the following two-stage test set out in **Hill and Hall (1988) 89 Cr. App. R. 74**:

1. What was the defendant's actual state of mind when he damaged the property, i.e. did he believe that the property was in immediate need of protection and that the damage caused was reasonable in the circumstances?
   (the subjective question)
   and
2. Was the damage capable of protecting the property?
   (the objective question, one of law for the judge)

The defendant in *Hill and Hall*, a nuclear protester, was arrested outside a US airbase with a hacksaw which she intended to use to cut through the wire fence around the base. She was tried under s.2 and argued that she honestly believed that she had a lawful excuse under s.5(2)(b) as she hoped her actions would persuade the Americans that their base was not secure so that they would leave, thereby reducing the threat from the Russians of a nuclear attack on properties in the area. Applying the two-stage test, the lawful excuse failed because the defendant did not believe that property was in immediate need of protection (that nuclear attack was imminent) nor was the intended damage (cutting the fence) capable of protecting property; it was too remote. Similarly, the defendant in *Blake* was unable to satisfy the two-stage test to rely on the s.5(2)(b) lawful excuse. His act of writing on the pillar was not capable of protecting property in the Gulf States; it was again too remote.

A case where the s.5(2)(b) lawful excuse did succeed was *Chamberlain v Lindon*. D, who knocked down a wall which was on his neighbour's land and which was obstructing his own right of access over the land, was able to rely on the s.5(2)(b) lawful excuse. The magistrates, in acquitting D, held that the s.5(2)(b) lawful excuse was still available even though the wall had been there several months and civil remedies had not been exhausted. They found that the requirement of "immediacy" was satisfied as the right to be protected was already being infringed.

Intoxication and Lawful Excuse

For the purposes of s.5 it is immaterial whether the belief is justified or not if it is honestly held (s.5(3)). Therefore, provided the belief is honest, it may be due to voluntary intoxication. Consequently, the defendant in **Jaggard v Dickinson [1980] 3 All E.R. 716** who, whilst intoxicated, caused damage whilst trying to force her way into someone's house, mistakenly believing that the house was the one in which she was staying that was owned by her friend, was able to rely on the s.5(2)(a) lawful excuse. D honestly believed she would have had her friend's consent to breaking in to her house and it was immaterial that her mistaken belief about which house she was breaking into was due to her intoxication.

Summary

1. The simple offence of criminal damage, contrary to s.1(1) of the Criminal Damage Act 1971, involves (a) damaging or destroying (b) property (c) belonging to another (d) intentionally or with (subjective) recklessness and (e) without lawful excuse.

2. In determining whether damage has been caused, relevant considerations are: effort and expense involved in restoration; whether there has been impairment of the value or usefulness of the property; the nature of the property concerned.

3. The aggravated offence of criminal damage, contrary to s.1(2), is committed where D has intentionally damaged or destroyed any property intending or being reckless as to whether life would thereby be endangered. Under s.1(2), D must intend or be reckless as to endangering life by the damage, not by his act which causes the damage.

4. Arson is criminal damage (simple or aggravated) by fire.

5. Section 5(2) provides two lawful excuses to the simple offence available where D damaged property (a) in the belief he would have the owner's consent or (b) in order to protect other property which he believed was in immediate need of protection.

6. The 1971 Act also provides offences of threatening to destroy or damage property (s.2) and possessing anything with intent to damage or destroy property (s.3).

7. Section 30 of the Crime and Disorder Act (as amended) also provides for an offence of racially or religiously aggravated criminal damage.

End of Chapter Question

Question

Barry lives adjacent to some allotments. He has never been bothered by them until Ted takes on the allotment next to Barry's back garden. A very keen vegetable grower, Ted often takes deliveries of horse manure as fertilizer. He also frequently burns rubbish in his allotment and the smoke drifts into Barry's garden. The smells and smoke coming from the allotment are often so bad that Barry and his family have to stay indoors and close the windows. Barry is concerned that the smoke is responsible for his son's asthma attacks. He puts his house up for sale but is soon told by his estate agent that he will have to considerably reduce the sale price of his house as the smells from the allotment have devalued it.

Barry decides to try to get Ted to leave. He tips a tin of paint over Ted's bike which has been left outside the allotment. He tells Ted that vandals must be responsible as it is a dangerous neighbourhood and he should move away, as he is doing. Ted buys some paint stripper for £5 and removes the paint himself in an hour. He does not give up the allotment. Barry then sprays weed killer into a patch of leeks Ted has been growing. He thinks that the weed killer is unlikely to be dangerous to humans and that, anyway, the leeks are probably intended as prize leeks, for show only, rather than consumption. Ted did, in fact, intend to make soup with the leeks but they start to turn brown before he can do so and he digs them up and throws them out. In a final attempt to drive Ted away, Barry sets fire to Ted's shed. Ted sees the fire before it can take hold and quickly hoses the fire out. The shed is left unstable, however, and has to be demolished.

Consider Barry's liability under the Criminal Damage Act 1971.

Points of Answer

Barry may be liable under the Act in respect of the following incidents:

- ♦ Painting the bike
  - • This could be the simple offence of criminal damage under s.1(1). Define. Damage can be temporary, as here. Whether there has been damage as the paint is so easily removed, is a question of fact and degree for the magistrates (*Roe v Kingerlee*), taking into account the effort (not much) and cost (again not much) of rectification (*Hardman*). Mens rea (MR) of intention to damage property belonging to another is satisfied.
- ♦ Weed killer in the leeks
  - • This could be the aggravated offence under s.1(2). Define. No one's life need be endangered (*Parker*) so it is irrelevant that the leeks are not eaten. Leeks are property under s.10. MR of intention to endanger life by the damage is difficult to establish on the facts but he may have been reckless. Recklessness is subjective (*R. v G*). He thinks the weed killer is "unlikely" to be dangerous to humans and the leeks are "probably intended for show." This suggests that

he may think there is still some chance that they will be eaten and, as he has taken this risk, he would be reckless. He was reckless as to endangering life *by the damage,* i.e. a brown leek contaminated by weed killer.

- Ted could also be liable for an offence under s.3 for possession of the weed killer with intent to damage property belonging to another.

♦ Starts the fire

- This could be arson or aggravated arson, contrary to ss.1(1) & 1(3) or s.1(2) & 1(3) respectively. Define. It is arson as he intentionally destroys the shed by fire. It would be aggravated arson if Ted intended to endanger life (unlikely) or was reckless in that regard because he foresaw the risk of endangering, for example, Ted's life or fire fighters' lives. Again, irrelevant that no one's life is actually endangered.

♦ Lawful excuse

- Barry may have a lawful excuse to the simple offences of criminal damage and arson, but not the aggravated offences, under s.5(2)(b) as he commits these offences because he feels his property is being devalued and his son's health is being affected. Damage must be done in order to protect property (*Hunt*). He must believe property is in immediate need of protection. Is a risk to the value of the property sufficient given that the house remains intact? The risk to his son is irrelevant as the lawful excuse relates only to the protection of property (*Baker*). There is a two-stage test to satisfy under s.5(2)(b) which is both subjective—he believed his house was in immediate need of protection and objective—the damage done was capable of protecting the property in immediate need of protection (*Hill & Hall*). If the court thinks that the property damaged (the bike, leeks and shed) and the property allegedly protected (Barry's house) are too "remote" from each other, i.e. the damage is not capable of protecting the house then the defence fails (*Hill & Hall*). Barry believed his house was in immediate need of protection and it was—it was at that time being devalued—so, as in *Chamberlain v Lindon*, the immediacy requirement may be satisfied.

Further Reading

I. Edwards, "Banksy's Graffiti: A Not-so-simple Case of Criminal Damage?" (2009) J.C.L. 345.
D.W. Elliott, "Endangering Life by Destroying or Damaging Property" [1997] Crim. L.R. 382.

Self Test Questions

To test your knowledge gained from this section go online to *http://www.sweetandmaxwell. co.uk* and take our online self test questions. Here you will also find key updates to ensure that you are only ever one click away from an instant update.

Inchoate Offences

10

CHAPTER OVERVIEW

In this chapter we:

- identify that the inchoate offences are those offences which generally precede the commission of the "full" offence, and that there are three types of inchoate offences; attempts, conspiracy and encouraging or assisting offence(s)

- explore the nature of the meaning of "more than merely preparatory" in the context of an attempted crime

- investigate whether an attempt has been committed even if the full offence is impossible physically, legally or due to the means adopted

- explain that conspiracy is an offence either contrary to the common law (conspiracy to defraud, to outrage public decency or to corrupt public morals) or under the Criminal Law Act 1977 (conspiracies charged under the 1977 Act are called statutory conspiracies)

- note that the common law offence of incitement has been abolished and has been replaced with three new offences involving encouraging or assisting another to commit offence(s) under the Serious Crime Act 2007.

Summary

End of Chapter Question

Further Reading

Self Test Questions

Introduction

The word inchoate means "just begun" or "undeveloped". An inchoate offence is therefore one which is preliminary to the completed offence and for which liability does not depend on the completion of the full offence. The justification for criminalising incomplete crimes is that the law penalises the threat of harm in D's wrongful conduct. Most substantive offences penalise *identifiable* harm, but the inchoate offences criminalise *potential* harm. Because what is "potential" is wide and sometimes unknowable, the study of inchoate liability is factually complex; and because of the way the law has sometimes developed, it is legally complex too. There are three inchoate offences, namely attempt, conspiracy and encouraging or assisting offence(s).

Attempt

What is an Attempt?

An attempt occurs where a defendant has been unsuccessful in completion of the offence he set out to commit, but he has progressed so far towards its completion that the criminal law imposes liability for the steps he has taken. The defendant is charged with attempting the relevant substantive offence, for example D may be charged with attempted murder, attempted arson or attempted theft. It is possible to attempt to commit an offence only if it is triable on indictment, not one which is summary only (Criminal Attempts Act 1981 s.1(4)). Nor is it possible to attempt to conspire or to attempt to commit an offence as an accessory (though it is possible to be an accessory to an attempt (**Dunnington [1984] Q.B. 472**)).

Attempts are governed by s.1(1) of the Criminal Attempts Act 1981 which provides:

> If, with intent to commit an [indictable] offence … a person does an act which is more than merely preparatory to the commission of the offence, he is guilty of attempting to commit the offence.

The Actus Reus of Attempt

This is an act (this precludes liability for attempt by omission) which is more than merely preparatory to the commission of the offence. There is no guidance in the statute as to the meaning of the term "more than merely preparatory" and it has, therefore, been left to case law to interpret, see below.

THE ROLE OF JUDGE AND JURY

The trial judge first determines whether an act is capable of being "more than merely preparatory" and if he determines that it cannot, he must withdraw the case from the jury. Once the evidence has gone before the jury, however, the judge cannot direct them on whether D's act was more than merely preparatory; it is the role of the jury to determine whether the defendant's actions were sufficient to amount to an attempt rather than a preparatory act (s.4(3)), with each case decided on its facts. This can, unfortunately, lead to inconsistent verdicts.

RELEVANCE OF THE OFFENCE CHARGED

In determining whether D's acts are capable of being more than merely preparatory, the judge must consider the essential nature of the substantive offence which it is alleged has been attempted, i.e. the essential act or transaction on which it is based and any consequence required to effect it (**Nash [1999] Crim. L.R. 308**). This approach was taken in **Toothill [1998] Crim. L.R. 876**. D appealed unsuccessfully against conviction for attempted burglary with intent to rape (now a different offence contrary to the Sexual Offences Act 2003 s.63). He had knocked on his victim's door at night and appeared to be masturbating. The Court of Appeal held that the trial judge had been correct to hold that there was evidence of attempted burglary which could go to the jury. D's contention that the offence required not only attempted entry as a trespasser but also attempted rape was rejected; the actus reus of attempted burglary required only an attempt to enter the building as a trespasser. As D had attempted to enter by knocking on the door, he had committed the actus reus of attempted burglary.

The importance of the nature of the offence was also stressed in **Qadir [1997] 9 Arch. News 1**. Potter L.J. stated:

> "Whether or not an act crosses the threshold between preparation and embarkation on the commission of the crime will always depend on an examination of the scope or substance of the crime aimed at … [I]n a case of [killing], wounding or causing actual bodily harm, it would be likely that any act leading up to the commission … of the crime but substantially anterior to it in time will be an act merely preparatory. In a case of deception … since the actus reus of the crime itself may take place over an extended period of time, the moment of embarkation upon it may be quite remote in time from the point of its anticipated successful outcome."

MORE THAN MERELY PREPARATORY

Prior to the commencement of the 1981 Act, attempts were governed solely by the common law. Various definitions of "an attempt" were put forward over the years. The two main tests were:

1. Has D completed the last act dependent on him? This was often restated as: Has D crossed the Rubicon, i.e., passed the point of no return? (**DPP v Stonehouse [1978] A.C. 55**).

2. The proximity test—acts immediately connected with the offence constitute an attempt whereas those which are remote from its commission do not (**Eagleton (1855) Dears. 515**).

With the failure of the Criminal Attempts Act 1981 adequately to define an attempt, it was unclear whether the courts would have regard to the pre-Act case law on attempts or would introduce a new test. For the first few years after its inception, the courts tended to rely on the pre-Act tests. However, this changed with **Gullefer [1990] 3 All E.R. 882**, in which the Court of Appeal stated that the 1981 Act did not enact the previous law but, instead, steered a middle course. D had bet on a greyhound at the racing track. The dog was losing as it reached the final bend in the track so the defendant rushed onto the track and began waiving his arms about to distract the other dogs. He failed to do so but, if he had succeeded, the race would have been declared void and his bet would have been returned to him.

The case was similar to a couple of pre-Act cases (**Robinson [1915] 2 K.B. 342** and **Comer v Bloomfield (1970) 55 Cr. App. R. 305**) in which the defendants fabricated events in order to set the scene to make a fraudulent insurance claim in the future. In each case, the defendant was not liable as he had not yet completed or sent in the insurance claim form. Similarly, *Gullefer's* appeal against a conviction for attempted theft was successful as what he had done was merely preparatory to theft-even if the race had been declared void, he would have still had to go to the bookmakers to ask for his money back. Lord Lane C.J. stated:

> "The words of the Act seem to steer a midway course. They do not provide … that the Eagleton test is to be followed, or that … D must have reached a point from which it is impossible for him to retreat before the actus reus of an attempt is proved … [An attempt] begins when the merely preparatory acts have come to an end and the defendant embarks on the crime proper [or] the actual commission of the offence."

In **Jones [1990] 1 W.L.R. 1057**, the Court of Appeal agreed that the Act did not enact the previous law and stated that trial judges should not refer to the old tests. D bought a shotgun and sawed off the barrel. He intended to use the gun to kill his love rival, A. In disguise, he lay in wait for A, jumped into the backseat of A's car and pulled the gun on A, who managed to escape. It later became apparent that D had intended to flee the country after the shooting and had already bought some foreign currency. His conviction for attempted murder was upheld. The court considered that obtaining the gun, sawing off the end, dressing in disguise and lying in wait were preparatory acts but getting into the car, taking out the loaded gun and pointing it at A provided sufficient evidence of attempted murder. It was not necessary to wait until D had done the last act, i.e. released the safety catch and put his finger on the trigger to begin squeezing it for an attempt to be committed.

In **Campbell (1991) 93 Cr. App. R. 350,** D's actions were found to be insufficient to amount to an attempt. D loitered one yard outside a sub-post office entrance for half an hour until he was arrested by the police. An imitation gun and a threatening note were found on his person. His conviction for attempted robbery was quashed as he had committed no acts which a jury could properly have concluded were more than merely preparatory. Watkins L.J. stated:

> "If a person in circumstances such as this, has not even gained the place where he could be in a position to carry out the offence, it is extremely unlikely that it could ever be said that he had performed an act which could be properly said to be an attempt".

The decision has been criticised as leaving the police in the unsatisfactory position of having to wait until D has entered the building and approached the counter before arresting him, with all the dangers to which this exposes people inside the building.

It is difficult to distinguish *Campbell* from **Attorney General's Reference (No.1 of 1992)** [1993] 1 W.L.R. 274 in which the court determined the actus reus of attempted rape had been committed despite the fact that D had not attempted to penetrate V's vagina. The court stated that the evidence of V's distress, the state of her clothing, the position in which she was seen, together with D's acts of dragging her up the stairs, lowering his trousers and interfering with her private parts showed that D had "embarked on committing the offence".

Campbell was, however, cited with approval in **Geddes [1996] Crim. L.R. 894** in which a test of: "has D actually tried to commit the offence?" was suggested to determine whether D's acts satisfied the actus reus of attempted false imprisonment. D, carrying a rucksack containing a knife, rope and masking tape, got into the boys' toilets at a school but did not get as far as encountering any of the pupils. He was convicted of attempted false imprisonment of a person unknown. Whilst expressing unease at their decision, the Court of Appeal quashed D's conviction. The court held that, although D's intentions were clear, he had not performed an act which was more than merely preparatory to the commission of the offence. Lord Bingham C.J. gave the judgment of the court. He stated that:

> "It is, we think, an accurate paraphrase of the statutory test and not an illegitimate gloss upon it to ask whether the available evidence, if accepted, could show that a defendant has done an act which shows that *he has actually tried to commit the offence in question,* or whether he has only got ready or put himself in a position or equipped himself to do so." (emphasis added)

The Court of Appeal followed the guidance in *Geddes* in **Tosti [1997] Crim. L.R. 746**. The defendants had taken oxyacetylene equipment with them to the farm they intended to burgle. On arrival at the farm buildings, they hid the equipment in a hedge and then went up to the barn door and bent down to look at the padlock on it. They got no further as they were disturbed by the farm owner. The Court of Appeal upheld the convictions for attempted burglary. The court stated that the jury might have concluded on the facts that the defendants had "actually tried to commit the offence [rather than] only got ready ... to do so." The court also considered the significance of "merely" in "more than merely preparatory" and stated that:

> "there may be actions which are preparatory which are not merely so and which are essentially the first steps in the commission of the offence."

In **Bowles and Bowles [2004] 8 Arch. News 2**, the court determined that there was no attempted forgery where the defendants prepared a will for a vulnerable elderly neighbour with themselves as beneficiaries but left it unexecuted in a drawer for several months. The defendants' conduct was considered merely preparatory towards making a false instrument. Thus, the approach taken in *Gullefer* and the pre-Act cases involving attempted fraud was adopted. However, more recently in **Moore v DPP, unreported, February 2, 2010**, the Divisional Court dismissed D's appeal for attempting to drink-drive his car on a public road. He had been stopped by a police officer around 15m from a public road. The road was the only place that D could have driven to. D was breathalysed and his breath was positive for alcohol. The Divisional Court reviewed the Law Commission proposals (considered in more detail on pp.321–323 below) for reform of the law governing attempts and held that D's act was sufficiently close to the final act before the full offence. It is, therefore, an attempt where D's act is part of the execution of the individual's plan to commit the full offence. An attempt is therefore an "executory" part of the full crime, and anything less does not suffice as *more* than merely preparatory.

The grid on p.319 summarises the distinctions drawn in each of the cases above.

The Mens Rea of Attempt

The mens rea for attempts is particularly important. Since the consequence required for the substantive offence has not occurred, it is D's mens rea which can turn what seems to be an innocuous act(s) into a crime. For example, if D throws some rubbish over his fence and it just misses smashing into his neighbour's greenhouse, this may or may not be attempted criminal damage—it is D's intention which determines whether he has committed an attempted offence.

The mens rea for attempts is the intention to commit the offence which it is alleged has been attempted. Thus, for example, for attempted criminal damage D must intend to damage property belonging to another; for an attempted s.18 OAPA offence D must intend to do GBH. It is unclear whether direct intent only applies in attempts or whether oblique intent also applies generally to attempts, see further Ch.3 p.57.

At this stage, it is important to distinguish intention as to acts and consequences required by the actus reus, and intention as to certain circumstances required by the actus reus.

FIGURE 10 When acts are merely preparatory

Case	Offence charged	Attempt?	Salient points
Gullefer (1990)	Attempted theft	No	1981 Act steers a midway course. An attempt begins when merely preparatory acts have come to an end and the defendant embarks on the crime proper.
Jones (1990)	Attempted murder	Yes	Agreed with *Gullefer* on the approach post-1981.
Campbell (1991)	Attempted robbery	No	If D has not even gained the place where he could be in a position to carry out the offence, it is extremely unlikely that he had committed an attempt.
Attorney General's Reference (No.1 of 1992)	Attempted rape	Yes	D had not attempted to penetrate V but had embarked on committing the offence of rape.
Geddes (1996)	Attempted false imprisonment	No	Guidance to jury: Has D actually tried to commit the offence or merely put himself in a position or equipped himself to do so?
Tosti (1997)	Attempted burglary	Yes	Followed guidance in *Geddes*.
Bowles and Bowles (2004)	Attempted forgery	No	No liability where Ds had not executed the document under which they could have inherited.
Moore v DPP (2010)	Attempted drink-driving	Yes	An attempt where D's act is part of the execution of the individual's plan to commit the full offence. Anything less than an "executory" part of the full crime will not suffice.

ACTS AND CONSEQUENCES

Where the actus reus of the substantive offence requires a certain consequence, it must be established that D intended both the act required by the substantive offence (e.g. stabbing in a murder case) and the consequence. Intention as to the consequence required by the actus reus can make the mens rea for the attempt more difficult to establish than the mens rea for the substantive offence. For example, the actus reus of murder is causing the death of a human being (i.e. killing). Hence, the mens rea for attempted murder is intention to *kill* (**Whybrow (1951) 35 Cr. App. R. 141**), notwithstanding that the mens rea for murder itself can be satisfied by intention to kill or intention to cause GBH.

Where the substantive offence may be committed by intention or recklessness, only intention as to the required consequence will suffice (**O'Toole [1987] Crim. L.R. 759**). However, where the defendant is charged with attempted aggravated criminal damage (the substantive offence is considered in Ch.9), he may be liable even if he was only reckless as to endangering life, provided he intended to do damage (**Attorney General's Reference (No.3 of 1992) [1994] 2 All E.R. 121**).

CIRCUMSTANCES

In relation to mens rea as to the circumstances required by the actus reus, the position is different. In **Khan [1990] 1 W.L.R. 815**, the court stated that for those offences where recklessness suffices as to circumstances so it would also suffice in attempts.

CONDITIONAL INTENTION

A conditional intention occurs where the defendant has not yet made up his mind whether to do something; he will only do so if a particular condition is satisfied. For example, a pickpocket puts his hand inside V's pocket intending to steal anything in there of value, finds only a handkerchief, leaves it and departs empty handed. Similarly, D may enter a building intending to cause serious injury if there is someone inside. We saw in Ch.7 on p.243 and Ch.8 on p.255 that where D's intention is conditional he may still be liable for burglary (so D could be liable for burglary in the above example even if the building is deserted) but not for theft, or robbery (which requires a theft). So, the pickpocket in the example above could not be liable for theft. Might he be liable for attempted theft (or attempted robbery if he used force)? The answer is yes, provided D does have the intention to steal if the condition is satisfied and care is taken in phrasing the charge. In the example of the pickpocket above, D should not be charged with attempted theft of the items he discards, i.e. the handkerchief, as such a charge will fail but, instead, should be charged with attempting to steal from the pocket (**Attorney General's References (Nos 1 and 2 of 1979) [1979] 3 All E.R. 143**).

Attempts and Impossibility

It may be impossible to carry out the full offence. Crimes can be impossible for three main reasons:

1. They are physically impossible. For example, D seeks to take money from a pocket or wallet which contains none, or D shoots at a pillow in a bed mistakenly believing it to be P whom D intends to kill.
2. They are legally impossible. For example, D receives goods he mistakenly believes to be stolen goods; or tries to take an article which is really his own property but which he believes belongs to P.

3. D's method of commission may render the offence impossible to commit. For example, D tries to kill someone with a dose of poison which is too small to kill; or to shoot someone out of the range of his gun; or to break into a safe with tools inadequate for this task.

Section 1(2) of the Act makes it clear that the fact that, in the circumstances, it is impossible to commit the substantive offence (whether physically, legally or due to the means adopted) is no bar to liability for attempting the offence. The effect of s.1(3) is that a person will be deemed to have had the requisite intent to commit the crime attempted even though, unknown to him, its commission was in fact impossible. This was confirmed in **Shivpuri [1987] A.C. 1.** D was convicted of attempting to be knowingly concerned in dealing with and harbouring a controlled drug, namely heroin. He was carrying a package containing a powdered substance which he admitted he suspected to be heroin, but the substance was actually a vegetable material akin to snuff. The House of Lords held that because the actus reus of the offence of attempt required an act which was more than merely preparatory to the commission of an offence, if D did that act with the intention of committing an offence, notwithstanding that the commission of the actual offence was, on the facts, impossible, D would have intended the offence. This was confirmed in **Jones [2008] Q.B. 460**. An undercover police officer, posing as a 12-year-old girl, had been in contact with D by text message, the subject matter of which included sexual acts D would perform on the "12 year old girl". D appealed against his subsequent conviction of attempting to incite a child under 13 years into penetrative sexual activity on the grounds that there was no actual child in this case. His appeal was dismissed because D had intention to incite a particular (even if not actual) child to engage in penetrative sexual activity and his acts were more than merely preparatory to commission of the offence.

There is one rider to this: D cannot be liable for an attempt if what he is attempting is not contrary to English law.

Attempts and Reform

In "Conspiracy and Attempts, A Consultation Paper", Law Com. CP No.183, 2007, the recommendations for reform include:

> Proposal 15: We propose that section 1(1) of the Criminal Attempts Act 1981 should be repealed and replaced by two separate inchoate offences, both of which would require an intention to commit the relevant substantive offence:
>
> **(1)** an offence of criminal attempt, limited to last acts needed to commit the intended offence; and
> **(2)** an offence of criminal preparation, limited to acts of preparation which are properly to be regarded as part of the execution of the plan to commit the intended offence.

FIGURE 10.1 **Requirements for an attempt**

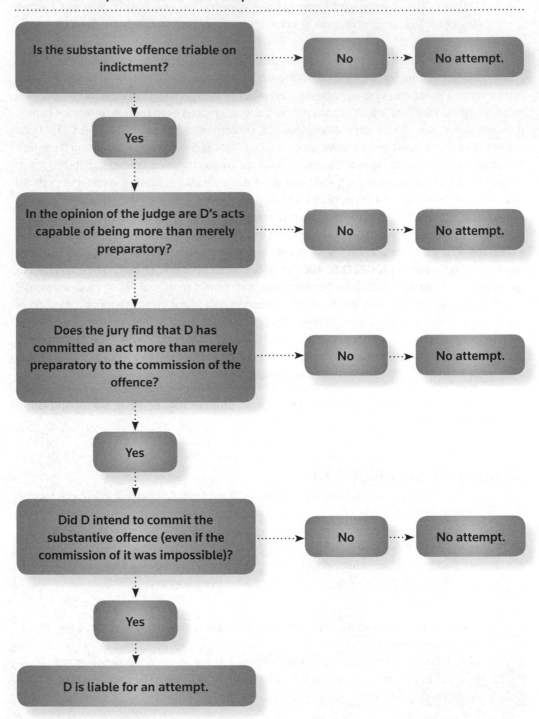

It was proposal 15(1) that was considered by the Divisional Court in *Moore v DPP* (above p.318) when dismissing D's appeal. D had gone beyond mere preparation. Had the police officer not intervened, it was clear D would have driven on the street.

In the Criminal Law Review Editorial of January 2008, Ian Dennis suggests that the two new offences are not necessarily any clearer or user-friendly than the old test:

> "This latest effort to resolve the classic issue of how to define the actus reus of an attempt may be as problematic as all its many predecessors. It would make the law more complex by introducing a new distinction between last acts and criminally preparatory acts, as well as preserving the existing distinction between merely preparatory and more than merely preparatory acts."

However:

> "As regards *mens rea* it is right to retain intention for an attempt to engage in criminal conduct and to cause a harmful result, and to provide that it should encompass direct and Woollin indirect intent. It is also right to provide that where subjective recklessness will suffice for a circumstantial element for the substantive offence it should also suffice for the attempt, and to insist on subjective recklessness as a minimum fault requirement for attempt even if a lesser fault or no fault is required for a circumstance of the substantive offence." ([2008] Crim. L.R. 1)

Over to you ...

In the Law Commission Consultation Paper 183 (2007), the Law Commission was very critical of the "widely divergent" views of the courts on what the test for "more than merely preparatory" should be and in particular criticised the outcome of the case of *Geddes* (above) (see Law Com. CP183 paras 1.71–1.76). The proposal reproduced above is designed to replace the test in the 1981 Act with two new offences. Which of the recommended offences covers the facts of *Geddes*?

Conspiracy

Conspiracy is an offence both under statute and at common law. At common law, only the offences of conspiracy to defraud, to outrage public decency and to corrupt public morals still exist. All other common law conspiracies were abolished by the Criminal Law Act 1977. Conspiracy to defraud was not abolished by the Fraud Act 2006, as Parliament intended to wait and see whether it was still necessary once the Act had been fully implemented, but its significance may now be severely limited. The offence is considered in Ch.8. Conspiracies to outrage public decency or to corrupt public morals do not generally feature on exam papers and are not considered further here.

Statutory Conspiracy

The statutory offence of conspiracy is defined in s.1(1) of the Criminal Law Act 1977 (as amended) which provides a person is liable for conspiracy if he:

> agrees with any other person or persons that a course of conduct shall be pursued which, if the agreement is carried out in accordance with their intentions … will necessarily amount to or involve the commission of any offence or offences by one or more of the parties to the agreement.

THE ACTUS REUS OF STATUTORY CONSPIRACY

The actus reus consists of the following:

1. an agreement;
2. between two or more parties;
3. that one or more of the parties will commit the substantive offence; and
4. the course of conduct to be committed in pursuance of the agreement necessarily amounts to a criminal offence.

■ An agreement between two or more parties to … commit the crime

The agreement must be to commit the same crime. Hence, in **Taylor [2002] Crim. L.R. 205**, where D1 agreed to import Class A drugs and D2 to import Class B drugs, there was no conspiracy. Where the parties do agree to commit the same crime, the offence is complete as soon as the agreement has been reached. It does not affect D's liability that the agreed offence is never carried out or that a party later changes his mind about carrying it out (**Barnard (1980) 70 Cr. App. R. 28**). Nor is it necessary that the parties meet, or even for every member to have communicated with each other, provided each conspirator has communicated with at least one other (**Scott (1979) 68 Cr. App. R. 164**). The agreement continues until the substantive offence is committed. So, parties can join an existing conspiracy at any time prior to its fruition (**DPP v Doot [1973] 1 All E.R. 940 HL**).

With at least two parties to the agreement

Certain parties are excluded by s.2(2) from inclusion in a conspiracy. Therefore, if there are only two parties and one of them is exempt by virtue of s.2(2) there is no conspiracy. The exempt categories are:

1. D's spouse/civil partner. (Although, if there is a third party to the conspiracy who is not exempt, D's spouse may liable for conspiracy (**Chrastny [1992] 1 All E.R. 189**). The Law Commission in its 2007 Consultation Paper 183 proposed removal of the spousal exemption as a "conspicuous anomaly" (para. 1.42)).
2. The victim of the conspiracy.
3. A person who is doli incapax (under the age of 10).

It is worth noting that the acquittal of one party is no bar to conviction of the other party unless, in the circumstances, D's conviction is inconsistent with the other's acquittal (s.5(8)).

The agreement must be that one or more of the parties will commit the substantive offence

An agreement that a third party will commit the offence is not a statutory conspiracy.

The course of conduct to be committed in pursuance of the agreement must necessarily amount to a criminal offence

The agreement must be to pursue a course of conduct which, if the agreement is carried out in accordance with their intentions, will necessarily amount to a crime. In result crimes, such as murder, this means both the defendants' actions and their consequences must be agreed. So, for example, if defendants are to be liable for a conspiracy to murder V in a terrorist attack, they must agree not only to fire bomb his car but also that he should die in the blast. "Necessarily" in this situation does not mean inevitably, i.e. that the offence will definitely be carried out in all circumstances. Hence, intention can be conditional for conspiracy. In **Jackson [1985] Crim. L.R. 442**, the defendants had agreed with X, who was on trial for burglary, that they would shoot him in the leg if he was convicted, in the hope that this would persuade the court to give him a lighter sentence. Their convictions for conspiracy to pervert the course of justice were upheld by the Court of Appeal which stated:

> "Planning was taking place for a contingency and if that contingency occurred the conspiracy would necessarily involve the commission of an offence. 'Necessarily' [does not] mean that there must inevitably be the carrying out of the offence; it means, if the agreement is carried out in accordance with the plan, there must be the commission of the offence referred to in the conspiracy count."

THE MENS REA OF STATUTORY CONSPIRACY

We have already seen that a conspiracy requires an agreement. This necessarily involves a mental element. In addition, it must be proven that the parties intend that the crime planned shall be committed.

Section 1(2) of the Criminal Law Act 1977 provides:

> Where liability for any offence may be incurred without knowledge on the part of the person committing it of any particular fact or circumstance necessary for the commission of the offence, a person shall nevertheless not be guilty of conspiracy to commit that offence by virtue of subsection (1) above unless he and at least one other party to the agreement intend or know that that fact or circumstance shall or will exist at the time when the conduct constituting the offence is to take place.

This is a notoriously difficult subsection to interpret. In **Saik [2007] 1 A.C. 18**, the House of Lords held that this means that the mens rea of any statutory conspiracy lies in:

1. making an agreement with co-conspirators; and
2. intention to pursue a course of conduct which would necessarily involve the commission of the crime in question by one or more of the conspirators; and
3. in addition, under s.1(2) of the 1977 Act, there is a further mental element which is the intention or knowledge that a fact or circumstances necessary for the commission of the crime would exist.

What the third point means is that the conspirator must intend or know of a fact or circumstances that shall or will (not suspect it might) exist at the time that the conspiracy is intended to be brought about. Any lesser mens rea that would suffice for the substantive offence (i.e. less than intend or know) is irrelevant to prove the conspiracy. This means that proving the mens rea of conspiracy may be more difficult than proving the mens rea for the full offence, a similar situation as for the mens rea of attempts (see above).

In its Consultation Paper 183, at para.1.22, the Law Commission uses the following example to illustrate the possible effect of the decision in *Saik*:

> "Accordingly, it is not sufficient that the alleged conspirators knowingly take an unjustified risk that the prohibited circumstances might exist at the time of the offence. Consider a hypothetical example involving an agreement by D1 and D2 to rape V. The circumstance element of the offence of rape is V's lack of consent. D1 and D2 agree to have sexual intercourse with V whether or not V consents. We consider that this ought

to be regarded as a conspiracy to commit rape but, following *Saik*, it will not necessarily be so regarded. The offence of rape does not require proof of knowledge that V will not consent and so section 1(2) applies. This means that the prosecution has to prove that D1 and D2 *knew* at the time of the agreement that V would not consent. However, it would be very easy for them plausibly to claim that they merely thought V 'might not' or 'probably would not' consent. That would not be an admission of fault sufficient to satisfy section 1(2), although we consider that it ought to be."

We will consider the recommendations in the Consultation paper further below.

Where one or more of the parties secretly wishes that the planned crime is not committed, because, for example, he is an undercover policeman, can he then be liable for conspiracy? In **Anderson [1985] 2 All E.R. 961**, the House of Lords stated obiter that he could. The position is less clear, however, in light of the Privy Council ruling in **Chiu-Cheung [1994] 2 All E.R. 924** which suggests that each party must intend the plan to be carried out. A further point made in *Anderson* also seems open to question. Lord Bridge suggested that D must also intend when he enters into the agreement to play some part in the planned crime. This would exclude the "Mr Big" who is involved in the planning stages but does not intend to get his hands dirty by participating in the crime itself. The Privy Council again cast doubt on this aspect of *Anderson* in **Siracusa (1990) 90 Cr. App. R. 340**, in which it was stated that "participation in a conspiracy … can be active or passive."

IMPOSSIBILITY

It is no bar to a statutory conspiracy that the offence planned is impossible to commit (s.1(1)(b) of the 1977 Act). Thus, for example, defendants can conspire to receive goods they mistakenly believe to be stolen goods.

REFORM

In its Consultation Paper "Conspiracy and Attempts", Law Com. CP No.183, 2007 the Law Commission makes the following recommendations for the reform of this inchoate offence:

Proposal 1: A conspiracy must involve an agreement by two or more persons to engage in the conduct element of an offence and (where relevant) to bring about any consequence element.

Proposal 2: A conspirator must be shown to have intended that the conduct element of the offence, and (where relevant) the consequence element, should respectively be engaged in or brought about.

Proposal 3: Where a substantive offence requires proof of a circumstance element, a conspirator must be shown to have been reckless as to the possible existence of a circumstance element at the time when the substantive offence was to be committed (provided no higher degree of fault regarding a circumstance is required by the substantive offence).

Proposal 4: As a qualification to proposal 3, where a substantive offence has a fault requirement more stringent than recklessness in relation to a circumstance element, a conspirator must be shown to have possessed that higher degree of fault at the time of his or her agreement to commit the offence.

Proposal 6: the defence of "acting reasonably" provided by [section 50] of the Serious Crime [Act 2007] should be applied in its entirety to the offence of conspiracy.

There is academic support for the proposals, but Ian Dennis in his Criminal Law Review editorial suggests the Law Commission clarifies:

"further the requirement that a conspirator must intend the conduct element of the agreed offence to be engaged in and any relevant consequence of the agreed offence brought about … and … give[s] further thought to exactly what offence a defendant in such a case can be charged with where he has not yet provided any actual assistance." ([2008] Crim. L.R. 89).

Incitement

Incitement was an offence at common law. Essentially, it involved intentionally persuading another, by threats, pressure, encouragement or inducement (**Invicta Plastics Ltd v Clare [1976] R.T.R. 251 DC**) to commit an offence. The common law offence has been abolished and replaced with the offences considered immediately below.

Encouraging or Assisting Crime(s)

Loosely based on some of the proposals in the Law Commission Report, *Inchoate Liability for Assisting and Encouraging Crime* (Law Com No.300, CM 6878, 2006), Pt 2 of the Serious Crime Act 2007 replaced the common law offence of incitement with three new offences relating to encouraging or assisting crime. The crimes are deceptive in their apparent simplicity:

FIGURE 10.2 **Encouraging or assisting crimes**

Section 44 Serious Crime Act 2007	**Doing an act capable of encouraging or assisting an offence, intending to encourage or assist**
Section 45 Serious Crime Act 2007	**Doing an act capable of encouraging or assisting an offence believing his act will encourage or assist**
Section 46 Serious Crime Act 2007	**Doing an act capable of encouraging or assisting one or more offences believing his act will encourage or assist one of more of them**

In the absence of case law on the new offences (a situation unlikely to be the status quo for very long), the most detailed analysis of the crimes can be found at D. Ormerod and R. Fortson, "Serious Crime Act 2007: the Part 2 offences" [2009] Crim. L.R. 389. The authors describe the three crimes as "some of the most convoluted offences in decades" with "excessive complexity" and "unwarranted incoherence".

The Elements of the Part 2 Offences

The three main offences in Pt 2 of the Serious Crime Act 2007 (SCA) are stated in ss.44–46.

Section 44 creates the offence of encouraging or assisting an offence. It provides:

> **(1)** A person commits an offence if—
>   **(a)** he does an act capable of encouraging or assisting the commission of an offence;
> and
>   **(b)** he intends to encourage or assist its commission.
>
> **(2)** But he is not to be taken to have intended to encourage or assist the commission of an offence merely because such encouragement or assistance was a foreseeable consequence of his act.

The crime is complete when D does the act capable of encouraging, etc. The same is also true of the ss.45 and 46 offences. This is the essence of the inchoate nature of the Pt 2 crimes.

The purpose of subs.(2) is to make intention in subs.(1) purposive or direct intention and exclude oblique/virtually certain/indirect/*Woollin* intent from the section.

Section 45 creates the offence of encouraging or assisting an offence believing it will be committed. It provides:

> A person commits an offence if—
> **(a)** he does an act capable of encouraging or assisting the commission of an offence; and
> **(b)** he believes—
> **(i)** that the offence will be committed; and
> **(ii)** that his act will encourage or assist its commission.

Note in respect of D's mens rea that the verb used is "will" not "might". Note further than "belief" is a difficult concept in the criminal law but it is not defined in the Act. A belief lies somewhere between a suspicion and knowledge.

Section 46 creates the offence of encouraging or assisting offences believing one or more will be committed. It provides:

> **(1)** A person commits an offence if—
> **(a)** he does an act capable of encouraging or assisting the commission of one or more of a number of offences; and
> **(b)** he believes—
> **(i)** that one or more of those offences will be committed (but has no belief as to which); and
> **(ii)** that his act will encourage or assist the commission of one or more of them.
>
> **(2)** It is immaterial for the purposes of subsection (1)(b)(ii) whether the person has any belief as to which offence will be encouraged or assisted.

There are certain elements which are common across the crimes. For example, in each, D (who is the encourager or assister) does an act capable of encouraging or assisting P (the would-be or actual principal to the offence) to commit an offence. It matters not whether P is actually influenced at all by D's act or even if P does commit the offence (s.49). The words "act", "capable", "encouraging" and "assisting" are not defined in the Act although marginal guidance is provided in s.65 insofar as "act" includes, inter alia, an omission where D is under a duty to act.

To have an understanding of the operation of the crimes, reference must also be made to ss.47 and 49; and it is here that the real complexities arise.

Section 47 relates to proving an offence under Pt 2. It provides:

... **(5)** In proving for the purposes of this section whether an act is one which, if done, would amount to the commission of an offence—

    (a) if the offence is one requiring proof of fault, it must be proved that—

        (i) D believed that, were the act to be done, it would be done with that fault;

        (ii) D was reckless as to whether or not it would be done with that fault; or

        (iii) D's state of mind was such that, were he to do it, it would be done with that fault; and

    (b) if the offence is one requiring proof of particular circumstances or consequences (or both), it must be proved that—

        (i) D believed that, were the act to be done, it would be done in those circumstances or with those consequences; or

        (ii) D was reckless as to whether or not it would be done in those circumstances or with those consequences.

(6) For the purposes of subsection (5)(a)(iii), D is to be assumed to be able to do the act in question.

(7) In the case of an offence under section 44—

    (a) subsection (5)(b)(i) is to be read as if the reference to "D believed" were a reference to "D intended or believed"; but

    (b) D is not to be taken to have intended that an act would be done in particular circumstances or with particular consequences merely because its being done in those circumstances or with those consequences was a foreseeable consequence of his act of encouragement or assistance.

(8) Reference in this section to the doing of an act includes reference to—

    (a) a failure to act;

    (b) the continuation of an act that has already begun;

    (c) an attempt to do an act (except an act amounting to the commission of the offence of attempting to commit another offence).

In ss.47(5) and (8), the word "act" refers to *P's* act; *not D's act*.

Section 49 further provides:

(1) A person may commit an offence under this Part whether or not any offence capable of being encouraged or assisted by his act is committed.

> **(2)** If a person's act is capable of encouraging or assisting the commission of a number of offences—
> **(a)** section 44 applies separately in relation to each offence that he intends to encourage or assist to be committed; and
> **(b)** section 45 applies separately in relation to each offence that he believes will be encouraged or assisted to be committed.

Section 47 might be regarded as the main mens rea section, but ss.44, 45 and 46 also contain mens rea elements. The sections are complicated because not only must D be proved to have a particular state of mind in respect of his own act(s) (outlined in the main sections themselves), s.47(5) provides that D must also be proved to have a particular state of mind about P's conduct, the circumstances in which D anticipates P will act, the consequences that will flow, *and* what P's state of mind will be when P commits the anticipated offence (an offence which of course need not be committed for liability to arise, s.49). The justification for s.47(5) can be found in the Explanatory Notes to the Act:

> 156. Requiring some degree of belief in relation to circumstances ensures that a person would not be guilty of an offence of encouraging or assisting a strict liability offence unless he believes or is reckless as to whether those circumstances exist. For example, D asks P to drive him home from the pub as he has had too much to drink. P is insured to drive D's car but unknown to D and P, P was disqualified from driving the day before. P is committing the principal offence of driving whilst disqualified, despite the fact he is not aware that he is disqualified, as this is an offence of strict liability. However it would not be fair to hold D liable in such circumstances.
>
> 157. Requiring some degree of belief in relation to consequences ensures that a person would not be guilty of an offence that requires certain consequences to arise for it to be committed, unless he believes or is reckless as to whether those consequences should arise. For example, D gives P a baseball bat and intends P to use it to inflict minor bodily harm on V. P however uses the bat to attack V and intentionally kills V. It would not be fair to hold D liable for encouraging and assisting murder, unless he also believes that, or is reckless as to whether, V will be killed.

Paragraph 157 above also illustrates that there is considerable overlap with the law governing accessorial liability considered in Ch.11. Bear in mind that the new SCA offences co-exist with the common law/s.8 of the Accessories and Abettors Act 1861. So a prosecutor can select which charge to bring where P has committed the principal offence because although inchoate in the sense that D's liability arises when he does "an act capable of" with the mens rea and liability is not derivative on the principal crime, D can be convicted of a Pt 2 SCA offence even where the principal crime has been committed. Ormerod and Fortson, in the article cited above, are critical of this overlap for a number of reasons, including the incoherence in the concurrent operation of criminal schemes of liability with very different aims dealing with different types of wrong (see also the Introduction to this chapter).

FIGURE 10.3 The elements of the Serious' Crime Act Offences

Section 44	Section 45	Section 46
D	D	D
Does an act	Does an act	Does an act
That is capable of	That is capable of	That is capable of
Encouraging or assisting	Encouraging or assisting	Encouraging or assisting
P	P	P
To commit an offence	To commit an offence	In the commission of one or more of a number of offences
Intending to encourage or assist P and intending that the offence will be committed	Believing that the offence by P will be committed and believing D's act will encourage or assist its commission	Believing one or more of those offences will be committed and his act will encourage or assist one or more of them (but has no belief as to which)
D must also believe that P will act with the requisite mens rea for the anticipated offence or D must be reckless whether P will do so (s.47(5)(a)).	D must also believe that P will act with the requisite mens rea for the anticipated offence or D must be reckless whether P will do so (s.47(5)(a)).	D must also believe that P will act with the requisite mens rea for the anticipated offence or D must be reckless whether P will do so (s.47(5)(a)).

Defence of Reasonableness

There is a defence of acting reasonably in s.50 which provides:

> **(1)** A person is not guilty of an offence under this Part if he proves—
> **(a)** that he knew certain circumstances existed; and
> **(b)** that it was reasonable for him to act as he did in those circumstances.

(2) A person is not guilty of an offence under this Part if he proves—

  (a) that he believed certain circumstances to exist;

  (b) that his belief was reasonable; and

  (c) that it was reasonable for him to act as he did in the circumstances as he believed them to be.

(3) Factors to be considered in determining whether it was reasonable for a person to act as he did include—

  (a) the seriousness of the anticipated offence (or, in the case of an offence under section 46, the offences specified in the indictment);

  (b) any purpose for which he claims to have been acting;

  (c) any authority by which he claims to have been acting.

The intended operation of this defence was neatly summarised by the Law Commission in Law Com 300 para. A.63:

"D, a motorist, changes motorway lanes to allow a following motorist (P) to overtake, even though D knows that P is speeding; D, a reclusive householder, bars his front door to a man trying to get into his house to escape from a prospective assailant (P); D, a member of a DIY shop's check-out staff, believes the man (P) purchasing spray paint will use it to cause criminal damage."

However, the burden of proof for the defence expressly lies on the defendant (see Ch.1 Introduction in respect of the burden of proof), a matter which will inevitably face a challenge for compatibility with art.6 ECHR.

(You may recall from pp.327–328 above that the Law Commission has recommended the introduction of a similar defence to a new offence of conspiracy in its Consultation Paper 183.)

. . . .

Limitation

As we have seen with conspiracy above, certain parties are excluded from the offence(s). Although unclear in scope, s.51 provides exclusion from liability in respect of "protective offences." Section 51 provides:

(1) In the case of protective offences, a person does not commit an offence under this Part by reference to such an offence if—

  (a) he falls within the protected category; and

(b) he is the person in respect of whom the protective offence was committed or would have been if it had been committed.

(2) "Protective offence" means an offence that exists (wholly or in part) for the protection of a particular category of persons ("the protected category").

The Act's Explanatory Notes provide assistance (paras 178–180):

> "This section sets out in statute the common law exemption from liability established in the case of *R v Tyrrell* (1894) 1 Q.B. 710. A person cannot be guilty of the offences in sections 44, 45 and 46 if, in relation to an offence that is a 'protective' offence (defined in subsection (2)), the person who does the act capable of encouraging or assisting that offence falls within the category of persons that offence was designed to protect and would be considered as the victim. For example, D is a 12 year old girl and encourages P, a 40 year old man to have sex with her. P does not attempt to have sex with D. D cannot be liable of encouraging or assisting child rape despite the fact it is her intent that P have sexual intercourse with a child under 13 (child rape) because she would be considered the 'victim' of that offence had it taken place and the offence of child rape was enacted to protect children under the age of 13."

Double Inchoate Liability

Section 44 is drafted in such a way that it is possible for D to be convicted under s.44 for assisting a s.45 or s.46 offence. The following example is taken from the Ormerod and Fortson article mentioned above:

> "P asks D to supply him with a weapon so that P can murder V: P is doing an act capable of encouraging (and intended to encourage) D to do an act that is capable of assisting P to commit the murder. P commits the s.44 offence. D commits the s.45 offence if, subject to s.47(5), he believes that P will use the weapon." ([2009] Crim. L.R. 389 at 392)

It is also possible to be convicted of attempting a s.44, s.45 or s.46 offences or even a statutory conspiracy to commit a s.44, s.45 or s.46 offence.

Impossibility

Physical and legal impossibility were potential defences to common law incitement but impossibility due to the means adopted was not (**DPP v Armstrong [2000] Crim. L.R. 379, R. v Fitzmaurice [1983] Q.B. 1083**, see pp.320–321 above for an explanation of these terms). It was the view of the Law Commission (Law Com No.300 para.6.61) that impossibility should not be a defence to offences under Pt 2 of the SCA, but it is at least arguable that if D does an act encouraging or assisting P in what P might later/could later/did later do, but that is itself not an offence in the criminal law, D should not be convicted of the SCA offence either. There is no provision in the Act to deal specifically with the question of impossibility.

Over to you...

A and B are next door neighbours. A, who has numerous previous convictions for violence, knocks at B's front door and asks B to lend him a hammer. B knows that A has previous convictions and that A had an argument with C, a mutual acquaintance, in the pub the night before. B thinks A is going to use the hammer in a violent attack on C (although it strikes B as odd that A has asked him for the hammer). B lends A the hammer, because B has also had an argument with C. In fact, A and C have settled their differences and A wants to borrow the hammer to put up a picture. Is B liable for an offence under Pt 2 SCA? If so, which?

Summary

1. **Attempt,** contrary to s.1 of the Criminal Attempts Act 1981 involves doing an act which is more than merely preparatory to the commission of the offence. Whether an act is more than merely preparatory is determined by the jury on a case by case basis. The mens rea for attempts is the intention to commit the offence which it is alleged has been attempted. The intention can be conditional. D may be liable for attempting the impossible whether the impossibility is physical, legal or due to the means adopted (s.1(2)).

2. **Conspiracy** is now primarily a statutory offence (under s.1(1) of the Criminal Law Act 1977). It involves an agreement between two or more parties that one or more of them will pursue a course of conduct which, if the agreement is carried out in accordance with their intentions, will necessarily amount to a crime. The mens rea for conspiracy requires agreement and that the parties intend that the crime

planned shall be committed. Certain parties are excluded by s.2(2) from inclusion in a conspiracy. Impossibility is no bar to conviction for conspiracy.

3. **Incitement** was a common law offence which involves trying to persuade another to commit an offence.

4. There are three new offences of *encouraging or assisting crime(s)* under the Serious Crime Act 2007. If D does an act capable of encouraging or assisting P to commit a crime, he is liable, even if P does not commit that crime, (a) under s.44, if D intends to encourage or assist and intends P to commit the anticipated offence, (b) under s.45 if D believes P will commit the offence and his encouragement or assistance will encourage or assist, or (c) under s.46 if D believes one or more of those offences will be committed and his act will encourage or assist one or more of them (but has no belief as to which), and in each case (d) D must also believe that P will act with the requisite mens rea for the anticipated offence or D must be reckless whether P will do so.

End of Chapter Question

Question

"There is no justification for criminalising an incomplete crime. No harm occurs; no injury is suffered until the defendant completes the offence."

Discuss the imposition of criminal liability for inchoate crimes in light of the above statement.

Point of Answer

♦   Start with a definition of inchoate as meaning an incomplete crime and identify the three main types;
   •   Attempt
   •   Conspiracy and
   •   Encouraging or assisting crimes.
♦   Concede that although the inchoate crimes do not result in the actus reus of the full offence, they do each have their own actus reus (for example, for an attempt, an act which is more than merely preparatory; for the SCA offences, an act capable of encouraging or assisting P to commit a crime) and mens rea (for example, for an attempt, intention to commit the full offence; for conspiracy, agreement and intent that the planned crime shall be committed).
♦   Each inchoate crime can be committed in circumstances of impossibility and
♦   are criminalised to penalise the potential for harm in D's conduct.
♦   Consider also that D's failure to succeed in the full offence, from say, an attempt, may be accidental; D's moral culpability is the same.
♦   Conclude (disagreeing with the quotation).

Further Reading

B. Hogan, "The Criminal Attempts Act and Attempting the Impossible" [1984] Crim. L.R. 584.

A. Jones, "Conspiracy, Attempt and Incitement" (Sweet and Maxwell, 1997).

D. Ormerod and R. Fortson, "Serious Crime Act 2007:the Part 2 offences" [2009] Crim. L.R. 389

K.J.M. Smith, "Proximity in Attempt: Lord Lane's Midway Course" [1991] Crim. L.R. 576.

J. Spencer and G. Virgo, "Encouraging and Assisting Crime" [2008] 9 Arch. News 7.

G.R. Sullivan, "Inchoate Liability for Assisting and Encouraging Crime—The Law Commission Report" [2006] Crim. L.R. 1047.

G. Williams, "Attempting the Impossible—The Last Round" (1985) N.L.J. 337; "The Lords Achieve the Legally Impossible" (1985) N.L.J. 502; "Impossible Attempts, Or Quis Custodiet Ipsos Custodes" (1986) 45 C.L.J. 33 and "Wrong Turnings on the Law of Attempt" [1991] Crim. L.R. 416.

Self Test Questions

To test your knowledge gained from this section go online to http://*www.sweetandmaxwell.co.uk* and take our online self test questions. Here you will also find key updates to ensure that you are only ever one click away from an instant update.

Participation in Criminal Offences

11

CHAPTER OVERVIEW

In this chapter we:

- distinguish the perpetrator (principal) from other parties who participate in the offence (accessories or secondary parties)

- explore the concept of innocent agency

- consider the requirements for the imposition of secondary liability

- consider joint enterprise liability

- consider how an accessory may withdraw their participation in an offence

- consider the scope of the doctrine of vicarious liability in the criminal law

- analyse the approach of the law to corporate criminal liability

Summary

End of Chapter Question

Further Reading

Self Test Questions

Introduction

Where the actus reus of a criminal offence is committed, persons other than the actual perpetrator may also be guilty of that offence because, for example, they gave advice, encouragement or assistance to the perpetrator. The following example provides an illustration. A plans a bank robbery. He obtains information from B, an employee of the bank, about the bank's security procedures and instructs C to carry out the robbery. C asks D to keep watch outside whilst he commits the robbery. C is the actual perpetrator of the robbery but A, B and D may also be liable for the same offence as C. This chapter primarily concerns the liability of such persons who are known collectively as accessories. It is for this reason that the topic is sometimes referred to as accessorial liability but you will also find it called the law of complicity and, more commonly, as secondary liability. The latter term will be used throughout this chapter. It must be borne in mind when studying this topic that, although the doctrine of secondary liability is of considerable importance in the criminal law, the subject is complex, not altogether certain and a clear and precise explanation of the law will not always be possible. Indeed, as Professor Ashworth has observed:

> "[The doctrine of secondary liability] is replete with uncertainties and conflicts. It betrays the worst features of the common law: what some would regard as flexibility appears here as a succession of opportunistic decisions by the courts, often extending the law, and resulting in a body of jurisprudence that has little coherence." (*Principles of Criminal Law*, 5th edn).

In addition to secondary liability, the liability of other parties on the basis of vicarious liability or corporate liability will also be considered in this chapter.

Secondary Liability

Distinguishing Accessories from Principals

Before considering the basis of secondary liability, it is first necessary to determine exactly who is an accessory by identifying the various parties to a criminal offence and the terminology used. Beginning with the person who actually commits the actus reus of an offence or causes it to be committed, he is sometimes known as the perpetrator but, more accurately, as the principal (see below) and it is as a principal (P) that he will be referred to throughout this chapter. The principal would, for example, be the person who stabs the victim in a wounding offence, penetrates the non-consenting victim in rape, damages another's property in criminal damage or causes the death of the victim in homicide. As more than one person may commit an actus reus or cause it to be committed, there may be more than one principal to an offence. For example, both P1 and P2 attack V with baseball bats and V dies from the combined effect of the blows from both defendants. Each defendant has caused the death and is liable in homicide as a joint principal (the exact offence for which each is liable will depend upon their individual mens rea).

Where it is clear that one of two people committed the offence but it is not possible to say which of them it was or that there was any agreement between them to commit the offence, neither of them can be convicted of that offence. In **Strudwick (1994) 99 Cr. App. R. 326**, X and Y were co-habitees who were jointly charged with the murder of X's child. Y admitted that he had been violent towards the child but this did not prove he had inflicted the fatal blows. The Court of Appeal quashed his conviction for murder. He might, however, now be liable for an offence under s.5 of the Domestic Violence, Crime and Victims Act 2004, see Ch.4. The person(s) who provides assistance to the principal either before or at the time of the offence is an accessory, but is also frequently referred to as a secondary party. To avoid confusion, the term accessory (A) will continue to be used in this chapter. A person who assists the principal after the commission of the crime is not an accessory but may be liable for an offence under s.4 of the Criminal Law Act 1967, see below.

. . . .

Principals and Innocent Agents

The term principal was defined above as the person who commits the actus reus of the offence in question or causes it to be committed. A person may not actually commit the actus reus himself but may still cause it to be committed and is, therefore, still a principal where he acts through what is known as an "innocent agent". In such circumstances, the perpetrator is the innocent agent and the principal is the person who causes the innocent agent to commit the actus reus. It is for this reason that it is preferable to use the word principal rather than perpetrator.

An innocent agent, as the title suggests, is someone who is innocent of the crime. A person may be an innocent agent in one of two ways. First, because he lacks the mens rea for the crime, as in the case of **Stringer [1991] Crim. L.R. 639**. The principal in this case was an employer who dictated a fraudulent letter to his secretary to type and post. The secretary was the innocent agent as she did not know the letter was to enable a fraudulent transfer.

Secondly, the perpetrator of an offence will be an innocent agent where he lacks the capacity to commit the offence itself because he is a minor under 10 years of age or is insane. In **Michael (1840) 9 Car. & P.** the principal was a mother who wished to kill her baby. She gave her nurse a bottle of poison, telling her it was medicine and asking her to administer it to the baby. The nurse did not do so and left the poison on a shelf. A child later removed the poison and gave it to the baby, killing him. The child was an innocent agent (as would the nurse have been, had she given the baby the poison, on the basis that she lacked mens rea).

The doctrine cannot be used to convict as a principal a party to an offence which is defined so as to require the principal to perform the act constituting the actus reus, for example bigamy and rape (although there is questionable dicta to the contrary concerning rape in **Cogan and Leak [1976] Q.B. 217**, see p.362).

Over to you...

A postman delivers a parcel bomb sent through the post by X to V's home. After the postman has handed the parcel to V it explodes, injuring V. Is the postman criminally liable for V's injuries?

Who is an Accessory?

Section 8 of the Accessories and Abettors Act 1861 (as amended) provides:

> Whosoever shall aid, abet, counsel or procure the commission of an indictable offence is liable to be tried, indicted and punished as a principal offender.

Thus, a person may be an accessory to an offence in one of four ways: by aiding, abetting, counselling or procuring. The charge against the accessory should be phrased in terms not only of aiding, abetting, counselling or procuring but of aiding, abetting, etc. a *specified offence* and, if convicted, A is convicted of the specified offence. For example, A might be *charged with aiding and abetting murder*, but if convicted, he is *convicted of murder*. Lord Widgery C.J. in **Attorney General's Reference (No.1 of 1975) [1975] 2 All E.R. 684** was of the opinion that the four words denoting secondary liability should be given their ordinary meaning if possible. He also said that there is a difference between each of them (though the difference was not explained) as Parliament would not have used four words if less would have sufficed. However, both aspects of this dictum are problematic. First, the four words are not commonly used words in the English language and so do not have an "ordinary" meaning. Secondly, there is some overlap between the meanings attributed to aiding, abetting and counselling. More recently, in **Bryce [2004] EWCA Crim 1231**, a contrary view was taken by Potter L.J. who stated that "the shades of difference ... are far from clear" so it might be more appropriate to charge an accessory using the catch-all phrase aid, abet, counsel or procure rather than attempt to specify in exactly which way the defendant was an accessory.

It may not be strictly necessary to distinguish between the four different modes of secondary liability but the following is a tentative attempt to do so based on the relevant case law.

AIDING

Aiding involves providing assistance, help or support to the principal before or at the time the offence is committed. So, for example, an "aider" would be someone who supplies the weapons, equipment or information to be used to commit a crime (**Bainbridge [1960] 1 Q.B. 129**) or acts as a look-out (**Betts and Ridley (1931) 22 Cr. App. R. 148**) or drives the principal to the place where the crime is to be committed (**DPP (for Northern Ireland) v Lynch [1975] 1 All E.R. 913 HL**). It is not, however, necessary that he agree with the principal to assist or that the principal is even aware of his assistance. Nor is it necessary to show that this assistance caused the offence. Consequently, it does not need to be established that the offence would not have been committed had such aid not been provided.

ABETTING

Abetting involves encouragement or instigating or inciting an offence. An example of abetting was **Wilcox v Jeffery [1951] 1 All E.R. 464**, in which A cheered and clapped at an unlawful concert. There is little difference between abetting and counselling (see below). In **N.C.B. v Gamble [1959] 1 Q.B. 11**, Devlin J. opined that the difference was that abetting required presence at the scene of the crime whereas counselling related to encouragement prior to the commission of the offence. Again, it is not necessary to show the abetting caused the offence and that without it the offence would not have been committed.

COUNSELLING

Counselling also involves encouragement or instigating or inciting an offence. Counselling (and abetting), unlike aiding, require the principal to be aware that he is being encouraged. It is not necessary to show that this encouragement caused the offence (**Calhaem [1985] Q.B. 808**). Consequently, a person may be a counsellor where he knows the principal has already determined to commit the offence (**Giannetto [1997] 1 Cr. App. R. 1**) or the principal would have committed the offence even without encouragement. However, it must be established that the offence actually committed was the offence encouraged, etc. and the principal was aware of that encouragement (*Calhaem*). The extent of the encouragement need not be great. Hence, in *Giannetto*, the Court of Appeal approved the trial judge's suggestion that if P said to a husband (A) that he was going to kill A's wife and A replied "Oh goody" and P then killed A's wife, A would have counselled the murder.

PROCURING

To procure means "to produce by endeavour" (*Attorney General's Reference (No.1 of 1975)*). There must be a causal link between A's act and the commission of the crime by P in the sense that P would not have committed the offence without A's assistance (*Attorney General's Reference (No.1 of 1975)*). So, A, the procurer, may produce an offence by putting someone up to committing a crime, either by persuasion or threats, or by taking some other action which will result in the commission of the offence by P as, for example, where A secretly spikes P's drink before he drives so that P then unwittingly drives over the legal limit. (P is not an innocent agent in this example as driving with a blood alcohol level over the legal limit is a crime of strict liability; so A is the procurer, not the principal.)

As we stated above, aiding, abetting and counselling do not require proof that A caused P to commit the principal offence, however, some causal link between A's actions and P's offence should be established (*Bryce*). The accessory in this case (A) drove P, who was carrying a gun, to a caravan near V's home. P lay in wait for V and shot him dead 12 hours later. A was held to have counselled V's murder. A's submission on appeal that his actions were too remote from the killing failed on the basis that, although some causal link is required, it is to be widely construed and was present on the facts. The court also stated that such a link could be broken only by "an overwhelming supervening event."

FIGURE 11 Summary of the four modes of secondary liability referred to in s.8 of the Accessories and Abettors Act 1861

	Brief definition	**Case example**	**Proof of causation required?**
Aid	Assisting or supporting P before or at the time the offence is committed.	*Bainbridge*	No*
Abet	Encouraging or instigating or inciting an offence at the time of its commission.	*Wilcox v Jeffery*	No*
Counsel	Encouraging or instigating or inciting an offence prior to its commission.	*Calhaem*	No*
Procure	Causing the commission of the offence.	*Attorney General's Reference (No.1 of 1975)*	Yes

* Although the prosecution need not prove that without the aiding, etc. the principal offence would not have occurred, some causal link between A's actions and P's offence should be made out.

PARTICIPANTS IN A JOINT ENTERPRISE

As we will see below, those who participate in a joint enterprise with P are also now considered to be accessories and they can be liable for the offence committed by P, just as those who aid, abet, counsel or procure can under s.8 of the Accessories and Abettors Act 1861.

Liability of Accessories

As s.8 above makes clear (as does s.44 of the Magistrates' Courts Act 1980 which applies to offences which are summary only), the principal and the accessory may be tried, convicted and punished for the same offence. Although it is preferable for the prosecution to specify in the indictment the capacity in which the defendant acted, it is sufficient for the prosecution merely to prove that he was either the principal or an accessory. Consequently, in *Giannetto*, it was enough for the prosecution to assert that the defendant either murdered his wife or was the accessory to her murder by a contract killer whom he had paid to carry out the killing. Despite this, it is still important to distinguish principals from accessories for the following reasons.

1. Secondary liability is often described as being "derivative"; it derives from the liability of the principal. Thus, a person will not be liable as an accessory unless, and until, the principal offence has been committed.
2. The requirements for the actus reus and mens rea of a crime may differ between a principal and an accessory.
3. Vicarious liability (see p.369 below) can only be imposed in relation to the principal's acts, not those of an accessory.
4. Where the principal offence is one of strict liability, the accessory will only be liable if he had mens rea (**Callow v Tillstone (1900) 83 L.T. 411**).

THE NEED FOR A PRINCIPAL OFFENCE

As explained above, the liability of the accessory derives from that of the principal. However, that is not to say that the liability of the accessory is contingent upon the conviction of the principal. The principal might be acquitted because, for example, he lacked the mens rea for the offence, is exempt from prosecution or has a defence not available to the accessory (see pp.362–364 below). All that is required for secondary liability to arise is the commission of the actus reus of the principal offence. This is illustrated by **Millward [1994] Crim. L.R. 527**. A instructed his employee, P, to drive a poorly-maintained vehicle which resulted in a car accident in which another road user was killed. P was charged with the offence of causing death by reckless driving, the actus reus of which offence was satisfied on the facts by P driving the defective vehicle on the road so as to cause death; the mens rea, recklessness, was not, as P was not aware of the vehicle's dangerous condition. As P's driving was not reckless, he was acquitted. A, however, was convicted of procuring the offence of causing death by reckless driving as the actus reus of the offence was committed and A ought to have realised that the vehicle was in a dangerous condition.

If P is found not to have even committed the actus reus of the principal offence, it follows that A cannot be liable as an accessory to it. (Liability may, however, be incurred for an inchoate offence, see Ch.10.) It was on this basis that A was acquitted of abetting careless driving in **Thornton v Mitchell [1940] 1 All E.R. 339**. A, a bus conductor, negligently indicated to the bus driver, P, to reverse, which P did, killing a pedestrian whom he had been unable to see. As P was acquitted of careless driving, an offence for which the only mens rea is an intention to drive, it must have been on the basis that he did not drive carelessly by relying on the conductor's direction. The absence of the actus reus of careless driving meant that there was no actus reus of a principal offence on which to base A's liability as an accessory. A further example is **Loukes [1996] Crim LR 341**, the facts of which were similar to *Millward*, above, but the offence charged was causing death by dangerous driving, rather than by reckless driving which had since been abolished. P was acquitted because his driving was not dangerous as the vehicle's poor condition would not have been obvious to a competent and careful driver. A was charged with procuring the offence of causing death by dangerous driving but, unlike in *Millward*, was acquitted as there was no actus reus of dangerous driving that A could be said to have procured.

ACTUS REUS OF SECONDARY LIABILITY

A will not be liable as an accessory (subject to the exception considered immediately below) unless he does something which, with the appropriate mens rea, would amount to aiding, abetting, counselling or procuring, i.e. A must actually provide the principal with advice, assistance, encouragement, etc. Consequently, where A is merely present at the scene of the crime and does nothing to encourage its commission, he will not normally be liable. In **Clarkson [1971] 3 All E.R. 344**, A, a soldier, was not liable as an accessory to rape where he encountered D, a fellow soldier, committing a rape and merely stood by watching whilst the rape took place, taking no action to either halt or encourage the offence. A situation in which A's presence alone may give rise to secondary liability is where his presence in itself amounts to encouragement. For example, A's presence at a prize-fight might amount to encouraging the fight as it would not go ahead without spectators (**Coney (1882) 8 Q.B.D. 534**).

Over to you...

A and his friends are in the pub after their football team has lost to their City rivals. A goes outside to have a cigarette and sees his friend P kicking V, a supporter from the winning team who is lying on the ground. P stops kicking V when he sees A. A gives P a "thumbs up" and smiles. P begins kicking V again and A goes back inside. P is later charged with s.47 assault. Could A be liable as an accessory to the s.47 offence?

SECONDARY LIABILITY BY OMISSION

As was seen above, secondary liability normally requires action on A's part. However, exceptionally, A may be liable as an accessory based on his omission. This will occur where A has the right of control over P's actions and deliberately chooses not to exercise it (**J F Alford Transport**

Ltd [1997] 2 Cr. App. R. 326). In **Tuck v Robson [1970] 1 All E.R. 1171**, a pub landlord was found guilty of aiding and abetting after hours drinking as he had stood by and watched his customers drinking after licensing hours. Similarly, in **Webster [2006] EWCA Crim 415**, the court held that A, the owner and front seat passenger in a car being driven dangerously by P, could be liable as an accessory to P's dangerous driving if he failed to take the opportunity to intervene to stop such driving.

MENS REA OF SECONDARY LIABILITY

There is some lack of precision and certainty as to the exact mental state required of an accessory though, essentially, what is required is:

1. an intention to do an act which aids, abets, counsels or procures; and
2. knowledge of the essential matters which constitute the principal offence (**Johnson v Youden [1950] 1 K.B. 544**).

In basic terms, this means that A contemplates what P is going to do and P's state of mind when he does it.

◼ The intention to aid, abet, etc.

A must provide deliberate assistance, i.e. D must intend to do the act which amounts to assisting, encouraging, etc. and also intend that the act will assist, encourage, etc. (*Bryce*). Thus, A can have the requisite intent where it is his aim or purpose that his acts will assist, etc. or has oblique intention to assist, etc. It is not a requirement that A intends that P will commit the offence (*Bryce*). Consequently, A can still be liable if he does not care whether the offence is committed or even if he actually hopes that it will not. In *N.C.B. v Gamble*, Devlin J. stated that:

> "[A]n indifference to the result of the crime does not itself negative abetting. If one man deliberately sells to another gun to be used for murdering a third, he may be indifferent about whether the third man lives or dies and interested only in the cash profit to be made out of the sale, but he can still be an aider and abettor. To hold otherwise would be to negative the rule that mens rea is a matter of intent only and does not depend on desire or motive."

On the facts of the case, A, a weighbridge operator employed by the Coal Board, was held liable as an accessory to the principal offence of driving an overloaded vehicle. A had informed a driver that his lorry was overloaded and was told by the driver that he was willing to take the risk of being caught with an overloaded vehicle. A then gave the driver a ticket so that he might leave the pit. A was liable as an accessory despite his indifference as to whether the driver would commit the offence.

Similarly, in *DPP for Northern Ireland v Lynch* where A drove P to somewhere he knew P was going to commit a murder, he was liable for aiding and abetting the subsequent murder even though "he regretted the plan or indeed was horrified by it" (per Lord Morris).

A case which on one interpretation appears to contradict the notion that motive is irrelevant, is the civil case of **Gillick v West Norfolk and Wisbech Area Health Authority [1985] 3 All E.R. 402** in which the House of Lords held that a doctor who provided contraceptive advice or treatment to a girl under 16 years of age knowing that it would encourage or facilitate unlawful sexual intercourse between the girl and a man (P) would, in certain circumstances, not be acting unlawfully. This would seem to be on the basis that the doctor would not aid and abet the crime of unlawful sexual intercourse because he did not intend to facilitate or encourage unlawful sexual intercourse but, rather, to protect the girl if she engaged in under age sex. However, as motive is irrelevant to intention, this interpretation is unsustainable. The better rationale for the decision is that the doctor would not be liable because he could rely upon the defence of necessity (see Ch.13).

■ Knowledge

A must have *knowledge* of the essential matters which constitute the offence, i.e. he must foresee, or choose to turn a blind eye to (**JR v Roberts and George [1997] R.T.R. 462**), the possibility of the offence being committed. In **Ferguson v Weaving [1951] 1 K.B. 814**, therefore, a pub licensee was not liable for aiding and abetting an offence of drinking alcohol on licensed premises after closing time because he did not know such after hours drinking was taking place. Where A's assistance, encouragement, etc. is provided prior to, rather than at the time of, the principal offence, the use of the term "knowledge" will not be appropriate as A cannot be said to have knowledge of something which has not yet happened. In such circumstances, it is more appropriate to ask whether A *contemplated* or *foresaw* that P might commit the offence.

■ The essential matters

Basically, knowledge of the *essential matters* of the principal offence means that A must at least foresee as a real possibility that P might commit the principal offence (**Powell and English [1997] 3 W.L.R. 959**, a case involving joint enterprise liability, but the principles set out in that case apply to accessories generally (*Bryce*)). Thus, A must know of, or foresee, the following:

1. The commission by P of the act which constitutes the actus reus. Thus, for example, A may be an accessory to murder where P shot and killed V if A foresaw that P might shoot V, or an accessory to the rape of V, if A foresaw that P might penetrate V.
2. Any circumstances required by the actus reus. For example, A may be an accessory to theft by P where he foresaw that P might appropriate property belonging to another or an accessory to a burglary committed by P where he foresaw that P might enter the building as a trespasser.
3. It has traditionally been a requirement that A foresees that P is acting (or *may* act, if the principal offence has not yet been committed) with the requisite mens rea for that offence.

There was a suggestion in **Rahman [2009] 1 A.C. 129**, however, that it is not necessary to consider A's foresight of the intention with which P might act, only his foresight of *what P might do*. (*Rahman* concerned a joint enterprise but the principles applicable to joint enterprise liability have been held to apply to secondary liability in general). In *Rahman*, the appellants were involved in a joint enterprise to injure V. During the course of the attack, V was stabbed and killed. They claimed, inter alia, that they should not be liable for murder because they had not foreseen that P might kill with intention to kill, only that he might kill with intention to do GBH. They were all convicted of murder and appealed ultimately to the House of Lords. According to Lord Bingham (who delivered the leading speech in a unanimous—in this respect—decision of the House), it was not necessary to establish the appellants' foresight of P's intention to kill in order to convict them of murder:

> "Given the fluid, fast-moving course of events in incidents such as that which culminated in the killing of the deceased, incidents which are unhappily not rare, it must often be very hard for jurors to make a reliable assessment of what a particular defendant foresaw as likely or possible acts on the part of his associates. It would be even harder, and would border on speculation, to judge what a particular defendant foresaw as the intention with which his associates might perform such acts. *It is safer to focus on the defendant's foresight of what an associate might do, an issue to which knowledge of the associate's possession of an obviously lethal weapon such as a gun or a knife would usually be very relevant.*" (emphasis added)

Lord Bingham's suggestion was subsequently applied by the Court of Appeal in **Badza [2009] EWCA 1363** in the context of joint enterprise liability for murder.

Over to you...

So, where does this leave us?

Lord Bingham's suggestion in *Rahman* and its subsequent application in *Badza* that the focus should be on A's foresight of what P might do rather than on the mens rea with which he might do it is, it is submitted, flawed given the judgment in *Powell and English* (see p.353) which was not overruled by *Rahman* and other statements in the speeches of the other Lordships in *Rahman* itself to the effect that A is liable if he foresees that P might kill or do GBH with *either* intention to kill or to do GBH and does not have to foresee P's precise mens rea. It is, perhaps then, the case that A's foresight of P's mens rea *is* relevant but that in murder it does not matter whether A foresees that P might intend to kill or to do GBH.

Must A's knowledge extend to knowing the exact offence which P is to commit?

If A aids, abets, counsels or procures P to commit a specified offence, clearly A knows the offence to be committed. However, if A, for example, provides P with tools or information to be used in a crime but P does not specify the exact offence to be committed, the intended victim or place for the commission of the offence, is A liable as an accessory for any offence which P then commits? Can it be said that he knows the essential elements of the principal offence? The issue was considered in *Bainbridge*. A supplied oxy-acetylene cutting equipment to P, suspecting it would be used for an illegal purpose, possibly to break up stolen property. The equipment was in fact used in a burglary—to break into and steal from a bank. The court held that it was not sufficient that A contemplated that an offence might be committed by P; it had to be proven that he foresaw that P might commit an offence of the type P actually committed. The court also stated that if A contemplated P committing a burglary, he would have been liable as an accessory even if he did not know when or where the burglary was to be committed.

In **DPP for Northern Ireland v Maxwell [1978] 3 All E.R. 1140**, the House of Lords extended the basis of liability beyond knowledge of the type of crime to be committed to include the situation where the offence committed was within the range of a limited number of crimes which the accessory had contemplated would be committed. This means that if A provides assistance to P, contemplating that P might commit an offence, but A is unsure whether P intends to commit offence X, Y or Z, A is liable if P commits any one of the offences X, Y or Z. The facts of *Maxwell* were as follows. A was the owner and driver of a car which guided P, a member of the Ulster Volunteer Force, to a pub. A thought that P either intended to shoot people in the pub or plant a bomb there. P planted a bomb, contrary to s.3(a) of the Explosive Substances Act 1883, and the House of Lords upheld A's conviction as an accessory to this offence because it was within the range of terrorist offences he had contemplated being committed.

Over to you...

Unfortunately, some questions concerning any possible limitations on liability remain unanswered following the above two decisions which pose potential problems for the courts in future. How do you think they would deal with, for example, the following?

A provides P with equipment which is used to commit several offences rather than just one. Will A be liable for all such offences?

A provides P with equipment but P does not use it to commit an offence (X) until several years later as he is sent to jail for another, unrelated, crime in the meantime. Will A be liable for offence X?

FIGURE 11.1 Summary of requirements of secondary liability

A is liable as an accessory where the following requirements are satisfied:		
Actus Reus of Principal Offence (X) is committed by P	+ Advice, encouragement or assistance, etc. by A (Actus reus)	+ A intends to aid or abet, etc. and knows or contemplates as a real possibility: (i) the commission of offence X by P; (ii) any circumstances required by the actus reus of offence X and (iii) that P acts or may act with the requisite mens rea for offence X (Mens rea)

Accessories and Transferred Malice

The doctrine of transferred malice (see p.66) applies to secondary liability. Thus, if A counsels P to commit an offence against X but P mistakenly commits that offence against V, A will still be liable as an accessory to the offence committed by P. However, if P were to deliberately commit the offence against V instead of X, the principle of transferred malice would not apply and A would not be liable (see below).

Joint Enterprise Liability

What is a Joint Enterprise?

A joint enterprise is where two or more parties embark upon the commission of a criminal offence with a common purpose. Essentially, under the doctrine of joint enterprise, participants in such an enterprise are liable not only for their own acts committed in furtherance of the enterprise but also for the acts of the other participants, even if the consequences of such acts are unforeseen. The common purpose involves agreement and consensus between the parties. This does not mean there has to be any formality involved. Consequently, although in many instances there will have been a plan to commit an offence, this is not required. Agreement may arise on the spur of the moment, with nothing being said at all. It can be made with a nod and a wink, or a knowing look or even inferred from the behaviour of the parties involved. Where there is no common purpose, there is no joint enterprise, merely two separate principals each liable for their own separate acts. Thus, in **Petters and Parfitt [1995] Crim. L.R. 501**, where two people independently came upon V in a car park, one of them attacked V and then the other joined in the attack, there was no joint enterprise; each was liable for their own actions.

Is Joint Enterprise a Separate Basis of Liability?

It is unclear whether joint enterprise is a separate form of liability or merely an aspect of secondary liability so that those who participate in a joint enterprise are accessories to it. The issue has never been clearly settled. A.P. Simester in "The mental element in complicity" (2006) 122 L.Q.R. 578, advocates taking the former approach and is supported by the Law Commission in their most recent report in 2007, "*Participating in Crime*" (Law Com. No.305). He argues:

> "Through entering into a joint [criminal venture], [A] changes her normative position. [A] becomes, by her deliberate choice, a participant in a group action to commit a crime. Moreover her new status has moral significance: she associates herself with the conduct of the other members of the group in a way that the mere aider and abettor, who remains an independent character throughout the episode does not. Whereas aiding and abetting doctrines are grounded in [A's] contribution to another's crime, joint [criminal venture] is grounded in *affiliation*. [A] voluntarily subscribes to a cooperative endeavour, one that is identified by its shared criminal purpose. As such, joint [criminal venture] doctrines impose a form of collective responsibility, predicated on membership of the unlawful concert … By offering allegiance to the enterprise, [A] implicitly condones its furtherance."

However, the latter approach has most support. In both the House of Lords' decisions on joint enterprise liability, *Powell and English* and *Rahman*, there was judicial support for the view that such people are indeed accessories. Further, in both **Reardon [1999] Crim. L.R. 392** and *Bryce*, the accessories were not involved in a joint enterprise but the court applied the principles set out in *Powell and English* concerning the mens rea of participants in a joint enterprise. Many academic commentators, including David Ormerod, writing in Smith and Hogan, *Criminal Law*, 12th edn, also take this approach. It is submitted that this is the better view and it is this approach which is taken in this chapter. If this is the case then, as Ormerod suggests, the common purpose will be sufficient evidence of aiding, abetting, etc. and the principles of mens rea which apply in respect of secondary liability (set out above) will apply to a joint enterprise and vice versa.

The only difference in mens rea between non-joint enterprise secondary liability and joint enterprise secondary liability is that to aid, abet, counsel or procure requires intention to assist, encourage, etc. (though it is likely that the participation in the joint venture itself provides sufficient evidence of this intention to aid, abet, etc.) and this is not required for accessories to a joint enterprise; foresight that P may commit the offence is sufficient.

Liability for Unintended Consequences

THE POSITION PRIOR TO POWELL AND ENGLISH

As explained above, where defendants participate in a joint enterprise, they are all liable for any offences committed by their accomplices in pursuance of the enterprise's common purpose. At one time this meant an accessory would be liable *only* for those offences committed by the principal to which there was express or tacit agreement (**Anderson and Morris [1966] 2 Q.B. 110**) or where there was a deliberate variation by P which did not differ from the common design in a matter of substance. The latter situation is illustrated by an example given by Hawkins at 2 PC c.29, s.20:

> "[I]f the felony committed be the same in substance with that which was intended, and variant only in some circumstance, as in respect of the time or place, at which, or the means whereby it was effected, the abettor of the intent is altogether as much an accessory as if there had been no variance at all between it and the execution of it; as where a man advises another to kill such a one in the night, and he kills him in the day, or to kill him in the fields, and he kills him in the town ..."

Where, however, there was a *deliberate* departure by the principal from the common purpose in a matter of substance, the accessory was not liable. As Hawkins explained (at s.21):

> "... [I]f a man command another to commit a felony on a particular person or thing and he do it on another; as to kill A and he kill B or to burn the house of A and he burn the house of B or to steal an ox and he steal a horse; or to steal such a horse and he steal another; or to commit a felony of one kind and he commit another of quite a different nature; as to rob JS of his plate as he is going to market, and he break open his house in the night and there steal the plate; it is said that the commander is not an accessory because the act done varies in substance from that which was commanded ..."

THE EFFECT OF THE DECISION IN POWELL AND ENGLISH

The law has now moved on considerably since *Anderson and Morris*. An accessory may now be liable not only for offences which he has agreed upon but also for those where there has been a deliberate departure by P in a matter of substance. However, in the latter situation A is only liable if he foresaw as a real possibility that P might commit the other offence (**Chan Wing-Siu [1985] 1 A.C. 168 PC**, where the risk was explained as being one not "so remote ... [as] to have been dismissed by [A] as altogether negligible", and confirmed by their Lordships in the joint appeals in *Powell and English*). Such consequences will still be within the scope of the common purpose. This is on the basis that the accessory continued to participate in the venture to commit offence X even though he foresaw that P might commit offence Y. So, for example, if A and P agree to commit a burglary and in the course of a burglary P, with malice aforethought, kills a security guard who disturbs them, P is liable for murder but will A also be liable? If it was not expressly or tacitly agreed to do this should they be disturbed, A will only be liable for murder if he foresaw that P might kill with malice aforethought. The facts of *Powell* illustrate the point. Three defendants went to V's house in order to buy drugs. One of the defendants (P) was carrying a gun and shot V when he answered the door. The House of Lords was required to consider the liability for murder of P's accomplices who had known P was carrying a gun. Their Lordships held that they were guilty of murder because they knew that P had a gun on him and had foreseen that he might use it to kill with the intention to kill or to cause GBH to V. According to Lord Hutton:

> "... participation in a joint criminal enterprise with foresight or contemplation of an act as a possible incident of that enterprise is sufficient to impose liability for the act carried out by another participant in the enterprise."

According to *Rahman*, the principle in *Powell and English* applies where an accomplice (A) is involved in a crime with others and realises that any one of them, not necessarily the actual killer, might use a weapon with malice aforethought. Hence, a trial judge's direction that A would be liable for murder only if he knew that the *actual knifeman* had a knife which he might use with intention to kill or to do GBH was considered too generous to A in **Yemoh [2009] EWCA Crim 930**.

CAN THE IMPOSITION OF LIABILITY IN SUCH CIRCUMSTANCES BE JUSTIFIED?

Although basing liability on A's foresight that P might commit a different offence is of general application, the cases in which this basis of liability evolved all concerned murder and it is in the context of murder that its potential unfairness is well illustrated. Where there is a joint enterprise to commit, for example, a robbery but someone is killed during the commission of that robbery, the person who took part in the joint enterprise but did not actually do the killing and did not intend such a result, would be liable if he foresaw that one of his accomplices might intentionally kill or intentionally inflict GBH. This harshness is even more obvious if one considers that the principal might only commit the killing with mens rea sufficient for a manslaughter conviction but his accessory foresees, for example, that he might kill with malice aforethought and so is liable for murder. This actually occurred in **Hui Chi-ming (1992) 94 Cr. App. R. 236**. An argument that this basis of liability contravened the art.6 right to a fair trial was rejected in **Concannon [2002] Crim. L.R. 213**: art.6 is concerned with the fairness of the trial, not of the substantive law.

Given the unfairness of this rule, there must be some justification for basing secondary liability merely on foresight. Two reasons, based on practical and policy considerations, were cited by Lord Steyn in the *English* appeal. The first is based on the practical difficulty in otherwise establishing that A had the necessary intention, even oblique:

> "... [I]t would in practice almost invariably be impossible for a jury to say that the secondary party wanted death to be caused or that he regarded it as virtually certain. In the real world proof of an intention sufficient for murder would be well nigh impossible in the vast majority of joint enterprise cases."

The second is the policy consideration—the need to control crimes committed by gangs:

> "The criminal justice system exists to control crime. A prime function of that system must be to deal justly but effectively with those who join with others in criminal enterprises. Experience has shown that joint criminal enterprises only too readily escalate into the commission of greater offences. In order to deal with this important social problem the accessory principle is needed and cannot be abolished or relaxed."

A FORESEES THAT P MIGHT ACT WITH APPROPRIATE MENS REA FOR AN OFFENCE BUT IS NOT LIABLE—"THE FUNDAMENTALLY DIFFERENT RULE"

In the appeal in *English*, their Lordships stated that even if A foresaw P might act with the mens rea for another offence, A would not be liable for that offence if P's "act" was "fundamentally different" from the acts A intended or foresaw P committing. This is sometimes referred to as the *English* qualification or, as here, the "fundamentally different rule". Recently, in **Parsons [2009] EWCA Crim 64**, the Court of Appeal emphasised that this "fundamentally different rule" applies to secondary liability generally and is not confined to homicide cases.

The "fundamentally different rule" was applied in **Rafferty [2007] EWCA Crim 1846**. P1 and P2 were engaged with A in a joint enterprise to attack V by punching, hitting and stamping on him. Subsequently, in A's absence, P1 and P2 caused V's death by drowning. The Court of Appeal held that causing V's death by drowning was fundamentally different from the joint enterprise to assault V so that A was not liable for the death. Hence, his conviction for manslaughter was quashed.

Rafferty provides a straightforward example of the application of the "fundamentally different rule". However, other cases have not been so straightforward due to difficulties in determining what constitutes P's "act" and what would be "fundamentally different", issues unfortunately left unexplored in *Powell and English*.

The difficulty in determining the relevant "act" and, therefore, any fundamentally different "act" was highlighted in **Attorney General's Reference (No.3 of 2004) [2006] Crim. L.R. 63)**.

P deliberately shot at and killed V with a firearm. A knew P had a firearm on him and intended that P use it in V's presence, but only to frighten him. The Court of Appeal was asked to consider how the "act" which caused death was to be defined; was it the deliberate shot by P aimed *at* V or the deliberate discharge of the firearm in circumstances where A did not foresee the possibility of death or physical injury to V? The Court of Appeal ruled that it was the former and that P's act was, therefore, fundamentally different from that which was contemplated by A; A was not liable for the death. In his commentary on the case in the Criminal Law Review, Ormerod observes how the case illustrates the "precarious position of the secondary party in a joint enterprise":

> "The scope of his liability can turn on extremely fine factual distinctions ... The language of the courts, including the House of Lords in Powell and English, rather obscures the degree of difficulty by describing [A]'s liability in vague terms of his foresight of P's 'act' A further dimension to the difficulty of ascertaining [A]'s liability is that whether P's conduct was 'fundamentally different' from what A foresaw as likely remains a question of fact. Again, the concept is vague with the courts providing little in the way of guidance. P's conduct might be regarded as sufficiently 'fundamentally different' where it involves a different act and/or where it involves P acting with a different mens rea. It is in the latter situation that the finest factual distinctions can determine [A]'s liability, yet in the case of murder and manslaughter, where the distinction for the principal is in terms only of mens rea, the liability of the secondary may well turn only on the foresight of a possibility of P's particular future state of mind."

Recently, in *Rahman*, Lord Bingham stated that "fundamentally different" has a "plain meaning" and is "not a term of art" which must be explained to the jury but, regrettably, this fails to introduce any clarity to the issue. The courts' failure to provide clear guidance on the term may result in inconsistent verdicts between factually similar cases as juries grapple with the issue of whether, on the facts, P's act was "fundamentally different". The difficulty facing the jury is particularly well illustrated by the fact that in *Rahman* their Lordships were themselves unable to agree on the correctness of the Crown Court decision in **Gamble [1989] N.I. 268**. A was a participant in a punishment beating of V with P and had agreed to "kneecapping" V (firing a bullet into V's kneecap) using a gun. P, however, used a knife to slit V's throat. Carswell J. found A not liable for murder. *Gamble* was approved in *Powell and English* but, in *Rahman*, three judges of the House of Lords doubted the correctness of the decision, a fourth, Lord Bingham, approved it on the basis that "the use of a knife suggested something different and, potentially, even more sinister" and cutting V's throat was "of an entirely different character in an entirely different context from that which [A] had foreseen and, in that sense, bargained for" (i.e. P's act was "fundamentally different") and the fifth judge thought it correct on the "very special" facts of the case, suggesting that there was in fact a break in the chain of causation between A's assault on V and P's act of slitting V's throat. If five House of Lords judges were unable to reach a consensus on A's liability, one can easily imagine the difficulties a jury would face.

■ Relevance of knowledge of the weapon used

Where the accessory knows that his principal is carrying a weapon, this is strong evidence that he foresaw that it might be used in the way it was, in fact, used. What is the position, though, where A thought his accomplice was carrying one weapon, for example, a club, and his accomplice was carrying, and used, a different weapon, for example, a gun? In such circumstances A's liability will depend upon whether the weapon used was "fundamentally different" from the weapon envisaged. If it is, A is not liable for P's offence (though A remains liable for any offence he himself has committed). However, if the weapon used is not "fundamentally different," A remains liable:

> "... If the weapon used by [P] is different to but *as dangerous as* the weapon that [A] contemplated he might use, [A] should not escape liability for murder because of the difference in the weapon, for example, if he foresaw that the primary party might use a gun to kill and [he] used a knife to kill or vice-versa." (emphasis added) (per Lord Hutton in *English*)

In *English*, during the course of a joint enterprise to attack V, a police officer, with wooden fence posts, P produced a knife, of which A was unaware, and stabbed V to death. A claimed that he had foreseen that P might cause GBH using the fence posts and that he might do so with intention to do GBH but that he had not foreseen death from stabbing. Their Lordships, in quashing English's conviction for murder, held that the use by P of a knife to kill the victim was fundamentally different from using wooden fence posts and was, therefore outside the scope of the joint enterprise. This was on the basis that a knife is a deadly weapon; a fence post is not.

The following cases illustrate the operation of the "fundamentally different rule" where a different weapon is used. In **Greatrex [1998] Crim. L.R. 733**, A and several other men set about V by kicking him. V was actually killed by one of them, P, using a metal bar which the others had not known he had brought with him. The Court of Appeal held that whether a weapon is fundamentally different is a question of fact, and therefore for the jury. The Court of Appeal ordered a retrial so that a jury could determine whether the use of the metal bar was in fact fundamentally different from kicking someone. In **Uddin [1998] 2 All E.R. 744**, A was involved in a joint enterprise to attack V with billiard cues but V was actually killed by P using a flick knife. The Court of Appeal stated that a jury might determine that a flick knife was fundamentally different from a billiard cue. **Jackson [2009] UKPC 28** concerned a joint enterprise to attack V with the flat of a machete blade in a "beating" rather than "chopping" motion. During the course of the attack P killed V by stabbing him with a long knife. The Privy Council stated that given the way the machete was used, the long knife was a "more lethal" weapon (adopting the terminology advocated in *Rahman*, below) and the stabbing was, therefore, fundamentally different from anything foreseen by A.

Conversely, in **Webb [2006] EWCA Crim 2496**, the Court of Appeal upheld A's conviction for murder where he knew P was carrying a knife but P killed V by asphyxiation using a handkerchief which he stuffed into V's mouth. A handkerchief might seem fundamentally different from a knife but, presumably, it is just as likely to cause death if it is stuffed into V's mouth. Similarly, an appeal argument based on the "fundamentally different rule" failed in *Yemoh*. During a fight involving A and several others, V was stabbed and killed with a knife with a pointed blade. It was unclear which of the defendants had fatally stabbed V. A was convicted of manslaughter, X of murder. There was evidence that X was carrying a Stanley knife but a pathologist considered it unlikely that a Stanley knife could inflict a fatal wound. A appealed against his manslaughter conviction on the basis that the stabbing was of a fundamentally different character to that intended or foreseen by the use of a Stanley knife. His appeal was rejected; a Stanley knife could cause serious injury or death when used in a slashing motion and there was not a fundamental difference between the infliction of serious injury by a Stanley knife and by a knife with a pointed blade.

■ A reformulation of the "fundamentally different rule"

A reformulation of the rule as it applies to weapons was advocated in *Rahman*. The appellants were involved in a joint enterprise to attack V using cricket bats and metal bars. During the course of the attack V was stabbed and killed. The appellants all claimed not to have used or have known of a knife. They were convicted of murder and appealed ultimately to the House of Lords. According to Lord Brown, with whom the majority agreed:

> "If [A] realises (without agreeing to such conduct being used) that [P] may kill or intentionally inflict serious injury, but nevertheless continues to participate with [P] in the venture, that will amount to a sufficient mental element for [A] to be guilty of murder if [P], with the requisite intent, kills in the course of the venture unless *(i) [P] suddenly produces and uses a weapon of which* [A] *knows nothing and which is more lethal than any weapon which* [A] *contemplates that* [P] *or any other participant may be carrying and (ii) for that reason* [P]'s *act is to be regarded as fundamentally different from anything foreseen by* [A])."

(The words in italics appear in the original and were stated to reflect the *English* qualification which, you will recall, takes P's actions outside the scope of the common purpose where he uses a weapon which is fundamentally different from that envisaged by A.)

Lord Brown's speech impacts on the application of the fundamentally different rule to weapons, in two ways:

1. It extends the rule so that A can rely on it if he foresees that P might kill with *intent to kill*, rather than with intent to do GBH as had been the position in *English*. In *Yemoh*, the

Court of Appeal stated that this would be the case only where A did not intend V to be killed but (a) realised that one of the attackers might kill with intent to kill or cause GBH; or (b) intended that GBH would be caused; or (c) realised that one of the attackers might cause GBH with intent to cause GBH.

2. It restricts the operation of the rule to the situation where P "suddenly produces ... a weapon ... of which [A] knows nothing and which is more lethal" than any weapon A contemplated being used and, even where this is the case, the wording suggests that it will not be in all such cases that the killing will be considered fundamentally different.

The principles set out above concerning the use of a weapon fit most easily into the situation where the principal and his accomplices are engaged in conduct where there was a plan to commit offence X and the principal deviated from the plan by committing offence Y. What is the position though where there is no such plan, where violence erupts spontaneously? In such circumstances, according to *Uddin*, if, once the principal has produced a weapon, the others then participate in the attack or continue to do so, they will be liable for the offence committed by the principal using that weapon.

■ Relevance of P's intention to the operation of the fundamentally different rule in murder

We saw above the impact of *Rahman* on the operation of the fundamentally different rule in murder where P uses a more lethal weapon to that envisaged. A can now rely on the rule where he foresaw that P might *kill* (subject to the clarification by the Court of Appeal in *Yemoh*, see above) but only where the weapon used is more lethal, is suddenly produced and is one of which A knows nothing. However, the main focus in *Rahman* was whether the "fundamentally different rule" would apply where P has killed *with intention to kill* but A only foresaw that he might kill or do GBH *with intention to do GBH*. The Court of Appeal presented two questions for their Lordships' consideration:

> "If in the course of a joint enterprise to inflict unlawful violence, the principal party kills with an intention to kill which is unknown to and unforeseen by a secondary party, is the principal's intention relevant, (i) to whether the killing was within the scope of a common purpose to which the secondary party was an accessory and (ii) to whether the principal's act was fundamentally different from the act or acts which the secondary party foresaw as part of the enterprise?"

Both questions were answered by their Lordships in the negative. Hence, if P kills with an intention to kill but A only foresaw that P might kill or do GBH with intention to do GBH, A remains liable for murder as an accessory; P's greater mens rea does not render his act fundamentally different so as to take the killing outside the scope of the joint enterprise.

Over to you...

See if you have understood the above principles by attempting to complete the flowchart below based on the following information:

During the course of a joint attack by A and P on V using wooden posts, P pulls out a flick knife and stabs V killing him. A did not know P was carrying a flick knife.

If you are stuck, there is some guidance in the flowchart contained in the summary to this chapter.

FIGURE 11.2 **Over to you flowchart**

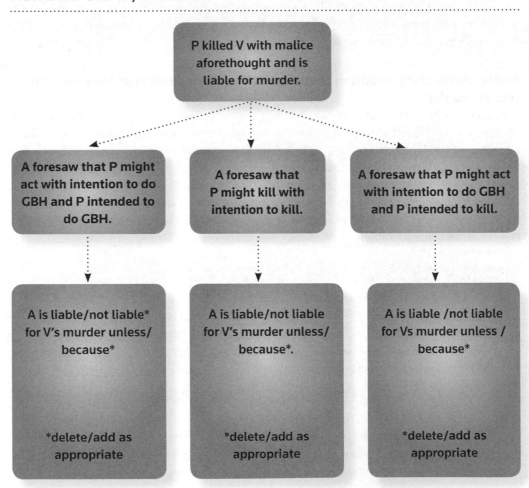

COMMISSION BY THE PRINCIPAL OF AN OFFENCE OF A DIFFERENT TYPE

Thus far, we have considered the liability of a participant in a joint enterprise where both the use of the weapon was foreseen and the particular type of offence committed was foreseen. One, as yet, unresolved matter concerns liability in the situation where the accessory knows that his accomplice in the joint enterprise will use a particular weapon but foresees it being used to commit a different offence from that which the principal actually commits.

There is no authority on the point, only obiter statements. In *Gamble*, Carswell J. was of the opinion that if A was a participant in a punishment beating of V with P and A agreed to, or foresaw, the kneecapping of V using a gun and P used the gun on V but used it to shoot V in the head, killing him, A would be liable if he foresaw this use of the gun but otherwise not. In *English*, however, Hutton L.J. left open the possibility that A might still be liable in the alternative situation:

> "... a secondary party who foresees grievous bodily harm caused by kneecapping with a gun should not be guilty of murder where, in an action unforeseen by the secondary party, another party to the criminal enterprise kills the victim by cutting his throat with a knife. The issue ... whether a secondary party who foresees the use of a gun to kneecap, and death is then caused by the deliberate firing of the gun into the head or body of the victim, is guilty of murder is *more debatable*." (emphasis added)

It is submitted that the view of Carswell J. is to be preferred. As Ormerod, Smith and Hogan, *Criminal Law*, 12th edn, point out:

> "Kneecapping, abominable though it is, is unlikely to cause death, whereas blowing a man's brains out is certain to do so. [A] should not be liable (for murder or manslaughter) simply because he foresaw the use of a gun with the intention of causing non-lethal grievous bodily harm in the course of the venture and a gun was used."

LIABILITY WHERE THE PRINCIPAL'S ACTIONS HAVE EXCEEDED THE SCOPE OF THE COMMON PURPOSE

Where P's actions exceed the scope of the joint enterprise because they are a deliberate departure from the joint enterprise and A did not foresee P might commit the actus reus of the offence with the appropriate mens rea or P's act is fundamentally different from that which was envisaged, we have seen that A is not liable for P's offence. But will A be liable for some lesser offence? In the appeal of *English* (see above), their Lordships chose not to substitute a manslaughter conviction. In doing so they appeared to accept that the accessory is not liable for a lesser offence. More recently in *Parsons*, the Court of Appeal took the same approach stating that where a murder is committed which is outside the scope of the joint enterprise, the accessory will not be guilty of manslaughter.

In **Gilmour [2000] 2 Cr. App. R. 407**, the Court of Appeal of Northern Ireland distinguished the situation where the principal's *actions* which cause death take him outside the scope of the joint enterprise from the situation where his actions which cause death are within the scope of the joint enterprise but he acts with a *greater mens rea* than that envisaged by the accessory. In the latter circumstances, the accessory is liable for manslaughter. This seems to be on the basis that P's act is not fundamentally different from that foreseen by A. *In Gilmour*, A accompanied P to a house where, as agreed, P petrol bombed the house. P did so with intention to kill. A had only foreseen arson to the house. Three boys were killed in the resulting fire. A was held liable for manslaughter as the principal had committed the very act which A had contemplated but with a greater mens rea than he had contemplated and A had acted with the mens rea for manslaughter.

The Court of Appeal took a similar line in **Day [2001] Crim. L.R. 984**, though without referring to *Gilmour*. Several men, including A and P, jointly attacked V. V died from one of the blows, a kick to the side of the head by P. P was convicted of murder and A of manslaughter on the basis that he had foreseen that P might kick V about the head causing some harm (not grievous bodily harm). The Court of Appeal held that such foresight was sufficient for a manslaughter conviction.

The Effect of the Acquittal or Reduction of Liability of the Principal

Where the Principal Lacked Mens Rea

We have already considered the situation where the perpetrator of an offence is not liable because he or she lacked mens rea but the person who instigated the offence is still liable because the actus reus of the principal offence was committed. This will often be on the basis that the perpetrator was an innocent agent. What is considered here is the situation where the perpetrator lacks mens rea, so is not liable, but is treated as the principal, not an innocent agent, and the effect, if any, of this on the liability of the accessory.

A person may lack mens rea but cannot be an innocent agent, only a principal, because the relevant offence cannot be committed by a principal acting via an innocent agent. For example, bigamy and possibly certain sexual offences which require penetration, such as rape, cannot be committed in this way even where a person is coerced into their commission.

A case which may cast doubt on this is *Cogan and Leak*. A forced his wife (V), to have sexual intercourse with P. P was convicted of raping V but his conviction was quashed on appeal on the basis that he may have lacked the mens rea for rape (he may have thought V consented). However, the Court of Appeal held that V had been raped:

> "… one fact is clear [C] had been raped … The fact that [P] was innocent of rape because he believed she was consenting does not affect the position that she was raped." (per Lawton L.J.)

and that A was an accessory to the rape. The Court of Appeal gave two reasons for upholding A's conviction. First, and primarily, because A was the principal acting through the innocent agent, P. However, reliance on the doctrine of innocent agency seems an inappropriate basis on which to convict A in the context of rape. Rape is an offence defined so as to require a man to intentionally penetrate V with his penis. The decision, in effect, suggests that a man can rape a woman using another man's penis and would even, if taken to its logical conclusion, allow for a woman to commit rape as a principal by using a man as an innocent agent although she cannot herself commit rape. A further problem with this basis for the court's decision is that, at that time, it was legally impossible for a husband to rape his wife during cohabitation (this principle was overruled in **R. v R [1991] 4 All ER 481**) so it ought to follow that it would also be legally impossible for a husband to rape his wife by means of an innocent agent.

The second reason given by the court was that A was liable for procuring a rape as, although P was acquitted due to lack of mens rea, this, as Lawton L.J. observed (see above), did not mean that V was not raped. No doubt a layman would consider that V had been raped but, in law she clearly had not because no *offence* of rape was committed. However, it is possible to say instead that A could be liable for procuring rape on the basis that P had committed the actus reus of rape; the approach taken in *Millward* in the context of causing death by reckless driving (see p.345 above). This seems the more sound rationale in terms of legal principle and it was on this basis that the defendants were convicted of procuring rape in **DPP v K [1997] 1 Cr. App. R. 36**. Two girls aged 11 and 14 were convicted of procuring rape by an unknown and untraceable boy who may have been between 10 and 14. The boy may have been doli incapax and, therefore, at the time legally incapable of committing rape, but the Divisional Court stated that this would not affect the defendants' liability for procuring rape.

Where the Principal has a Defence not Available to the Accessory

Where the principal has a defence available to him which the accessory cannot rely upon, this will not affect the liability of the accessory. Thus, in **Bourne (1952) 36 Cr. App. R. 125**, where A compelled his wife, P, to commit an act of bestiality with a dog, A was liable as an accessory even though P was not liable because she had a defence of duress. Similarly, as was seen above in *DPP v K*, the fact that the principal is doli incapax will also have no effect on A's liability.

Where P commits the actus reus of murder with intent to kill or to do GBH but has the partial defence of diminished responsibility or loss of control available to him so as to reduce his liability to that for manslaughter, A, the accessory, remains liable for murder (Homicide Act 1957 s.2(4) and Coroners and Justice Act 2009 s.54(8) respectively).

Can an Accessory be Liable for a Graver Offence than the Principal?

The answer is yes (**Howe [1987] A.C. 417**). This could occur where A had the mens rea for a more serious offence than that for which the principal had mens rea and the actus reus of both offences is the same. For example, P might be liable for wounding contrary to s.20 of the Offences Against the Person Act 1861 and the accessory, A, for wounding contrary to s.18 of the same Act, if A foresees that P might wound with the intent to do GBH but P actually wounds with the intent only to do some harm (see Ch.5 for the mens rea of ss.18 and 20 OAPA 1861).

Withdrawal of Participation by an Accessory

Here we consider the position of someone who has aided, abetted or counselled another, or has embarked on a joint enterprise, and then has a change of heart prior to the commission of the principal offence so that he no longer wishes to be involved. Can such a person effectively withdraw, thereby preventing liability arising in respect of the principal offence? The answer is that an effective withdrawal is possible, though in the limited circumstances set out below. To hold otherwise would mean there was no incentive to change one's mind. Further, a person who no longer wishes to be involved is morally less culpable than the principal offender and this ought to be recognised by the criminal law. Even where withdrawal is effective, however, this will not negate liability for any offence which has already been committed by the accessory up to that point, for example, for conspiracy, attempt or an offence under the Serious Crime Act 2007 (see Ch.10).

What Constitutes an Effective Withdrawal?

It is clear that repentance alone, without any action on the accessory's part, will not be sufficient to constitute an effective withdrawal and negation of liability (**Beccera (1975) 62 Cr. App. R. 212**)). Nor will staying away when the principal offence is to be committed or running away from the scene prior to its commission; the principles of secondary liability explained above apply whether or not the accessory is present at the time the principal offence is committed

(**Rook (1993) 97 Cr. App. R. 327**). Whether a withdrawal is effective is a question of fact and degree for the jury, account being taken of, inter alia, the nature of the assistance and encouragement already given, how imminent the commission of the principal offence is and the method by which withdrawal is attempted (**O'Flaherty [2004] 2 Cr. App. R. 20**).

THE NEED FOR COMMUNICATION

It seems that, as a bare minimum, the accessory must communicate his withdrawal. A timely, unequivocal communication by the accessory that he no longer wishes to be involved is required, i.e.:

> "... such communication verbal or otherwise, that will serve unequivocal notice upon the other party to the common unlawful cause that if he proceeds upon it he does so without the further aid and assistance of those who withdraw." (per Sloan J.A. in Whitehouse [1941] 1 W.R.R. 112 Court of Appeal of British Columbia, quoted and approved in *Beccera*).

Whether the communication is unequivocal is determined strictly. Thus, in **Baker [1994] Crim. L.R. 444**, the accessory had not effectively withdrawn when he used the words: "I'm not doing it" as the words used were equivocal; they could merely mean that A would not strike any more blows rather than that he wished to disassociate himself from the offence.

Where an accessory tries unsuccessfully to dissuade his accomplice from committing the principal offence, this may amount to withdrawal. Thus, in **Grundy [1977] Crim. L.R. 543**, where A gave burglars information to assist them in the commission of a burglary and then tried in vain for two weeks to dissuade them from breaking into the premises, the Court of Appeal held that A's attempts at dissuasion amounted to evidence of withdrawal which should have been left to the jury.

Whether an accessory who is unable or unwilling to communicate his withdrawal to his accomplices can withdraw by other means such as informing the police has not yet been determined by the courts though such efforts ought to be sufficient, especially if they prevent the commission of the offence. It is also unclear whether, in the situation where there is more than one principal, the accessory may communicate his withdrawal to only one or whether he must inform all of them. Where, however, the accessory has counselled more than one person to commit an offence, he is required to communicate his withdrawal to all those whom he has counselled (**State v Kinchen (1910) 52 So. 185**).

IS COMMUNICATION ALWAYS REQUIRED?

In **Mitchell [1999] Crim. L.R. 496**, the Court of Appeal stated that where the violence used is spontaneous, rather than pre-planned, communication of withdrawal is not required. The facts were as follows. A and P had been involved in a spontaneous attack on V. They then walked away, A throwing down his weapon. P then turned around, picked up a stick and hit V with it several times, killing him. A was held to have withdrawn by the time of the fatal blow. Communication by him of withdrawal was not required; he had withdrawn merely by walking away. *Mitchell* was heavily criticised because merely leaving the scene does not indicate a countermanding of one's prior encouragement and assistance and the principal may continue to be encouraged, unaware that the accessory has left. Following this criticism, the status of the case was clarified in **Robinson [2000] 5 Arch. News 2**, which described the case as exceptional. According to the court, communication of withdrawal must normally be given even in cases of spontaneous violence unless it is not reasonable and practicable to do so. They gave as an example of where it would not be reasonable and practicable to communicate withdrawal:

> "The exceptional circumstances pertaining in *Mitchell* where [the original violence had ended and A] threw down his weapon and moved away before the final and fatal blows were inflicted."

This approach was approved in *O'Flaherty*, where Mantell L.J. stated:

> "… in a case of spontaneous violence, in principle it is possible to withdraw by ceasing to fight, throwing down one's weapons and walking away"

and recently in **Mitchell & Ballantyne [2009] 1 Cr. App. R. 31.**

WILL COMMUNICATION ALWAYS BE SUFFICIENT?

In those instances where communication alone is sufficient evidence of withdrawal, no further action on the part of the accessory is required. Thus, he does not have to also attempt to prevent the principal committing the offence (*O'Flaherty*). Withdrawal by communication alone is more likely to be effective during the preparatory stages of an offence but, once the offence is in the course of being committed, nothing less than A interceding to prevent the commission of the crime may be required. In *Beccera*, A broke into a house with P and X intending to steal. A gave a knife to P to use if necessary on anyone interrupting them. The tenant of the upstairs flat, V, came down to investigate the noise. A said, "Come on let's go." A then jumped out of the window and ran away. P stabbed V with the knife, killing him. A was tried for murder and contended that he had withdrawn from the joint enterprise before the attack on V. The Court of Appeal held that A's words of withdrawal, coupled with leaving the scene of the crime were not sufficient to amount to withdrawal; withdrawal at that stage required a countermanding in some manner more effective than A's words and actions had been. Unfortunately, the court did not specify what would have been required for effective withdrawal but it is likely that A would have to have physically intervened between P and V to prevent the attack.

Over to you...

A and P plan to burgle V's home but A's girlfriend finds out about the plan and warns him that she will end their relationship if he participates in the burglary. A decides not to go ahead and, at the time they are due to commit the burglary, he sends a text message to P to say that he "Can't do it. Will explain later." P does not see the text as he has left his mobile phone at home. P commits the burglary on his own.

Has A withdrawn from the burglary? If yes, why? If not, why not?

Can a Victim be an Accessory?

The victim of an offence is not per se excluded from liability as an accessory to it. For example, the "victim" of a sexual offence may have been a willing participant, providing encouragement to the principal, but the principal is liable because the consent is invalid, the activity in question not being one to which a person can validly consent (see, further, Chs 5 and 6). Where, however, an offence is specifically designed to protect a class of persons, the victim of such an offence who belongs to that class of persons cannot be convicted as an accessory to it, notwithstanding that they may have aided or abetted its commission. Thus, in **Tyrell [1894] 1 Q.B. 710**, a girl under 16 who willingly allowed P to have sexual intercourse with her was not liable for aiding and abetting the offence under s.5 of the Criminal Law Amendment Act 1885 (now replaced with an offence under the Sexual Offences Act 2003 s.9) as the statute was passed to protect such girls from themselves.

Reform

The Serious Crime Act 2007 created three new inchoate offences of encouraging or assisting an offence(s) which arise whether or not the principal commits the offence which D had assisted or encouraged. These offences were considered in Ch.10. Also in 2007, the Law Commission published its Report, "Participating in Crime" (Law Com. No.305) which can be viewed online at *http://www.lawcom.gov.uk/docs/lc305.pdf*. The report made several recommendations for reform of secondary liability in murder which would apply where the principal *does* commit the offence assisted or encouraged. In summary, their proposals are as follows:

■ Secondary liability

1.   Section 8 of the Accessories and Abettors Act 1861 and s.44(1) of the Magistrates' Courts Act 1980 would be amended to limit secondary liability to assisting or encouraging the principal.

2. A would be liable for assisting or encouraging P to perpetrate the conduct element of an offence committed by P if he *intended* that the conduct element should be perpetrated.

3. Liability for procuring would be abolished and replaced with liability as a principal for intentionally causing a person to do a criminal act.

■ Joint criminal ventures

1. This would occur where A either agrees with P to commit an offence or shares a common intention with P to commit an offence.

2. Where A and P are parties to such a venture, A is liable for any offence committed by P whether agreed or collateral if he foresaw that the offence might be committed.

■ Innocent agency

The doctrine of innocent agency would be replaced by a statutory regime under which A would be liable for an offence as a principal if he intentionally causes P, an innocent agent, to commit the conduct element of an offence but P does not commit the offence because P: is under the age of 10 years; has a defence of insanity; or acts without the fault required to be convicted of the offence.

■ Causing the commission of a no-fault offence

There should be a statutory offence of causing another person to commit a no-fault (strict liability) offence by virtue of which A would be convicted as a principal rather than as a secondary party.

In 2008 the Government produced a Consultation Paper, *"Murder, Manslaughter and Infanticide: proposals for reform of the law"* in which, inter alia, they sought opinions on reform of secondary liability in murder only. The majority of the responses received were against such limited reform and the Government chose not to proceed, stating that they accepted that any reform should be a comprehensive reform of secondary liability generally.

Assistance After the Principal Offence

The focus of this chapter has been the liability of accessories, of persons who assist the principal prior to, or at the time, the principal offence is committed. A person who assists the principal after the commission of the offence, for example by acting as the getaway driver, harbouring the principal or removing evidence, although not an accessory, may still be liable under s.4 of the Criminal Law Act 1967. Section 4 provides:

> (1) Where a person has committed a relevant offence, any other person who, knowing or believing him to be guilty of the offence or of some other relevant offence, does without lawful authority or reasonable excuse any act with intent to impede his apprehension or prosecution shall be guilty of an offence.

The actus reus of the offence is phrased in terms of doing "any act". Thus, it cannot be committed by omission. It is not necessary that the act committed actually impedes the arrest or prosecution of the principal as the offence requires proof only of an intention to impede. The mens rea is the intention to impede coupled with the knowledge or belief of the principal's guilt in respect of a relevant offence although it is not necessary to prove knowledge of the exact relevant offence committed. Nor is it necessary to prove that the defendant knew the principal's identity (**Brindley [1971] 2 Q.B. 300**).

A person may also be liable under s.5 of the 1967 Act for accepting a payment in return for not disclosing information which might secure the prosecution of an offender. Section 5 provides:

> **(1)** Where a person has committed a relevant offence, any person who, knowing or believing that the offence or some [other relevant offence] has been committed, and that he has information which might be of material assistance in securing the prosecution or conviction of an offender for it, accepts or agrees to accept for not disclosing that information, any consideration other than the making good of loss or injury caused by the offence, or the making of reasonable compensation for that loss or injury, shall be liable ...

The actus reus of the offence consists of accepting, or agreeing to accept, consideration for not providing information which might assist in the prosecution or conviction of the principal. Consideration bears the meaning attributed to it in Contract law and includes money as well as payment in kind. The mens rea involves knowledge or belief that a relevant offence has been committed and the intention to accept the consideration.

Vicarious Liability

What is Vicarious Liability in the Criminal Law?

Vicarious liability is a doctrine commonly associated with the law of torts where one person (D) is held liable for the acts of another (A). It is worth emphasising that in the criminal law, this means D is criminally liable for the acts of another. Because of the serious consequences which flow from a criminal conviction, the law is very reluctant to impose criminal vicarious liability, and, as we shall see, it is the exception rather than the rule.

Vicarious liability exists in the law of torts in order, inter alia, to provide the victim of a tort with the best opportunity to gain compensation. That is from the employer who, in law, should be insured. The same parallel cannot be drawn in the criminal law because it is impossible to insure against criminality, whether one's own or another's. Further, the imposition of tortious vicarious liability exists to ensure that an employer maintains the highest standards of safety for his employees and customers. This purpose is most commonly served in the criminal law through a broad framework of strict liability regulatory crimes which is designed to deter breach of the rules, such as the Health and Safety at Work, etc. Act 1974. For a detailed rationale of the doctrine of vicarious liability in the law of torts, see the speech of Lord Nicholls in **Majrowski v Guy's and St Thomas's NHS Trust [2006] UKHL 34**.

It is one of the principles of criminal law that D is liable for his own personal acts but not those of another. So, as a general rule, the criminal law does not impose vicarious liability. Where it does exist, judges have justified it by saying the legislation would be rendered nugatory (see *Coppen v Moore No.2* below) if D was not held liable for the crimes of A.

As in the law of torts, the operation of vicarious liability is broadly confined to the situation where an employer is liable for the acts of the employee committed during the course of employment (**Lister and Others v Hesley Hall Ltd [2001] UKHL 22**; **Mattis v Pollock (t/a Flamingo's nightclub) [2002] EWHC 2177 Q.B.**). Unlike the law of torts, however, the doctrine in the criminal law is not limited to the employer/employee relationship (**Cobb v Williams [1973] Crim. L.R. 243**; **Clode v Barnes [1974] 1 All E.R. 1166**).

· ·

Vicarious Liability for Crimes of Strict Liability

Although referred to as vicarious liability, this is where D is liable because the act of A is the act of D. This is often called the attributed act doctrine because the act of A is attributed to D; in fact, it is D's act.

VICARIOUS LIABILITY FOR CRIMES OF STRICT LIABILITY AT COMMON LAW

The only common law offences where vicarious liability is a possibility are public nuisance and criminal libel, for both of which an employer can be held vicariously liable for the acts of his employees (see p.68).

VICARIOUS LIABILITY FOR STATUTORY CRIMES OF STRICT LIABILITY
■ **Express statutory provisions**

Parliament sometimes specifically imposes vicarious liability in the statutory definition of the offence. For example, s.1 of the Property Misdescriptions Act 1991 provides:

> **(1)** Where a false or misleading statement about a prescribed matter is made in the course of an estate agency business or a property development business, otherwise than in providing conveyancing services, the person by whom the business is carried on shall be guilty of an offence under this section.
>
> **(2)** Where the making of the statement is due to the act or default of an employee the employee shall be guilty of an offence under this section; and the employee may be proceeded against and punished whether or not proceedings are also taken against his employer.

The crime of misdescription is therefore committed by both the employee and the employer.

■ Implied statutory provisions

In **Coppen v Moore (No.2) [1898] 2 Q.B. 306**, D owned a chain of grocery shops. He sent written instructions to each of his shops that the hams offered for sale should be correctly labelled, but an assistant in one of the shops sold a "breakfast" ham as a "Scotch" ham. D was convicted of selling goods to which a false trade description had been applied under the Merchandise Marks Act 1887 (it is now an offence contrary to the Trade Descriptions Act 1968). The Divisional Court found that D was the seller, even if not the actual salesman, and also that:

> "When the scope and object of the Act are borne in mind, any other conclusion would to a large extent render the Act ineffective for its avowed purposes ... It is obvious that, if sales with false trade descriptions could be carried out ... with impunity so far as the principal is concerned, the Act would to a large extent be nugatory."

This reasoning was applied in **Harrow London Borough Council v Shah [2000] 1 W.L.R. 83**, to convict the owner of a shop of selling a national lottery ticket to someone under 16. The owner (D) was actually in the back room when his employee (A) sold a ticket to a boy of 13-and-a-half, honestly believing him to be at least 16-years-old. The owner had trained his assistant, and warned him not to sell if in any doubt as to the purchaser's age. However, D was convicted as the "seller" of the ticket. The act of A was the act of D.

Where the offence is satisfied on a proof of an act such as selling, the courts have construed the word "sell" extensively to cover the situation where the employee is the salesman, but D is the seller. This is therefore called the extensive construction principle.

A similar approach has been taken to offences phrased in terms of "using" a vehicle (**Griffiths v Studebakers Ltd [1924] 1 K.B. 102**) and "being in possession" of goods (**Melias Limited v Preston [1957] 2 Q.B. 380**), but not to verbs such as "driving" because the employer cannot "drive" through the act of another, although he can "sell" and "use" (**Richmond upon Thames LBC v Pinn and Wheeler Ltd [1989] R.T.R. 354**).

The verb "causing" has also been construed extensively. In **National Rivers Authority v Alfred McAlpine Homes East Ltd [1994] 4 All E.R. 286**, D was a company which was building houses on a residential development. A nearby stream became polluted when cement was washed into it, and the company was charged with causing polluting matter to enter controlled waters contrary to s.85 of the Water Resources Act 1991. At first instance, the magistrates held that there was no case to answer because the identification doctrine (see p.375) was not satisfied. However, the authority's appeal was allowed. The Divisional Court held that D's employees had caused the pollution in the course of their employment, so therefore the company had also caused it.

Only the acts of A can be attributed to D, not mens rea, so if the offence requires mens rea, D cannot be vicariously liable under the extensive construction principle (**Vane v Yiannopolous [1965] A.C. 486**, below).

Vicarious Liability for Crimes with Mens Rea

The circumstances in which D can be criminally vicariously liable for a crime with mens rea are limited to where D is the holder of a licence and he has delegated the activities in that licence to A, or where he has delegated the activities imposed by a statutory duty to A. Even though D should normally be liable only for his own acts and omissions, the imposition of vicarious liability is justified because if D tries to avoid liability by delegating it to another, he can still be convicted in certain circumstances.

This is the delegation principle and it operates by imputing both the actus reus and the mens rea of the delegate (A) to the person under the duty or the holder of the licence (D). For example, in **Allen v Whitehead [1930] 1 K.B. 211**, the owner and licensee of a cafe (D) delegated the operation of the cafe to a manager (A). D had expressly instructed A that no prostitutes were to be allowed to congregate on the premises, as it was an offence under s.44 of the Metropolitan Police Act 1839, knowingly to suffer prostitutes to meet together on such premises. A, however, allowed a number of women he knew to be prostitutes to use and stay in the premises. D only visited the premises once or twice a week and had no personal knowledge of what had taken place. D's liability could not be imposed via the extensive construction principle above as the crime had mens rea ("knowingly"), yet because he had delegated the duty to A, A's knowledge was imputed to D.

Had A sub-delegated the operation of the cafe to another, B, then D could be liable for B's acts and knowledge in the same way (**Sopp v Long [1969] 1 All E.R. 855**), but D would not be liable for B's acts and knowledge if control of the premises had not been delegated to B, because he was, say, merely an employee (**Allchorn v Hopkins (1905) 69 J.P. 355**). For D to be liable for a delegate's acts and knowledge, there must have been a complete delegation of the functions and responsibilities of the licence or duty. In **Vane v Yiannopolous [1965] A.C. 486**, D was the licensee of a restaurant, which had a licence to sell alcohol only to persons ordering meals. D had instructed his waitress accordingly. However, on one occasion, without D's knowledge, the waitress served drinks to two people who did not order a meal. D was not vicariously liable. He had not made full delegation of the licence's activities.

A person cannot be held vicariously liable for aiding and abetting another to commit an offence (**Ferguson v Weaving [1951] 1 K.B. 814 DC**) nor for attempting to commit an offence (**Gardner v Akeroyd [1952] 2 Q.B. 743 DC**).

Reform

Clause 29 of the Draft Criminal Code Bill recommended the abolition of the delegation principle but the retention of vicarious liability for strict liability under the extensive construction principle (Law Com. No.177).

FIGURE 11.3 Criminal Vicarious Liability

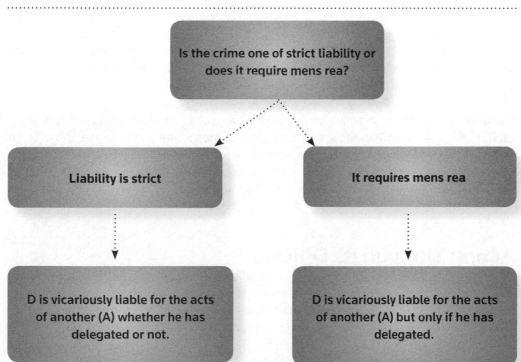

Corporate Liability

. . . .

Introduction

Corporations, such as limited companies and Plc's, are legal persons. A company has a legal identity, separate from that of its directors or members (**Salomon v Salomon and Co Ltd [1897] A.C. 22**). It can enter into contracts, commit torts and, in most circumstances, be convicted of criminal offences. In principle, corporations (and companies; we use the terms interchangeably here) can be criminally liable to the same extent as individual persons subject to two exceptions;

1. corporations cannot commit some offences because their very nature precludes it, e.g. wounding with intent to cause GBH, rape, etc. and

2. corporations cannot be convicted of offences for which the only punishment is imprisonment, e.g. murder and treason.

. . . .

Vicarious or Corporate Liability?

As explained above, vicarious liability is where D is liable for A's acts, and A may also be liable. Corporate liability, on the other hand, is not where a company or corporation is liable for another's crime, but where it is liable for its own criminal offence. There is confusion, of course, because a company, whilst being a legal person, is not a human being and can act only through its human officers. That is the reason corporate liability is covered in this chapter. The notion of acting through another's action is examined in more detail below.

The distinction between vicarious and corporate liability is important because the bases of liability differ. Also, an individual employer may be vicariously liable for the crime of his employee, but if he is not a company, the question of corporate liability never arises. That is not to say a company cannot be vicariously liable, because it can, if either the extensive construction principle or the delegation principle is satisfied, see above.

. . . .

Acting Through its Officers

One of the reasons corporate liability is conceptually difficult is because the discussion centres on the personal liability of a company, but necessarily involves an examination of the liability of the human individuals within that organisation. It is the law that the "controlling mind" of the company, made up of one of the senior managers or directors of the company, is the mind of the company itself. Lord Denning illustrated this by metaphor in **HL Bolton (Engineering) Co Ltd v PJ Graham and Sons Ltd [1957] 1 Q.B. 159**:

"A company may in many ways be likened to a human body. It has a brain and nerve centre which controls what it does. It also has hands which hold the tools and act in accordance with directions from the centre. Some of the people in the company are mere servants and agents who are nothing more than hands to do the work and cannot be said to represent the mind or will. Others are directors and managers who represent the directing mind and will of the company, and control what it does. The state of mind of these managers is the state of mind of the company and is treated by law as such."

In the leading case, **Tesco Supermarkets Ltd v Nattrass [1972] A.C. 153**, Lord Reid emphasised the difference between the personal liability of a corporation and its vicarious liability as an employer:

"A living person has a mind which can have knowledge or intention or be negligent and he has hands to carry out his intentions. A corporation has none of these: it must act through living persons, though not always one and the same person. Then the person who acts is not speaking or acting for the company. He is acting as the company and his mind which directs his acts is the mind of the company. There is no question of the company being vicariously liable. He is not acting as a servant, representative, agent or delegate. He is an embodiment of the company, or, one could say, he hears and speaks through the persona of the company, within his appropriate sphere, and his mind is the mind of the company. If it is a guilty mind then that guilt is the guilt of the company."

The doctrine of corporate liability therefore operates by imputing the actus reus and mens rea of a senior manager identified with the company to the corporation itself. This is called the identification doctrine.

This part of the text should be read alongside pp.128–132 where the offence of corporate manslaughter is discussed. We have attempted to ensure there is no overlap, so for a comprehensive understanding of the topic, these two parts of the book should be read together.

The Identification Doctrine

THE DIRECTING MIND

As Lord Denning explained above, the doctrine requires that the "directing mind and will" of the company is identified. The House of Lords in *Tesco* made it clear that only those exercising very senior management functions would suffice. The difficulty is in stating when a person is sufficiently senior in a company to be considered the controlling mind of it. In *Tesco*, there was divergence even among their Lordships. Lord Reid held that the controlling minds were:

> "The board of directors, the managing director and perhaps other superior officers of a company [who] carry out the functions of management and speak and act as the company."

Viscount Dilhorne said that such a person would be one:

> "[W]ho is in actual control of the operations of a company or of part of them and who is not responsible to another person in the company for the manner in which he discharges his duties in the sense of being under his orders."

However, according to Lord Diplock, the process consists of:

> "[I]dentifying those natural persons who by the memorandum and articles of association or as a result of action taken by the directors or by the company in general meeting pursuant to the articles are entrusted with the exercise of the powers of the company."

In *Tesco* itself, all agreed on the facts that the manager of one of 800 branches of the grocery store was far too junior to be identified with the corporation. Similarly, in **Magna Plant Ltd v Mitchell [1966] Crim. L.R. 394**, a car hire company's depot engineer, even though he was the only manager, was too junior. On the other hand, a traffic manager, who was self-employed, was the responsible person and his knowledge could be imputed to the company in **Worthy v Gordon Plant (Services) Ltd [1989] R.T.R. 7**.

Whether a person is identified with the company in this way is a question of law. If no one can be identified, the prosecution fails. It is far easier, therefore, to find a controlling mind within a small company than a larger one with a complex managerial or directorial structure, or where decision making and responsibility are delegated throughout the management hierarchy, see in particular the discussion on p.130.

Over to you...

If the charge being considered is manslaughter by the corporation, you must refer to the provisions of the Corporate Manslaughter and Corporate Homicide Act 2007 which is examined in Ch.4. The identification doctrine, which is a common law doctrine, has been replaced *in respect of manslaughter only* by the provisions of the Act. Where relevant (i.e. the crime is one which can be committed by a corporation but is not manslaughter), the identification doctrine continues to be used.

ATTRIBUTION NOT IDENTIFICATION?

Because, where it applies, the identification doctrine limits the controlling mind to those in very senior positions, this can severely restrict the scope of corporate liability. Lord Hoffmann made a brave attempt to circumvent the rigidity of the doctrine in the Privy Council decision in **Meridian Global Funds Management Asia Limited v Securities Commission [1995] 2 A.C. 500**. K was the chief investment officer of an investment management company. Unknown to anyone who was the "directing mind and will" of the defendant company, K acquired a shareholding in another company, as part of his scheme to acquire control of the target company for his personal benefit. However, no notice was given as required under statute. Lord Hoffmann held that a special rule of attribution would be necessary to attribute K's act and knowledge to the company, and further that it applied irrespective of whether K could properly be described as the directing mind and will of the company. He considered the purpose of the relevant New Zealand statute was to enable immediate identification of substantial shareholdings. This aim would be defeated unless corporate holders were identified with the employee (K) who had acquired the holding. K's knowledge of the holding was attributed to the defendant company, which was therefore guilty.

The case is, however, probably limited in application to statutory provisions with a similar purpose. Certainly it has not been adopted in other areas of the law.

AGGREGATION NOT IDENTIFICATION?

A company's "fault" cannot be found by grouping the conduct and blameworthiness of more than one individual employee, even more than one controlling mind. Such aggregation was held to be of no application to the common law (and therefore at that time, to the offence of manslaughter) in **Attorney General's Reference (No.2 of 1999) [2000] Q.B. 796**. For the current offence of corporate manslaughter, the requirement is that there was a "senior management failure". This is considered in Ch.4 but it is worth noting here that liability is based on a form of aggregation.

So, the common law identification doctrine is the only test which allows personal corporate liability, and this can arise only if an individual identifiable with the company also commits the offence.

◄ ···

Summary

1. The principles of secondary liability mean that it is not only the person who commits an offence (the principal) who may be liable for it but also the person who has in some way assisted them in its commission (the accessory).

2. The principal may act through an innocent agent.

3. An accessory is someone who aids, abets, counsels or procures the commission of an offence by the principal.

4. The principal and the accessory may be tried, convicted and punished for the same offence.

5. Secondary liability is contingent on the commission of the actus reus of the offence by the principal. The principal may, therefore, avoid conviction because he lacked mens rea or has a defence not available to the accessory but the accessory will remain liable.

6. The actus reus of secondary liability involves doing something which amounts to aiding, abetting, counselling or procuring. The mens rea consists of an intention to aid, abet, counsel or procure together with knowledge of the essential matters which constitute the principal offence.

7. Where two or more parties embark upon the commission of a criminal offence with a common purpose then, under the doctrine of joint enterprise, the parties may be liable not only for their own acts in furtherance of the enterprise but also for the acts of the other participants in the enterprise. A person will be liable as an accessory to any offence committed by the principal during a joint enterprise that was either agreed upon or which he foresaw the principal might commit with the appropriate mens rea.

8. Where a participant in a joint enterprise thought his accomplice was carrying one weapon and his accomplice was carrying, and used, a different weapon, his liability will depend upon whether the weapon used was fundamentally different from the weapon envisaged.

9. An accessory may withdraw from liability if he makes an unequivocal communication of withdrawal prior to the commission of the principal offence. Where the principal has actually embarked on the commission of the offence, more than communication may be required of the accessory, for example, taking steps to intercede to prevent the commission of the offence.

10. Where an accessory effectively withdraws, he remains liable for any offences he had committed up to that point.

11. A person who assists the principal after the commission of the offence or accepts payment in return for not disclosing information which might secure their prosecution may commit an offence under s.4 or s.5 of the Criminal Law Act 1967.

12. D may be exceptionally vicariously liable for the acts of A where (a) the crime is one of strict liability and the extensive construction principle allows it, or (b) where the

crime has mens rea through the delegation principle, but only if there is complete delegation.

13. Corporate liability—A company is a separate legal entity and is criminally liable to the same extent and on the same basis as an individual. It can also be "personally" liable under the common law identification principle provided a "directing mind and will" of the company is also convicted.

FIGURE 11.4 **Summary of A's liability for the murder of V committed by P during a joint enterprise to commit offence X**

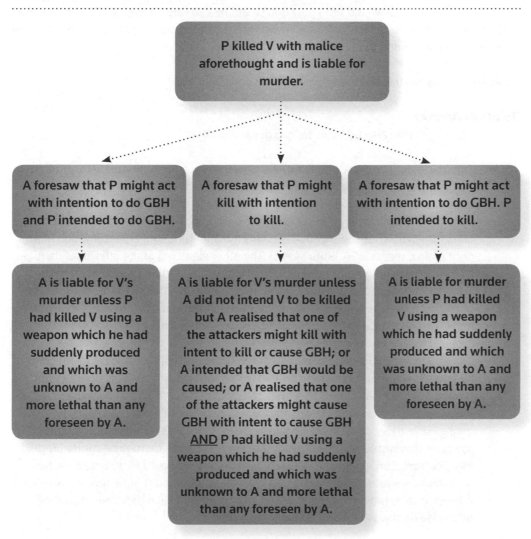

End of Chapter Question

Question

Dave, Tim, Bob and Nick plan to commit a burglary at a stately home owned by John, a wealthy businessman. They intend to commit the burglary when John is asleep in bed but have the information to disable the alarm system as Dave recently fitted the system at the house. On the night of the burglary, Nick has cold feet. He stays at home and sends Tim a text message saying that he "won't do it". Tim has his phone turned off and does not get the message. When Nick fails to turn up the others go ahead without him. They are busy helping themselves to silverware when they are disturbed by John. Bob pulls out a gun and shoots John in the head, killing him instantly. Tim and Dave did not know Bob would be carrying a weapon. Dave knows Bob well and knows that he is a violent thug who always carries a metal cosh with him. Bob has been convicted of murder and burglary.

Consider the criminal liability, if any, of Dave, Tim and Nick.

Points of Answer

Tim, Nick and Dave may also be liable for murder and burglary.

- ♦ The four (Bob, Tim, Nick and Dave) were involved in a joint enterprise to commit burglary at John's house. Burglary under s.9(1)(a) of the Theft Act 1968 (entering the building as trespassers with intent to steal) and s.9(1)(b) (having entered the building as trespassers, then stealing) is committed. The theft occurs as soon as one of them touches the silverware as this the appropriation; an assumption of a right of an owner (s.3 TA 1968; *Morris*). The other elements of the offence of theft, i.e. property; belonging to another; dishonesty and intention permanently to deprive can be satisfied on the facts. Nick can be liable even though he is not there as presence at the scene is not required for joint enterprise liability (*Rook*). Tim, Nick and Dave will also be liable for the death as accessories if the killing was within the scope of the joint enterprise.
- ♦ Murder was not expressly or impliedly agreed upon so Tim, Nick and Dave will only be liable for murder if they foresaw that Bob might kill with malice aforethought (*Powell & English*) although Nick may still not be liable if he has withdrawn by this stage, see below. It is unlikely that Tim or Nick would have foreseen that Bob might kill as they do not know about the weapon or Bob's violent nature. If this is the case, they would not be liable for the death; not even for manslaughter (*English; Pearson*). Tim would still be liable for burglary as would Nick, unless he has withdrawn, see later. Dave knows Bob is a violent thug and that he always carries a weapon so he may well have foreseen that Bob might kill if they were disturbed, otherwise he also would only be liable for burglary.

◆ Dave would be liable for murder if he foresaw Bob might kill whether he foresaw that Bob might kill with intent to kill or only with intent to do GBH (*Rahman*).

◆ Dave may escape liability for murder if the use of the gun was fundamentally different from that which was envisaged (*English*). He can rely on the "fundamentally different weapon rule" (the rule) even if he foresaw that Bob might kill with intent to kill rather than with intent to do GBH (*Rahman*). However, if he foresaw that Bob might kill with intent to kill, he can only rely on the rule if he did not intend John to be killed but (a) realised that one of the group might kill with intent to kill or cause GBH; or (b) intended that GBH would be caused; or (c) realised that one of the group might cause GBH with intent to cause GBH (*Yemoh*). The rule requires the principal to (i) suddenly produce a weapon of which the accessory knows nothing and which (ii) is more lethal than any weapon the accessory contemplated being used—this is a jury question (*Greatrex*). Applied to the facts, Dave thought Bob was carrying a cosh. If the jury consider this fundamentally different, i.e. less dangerous (the terminology used in *English*) / lethal (the wording used in *Rahman*) than a gun he might rely on the rule, otherwise he would remain liable for murder.

◆ If Nick is not liable for the death, he may still be liable for burglary unless he has effectively withdrawn. Failure to turn up is not withdrawal; as a minimum, unequivocal (*Baker*) and effective communication (*Beccera*) of withdrawal is required. Is a text to one member sufficient and are the words he uses unequivocal? Is the text enough at this late stage? Something more might be required (*Beccera*) e.g. intervening to stop the crime or alerting the police. If he has withdrawn, he would still be liable for conspiracy to commit burglary.

Further Reading

P. Alldridge, "The doctrine of Innocent Agency" (1990) Criminal Law Forum 45.

R. Buxton, "Joint enterprise" [2009] Crim. L.R. 233.

J. Gobert, "Corporate Criminality: New Crimes for the Times" [1994] Crim. L.R. 722.

J. Gobert and M. Punch, "Rethinking Corporate Crime" (2003).

P. Pace, "Delegation—A Doctrine in Search of a Definition" [1982] Crim. L.R. 627.

A.P. Simester, "The mental element in complicity" (2006) 122 L.Q.R. 578.

G.R. Sullivan, "Participation in Crime: Law Com No 305—Joint Criminal Ventures" [2008] Crim. L.R. 19.

R.D. Taylor, "Complicity, legal scholarship and the law of unintended consequences" (2009) L.S. 1

and "Procuring, causation, innocent agency and the Law Commission" [2008] Crim. L.R. 32

G. Virgo, "Making Sense of Accessorial Liability" [2006] Arch. News 6.

C. Wells, Corporations and Criminal Responsibility, 2nd edn (Clarendon, 2001).

W. Wilson, "A Rational Scheme of Liability for Participation in Crime" [2008] Crim. L.R. 3.
http://www.lawcom.gov.uk/docs/lc305.pdf.

 ## Self Test Questions

To test your knowledge gained from this section go online to http://*www.sweetandmaxwell.co.uk* and take our online self test questions. Here you will also find key updates to ensure that you are only ever one click away from an instant update.

Defences I—Defences Negating the Offence or Affecting Capacity

12

CHAPTER OVERVIEW

In this chapter we:

- analyse the defences of mistake, intoxication, automatism, insanity, unfit to plead and doli incapax

- consider the mechanism by which each defence operates

- evaluate the distinction between specific and basic intent, where the distinction is relevant

- explore the policy arguments limiting the availability of intoxication as a defence

- compare the defences of automatism and insanity and comment on the operation of the rules.

Summary

End of Chapter Question

Further Reading

Self Test Questions

Introduction

As explained in Ch.2, criminal liability requires proof that the defendant committed the actus reus of the relevant offence with the appropriate mens rea and in the absence of any defence. We have already considered (in Ch.4) some defences specific to murder alone, namely diminished responsibility, provocation (and the defence of loss of self-control which replaces it) and suicide pact. In this and the following chapter, we will consider some defences which apply to crimes in general. Such general defences may operate in different ways. Some defences arise independently of the actus reus and mens rea; here the defendant is seeking either to *justify* his actions or to *excuse* himself from liability. Such defences are discussed in Ch.13. Other defences operate to negate the actus reus or mens rea. In reality, they are a denial that the prosecution has proved one of the constituent elements of the offence but they are still commonly referred to as defences. This chapter considers some of these defences, namely, mistake, intoxication and automatism. The final category of defences is that which affects the defendant's capacity to commit the crime; they render him exempt from criminal liability. These are the defences of insanity and doli incapax (being under the age of criminal responsibility). These "capacity" defences are also discussed in this chapter.

Mistake

· ·

Introduction

Before examining the scope of the defence of mistake, it is first necessary to consider those situations where the defendant's mistake will *not* assist him. Briefly, a mistake which involves ignorance of the criminal law will not afford a defence. Thus, for example, a defendant who comes to England from a country where a certain act, such as taking more than one spouse, is legal, cannot plead ignorance of the law as a defence if he then commits that act which is unlawful under English law. Similarly, as we saw in Ch.3, it is no defence to injuring B that D intended to injure A but attacked B by mistake; the principle of transferred malice applies. There is, in fact, no defence of mistake per se. As we shall see, however, a defendant may be able to rely successfully on his mistake where it meant he lacked the mens rea for the particular crime or where the mistake is as to a fact which, if true, would provide a defence.

· ·

Mistakes which Negate the Mens Rea

MISTAKE AS TO THE CIVIL LAW

We saw above that a mistake as to the criminal law is no defence. However, the position differs where the mistake is as to the civil law. Where a defendant makes such a mistake as to an element of the actus reus requiring mens rea, to the effect that he lacked the mens rea for the crime, he is not liable. A defendant may act under a mistake as to the civil law where, for example, he damages property in the mistaken belief that it is his own, unaware that it has become someone else's property under property law. Such a mistake arose in **Smith [1974] Q.B. 354**, discussed on p.297, and led to the acquittal of the defendant for criminal damage as his mistake meant that he did not intend to damage property belonging to another.

MISTAKE OF FACT

In **DPP v Morgan [1976] A.C. 182**, the House of Lords held that a defendant who acted under a mistake of fact as to an element of the actus reus of a crime which meant that he lacked the mens rea for that offence would not be liable whether or not his mistake was a reasonable one to make; mens rea is negated as much by an unreasonable mistake as by a reasonable one. (The reasonableness of the mistaken belief is not irrelevant, however, as the more reasonable the belief the more likely it is that the jury will believe that the defendant held such a belief). Morgan (D), a senior member of the RAF, invited three men back to his house to have sexual intercourse with his wife (V). D told the three men that, if V screamed, it was merely her way of demonstrating her sexual pleasure. The three men forced V to have sex with them. They were convicted of rape and D was convicted of being an accessory to rape. On appeal, their Lordships held that the three men could not be liable for rape (as defined prior to the Sexual Offences Act 2003) if they lacked the mens rea because they believed, albeit unreasonably, that their victim had consented to sexual intercourse (the mens rea for rape at the time being intention or recklessness not merely as to having sexual intercourse but as to having sexual intercourse *without consent*). However, the convictions were upheld as the House considered that no properly directed jury would have believed the men's story that they honestly believed Mrs Morgan had consented.

Although there was some dicta in subsequent cases to the effect that the *Morgan* principle was confined to rape only, the general applicability of the principle was confirmed by the Court of Appeal in the indecent assault case of **Kimber [1983] 3 All E.R. 316**, the s.47 assault case of **Gladstone Williams [1987] 3 All E.R. 411**, and by their Lordships in **B v DPP [2000] 2 A.C. 428**. In fact, the *Morgan* principle now applies to all offences where a mistake of fact is capable of negating the mens rea. Thus, it does not apply to offences of strict liability nor, interestingly, to offences under ss.1–4 of the Sexual Offences Act 2003 such as rape and sexual assault (see Ch.6) as the mens rea for such offences is phrased in terms of a *reasonable* belief in consent.

Mistakes which do not Negate the Mens Rea

A mistake of fact which does not negate the mens rea and, consequently, to which the *Morgan* principle does not apply, may be either irrelevant or one as to facts which, if true, would provide a defence.

IRRELEVANT MISTAKES

A mistake which is irrelevant does not assist the defendant in any way. Thus, in **Forbes (Giles) [2001] UKHL 40**, the defendant was correctly convicted under s.170(2) of the Customs and Excise Management Act 1979 in respect of the importation of prohibited goods where he had imported child pornography (prohibited goods) even though he had mistakenly believed he had imported adult pornography (also prohibited goods); his mistake was irrelevant.

MISTAKE AS TO A DEFENCE

Traditionally, a mistake of fact which, if true, would afford a defence had to be a reasonable mistake to excuse criminal liability. This was unchanged by *Morgan* which was concerned only with mistakes as to an element of the actus reus which negates the mens rea. Thus, for example, D's assertion that he injured V in the mistaken belief that he did so under duress will only provide D with a defence if the mistake was a reasonable one to make in the circumstances (**Hasan [2005] 2 A.C. 467**, see Ch.13).

. . . .

Mistake as to the Need to Act in Self-defence or Prevention of Crime

The effect of the *Morgan* principle is that, for example, a defendant who shoots and kills what he mistakenly believes to be an animal is not liable for murder if it turns out to be a human that he has killed as he lacked the mens rea; he did not intend to kill a human. But what of the situation where the defendant shoots and kills V, intending to kill V, but intends to kill only because he mistakenly believes he is acting to defend A from V when, in reality, A is not in any danger from V? At common law, a mistaken belief in the need to use force, even fatal force, in self-defence or prevention of crime was not treated as one of mistaken belief in a defence (see above), so the mistake did not have to have been based on reasonable grounds (*Gladstone Williams*), although the force used had to be objectively reasonable in the circumstances as the defendant believed them to be. A possible rationale was given by the Privy Council in **Beckford [1988] A.C. 130**: in crimes of violence, both fatal and non-fatal, it is an essential requirement of liability that the violence used was *unlawful*; "unlawful" is, in fact, part of the definition (specifically the actus reus) of such offences. Thus, D, for example, must intend not only to kill or cause GBH but *unlawfully* to kill or cause GBH (for murder) or intend or be reckless as to the infliction of *unlawful* force (for a battery). Consequently, where D injured V mistakenly believing he was acting in self-defence or prevention of crime he did not intend to act unlawfully and, therefore, lacked the mens rea for the crime, whether or not his mistake was reasonable.

The common law position has now been put onto a statutory footing by s.76(4) of the Criminal Justice and Immigration Act 2008 which provides that a defendant can rely on a genuine, mistaken belief in the need to act in self-defence or prevention of crime whether or not the mistake was a reasonable one to have made. Section 76 is explored in Ch.13.

Mistaken Belief in Consent

Where a defendant harms V, mistakenly believing that he has V's consent to do so, it is unclear whether he lacks mens rea for an assault offence because the status of consent as either a "definitional" element of an offence or as merely a defence has not yet been resolved (see further Ch.5). If the absence of consent is a definitional element of an offence involving the use of force on a victim, a mistaken belief in consent will negate the mens rea of such an offence. However, if consent is merely a defence, a mistaken belief in consent will not negate mens rea and will only afford a defence if it is based on reasonable grounds. Though the exact mechanism by which consent operates has not yet been determined, the Court of Appeal in **Jones (1986) 83 Cr. App. R. 375**, without discussing in detail the status of consent (though approving those cases which treated consent as a definitional element), held that a genuine, albeit mistaken, belief that a victim was consenting to rough and undisciplined horseplay was a defence *even if that belief was an unreasonable belief*. Similarly, the Court of Appeal in **Richardson and Irwin [1999] 1 Cr. App. R. 192** appeared to treat a (drunken) mistaken belief in consent to rough horseplay as negating mens rea and, therefore, by implication, consent as a definitional element (see pp.404–405).

Mistake in Bigamy

A special rule concerning mistake exists in the context of bigamy. Bigamy, contrary to s.57 of the Offences Against the Person Act 1861, is committed by a defendant who, whilst already married, marries another person. The mens rea is an intention to go through a second ceremony of marriage. In **Tolson (1889) 23 Q.B.D. 168**, the defendant remarried, mistakenly believing that her first husband had died. Mrs Tolson's conviction for bigamy was quashed as her mistake was based on reasonable grounds. Subsequent cases (see, for example, **Gould [1968] 1 All E.R. 849**) confirmed that a reasonable belief that one was no longer married would be a defence to a bigamy charge.

The decision in *Tolson* was unaffected by *Morgan* which, in fact, distinguished *Tolson* as Mrs Tolson's mistake was not one which would negate the mens rea for bigamy as she did intend to go through a marriage ceremony; mens rea is not required as to the actus reus requirement of "being married." It is unclear whether the *Tolson* rule survives the decisions in **B v DPP [2000] 2 A.C. 428** and **K [2002] 1 A.C. 462** (see Ch.3) and, therefore, whether an unreasonable belief that one is no longer married would now suffice.

FIGURE 12 **Summary of mistake**

FIGURE 12 **Summary of mistake**

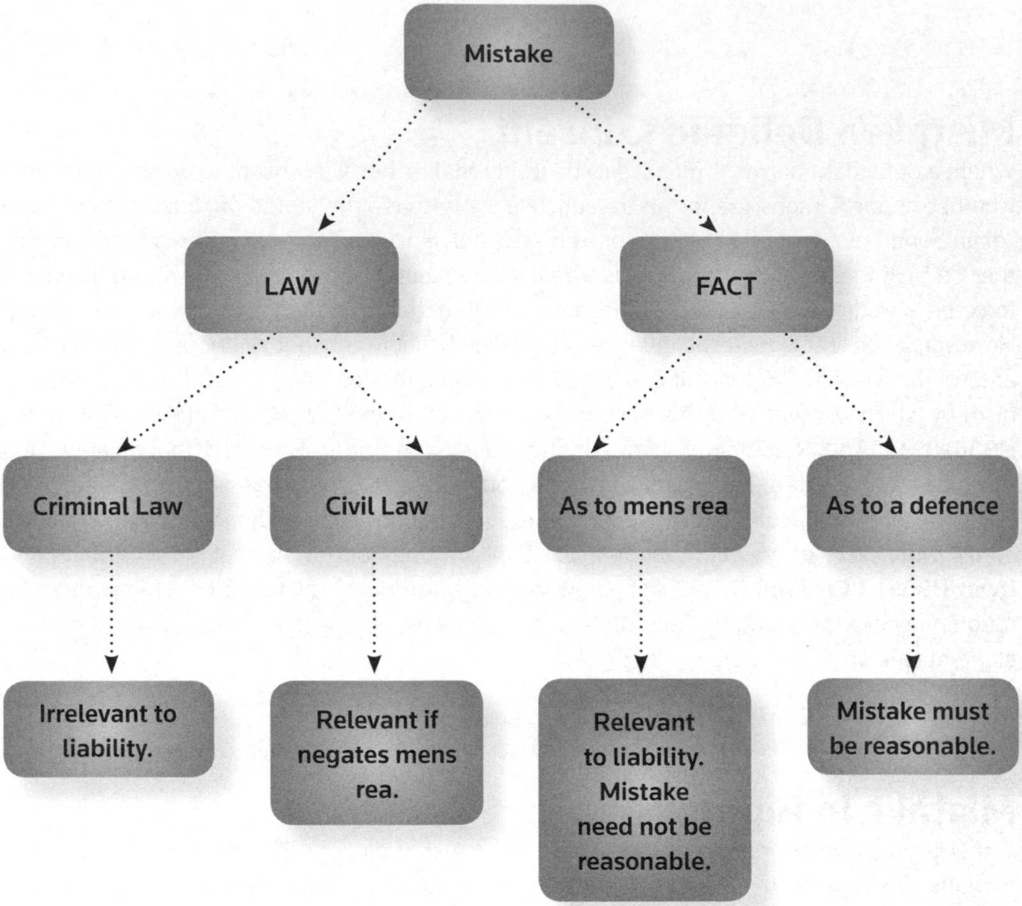

Intoxication

Introduction

A defendant may seek to explain his actions on the basis that he was drunk or "high" on drugs at the time he committed the actus reus of the offence with which he is charged. As we shall see, however, intoxication from drink or drugs is not, per se, a defence. It may, however, in certain circumstances, support an argument that the defendant should not be liable because he was so intoxicated that he lacked the mens rea for the offence. Where intoxication cannot be relied upon in relation to liability, it may be taken into consideration on sentencing. The relevant law has been developed entirely by the judiciary who have been heavily influenced by public policy considerations which must always be borne in mind when considering the current rules which are inconsistent and frequently contrary to legal principle.

What is Intoxication?

There is no legal definition of intoxication under English law but what is clear is that intoxication must be "very extreme" to be relied upon (**Stubbs (1989) 88 Cr. App. R. 53**). Each case is decided on its facts; a consumption of several pints of beer may render one person "legless" but have little impact on another.

Intoxication may be *voluntary* (often described as self-induced) or *involuntary*. As will be seen, different rules apply depending on whether the intoxication is voluntary or involuntary. Again, neither term is defined but voluntary intoxication is generally considered to be the ingestion of an intoxicant, knowing it to be an intoxicant, and involuntary intoxication as unintentionally ingesting an intoxicant. The classic example of involuntary intoxication is one where the defendant's non-alcoholic drink is laced with an intoxicant. It does, however, also encompass self-induced intoxication by taking drugs for prescribed medical purposes, taking a dangerous drug mistakenly believing it to be a non-dangerous one or taking a sedative drug without foreseeing that it might make one aggressive or uncontrolled.

Over to you...

Do you think we should have a legal definition of intoxication and why do you think we do not?

Voluntary Intoxication

THE POLICY ARGUMENTS AGAINST TAKING VOLUNTARY INTOXICATION INTO CONSIDERATION

There is a perception amongst the public and the judiciary that intoxication lies behind the commission of many violent crimes, a view which seems borne out by crime statistics. According to the 2008/09 British Crime Survey, 47 per cent of all victims of violent crime believed their assailant to have been under the influence of alcohol at the time of the offence and 17 per cent believed their assailant was under the influence of drugs. Similar figures can be derived from previous surveys. Victims' perceptions may not necessarily represent the true figures for the number of offenders intoxicated at the relevant time and nor do the figures establish a causal link between intoxication and violent offending but, nevertheless, the figures suggest a strong relationship between the two which has long been accepted by the courts and continues to be so:

> "It is common knowledge that those who take alcohol to excess or certain sorts of drugs may become aggressive or do dangerous or unpredictable things, they may be able to foresee the risks of causing harm to others but nevertheless persist in their conduct". (per Griffiths L.J. in **Bailey (1983) 77 Cr. App. R. 76**).

This view of the effects of intoxication has influenced the courts' approach to intoxication as a defence and led to a policy aimed at protecting the public from those who, by becoming intoxicated, render themselves a danger to society. The aim of public protection is achieved by refusing to allow an intoxicated offender to be treated more favourably than a sober one, even where he lacked the mens rea for the crime, save only in certain limited circumstances. As Lord Birkenhead L.C. stated in **DPP v Beard [1920] A.C. 479**:

> "A man who by his own voluntary act debauches and destroys his will power, shall be no better situated in regard to criminal acts than a sober man."

The message from the courts is clear, if you become voluntarily intoxicated you must answer for the consequences:

> "If a man of his own volition takes a substance which causes him to cast off the restraints of reason and conscience, no wrong is done to him by holding him answerable criminally for any injury he may do while in that condition" (per Lord Elwyn-Jones L.C. in **DPP v Majewski [1977] A.C. 443**).

The judiciary has readily admitted that policy considerations underpin the law on intoxication. For example, in *Majewski*, Lord Simon stated that:

> "One of the prime purposes of the criminal law, with its penal sanctions, is the protection from certain proscribed conduct of persons who are pursuing their lawful lives. Unprovoked violence has, from time immemorial, been a significant part of such proscribed conduct. To [permit intoxication as a defence] would leave the citizen legally unprotected from unprovoked violence where such violence was the consequence of drink or drugs having obliterated the capacity of the perpetrator to know what he was doing or what were its consequences."

Similarly, in **Kingston [1994] 3 All E.R. HL**, Lord Mustill stated:

"... in at least some cases a defendant cannot say that he was so drunk that he could not form the required intent. ... Why is this so? The answer must, I believe, be the same as that given in other common law jurisdictions: namely that such evidence is excluded as a matter of policy."

As noted above by Lord Mustill, such policy considerations have not just influenced the courts of England and Wales; many other jurisdictions have adopted a similar, policy-driven approach to ours. But what is the approach of the courts of England and Wales? Originally, the common law refused to allow intoxication as an excuse at all; if anything, it was viewed as an aggravating factor but this approach was gradually relaxed during the 19th century to the position we have today which is, essentially, a compromise. The aim is now to balance, on the one hand, public policy considerations against, on the other hand, the legitimate defence argument that both elements of criminal liability cannot be established by the prosecution because the defendant's intoxication meant he did not form the mens rea at the time he committed the actus reus. The common law achieves this by allowing intoxication to sustain an argument of no mens rea but, at the same time, imposing restrictions on the availability of this argument to certain crimes only, crimes categorised as ones of specific intent.

INTOXICATION NEGATING MENS REA

■ The rule in Majewski

Evidence that the defendant was voluntarily intoxicated at the time he committed the actus reus of an offence may, in certain circumstances, result in a finding that the intoxication so affected the defendant's awareness of his actions and their consequences that he lacked the relevant mens rea and is, therefore, not liable. The leading authority is *Majewski*. D was charged with, inter alia, a s.47 assault on a police officer. He was intoxicated at the time, having consumed a large quantity of barbiturates, amphetamines and alcohol. The trial judge refused to allow evidence of D's intoxication to be relied on to support a submission of no mens rea. D appealed against conviction, ultimately to the House of Lords. Their Lordships, in dismissing the appeal, set out what has become known as the rule in *Majewski*: voluntary intoxication may be used as a "defence" (i.e. to assert that the prosecution cannot prove mens rea) in crimes of "*specific intent*" but not in crimes of "*basic intent.*" Applying this rule to the facts of the case, their Lordships held that as s.47 is a crime of basic intent intoxication was not available as a defence.

■ Is the rule in Majewski contrary to legal principle?

The reason given in *Majewski* for permitting intoxication as a defence to crimes of specific intent only was given by Lord Elwyn Jones L.C. as that the defendant is presumed to be reckless in voluntarily becoming intoxicated and this recklessness is sufficient mens rea for an offence of basic intent:

> "[The defendant's] course of conduct in reducing himself by drugs and drink to that condition in my view supplies the evidence of mens rea, of guilty mind certainly sufficient for crimes of basic intent. It is a reckless course of conduct and recklessness is enough to constitute the necessary mens rea in assault cases ... The drunkenness is itself an intrinsic integral part of the crime."

However, this rationale for rejecting intoxication as a defence in crimes of basic intent is, it is submitted, deeply flawed in respect of legal principle for the following reasons:

1. It conflicts with s.8 of the Criminal Justice Act 1967 which directs the court to have regard to *all the evidence* in deciding whether a person intended or foresaw the natural and probable result of his actions. Evidence that the defendant was intoxicated at the time of commission of the actus reus should, therefore, be taken into account in determining his mens rea. Lord Elwyn-Jones L.C. found a way around the potential conflict, however, by suggesting that the reference to "all the evidence" meant all the relevant evidence and, as there is a substantive rule of law that in crimes of basic intent evidence of intoxication is *irrelevant*, it cannot be taken into consideration under s.8.

2. There is no coincidence of actus reus and mens rea; the recklessness in becoming intoxicated does not coincide with the commission of the actus reus of the offence—it precedes it.

3. Lord Elwyn-Jones L.C. was attempting to equate two entirely different notions of recklessness; the defendant's recklessness in becoming intoxicated is in relation to the effects of the intoxicant, for example, his foresight that it will render him unable to control his actions, whereas the recklessness required for an offence involves foresight as to a particular consequence of one's actions, for example, foresight as to causing some harm.

Over to you...

Do you think it is correct to assume, as *Majewski* does, that a defendant whilst getting drunk is reckless; and that he is reckless even if he does not actually foresee the type of conduct in which he might later indulge?

The scope of the rule in Majewski

The rule in *Majewski* applies to:

1. voluntary intoxication only;
2. by drink or dangerous drugs; where

3. the defendant lacks mens rea; and
4. the crime is one of specific intent.

The rule applies to voluntary intoxication only

A defendant is voluntarily intoxicated where he knows he is ingesting an intoxicant, irrespective of whether he knows its precise nature or strength. Consequently, in **Allen [1988] Crim. L.R. 698**, the defendant was still treated as voluntarily intoxicated where he thought he was drinking low alcohol wine but had, in fact, been drinking wine with a high alcohol content.

Over to you...

Do you think the *Allen* decision is fair or too harsh and merely another policy decision? Ought a defendant who commits a crime having drunk two pints of lager, believing he was drinking low alcohol lager which would have little effect on him, but was in fact drinking extra strength lager, to be treated as voluntarily intoxicated? Is he truly reckless in such circumstances?

The rule applies to intoxication by alcohol or dangerous drugs

The rule in *Majewski* applies to voluntary intoxication by alcohol or by dangerous drugs (**Lipman [1970] 1 Q.B. 152**). In this case, the defendant had taken LSD and, during the "trip" that resulted, he killed his girlfriend, believing her to be a snake. He was found not liable for murder (a specific intent crime) though he was convicted of manslaughter (a basic intent crime) according to the rules (explained below on p.397) in respect of reducing liability. The rules relating to non-dangerous drugs are considered on p.398.

The defendant must lack mens rea

Majewski only assists a defendant who actually lacked the mens rea because of his intoxication; a drunken or drugged intent is still an intent (*Kingston*). The burden of proof lies on the prosecution to prove that, despite his intoxication, the defendant still formed the mens rea (**Sheehan [1975] 2 All E.R. 960**). It is not necessary for the jury to be satisfied that the defendant was incapable of forming the mens rea, merely that he did not form it (**Pordage [1975] Crim. L.R. 575**).

The crime charged must be one of specific intent

Voluntary intoxication may be used to support a submission of no mens rea in respect of crimes of specific intent but not crimes of basic intent. This raises two important issues:

1. how have the courts sought to define a crime of specific intent and
2. is it really logical to distinguish crimes in this way?

Distinguishing specific intent crimes from those of basic intent

Although the distinction between specific intent crimes and basic intent crimes is crucial to the operation of the *Majewski* Rule, there is, in fact, no general agreement on a single test for determining whether a crime is one of specific intent. Although the following tests have been suggested, it must be borne in mind that the classification of any individual offence is not completely settled until decided by the courts.

1. Lord Simon in *Majewski* suggested that specific intent requires "purposive intent"; i.e. direct intent. However, murder does not require a purposive intent but is classified as a specific intent offence.

2. A specific intent offence is one of "ulterior intent" (as suggested by dicta of Lord Simon in *Morgan*). An ulterior intent offence is one for which the mens rea extends beyond the actus reus, for example s.18 wounding for which the mens rea is intention to do grievous bodily harm. However, this test does not always produce a correct result (as Lord Simon himself acknowledged) as, for example, murder and causing GBH with intent to do so contrary to s.18 OAPA 1861 are crimes of specific intent but not of ulterior intent.

Despite the problems with each of the above two tests, Hughes L.J. in **Heard [2007] EWCA Crim 125** Heard curiously chose to define crimes of specific intent in such a way as to encompass both tests:

> "… Crimes of specific intent are those where the offence requires proof of purpose or consequence, which are not confined to, but amongst which are included, those where the purpose goes beyond the actus reus (sometimes referred to as cases of 'ulterior intent')."

3. In *Majewski*, it was suggested by three of their Lordships that, if recklessness suffices, the offence is one of basic intent whereas, if intention only suffices as to at least one element of the offence, the offence is one of specific intent. This approach gained support in **DPP v Caldwell [1981] 1 All E.R. 961** and is the test which produces a correct classification most often. Applying it does, for example, classify murder; s.18 wounding or causing GBH with intent to do GBH; theft; robbery; handling stolen goods and attempts as specific intent offences because they are not satisfied by recklessness and, indeed, the courts have agreed that each of these crimes is one of specific intent. Conversely, manslaughter; s.20; s.47; battery and assault, for example, are crimes of basic intent because they can be satisfied by recklessness and, again, the courts have stipulated that these are all crimes of basic intent. There are two categories of offences, however, where the test is either not conclusive or inapplicable; these are:

   (a) Criminal damage offences.
   (b) Certain sexual offences.

The mens rea for criminal damage offences is phrased in terms of intention or recklessness. As recklessness will suffice, they should all be categorised as crimes of basic intent. However, this is not the case. In the past, the courts have distinguished between criminal damage offences where the *charge* is phrased in terms of intention only and those where the charge is phrased in terms of intention or recklessness or recklessness only; the former have been treated as crimes of specific intent and the latter as crimes of basic intent. Following *Heard*, however, this distinction may only apply to the simple, not the aggravated offences. In *Heard*, the court suggested that criminal damage being reckless as to endangering life which, based on the above analysis ought to be classified as a crime of basic intent, is actually a crime of specific intent because it is one of ulterior intent (see above).

The test above falls down in respect of sexual offences contrary to ss.1–4 of the Sexual Offences Act 2003 because they are not phrased in terms of intention only or recklessness. Rape (definition amended by the 2003 Act) and indecent assault (replaced with the offence of sexual assault under s.3 of the Act) were formerly crimes of basic intent. It was unclear when the 2003 Act came into force whether rape would continue to be a crime of basic intent and whether sexual assault and the offences contrary to ss.2 and 4 (assault by penetration and causing a person to engage in sexual activity) would also be crimes of basic intent. For such offences, the mens rea in relation to the act constituting the actus reus of the offence is intention, for example intentional penetration or touching, but the mens rea requirement in relation to V's consent is phrased in terms of a lack of reasonable belief in consent. A belief in consent which is induced by intoxication is very unlikely to be considered a *reasonable* belief so it is unlikely that intoxication would actually be able to negate mens rea anyway but, in any event, reasonable belief does connote basic intent. It is an objective test (although with a subjective element to it also; see p.176), so this aspect of the mens rea is something between recklessness and negligence. If a mens rea of recklessness renders a crime one of basic intent, it must logically follow that if something less than recklessness suffices the crime is also one of basic intent.

However, will an offence phrased in terms of intention as to one element of the actus reus, but in terms of reasonable belief in respect of another, be one of specific or basic intent? This question was considered in *Heard*. D, whilst drunk, had exposed his penis and rubbed it against a police officer's leg. He was charged with sexual assault and argued that due to his voluntary intoxication he lacked the intention to touch. The Court of Appeal stated that:

"it is ... of very limited help to attempt to label [such offences] as a whole [as] of either basic or specific intent, because the state of mind which must be proved varies with the issue."

So, it would seem more helpful to consider whether an *element* of an offence requires no more than basic intent. However, the court held that intoxication was not available to negate mens rea, even in respect of the intention to touch, for the offence of sexual assault as "intentionally" in s.3 meant no more than that D's touching was not an accident. This means that both elements of the mens rea of sexual assault require basic intent only. It must follow that a defendant will also not be able to rely on his intoxication to plead no mens rea for rape and the other sexual offences under ss.2 and 4 SOA 2003.

Over to you...

Consider the impact of *Heard* on the classification of crimes as specific or basic intent. Do you think it has brought clarity to the law or made more pressing the need for statutory reform?

The Law Commission in Law Com. No.229, 1995 acknowledged the difficulties that a lack of a single, agreed test for crimes of specific intent can cause:

"[This] must inevitably lead to uncertainty, wasted court time and the unnecessary incurring of legal costs when a new offence is introduced, since, until the matter is decided by the courts, it will not be possible to ascertain into which category it falls."

It therefore recommended the abolition of the distinction between crimes of specific and basic intent (and did so again in its subsequent report in 2009, see further p.407).

Is the specific intent/basic intent distinction logical?

We saw above the various attempts to distinguish crimes of specific intent from those of basic intent but is the distinction itself a valid one to make? Is it not purely arbitrary to say that one offence is specific intent, for which the defendant can rely on his intoxication to negate mens rea, yet another is basic intent for which he cannot? Take, for example, non-fatal offences against the person. Section 18 wounding or causing GBH with intent is a crime of specific intent, whereas s.20 wounding or inflicting GBH is not. The only difference between these offences is that the latter can be satisfied by recklessness. However, a defendant may commit s.20 with a mens rea of intention to do some harm, rather than recklessness in that regard. Why should such a defendant be treated less favourably than a defendant who intended grievous bodily harm? Why should intoxication excuse one type of intention and not another? Many academics have criticised the specific/basic intent distinction. Ormerod, Smith and Hogan, *Criminal Law*, 12th edn, for example, describes it as "over-simplified." Jefferson, in his Textbook on Criminal Law, 9th edn, describes it as "capricious." The main problem with the distinction is the absence of any logic to it. This was recognised by Lord Salmon in *Majewski* but justified on the basis that, "... this is the view adopted by the common law of England, which is founded on common-sense and experience rather than strict logic." He was prepared to accept this illogicality:

". . Because the benevolent part of the rule [allowing intoxication to negate mens rea] removes undue harshness without imperilling safety and the stricter part of the rule [limiting the availability of the defence] works without imperilling justice. It would be just as ridiculous to remove the benevolent part of the rule (which no one suggests) as it would be to adopt the alternative of removing the stricter part of the rule for the sake of preserving absolute logic. Absolute logic in human affairs is an uncertain guide and a very dangerous master."

The specific/basic intent distinction does have some academic support. William Wilson, *Criminal Law Doctrine and Theory*, 3rd edn, paraphrasing Professor Ashworth, sees the distinction as, "a neat reconciliation ... between the mens rea principle and the policy of social defence" because, in practice, it is often the case that a defendant who relies on intoxication to negate mens rea in a crime of specific intent will still be convicted of a lesser basic intent offence (see below). But this justification does not apply to all crimes as it is not always the case that there is a lesser basic intent offence for which the defendant can be convicted; specific intent offences:

"are not restricted to those crimes in which the absence of a special intent leaves available a lesser crime embodying no special intent, but embraces all cases of special intent even though no alternative lesser criminal charge is available" (per Lord Russell in *Majewski*).

■ The operation of the rule in Majewski

Crimes of specific intent
Where a defendant successfully pleads no mens rea in relation to a crime of specific intent he will only be acquitted if there is no lesser included basic intent offence; if there is, he will be convicted of that offence instead. Thus, for example, a defendant who successfully raises his intoxication to a charge of murder will be convicted of manslaughter whereas a defendant who successfully raises his intoxication to a charge of theft will be acquitted.

Crimes of basic intent
It has already been established that intoxication may not be used to support a defence of no mens rea in crimes of basic intent. But what would be the consequence of attempting to do so? You will recall that Lord Elwyn-Jones L.C. stated in *Majewski* that the defendant's recklessness in becoming intoxicated constituted the necessary mens rea in offences of basic intent. Following *Majewski*, the view developed that a defendant who adduced evidence of his intoxication on a basic intent crime would in fact relieve the prosecution of the burden of proving mens rea; his recklessness in getting drunk would be sufficient. In effect, the offence became one of strict liability. It was always unclear whether, if this view was correct, the prosecution

might adduce evidence to prove the defendant's intoxication from the outset in order to satisfy the mens rea.

An alternative view has been taken more recently to the effect that evidence of intoxication is legally irrelevant in crimes of basic intent (**Woods (1981) 74 Cr. App. R. 312**)). Once intoxication is deemed irrelevant, the question then becomes: would the defendant have had the requisite mens rea had he not been intoxicated? This was the approach taken in **Aitken [1992] 1 W.L.R. 1006** and again in *Richardson and Irwin*. In the latter case, the defendants and V were university students. After drinking in the Students' Union, they went to the flat of one of the defendants. There was some horseplay and the defendants lifted V over the edge of the balcony and dropped him. He fell several feet and sustained GBH. The defendants were convicted of s.20 and appealed. The Court of Appeal quashed their convictions on the basis of a misdirection by the recorder at the trial to the effect that the jury should decide whether the reasonable sober man would have foreseen some harm; the correct direction to the jury ought to have been that they had to be sure the defendants would have foreseen this risk had they been sober. (See p.404 below where this case is also considered in relation to mistaken belief in consent.)

It follows from *Richardson and Irwin* that if there was some special factor or circumstance other than intoxication which could have caused the defendant to make the same mistake or fail to appreciate the risk involved in his actions, so that he would not have foreseen the risk even if he had been sober, the defendant would not be liable. An example of such a factor would seem to be the low IQ of the defendant.

Over to you...

Do you think the initial convictions of *Richardson and Irwin* were unsafe despite the misdirection? Is it not likely that if they were sober they would have foreseen that dangling V over the edge of a balcony posed a risk of some harm to him?

THE DISTINCTION BETWEEN "DANGEROUS" AND "SOPORIFIC" DRUGS

Following the case of **Hardie [1985] 1 W.L.R. 64**, the rule in *Majewski*, disallowing evidence of intoxication to negate mens rea in crimes of basic intent, does not apply to cases where the self-induced intoxication is caused by a non-dangerous drug (i.e. one which is not likely to cause aggression, unpredictability or uncontrolled conduct) such as a sedative or soporific type drug. The reason given by the Court of Appeal for treating sedative drugs differently from dangerous drugs was that the former type is wholly different in kind from the latter and the effects of such drugs are not generally known.

Hardie had become upset after his girlfriend left him and took several of his girlfriend's old Valium tablets. He was told that the Valium (a sedative drug) would calm his nerves and do no harm. However, he became intoxicated and started a fire in his girlfriend's flat when she was inside. He was charged with criminal damage with intent or recklessness as to endangering life (then classified as a basic intent offence) and argued that the effect of taking the Valium was that he lacked the requisite mens rea. He was convicted and his conviction was quashed by the Court of Appeal which stated that if the defendant's intoxication was self-induced at the time of the actus reus due to taking a soporific drug e.g. Valium, so that he lacked the mens rea for the offence, he ought to be acquitted provided he was not reckless in taking the drug. The type of recklessness was not specified but is, it is submitted, subjective given the court's reference to *Bailey* (pp.411–412) and in light of the decision in *R. v G* (p.61) highlighting the general trend in the criminal law towards subjectivism. Recklessness in this context relates to the effect of the drug on the defendant, not as to foresight of the commission of any offence. Hence, the defendant must be aware that taking the drug may lead to aggressive, unpredictable and uncontrolled conduct (exactly the same as in self-induced automatism, see p.411).

The effect of *Hardie* would seem to be that a defendant who *recklessly* ingests a soporific drug will be treated as voluntarily intoxicated but the defendant who is not reckless in taking such a drug will be treated as involuntarily intoxicated, even though his intoxication is self-induced.

Hardie was charged with a basic intent offence but what would be the position if a defendant in similar circumstances was charged with a specific intent offence? If the defendant's intoxication is not voluntary because he is not reckless it should not matter whether he is charged with a basic intent offence or a specific intent offence (see p.401 below). To hold otherwise, would mean that a defendant charged with a specific intent crime for which there is a lesser basic intent offence would, under the *Majewski* Rule, be convicted of that instead whereas, had he been charged with a basic intent offence, he would have been acquitted under *Hardie*. It is possible to argue that, like *Bailey*, *Hardie* was actually a case of self-induced automatism caused by a non-dangerous drug (see pp.411–412) rather than, as most commentators suggest, a case of involuntary intoxication. However, even if the correct defence was self-induced automatism, applying the rules set out in *Bailey* (see p.411) would result in a complete acquittal on a specific intent offence charge. Thus, it is submitted that whatever the exact nature of the defence, be it involuntary intoxication or self-induced automatism, the principle in *Hardie* applies to both basic intent and specific intent offences.

Over to you...

Hardie poses potential problems for the courts in future. How do you think they would deal with the following, for example:

1. **Classifying a drug which is normally considered dangerous but which has a soporific effect and does not make the user aggressive and unpredictable, for example heroin?**
2. **The situation where the defendant has taken a cocktail of drugs, some of which are dangerous and some of which are merely soporific, for example, tranquillizers taken in conjunction with alcohol?**

Do you think public policy considerations would most likely favour applying the rule in *Majewski*?

INTOXICATION INDUCED TO GIVE "DUTCH COURAGE"

The rule in *Majewski* does not assist a defendant who, having decided to commit an offence, deliberately becomes intoxicated in order to give himself the courage to commit it. In such circumstances, even if the crime is one of specific intent, the defendant cannot use evidence of his intoxication to plead no mens rea (**Attorney General for Northern Ireland v Gallagher [1963] A.C. 349**). As Lord Denning stated in *Gallagher* (a case involving a defendant who, having first decided to kill his wife, drank a bottle of whisky before killing her):

"If a man, whilst sane and sober, forms an intention to kill and makes preparation for it, knowing it is a wrong thing to do, and then gets himself drunk so as to give himself Dutch courage to do the killing, and whilst drunk carries out his intention, he cannot rely on this self-induced drunkenness as a defence to a charge of murder, nor even as reducing it to manslaughter. He cannot say that he got himself into such a stupid state that he was incapable of an intent to kill ... The wickedness of his mind before he got drunk is enough to condemn him, coupled with the act which he intended to do and did do."

Although the decision in *Gallagher* conflicts with the basic principle of contemporaneity of actus reus and mens rea (D's mens rea precedes the actus reus), it is thought that it can be justified on policy grounds. Ormerod, Smith and Hogan, *Criminal Law*, 12th edn, argues that the defendant in such circumstances is akin to someone who is liable as principal where he induces an innocent agent, an irresponsible person, to commit an offence; the defendant who has formed the mens rea whilst sober and is, therefore, responsible, should be liable for the foreseen and intended acts of the irresponsible defendant he becomes.

INTOXICATION AND ACCIDENTS

There is no ratio on whether a defendant, who accidentally commits what would otherwise be an offence if committed deliberately, is liable if he did so whilst intoxicated. In an obiter statement in *Heard*, Hughes L.J. suggested that as "a drunken intent is still an intent", the corollary [is] that a drunken accident is still an accident." Hughes L.J. cited as an example, the intoxicated defendant whose control of his limbs is unco-ordinated or impaired so that, as a result, he accidentally stumbles against another person touching him/her in a way which, objectively viewed, is sexual. His view was that if this would not be an offence if committed whilst sober, it would not be an offence to do so whilst intoxicated as,

> "[t]he intoxication, in such a situation, has not impacted on intention. Intention is simply not in question. What is in question is impairment of control of the limbs."

Hughes L.J.'s example related to liability for sexual assault but presumably is not limited to this offence.

Involuntary Intoxication

The position with regard to involuntary intoxication where the defendant's drink is "spiked" was set out by the House of Lords in *Kingston*. X, in order to blackmail D, a homosexual paedophile, invited him to his flat where he laced his drink. X had also lured back to the flat a 15-year-old boy whom he had then drugged. Whilst the boy was asleep, X invited D to sexually abuse the boy. D did so and was photographed and taped by X. D was charged with indecent assault and asserted that he remembered nothing after seeing the boy lying on the bed. He was convicted on the basis that, notwithstanding his involuntary intoxication, he had still formed the mens rea for indecent assault. His conviction was quashed by the Court of Appeal on the basis that a defendant who is not to blame for becoming intoxicated should not be liable for an offence he commits with mens rea if he would not have formed the mens rea had he been sober; he should be excused "because the operative fault is not his." The prosecution then appealed to the House of Lords which reinstated the conviction. Their Lordships considered it irrelevant that the defendant had been unable to resist his paedophilic impulses or was involuntarily intoxicated; he had formed the mens rea and was, therefore, liable—a drugged intent is still an intent. The court stated that involuntary intoxication would be a defence, however, to any crime, be it of specific or basic intent, provided that it meant the defendant did not form the mens rea for the offence.

As was seen above on pp.398–399, self-induced intoxication by a soporific drug may also be treated as involuntary intoxication, the relevant question being whether the defendant was reckless in becoming intoxicated. Similarly, self-induced intoxication by taking drugs for prescribed medical purposes or taking a dangerous drug mistakenly believing it to be a non-dangerous one is treated as involuntary intoxication, the position being the same as that set out in *Kingston*.

FIGURE 12.1 **Intoxication**

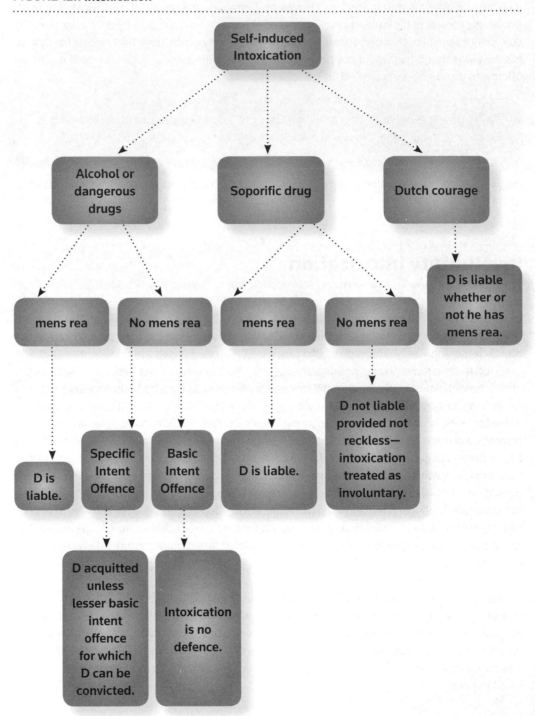

Intoxicated Mistaken Beliefs

Thus far, we have considered the availability of intoxication as a defence. We now consider the situation where the intoxication has given rise to a mistaken belief upon which the defendant has acted.

MISTAKES DUE TO VOLUNTARY INTOXICATION

■ Mistake as to identity

An intoxicated mistaken belief as to the identity of one's victim is no defence even if no offence would have been committed had the facts been as the defendant assumed them to be. In **Fotheringham (1988) 88 Cr. App. R. 206**, following an evening of heavy drinking, D got into bed and without her consent had sex with the woman lying there. D believed the woman was his wife but she was, in fact, the 14-year-old babysitter whom his wife had told to sleep in the marital bed. He was convicted of rape even though, had the victim been, as he believed, his wife, no offence would have been committed as, at that time, it was not possible to rape one's wife.

■ Mistake as to duress

D's assertion that he injured V in the mistaken belief that he did so under duress will only provide D with a defence if the mistake was a reasonable one to make in the circumstances (*Hasan*). Hence, an intoxicated, and therefore unreasonable, mistaken belief as to duress will not excuse a defendant.

■ Mistake which provides a lawful excuse under the Criminal Damage Act 1971

Section 5(2) of the Criminal Damage Act 1971 provides the defendant with a lawful excuse to criminal damage where he believed he had consent to damage the property in question or believed he did so in order to protect property in immediate need of protection. Section 5(3) further provides that it is irrelevant whether such a belief is justified, provided it is honestly held. This means that it does not have to be a sober belief (**Jaggard v Dickinson [1980] 3 All E.R. 716**, see p.309). So, voluntary intoxication may be used to explain why the defendant held a belief sufficient for a lawful excuse to criminal damage but voluntary intoxication can not be used to negate the mens rea for criminal damage as this is a crime of basic intent (unless the prosecution alleges intentional damage only, see p.396)!

■ Mistake as to a justificatory defence

Jaggard v Dickinson concerned a statutory excuse. The courts (and now statute) have adopted a different approach where voluntary intoxication gives rise to a belief which, if held by a sober person, would provide a justificatory defence at common law, for example a belief in the need to use force in self-defence (this defence is considered in Ch.13).

In **O'Grady [1987] Q.B. 995**, D, who had fallen asleep in his flat after drinking heavily with his friend, V, awoke, he claimed, to find V attacking him with a piece of glass. D, believing he was acting in self-defence, picked up a piece of glass and attacked V with it. V died from the injuries he sustained in the attack. D was convicted of V's manslaughter and appealed. He argued that the reasonableness of the force used to act in self-defence should be assessed on the basis of his drunken mistaken belief as to the amount of force required. He was unsuccessful. The Court of Appeal stated that a mistaken belief induced by voluntary intoxication that one is being attacked, or as to the severity of an attack, will not afford a defence even to a crime of specific intent. The statement was, presumably, obiter because the defendant was appealing against his conviction for manslaughter, a basic intent offence.

However, *O'Grady* was followed by the Court of Appeal in **O'Connor [1991] Crim. L.R. 135** and in **Hatton [2006] 1 Cr. App. R. 16**, in which the court rejected the suggestion that the statements in *O'Grady* were simply obiter and applied the principle therein to the specific intent offence of murder.

The decision in *O'Grady* was difficult to justify for the following reasons:

1. Its effect was that if the defendant was so intoxicated that he lacked the mens rea for a crime of specific intent such as murder, he was not liable for that offence but, if he was drunk and believed that he was defending himself when he killed, he could not rely on his mistaken belief in self-defence.
2. We saw on p.386 that the word "unlawful" is part of the definition of offences of violence. Consequently, where D injures V, mistakenly believing he is acting in self-defence, he does not intend to act unlawfully and, therefore, lacks the mens rea for the crime, whether or not his mistake is reasonable. On this basis, it should be irrelevant that D's mistake arose from his voluntary intoxication. The intoxicated defendant should still be able to argue that, although he intended, for example, to kill he did not intend to unlawfully kill and so lacked the mens rea for murder.

In spite of the criticisms of *O'Grady* Parliament, in its recent review of self-defence and the statutory defence of prevention of crime (Criminal Law Act 1967 s.3), chose to maintain the status quo and enacted s.76(5) of the Criminal Justice and Immigration Act 2008 which restates the common law position that a mistaken belief in the need to act in self-defence which is due to voluntary intoxication cannot be relied upon. The Act makes clear that this is also the case where the defendant relies upon a mistaken belief in the need to act in prevention of crime.

■ Mistake as to consent

In *Richardson and Irwin* (see p.398), the defendants argued that in their intoxicated state they mistakenly believed the victim had consented to their horseplay. The Court of Appeal, without considering *O'Grady*, stated, obiter, that evidence of intoxication could be taken into account on the issue of the defendants' mistaken belief in the victim's consent, even though they were charged with a basic intent offence. This must surely be on the basis that a mistaken belief in consent would negate the mens rea (of foresight of *unlawful* harm) but this was precisely what the court in *O'Grady* said would not be permitted in relation to self-defence!

The foregoing analysis of intoxicated mistakes illustrates that the courts adopt differing approaches depending on the nature of the mistaken belief. There is clearly a need for a consistent approach. The Law Commission recognise this and their most recent reform proposals, "Intoxication and Criminal Liability" (Law Com. No.314), would prevent D relying on a genuine mistake of fact arising from voluntary intoxication in support of *any* defence unless D would have held the same belief had he not been intoxicated. (This approach is in line with that taken in *Richardson* and *Irwin* in respect of a voluntarily intoxicated defendant charged with an offence of basic intent.)

MISTAKES DUE TO INVOLUNTARY INTOXICATION

There is no case law on the point but, clearly, the policy arguments against allowing such mistakes are much less strong than for voluntary intoxication. Even s.76.(5) of the Criminal Justice and Immigration Act 2008 (see above) which confirms the harsh position in *O'Grady* concerning an intoxicated mistake as to self-defence or prevention of crime refers specifically to a mistake of fact which is due to *voluntary* intoxication. Presumably, therefore, such an intoxicated mistake caused by involuntary intoxication would afford a defence. Where the law allows D to rely on a mistake due to voluntary intoxication, as in the case of consent, it will, no doubt, also allow D to rely on one due to involuntary intoxication. Further, where the law requires a mistake to have been based on reasonable grounds, such as in duress, the courts have only specified that a mistake which is due to voluntary intoxication is unreasonable. We would submit, therefore, that D can rely on any mistake of fact which is due to involuntary intoxication. This would be in line with the Law Commission's recent proposals (Law Com. No. 314) which recommend that any mistake of fact due to involuntary intoxication can be relied upon to support a defence.

Intoxication Giving Rise to Automatism or Insanity

Where the defendant's intoxication renders him an automaton, his defence is intoxication, not automatism. Similarly, where intoxication brings on a "disease of the mind", for example delirium tremens, so that the defendant is insane as defined by the *M'Naghten* Rules (see p.414), his defence is insanity rather than intoxication (**Davis (1881) 14 Cox C.C. 563**).

Reform

As can be seen from the foregoing analysis of the rules concerning intoxication as a defence under the English criminal law, the law is a mass of inconsistency, lacks any logic and is rooted firmly in policy. The theoretical difficulties with the current law (they may not be recognised in practice, see below) have been acknowledged by the judiciary—Lord Mustill, for example, speaking in *Kingston* said:

> "This area of the law is controversial, as regards the content of the rules, their intellectual foundations, and their capacity to furnish a practical and just solution"

—and by the Law Commission which has reported on intoxication on several occasions but without any sign, as yet, from Parliament of a willingness to implement its suggestions. The following is a summary of the main reform proposals.

ABOLITION OF THE MAJEWSKI RULE

Abolishing the *Majewski* Rule on intoxication might sound radical but is not entirely untested or without merit. Some Australian states, New Zealand and South Africa have all taken just such an approach without any apparent descent into lawlessness. Abolition would remove the distinction between crimes of specific and basic intent, leaving the only question being one for the jury to consider: did the defendant, whatever his state of intoxication, perform a voluntary act and do so with the mens rea for that crime? Academic support for such an approach comes from C.N. Mitchell, "The Intoxicated Offender—Refuting the Legal and Medical Myths" (1988) Int J Law and Psych 77. Mitchell argues that the intoxication rules are unnecessary as they are all based on the fallacy that intoxication causes aggression and negates intent whereas scientific research actually demonstrates that intoxicated people almost always know what they are doing and do exactly what they intend. This view seems to be borne out in practice in those jurisdictions which have abolished the rules on intoxication. It appears that complete acquittal due to intoxication is very uncommon there. Orchard, "Surviving Without Majewski—A View from Down Under" [1993] Crim. L.R. 427, suggests that this may be due partly to judges and juries being unwilling to:

> "... Give effect to what they regard as an unmeritorious principle, but it also reflects the reality that while intoxication may often contribute to and explain intentional offending it will seldom result in the absence of the modest mental requirements of intention, awareness and foresight that generally suffice for mens rea."

The Law Commission briefly flirted with the idea of abolition in its 1993 Consultation Paper, "Intoxication and Criminal Liability", but had changed its mind by the time its 1995 Report, "Legislating the Criminal Code: Intoxication and Criminal Liability" (Law Com. No.229), was published. This was due to a negative response to the proposals from the judiciary who considered the general public would not accept acquittals on grounds of no mens rea and that the current law actually worked well and fairly in practice.

CREATION OF AN OFFENCE OF DANGEROUS OR CRIMINAL INTOXICATION

In 1975, the Butler Committee suggested creation of the strict liability offence of dangerous intoxication. The Law Commission, in its 1993 Consultation Paper, suggested reform along similar lines with the creation of an offence of criminal intoxication but accompanied by abolition of the *Majewski* Rule. Such reform would have permitted a defendant to plead lack of mens rea due to intoxication as a defence to any crime. If believed, he would be acquitted but convicted of criminal intoxication instead. However, as explained above, such reform proposals failed to make it into the final report.

CODIFICATION

The Law Commission in its 1995 Report suggested codification, essentially of the status quo, but with some clarification and minor modifications: the distinction between specific and basic intent offences would be abolished and voluntary intoxication would only be capable of negating the mens rea of offences of intention but not those offences which could be satisfied by recklessness. A major criticism of the report was that, in seeking to produce a comprehensive Code for intoxication, the Law Commission's proposals were too complex.

In 2009, the Law Commission produced a further report on reform of intoxication entitled "Intoxication and Criminal Liability" (Law Com. No.314) which can be viewed online at *http://www.lawcom.gov.uk/docs/lc314.pdf*. The report proposed a "Criminal Liability (Intoxication) Bill" which would, in the words of the Law Commission:

> "Have the great merit of making the law consistent, coherent and much easier to apply, in cases where at present it is uncertain."

The Law Commission state that they still consider codification, clarification and modification is the correct approach but attempt to address the criticism of their 1995 report by not seeking legislative reform of *all* aspects of the law of intoxication. The proposals contained in the Bill would have the following effect:

■ Voluntary Intoxication

1. Voluntary intoxication is defined as any intoxication which is not involuntary or almost entirely involuntary.
2. Where D takes a drug as a result of addiction, his intoxication would be treated as voluntary.
3. The classification of offences as either specific or basic intent would cease.
4. Where the *prosecution* allege that D was voluntarily intoxicated at the material time, D would be presumed not to be so and the prosecution would have to prove beyond a reasonable doubt that D was intoxicated at that time. Where it is proved by the prosecution (or admitted) that D was intoxicated, there would be a further presumption that the intoxication was voluntary.

5. Where the *defendant* claims to have been intoxicated at the material time, D would be presumed not to have been so and would bear an evidential burden in support of his/her claim to have been intoxicated at that time.

6. The *Majewski* Rule would become a "general rule" that if D is charged with committing an offence as principal and the fault element (mens rea) is not an "integral fault element", for example it merely requires proof of recklessness, and D was voluntarily intoxicated at the relevant time, D should be treated as having been aware of anything which he/she would have been aware of but for the intoxication. Certain "integral fault elements" would be excluded from the general rule. These are: intention, knowledge, belief (where it is equivalent to knowledge), fraud, and dishonesty. Where the integral fault element is phrased in such terms, the prosecution would have to prove D acted with that relevant state of mind.

7. There would no longer be a distinction drawn between soporific and dangerous drugs. Hence, a defendant in the position of *Hardie* would now be treated as voluntarily intoxicated.

8. D would not be able to rely on a genuine mistake of fact arising from voluntary intoxication in support of a defence unless D would have held the same belief had he not been intoxicated. This would be so even in the case of a statutory provision phrased in terms of "honest belief" such as s.5 of the Criminal Damage Act 1971.

9. The report also makes recommendations in respect of secondary liability, liability under Pt 2 of the Serious Crime Act 2007 and inchoate liability which are beyond the scope of this text.

■ Involuntary Intoxication

1. Involuntary intoxication is defined as any intoxication which is entirely, or almost entirely, involuntary.

2. Where the prosecution allege that D was voluntarily intoxicated at the material time and D contends that the intoxication was involuntary, it is for D to prove this on the balance of probability.

3. Where the defence contends that D was intoxicated at the material time, discharges the evidential burden and D is subsequently taken to be so, it would be presumed that the intoxication was voluntary. If D wished then to contend that the intoxication was involuntary, it would be for D to prove this on the balance of probability.

4. The current position on the availability of the defence (the rule in *Kingston*) would be maintained.

5. D would be able to rely on any mistake of fact which was due to involuntary intoxication to support a defence.

6. There would be a non-exhaustive list of situations which would count as involuntary intoxication. This list would include those situations where: D reasonably believed: what he had taken was not an intoxicant; the substance was administered without consent or under duress and the substance was taken for a "proper medical purpose" i.e. it was a properly authorised/licensed drug taken on medical advice or in accordance with

the accompanying instructions or, if not so taken, it was reasonable for D to have taken it.

Over to you...

Do you think such reforms if implemented would achieve their stated aim of making the law on intoxication "consistent, coherent and much easier to apply"?

Automatism

Introduction

Almost always, the actus reus of a crime involves conduct on the part of the defendant. Such conduct must be willed, or voluntary, before it can form the basis of criminal liability. Therefore, where such conduct is involuntary, the defendant may escape liability. Conduct may be involuntary where it is caused by a state of automatism. Automatism may be classified as either sane automatism (normally referred to simply as *automatism*) which, subject to any argument that the defendant was responsible for his state of automatism, will result in a complete acquittal, or insane automatism (normally referred to as *insanity*) which results in a finding of not guilty by reason of insanity (see p.413).

What is Automatism?

In **Bratty v Attorney General, for N Ireland [1963] A.C. 386**, Lord Denning stated that automatism means:

"... An act which is done by the muscles without any control by the mind, such as a spasm, a reflex action or a convulsion; or an act done by a person who is not conscious of what he is doing, such as an act done whilst suffering from concussion or whilst sleepwalking."

Essentially, what is required is that the defendant's mind has no control over his limbs.

A Denial of Actus Reus or Mens Rea?

Where a defendant claims automatism, what is the basis of his claim: that he lacked mens rea or committed no actus reus or is it both? The answer depends upon whether voluntariness is viewed merely as a mental concept—no mens rea—because the defendant's mind did not control his body—or as an actus reus concept—because the defendant's actions were not willed—or as both. Unfortunately, there is no definitive answer. It is submitted that the defence is one of denial of actus reus only. As automatism is thought to be available as a defence to crimes of strict liability, this supports the argument that the defence does not involve a denial of mens rea; mens rea not being required for crimes of strict liability.

Requirements for the Defence to Succeed

The defence of automatism is only available where the following two conditions are satisfied:

1. there was a total loss of voluntary control; and
2. this was caused by an external factor.

TOTAL LOSS OF VOLUNTARY CONTROL

Automatism requires a total destruction of voluntary control; it is insufficient that the defendant still retained impaired or partial control over his actions. Consequently, the defence failed in **Broome v Perkins [1987] Crim. L.R. 271** where the defendant still maintained some control over his driving. The defendant was charged with driving without due care and attention and claimed that he had been in a hypoglycaemic condition (this is very low blood sugar levels) when he committed the offence. The Court of Appeal held that the evidence showed that his actions had only been automatic at intervals and at other times they had not as his mind had been controlling his limbs. Because he had not been in a state of automatism throughout his journey, he could not rely on the defence. Although this seems harsh, the decision was followed in **Attorney General's Reference (No.2 of 1992) [1994] Q.B. 91** in which a defendant who had driven in a trance-like state was unable to rely on automatism as a defence because his awareness was merely reduced.

CAUSED BY AN EXTERNAL FACTOR

Where automatism is caused by a disease of the mind, the defence is one of insane automatism (insanity) rather than sane automatism. Consequently, it is important to determine the cause of the automatism. The current test for distinguishing the two defences stems from the case of **Quick [1973] Q.B. 910**, in which the Court of Appeal explained what would not constitute a disease of the mind and, by implication, what *would* constitute sane automatism:

"A malfunctioning of the mind of transitory effect caused by the application to the body of some external factor such as violence, drugs, including anaesthetics, alcohol and hypnotic influences cannot fairly be said to be due to disease."

Hence, the courts draw a distinction between an external factor such as a blow to the head, anaesthetic, an attack by a swarm of bees resulting in a reflex spasm (**Hill and Baxter [1958] 1 Q.B. 277**), injecting insulin (*Quick*) or hypnosis (*Quick*) which gives rise to a defence of sane automatism, and factors which are internal or inherent in the form of disease, such as epilepsy, which give rise to a finding of insanity. The distinction, and its implications, are explored further under the defence of insanity.

Self-induced Automatism

Where the defendant is in some way responsible for becoming an automaton, for example, he takes a non-prescribed drug or takes too much of one which has been prescribed; is a diabetic who fails to eat after taking insulin; or takes alcohol against medical advice whilst on medication, the automatism is classified as being self-induced and the following rules apply.

AUTOMATISM CAUSED BY ALCOHOL OR DANGEROUS DRUGS

Where the ingestion of alcohol or dangerous drugs causes the automatism, the defence is one of intoxication to which the intoxication rule in *Majewski* applies (see p.392).

AUTOMATISM CAUSED BY OTHER EXTERNAL FACTORS

◼ Crimes of specific intent

In *Bailey*, the court held that where the defendant's automatism is self-induced and he is charged with a specific intent offence, he must be acquitted; the crime is not reduced to a lower basic intent alternative (unlike under *Majewski*). This is the rule even if the defendant is reckless in becoming an automaton.

As we noted on p.399, it is not completely clear whether the correct defence in respect of a defendant who commits an offence whilst intoxicated by a non-dangerous drug such as the sedative drug Valium (as was the case in *Hardie*) is self-induced automatism or involuntary intoxication. If it is the former, the operation of the rule in *Bailey* set out immediately above would result in an acquittal for an offence of specific intent whether or not D was reckless in taking the drug. If it is the latter, although the position is not settled, it is also likely to lead to an acquittal (see further the discussion on p.399).

◼ Crimes of basic intent

Where the defendant's automatism is self-induced and he is charged with a basic intent offence, he will not be convicted unless he was reckless as to becoming aggressive, unpredictable or uncontrolled (*Bailey*).

The facts of *Bailey* illustrate the operation of the rules where the automatism is caused by an external factor other than alcohol or dangerous drugs. D struck V on the head with a metal bar and was charged with wounding under both ss.18 and 20 of the Offences Against the Person Act 1861. His defence was automatism—that he was suffering from hypoglycaemia (low blood sugar) at the relevant time, caused by failing to eat sufficient food after taking insulin. The Court of Appeal stated obiter (the court found that insufficient evidence was adduced that D was actually in a state of automatism) that, if D was an automaton, he ought not to be convicted of the s.18 offence as this was one of specific intent. Further, he ought also to be able to rely on the defence in relation to the s.20 wounding (a basic intent offence) as it was not common knowledge amongst diabetics that a failure to eat sufficient food after taking insulin could lead to aggressive, unpredictable or uncontrolled behaviour. This being the case, D would not be reckless if he himself did not appreciate this risk.

It is not completely settled which type of recklessness is required to exclude the defence. In *Bailey*, the type of reckless referred to was subjective (did he foresee the risk?). However, in *Quick*, the court had previously applied a test of objective recklessness in self-induced automatism (should he have foreseen the risk?). There is, therefore, no clear authority on the point but, following the decision of their Lordships in *R. v G* highlighting the general trend in the criminal law towards subjectivism, it is submitted that the test would be one of subjective recklessness.

Over to you...

In 1983 when *Bailey* was decided, the court was of the view that the defendant was not reckless because the possible consequences of a failure to eat after taking insulin were not then common knowledge amongst diabetics. Is that still likely to be the case and might a defendant in *Bailey's* position today be convicted?

Reform

The Draft Criminal Code (Law Com. No.177, 1989) proposes, essentially, maintaining the status quo though with a move from a requirement of total loss of control to loss of *effective* control. The Code would define a state of automatism as:

1. a reflex, spasm or convulsion; or
2. [one which] occurs while [the defendant] is in a condition (whether of sleep, unconsciousness, impaired consciousness or otherwise) depriving him of effective control of his act;

and the act or condition is the result neither of anything done or omitted with the fault required for the offence nor of voluntary intoxication.

Insanity

Introduction

Where the defendant asserts he was insane at the time of commission of the relevant offence, he may rely on the common law defence of insane automatism, or insanity as it is more commonly known. The defence is available to all crimes. The Divisional Court held in **DPP v Harper [1997] 1 W.L.R. 1406** that the defence does not apply to crimes of strict liability but that contradicts the Court of Appeal's decision in *Hennessey* and, therefore, must be wrongly decided. A successful plea results in a finding of not guilty by reason of insanity (Criminal Procedure (Insanity) Act 1964 s.1). Where the defendant asserts that he is insane by the time of the trial itself, the defence is one of "unfitness to plead" rather than insanity. This defence is discussed on p.423.

The Burden of Proof

As all defendants are presumed sane (see the *M'Naghten* Rules below), the defendant bears the burden of proving (as an exception to the rule in *Woolmington*) that he was insane when he committed the offence, the standard of proof being on the balance of probability.

The Importance of the Distinction between Sane and Insane Automatism

A defendant who successfully relies upon sane automatism will be acquitted (subject to any argument that the automatism was self-induced). Where, however, the defendant is found to have suffered from insane automatism, the correct verdict is the "special verdict" of not guilty by reason of insanity. The latter verdict can result in severe consequences for a defendant. Prior to the Criminal Procedure (Insanity) and Unfitness to Plead Act 1991, the trial judge had no discretion on sentencing the insane offender; he had to order an indefinite period of detention in a secure mental hospital. The 1991 Act now gives the trial judge a range of sentencing options ranging from an absolute discharge, a guardianship order or a supervision and treatment order but still extending to include compulsory, indefinite detention in a secure mental hospital. However, under s.5(3) of the Criminal Procedure (Insanity) Act 1964 (as amended by the Domestic Violence, Crime and Victims Act 2004) the court may only impose such an indefinite period of detention (even for murder) if there is medical evidence which justifies detention in hospital, i.e. evidence that the defendant suffers from a mental disorder which requires specialist treatment. Despite these recent sentencing reforms, an acquittal on grounds of automatism is still preferable to a finding of not guilty by reason of insanity and a defendant will always seek to argue that he was a sane, not an insane, automaton.

The Legal Definition of Insanity

Insanity is governed by the terms of the **M'Naghten Rules (1843) 4 St.Tr.(N.S.) 847**. These provide the *legal* definition of insanity. This definition is so narrow that, in many instances, a defendant who is mentally disordered will not be able to bring himself within the scope of the defence. The narrow definition, the possibility of a harsh sentencing outcome (see above) and also the availability of diminished responsibility as a defence to murder, mean that insanity is infrequently pleaded. It is worth noting, however, that since the more flexible sentencing regime came into operation there has been a slight gradual increase in insanity pleas (see R.D. Mackay, B.J. Mitchell and Leonie Howe: "Yet More Facts about the Insanity Defence" [2006] Crim. L.R. 399).

Before the jury may make a finding as to insanity, the court must hear evidence from at least two medical practitioners, one of whom must be an expert in mental disorder approved by the Home Secretary (Criminal Procedure (Insanity) and Unfitness to Plead Act 1991 s.1).

THE M'NAGHTEN RULES

The *M'Naghten* Rules were set out by House of Lords' judges in 1843 following public outrage over the successful appeal on grounds of insanity of Daniel M'Naghten. *M'Naghten* had intended to kill Robert Peel but, by mistake, killed Peel's secretary. The Rules are not strictly binding but have been followed ever since. They provide that a defendant wishing to rely on the defence of insanity must prove that:

1. he laboured under a defect of reason;
2. caused by a disease of the mind; so that *either*
3. he did not know the nature and quality of his act or, ***alternatively,*** he did not know what he was doing was wrong.

■ Defect of reason

The disease of the mind must have prevented the defendant, or made him incapable of, exercising his powers of reasoning; mere failure to exercise such powers due to absent-mindedness or lack of concentration is insufficient (**Clarke [1972] 1 All E.R. 219**).

■ Disease of the mind

The issue of whether a particular condition is a disease of the mind is one of law for the trial judge (**Kemp [1957] 1 Q.B. 399**). In *Quick*, the court suggested that a disease of the mind is any disease which produces a malfunctioning of the *mind* (in the sense of the faculties of reason, memory and understanding (**Sullivan [1984] A.C. 156**)). So, the condition need not be a disease of the brain. Nor is it relevant that the condition is curable or even temporary (*Kemp*). Conditions which have been held to constitute a disease of the mind include epilepsy, arteriosclerosis, brain tumour, manic depression, schizophrenia, diabetes and sleepwalking. The inclusion in the list of conditions such as epilepsy, diabetes and sleepwalking might seem surprising. The reason for their classification as diseases of the mind is, however, due to the operation of the external/internal factor test which was discussed briefly on p.411 and is now explored more fully.

The External/Internal Factor Test

As explained on p.412 the courts distinguish sane automatism from insanity by the operation of the external/internal factor test. This means that a condition caused by an *external* factor may give rise to the defence of *automatism* and a condition caused by an *internal* factor will constitute a *disease of the mind*, bringing the defendant within the scope of the defence of *insanity*. The facts of *Quick*, in which the test was developed, illustrate the distinction. D was a diabetic who assaulted V whilst suffering from a hypoglycaemic episode. The hypoglycaemia was caused by his taking insulin (an external factor) and then failing to eat. D claimed that he had been a sane automaton at the time of the assault. The Court of Appeal quashed D's conviction for assault occasioning actual bodily harm, holding that he had been a sane automaton due to the external factor of the insulin injection, rather than the internal factor of the disease of diabetes itself (which would have constituted a disease of the mind).

The courts' rigid adherence to the external/internal factor test has led to some bizarre distinctions and decisions, as illustrated below.

Diabetes

As we saw in *Quick*, a defendant who takes his insulin but fails to eat is treated by the courts as a sane automaton. However, a defendant who takes insufficient insulin is treated as having been an insane automaton (**Hennessey [1989] 1 W.L.R. 287**). Hennessey was charged with taking a conveyance without authority and driving whilst disqualified. He had been suffering from stress and depression which, he argued, was the reason he had failed to eat or take his proper dose of insulin which, in turn, had caused a rise in his blood sugar level and the condition known as hyperglycaemia. The Court of Appeal refused to treat the stress or depression as external factors and held that the hyperglycaemia was caused by the internal factor of the diabetes; the correct defence was insanity, not sane automatism. The Criminal Procedure (Insanity) and Unfitness to Plead Act 1991 was not then in force and a finding of insanity would have resulted in an indefinite period of detention in a mental institution. Therefore, rather than face such a consequence, the defendant changed his plea to guilty. The justification for the external/internal factor test is the assumed danger of recurrence: the internal factor is often a condition which will recur whereas an external factor such as the administration of anaesthetic is unlikely to do so. However, the effect of the distinction on diabetics, resulting in the hypoglycaemic offender falling within automatism and the hyperglycaemic offender being classified as an insane automaton, neither of whom is more likely than the other to suffer a recurrence, illustrates the weakness of this argument. Further, the classification of some diabetics as insane, rather than sane, automatons is quite bizarre and an affront to common sense. As Lawton L.J. stated in *Quick*:

"Common sense is affronted by the prospect of a diabetic being sent to [a secure mental] hospital when in most cases the disordered mental condition can be rectified quickly by pushing a lump of sugar ... into the patient's mouth."

Epilepsy

In **Sullivan [1984] A.C. 156**, the court held that an epileptic who committed a s.20 assault whilst recovering from an epileptic seizure would be treated as an insane automaton, epilepsy being an internal factor. As with *Hennessey*, following such a finding by the court, the defendant changed his plea to guilty.

Sleepwalking

In **Burgess [1991] 2 Q.B. 92**, the defendant attacked a friend by hitting her with a video recorder whilst sleepwalking and was charged with s.20 wounding. He pleaded automatism as a defence but the court held, despite the dicta in *Bratty* to the effect that sleepwalking constituted the defence of automatism (see p.409), and the fact that external triggers such as intoxicants, sleep deprivation, stress and being aroused from a deep sleep can all trigger sleepwalking, that the tendency to sleepwalk is an internal factor constituting a disease of the mind; the correct defence was insanity.

Although *Burgess* has not been overruled, the courts have, on occasion, been willing to take into account the presence of an external factor which triggers the episode of sleepwalking, so permitting the defence of sane-automatism to go before the jury. In **Pooley ((unreported) January 16, 2007, Aylesbury Crown Court**, referred to by R.D. Mackay and M. Reuber in "Epilepsy and the defence of insanity: time for change?"), for example, on a charge of sexual assault committed whilst D was sleepwalking, the trial judge treated the "concurrent causes" of the sleepwalking—self-induced intoxication and environmental change—as external factors, so permitting the defence of sane-automatism to be left to the jury who then acquitted D.

More recently, a particularly sympathetic approach was taken by prosecutors in the case of Brian Thomas who was tried at Swansea Crown Court in November 2009 for murdering his wife, to whom he had been happily married for 40 years, during a nightmare in which he thought he was attacking an intruder. Mr Thomas had been a sleepwalker for many years and had suffered from a variety of sleep disorders. Initially, the prosecution sought a verdict of not guilty on the grounds of insanity (there being no external factor only the internal factor of the sleep disorder) and argued for detention in a mental hospital. The defence sought a verdict of not guilty on the grounds of sane automatism. However, the prosecution then changed their stance and withdrew the case on the basis of expert psychiatric evidence that sending Mr Thomas to a psychiatric hospital would serve "no useful purpose" because the risk of recurrence was so slight, following which the jury were directed to acquit.

In "Violence, Sleepwalking and the Criminal Law Part 2: The Legal Aspects" [2005] Crim. L.R. 614 by W. Wilson, I. Ebrahims, P. Fenwick and R. Marks, the authors suggest that English criminal law:

> "Remains bereft of a satisfactory method of dealing with defendants [such as diabetics, epileptics and sleepwalkers] who, although lacking fault, have a condition which poses a potential threat to the public."

At the time of the decisions in *Hennessy*, *Sullivan* and *Burgess*, the trial judge had no discretion in sentencing the insane offender; he had to impose an indefinite period of detention in a secure mental unit. Nowadays, the trial judge has a range of sentencing options at his disposal and is very unlikely to detain indefinitely a diabetic, epileptic or sleepwalker. In the view of the authors, therefore:

> "Insanity is likely to present an increasingly popular defence in those relatively rare cases where supporting evidence is raised that the defendant committed criminal wrongdoing in the absence of conscious awareness or volitional intent."

It is hard to say whether this will happen. The defendant in such circumstances would still have to deal with the dreadful stigma of being labelled "insane". The possibility of a sympathetic trial judge willing to treat the case as one of sane automatism due to the presence of some external factor such as alcohol or stress or a prosecutor exercising discretion not to proceed, as in the above-mentioned first instance decisions, may mean it is still worth the defendant taking a chance on sane automatism.

Violence resulting in post traumatic stress disorder

In **T [1990] Crim. L.R. 256**, the application of the external/internal factor test led, for once, to a decision which was just and sensible. The defendant, who suffered from post-traumatic stress disorder as a consequence of being raped, stabbed V during a robbery. The Crown Court judge held that the post traumatic stress was caused by the external factor of the rape and, therefore, the defence was one of sane automatism.

Over to you...

Given the often absurd and harsh consequence of the internal/external factor test and the inability of the courts to come up with a fairer test might it be time to dispense with a legal definition of insanity altogether? Could we instead ask psychiatrists to determine whether D's medical condition meant that he was not responsible for his actions, i.e. leave the question to be decided entirely by medical experts?

If a defect of reason caused by a disease of the mind can be established, the defendant must then prove *either* that he did not know the nature and quality of his act *or* that his act was wrong. This requirement will often exclude a defendant who, in the opinion of medical practitioners, is suffering from a mental disorder. The Yorkshire Ripper, Peter Sutcliffe, for example, was schizophrenic but failed both tests as he knew he was killing his victims (nature and quality of his act) and that killing was against the law.

■ Not knowing the nature and quality of his act

The defendant must not have known what he was physically doing and what the physical consequences of his actions would be (**Codere (1916) 12 Cr. App. R. 21**). This will usually be very difficult to establish. An oft-cited example is where a man cuts a woman's throat believing, due to his mental disorder, that he is cutting a loaf of bread.

If the defendant cannot prove he did not know the nature and quality of his act, he can try to rely on the alternative requirement for the insanity defence, i.e. that he did not know that his act was wrong.

■ Not knowing his act was wrong

The defendant must have failed to realise that his actions were legally wrong rather than simply morally wrong (**Windle [1952] 2 Q.B. 826** and confirmed more recently by the Court of Appeal in **Johnson [2007] EWCA Crim 1978**). *Windle*, who suffered from the medical condition known as folie à deux, murdered his wife with a fatal dosage of aspirin. On arrest, he told the police that he supposed he would hang for what he had done. This comment showed that he understood he had committed a crime and his defence of insanity failed.

Research by Mackay, Mitchell and Howe for their article "Yet More Facts about the Insanity Defence" suggests that, despite the strict test in the *M'Naghten* Rules, some psychiatrists seem, in practice, to be adopting a pragmatic approach in their court reports in support of an insanity plea. They rely on the defendant's belief that although he recognised his actions were unlawful he thought they were morally justified. It appears that this is being accepted by the courts as an insanity defence. This "more relaxed" approach by the courts was acknowledged by Latham L.J. in *Johnson*, though not adopted in the case itself (because both psychiatrists at D's trial agreed that D had known what he did was legally wrong). Latham L.J. considered that there was scope for a re-examination of the insanity rules but not "at this level in this case". The English courts are currently out of step with those in most common law jurisdictions that still impose a test of "wrongfulness" but have expanded the meaning of the term to encompass "moral wrongness" (for example, Australia, Canada and New Zealand) and it is likely to be only a matter of time before the English courts follow suit.

Irresistible Impulse

Insanity (unlike diminished responsibility) does not encompass acting under an uncontrollable impulse per se (**Kopsch (1925) 19 Cr. App. R. 50**). The fact that a defendant acted under an irresistible impulse might, however, lend weight to a submission that the defendant did not know either what he was doing or that it was wrong.

Insane Delusions

The issue of the significance of insane delusions was considered by the judges who formulated the *M'Naghten* Rules. Essentially, the test they suggested is that the responsibility of the deluded defendant is the same as it would have been had the facts been as he assumed them to be. The judges gave the following examples:

> "... If under the influence of his delusion he supposes another man to be in the act of attempting to take away his life, and he kills that man, as he supposes in self-defence, he would be exempt from punishment. If his delusion was that the deceased had inflicted a serious injury to his character and fortune, and he killed him in revenge for such supposed injury, he would be liable to punishment."

The test seems flawed in that, depending on the defendant's delusion, it is possible that he has not committed the actus reus of the offence he intends to commit. For example, a defendant whose delusion means that he believes he is killing his wife's lover but is in fact killing her pet, could not be liable for murder as it is only possible to murder a human being or, indeed, for criminal damage to the pet, as he does not intend to damage property belonging to another.

Criticism and Reform

Although some criticisms of the insanity defence will have become apparent during your reading of this chapter, it is worth briefly considering them again together with others not previously mentioned in order to consider whether there is a pressing need for reform. What follows is a summary of the main academic and practical criticisms of the current insanity defence.

1. It does not follow the rule in *Woolmington*; the burden of proof is on the defendant rather than the prosecution.
2. It is a legal defence, not a medical one. The judge determines whether there is evidence of insanity and then the jury, not psychiatrists, determine whether the defendant

was insane. They do so having heard expert medical testimony but can choose to disregard it.

3. The operation of the internal/external factor test means that the defence is too broadly defined, encompassing people who present little danger to the public, for example the diabetic who is hyperglycaemic, the epileptic and the sleepwalker; conversely, it could be said to be too narrowly defined because the requirements can exclude the mentally disordered who might have benefitted from detention in a mental hospital.

4. It is irrelevant that the condition can be cured.

5. It does not encompass knowing one's act was morally wrong.

6. It excludes irresistible impulse.

7. The label "insane" and the possibility of detention in a mental hospital deter defendants from pleading the defence.

8. In the case of murder, if detention in a mental hospital is imposed it will be for an indeterminate time whereas a conviction for murder will result in a life sentence which is normally between 10 and 15 years, so a guilty plea may well be preferable.

9. A defendant whose insanity plea results in detention in a mental hospital and who was not a significant danger to the public when he went in may well be so when he comes out.

In 1975, the Butler Committee on Mentally Abnormal Offenders produced a report (Cmnd 6244) which concluded that there was a need for significant reform. The report proposed a change of terminology away from the stigmatising verdict of "not guilty by reason of insanity" to one of "not guilty on evidence of mental disorder" with the burden of proof on the prosecution. The verdict would be returned in either of two situations:

1. the defendant was unable to form the mens rea (this would replace the "nature and quality" test); or

2. the defendant was aware of his actions but suffered from severe mental disorder at the relevant time (this would replace the "wrongfulness" test).

The report was largely ignored but in 1989 a Draft Code Bill was produced by the Law Commission (Law Com. No.177) which adopts these proposals with amendments. The Bill also set out two circumstances which would result in a "not guilty on evidence of mental disorder" verdict:

1. If the defendant is proved to have committed the offence but it is proved on the balance of probability (whether by the prosecution or by the defendant) that he was at the time suffering from severe mental illness or severe mental handicap.

   This would cover the defendant who acted with mens rea but whose mental disorder meant that he was not responsible for his actions. The verdict could not be returned in this situation if the court or jury is satisfied beyond reasonable doubt that the offence was not attributable to the severe mental illness or severe mental handicap, i.e. there must be a causal connection between the disorder and the act which the defendant has committed.

Severe mental illness is one which has one or more of the following characteristics—

(a) lasting impairment of intellectual functions shown by failure of memory, orientation, comprehension and learning capacity;

(b) lasting alteration of mood of such degree as to give rise to delusional appraisal of the defendant's situation, his past or his future, or that of others, or lack of any appraisal;

(c) delusional beliefs, persecutory, jealous or grandiose;

(d) abnormal perceptions associated with delusional misinterpretation of events;

(e) thinking so disordered as to prevent reasonable appraisal of the defendant's situation of reasonable communication with others.

Severe mental handicap means: "a state of arrested or incomplete development of mind which includes severe impairment of intelligence and social functioning."
Or

2. **(a)** The defendant is acquitted of an offence *only* because, by reason of evidence of mental disorder or a combination of mental disorder or intoxication, it is found that he acted or may have acted in a state of automatism, or without the fault (mens rea) required for the offence, or believing that an exempting circumstance (for example self-defence) existed; and

(b) it is proved on the balance of probability (whether by the prosecution or by the defendant) that he was suffering from mental disorder at the time of the act.

Over to you...

Would these reforms address the major criticisms of the defence outlined above?

In 2008, the Law Commission announced that a review of the insanity defence and unfitness to plead would form part of their Tenth Programme of Law Reform (Law Com. No.311) but the Commission had not reported on their findings at the time of writing this book.

FIGURE 12.2 **Sane and Insane Automatism**

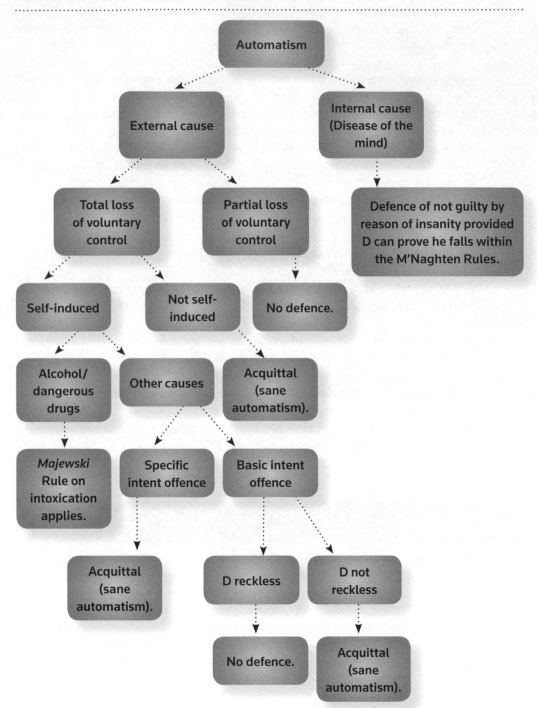

Unfit to Plead

The defence of unfit to plead is available to a defendant who, by the time of the trial, cannot, because of his disorder, comprehend the proceedings so as to make a proper defence, instruct counsel or follow the evidence against him. The defence applies not only to those whose mental impairment has this effect; a mute defendant may also plead the defence. Unfitness to plead is governed by the Criminal Procedure (Insanity) Act 1964 as substituted by the Criminal Procedure (Insanity) and Unfitness to Plead Act 1991 and amended by the Domestic Violence, Crime and Victims Act 2004.

Either side or even the judge may raise the issue of unfit to plead. Where it is the defence who raises it, the burden is on D to the civil standard of proof; where it is the prosecution or trial judge, the burden is on the prosecution to the criminal standard of proof.

If the defence is raised on arraignment, it is for the judge, in the absence of the jury, to determine whether the defendant is fit to plead. The decision on fitness to plead is reached following evidence from two doctors, one of whom must be approved by the Home Secretary as a specialist in the relevant field. What happens next depends on the judge's verdict.

Judge Determines the Defendant is Fit to Plead

In such circumstances, a jury will be empanelled and the trial proceeds as normal.

Judge Determines the Defendant is Unfit to Plead

In such circumstances, the court undertakes a "trial of the facts" to determine whether the defendant committed the actus reus of the offence charged. It does not consider whether the defendant had the requisite mens rea (**Antoine [2001] 1 A.C. 340 HL**) or the defence of provocation (**Grant [2002] Q.B. 1030** (presumably, the position will be the same with the new defence of loss of control)). The court must be satisfied beyond reasonable doubt that the defendant did commit the actus reus; if not so satisfied, he is released. If satisfied of this, a range of sentencing options is available to the judge (the same as for a verdict of not guilty by reason of insanity, see p.414) ranging from an absolute discharge, a guardianship order or a supervision and treatment order extending to include compulsory, indefinite detention in a secure mental hospital.

Doli Incapax

Under s.50 of the Children and Young Persons Act 1933 (as amended), children below 10 years of age are conclusively presumed to be legally incapable of committing a crime; they are said to be doli incapax. At common law, there was also a rebuttable presumption of doli incapax in respect of children aged between 10 and 14 which could be rebutted by evidence that the child knew his actions were wrong. This presumption was abolished by s.34 of the Crime and Disorder Act 1998. In **JTB [2009] 2 W.L.R. 1088**, the 12-year-old appellant submitted that the defence of doli incapax had survived the abolition of the presumption so that it was still open to him to adduce evidence that at the relevant time he was doli incapax. The House of Lords rejected this submission; s.34 abolished both the presumption and the defence of doli incapax for those aged 10–14.

Summary

1. A mistake as to the civil law or as to a fact in relation to an element of the actus reus may afford a defence if it negates the mens rea for the offence, such a mistake does not also have to be a reasonable one to make. A mistake which does not negate the mens rea must be a reasonable mistake if it is to afford a defence.

2. Intoxication may be voluntary or involuntary.

   Voluntary intoxication by alcohol or dangerous drugs is a "defence" only if it negates the mens rea for the offence. The defence is only available to crimes of specific intent, not those of basic intent. This is known as the rule in *Majewski*. Where the defendant has become intoxicated due to ingesting soporific drugs, the rule in *Majewski* does not apply; the court will consider whether the defendant lacked mens rea and, if he did, was he reckless in becoming intoxicated. Where the defendant has deliberately become intoxicated in order to give him the courage to commit an offence, he cannot rely on his intoxication to negate mens rea. Involuntary intoxication is a defence to all crimes provided the defendant lacked the mens rea.

   A defendant may act upon an intoxicated mistaken belief. The courts' approach to such a belief depends upon the nature of the mistake.

3. Automatism is a defence where the defendant suffered a total loss of voluntary control and this was caused by an external factor.

   Where the defendant's automatism is self-induced and he is charged with a specific intent offence, he must be acquitted. Where the defendant's automatism is self-induced and he is charged with a basic intent offence, he will not be convicted unless he was reckless as to becoming aggressive, unpredictable or uncontrolled.

4. Insanity is a defence proscribed by the *M'Naghten* Rules. These require the defendant to have laboured under a defect of reason from a disease of the mind so that either he did not know the nature and quality of his act or, alternatively, so that he did not know that what he was doing was wrong.

A defendant who has become insane by the time of the trial itself may assert he is unfit to plead.

5. Children under the age of ten are legally incapable of committing a crime, they are *doli incapax.*

End of Chapter Question

Question
Questions 2. and 3. relate to the facts of the question on p.170, pt 1. of which required you to consider the criminal liability of Dean. You are now asked to consider possible defences for Dean.

2. How would your answer to question 1. differ if Dean had had several pints of beer before arriving at the nightclub?

3. Alternatively, how would your answer to question 1. differ if Dean was a diabetic who had taken his daily dose of insulin but had failed to eat anything since his breakfast that day, this had altered the levels of sugar in his blood and he was feeling lightheaded at the time of the incidents in the nightclub?

Points of Answer
Pt 2.

1. The answer would differ in that Dean may now have a defence of (voluntary) intoxication as he had been drinking beer.
2. Voluntary Intoxication would be available as a "defence", i.e. to argue no mens rea, on a charge of s.18 assault as that is a specific intent offence but not on a charge of s.20 or s.47 assault as they are both basic intent offences (*Majewski*).
3. If successfully pleaded to s.18, he would be liable for the lesser basic intent offence of s.20. If Dean's intoxication were raised on the basic intent charges, the issue would be whether he would have been aware of the relevant risk had he been sober (*Richardson and Irwin*) and the answer is likely to be "yes."

Pt 3.

1. The answer would differ in that Dean may now have a defence of automatism.
2. At issue here is whether the altered blood sugar levels give rise to a defence of (sane) automatism or insane automatism (insanity). Which of these two defences would be available is determined by the operation of the internal/external factor test (*Quick*). Diabetes may give rise to a hypoglycaemic episode (low blood sugar) or a hyperglycaemic episode (high blood sugar). The defence is automatism if Dean suffered from hypoglycaemia at the time of the assaults caused by the external factor of taking the

insulin without eating (as in *Quick*); if there was no external factor, i.e. the episode was hyperglycaemia caused by the internal factor of the diabetes itself the only defence is insanity (as in *Hennessey*). On the facts, the defence would be sane automatism caused by taking the insulin.

3. A successful plea of automatism normally results in an acquittal but Dean's automatism was self-induced because he failed to eat. The outcome of such a plea here will depend on the nature of the offences with which he is charged. If Dean is charged with s.18 offences, he would be acquitted as s.18 is a crime of specific intent (*Bailey*). In respect of the s.20 and s.47 charges (both crimes of basic intent), he will acquitted unless he was subjectively reckless as to becoming aggressive, unpredictable or uncontrolled (*Bailey*). As the effects for a diabetic of not eating following the digestion of insulin are pretty well known now amongst diabetics, unlike in 1983 when *Bailey* was decided, Dean may well have known the consequences of not eating and be considered reckless. If reckless, he would still be liable for the ss.20 and 47 offences.

Further Reading

N. Barlow, "Drug Intoxication and the Principle of Capacitas Rationalis" (1984) 100 L.Q.R. 639.

F. Bennion, "Mens rea and defendants below the age of discretion" [2009] Crim. L.R. 757

J. Child, "Drink, Drugs and Law Reform: a Review of Law Commission Report No.314" [2009] Crim. L.R. 488.

S. Dell, "Wanted: An Insanity Defence that Can Be Used" [1984] Crim. L.R. 431.

G. Dingwall, "Intoxicated mistakes about the need for self-defence" (2007) 70 M.L.R. 127.

S. Gardner, "The Importance of Majewski" [1984] O.J.L.S. 279.

S. Gough, "Surviving Without Majewski?" [2002] Crim. L.R. 719.

J. Horder, "Pleading Involuntary Lack of Capacity" (1993) 52 Camb. L.J. 298

A. Loughnan, "Manifest Madness: towards a new understanding of the insanity defence" M.L.R. (2007) Vol.70 No.3 pp.379–401.

R.D. Mackay, "Righting the Wrong?—Some Observations on the Second Limb of the M'Naghten Rules" [2009] Crim. L.R. 80.

R.D. Mackay, B. J. Mitchell and Leonie Howe, "Yet More Facts about the Insanity Defence" [2006] Crim. L.R. 399.

R.D. Mackay and B. J. Mitchell, "Sleepwalking, Automatism and Insanity" [2006] Crim. L.R. 901.

R.D. Mackay & M. Reuber, "Epilepsy and the Defence of Insanity: Time for Change?" [2007] Crim. L.R. 782.

C.N. Mitchell, "The intoxicated offender—refuting the legal and medical myths" (1988) Int. J. Law and Psych 77.

G. Orchard, "Surviving without Majewski – a view from down under" [1993] Crim. L.R. 427.

J. Rogers, "Let the Drunkard Lie" (2005) 155 N.L.J. 1892.

A.P. Simester, "Intoxication is Never a Defence" [2009] Crim. L.R. 3.

A.T.H. Smith, "Error and Mistake of Law in Anglo-American Criminal Law" (1985) 14 Anglo-Am L.R. 3.

G.R. Sullivan, "Involuntary Intoxication and Beyond" [1994] Crim. L.R. 272.

W. Wilson, I. Ebrahims, P. Fenwick and R. Marks, "Violence, Sleepwalking and the Criminal Law Part 2: The Legal Aspects" [2005] Crim. L.R. 614.

http://www.lawcom.gov.uk/docs/lc314.pdf.

Self Test Questions

To test your knowledge gained from this section go online to *http://www.sweetandmaxwell. co.uk* and take our online self test questions. Here you will also find key updates to ensure that you are only ever one click away from an instant update.

Defences II—Defences which Justify or Excuse the Offence

13

CHAPTER OVERVIEW

In this chapter we:

- analyse the defences of consent (briefly), self-defence and the prevention of crime, duress and necessity

- explore the concept of justificatory and excusatory defences

- consider the effect of a mistake on each of the defences

- consider whether necessity exists as a defence at all or is, where it is available, another form of duress.

Summary

End of Chapter Question

Further Reading

Self Test Questions

Introduction

In this chapter we deal with the defences of consent, self-defence and prevention of crime, duress and necessity. These are the defences which might be said to arise independently of the actus reus or mens rea of the crime, where D is seeking to excuse or justify his actions. For example, duress is a defence which leads to a complete acquittal despite the prosecution being able to establish both the actus reus and mens rea. D is not guilty because he is excused of his actions by reason of the duress. In this chapter we also consider consent and self-defence. Prevailing wisdom has it that each of these defences is actually part of the definition of the crime, i.e. they are not defences so much as the failure of the prosecution to establish an element of the offence (notably the unlawfulness of the conduct). However, it is not uniformly accepted that such defences are part and parcel of the crime (see, e.g. the arguments concerning the operation of consent in Ch.5 on p.160), so they are also dealt with here.

Another reason for grouping consent, self-defence and duress into the same chapter is that a common way of categorising defences is into those which are elements of the offence (see Ch.12), and those which are either justificatory or excusatory. The distinction between justificatory and excusatory defences, in very basic terms, is that a defence which is justificatory is one where D's conduct is approved by society in general, but an excusatory defence is one without such approval, but punishment is not considered to be appropriate. To a defendant, the distinction is irrelevant. On the whole, he will not care, provided he is acquitted. Legal commentators and judges do care about the distinction, but are not in agreement as to the differences or the practical consequences between them. However, as the distinction has received judicial recognition (**Hasan [2005] 2 W.L.R. 709**, per Lord Bingham), it must also be considered, albeit briefly, here.

Unlike age and insanity (which affect capacity), or mistake (which negates mens rea), or intoxication (which is the reason D did not form mens rea), consent and self-defence are defences which, if successful, justify D's conduct. On the other hand, duress is not a justification for action, but an excuse. Necessity, to the extent that it differs from duress, is probably justificatory, but, as will be seen, it is difficult to define and categorise this defence with any certainty whatsoever.

The argument runs that justificatory defences negate the unlawfulness of the actus reus, which brings us back to the view in the first paragraph above, so consent, self-defence and necessity do negate a definitional element of a crime, but excusatory defences, such as duress, do not.

Consent

Many offences against the person, including the non-fatal assaults and certain sexual offences, cannot be committed where V consents. Many factors affect the validity of consent, such as the age of V, his mental capacity, mistake, fraud, the degree of harm and public policy considerations, see Ch.5.

Consent negates the unlawfulness of the assault (**Kimber [1983] 1 W.L.R. 1118, B v DPP [2000] 2 A.C. 428 HL**, cf. obiter in **Brown [1994] 1 A.C. 212 HL**) and the burden of proving unlawfulness lies on the prosecution. Therefore, if there is evidence that the victim gave valid consent, D is entitled to be acquitted unless the prosecution proves beyond reasonable doubt that the assault was unlawful. It is incorrect to assert, as judges and students sometimes do, that it is for the defendant to prove the victim consented.

Self-defence and the Prevention of Crime

. . . .

Introduction

The term self-defence is typically used to denote the situation in which D reacts to an attack from P, but in fact the defences (there is more than one) are far wider and cover the use of force against P who is threatening a third party, where P is damaging D's or another's property, or is committing or is about to commit any crime, whether one of violence or not. For ease of reference, we will use the term self-defence to apply to all of the above, and the same law applies unless we expressly state otherwise.

As with consent above, self-defence negates the unlawfulness of the actus reus. The burden of proving unlawfulness is on the prosecution, so where evidence is adduced that D acted in self-defence, he is entitled to be acquitted unless the prosecution proves beyond reasonable doubt that the attack was unlawful (**Palmer v R [1971] A.C. 814 PC**).

SOURCES OF LAW

Self-defence is a common law defence which allows a person to use reasonable force to defend himself from an attack, to defend another person from attack, and to defend his property. There is, however, another defence governed by s.3 of the Criminal Law Act 1967 which provides:

> **(1)** A person may use such force as is reasonable in the circumstances in the prevention of crime, or in effecting or assisting in the lawful arrest of offenders or suspected offenders or of persons unlawfully at large.
> **(2)** Subsection (1) above shall replace the rules of the common law on the question when force used for a purpose mentioned in the subsection is justified by that purpose.

Generally, the statutory defence is wider because it entitles D to use force to prevent *any* crime. This includes using force to prevent violent, non-violent crimes, crimes against property and the person. The common law defence is limited to using force against violent assaults and to defend one's own property from damage. However, the statutory defence operates only to cover the prevention of actual crime, so if D *thought* a crime was being committed, but none was, or what would be a crime was being conducted by a child under the age of 10, or an insane automaton, the common law defence would apply where the statute does not. Section 3 would be inapplicable because, technically, no crime would be being prevented. Where s.3 overlaps with the common law defence, the statutory defence is to be preferred (s.3(2)), and the same rules apply to the operation of each defence (**McInnes [1971] 1 W.L.R. 1600 CA**).

REASONABLE FORCE

There is a single test applicable to either defence (common law or s.3) and that is whether the force used is reasonable. Card, Card, Cross and Jones, *Criminal Law*, 17th edn, suggests that the reasonableness of the force used is assessed according to whether (a) the use of *any* force was justified, and (b) whether the force used was *excessive* in all the circumstances. In **Scarlett [1993] 4 All E.R. 629**, the Court of Appeal stated that D would be judged on the facts as he perceived them, including his belief as to the amount of force that was needed. The same court later expressly rejected the very subjective nature of this approach. It is therefore the law that D is judged on the facts as he saw them, but the force used must be objectively reasonable, in the light of D's belief (**Owino [1996] 2 Cr. App. R. 128 CA**). In this case, D was convicted of assaulting his wife occasioning her actual bodily harm. His defence was that the injuries were caused by his use of reasonable force to restrain her from assaulting him. The judge directed the jury to the effect that the prosecution must prove that D did not believe he was using reasonable force. The Court of Appeal held that the law is, instead, that a person may use such force as is (objectively) reasonable in the circumstances as he (subjectively) believes them to be.

The case law on the question of reasonableness has recently been consolidated into statute under s.76 of the Criminal Justice and Immigration Act 2008 (CJ&IA 2008) which provides:

> **(1)** This section applies where in proceedings for an offence—
>   **(a)** an issue arises as to whether a person charged with the offence ("D") is entitled to rely on a defence within subsection (2), and
>   **(b)** the question arises whether the degree of force used by D against a person ("V") was reasonable in the circumstances.
>
> **(2)** The defences are—
>   **(a)** the common law defence of self-defence; and
>   **(b)** the defences provided by section 3(1) of the Criminal Law Act 1967 ...

(3) The question whether the degree of force used by D was reasonable in the circumstances is to be decided by reference to the circumstances as D believed them to be, and subsections (4) to (8) also apply in connection with deciding that question.

(4) If D claims to have held a particular belief as regards the existence of any circumstances—

    (a) the reasonableness or otherwise of that belief is relevant to the question whether D genuinely held it; but

    (b) if it is determined that D did genuinely hold it, D is entitled to rely on it for the purposes of subsection (3), whether or not—

        (i) it was mistaken, or

        (ii) (if it was mistaken) the mistake was a reasonable one to have made.

(5) But subsection (4)(b) does not enable D to rely on any mistaken belief attributable to intoxication that was voluntarily induced.

(6) The degree of force used by D is not to be regarded as having been reasonable in the circumstances as D believed them to be if it was disproportionate in those circumstances.

(7) In deciding the question mentioned in subsection (3) the following considerations are to be taken into account (so far as relevant in the circumstances of the case)—

    (a) that a person acting for a legitimate purpose may not be able to weigh to a nicety the exact measure of any necessary action; and

    (b) that evidence of a person's having only done what the person honestly and instinctively thought was necessary for a legitimate purpose constitutes strong evidence that only reasonable action was taken by that person for that purpose.

(8) Subsection (7) is not to be read as preventing other matters from being taken into account where they are relevant to deciding the question mentioned in subsection (3).

(9) This section is intended to clarify the operation of the existing defences mentioned in subsection (2).

(10) In this section—

    (a) "legitimate purpose" means—

        (i) the purpose of self-defence under the common law, or

        (ii) the prevention of crime or effecting or assisting in the lawful arrest of persons mentioned in the provisions referred to in subsection (2)(b);

    (b) references to self-defence include acting in defence of another person; and

    (c) references to the degree of force used are to the type and amount of force used.

As is clear from subs.(2), the sources of law for the defences are still the common law and s.3, so it is wrong to suggest self-defence and prevention of crime are now governed by the 2008 Act. What s.76 does is put onto a statutory footing the previous case law (which we examine below) on the test of "reasonable" force. The Explanatory Notes to the Act explain:

> "Section 76 provides a gloss on the common law of self-defence and the defence provided by section 3(1) of the Criminal Law Act 1967 … It is intended to improve understanding of the practical application of these areas of the law. It uses elements of case law to illustrate how the defence operates. It does not change the current test that allows the use of reasonable force."

There are two elements involved in the question of reasonableness:

1. D's actual belief that force is necessary; and
2. in the light of that belief, that the amount of force is objectively proportionate to the threat.

Each of these is explored further below.

■ The need to act

In **Palmer v R [1971] A.C. 814 PC,** Lord Morris explained that:

> "If there has been an attack so that the defence is reasonably necessary, it will be recognised that a person defending himself cannot weigh to a nicety the exact measure of his necessary defensive action. If a jury thought that in a moment of unexpected anguish a person attacked had only done what he honestly and instinctively thought was necessary that would be most potent evidence that only reasonable defensive action had been taken."

This has been adopted almost word for word into s.76(7) of the CJ&IA 2008 (see above). The effect of ss.76(3) and (7) and case law is that D's honest and instinctive thought must be judged *subjectively*. In **Williams [1987] 3 All E.R. 411**, D watched a third party called M arrest a youth, X. M said he was a police officer but failed to produce a warrant card. W, honestly believing that X was being unlawfully assaulted by M, himself assaulted M. His appeal against conviction was allowed. D was to be judged according to his view of the facts, mistaken or not, and it was irrelevant whether that mistake was reasonable (see p.436 below).

■ Proportionality

The amount (or the degree) of force used by D must be judged objectively. The jury or magistrates must bear in mind that D is often the initial victim of the attack, and he may not have been able to judge accurately the severity of the threat nor, as the Privy Council said above, "weigh to a nicety the exact measure of his necessary defensive action". However, the degree of force used is judged, in light of what D actually believed, *objectively*. The relative size and strength, and skill, of the parties are also relevant. So if D were a slightly built person who was attacked on his own by two or more well-built, but unarmed, aggressors, the jury may find the reaction by D to be proportionate if he picked up a bar and forcefully hit each of his attackers. That said, if D continued to hit the aggressors after the threat had abated, and for some time after they had ceased the attack, the force used would no longer be proportionate. A defendant who is an expert in hand-to-hand combat may be tempted to cause serious injuries to "punish" an aggressor who has picked his pocket, but should resist the temptation as a jury would almost certainly conclude his reaction to be disproportionate.

■ Is there a duty to retreat?

There was a duty to retreat at common law (**Julien [1969] 1 W.L.R. 839**) but, in **Bird [1985] 1 W.L.R. 816**, the Court of Appeal held that D does not have to display an unwillingness to fight in order for the plea of self-defence to succeed (although it was a factor to be taken into account). In **McInnes [1971] 1 W.L.R. 1600 CA**, a fight between rival gangs led to the death of one of the gang members. D claimed at trial that he brandished the fatal weapon, a knife, because he was frightened of the other gang and that the injury occurred accidentally when the deceased ran onto the knife. His conviction for murder was quashed. The Court of Appeal held that it was not necessary for D to have retreated as far as he could; but failure to retreat was a material factor in considering the reasonableness of the defendant's conduct.

■ Is D allowed to make a pre-emptive strike?

Provided D's act is immediately, or imminently, preparatory to self-defence, he may have a defence, but just how far in advance the threat must be is unclear. The jury acquitted the defendant in **Attorney General's Reference (No.2 of 1983) [1984] 1 All E.R. 988**. During rioting D's property had been attacked and damaged. He feared further attack and made some petrol bombs which he intended to use only to repulse raiders from his property. He was charged with having made an explosive substance in such circumstances as to give rise to a reasonable suspicion that he had not made it for a lawful object, contrary to s.4(1) of the Explosive Substances Act 1883. A prosecution submission that self-defence was not open to D was rejected and the jury, directed to consider the reasonableness of the means adopted for self-defence, acquitted D. The question of whether the threat had to be immediate or imminent was not clarified, however.

On the same facts today, the defence of duress of circumstances may be a suitable alternative (see p.440 below) but that defence fails unless D acts to avoid personal injury or death, and a threat to property damage is insufficient.

It may even be self-defence if D's motivation to act is revenge. In **Rashford [2005] EWCA Crim 3377**, D had argued with his friend, V, and later, during a fight, stabbed him. At trial, it was the prosecution's case that D had been the aggressor looking for revenge following the earlier argument. The Court of Appeal held self-defence was not unavailable just because D was the initial aggressor, by provoking or willingly entering into an argument. The mere fact that D wished to exact revenge from V did not per se rule out self-defence. That said, the defence was unsuccessful on the facts.

THE EFFECT OF THE DEFENCE

If the defence succeeds, whether common law or statutory, D's conduct is regarded as lawful and he is completely acquitted. It can be a defence to any crime including murder. If the defence fails, D is guilty.

An unsuccessful argument of self-defence can have a bearing on sentence where it is regarded as a mitigating factor. Of course, this cannot affect the life sentence on a murder charge. If D is charged with murder, and the defence has failed because the amount of force used was excessive, the offence is not reduced to manslaughter (**Clegg [1995] 1 All E.R. 334**). Many students make the error of thinking self-defence operates in the same way as the partial defences to murder (provocation/loss of self-control or diminished responsibility), and the Nathan Committee (House of Lords, 1989) proposed that excessive force self-defence should reduce murder to manslaughter. Although this has not been enacted in terms, it is at least arguable *where D has lost self-control* that the new defence under the Coroners and Justice Act 2009 allows for excessive force self-defence to reduce murder to manslaughter. The sticking point will, however, be the loss of self-control requirement; see Ch.4.

MISTAKE AND SELF-DEFENCE

The effect of a mistake in circumstances where D thought he was acting in self-defence has been mentioned above on p.386. The effect of D's mistake depends on the mistake he made. If it relates to the *need* to use force, it is viewed subjectively, and following **DPP v Morgan [1976] A.C. 182**, the reasonableness of the mistake is irrelevant. **Williams [1987] 3 All E.R. 411** was also considered at p.386 above. This case established that if D makes a mistake as to the facts, he is to be judged according to his mistaken view of the facts, whether or not that mistake was, on an objective view, reasonable. This mistake relieves D of liability because his mistake prevented him forming the mens rea of the offence in question. This is now contained in ss.76(4) and (5) of the CJ&IA 2008.

However, if D makes a mistake about the *amount* of force which needs to be used, the degree of force is assessed objectively in light of the subjectively assessed circumstances (*Owino* above). David Ormerod has neatly summarised the test as follows:

> "It is well established that the defence applies where (1) D genuinely believes in the need for force to protect himself, others or his property (even if D is mistaken in that belief and his mistake is an unreasonable one) and (2) the degree of force used in the circumstances as D believed them to be is reasonably necessary." ([2010] Crim. L.R. 202)

It was held in **Martin (Anthony) [2002] Crim L.R. 136**, that if D perceived the degree of danger as being far greater than would be perceived by a reasonable person, D's mistake must be ignored and he must be judged on the normal person's assessment of the degree of danger. *Martin* was a controversial case which attracted a great deal of media attention. D was charged with murder and wounding with intent, having shot two people who were burgling his home. At trial, he unsuccessfully pleaded self-defence. Following conviction, however, it was found by a psychiatrist that D had been suffering from a long-term paranoid personality disorder, which, it was contended on appeal, had affected his perception of the *amount* of force that had to be used in the circumstances. The Court of Appeal held, however, that the jury could not, save in exceptional circumstances (no guidance was given as to when such circumstances might exist), take into account a psychiatric condition which affected his view of the amount of force which was needed. The decision is very harsh and it conflicts with the subjective assessment of the facts as D believed them to be (*Williams* above and **Beckford v R [1988] A.C. 130 PC**) and similar tests in other defences (for example, within the common law defence of provocation, the defendant's characteristics which affect the gravity of the provocation are relevant, even if they amount to a psychiatric condition; it remains to be seen whether the new loss of self-control defence under the Coroners and Justice Act 2009 which will replace provocation will permit the jury to take this evidence into account as relevant to the circumstances of D.) Further, the decision lacks sense, because a jury can take into account a defendant's physical characteristics which affect D's view of the amount of necessary force.

Over to you ...

Section 76 of the CJ&IA 2008 has not changed the law from the *Martin* case. In Committee in the House of Lords on the Bill for this Act the Advocate-General for Scotland (Lord Davidson of Glen Clova) said as follows:

"[What is now s.76] and its handling of the circumstances is, I submit, a faithful reflection of the common law position. Nothing in case law suggests that the reference to 'all the circumstances' in the *Martin* judgment should be elevated into an element of the established common law principle that the degree of force used must be reasonable in the circumstances as the defendant believed them to be."

As to the situation where D has made an intoxicated mistake as to self-defence, see s.76(6) and Ch.12.

FIGURE 13 **The defence of self-defence**

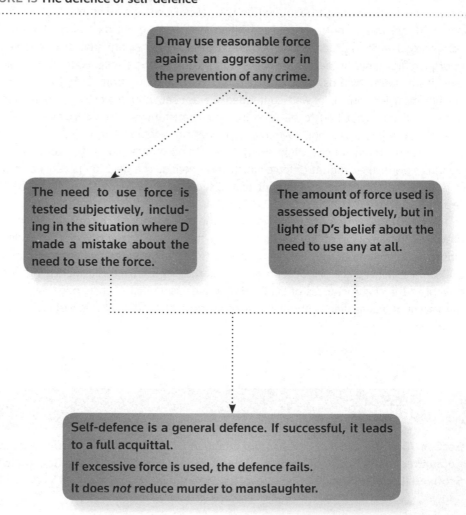

D may use reasonable force against an aggressor or in the prevention of any crime.

The need to use force is tested subjectively, including in the situation where D made a mistake about the need to use the force.

The amount of force used is assessed objectively, but in light of D's belief about the need to use any at all.

Self-defence is a general defence. If successful, it leads to a full acquittal.

If excessive force is used, the defence fails.

It does *not* reduce murder to manslaughter.

THE EUROPEAN CONVENTION ON HUMAN RIGHTS

Article 2(1) states that everyone's right to life shall be protected by law and no-one shall be deprived of his life intentionally save in the execution of a sentence of a court following his conviction of a crime for which this penalty is provided by law. Article 2(2) provides, however, that the deprivation of life shall not be regarded as inflicted in contravention of this article when it results from the use of force which is no more than absolutely necessary:

1. in defence of any person from unlawful violence;
2. in order to effect a lawful arrest or to prevent the escape of a person lawfully detained;
3. in action lawfully taken for the purpose of quelling a riot or insurrection.

It may be difficult to imagine, but say D killed P in defence of property, or in the more general prevention of any crime, and the jury agrees the amount of force used was proportionate (a leap of faith on the reader's part may be required as it is difficult to imagine where a proportionate response to a threat to property is to kill). Under English law, D is entitled to be acquitted, but that acquittal would surely violate art.2. Such a violation is even more extreme if D made an honest but unreasonable mistake as to the facts. This simply cannot be "absolutely necessary" force. The European Court of Human Rights held in **McCann v UK (1995) 21 E.H.R.R. 97** that D's mistake must be judged on reasonable grounds, and the liberal subjective approach of English law where D has acted in mistaken self-defence with fatal consequences needs to be remodeled to comply with the ECHR.

REFORM OF SELF-DEFENCE

Any change to the law governing self-defence would have to take into account the conflict between the English law and art.2, considered above.

The Nathan Committee (House of Lords, 1989) proposed that excessive force self-defence should reduce murder to manslaughter, but this has not been enacted, subject to the comment we made above in respect of loss of self-control (above and Ch.4).

Duress

Introduction

The law has long recognised a defence where D commits a crime under threat of death or serious injury. Over the past 30 or so years, the law has also recognised that the situation in which D found himself could cause fear of death or serious injury, rather than there being a human threat. This is the defence of duress. There is one defence of duress, but two types; duress by threats and duress of circumstances. The two types have the same rules and availability as each other, and are conveniently referred to by the cause of the fear (the threats or the circumstances).

There is an unanswered question of whether there is a third defence, that of necessity, either born out of or existing wholly separately to the defence of duress of circumstances. Certainly, Lord Bingham in **Hasan [2005] 2 A.C. 467** used the terms duress of circumstances and necessity interchangeably indicating they are the same defence. In many of the cases examined below as part of the duress defence, the term necessity is used, probably synonymously, yet there are cases where the defence of necessity arises where duress appears not to. This issue is explored further on pp.451–457 below.

Duress by Threats or of Circumstances?

Each type of the duress defence requires that a crime is committed in order to avoid death or serious injury, where a reasonable person would do the same. D is compelled to act. His will is overborne and he feels he has no choice. Duress by threats is where there is a coercer whose purpose is to force D into committing the crime. Duress of circumstances recognises that D might face death or serious harm if he does not commit a crime, but there is no human agent directing the crime to be committed. For example, if D drove dangerously away from an aggressor, he may plead duress of circumstances in that he felt compelled to break the driving laws to avoid death or serious injury, but a plea of duress by threats would fail because the aggressor did not threaten D with death or injury unless he committed the offence of dangerous driving.

Aside from the difference in the source of the fear, the conditions for a successful plea are the same for each type of the defence. The case law which follows can be from either type of the defence to illustrate its operation. First, though, we will consider how the second type developed.

THE DEVELOPMENT OF THE DEFENCE OF DURESS OF CIRCUMSTANCES

Duress of circumstances was accidentally invented by the Court of Appeal in **Willer (1986) 83 Cr. App. R. 225** when it quashed D's conviction on a procedural irregularity, but in circumstances which could be viewed as being duress, without a human coercer. The case was, however, quickly approved in **Conway [1989] Q.B. 290**. D was charged with reckless driving. D's passenger, T, had previously been the target of an attack with a shotgun. When two plain clothes police officers approached D's car, he feared that T was about to be shot at again. D drove off, and he admitted at trial his driving had been reckless, but he claimed he only discovered that the chasers were police officers after T had been dropped off and the officers caught up with him. Allowing his appeal against conviction, the Court of Appeal recognised the existence of the defence where a person felt constrained to act as he did to avoid death or serious bodily harm to himself or another, and a reasonable man would have driven as D did in the circumstances.

Curiously and coincidentally, the early cases on duress of circumstances involved road traffic laws. In **Martin (1989) 88 Cr. App. R. 343**, D drove his car while disqualified but said he did so only because his wife, who was suicidal, had threatened to kill herself if he had not driven at the time in question. The Court of Appeal held that the defence of duress could arise equally from objective dangers threatening the defendant or others as well as from a human coercer.

The application of duress of circumstances to non-road traffic crimes was confirmed in **Pommell [1995] 2 Cr. App. R. 607**, where D had been convicted of possessing a submachine gun contrary to s.5 of the Firearms Act 1968. D had persuaded another (whom D thought likely to commit an offence) to give him the weapon so that it could be surrendered. The Court of Appeal saw no reason to limit the defence to road traffic offences, and ordered a retrial.

Even though the defence of duress is now well established, each type is very limited and very difficult to plead successfully. Ormerod, Smith and Hogan, *Criminal Law*, 11th edn, puts this down to judicial scepticism. According to Lord Simon in **DPP for Northern Ireland v Lynch [1975] A.C. 653**, "your Lordships should hesitate long lest you may be inscribing a charter for terrorists, gang-leaders and kidnappers." Although the burden of proof rests on the prosecution, there are so many requirements of the defence that it is exceedingly difficult to plead.

The Elements of the Defence

Conway (above) adopted the test for duress laid down by the Court of Appeal in **Graham [1982] 1 W.L.R. 294** and this was approved by the House of Lords in **Howe [1987] 1 A.C. 417 HL**. Based on the common law test for the defence of provocation (Ch.4), there are two stages:

1. whether D was or might have been induced to act as he did because, as a result of what he reasonably believed, D had good cause to fear that if he did not act [the coercer] would kill him or cause him serious physical injury [or in the circumstances, death or serious injury would result]; and, if the answer was in the affirmative,
2. whether a sober person of reasonable firmness sharing D's characteristics would [have done the same].

In **Hasan [2005] 2 A.C. 467**, the House of Lords summarised the elements of the defence of duress as:

1. the threat relied on (which we will see has to be immediate) must be to cause (or the circumstances must cause fear of) death or serious injury;
2. the threat must be directed against (or the circumstances produce fear for) the defendant or his immediate family, or someone close to him, or if not to the defendant or a member of his immediate family, to a person for whose safety the defendant would reasonably regard himself as responsible;

3. the jury must have regard to the reasonableness of the defendant's perceptions and his conduct;
4. the defence is available only where the criminal conduct which it is sought to excuse has been directly caused by the threats which are relied upon;
5. there was no evasive action he could reasonably have been expected to take; and
6. the defendant may not rely on duress to which he has voluntarily laid himself open.

We will adopt this declaration of the law governing duress as the structure for the following explanation of the operation of the defence.

DEATH OR SERIOUS INJURY

The defence is available only to avoid death or serious injury. Anything less (a threat of pain but not injury was not enough in **Quayle [2005] 2 Cr. App. R. 34**) is insufficient. However, in a case of duress by threats, if D would not have done the crime if it were not for the threats of death or serious harm, the defence is open to him even if he in fact acted because of the cumulative effect of all the threats—the permitted ones as well the prohibited ones. In **Valderrama-Vega [1985] Crim. L.R. 220**, D was charged with being knowingly concerned in the fraudulent evasion of the prohibition on importation of a controlled drug. His defence was that he, his wife and his family had been threatened by a Mafia-type organisation with injury or death. He was under severe financial pressure, and he had also been threatened with disclosure of his homosexuality. The judge's direction was therefore incorrect when he said that duress was a defence if the defendant acted "solely" as a result of threats of death or serious injury.

Logically, the prime motivation in a duress of circumstances case would be to avoid death or serious injury, but if there were other motivating factors, presumably the same rules would apply.

As explained in Ch.5, the law has recognised that the term "bodily harm" under the Offences against the Person Act 1861 encompasses clinical or psychiatric injury. One would therefore speculate that if a person were under a threat of serious psychiatric injury, one would have, subject to the other elements, a defence. In **Baker and Wilkins [1997] Crim. L.R. 497**, D had an argument with her ex-partner and the father of her child. Their daughter was in her father's house and D was outside. The father was refusing to return the child after a contact visit. D damaged the front door and pleaded duress on a charge of criminal damage. There was no threat or fear of death or any physical injury to either D or the child, but D argued she feared her daughter would suffer psychiatric harm. However, the Court of Appeal refused to extend the defence to circumstances where the defendant had feared serious psychological injury. There was a lot of criticism of this decision, and the criticism was seen as carrying "a great deal of force" in **DPP v Rogers [1998] Crim. L.R. 202**. It is therefore to be hoped that it will not be followed.

The threat must be external to D. Obviously, this will always be the case for duress by threats, but it is not so obvious for duress of circumstances. In **Rodger and Rose [1998] 1 Cr. App. R. 143**, the defendants made an imaginative plea for duress of circumstances, but it ultimately failed. They were convicted of breaking out of prison. They had previously been convicted of murder and were subsequently informed that the tariff of their sentence had been increased. They became depressed and suicidal. They maintained that, had they not escaped, they would have committed suicide. The Court of Appeal upheld their convictions, stating the defence was only open where the causative feature of the commission of the offence was extraneous to the offender.

IMMEDIATE OR IMMINENT?

In **Abdul-Hussain [1999] Crim. L.R. 570 CA**, the defendants were Shiite Muslims, originally from Southern Iraq, then living in Sudan and fearing (legal) deportation to Iraq, where they believed they would face death. They hijacked an aeroplane, which eventually landed at Stansted airport. The defendants released the hostages and surrendered. At their trial they admitted the hijacking but pleaded duress, contending they only did it to escape death, either of themselves or of their families, at the hands of the Iraqi authorities. The trial judge ruled that the defence of necessity or duress of circumstances should not be left to the jury because the threat was insufficiently close and immediate to give rise to a virtually spontaneous reaction to the physical risk arising. The Court of Appeal quashed their convictions: an imminent peril of death or serious injury to D or his dependants was one that operated on his mind so as to over-bear his will. The period of time which elapsed between the inception of the peril and the defendant's act was a relevant but not conclusive factor. The court provided what Professor Smith described as "a vivid and persuasive example to support its decision":

> "If Anne Frank had stolen a car to escape from Amsterdam and been charged with theft, the tenets of English law would not, in our judgment, have denied her a defence of duress of circumstances, on the ground that she should have waited for the Gestapo's knock on the door." ([1999] Crim. L.R. 570)

The House of Lords in *Hasan* (considered further below) clearly preferred immediacy to imminence however; per Lord Bingham:

> "It should however be made clear to juries that if the retribution threatened against the defendant or his family or a person for whom he reasonably feels responsible is not such as he reasonably expects to follow *immediately or almost immediately* on his failure to comply with the threat, there may be little if any room for doubt that he could have taken evasive action, whether by going to the police or in some other way, to avoid committing the crime with which he is charged." (emphasis added)

A THREAT TO WHOM?

In *Conway* and *Pommell* above, the defendants acted as they did due to fear for the life or safety of another. In *Hasan*, Lord Bingham directed that the threat must be directed against (or, it is submitted, the circumstances must produce fear for) D or his immediate family, or someone close to him, or if not, to a person for whose safety D would reasonably regard himself as responsible. In **Wright [2000] Crim. L.R. 510 CA**, both D and her boyfriend had been threatened by her drug dealer with having their throats cut if she failed to travel to the West Indies and bring back a quantity of cocaine. The trial judge directed the jury, as to the threat against the boyfriend, to consider his proximity to D, being neither married to nor related by blood to D. On appeal, however, the boyfriend was held to come within a category of "some other person for whose safety the defendant would reasonably regard herself as responsible." In *Conway*, D and his passenger had no familial or other relationship, but it is clearly reasonable for a driver of a vehicle to regard himself as responsible for the safety of his passenger.

THE OBJECTIVE ELEMENTS

In *Graham* (above), the test of duress was based on the common law test of provocation in that it also has a subjective and an objective test. However, the subjective test in duress is not without its objectivity, as shown below:

1. whether D was or might have been induced to act as he did because, as a result of what he *reasonably believed*, D had *good cause* to fear that if he did not so act the [coercer] would kill him or cause him serious physical injury [or in the circumstances, death or serious injury would result]; and, if the answer was in the affirmative,
2. whether a *sober person of reasonable firmness* sharing D's characteristics would [have done the same] (emphasis added).

■ Good cause to believe

Mantell J. attempted in **Cairns [1999] 2 Cr. App. R. 137 CA** and **Martin (David) [2000] 2 Cr. App. R. 42** to draw an analogy between self-defence and duress, in order to make the first test entirely subjective. In *Martin (David)*, D had a schizoid-affective disorder which meant that he was more likely to regard things said to him as being threats, and to believe that such threats would be carried out, than a reasonable person would. These decisions cannot, however, survive the opinion of Lord Bingham in *Hasan*:

> "It is of course essential that the defendant should genuinely, i.e. actually, believe in the efficacy of the threat by which he claims to have been compelled. But there is no warrant for relaxing the requirement that the belief must be reasonable as well as genuine."

Provided D's belief that there is a threat is reasonable, there does not in fact have to be such a threat (**Safi [2003] Crim. L.R. 721**). Another hijacking case, D contended that he had acted under an imminent threat of death or serious injury from the Taliban regime in Afghanistan. The judge had directed that there had to be a threat in fact, but the Court of Appeal held this was a misdirection and the judge should have directed the jury to consider whether D's belief was reasonable.

■ The person of reasonable firmness

The second element of the *Graham* test is that a sober person of reasonable firmness, sharing D's characteristics, would have done the same. Whenever the law uses the reasonable person, with D's characteristics, as the objective comparator of D's acts, we must determine which of D's characteristics are relevant. The answer is never "all of them", otherwise there would be no objectivity at all.

Because the person in this test is one of reasonable firmness, the jury cannot consider any characteristics of the defendant which show that he is not such a person. Thus, in **Horne [1994] Crim. L.R. 584**, evidence of particular vulnerability and pliancy was not admissible. Similarly in **Hegarty [1994] Crim. L.R. 353**, the jury could take account of characteristics such as age, sex and physical health, but there was no scope for attributing to the hypothetical person the characteristic of being "emotionally unstable".

The Court of Appeal in **Bowen [1996] 2 Cr. App. R. 157** delivered a very useful summary of the key principles with respect to the characteristics of the person of reasonable firmness. There is recognition therein that characteristics peculiar to D are unlikely to be admissible, but where D falls within a category accepted by the law to be more vulnerable, or less able to resist the threat, that may be relevant:

> "Obvious examples are age, where a young person may well not be so robust as a mature one; possibly sex, though many women would doubtless consider they had as much moral courage to resist pressure as men; pregnancy, where there is added fear for the unborn child; serious physical disability, which may inhibit self protection; recognised mental illness or psychiatric condition, such as post traumatic stress disorder leading to learned helplessness."

Therefore on the facts, D's low intelligence quotient (IQ) short of recognised mental incapacity was not a relevant factor. The court recognised that duress is unlike the defence of provocation in this regard. Under s.3 of the Homicide Act 1957, individual characteristics such as homosexuality (where the taunt is directed at D's sexual orientation) could be significant in causing D to act in a certain way, but a strictly objective test has to be applied by a jury considering duress. This is for the policy reasons mentioned above on p.441.

The mention of "learned helplessness" in *Bowen* above is a reference to **Emery (1993) 14 Cr. App. R. (S.) 394** where the Court of Appeal was prepared to view the effects of long term abuse as relevant to D's will being crushed by the abuse. However, in **Flatt [1996] Crim. L.R. 576**, the Court of Appeal directed that drug addiction was not a characteristic but a self-induced condition, and was therefore irrelevant.

NOMINATED OFFENCE

This requirement applies to duress by threats only. The requirement is that the coercer must direct D to commit a particular crime (**Cole [1994] Crim. L.R. 582**). If, for example, a coercer says "Pay me the money you owe me or I'll kill you/your wife/your children", the defence of duress by threats is not available because he has not directed a crime be committed. D might have been able to raise the money legally. In *Cole*, the Court of Appeal held that D must commit "the very offence" nominated by the person making threats. So, would the threatener need to direct D to rob a particular bank on a particular street, or would "do a robbery to get the money" suffice? In **Ali (1994) 16 Cr. App. R. 692**, the court assumed that a demand to steal money from a bank/building society would be sufficient and it was not a requirement that a particular bank/building society be nominated by the person making the threats.

EVASIVE ACTION

This requirement ties in with the threat of immediate harm considered above on p.443. If the threatened harm will not ensue until later, the defence may fail for lack of immediacy, or there may not be a compulsion to commit the crime there and then, or D may have an opportunity to avoid the harm. D must take any opportunity to take evasive action, for example to run away or alert the police. In **Hudson and Taylor [1971] 2 Q.B. 202**, the defendants were two teenage girls who were on trial for perjury arising out of a previous trial in which they had lied. They pleaded duress on the basis that they had been warned by a man with a reputation for violence, and who was in the public gallery as they gave their evidence, that if they told the truth, they would be "cut up". At the perjury trial, the judge ruled that the threats were not sufficiently present and immediate to support the defence of duress, but it was held by the Court of Appeal that, although the threats could not be executed in the courtroom, they could have been carried out in the streets of Manchester that same night. The Court of Appeal's decision was described by Professor Glanville Williams, *Textbook of Criminal Law*, 2nd edn, as "an indulgent decision", and by Lord Bingham in *Hasan* as having had:

> "the unfortunate effect of weakening the requirement that execution of a threat must be reasonably believed to be imminent and immediate if it is to support a plea of duress … I can understand that the Court of Appeal had sympathy with the predicament of the young appellants but I cannot, consistently with principle, accept that a witness testifying in the Crown Court at Manchester has no opportunity to avoid complying with a threat *incapable of execution then or there*." (emphasis added)

In **Heath [2000] Crim. L.R. 109**, D was a heroin user who owed his supplier £1500. The supplier passed the debt to someone else, X. D was contacted and threatened by X. X refused D's offer to pay by installments or to pay him by D selling his car, but D was told that £1000 would be wiped off his debt if he collected a van containing a consignment of shampoo and drove it to Bristol. D met X, whom he recognised as a man of violence. D claimed that he had agreed to drive the van (which in fact contained drugs) out of fear. X knew where D lived and about D's girlfriend and X had a reputation for violence. D also said he had not contacted the police or his family because he was a heroin addict. The court held that duress was not available as there were safe avenues of escape available to D but he had chosen not to take them.

VOLUNTARY ASSOCIATION WITH VIOLENT CRIMINALS

A person may bring the duress upon himself and, where he does, the defence fails. This is called self-induced duress. For example, in **Fitzpatrick [1977] N.I. 20**, an IRA case, the Court of Criminal Appeal in Northern Ireland held:

> "A person may become associated with a sinister group of men with criminal objectives and coercive methods of ensuring that their lawless enterprises are carried out and thereby voluntarily expose himself to illegal compulsion ... if a person voluntarily exposes and submits himself ... to illegal compulsion, he cannot rely on the duress to which he has voluntarily exposed himself as an excuse either in respect of the crimes he commits against his will or in respect of his continued but unwilling association with those capable of exercising upon him the duress which he calls in aid."

Some of the issues involved here include:

1. Does D have to join an organised "gang"?
2. Does D have to know he may be subject to threats by others?
3. If no to 2. is the defence available if D did not know, but he should have known?
4. In either case, does D have to know, or ought to know, he may be subjected (a) to coercion to commit crimes in general, or (b) to coercion to commit the type of crime with which he is now charged?

The conflicting decisions of the Court of Appeal in **Sharp [1987] Q.B. 853**, **Shepherd (1987) 86 Cr. App. R. 47**, *Heath* (above) and **Baker [1999] 2 Cr. App. R. 335** were clarified in **Hasan [2005] UKHL 22**. D was charged with aggravated burglary and his defence was duress. He claimed that he had been coerced into committing the burglary by S, a man with a reputation of being violent and a drug dealer. The judge directed the jury that the defence would not be available to D if it found that by associating with S he had voluntarily put himself in a position in which he knew that he was likely to be subjected to threats. Lord Bingham, with whom Lords Steyn, Rodger and Brown agreed, explained:

"The defendant is, ex hypothesi, a person who has voluntarily surrendered his will to the domination of another. Nothing should turn on foresight of the manner in which, in the event, the dominant party chooses to exploit the defendant's subservience ... In holding that there must be foresight of coercion to commit crimes of the kind with which the defendant is charged, R v Baker mis-stated the law."

Following *Hasan*, it is now the law that if a person voluntarily becomes or remains associated with others engaged in criminal activity in a situation where he knows or ought reasonably to know that he may be the subject of compulsion by them or their associates, he cannot rely on the defence of duress. The questions 1.–4. above are therefore answered no, no, no and (b).

Availability of the Defence

In **DPP for Northern Ireland v Lynch [1975] A.C. 653**, the House of Lords held by a 3:2 majority that duress could be a defence to an accessory to murder, but this part of the decision was overruled in **Howe [1987] 1 A.C. 417**. In **Gotts [1992] 2 A.C. 412**, their Lordships took *Howe* to a logical conclusion and held that duress was not available as a defence to attempted murder.

The rationale for a blanket exclusion of duress as a defence to a charge of murder (and being an accessory to murder) was stated by Lord Griffiths:

"It is based upon the special sanctity that the law attaches to human life and which denies to a man the right to take an innocent life even at the price of his own or another's life."

Howe attracted much criticism because it required D to be a hero, to sacrifice himself or another for whom he is responsible, rather than take another's life. But it fails to give any thought at all to an argument, as offensive as it might be, as to quantity; take one life to spare many? Or the quality argument; take the life of an old person to spare the life of a child? Neither do these examples have simple solutions, but when one considers the amount of morally complex, ethically challenging issues currently left to the jury, it is illogical that duress is embargoed on a murder charge. Consider further the nature of implied malice in the mens rea of murder (see Ch.4). If D stabs V with intent to cause GBH only, and V survives, D is entitled to plead duress and have it left to the jury. But say V is, unknown to D, a haemophiliac and dies, D has no such defence. The availability of the defence should not be down to such matters of chance when the mens rea is the same.

The sanctity of life reason proffered by Lord Griffith above cannot be true with respect to attempted murder, where V has not died. So what of a defendant who is charged with attempted murder for causing serious, but non-fatal injuries where he intended to cause serious harm, but the prosecution thinks it can prove intent to kill (the mens rea for attempted murder)? The jury is not allowed to hear evidence of duress. But if on the same facts, the prosecution thought that it could only prove intent to cause GBH, the jury will consider the defence.

Over time, the Law Commission has made several recommendations concerning the availability of the defence. The most recent in "Murder, Manslaughter and Infanticide" (Law Com. No.304, 2006) recommends making the defence generally available, and in *Hasan*, Lord Bingham noted that "the logic of this argument is irresistible."

There is uncertainty as to whether duress is available as a defence to treason. The Court of Appeal in both *Pommell* and *Shayler* (below) commented that duress was potentially a defence to all crimes except "murder, attempted murder and some forms of treason". This is probably because in **Steane [1947] K.B. 997 CCA** Lord Goddard was of the opinion that duress was never a defence to treason. *Steane* is probably per incuriam, however, because a recent decision to the contrary (**Purdy (1945) 10 J.C.L. 182**) was not cited.

Reform of Duress

AVAILABILITY
The Law Commission Report, "Murder, Manslaughter and Infanticide" (Law Com. No.304, 2006) recommends that duress should be a full defence to all crimes (Pt 6). The person of reasonable firmness is replaced with a person of ordinary courage.

■ Proof
It is current law that the burden of proving duress lies on the prosecution. Therefore, if there is evidence of duress, the defence succeeds unless the prosecution proves beyond reasonable doubt any of the elements explained above. However, in its report, "Legislating the Criminal Code: Offences against the Person and General Principles" (Law Com. No.218, 1993), the Law Commission recommended that the legal burden of proving duress should be placed on D. Placing a proof burden on D has always been something strongly resisted by the Law Commission, but, as it points out in para.33 of this report, the defence of duress is peculiarly difficult for the prosecution to investigate and disprove beyond reasonable doubt. This recommendation has been included in the 2006 report, in which the Law Commission suggests a reverse proof burden would not be incompatible with art.6 of the European Convention on Human Rights. However, Lord Bingham in *Hasan* seems unconvinced of the "merits of doing so".

FIGURE 13.1 **The requirements and limitations imposed in the defence of duress**

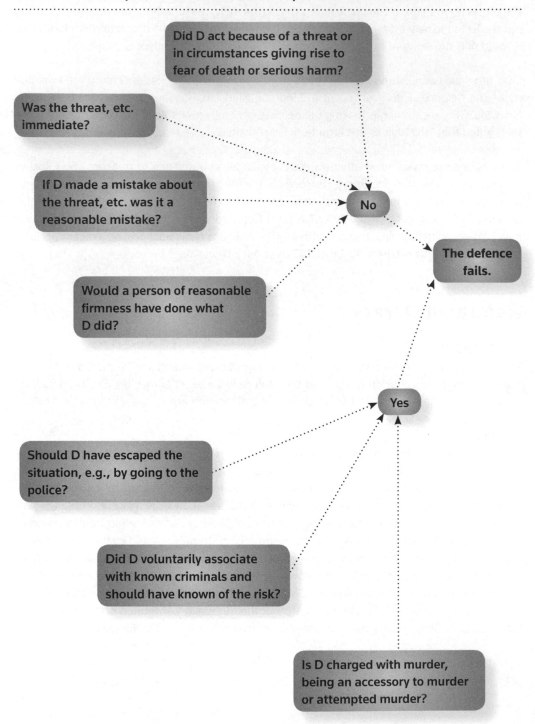

Over to you...

Duress is a complex defence and there is much to revise. You should learn the elements (you might think of them as hurdles that D must jump successfully in order for the defence to succeed) but at all times keep your eye on the burden of proof. D must adduce evidence of duress (enough to meet the evidential burden, see Ch.1) and the prosecution bears the proof burden; i.e. that, for example, D was not subjected to the "right" sort of threat, or the situation lacked immediacy, or he associated with the "wrong" people and so on. Try to revise at least one authority for each "hurdle".

Necessity

In many of the cases above, especially those concerned with duress of circumstances, the Court of Appeal and House of Lords have treated the defence as synonymous with the term "necessity".

In *Shayler*, D was a former employee of the security service, and faced trial for disclosing information in breach of the Official Secrets Act 1989. He contended, inter alia, that the defences of duress and necessity were available to him on the basis that the disclosure was necessary in the public interest to avert damage to life and limb or serious damage to property, or to expose serious and pervasive illegality. The Court of Appeal held ([2001] 1 W.L.R. 2206) that duress and necessity were one and the same defence, but D could not rely on it as he was not in a position to identify any external action which created an imminent threat to life and limb of members of the general public.

The Court of Appeal's reasoning in *Shayler* has been forcefully criticised for making one from two separate defences. Gardner argues ([2005] Crim. L.R. 371):

"It is striking that the judgment of the Court of Appeal in Shayler contains no real argument for its position that justificatory necessity has little currency in English law, and that the phenomenon referred to as 'the defence of necessity' thus consists almost entirely in the excusatory defence of duress of circumstances. The passage in question ([2001] 1 W.L.R. 2206 at [52]–[56]) merely draws together what are really no more than a few incautious remarks in other sources, (The judgment overlooks the more satisfactorily reasoned previous statement of the same position, by the Court of Appeal in Pommell [1995] 2 Cr. App. R. 607 at 614), before asserting that the distinction ... has 'correctly, been by and large ignored or blurred by the courts', and depicting the upshot wholly in terms of the excusatory form."

On appeal to the House of Lords ([2003] 1 A.C. 247), their Lordships refused to consider the defence at all, and Lord Bingham specifically said he would not endorse all that the Court of Appeal had said on the matter. Because the defence was not available on the facts, anything said would have been obiter, but the House of Lords missed an opportunity to clarify whether the defence does actually exist, and if so, what its boundaries might be.

Medical Necessity

There is no doubt that the defence of necessity exists within the medical field, something accepted even by the Court of Appeal in *Shayler*. For example, in **F v West Berkshire HA [1990] 2 A.C. 1**, the House of Lords allowed the sterilisation of a 36 year old woman who had severe learning disabilities, holding it was in the patient's best interest. There is little by way of detailed guidance on the limits of the operation of the defence, but it has been considered in **Airedale NHS Trust v Bland [1993] 1 All E.R. 821, R. v Bournewood Community and Mental Health NHS Trust ex parte L [1998] 3 All E.R. 289, A (Medical Treatment: Male Sterilisation), Re [2000] 1 F.C.R. 193; S (Adult Patient: Sterilisation), Re [2001] Fam 15, NHS Trust v T (Adult Patient: Refusal of Medical Treatment) [2005] 1 All E.R. 387**, to name a few.

However, as Gardner points out ([2005] Crim. L.R. 371), what appear to be necessary medical acts are, on closer analysis, necessary and lawful acts within a medical context. These cases are not limited to emergency medical treatment, for example, so it would not be a huge leap for the judiciary to expand the defence, if they were so minded (see p.455 below). Many judges feel constrained, however, and resist the expansion of the defence, by two previous cases:

1. In **London Borough of Southwark v Williams [1971] 2 All E.R. 175 CA**, Lord Denning warned that "necessity would open a door which no man could shut ... if hunger were once allowed to be an excuse for stealing, it would open a way through which all kinds of disorder and lawlessness would pass".
2. The apparently incontrovertible decision in *Dudley and Stephens*, to which we now turn our attention.

Necessity and Murder

One of the most famous criminal law cases of all time is **Dudley and Stephens (1884–85) L.R. 14 Q.B.D. 273**. At a murder trial, the jury returned a "special" verdict. This means they heard the evidence and made a statement as to the facts of the case, but did not come to a verdict of guilt or innocence. The Lord Chief Justice, Lord Coleridge, then applied the facts as found by the jury to the law, and held that necessity was not a defence to murder. *Dudley and Stephens* were sailors who, with two others, had been shipwrecked and were all together in a life boat. After 18 days at sea, and seven days without food and five without water, Dudley suggested to Stephens that they should kill and eat the cabin boy who was ill and delirious from drinking salt water. They were later rescued and were brought back to England to face trial for murder. Lord Coleridge's judgment seemed to demand that the defendants had the benefit of hindsight in advance, in that they apparently should have known they were going to be rescued:

> "The prisoners put to death a weak and unoffending boy upon the chance of preserving their own lives by feeding upon his flesh and blood after he was killed, and with the certainty of depriving him of any possible chance of survival. The verdict finds in terms that 'if the men had not fed upon the body of the boy they would probably not have survived,' and that 'the boy being in a much weaker condition was likely to have died before them.' They might possibly have been picked up next day by a passing ship; they might possibly not have been picked up at all; in either case it is obvious that the killing of the boy would have been an unnecessary and profitless act. It is found by the verdict that the boy was incapable of resistance, and, in fact, made none; and it is not even suggested that his death was due to any violence on his part attempted against, or even so much as feared by, those who killed him."

If it was not necessary to kill the cabin boy because he was not a threat to the defendants, and they were later rescued, arguably, the judgment leaves a lacuna in which the defence could succeed if the victim was killed because he was putting the lives of others in danger. Although there is no decision of a criminal court to this effect, the following events give us pause for thought. In 1987, the ferry, The Herald of Free Enterprise, sank after leaving the port of Zeebrugge with its bow doors open. 197 people died. At the coroner's inquest a man, X, testified that he had been on the ferry and he and dozens of other people had been in the water near the foot of a rope ladder leading to a life boat. A young man, Y, who was petrified by cold or fear was on the ladder and, for at least ten minutes he was unable to move up or down. Eventually X instructed those nearest to push Y off the ladder, which they did, and Y was never seen again. The others were then able to climb up the ladder to safety. X was not prosecuted for murder, but it is generally thought (see, e.g. Lectures on "Necessity and Duress", J.C. Smith) that he could have pleaded necessity and the court could have distinguished *Dudley and Stephens* on the grounds that X had not made a choice as to who had to die, because the unfortunate young man on the ladder had chosen himself by his immobility there. The second was that, unlike the ship's boy ... the young man, although in no way at fault, was preventing others from going where they had a right, and a most urgent need, to go, and was thereby unwittingly imperiling their lives.

We can infer from this then that because in *Dudley and Stephens* the defendants elected to kill the cabin boy, who was no threat to them, the defence failed. In (**A (Children), Re [2001] 2 W.L.R. 480**), Brooke L.J. (with whom Ward and Walker L.JJ. agreed on this point) also cited the example of:

"A pilotless aircraft, out of control and running out of fuel ... heading for a densely populated town. Those inside the aircraft were in any event 'destined to die'. There would be no question of human choice in selecting the candidates for death, and if their inevitable deaths were accelerated by the plane being brought down on waste ground the lives of countless other innocent people in the town they were approaching would be saved."

The case of the conjoined twins (A, Re) is the most recent pronouncement on the defence, but it is not a criminal case. An analysis of the decision follows a brief explanation of the tragic facts of the case. Jodie and Mary were conjoined twin girls who were born to devout Roman Catholic parents. They were joined at the pelvis. Each girl had her own brain, heart and lungs and other vital organs and her own arms and legs. However, Mary's heart and lungs were too weak to oxygenate and pump blood through her own body, so Jodie, the stronger twin, sustained Mary's life. Medical evidence was given that if they were not separated Jodie's heart would eventually fail and they would both die within a few months of their birth. However, if they were separated the doctors were convinced that Jodie would have a life which was worthwhile although Mary would die within minutes. The parents refused to consent to the operation on religious grounds. The hospital sought an application for a declaration that it could lawfully carry out separation. This was granted at first instance, and this decision was upheld on appeal. The operation would cause the inevitable death of Mary, but it was an act of necessity. Brooke L.J. adopted a test of necessity proffered by Sir James Stephen, a 19th century judge, (History of the Criminal Law of England (1883), vol.2) that necessity is a defence if:

1. the act is needed to avoid inevitable and irreparable evil;
2. no more should be done than is reasonably necessary for the purpose to be achieved; and
3. the evil inflicted must not be disproportionate to the evil avoided.

So, does A, Re, change the rule in *Dudley and Stephens* that necessity is no defence to murder? The answer is, simply, no. First, it must be noted that A, Re is not a criminal case, but a civil action by a hospital seeking a declaration to perform an operation.

Second, there was no charge of murder. Third, it is a decision of the Court of Appeal, Civil Division, which has only persuasive effect on criminal courts. Following Lord Coleridge's dicta to the letter, necessity is no defence to murder. However, perhaps there is an argument that *Dudley and Stephens* was not a case of necessity at all. Because the choice as to victim was made by the sailors, this was a case of (unsuccessful) duress of circumstances rather than necessity (if they are separate defences, see below). In order to avoid death or serious injury, the defendants killed the cabin boy. Because it did not matter which of the four died to save the others, it is unlike the conjoined twins case. The cabin boy was not by his conduct directly or indirectly bringing the others near death, but Mary was causing Jodie's death (and Y would have caused the death of X and the others had they not pushed him from the ladder). The reason the defence failed in *Dudley and Stephens* could be because no reasonable person would have done as they did.

Necessity and other Crimes

The defence of necessity has been rarely argued before the courts, but has occasionally been successful. For example, in **Johnson v Phillips [1976] 1 W.L.R. 65**, the Court of Appeal held that a police officer may, in the execution of his duty, order a motorist to disobey traffic regulations if such a direction is reasonably necessary for the preservation of life or property. D was waiting in his vehicle behind an ambulance. A police officer told him to reverse about 10 to 15 yards the wrong way down a one-way street. D refused and was arrested for obstructing a police officer in the execution of his duty. The Court of Appeal stated that D would have been able to reply on the defence of necessity had he committed the traffic violations.

However, some more recent attempts have failed. In **Altham [2006] EWCA Crim. 7**, the Court of Appeal held that a person who used cannabis for pain relief and who was charged with possessing a controlled drug could not raise a defence of necessity by relying on art.3 of the European Convention on Human Rights (inhuman or degrading treatment or punishment). A similar argument had been rejected based on art.8 (private life) in **Quayle [2005] 1 W.L.R. 3642**. In *Quayle*, the Court of Appeal had to consider, inter alia, whether the defence of necessity could be left to the jury in respect of the possession of cannabis under the Misuse of Drugs Act 1971. D believed that using cannabis was necessary to avoid suffering pain arising from a pre-existing medical condition. The court's answer was no. The decision was particularly unhelpful, it lacked full reasoning, but worse, it did not deal with either duress or necessity, but "a novel hybrid: 'necessity of circumstances'." (David Ormerod in his commentary on *Quayle* at [2006] Crim. L.R. 148.)

Arguments against the Existence of the Defence of Necessity

Lord Denning argued forcefully (above in *London Borough of Southwark v Williams*) that a defence of necessity would be an excuse for crime and there would be no end to its use. The decision in *Dudley*, although not without criticism, certainly suggests there is no such defence, or none to murder. In **Buckoke v Greater London Council [1971] Ch. 655** the Court of Appeal (Lord Denning again) suggested obiter that where, for example, a fire engine driver drove through a red light to get to a burning building, the prosecution had a discretion not to prosecute (similarly the CPS declined to prosecute in the Herald of Free Enterprise "necessity" example given on p.453 above). Finally, the defence of necessity may simply be the defence of duress of circumstances under another name and the rules governing the defence are well established by the common law, including those as to its availability.

Why should the Defence be Recognised?

In his commentary on *Quayle*, Ormerod argues forcefully that duress and necessity are, or at least should be, separate defences:

> A plea of necessity avoids many of the restrictions which constrain duress of circumstances: there is no requirement of a threat of death or serious injury and thus no need to inquire into the equivalence of pain and injury; the defence is potentially available to all crimes, even murder (*A Re*); and, there is no requirement of immediacy: "the principle is one of necessity not emergency", per Lord Goff in **F v West Berkshire HA [1990] 2 A.C. 1 at 75**.

There seems to be a wide-spread judicial reluctance to acknowledge the existence of the defence outside medical cases. Certainly, it could never be a subjective test of whether D thought his acts were necessary but, even assessed objectively as it was in *A, Re* judges appear to be very uncomfortable with the task of balancing competing rights and interests. The task is inherently complex and necessarily involves making difficult judgments about the relative strength of economic, ethical, medical or "human" rights. Rather than do so, the appellate courts simply say the defence does not exist, or if it does, it is the same as duress of circumstances but by a different name. This is, however, unsatisfactory:

> "... in some instances it may produce illogical results: D who sees V in pain can act to save him and rely on necessity (e.g. when driving while disqualified to rush V to hospital), but cannot act similarly to save himself from identical pain. As a matter of evidence, for the defence to be credible may well require the source of the threat to be from an external source, but that does not mean that as a matter of substantive law the threat must have manifested itself externally for it to be well founded" ([2006] Crim. L.R. 148).

There is a difference, one perhaps missed by all courts since *Dudley and Stephens*, between the theoretical acknowledgement of the existence of a defence, and the defence failing on the facts of the case. For example, if we accept the argument above as right, that in *Dudley and Stephens* the defence pleaded was actually duress (albeit in the name of necessity), rather than accepting that it was unsuccessful on the facts (notably the objective test), Lord Coleridge C.J. concluded the defence of necessity did not exist on a charge of murder. To say it is enough to leave the defence in the hands of the CPS is to under-estimate the importance of certainty in the criminal law; prosecutorial discretion is not sufficient because it can lead to inconsistency. In *Buckoke v Greater London Council* (above), Buckley L.J. suggested obiter that citizens should not be left to decide for themselves whether to commit offences which may as the law stands involve them in difficulties. Also, it could be said as a matter of principle that people who have not acted in a morally wrong way or for the good of others should not be said to have committed a crime.

To avoid a moral, social or ethical conundrum, with which a trial judge may be unable to deal, Gardner suggests ([2005] Crim. L.R. 371) a test not based on Stephen's view of competing evils (*A, Re*) but on competing rights:

1. the conduct that would otherwise be a crime is necessary to vindicate a legal right, and
2. that right is superior to any right that the offence itself was designed to protect, and
3. a no less aggressive course of action was open to D.

He gives the example of D ruining another's coat when, there being no less aggressive alternative, he uses the coat to save a child from drowning. This child's right to life under art.2 ECHR is vindicated, so the act is justified.

Marital Coercion and Superior Orders

These defences rarely appear in exam papers and a detailed examination of each is beyond the scope of this text. Briefly, marital coercion is a common law defence available to a married woman who commits a crime in the presence of her husband and under his coercion to the extent that her will is overborne. There is no requirement that D was threatened with physical force to rely on the defence; "moral force or emotional threats will suffice" (**Cairns [2002] EWCA Crim 2838**). Unlike with duress, the burden of proof, to the civil standard, is on D so, if available, duress will normally be the preferred defence.

According to obiter in **Clegg [1995] 1 All E.R. 334**, there is no defence of superior orders, i.e. D cannot rely on the defence that he was merely following the orders of someone with authority over him, either in civilian life or in the military.

◄···

Summary

1. **Consent.** Many offences against the person, including the non-fatal assaults and sexual offences, cannot be committed where V consents, see Ch. 5.

2. **Self-defence and prevention of crime.** A complete defence either under the common law defence or s.3 of the Criminal Law Act 1967, a person may use reasonable force (the test is now contained in the CJ&IA 2008 s.76). It is a two part test. A person may use such force as is (objectively) reasonable in the circumstances as he (subjectively) believes them to be, even if he is mistaken. There is no legal duty to retreat, and D may make a pre-emptive strike against an imminent threat.

3. **Duress.** This is one defence of two types; by threats and circumstances. Traditionally, the defence is expressed as having two stages:

   (a) whether D was induced to act as he did because, as a result of what he reasonably believed, D had good cause to fear that if he did not so act the [coercer] would immediately kill him or cause him (or someone close or for whom he reasonably regarded himself as responsible) serious physical injury [or in the circumstances, death or serious injury would result]; and, if so,

   (b) whether a sober person of reasonable firmness sharing D's characteristics would [have done the same];

   D must not fail to take an opportunity to take evasive action; if D voluntarily becomes or remains associated with others engaged in criminal activity in a situation where he knows or ought reasonably to know that he may be the subject of compulsion by them or their associates, he cannot rely on the defence of duress; The defence is currently not available on a charge of murder nor attempted murder.

4. **Necessity**. Outside the medical field, the defence's existence is not clear nor, if it does exist, are its boundaries.

End of Chapter Question

Question
"The courts seem unable to decide whether the defence of necessity does exist as a form of duress, or does not exist at all."

Consider the truth of the above statement.

Points of Answer
- Start with a simple definition of duress (*Conway, Pommell,* etc.) and attempt a definition of necessity (perhaps citing the Stephen test, above).
- Cite the facts and decision in *Dudley and Stephens*. Explain it is possible it is a (failed) duress case rather than a true necessity case (if they differ).

- ◆ Explain the decision in *A, Re* noting it is a medical case and was decided in the Court of Appeal (Civil Division), but nevertheless held that a defence of necessity would shield the doctors from liability for murder.
- ◆ Provide an explanation that the defence of necessity has detractors; use the arguments provided above.
- ◆ Note on the other hand that current academic writings argue they are separate— duress reflects urgency, necessity reflects inevitable and avoidable harms (*A, Re*), and, perhaps, also mention the other medical cases such as *F, Re* (although not criminal).
- ◆ Answers should conclude with some arguments about whether or not they do, or should, exist separately.

Further Reading

I. Dennis, "A Pointless Exercise" [2008] Crim. L.R. 507; "Defending self-defence" [2010] Crim. L.R. 167 and "Duress, Murder and Criminal Responsibility" (1980) 96 L.Q.R. 208.

S. Gardner, "Direct Action and the Defence of Necessity" [2005] Crim. L.R. 371.

D. Lanham, "Offensive Weapons and Self Defence" [2005] Crim. L.R. 85.

D. Ormerod, "Necessity of circumstance" [2006] Crim. L.R. 148.

P. Reed, "Rashford—Self-defence and Motive for Revenge" (2006) 166 Crim. Law. 1.

P. Robinson, "Criminal Law defences: A Systematic Analysis" (1982) 82 Col. L.R. 199.

J.C. Smith, "Justifications and Excuses in Criminal Law" (1989).

J.C. Smith and T. Rees, "Homicide: Murder—Excessive Force in Self-Defence" [2002] Crim. L.R. 136.

K.J.M. Smith, "Must Heroes Behave Heroically?" [1989] Crim. L.R. 622.

G. Williams, "The Theory of Excuses" [1982] Crim. L.R. 732.

W. Wilson, "The Structure of Criminal Defences" [2005] Crim. L.R. 122.

Self Test Questions

To test your knowledge gained from this section go online to *http://www.sweetandmaxwell. co.uk* and take our online self test questions. Here you will also find key updates to ensure that you are only ever one click away from an instant update.

LEGAL TAXONOMY
FROM SWEET & MAXWELL

This index has been prepared using Sweet & Maxwell's Legal Taxonomy. Main index entries conform to keywords provided by the Legal Taxonomy except where references to specific documents or non-standard terms (denoted by quotation marks) have been included. These keywords provide a means of identifying similar concepts in other Sweet & Maxwell publications and online services to which keywords from the Legal Taxonomy have been applied. Readers may find some minor differences between terms used in the text and those which appear in the index.

Suggestions to **sweet&maxwell.taxonomy@thomson.com**.

Index

Absolute liability
see **Strict liability**
Abstraction of electricity
generally, 223
Abuse of position of trust
child sex offences, 192–194
fraud by abuse of position, 284
Accessories
see also **Assisting offenders;**
Encouraging or assisting crime;
Joint enterprise
acquittal or reduction in liability of principal
principal having defence unavailable to accessory, 363–364
principal lacking mens rea, 362–363
actus reus, 346
aiding, abetting, counselling or procuring, 342–344
definition, 342
innocent agents, 341–342
intention, 347–348
introduction, 340
joint enterprise, 344
knowledge, 348–350
liability, 345, 351
liability for more serious offence than principal, 364
mens rea, 347–350
omissions, 346–347
principal offence, need for, 345–346
principals distinguished, 340–341
reform, 367–368
summary, 377–379
transferred malice, 351
victims, 367
withdrawal of participation
communication of withdrawal, 365–366

effective withdrawal, 364–365
introduction, 364
Accomplices
see **Accessories; Assisting offenders; Joint enterprise**
Acts of Parliament
sources of law, 4–5
statutory interpretation, 6
Actual bodily harm
see **Assault**
Actus reus
acts, 13–14
attempts, 13
causation
breaking chain of causation, 26–36
establishing chain of causation, 25
factual causation, 25
legal causation, 25–26
reform, 36–37
result crimes, 23–24
circumstances, 23
coincidence with mens rea, 37–38
continuing acts, 21, 37–38
definition, 12–13
introduction, 12
omissions
assumption of responsibility, 19–21
contractual duties, 16–17
creation of dangerous situation, 21–22
duties arising out of public office, 17–18
establishing a legal duty, 22
general principles, 14–15
offences capable of being committed by omission, 15–16
relationships, 18
statutory duties, 22
supervening fault, 21–22

state of affairs offences, 22–23
summary, 38–40
Administering substances with intent
sexual offences, 186–187
Aggravated burglary
generally, 256–257
Aggravated criminal damage
actus reus, 299–300
basic offence distinguished, 299
definition, 299
endangerment of life, 299
lawful excuse, 301
mens rea, 300–301
sentence, 299
Aggravation on racial or religious grounds
see **Racially aggravated offences; Religiously aggravated offences**
Aiding and abetting
see **Accessories**
Animals
criminal damage, 295
theft, 222–223
Appeals
generally, 6–8
Arson
see **Criminal damage**
Assault
see also **Battery; Sexual offences**
actual bodily harm
actus reus, 145–146
mens rea, 147
actus reus
acts, 140–141
apprehension of unlawful force, 139–140
immediate harm, 141–142
words, 140–141
assault with intent to rob, 250
consent
fraud, 165–166

horseplay, 163
informed consent, 166–167
introduction, 160
mistake, 160, 165–166
public interest, 161–167
sadomasochism, 164–165
sexual activity, 163–165
sports, 162–163
status as a defence, 160
valid consent, 160–161
definition, 139
introduction, 138–139
mens rea, 142
racially or religiously aggravated
offences, 152–154
reform proposals, 151–152
summary, 168–169
Assisting offenders
generally, 368–369
Attempts
actus reus
generally, 13, 314
more than merely preparatory,
315–318, 319
questions of fact and law, 315
relevance of offence charged, 315
definition, 314
impossibility, 320–321
introduction, 314
mens rea
acts and consequences, 319–320
circumstances, 320
conditional intention, 320
generally, 318
reform proposals, 321–323
summary, 337
summary of requirements, 322
Attorney-General's references
generally, 7
Automatism
see also **Insanity**
actus reus, 13–14
definition, 409
intoxication, 405
introduction, 409
lack of actus reus and/or mens rea,
409–410
reform proposals, 412
requirements of defence, 410–411
self-induced automatism, 411–412
Battered woman syndrome
provocation, 108–109
Battery
see also **Assault**

actus reus
indirect force, 143–144
omissions, 144
unlawful force, 143
consent
fraud, 165–166
horseplay, 163
informed consent, 166–167
introduction, 160
mistake, 160, 165–166
public interest, 161–167
sadomasochism, 164–165
sexual activity, 163–165
sports, 162–163
status as a defence, 160
valid consent, 160–161
definition, 143
introduction, 138–139
mens rea, 145
reform proposals, 151–152
summary, 168–169

Bigamy
mistake, 387
Bilking
see **Making off without
payment**
Blackmail
actus reus, 257–259
definition, 257
demands, 258
menaces, 258–259
mens rea, 259–261
sentence, 257
unwarranted demands, 259–260
view to gain or intent to cause loss,
260–261
Burden of proof
see also **Standard of proof**
defence, 8–9
prosecution, 8
Burglary
actus reus
entry, 252–253
building or part of building,
254–255
trespass, 253–254
aggravated burglary, 256–257
definition, 251–252
mens rea, 255–256
sentence, 251

Case law
sources of law, 4–5

Causation
breaking chain of causation
drug users, 33–35
egg shell skull, 35–36
flight by victim, 31–32
introduction, 26–27
naturally occurring events, 27
neglect of victim to treat injuries,
32–33
negligent medical treatment,
29–31
third party conduct, 27–29
victims' conduct, 31–35
establishing chain of causation, 25
factual causation, 25
legal causation, 25–26
reform proposals, 36–37
result crimes, 23–24
summary, 40
Children
child sex offences
abuse of position of trust,
192–194
arranging or facilitating, 195
familial child sex offences,
195–196
generally, 189–193
introduction, 189
sexual grooming, 194–195
doli incapax, 423–424
homicide
causing death of children or
vulnerable adults, 127–128
infanticide, 126
necessity, 454–455
unborn children, 85
innocent agents, 341–342
Choses in action
theft, 220–221
Civil proceedings
criminal proceedings distinguished, 3
Coercion
defences, 457
Common law
sources of law, 4–5
Companies' liability
see **Corporate liability**
Complicity
see **Accessories; Assisting
offenders; Joint enterprise**
Confidential information
theft, 223
Conjoined twins
necessity, 454–455

Consent
  criminal damage, 306–307
  defences, 430–431
  offences against the person
    fraud, 165–166
    horseplay, 163
    informed consent, 166–167
    introduction, 160
    mistake, 160, 165–166
    public interest, 161–167
    sadomasochism, 164–165
    sexual activity, 163–165
    sports, 162–163
    status as a defence, 160
    valid consent, 160–161
  sexual offences
    background to SOA 2003, 197
    deception, 200–202
    definition, 197–198
    impersonation, 202
    intoxication, 202–204
    introduction, 196–197
    presumptions, 198–202
  theft, 213–216
Conspiracy
  actus reus, 324–325
  common law offences, 323–324
  conspiracy to defraud, 278–281
  definition, 324
  impossibility, 327
  introduction, 314
  mens rea, 326–327
  reform proposals, 327–328
  summary, 337
Continuing acts
  actus reus, 21, 37–38
  theft, 219
Corporate liability
  acting through company officers,
    374–375
  aggregation, 377
  attribution of acts and knowledge,
    377
  identification doctrine, 375–377
  introduction, 374
  vicarious liability distinguished, 374
Corporate manslaughter
  see **Manslaughter**
Corpses
  see **Human remains**
Counselling and procuring
  see **Accessories**
Courts
  overview of structure, 6–8

Crime
  definition, 2–3
Crime prevention
  burden of proof, 431
  definition, 431
  effect of defence, 436
  human rights, 439
  mistake, 386–387, 436–438
  reasonable force
    duty to retreat, 435
    generally, 432–434
    need to act, 434–435
    pre-emptive strikes, 435–436
    proportionality, 435
  reform proposals, 439
  sources of law, 431–432
Criminal damage
  actus reus
    belonging to another,
      296–297
    damage, 293–294
    destruction, 295
    property, 295
    removal of machine parts, 294
    wheel clamping, 294
  aggravated criminal damage
    actus reus, 299–300
    basic offence distinguished, 299
    definition, 299
    endangerment of life, 299
    lawful excuse, 301
    mens rea, 300–301
    sentence, 299
  arson, 301–302
  basic offence, 292–293
  intention, 297
  introduction, 292
  lawful excuse
    belief in consent, 306–307
    belief in protection of property,
      307–308
    generally, 305–306
    intoxication, 309, 403
  machine parts, removal of, 294
  mens rea
    intention, 297
    recklessness, 298
  possession with intent to
    damage, 304
  racially or religiously aggravated
    offences, 305
  recklessness, 298
  sentence, 292
  summary, 309

  threatening to commit criminal
    damage, 303
  wheel clamping, 294
Criminal law
  nature and function, 2–3
  objectivism/subjectivism
    compared, 3–4

Deception
  see also **Fraud**
  consent
    offences against the person,
      165–166
    sexual offences, 200–202
  former offences, 277–278
  theft, 213–216
Declarations of incompatibility
  human rights, 6
Diabetes
  insanity, 415–416
Diminished responsibility
  see also **Manslaughter**
  abnormality of mind, 92–94, 96–97
  burden of proof, 91–92, 98
  intoxication, 94–96
  introduction, 91
  revised definition, 96–98
  substantial impairment, 94–96, 97
Disease of the mind
  see **Insanity**
Dishonesty
  see also **Fraud**
  handling stolen goods, 271
  obtaining services dishonestly,
    285–286
  theft
    exceptions, 231–232
    Ghosh test, 234–237
    question of fact or law, 233–237
    reform proposals, 237, 239
    "Robin Hood defence", 236–237
    summary, 238
    willingness to pay, 232–233
Doli incapax
  defences, 423–424
Double jeopardy
  retrials following acquittal, 7–8
Drugs
  see also **Intoxication**
  causation, 33–35
  unlawful act manslaughter, 125–126
Duress
  see also **Necessity**
  availability of defence, 448–449

burden of proof, 449
duress of circumstances, 440–441
elements of defence
    death or serious injury, 442–443
    good cause to believe, 445–446
    immediate or imminent threat,
      442–443
    introduction, 441–442
    objective elements, 445–448
    person of reasonable firmness,
      446–44
    to whom threats directed, 444
evasive action, 446–447
introduction, 439–440
nominated offence, 446
reform proposals, 449
self-induced duress, 447–448
types, 440
voluntary association with violent
    criminals, 447–448

Duty of care
manslaughter by gross negligence
    breach of duty, 119
    causation, 120
    criticisms of law, 120–121
    current law, 116–117
    development of law, 115–116
    duty, 117–118
    gross negligence, 120
    human rights, 120–121
    reform proposals, 121
    risk of death, 119
omissions as actus reus
    assumption of responsibility, 19–21
    battery, 144
    contractual duties, 16–17
    creation of dangerous situation,
      21–22
    duties arising out of public office,
      17–18
    establishing a legal duty, 22
    general principles, 14–15
    offences capable of being
      committed by omission, 15–16
    relationships, 18
    statutory duties, 22
    supervening fault, 21–22

Egg shell skull
causation, 35–36
Electricity
theft, 223
Encouraging or assisting crime
see also **Accessories**

abolition of incitement, 328
defence of reasonableness, 333–335
double inchoate liability, 335
elements of offences, 328–333
exclusion of protective offences,
    334–335
impossibility, 336
introduction, 314
summary, 336–337
Epilepsy
insanity, 416

Fitness to plead
defences, 423
Fixtures
theft, 221–222
Foreseeability
intention, 48–59
joint enterprise
    actions of principal exceeding
      scope of common purpose,
      361–362
    commission by principal of
      different type of offence, 361
    "fundamentally different" rule,
      355–360
    generally, 353–354
    intention of principal, 359
    justification for imposing liability,
      354–355
    knowledge of weapon used,
      357–358
recklessness
    introduction, 60
    subjective/objective approach,
      60–64
    unjustified risk, 60
Fraud
common law offences, 277
consent to assault, 165–166
conspiracy to defraud, 278–281
deception offences, 277–278
definition, 281
fraud by abuse of position, 284
fraud by failing to disclose
    information, 283
fraud by false representation, 281–283
inchoate liability, 285
mens rea, 284
obtaining services dishonestly,
    285–286
possession of articles for use in
    fraud, 274
sentence, 281

Function of criminal law
see **Criminal law**
Fungi
criminal damage, 295
theft, 222

Going equipped to steal
generally, 272–274
Grievous bodily harm
causing GBH with intent,
    150–151
consent
    fraud, 165–166
    horseplay, 163
    informed consent, 166–167
    introduction, 160
    mistake, 160, 165–166
    public interest, 161–167
    sadomasochism, 164–165
    sexual activity, 163–165
    sports, 162–163
    status as a defence, 160
    valid consent, 160–161
definition, 148
inflicting GBH, 147–149
racially or religiously aggravated
    offences, 152–154
reform proposals, 151–152
summary, 168–169

Handling stolen goods
actus reus
    continuing nature of theft, 267
    handling, 262–267
    otherwise than in the course of
      stealing, 267
    stolen goods, 267–270
definition, 261–262
dishonesty, 271
handling
    definition, 262
    otherwise than in the course of
      stealing, 267
    receiving, 262–263
    undertaking or assisting in
      retention, etc., 263–267
knowledge or belief that goods are
    stolen, 271
mens rea, 271–272
sentence, 261
stolen goods
    goods, 267
    goods ceasing to be stolen,
      268–269

goods representing those
        originally stolen, 269–270
    stolen, 267–268
Harassment
    charging under different statutory
        provisions, 158–159
    course of conduct, 156
    defences, 158
    generally, 155–156
    mens rea, 157–158
    putting people in fear of violence,
        156–157
    racially or religiously aggravated
        offences, 152–154
HIV
    assault, 166–167
Homicide
    see **Causing death of children or
        vulnerable adults; Infanticide;
        Manslaughter; Murder**
Horseplay
    assault, 163
Human remains
    theft, 224
Human rights
    crime prevention, 439
    declarations of incompatibility, 6
    incorporation into domestic law, 5–6
    manslaughter by gross negligence,
        120–121
    retrospective legislation, 4–5
    self-defence, 439
    statutory interpretation, 6
    strict liability, 76

Impossibility
    attempts, 320–321
    conspiracy, 327
    encouraging or assisting crime, 336
Inchoate offences
    see **Attempts; Conspiracy;
        Encouraging or assisting crime**
Incitement
    see also **Encouraging or assisting
        crime**
    abolition, 328
Incorporeal moveable property
    theft, 221
Infanticide
    generally, 126
Insanity
    see also **Automatism**
    burden of proof, 413
    criticism of defence, 419–420

definition, 414
disease of the mind
    diabetes, 415–416
    epilepsy, 416
    generally, 414–415
    post-traumatic stress disorder, 417
    sleepwalking, 416–417
insane delusions, 419
intoxication, 405
introduction, 413
irresistible impulse, 419
M'Naghten rules
    defect of reason, 414
    disease of the mind, 414–418
    introduction, 414
    knowledge of nature and quality
        of acts, 418
    knowledge of wrongfulness of
        acts, 418
    murder, 91
    reform proposals, 419–421
    sane/insane automatism
        distinguished, 413, 422
Intangible property
    see **Incorporeal moveable property**
Intention
    direct intention, 47–48
    introduction, 46–47
    oblique intention, 48–59
    reform proposals, 59–60
Intoxication
    automatism, 405
    consent in sexual offences, 202–204
    definition, 389
    diminished responsibility, 94–96
    insanity, 405
    introduction, 388–389
    involuntary intoxication, 401–402
    mistaken belief
        consent, 404–405
        criminal damage, 403
        duress, 403
        identity, 403
        involuntary intoxication, 405
        mistake as to a defence, 403–404
        voluntary intoxication, 403–405
    provocation, 103
    reform proposals, 405–409
    voluntary intoxication
        accidents, 400–401
        basic/specific intent crimes
            distinguished, 394–398
        dangerous/soporific drugs
            distinguished, 397–399

"Dutch courage", 400
    intoxication negating mens rea,
        391–399
    mistake, 403–405
    policy arguments, 389–391
Involuntary manslaughter
    see **Manslaughter**

Joint enterprise
    acquittal or reduction in liability of
        principal
        principal having defence
            unavailable to secondary
            party, 363–364
        principal lacking mens rea,
            362–363
    definition, 351–352
    liability for more serious offence than
        principal, 364
    nature of liability, 352–353
    reform, 367–368
    summary, 377–379
    unintended consequences
        actions of principal exceeding
            scope of common purpose,
            361–362
        commission by principal of
            different type of offence, 361
        "fundamentally different" rule,
            355–360
        generally, 353–354
        intention of principal, 359
        justification for imposing liability,
            354–355
        knowledge of weapon used,
            357–358
    withdrawal of participation
        communication of withdrawal,
            365–366
        effective withdrawal, 364–365
        introduction, 364

Land
    see **Real property**
Law reform
    generally, 9–10
Liability
    see **Accessories; Corporate liability;
        Joint enterprise; Vicarious
        liability**
Loss of control
    see also **Manslaughter**
    burden of proof, 113
    definition, 110–111

introduction, 109–110
objective test, 112
provocation compared, 113
qualifying trigger, 111–112

M'Naghten rules
see **Insanity**
Making off without payment
actus reus, 275–276
definition, 274–275
mens rea, 276–277
sentence, 275
Manslaughter
actus reus
causation, 86
death, 85
introduction, 84
jurisdiction, 84
living persons, 85
Queen's peace, 85
unlawful killing, 86
victims, 84
year and a day rule, 85–86
corporate manslaughter
common law, 128–130
statutory provisions, 130–132
definition, 88–89
diminished responsibility
abnormality of mind, 92–94,
96–97
burden of proof, 91–92, 98
intoxication, 94–96
introduction, 91
revised definition, 96–98
substantial impairment,
94–96, 97
introduction, 84
involuntary manslaughter
introduction, 114
manslaughter by gross
negligence, 115–121
recklessness, 114–115
unlawful act manslaughter,
121–126
jurisdiction, 84
loss of control
burden of proof, 113
definition, 110–111
introduction, 109–110
objective test, 112
provocation compared, 113
qualifying trigger, 111–112
manslaughter by gross negligence
breach of duty of care, 119

causation, 120
criticisms of law, 120–121
current law, 116–117
development of law, 115–116
duty of care, 117–118
gross negligence, 120
human rights, 120–121
reform proposals, 121
risk of death, 119
provocation
battered woman syndrome,
108–109
circumstances, 107
cumulative provocation, 99–100
definition, 98–99
intoxication, 103
introduction, 98
loss of control, 100–101
misdirected retaliation, 99
mistake of fact, 108
proportionality, 107
provocative conduct, 99–100
reasonable person, 101–107
reform, 109–113
self-induced provocation, 100
recklessness, 114–115
suicide pacts, 114
summary, 132–134
types, 88–89, 90–91
unlawful act manslaughter
causation, 125
dangerousness of acts, 123–124
directing of acts at others,
125–126
intentional acts, 122
introduction, 121–122
reform proposals, 126
supply of drugs, 125–126
unlawfulness of acts, 122–123
voluntary manslaughter
diminished responsibility, 91–98
introduction, 89–90
loss of control, 109–113
provocation, 98–109
sentence, 89
suicide pacts, 114
Marital coercion
see **Coercion**
Medical treatment
assault, 165–166
causation, 29–31
necessity, 452, 454–455
Mens rea
see also **Strict liability**

coincidence with actus reus, 36–37
definition, 44
determining mens rea, 44–45
intention
direct intention, 47–48
introduction, 46–47
oblique intention, 48–59
reform proposals, 59–60
introduction, 44
miscellaneous forms, 65
motive distinguished, 45
negligence, 65
proof, 45–46
recklessness
introduction, 60
subjective/objective approach,
60–64
unjustified risk, 60
reform proposals, 65
summary, 79–80
transferred malice, 66–67
Mental disorder
see **Insanity**
Mistake
belief in consent
assault, 160, 165–166, 387
intoxication, 404–405
bigamy, 387
civil law, 384–385
intoxication
consent, 404–405
criminal damage, 403
duress, 403
identity, 403
involuntary intoxication, 405
mistake as to a defence, 403–404
voluntary intoxication, 403–405
introduction, 384
irrelevant mistakes, 386
mistake as to a defence, 386
mistake of fact, 385
mistakes negating mens rea,
384–385
mistakes not negating mens rea,
385–386
need to act in self-defence or
prevention of crime, 386–387,
436–438
provocation, 108
sexual offences, 176–177
summary, 388
theft, 229–230
Motive
mens rea distinguished, 45

Murder
  actus reus
    causation, 86
    death, 85
    introduction, 84
    jurisdiction, 84
    living persons, 85
    Queen's peace, 85
    unlawful killing, 86
    victims, 84
    year and a day rule, 85–86
  definition, 86
  introduction, 84
  jurisdiction, 84
  mens rea
    implied malice, 87
    introduction, 86
    malice aforethought, 87
  necessity, 452–455
  reform proposals, 88
  sentence, 86
  summary, 132
Mushrooms
  see **Fungi**

Nature of criminal law
  see **Criminal law**
Necessity
  see also **Duress**
  criticism of defence, 455–457
  generally, 451–452
  medical treatment, 452, 454–455
  murder, 452–455
  other offences, 455
Negligence
  medical treatment, 29–31
  mens rea, 65

Objectivism/subjectivism compared
  see **Criminal law**
Oblique intention
  see **Intention**
Obtaining by deception
  see also **Fraud**
  former offences, 277–278
Obtaining services dishonestly
  generally, 285–286
Omissions
  assumption of responsibility, 19–21
  battery, 144
  contractual duties, 16–17
  creation of dangerous situation, 21–22
  duties arising out of public office, 17–18

  establishing a legal duty, 22
  general principles, 14–15
  offences capable of being committed by omission, 15–16
  relationships, 18
  statutory duties, 22
  supervening fault, 21–22

Parties
  see **Accessories; Joint enterprise**
Plants
  criminal damage, 295
  theft, 222
Possession of articles for use in fraud
  generally, 274
Possession with intent to damage
  generally, 304
Post-traumatic stress disorder
  insanity, 417
Precedent
  sources of law, 5
Presumption of innocence
  strict liability, 76
Prevention of crime
  see **Crime prevention**
Protection from harassment
  see **Harassment**
Provocation
  see also **Manslaughter**
  battered woman syndrome, 108–109
  circumstances, 107
  cumulative provocation, 99–100
  definition, 98–99
  intoxication, 103
  introduction, 98
  loss of control, 100–101
  misdirected retaliation, 99
  mistake of fact, 108
  proportionality, 107
  provocative conduct, 99–100
  reasonable person, 101–107
  reform, 109–113
  self-induced provocation, 100
Psychiatric harm
  grievous bodily harm, 148–149
Putting people in fear of violence
  harassment, 156–157

Racially aggravated offences
  criminal damage, 305
  offences against the person, 152–154
Rape
  actus reus, 175–176
  consent

    background to SOA 2003, 197
    deception, 200–202
    definition, 197–198
    impersonation, 202
    intoxication, 202–204
    introduction, 196–197
    presumptions, 198–202
  definition, 174–175
  mens rea, 176–177
  penetration, 175
  persons capable of committing rape, 175
  sentence, 175
Real property
  criminal damage, 295
  theft, 221–222
Reasonable force
  see **Crime prevention; Self-defence**
Recklessness
  introduction, 60
  subjective/objective approach, 60–64
  unjustified risk, 60
Reform
  see **Law reform**
Regulatory offences
  see **Strict liability**
Religiously aggravated offences
  criminal damage, 305
  offences against the person, 152–154
Retrials
  retrials following acquittal, 7–8
Reverse burdens
  generally, 9
Robbery
  actus reus, 248–250
  assault with intent to rob, 250
  definition, 248
  mens rea, 250
  sentence, 248
  theft, 248–249
  use or threat of force, 249–250

Sadomasochism
  assault, 164–165
Secondary liability
  see **Accessories; Assisting offenders; Corporate liability; Joint enterprise; Vicarious liability**
Self-defence
  burden of proof, 431
  definition, 431
  effect of defence, 436
  human rights, 439

mistake, 386–387, 436–438
reasonable force
    duty to retreat, 435
    generally, 432–434
    need to act, 434–435
    pre-emptive strikes, 435–436
    proportionality, 435
reform proposals, 439
sources of law, 431–432
transferred malice, 67
Sexual activity
    see **Assault; Sexual offences**
Sexual offences
administering substances with intent, 186–187
assault by penetration
    actus reus, 181–182
    definition, 181
    mens rea, 182
    penetration, 181–182
    sentence, 181
    sexual nature of penetration, 182
causing sexual activity without consent, 183–184
child sex offences
    abuse of position of trust, 192–194
    arranging or facilitating, 195
    familial child sex offences, 195–196
    generally, 189–193
    introduction, 189
    sexual grooming, 194–195
committing an offence with intent to commit a sexual offence, 188
consent
    background to SOA 2003, 197
    deception, 200–202
    definition, 197–198
    impersonation, 202
    intoxication, 202–204
    introduction, 196–197
    presumptions, 198–202
introduction, 174
preparatory offences
    administering substances with intent, 186–187
    committing an offence with intent to commit a sexual offence, 188
    introduction, 186
    trespass with intent, 188–189
rape
    actus reus, 175–176

definition, 174–175
mens rea, 176–177
penetration, 175
persons capable of committing rape, 175
sentence, 175
sex with adult relatives, 184–186
sexual assault
    actus reus, 177–180
    definition, 177
    mens rea, 180–181
    sentence, 177
    sexual nature of touching, 178–180
    touching, 178
summary, 204–205
trespass with intent, 188–189
Silent telephone calls
    assault, 140
Sleepwalking
    insanity, 416–417
Sources of law
    generally, 4–5
Sports
    assault, 162–163
Stalking
    see **Harassment**
Standard of proof
    see also **Burden of proof**
    defence, 9
    prosecution, 8
State of affairs offences
    see **Strict liability**
Statutes
    see **Acts of Parliament**
Statutory interpretation
    human rights, 6
    presumption of mens rea
        defences, 73
        encouraging vigilance and compliance, 74–75
        generally, 69–70
        necessary implication to displace presumption, 72–74
        public safety, 74
        seriousness of offence, 71–72
        social concern, 74
        true crimes and regulatory crimes distinguished, 70–72
Strict liability
    absolute liability
        actus reus, 22–23
        mens rea, 67–68

alternatives, 79
common law, 68
definition, 67
human rights, 76
justification, 76–78
presumption of mens rea
    defences, 73
    encouraging vigilance and compliance, 74–75
    generally, 69–70
    necessary implication to displace presumption, 72–74
    public safety, 74
    seriousness of offence, 71–72
    social concern, 74
    true crimes/regulatory crimes distinguished, 70–72
state of affairs offences
    actus reus, 22–23
    mens rea, 67–68
vicarious liability, 370–372
Subjectivism/objectivism compared
    see **Criminal law**
Suicide pacts
    manslaughter, 114
Superior orders
    defences, 457

Telephone calls
    assault, 140
Theft
    see also **Handling stolen goods; Robbery**
actus reus
    appropriation, 211–219
    belonging to another, 224–230
    property, 219–224
appropriation
    appropriation without taking possession, 212
    assumption of rights of owner, 211–212
    bona fide purchasers, 218
    cheques and bank credits, 212–213
    consent, 213–216
    continuing acts, 219
    gifts, 216–218
    later assumption of rights, 218
belonging to another
    abandoned property, 226
    company property, 225–226
    co-ownership, 225

definition, 224
equitable interests, 226
ownership, possession and
control, 224–225
partnership property, 225
property obtained by another's
mistake, 229–230
property received for particular
purpose, 227–229
proprietary rights and interests,
225–226
time when mens rea formed,
227–230
trust property, 226
definition, 210–211
dishonesty
exceptions, 231–232
Ghosh test, 234–237
question of fact or law, 233–237
reform proposals, 237, 239
"Robin Hood defence", 236–237
summary, 238
willingness to pay, 232–233
intention permanently to deprive
borrowing, 241–242
conditional intention, 243
generally, 239–240
intention to treat as own property
to dispose of, 240–241
lending, 242
parting with property under
condition as to return,
242–243
mens rea

dishonesty, 231–239
intention permanently to deprive,
239–243
property
animals, 222–223
confidential information, 223
corpses, 224
definition, 220
electricity, 223
exclusions, 221–224
fixtures, 221–222
intangible property, 221
introduction, 219–220
land, 221–222
mushrooms, plants, fruit, etc., 222
things in action, 220–221
trade secrets, 223
sentence, 211
summary, 243–244
**Threatening to commit criminal
damage**
generally, 303
Trade secrets
theft, 223
Transferred malice
accessories, 351
mens rea, 66–67
Trespass with intent
sexual offences, 188–189

Unborn children
homicide, 85
Unfitness to plead
see **Fitness to plead**

Unlawful act manslaughter
see **Manslaughter**

Vicarious liability
corporate liability distinguished, 374
nature, 369–370
offences with mens rea, 372–373
reform proposals, 373
strict liability offences, 370–372
Voluntary intoxication
see **Intoxication**
Voluntary manslaughter
see **Manslaughter**

Wounding
consent
fraud, 165–166
horseplay, 163
informed consent, 166–167
introduction, 160
mistake, 160, 165–166
public interest, 161–167
sadomasochism, 164–165
sexual activity, 163–165
sports, 162–163
status as a defence, 160
valid consent, 160–161
definition of wound, 148
racially or religiously aggravated
offences, 152–154
reform proposals, 151–152
summary, 168–169
unlawful wounding, 147–149
wounding with intent, 150–151